D1455249

Microsoft®
SQL Server™ 7.0
System
Administration
Training

PUBLISHED BY
Microsoft Press
A Division of Microsoft Corporation
One Microsoft Way
Redmond, Washington 98052-6399

Copyright © 1999 by Microsoft Corporation

All rights reserved. No part of the contents of this book may be reproduced or transmitted in any form or by any means without the written permission of the publisher.

Library of Congress Cataloging-in-Publication Data
Microsoft SQL Server 7.0 System Administration Training Kit /
   Microsoft Corporation.
       p.   cm.
    ISBN 1-57231-827-9
    1. SQL server.   2. Client/server computing.   I. Microsoft
Corporation.
  QA76.9.C55M534 1999
  005.75'85--dc21   99-13556
                                       CIP

Printed and bound in the United States of America.

3 4 5 6 7 8 9 WCWC 4 3 2 1 0 9

Distributed in Canada by Penguin Books Canada Limited.

A CIP catalogue record for this book is available from the British Library.

Microsoft Press books are available through booksellers and distributors worldwide. For further information about international editions, contact your local Microsoft Corporation office or contact Microsoft Press International directly at fax (425) 936-7329. Visit our Web site at mspress.microsoft.com.

ActiveX, BackOffice, JScript, Microsoft, Microsoft Press, MS-DOS, Outlook, PivotTable, Visual Basic, Visual FoxPro, Windows, and Windows NT are either registered trademarks or trademarks of Microsoft Corporation in the United States and/or other countries. Other product and company names mentioned herein may be the trademarks of their respective owners.

The example companies, organizations, products, people, and events depicted herein are fictitious. No association with any real company, organization, product, person, or event is intended or should be inferred.

For The Information Management Group
Writers: Sean Nolan, Tom Huguelet
Graphic Artist: Jesse Wolfe
Technical Contributors: Jodi Allen, Dan Christie

For Microsoft (Original Instructor-Led Course Content)
Dan Basica, Homer Christensen, Wendy Cleary, Margo Crandall, Karl Dehmer, Stacey Dickinson, Xandria Eykel, Cheryl Hoople, Marilyn McGill, Lori Oviatt, Carl Rabeler, Adam Shapiro

For Microsoft Press
Program Manager: Jeff Madden
Project Editor: Michael Bolinger
Technical Editor: Nick Cavalancia

Part No. 097-0002093

Contents

About This Book

Welcome to *Microsoft SQL Server 7.0 System Administration Training Kit*. This book provides you with the knowledge and skills required to install, configure, administer, and troubleshoot Microsoft SQL Server client/server database management system version 7. The contents of this book reflect the significant changes in the product from previous versions and provide a task-oriented discussion of all of the important features that SQL Server provides for administrators.

Note For more information on becoming a Microsoft Certified Systems Engineer, see the "The Microsoft Certified Professional Program" section later in "About This Book."

Each chapter in this book is divided into lessons. Most lessons include hands-on procedures that allow you to practice or demonstrate a particular concept or skill. Each lesson ends with a short summary, and each chapter ends with a set of review questions to test your knowledge of the chapter material.

The "Getting Started" section of this introductory section provides important setup instructions that describe the hardware and software requirements to complete the procedures in this course. It also provides information about the networking configuration necessary to complete some of the hands-on procedures. Read through this section thoroughly before you start the lessons.

Intended Audience

This book has been developed for information system (IS) professionals and database administrators who need to install, administer, and support Microsoft SQL Server 7 or who plan to take the related Microsoft Certified Professional exam 70-028, *Administering Microsoft SQL Server 7.0*.

Prerequisites

Before you begin to work with the material in this Training Kit, it is recommended that you have

- Completed Course 922, *Supporting Microsoft Windows NT 4.0 Core Technologies,* or equivalent knowledge, including knowing how to
  - Share and access network resources
  - Configure Microsoft Windows NT disk mirroring and striping with parity
  - Describe the difference between a domain and a workgroup (this is important in order to understand how security is administered)
  - Change network and international settings (default language and default date) with the Control Panel
  - View and interpret data from the Windows NT application log
  - View and interpret data from Windows NT Performance Monitor
  - Use the User Manager for Domains to set up Windows NT user accounts
  - Edit the registry
- An understanding of basic relational database concepts, including
  - Logical and physical database design
  - Data integrity
  - Relationships between tables and columns (primary and foreign keys, one-to-one, one-to-many, and many-to-many)
  - How data is stored in tables (rows and columns)
- Knowledge of basic Transact-SQL syntax (SELECT, INSERT, and UPDATE statements)
- An understanding of the role of the database administrator

Reference Materials

You might find the following reference material useful:

- SQL Server white papers and case studies, available online at http://www.microsoft.com/sql/index.htm
- SQL Server Books Online, available on the product CD-ROM

About the CD-ROMs

The Supplemental Course Materials CD-ROM contains a variety of informational aids that can be used throughout this book. These include multimedia presentations, sample data, demonstrations, and files used in hands-on procedures.

The multimedia presentations supplement some of the key concepts covered in the book. You should view these presentations when suggested and then use them as a review tool while you work through the material. A complete version of this book is also available online, with a variety of viewing options. For instructions on running the online book, see the section "Installing the Online Book" later in this introduction. (The other CD-ROM contains Microsoft SQL Server version 7.0 120-day Evaluation Edition.)

The Supplemental Course Materials CD-ROM also contains files required to perform the hands-on procedures and information designed to supplement the lesson material. These files can be used directly from the CD-ROM or copied onto your hard disk by using the Setup program. The files include demonstrations of key concepts, practice files for the procedures, and additional sample files.

The demonstrations require Microsoft Media Player and an HTML browser. If Microsoft Internet Explorer and Media Player are installed on your system, simply double-click on any of these files to view them.

Features of This Book

Each chapter opens with a "Before You Begin" section, which prepares you for completing the chapter.

▶ Whenever possible, lessons contain procedures that give you an opportunity to use the skills being presented or to explore the part of the application being described. All procedures are identified with a bullet symbol like the one to the left of this paragraph.

The "Review" section at the end of each chapter allows you to test what you have learned in the lesson.

Appendix A, "Questions and Answers," contains all of the book's practice and review questions and the corresponding answers.

Notes

Notes appear throughout the lessons.

- Notes marked **Tip** contain explanations of possible results or alternative methods.
- Notes marked **Important** contain information that is essential to completing a task.
- Notes marked **Note** contain supplemental information.
- Notes marked **Caution** contain warnings about possible loss of data.

Notational Conventions

- Characters or commands that you type appear in **bold** type.

- *Italic* in syntax statements indicates placeholders for variable information. *Italic* is also used for book titles.

- Names of files and folders appear in Title Caps, except when you are to type them directly. Unless otherwise indicated, you can use all lowercase letters when you type a filename in a dialog box or at a command prompt.

- Filename extensions appear in uppercase.

- Acronyms appear in all uppercase.

- Monospace type represents code samples, examples of screen text, or entries that you might type at a command prompt or in initialization files.

- Square brackets [ ] are used in syntax statements to enclose optional items. For example, [*filename*] in command syntax indicates that you can choose to type a filename with the command. Type only the information within the brackets, not the brackets themselves.

- Braces { } are used in syntax statements to enclose required items. Type only the information within the braces, not the braces themselves.

- Icons represent specific sections in the book, as follows:

Icon	Represents
	A multimedia presentation. You will find the applicable multimedia presentation on the Supplemental Course Materials CD-ROM.
	A file contained on the CD-ROM. Some files are needed to complete a hands-on practice; others contain supplemental information about the topic being discussed. The purpose of the file and its location are described in the accompanying text.
	A hands-on practice containing exercise(s). You should perform the practice to give yourself an opportunity to use the skills being presented in the lesson.
	Chapter review questions. These questions at the end of each chapter allow you to test what you have learned in the lessons. You will find the answers to the review questions in the Questions and Answers appendix at the end of the book.

Keyboard Conventions

- A hyphen (-) between two key names means that you must press those keys at the same time. For example, "Press Alt-Tab" means that you hold down Alt while you press Tab.

- You can choose menu commands with the keyboard. Press the Alt key to activate the menu bar, and then sequentially press the keys that correspond to the highlighted or underlined letter of the menu name and the command name. For some commands, you can also press a key combination listed in the menu.

- You can select or clear check boxes or option buttons in dialog boxes with the keyboard. Press the Alt key, and then press the key that corresponds to the underlined letter of the option name. Or you can press Tab until the option is highlighted, and then press the Spacebar to select or clear the check box or option button.

- You can cancel the display of a dialog box by pressing the Esc key.

Chapter and Appendix Overview

This course combines notes, hands-on procedures, multimedia presentations, and review questions to teach you system administration methods for using SQL Server 7. It is designed to be completed from beginning to end, but you can choose to complete only the sections that interest you. (See the next section, "Finding the Best Starting Point for You" for more information.) If you choose the customized track option, see the "Before You Begin" section in each chapter. Any hands-on procedures that require preliminary work from preceding chapters refer to the appropriate chapters.

The self-paced training book is divided into the following chapters:

- "About This Book" (this chapter) contains a self-paced training overview and introduces the components of this training. Read this section thoroughly to get the greatest educational value from this self-paced training and to plan which lessons you will complete.

- Chapter 1, "Overview of SQL Server," introduces SQL Server. It defines some of the important characteristics of SQL Server and explains the environments in which it has been designed to work. You will be introduced to the different parts of the product and given some idea as to the role played by these parts.

- Chapter 2, "Installation," explains how to install SQL Server 7. It lists the hardware and software requirements of the program, and it explains the specific information you have to supply and the decisions you have to make during the installation process. The chapter concludes with a discussion of the steps that you should take to test your new installation to be sure that the setup has completed correctly.

- Chapter 3, "Upgrading to SQL Server 7.0," explains how to upgrade a complete SQL Server 6.*x* installation to SQL Server 7. In this chapter you will learn how to use the SQL Server Upgrade Wizard and how to perform other tasks associated with cleanly upgrading your existing SQL Servers.

- Chapter 4, "System Configuration and Architecture," shows you how to use some of the client administration utilities and how to configure SQL Server. You will also learn some of the background you will need to create and manage SQL Server databases.

- Chapter 5, "Database Files," discusses SQL Server databases. Databases are stored in primary and secondary data files and use log files to ensure data integrity. The chapter shows how to create databases and discusses ways to manage them, estimate space requirements, and use advanced management techniques such as using multiple files and disks.

- Chapter 6, "Transferring Data," shows you how to transfer data and database objects into and out of SQL Server databases. SQL Server provides a number of data transfer mechanisms. Most of the chapter focuses on one of these—Data Transformation Services. The others are briefly introduced.

- Chapter 7, "Web Publishing and Full-Text Indexing," explains how to automatically generate Web pages from your SQL Server databases. The chapter also discusses full-text indexing and searching in SQL Server 7, which gives you the ability to perform complex linguistic searches not normally possible on text or character data in a relational database.

- Chapter 8, "Backup and Restore Overview and Strategy," presents an overview of the SQL Server backup and restore processes and discusses issues that you should consider when planning a backup and restore strategy for a SQL Server database.

- Chapter 9, "Backing Up Databases," discusses the media that you can use when creating SQL Server backups and how to perform backups using SQL Server Enterprise Manager or the Transact-SQL BACKUP statement.

- Chapter 10, "Restoring Databases," teaches you how to restore backups in case of database or server failure. You will learn about the SQL Server recovery process and how to restore user and system databases, back up the transaction log in case of a database failure, rebuild the system databases, and implement a standby SQL Server.

- Chapter 11, "Logins, User Accounts, and User Roles," introduces three levels of access that are verified before a user can access data in a SQL Server database. The chapter explains how to create and manage logins, users, and roles. The important difference between logins that are authenticated by Windows NT and those that are authenticated by SQL Server is also discussed in this chapter.

- Chapter 12, "Permissions and Security Planning," discusses how SQL Server checks permissions every time you attempt to execute statements or use objects in a database. In this chapter, you will learn how to grant and deny permissions to users and roles in a database and how to plan the permissions for each user or role.

- Chapter 13, "Automating Administrative Tasks," discusses the SQL Server 7 tools that you can use to automatically perform repetitive maintenance, respond to the ongoing demands of the server, and be alerted to problems as they occur. The chapter explains how these tools are implemented and teaches you how to use them.

- Chapter 14, "Monitoring and Maintaining SQL Server," shows you how to monitor SQL Server to find out when things are not occurring normally and thereby take steps to rectify the problem before alerts fire. The chapter also introduces the Database Maintenance Plan Wizard, which you can use to automatically create all of the jobs and tasks that should be part of your database maintenance plan.

- Chapter 15, "Introducing Replication," is the first of three chapters that deal with SQL Server replication. In this chapter, you will learn about the concepts and terminology associated with replication.

- Chapter 16, "Planning and Setting Up Replication," discusses planning a replication implementation and performing a number of replication tasks, including setting up servers, creating publications, and setting up subscriptions.

- Chapter 17, "Managing Replication," shows you how to monitor the replication agents and use various tools in SQL Server to troubleshoot replication problems. The chapter also explains how to publish data to non–SQL Server Subscribers, replicate data from non–SQL Server databases, and make a publication available for subscription on the Internet.

- Appendix A, "Questions and Answers," lists all of the practice and review questions from the book, showing suggested answers.

- Appendix B, "Database Schemata," gives you graphical schema diagrams of the SQL Server 7 sample databases, Northwind and pubs, that show the tables, columns, and relationships in these databases.

Finding the Best Starting Point for You

Because this book is self-paced, you can skip some lessons and revisit them later. Note, however, that you must complete the procedures in Chapter 2, "Installation," before you can perform procedures in the other chapters. Use the following table to find the best starting point for you:

If you	Follow this learning path
Are preparing to take the Microsoft Certified Professional exam 70-028, *Administering Microsoft SQL Server 7.0*.	Work through all chapters, 1 through 17, in order.
Want to review information about specific topics from the exam.	Use the "Where to Find Specific Skills in This Book" section that follows this table.

Where to Find Specific Skills in This Book

The following tables provide a comprehensive list of the skills measured on certification exam 70-028, *Administering Microsoft SQL Server 7.0*. The tables list the skill and indicate where in this book you will find the lesson relating to that skill.

Note Exam skills are subject to change without prior notice and at the sole discretion of Microsoft.

Planning

Skill being measured	Location in book
Develop a security strategy.	
Assess whether to use Microsoft Windows NT or Microsoft SQL Server accounts.	Chapter 11, Lessons 1 and 2
Assess whether to leverage the Windows NT group structure.	Chapter 11, Lessons 1 and 2
Plan the use and structure of SQL Server roles. Server roles include fixed server, fixed database, and user-defined database.	Chapter 11, Lesson 3
Assess whether to map Windows NT groups directly into a database or to map them to a role.	Chapter 11, Lesson 3
Assess which Windows NT accounts will be used to run SQL Server services.	Chapter 2, Lesson 1
Plan an *n*-tier application security strategy, determining whether to use application roles or other mid-tier security mechanisms such as Microsoft Transaction Server.	Chapter 1, Lesson 3
Plan the security requirements for linked databases.	Chapter 6, Lesson 4

Skill being measured	Location in book
Develop a SQL Server capacity plan.	
Plan the physical placement of files, including data files and log files.	Chapter 5, Lessons 1 and 4
Plan the use of filegroups.	Chapter 5, Lesson 4
Plan for growth over time.	Chapter 5, Lesson 5
Plan the physical hardware system.	Chapter 2, Lesson 1, and Chapter 5, Lesson 4
Assess the communication requirements.	Chapter 1, Lesson 3, and Chapter 2, Lesson 1
Develop a data availability solution.	
Choose the appropriate backup and restore strategy. Strategies include full backup, full backup and transaction log backup, differential backup with full backup and transaction log backup, and database files backup and transaction log backup.	Chapter 8, Lessons 1 and 2
Assess whether to use a standby server.	Chapter 10, Lesson 4
Assess whether to use clustering.	Chapter 10, Lesson 4
Develop a migration plan.	
Plan an upgrade from a previous version of SQL Server.	Chapter 3, Lesson 1
Plan the migration of data from other data sources.	Chapter 6, Lessons 1 and 2
Develop a replication strategy.	
Given a scenario, design the appropriate replication model. Replication models include single Publisher, multiple Subscribers; single Subscriber, multiple Publishers; multiple Publishers, multiple Subscribers; and remote distribution server.	Chapter 15, Lessons 1, 2, and 4
Choose the replication type. Replication types include snapshot, transactional, and merge.	Chapter 15, Lessons 1, 2 and 3

Installation and Configuration

Skill being measured	Location in book
Install SQL Server 7.	
Choose the character set.	Chapter 2, Lesson 1
Choose the Unicode collation sequence.	Chapter 2, Lesson 1
Choose the appropriate sort order.	Chapter 2, Lesson 1
Install network libraries and protocols.	Chapter 2, Lesson 1
Install services.	Chapter 2, Lessons 1 and 2

(continued)

Skill being measured	Location in book
Install and configure a SQL Server client.	Chapter 4, Lesson 1
Perform an unattended setup.	Chapter 2, Lesson 3
Upgrade from a SQL Server 6.x database.	Chapter 3, Lessons 1 and 2
Configure SQL Server.	
Configure SQL Mail.	Chapter 13, Lessons 1 and 2
Configure default ANSI settings.	Chapter 4, Lesson 1
Install and configure the Full-Text Search service.	
Install the Full-Text Search service.	Chapter 7, Lesson 2
Enable full-text searches for specific columns and tables.	Chapter 7, Lesson 2
Create and manage indexes to support full-text searches.	Chapter 7, Lesson 2

Configuring and Managing Security

Skill being measured	Location in book
Assign SQL Server access to Windows NT accounts, SQL Server login accounts, and built-in administrator accounts.	Chapter 11, Lesson 1
Assign database access to Windows NT accounts, SQL Server login accounts, the guest user account, and the dbo user account.	Chapter 11, Lesson 3
Create and assign SQL Server roles. Server roles include fixed server, fixed database, public, user-defined database, and application.	Chapter 11, Lesson 3
Grant to database users and roles the appropriate permissions for database objects and statements.	Chapter 12, Lessons 1 and 2
Audit server and database activity by using the SQL Server Profiler.	Chapter 14, Lesson 2

Managing and Maintaining Data

Skill being measured	Location in book
Create and manage databases—create data files, filegroups, and transaction log files.	Chapter 5, Lessons 1, 2, and 3
Create and manage databases—specify growth characteristics.	Chapter 5, Lesson 2
Load data by using various methods. Methods include the INSERT statement, the SELECT INTO statement, bcp, Data Transformation Services (DTS), BULK INSERT, Host Data Replicator (HDR), and Transfer Manager.	Chapter 6, Lesson 1

Skill being measured	Location in book
Back up system and user databases by performing a full backup, a transaction log backup, a differential backup, and a filegroup backup.	Chapter 9, Lessons 1 and 2
Restore system and user databases from a full backup, a transaction log backup, a differential backup, and a filegroup backup.	Chapter 10, Lessons 1, 2, 3, and 5
Manage replication.	
Configure servers, including distribution, publishing, and subscribing servers.	Chapter 16, Lessons 1 and 2
Create publications.	Chapter 16, Lesson 3
Set up and manage subscriptions.	Chapter 16, Lesson 4
Automate administrative tasks.	
Define jobs.	Chapter 13, Lesson 2
Define alerts.	Chapter 13, Lesson 3
Define operators.	Chapter 13, Lesson 2
Set up SQL Server Agent Mail for job notification and alerts.	Chapter 13, Lessons 1 and 2
Enable access to remote data.	
Set up linked servers.	Chapter 6, Lesson 4
Set up security for linked databases.	Chapter 6, Lesson 4

Monitoring and Optimization

Skill being measured	Location in book
Monitor SQL Server performance by using Performance Monitor and Profiler.	Chapter 14, Lesson 2
Tune and optimize SQL Server memory and CPU usage.	Chapter 14, Lessons 1 and 2
Limit resources used by queries by using the Query Governor.	Chapter 14, Lesson 1

Troubleshooting

Skill being measured	Location in book
Diagnose and resolve problems when upgrading from SQL Server 6.*x*.	Chapter 3, Lesson 3
Diagnose and resolve problems with backup and restore operations.	Chapter 9, Lesson 2, and Chapter 10, Lesson 5
Diagnose and resolve replication problems.	Chapter 17, Lesson 1
Diagnose and resolve job or alert failures.	Chapter 13, Lesson 4

(continued)

Skill being measured	Location in book
Diagnose and resolve distributed query problems.	Chapter 6, Lesson 4
Use the Client Configuration Utility to diagnose and resolve client connectivity problems.	Chapter 4, Lesson 1
Diagnose and resolve problems with access to SQL Server, databases, and database objects.	Chapter 4, Lesson 1

Getting Started

This self-paced training course contains hands-on procedures to help you learn about Microsoft SQL Server 7.

Caution   Several procedures may require you to make changes to your server. This may have undesirable results if you are connected to a larger network. Check with your Network Administrator before attempting these procedures.

Hardware Requirements

Each computer must have the following minimum configuration. All hardware should be on the Microsoft Windows NT Server 4.0 Hardware Compatibility List.

- Intel or compatible (Pentium 166 MHz or higher, Pentium PRO, or Pentium II) computer
- At least 64 MB of memory
- At least 300 MB of free hard disk drive space
- Sound card and speakers
- CD-ROM drive

Software Requirements

The following software is required to complete the procedures in this course. A 120-day evaluation copy of SQL Server 7.0 is included on CD-ROM in this kit.

- Microsoft Windows NT Server 4.0 with Service Pack 4, preferably installed as a Primary Domain Controller
- Microsoft SQL Server 7.0 Standard Edition

Caution The 120-day Evaluation Edition provided with this training is not the full retail product and is provided only for the purposes of training and evaluation. Microsoft Technical Support does not support this evaluation edition. For additional support information regarding this book and the CD-ROMs (including answers to commonly asked questions about installation and use), visit the Microsoft Press Technical Support Web site at http: //mspress.microsoft.com/ mspress/support/. You can also e-mail TKINPUT@MICROSOFT.COM, or send a letter to Microsoft Press, Attn: Microsoft Press Technical Support, One Microsoft Way, Redmond WA, 98052-6399.

Setup Instructions

Set up your computer according to the manufacturer's instructions.

Caution If your computer is part of a larger network, you *must* verify with your network administrator that the computer name, domain name, and other information used in setting up Microsoft SQL Server 7 as described in Chapter 2 does not conflict with network operations. If it does conflict, ask your network administrator to provide alternative values, and use those values throughout all of the procedures in this book.

Microsoft SQL Server 7.0 120-day Evaluation Edition

You will install Microsoft SQL Server 7.0 in Chapter 2, "Installation." You can perform the procedures in the rest of the chapters only after you have installed SQL Server as instructed in Chapter 2. You should not perform the procedures in the chapters of this book on a SQL Server that is being used by other users.

Installing the Exercise Files

The Supplemental Course Materials CD-ROM contains a set of exercise files that you will need to install on your hard disk drive to complete many of the procedures in this book.

▶ **To install the exercise files to your hard disk drive**

1. Insert the Supplemental Course Materials CD-ROM in to your CD-ROM drive.

2. Select Run from the Start menu on your desktop, and type **D:\Setup.exe** (where D is the name of your CD-ROM drive).

   This will initiate the setup process that will install the exercise files to your hard disk drive.

3. Follow the instructions of the Setup wizard.

Important This book operates on the assumption that your hard disk is named C, and the Setup wizard installs the exercise files to a default folder named C:\Sqladmin. If you alter the name of this default folder during the setup, the references to exercise files in this book will differ from the true location of files on your hard disk drive.

Installing the Media Files

The Supplemental Course Materials CD-ROM contains a set of audio visual demonstration files that you can view by running the files from the CD-ROM. You will find prompts within the book indicating when the demonstrations should be run. You must have installed Media Player and an Internet browser on your computer to view these files. (Microsoft Internet Explorer and Media Player are included on this CD-ROM. To install either of these software programs, see the installation instructions in the Readme.txt files on the CD-ROM.)

▶ **To view the demonstrations**

1. Insert the Supplemental Course Materials CD-ROM into your CD-ROM drive.

2. Select Run from the Start menu on your desktop, and type **D:\Media\\demon-stration_filename** (where D is the name of your CD-ROM drive).

   This will run the appropriate demonstration in your Internet browser.

Using the StudyNwind Database

The Northwind sample database is supplied with SQL Server 7. The StudyNwind database is a copy of the Northwind database. There are minor changes to some of the data in StudyNwind, but the database schema is the same as Northwind. Chapter 6 and many of the chapters that follow it in this book use the StudyNwind database.

To install the StudyNwind database on your server, run the C:\Sqladmin\Exercise\Setup\Maknwind.cmd batch file that you installed to your hard disk drive from the Supplemental Course Materials CD-ROM at a command prompt. You must specify the name of your server and the password of the sa login (if any) as command-line parameters when you run the batch file. For example, if your server name is SQLSERVER and the sa password is blank, you would execute the following command:

```
maknwind SQLSERVER
```

As another example, if the name of your server is SQLSERVER and the sa password is database, you would execute the following command:

```
maknwind SQLSERVER database
```

You can install the database more than once. If you modify data in the database or even modify the database—for example, if you delete a table or an index—you can reinstall the database to return it to its original state. Before you try to reinstall the database, make sure that it is not the current database in a SQL Server Query Analyzer or SQL Server Enterprise Manager window, or just close those applications. Otherwise the database is open and the batch file cannot remove and reinstall it.

Installing the Online Book

The CD-ROM also includes an online version of the book that you can view on screen by using Microsoft Internet Explorer 4.01 with SP1.

▶ **To use the online version of this book**

1. Insert the Supplemental Course Materials CD-ROM into your CD-ROM drive.

2. Select Run from the Start menu on your desktop, and type **D:\Ebook\Setup.exe** (where D is the name of your CD-ROM drive).

   This will install the online book to your hard disk drive.

3. Click OK to exit the Installation wizard.

The Microsoft Certified Professional Program

The Microsoft Certified Professional (MCP) program provides the best method to prove your command of current Microsoft products and technologies. Microsoft, an industry leader in certification, is in the forefront of testing methodology. Our exams and corresponding certifications are developed to validate your mastery of critical competencies as you design and develop, or implement and support, solutions with Microsoft products and technologies. Computer professionals who become Microsoft certified are recognized as experts and are sought after industrywide.

The Microsoft Certified Professional program offers six certifications, based on specific areas of technical expertise:

- *Microsoft Certified Professional (MCP).* Demonstrated in-depth knowledge of at least one Microsoft operating system. Candidates may pass additional Microsoft certification exams to further qualify their skills with Microsoft BackOffice products, development tools, or desktop programs.

- *Microsoft Certified Professional + Internet.* MCPs with a specialty in the Internet, qualified to plan security, install and configure server products, manage server resources, extend servers to run CGI scripts or ISAPI scripts, monitor and analyze performance, and troubleshoot problems.

- *Microsoft Certified Systems Engineer (MCSE).* Qualified to effectively plan, implement, maintain, and support information systems in a wide range of computing environments with Microsoft Windows 95, Windows 98, Microsoft Windows NT, and the Microsoft BackOffice integrated family of server software.

- *Microsoft Certified Systems Engineer + Internet (MCSE + Internet).* MCSEs with an advanced qualification to enhance, deploy, and manage sophisticated intranet and Internet solutions that include a browser, proxy server, host servers, database, and messaging and commerce components. In addition, an MCSE+ Internet-certified professional is able to manage and analyze Web sites.

- *Microsoft Certified Database Administrator (MCDBA).* Qualified to derive physical database designs, develop logical data models, create physical databases, create data services by using Transact-SQL, manage and maintain databases, configure and manage security, monitor and optimize databases, and install and configure Microsoft SQL Server.

- *Microsoft Certified Solution Developer (MCSD).* Qualified to design and develop custom business solutions with Microsoft development tools, technologies, and platforms, including Microsoft Office and Microsoft BackOffice.

- *Microsoft Certified Trainer (MCT).* Instructionally and technically qualified to deliver Microsoft Official Curriculum through a Microsoft Authorized Technical Education Center (ATEC).

Microsoft Certification Benefits

Microsoft certification, one of the most comprehensive certification programs available for assessing and maintaining software-related skills, is a valuable measure of an individual's knowledge and expertise. Microsoft certification is awarded to individuals who have successfully demonstrated their ability to perform specific tasks and implement solutions with Microsoft products. Not only does this provide an objective measure for employers to consider, it also provides guidance for what an individual should know to be proficient. And as with any skills-assessment and benchmarking measure, certification brings a variety of benefits to the individual and to employers and organizations.

Microsoft Certification Benefits for Individuals

As a Microsoft Certified Professional, you receive many benefits:

- Industry recognition of your knowledge and proficiency with Microsoft products and technologies

- Access to technical and product information directly from Microsoft through a secured area of the MCP Web Site

- Logos to enable you to identify your Microsoft Certified Professional status to colleagues or clients

- Invitations to Microsoft conferences, technical training sessions, and special events

- A Microsoft Certified Professional certificate

- Subscription to *Microsoft Certified Professional Magazine* (North America only), a career and professional development magazine

Additional benefits, depending on your certification and geography, include

- A complimentary one-year subscription to the Microsoft TechNet Technical Information Network, providing valuable information on monthly CD-ROMs.

- A one-year subscription to the Microsoft Beta Evaluation program. This benefit provides you with up to 12 free monthly CD-ROMs containing beta software (English only) for many of Microsoft's newest software products.

Microsoft Certification Benefits for Employers and Organizations

Through certification, computer professionals can maximize the return on investment in Microsoft technology. Research shows that Microsoft certification provides organizations with

- Excellent return on training and certification investments by providing a standard method of determining training needs and measuring results

- Increased customer satisfaction and decreased support costs through improved service, increased productivity, and greater technical self-sufficiency

- A reliable benchmark for hiring, promoting, and career planning
- Recognition and rewards for productive employees by validating their expertise
- Retraining options for existing employees so they can work effectively with new technologies
- Assurance of quality when outsourcing computer services

Requirements for Becoming a Microsoft Certified Professional

The requirements for becoming a Microsoft Certified Professional differ for each certification and are specific to the products and job functions addressed by the certification.

To become a Microsoft Certified Professional, you must pass rigorous certification exams that provide a valid and reliable measure of technical proficiency and expertise. These exams are designed to test your expertise and ability to perform a role or task with a product, and are developed with the input of professionals in the industry. Questions in the exams reflect how Microsoft products are used in actual organizations, giving them "real-world" relevance.

Microsoft Certified Product Specialists are required to pass one operating system exam. Candidates may pass additional Microsoft certification exams to further qualify their skills with Microsoft BackOffice products, development tools, or desktop applications.

Microsoft Certified Professional – Specialist: Internet candidates are required to pass the prescribed Microsoft Windows NT Server 4.0, TCP/IP, and Microsoft Internet Information System exam series.

Microsoft Certified Systems Engineers are required to pass a series of core Microsoft Windows operating system and networking exams and BackOffice technology elective exams.

Microsoft Certified Solution Developers are required to pass two core Microsoft Windows operating system technology exams and two BackOffice technology elective exams.

Microsoft Certified Trainers are required to meet instructional and technical requirements specific to each Microsoft Official Curriculum course they are certified to deliver. In the United States and Canada, call Microsoft at (800) 636-7544 for more information on becoming a Microsoft Certified Trainer. Outside the United States and Canada, contact your local Microsoft subsidiary.

Technical Training for Computer Professionals

Technical training is available in a variety of ways, with instructor-led classes, online instruction, or self-paced training available at thousands of locations worldwide.

Self-Paced Training

For motivated learners who are ready for the challenge, self-paced instruction is the most flexible and cost-effective way to increase your knowledge and skills.

A full-line of self-paced print and computer-based training materials are available direct from the source—Microsoft Press. Microsoft Official Curriculum courseware kits from Microsoft Press are designed for advanced computer system professionals and are available from Microsoft Press and the Microsoft Developer Division. Self-paced training kits from Microsoft Press feature print-based instructional materials, along with CD-ROM-based product software, multimedia presentations, procedural exercises, and practice files. The Mastering Series provides in-depth, interactive training on CD-ROM for experienced developers. They're both great ways to prepare for Microsoft Certified Professional exams.

Online Training

For a more flexible alternative to instructor-led classes, turn to online instruction. It's as near as the Internet, and it's ready whenever you are. Learn at your own pace and on your own schedule in a virtual classroom, often with easy access to an online instructor. Without ever leaving your desk, you can gain the expertise you need. Online instruction covers a variety of Microsoft products and technologies. It includes options ranging from Microsoft Official Curriculum to choices available nowhere else. It's training on demand, with access to learning resources 24 hours a day.

Online training is available through Microsoft Certified Technical Education Centers.

Microsoft Certified Technical Education Centers

Microsoft Certified Technical Education Centers (CTECs) are the best source for instructor-led training that can help you prepare to become a Microsoft Certified Professional. The Microsoft CTEC program is a worldwide network of qualified technical training organizations that provide authorized delivery of Microsoft Official Curriculum courses by Microsoft Certified Trainers to computer professionals.

For a listing of CTEC locations in the United States and Canada, call the Microsoft fax service at (800) 727-3351. Outside the United States and Canada, call the fax service at (206) 635-2233.

Technical Support

Every effort has been made to ensure the accuracy of this book and the contents of the companion disc. If you have comments, questions, or ideas regarding this book or the companion disc, please send them to Microsoft Press, using either of the following methods:

E-mail:
TKINPUT@MICROSOFT.COM

Postal Mail:
Microsoft Press
Attn: Microsoft SQL Server 7.0 System Administration Training Kit Editor
One Microsoft Way
Redmond, WA 98052-6399

Microsoft Press provides corrections for books through the World Wide Web at the following address:

http://mspress.microsoft.com/support/

Please note that product support is not offered through the above mail addresses. For further information regarding Microsoft software support options, please connect to http://www.microsoft.com/support/ or call Microsoft Support Network Sales at (800) 936-3500.

Evaluation Edition Software Support

The Evaluation Edition of Microsoft SQL Server 7.0 included with this book is unsupported by both Microsoft and Microsoft Press, and should not be used on a primary work computer. For online support information relating to the full version of Microsoft SQL Server 7.0 that might also apply to the Evaluation Edition, you can connect to http://support.microsoft.com/.

For information about ordering the full version of any Microsoft software, please call Microsoft Sales at (800) 426-9400 or visit http://www.microsoft.com. Information about issues relating to the use of the evaluation edition with this Training Kit is posted to the Support section of the Microsoft Press Web site (http://mspress.microsoft.com/support/).

C H A P T E R   1

Overview of SQL Server

About This Chapter

This chapter introduces Microsoft SQL Server. It defines some of the key characteristics of SQL Server and explains the environments in which it has been designed to work. You will be introduced to the different parts of the product and be given some idea as to the role played by these parts. Most of the topics introduced in this chapter will be covered in detail later in this book. Databases are not introduced in this chapter; you will first read about databases in Chapter 3, "System Configuration and Architecture," after you have installed SQL Server.

Before You Begin

To complete the lessons in this chapter you must have

- A computer running Microsoft Windows 95, Windows 98, or Microsoft Windows NT and Microsoft Internet Explorer 4.01 with SP1 or later.

- The Microsoft SQL Server version 7.0 Evaluation Edition CD-ROM included in this kit or a copy of the Microsoft SQL Server version 7.0 CD-ROM.

Lesson 1: What Is SQL Server?

SQL Server is a client/server relational database management system (RDBMS) that uses Transact-SQL to send requests between a client and SQL Server. The following sections define and explain these terms.

After this lesson, you will be able to

- Describe Microsoft SQL Server
- List the operating system platforms supported by SQL Server
- Describe how SQL Server takes advantage of the features of the Windows NT operating system
- Describe how SQL Server integrates with other Microsoft BackOffice products

Estimated lesson time: 30 minutes

Client/Server Architecture

The terms *client*, *server*, and *client/server* can be used to refer to very general concepts or to specific items of hardware or software. At the most general level, a *client* is any component of a system that requests services or resources from other components of a system. A *server* is any component of a system that provides services or resources to other components of a system.

For example, when you print a document from your workstation on a network, the workstation is the client and the machine that does the print spooling is the server.

Any client/server data-based system consists of the following components:

- **The server**—A collection of data items and supporting objects organized and presented to facilitate services, such as searching, sorting, recombining, re-trieving, updating, and analyzing data. The database consists of the physical storage of data and the database services. All data access occurs through the server; the physical data is never accessed directly by the client.
- **The client**—A software program that might be used interactively by a person or that could be an automated process. This includes all software that interacts with the server, either requesting data from or sending data to the database. Examples are management utilities (those that are part of the SQL Server product as well as those bought separately), ad hoc query and reporting soft-ware, custom applications, off-the-shelf applications, and Web server-based applications.
- **The communication between the client and the server**—The communica-tion between the client and the server depends largely on how the client and server are implemented. Both physical and logical layers of communication can be identified.

When you communicate with someone using the telephone, the telephone system is the physical layer and a spoken natural language is the logical layer of communication. For a data-based system, the physical layer can be a network if the server and the client are on different computers. It can be interprocess communication if the server and the client are on the same computer. The logical communication structure of the physical layer may be low-level operating system calls, a proprietary data access language, or the open Structured Query Language (SQL).

All implementations of data-based systems fall into one of three categories:

- **File-based systems**—Commonly found on personal computers, these systems use an application that directly accesses data files on a local hard drive or on a network file server. These systems implement the database services and the logical layer of communication as part of the client application; only the physical layer of communication and the physical storage of data are external to the client application. In this implementation, the client application fulfills both the role of client and the role of server. Figure 1.1 illustrates a file-based system.

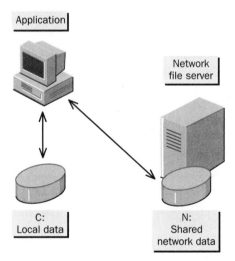

Figure 1.1   A file-based system

- **Host-based systems**—Typically used in legacy mainframe and minicomputer environments, these systems implement all or most of the database services and client functionality on a large central computer. The user views and interacts with the client application remotely, using a terminal. The communication between the client and the database occurs on the host computer, and both the logical layer and the physical layer are implemented in the software and hardware on the host. In this implementation, the host computer fulfills both the role of client and the role of server. Figure 1.2 illustrates a host-based system.

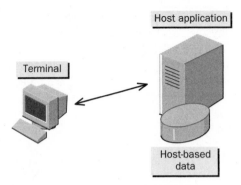

Figure 1.2   A host-based system

- **Client/server systems**—These systems are designed to separate database services from the client, allowing the communication between them to be more flexible and open. Database services are implemented on a powerful computer, permitting centralized management, security, and shared resources. So the *server* in *client/server* is the database and its services. Client applications are implemented on a variety of platforms using a variety of tools, allowing flexibility and high-quality user applications; this is the *client* in *client/server*. The client communicates logically with the database through a database application programming interface (API), and the server performs the physical database access, usually in the file system of the server. Figure 1.3 illustrates the client/server model.

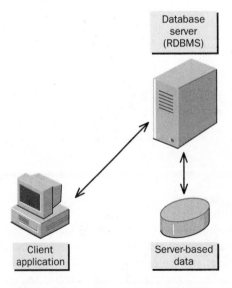

Figure 1.3   A client/server system

The following table compares some of the advantages and disadvantages of file-based, host-based, and client/server systems. Many organizations now use a mix of these systems. For example, data capture may be performed on a host-based system with thousands of terminals. The data may then be queried, manipulated, and analyzed by a client/server system, either directly on the host or after the data has been transferred to another database.

File-based	Host-based	Client/server
Low cost	High initial cost	Variable cost
Low security	High security	Medium to high security
Low reliability	High reliability	Medium to high reliability
Application development possible with few skills	Application development requires skilled staff	Application development requires skilled staff
Well suited to small databases and end-user databases	Not appropriate for small databases or end-user databases	Can be used for small databases; not appropriate for end-user databases
Scalable to medium databases (± 50 MB)	Scalable to very large databases (1000s of GB)	Scalable to very large databases (1000s of GB)
Minimal centralized management	Excellent centralized management	Excellent centralized management
Highly flexible end-user interface	Inflexible end-user interface	Flexible end-user interface
Low-to-medium vendor lock-in	High vendor lock-in	Medium vendor lock-in
Uses network inefficiently	Uses network efficiently	Can use network efficiently

Thousands of commercial data-based systems are available, ranging from those comprising a single application running on a single personal computer to those comprising hundreds of applications running on complex networks of mainframe computers, minicomputers, and personal computers. All have the three basic components listed earlier: a server (the database), a client, and some means of communication between the two. Try to identify these components whenever you encounter a data-based system. In a large system, each component may consist of further layers, but you should always be able to distinguish the three basic components.

Note The key to understanding client/server systems (and specifically SQL Server) is to realize that the database server (SQL Server) is a fully functional process or application that provides database services, as opposed to a file on a network file server, which is a static storage structure only. Clients interact with these database services via a clearly defined communication interface, allowing for tight control and security. Clients do not have direct access to data; they always communicate with the database server, which in turn interacts with the physical data. SQL Server's own management utilities are clients that can run on the same computer or on another computer; they have no more direct access to data than other clients do.

Relational Database Management Systems

A *relational database* is a collection of data organized in two-dimensional tables consisting of named columns and rows. Each table represents the mathematical concept of a *relation* as defined in set theory. In set theory, columns are known as *attributes* and rows are known as *tuples*. The operations that can be performed on tables are similarly based on the manipulation of relations to produce new relations, usually referred to as queries or views.

Relational databases differ from nonrelational databases in that the database user is not aware of system dependencies, if any, stored within the data. No knowledge of the underlying database is required; data can be queried and updated using standard languages (these languages together make up the Structured Query Language, or SQL), which produce a consistent result. SQL Server databases are relational.

A relational database management system (RDBMS) is responsible for

- Storing and making data available in tables
- Maintaining the relationships between tables in the database
- Ensuring the integrity of data by making certain that rules governing the data values and defining the relationships between tables are not violated
- Recovering all data to a point of known consistency in case of a system failure

Transact-SQL

SQL Server uses Transact-SQL, a version of SQL, as its database query and programming language. SQL is a set of commands that allow you to specify the information that you want to retrieve or modify. With Transact-SQL, you can access data and query, update, and manage relational database systems.

The American National Standards Institute (ANSI) and the International Standards Organization (ISO) have defined standards for SQL. Transact-SQL supports the latest ANSI SQL standard published in 1992, called ANSI SQL-92, plus many extensions to provide increased functionality.

SQL Server Platforms

SQL Server runs on the operating systems shown in Figure 1.4. The SQL Server version 7 server software runs only on the Windows 32-bit API-based operating systems, but you can use all of the operating system platforms to create and execute client applications.

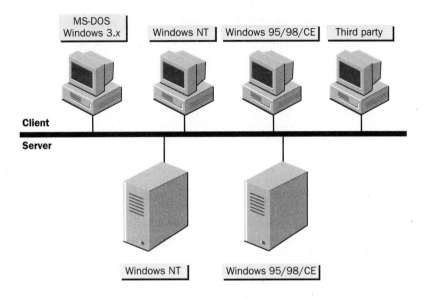

Figure 1.4   Operating systems on which the SQL Server client and server software can run

The following table gives more detail about operating systems and how they do or do not support SQL Server 7.

Platform	Server software	Client software
Microsoft Windows 95 or later	Yes; runs as an application	Yes
Microsoft Windows NT Workstation 4.0 or later	Yes; runs as a service	Yes
Windows NT Server	Yes; runs as a service	Yes
Windows NT Server Enterprise Edition	Yes; runs as a service	Yes
Windows 3.x	No	Yes (only via SQL Server versions 6.0 and 6.5)
MS-DOS	No	Yes (only via SQL Server versions 6.0 and 6.5)
Third party	No	Yes, such as UNIX and Apple Macintosh

SQL Server Integration with Windows NT

SQL Server is tightly integrated with the Windows 32-bit platform. In particular, it is designed to take advantage of the features of the Windows NT operating system for large-scale organization and enterprise databases.

Security

SQL Server is integrated with the security system in Windows NT. This integration allows a user to access both SQL Server and Windows NT with a single username and password. SQL Server provides its own security for non–Microsoft clients.

SQL Server can also use the Windows NT encryption features for network security by using the Multiprotocol Net-Library.

Note SQL Server 7 security is more integrated with Windows NT and more flexible than previous versions. Database permissions can now be assigned directly to Windows NT users. You can also now manage database access and permissions using Windows NT groups.

Multiprocessor Support

SQL Server supports the symmetric multiprocessing (SMP) capabilities of Windows NT. It automatically takes advantage of any additional processors that are added to the server computer.

Microsoft Event Viewer

SQL Server writes messages to the Windows NT application, security, and system event logs, providing a consistent mechanism for viewing and tracking problems.

Windows NT Services

SQL Server runs as a service on Windows NT, allowing you to start and stop SQL Server remotely.

Windows NT Performance Monitor

SQL Server sends performance metrics to the Windows NT Performance Monitor, enabling you to monitor the system performance of SQL Server.

Microsoft Index Server

SQL Server uses Microsoft Index Server; a full-text indexing and search engine supported by various Microsoft BackOffice products.

Microsoft Cluster Server

Microsoft Cluster Server (MSCS), a feature of Microsoft Windows NT Server
Enterprise Edition, supports the connection of two servers, or nodes, into a cluster
for greater availability and better manageability of data and applications. SQL
Server works in conjunction with MSCS to switch automatically to the secondary
node if the primary node fails.

SQL Server Integration with Microsoft BackOffice

SQL Server integrates well with other Microsoft BackOffice products. BackOffice
is a group of server applications that work together to help you build business
solutions, as illustrated in Figure 1.5.

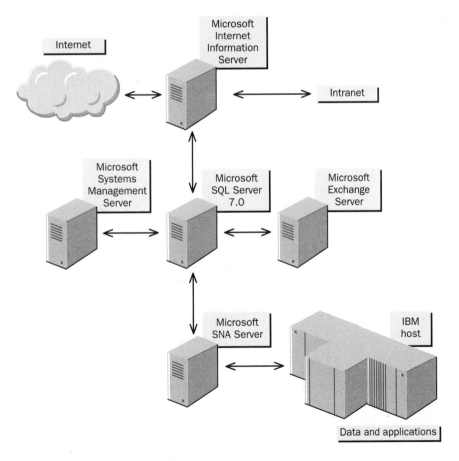

Figure 1.5 Integration of SQL Server with other BackOffice products

The following table describes some commonly used BackOffice applications that work with or use SQL Server.

BackOffice application	Description
Microsoft Internet Information Server (IIS)	Allows Internet browser clients access to data via SQL Server.
Microsoft Exchange Server	SQL Server can send e-mail messages using Microsoft Exchange Server or other Messaging Application Programming Interface (MAPI) compliant providers.
	SQL Server can send messages when an error occurs or when a scheduled task (such as a database backup) succeeds or fails.
Microsoft SNA Server	Links IBM environments running the Systems Network Architecture (SNA) protocol with PC-based networks.
	You can integrate SQL Server with IBM mainframe or AS/400 applications and data using SNA Server.
Microsoft Systems Management Server (SMS)	Manages computer software, hardware, and inventory. SMS requires SQL Server to store its databases.

Lesson Summary

SQL Server is a client/server relational database management system that is highly integrated with the Windows NT operating system. Using SQL Server, you can develop modern applications that separate the client application and the database services. SQL Server Transact-SQL supports the ANSI SQL-92 standard and provides extensions to the SQL language.

Lesson 2: SQL Server Components

SQL Server provides database, client, and communication components:

- The database component of SQL Server is implemented as a group of 32-bit Windows applications or Windows NT services. Tools for installing, configuring, and managing these applications and services are also supplied.

- The client component of SQL Server includes Windows 32-bit-based and command-prompt-based server and database management utilities as well as Transact-SQL query utilities. A number of APIs and object models are supplied to enable custom application development.

- The client-to-database communication for SQL Server is accomplished by two pieces of software: the database interface and a Net-Library. These are installed on the client and are included as part of the server installation. A utility for configuring the installed Net-Library client software is provided.

After this lesson, you will be able to

- Describe the components that make up the SQL Server database services
- Describe the SQL Server client components
- Use the SQL Server Help and Books Online

Estimated lesson time: 45 minutes

SQL Server Services

The SQL Server services are MSSQLServer, SQL Server Agent, and Microsoft Distributed Transaction Coordinator (MS DTC). Figure 1.6 shows these services and the main functions they provide. The Microsoft Search Service is an optional service that can be installed during initial setup, later, or not at all. All SQL Server services run as services on Windows NT or as applications on Windows 32-bit platforms.

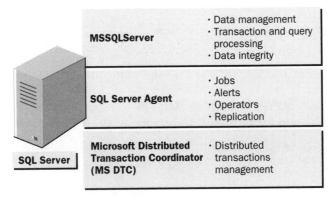

Figure 1.6   The SQL Server services

The MSSQLServer Service

The MSSQLServer service is the RDBMS. It is the component that processes all Transact-SQL statements and manages all files that are part of the databases on the server. All of the other SQL Server services are dependent on the MSSQLServer service, and they exist to extend or complement the functionality of the MSSQLServer service. The MSSQLServer service

- Allocates computer resources among multiple concurrent users
- Prevents logical problems, such as timing requests from users who want to update the same data at the same time
- Enforces data consistency and integrity
- Enforces security

The SQL Server Agent Service

SQL Server Agent is a service that works in conjunction with SQL Server to create and manage local or multiserver jobs, alerts, and operators.

The Microsoft Distributed Transaction Coordinator Service

Microsoft Distributed Transaction Coordinator (MS DTC), also a component of Microsoft Transaction Server, is a transaction manager that allows clients to include several different sources of data in one transaction. MS DTC coordinates the proper completion of distributed transactions to ensure that all updates on all servers are permanent—or, in the case of errors, that all modifications are canceled. This is achieved using a process called two-phased commit. MS DTC is an X/Open XA–compliant transaction manager. (X/Open XA is an open transaction standard.)

The Microsoft Search Service

The Microsoft Search Service provides full-text search capabilities for text column data. This optional service can be installed during the standard SQL Server installation or later.

SQL Server Client Software

SQL Server includes a variety of client software for designing and creating databases, querying data, and administering the server.

SQL Server Enterprise Manager
Snap-in for Microsoft Management Console

SQL Server Enterprise Manager is a server administration and database management client. It is a Microsoft Management Console (MMC) snap-in. MMC is a shared user interface for BackOffice server management. This shared console provides a convenient and consistent environment for administrative tools.

SQL Server Query Analyzer

The SQL Server Query Analyzer is a Transact-SQL query tool used to send individual or batched Transact-SQL statements to SQL Server. It also provides query analysis, statistical information, and the ability to manage multiple queries in different windows simultaneously.

Note SQL Server Query Analyzer replaces ISQL/w found in previous versions of SQL Server.

SQL Server Administrative Tools and Wizards

SQL Server provides a number of administrative tools and wizards that assist with particular aspects of SQL Server. The following table describes these tools and wizards.

Graphical tool	Purpose
SQL Server Client Configuration	Utility used to manage the communication components on SQL Server clients
SQL Server Performance Monitor	Windows NT Performance Monitor settings file; provides a preconfigured view of some of the common SQL Server counters
SQL Server Profiler (previously named SQL Trace)	Utility used to capture a continuous record of server activity and provide auditing capability
SQL Server Service Manager	Graphical utility used for starting, stopping, and pausing SQL Server services
SQL Server Setup	Application used to install and reconfigure SQL Server and SQL Server clients
SQL Server wizards	Collection of tools that guide users through complex tasks
Data Transformation Services	A set of components that allow you to import, export, and transform data between multiple heterogeneous sources, using an OLE DB-based architecture

SQL Server Command-Prompt Management Tools

SQL Server command-prompt management tools allow you to enter Transact-SQL statements and execute script files. The next table describes the most frequently used command-prompt utilities provided with SQL Server. Each file is an executable program.

Utility	Description
osql	Utility that uses Open Database Connectivity (ODBC) to communicate with SQL Server. Primarily used to execute batch files containing one or more SQL statements.
bcp	Batch utility used to export and import data to and from SQL Server and non–SQL Server databases. Copies data to or from a standard text or binary data file.

Note The osql utility replaces the isql utility found in previous versions of SQL Server. The isql utility, which uses DB-Library to communicate with SQL Server, is available for backward compatibility.

SQL Server Help and SQL Server Books Online

SQL Server offers extensive documentation and different types of help to assist you. The following table describes each type of help provided by SQL Server.

Type of help	Description
Application help	Several SQL Server tools—including SQL Server Enterprise Manager, SQL Server Profiler, and SQL Server Query Analyzer—provide context-sensitive help on the application interface.
	Click the Help button, select a command from the Help menu, or (sometimes) press F1 to open application help.
Transact-SQL help	When using SQL Server Query Analyzer, highlight a statement name and press Shift-F1.
SQL Server Books Online	SQL Server Books Online provides online indexed, searchable access to all of the SQL Server documentation.

You can use SQL Server Books Online directly from the Microsoft SQL Server 7 CD-ROM on any Windows 32-bit-based computer without first installing SQL Server. Internet Explorer 4.01 with SP1 or later must be installed on the computer to use SQL Server Books Online. If Internet Explorer 4.01 with SP1 or later is not installed on the computer, you can install it by selecting Install SQL Server 7.0 Prerequisites in the Microsoft SQL Server dialog box when you insert the Microsoft SQL Server 7 CD-ROM.

Practice: Using SQL Server Books Online

In this practice, you will view and search the contents of SQL Server Books Online and familiarize yourself with conventions used in the documentation.

▶ **To view the contents of SQL Server Books Online**

1. Insert the Microsoft SQL Server version 7.0 CD-ROM into the CD-ROM drive, and when the Microsoft SQL Server dialog box appears, click Browse Books Online.

2. In the console tree, review the organization of SQL Server Books Online.

3. On the Contents tab, expand Getting Started.

4. In the details pane, review the listed topics.

5. Click Documentation Conventions and review the contents.

6. In the console tree, click Finding Information On The Internet, and then review the contents in the details pane.

▶ **To use the SQL Server Books Online index**

1. On the Index tab, type **system tables**.

2. Double-click the word Functions in the list of topics, and then view the information in the details pane.

▶ **To search SQL Server Books Online for a word or phrase**

1. On the Search tab, type a few words to find the topic "How to configure a client to use TCP/IP (Client Configuration)."

   You do not have to type all of the words in the phrase to search for the topic. For example, you can type **TCP/IP client** to find the topic.

2. Click List Topics or press Enter to execute the search.

3. Double-click "How to configure a client to use TCP/IP (Client Configuration)" to open the topic.

▶ **To find a word or phrase in a SQL Server Books Online topic**

1. On the Contents tab, expand Getting Started and click "Using the HTML Help Viewer."

2. Click in the details pane to make it the active pane.

3. Press Ctrl-F.

4. In the Find What box, type **operators**.

5. Click Find Next.

6. Notice that the word *operators* is highlighted.

7. Repeat steps 5 and 6 to find each occurrence of the word *operators*.

8. Click Cancel to close the Find dialog box. Close SQL Server Books Online.

Lesson Summary

SQL Server has a number of server components that run as services on Windows NT and as applications on Windows 95 or Windows 98. The server components provide the database services of SQL Server.

SQL Server client components run as applications on Windows 32-bit platforms. The client components are utilities for managing, programming, and analyzing the functionality of SQL Server. Client utilities can be installed on any Windows 32-bit computer on the network to allow remote administration and programming of the SQL Server computer.

Lesson 3: Overview of SQL Server Architecture

SQL Server provides a number of structured architectures that hide underlying technical details, simplifying the development, maintenance, and management of your database applications. This lesson provides an overview of how SQL Server clients communicate with the server, the structure of SQL Server client applications, and the administration model of SQL Server.

After this lesson, you will be able to

- Describe how SQL Server communicates with clients
- Describe the database interfaces available to application developers
- Describe the administrative components of SQL Server
- Describe SQL Server application design

Estimated lesson time: 30 minutes

Communication Architecture

SQL Server uses a layered communication architecture to isolate applications from the underlying network and protocols (see Figure 1.7). This architecture allows you to deploy the same application in different network environments.

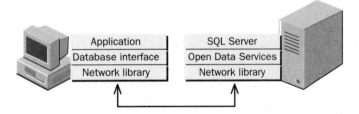

Figure 1.7   The layered communication architecture

The components of the communication architecture include applications, database interfaces, network libraries, and Open Data Services.

Applications

An application is developed using a database application programming interface (API) or object model. The application has no knowledge of the underlying network protocols used to communicate with SQL Server. Examples of client applications include SQL Server Enterprise Manager, SQL Server Query Analyzer, osql, ad hoc query and report writers, Web server-based applications, and business applications.

Database Interfaces

The database interface is used by the application to send requests to SQL Server. It also receives results returned by SQL Server and passes them to the application, sometimes processing the results first. The database interfaces for SQL Server are OLE DB, ODBC, and DB-Library.

Network Libraries

A network library is a communication software component that packages the database requests and results for transmission by the appropriate network protocol. A network library, also known as a Net-Library, must be installed on both the client and the server.

Clients and servers can use more than one Net-Library concurrently, but they must use a common network library in order to communicate successfully. SQL Server has Net-Libraries that support network protocols such as TCP/IP, Named Pipes, Novell IPX/SPX, Banyan VINES/IP, and AppleTalk ADSP.

Some Net-Libraries support only one network protocol; for example, the TCP/IP Sockets Net-Library supports only the TCP/IP network protocol. Other Net-Libraries, such as the Multiprotocol Net-Library, support multiple network protocols. All of the SQL Server database interfaces work on any of the Net-Libraries.

Consider two main criteria when choosing a Net-Library. First, review the capabilities of the Net-Libraries and match them to your needs. For example, the Multiprotocol Net-Library supports encrypting data sent across the network, but it does not support server name enumeration. Second, match the Net-Library to your network infrastructure and client network software.

Open Data Services

Open Data Services functions as the interface between server Net-Libraries and server-based applications. SQL Server itself and extended stored procedure DLLs are examples of server-based applications. This component handles network connections, passing client requests to SQL Server for processing and returning any results and replies to SQL Server clients. Open Data Services automatically listens on all server Net-Libraries that are installed on the server.

Data Access Architecture

Users use SQL Server databases through an application that uses a data object interface or an API to gain access to SQL Server (see Figure 1.8).

SQL Server supports commonly used and emerging database interfaces. It supports low-level native APIs as well as easy-to-use data object interfaces.

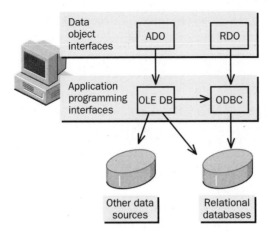

Figure 1.8   The data access architecture

Application Programming Interfaces

A database API defines how to write an application to connect to a database and pass commands to the database. SQL Server provides native support for two main classes of database APIs, which in turn determine the data object interface that you can use. Use the database APIs to have more control over application behavior and performance. Full access to SQL Server 7 is supported by the ODBC and OLE DB database APIs. The DB-Library API used in previous versions of SQL Server provides backward compatibility but does not support the new functionality found in SQL Server 7.

OLE DB

The OLE DB interface is a Component Object Model (COM) based data access interface. It supports applications written to use OLE DB or data object interfaces that use OLE DB. OLE DB is designed to work with relational databases (such as those in SQL Server) as well as with nonrelational data sources (such as a full-text index or an e-mail message store).

OLE DB uses a provider to gain access to a particular data source. Providers for SQL Server, Oracle, Jet (Microsoft Access databases), and ODBC are supplied with SQL Server. Using the OLE DB provider for ODBC, you can use OLE DB to gain access to any ODBC data source.

ODBC

The ODBC interface is a call-level interface. It directly accesses the SQL Server TDS protocol and supports applications or components that are written to use ODBC or data object interfaces that use ODBC. ODBC is designed to work with relational databases (such as those in SQL Server) only, although there are limited ODBC drivers available for some nonrelational data sources.

ODBC uses a driver to gain access to a particular data source.

Data Object Interfaces

In general, data object interfaces are easier to use than database APIs but may not expose as much functionality as an API. ADO (ActiveX Data Objects) is the data object interface for OLE DB, and RDO (Remote Data Objects) is the data object interface for ODBC.

ActiveX Data Objects

ActiveX Data Objects (ADO) encapsulates the OLE DB API in a simplified object model that reduces application development and maintenance costs. It can be used from Microsoft Visual Basic, Visual Basic for Applications, Active Server Pages (ASP), and the Microsoft Internet Explorer scripting object model.

Remote Data Objects

Remote Data Objects (RDO) maps over and encapsulates the ODBC API. It can be used from Microsoft Visual Basic and Visual Basic for Applications.

Administrative Architecture

SQL Server provides a variety of management tools that minimize and automate routine administrative tasks. Figure 1.9 shows how the administrative tools use different interfaces to communicate with SQL Server.

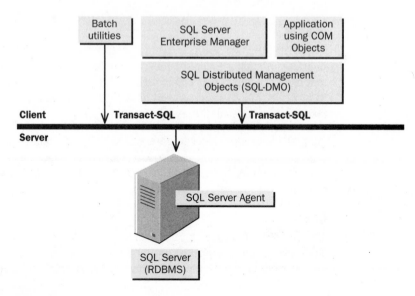

Figure 1.9   The administrative architecture

SQL Server Administration

You can administer SQL Server using

- Batch utilities provided with SQL Server, such as osql and bcp
- Graphical administrative tools provided with SQL Server (SQL Server Enterprise Manager, SQL Server Query Analyzer, and SQL Profiler)
- COM-compatible applications, written in languages such as Visual Basic

All of these tools use Transact-SQL statements to initiate actions on SQL Server. In some cases you will specify the Transact-SQL statements explicitly; in others the tool will generate the Transact-SQL statements for you.

SQL Distributed Management Objects

SQL Distributed Management Objects (SQL-DMO) is a COM-based object model provided by SQL Server. SQL-DMO hides the details of the Transact-SQL statements; it is suitable for writing administrative applications and scripts for SQL Server. The graphical administrative tools provided with SQL Server are written using SQL-DMO. SQL-DMO is not a data interface model; it should not be considered for writing standard database applications.

SQL Server Agent

SQL Server Agent is a service that works in conjunction with SQL Server to enable the following administrative capabilities: alert management, notification, job execution, and replication. Each of these is discussed in the sections that follow.

Alert Management

Alerts provide information about the status of a process, such as when a job is complete or when an error occurs. SQL Server Agent monitors the Windows NT application event log for events, generating alerts based on them.

Notification

SQL Server Agent can send e-mail messages, page an operator, or start another application when an alert occurs. For example, you can set an alert to occur when a database or transaction log is almost full and then have the alert generate a notification to inform someone that the alert has occurred.

Job Execution

SQL Server Agent includes a job creation and scheduling engine. Jobs can be simple, single-step operations, or they can be complex, multistep tasks that require scheduling. You also can create job steps with Transact-SQL, scripting languages, or operating system commands.

Replication Management

Replication is the process of copying data or transactions from one SQL Server to another. SQL Server Agent is responsible for managing this process by synchronizing data between servers, monitoring the data for changes, and replicating the information to other servers.

Application Architecture

Before you design an application for SQL Server, it is important to spend time designing a database to model the business accurately. A well-designed database requires fewer changes and generally performs more efficiently. Planning a database design requires knowledge of the business functions you want to model and the database concepts and features you will use to represent those business functions.

A number of application architectures can be used with SQL Server. The application architecture you select depends on your database design and your business needs and affects how you develop, deploy, and manage your software application. This section presents some of the most common architectural designs and deployment options.

Application Layering

Selecting a layered application approach affords flexibility and a choice of management options. You can divide software applications into three logical layers. Each layer, which can physically reside on one or more servers, provides clearly defined services, as shown in Figure 1.10. The three layers are as follows:

- **Presentation services**—Format and present information to users and provide an interface for data entry.
- **Business services**—Implement business rules by, for example, checking limits, validating data, and providing calculated or summarized data.
- **Data services**—Provide storage, retrieval, security, and integrity for data.

Once these layers have been defined, they can be implemented in various ways, as described in the sections that follow.

Intelligent Server (Two-Tier)

With a two-tiered architecture using an intelligent server, most processing occurs on the server, with presentation services handled on the client. In many instances, most of the business services logic is implemented in the database. This design is useful when clients do not have sufficient resources to process the business logic. However, the server can become a bottleneck because database and business services compete for the same hardware resources. Network use can be inefficient because the client has to send all data to the server for verification, sometimes re-sending the same data many times until it is approved by the server.

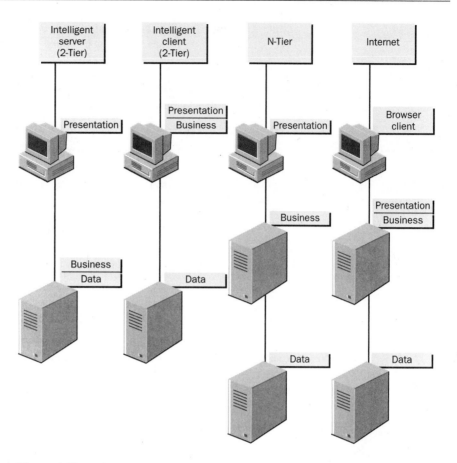

Figure 1.10   A layered application architecture

Corporate applications designed from a database-centric point of view are an example of this design.

Intelligent Client (Two-Tier)

With a two-tiered architecture using an intelligent client, most processing occurs on the client, with data services handled on the server. This design is the traditional client/server environment that is widely used. However, network traffic can be heavy and transactions longer (that is, clients may lock data for lengthy periods), which can in turn affect performance.

Applications developed for small organizations with products such as Microsoft Access are an example of this design.

N-Tier

In an *n*-tier approach, processing is divided among a database server, an application server, and clients. This approach separates logic from data services, and you can easily add more application servers or database servers as needed. However, the potential for complexity increases, and this approach may be slower for small applications.

Multitiered enterprise applications and applications developed with transaction processing monitors are examples of this design.

Internet

In the Internet architecture, processing is divided into three layers, with the business and presentation services residing on the Web server and the clients using simple browsers. Any client that has a browser is supported, and software does not need to be maintained on the client.

A Web site that uses several Web servers to manage connections to clients and a single SQL Server database that services requests for data is an example of this architecture.

Lesson Summary

SQL Server has many components, so it is important to understand how they work together.

Database interfaces provide a consistent interface to database services for programmers developing client applications for SQL Server. The administrative architecture of SQL Server allows administrators to easily create complex maintenance plans for SQL Server databases, including automated job schedules and response to events.

Applications should be designed using a layered architecture that clearly defines where the different services in the application will be implemented.

Lesson 4: Overview of SQL Server Security

SQL Server validates users at two levels: login authentication and permissions validation. Login authentication ensures that the user is a known, valid user of the SQL Server. Permissions validation checks that the user is authorized to use a particular statement or object in a database. This lesson describes these two levels of security.

After this lesson, you will be able to

- Describe login authentication
- Describe permission validation
- Describe SQL Server database users and roles

Estimated lesson time: 30 minutes

Login Authentication

A user must have a login account to connect to SQL Server. SQL Server recognizes two login authentication mechanisms—SQL Server authentication and Windows NT authentication—both of which have a different type of login account (see Figure 1.11).

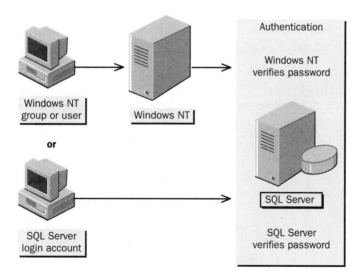

Figure 1.11 Two types of login authentication

SQL Server Authentication

When using SQL Server authentication, a SQL Server system administrator defines a SQL Server login account and password. Users must supply both the SQL Server login and the password when they connect to SQL Server.

Windows NT Authentication

When using Windows NT authentication, a Windows NT user or group account controls user access to SQL Server—a user does not provide a SQL Server login account when connecting. A SQL Server system administrator must grant either the Windows NT user account or the Windows NT group account access to SQL Server.

Authentication Modes

When SQL Server is running on Windows NT, a system administrator can specify that it run in one of two authentication modes: Windows NT Authentication Mode or Mixed Mode.

Note Previous versions of SQL Server supported three authentication modes. In SQL Server 7, Standard Mode is no longer supported.

Windows NT Authentication Mode

When the SQL Server is using Windows NT Authentication Mode, only Windows NT authentication is allowed. Users cannot specify a SQL Server login account. This mode is not supported by a SQL Server installed on Windows 95 or Windows 98.

Mixed Mode

When the SQL Server is using Mixed Mode, users can connect to SQL Server with Windows NT authentication or SQL Server authentication.

Note Clients connecting to a server running in Windows NT Authentication Mode must use a Windows NT–authenticated connection. Clients connecting to a server running in Mixed Mode can choose an authentication mechanism.

Permission Validation

SQL Server accepts Transact-SQL statements after a user's login has been successfully authenticated. Each time a user sends a statement, SQL Server checks that the user has permission to carry out the action requested by the statement. If the user has permission, the action is carried out; if the user does not have permission, an error is returned to the user. Figure 1.12 illustrates this process.

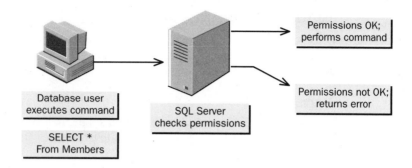

Figure 1.12 Permission validation in SQL Server

Note In most cases, users will be interacting with an application user interface, unaware of the Transact-SQL statements that their actions are generating.

Database User Accounts and Roles

User accounts and roles, which identify a successfully logged-on user within a database, are used to control ownership of objects. Permissions to execute statements and to use objects in a database are granted to users and roles. Each user account is mapped to a SQL Server login (see Figure 1.13).

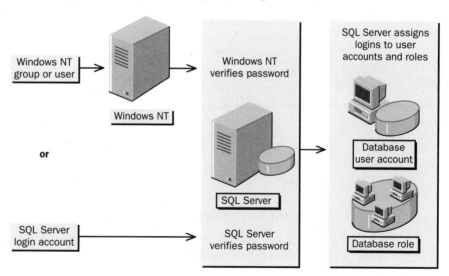

Figure 1.13 Database users and roles

Database User Accounts

The user accounts used to apply security permissions are mapped to Windows NT user or group accounts or to SQL Server login accounts. User accounts are specific to a database and cannot be used in other databases.

Database Roles

Roles enable you to assemble users into a single unit to which you can apply permissions. Both server-level and database-level roles exist. A user can be made a member of more than one role.

SQL Server provides predefined server and database roles for common administrative functions, so that you can easily assign a selection of administrative permissions to a particular user simply by making the user a member of the appropriate roles. You can also create your own user-defined database roles.

Note Roles replace the SQL Server version 6.5 concepts of aliases and groups.

Fixed Server Roles

Fixed server roles provide groupings of administrative privileges at the server level. They are managed independently of databases. Examples of fixed server roles are roles for system administrators, database creators, and security administrators.

Fixed Database Roles

Fixed database roles provide groupings of administrative privileges at the database level. Examples of fixed database roles are roles for backing up and restoring a database, for security administrators, for reading data, and for modifying data.

User-Defined Roles

You also can create your own database roles to represent work performed by a group of employees in your organization. You do not have to grant, revoke, or deny permissions for each person. If the function of a role changes, you can easily change the permissions for the role, and the changes apply automatically to all members of the role.

Lesson Summary

SQL Server accepts connections from users that it can authenticate or those that have already been authenticated by Windows NT. After user logins are authenticated, they are mapped to user accounts and roles in one or more databases. A login must be mapped to a user account in a database in order to use that database. A login cannot be mapped to more than one user in a database but can be a member of many roles. Permissions are granted to user accounts and roles in each database.

Review

The following questions are intended to reinforce key information presented in the chapter. If you are unable to answer a question, review the appropriate lesson and then try the question again. Answers to the questions can be found in Appendix A, "Questions and Answers."

1. You have an existing application that uses SQL Server and Windows 95 and Windows NT Workstation client computers. Another department that uses a Novell network wants access to the database. Is this possible?

2. You want to develop a SQL Server application using ADO or OLE DB. What are some of the factors to consider?

C H A P T E R 2

Installation

About This Chapter

Before installing Microsoft SQL Server 7, you should make sure that you are aware of the hardware and software requirements of the program. During installation, you will be prompted for specific information and will need to make decisions based on the options provided. Finally, you need to test your new installation to be sure that the setup has completed correctly. This chapter will lead you through these phases to help you successfully install SQL Server 7.

Before You Begin

To complete the lessons in this chapter you must have

- Microsoft Windows NT Server version 4.0 with SP4 or later running on your computer. (The computer must be configured as the Primary Domain Controller of the STUDYSQL domain. If this is not the case, you will have to make allowance for your configuration when performing the exercises in the chapters of this training kit.)

- At least 180 MB of unused hard disk space available on your computer.

Lesson 1: Preparing to Install SQL Server

Knowing the hardware and software installation requirements before you install SQL Server enables you to select the appropriate platform on which to install it.

The Setup program presents several installation options. Identifying the appropriate settings for these options ensures that your system is configured to meet your needs.

After this lesson, you will be able to

- Determine hardware and software requirements for SQL Server version 7 and the SQL Server management tools
- Determine the SQL Server installation options that are appropriate for your system

Estimated lesson time: 60 minutes

Hardware and Software Requirements

The following table describes the hardware and software requirements for a SQL Server installation. For more information about supported hardware, see the Microsoft Windows NT Hardware Compatibility List (HCL) at http://www.microsoft.com/isapi/hwtest/hcl.idc.

Component	Requirements
Computer	Intel and compatible systems. DEC Alpha and compatible systems.
Memory	A minimum of 32 MB—additional memory is recommended for large databases and replication.
Hard disk space	An installation of a new server only, with no management tools, requires 65 MB. A Typical installation requires 170 MB, and a full installation requires 180 MB. An installation of only management tools requires 90 MB.
File system	NTFS or FAT—NTFS is recommended for server installation because of the security and recovery advantages that this file system offers.
Operating system	Windows NT Server 4 or Windows NT Workstation 4 with Service Pack 4, or a later service pack, Microsoft Windows 95, or Windows 98.
Other software	All operating systems require Microsoft Internet Explorer 4.01 with SP1 or later.

Note You must install Microsoft Internet Explorer 4.01 with SP1 or later in order to use SQL Server Enterprise Manager.

Caution In general, if the hard disk of the computer has a write-caching disk controller, disable it. Unless a write-caching disk controller is designed specifically for a database, it can seriously threaten SQL Server data integrity.

SQL Server Installation Options

When installing SQL Server 7, the following options are available. Many of these options are bypassed if you perform a Typical installation, but you can set all of them if you perform a Custom installation.

Licensing Mode

During installation, the Setup program requires you to select a licensing mode and then to accept the terms of the license agreement. You have a choice of two licensing modes—Per Server and Per Seat:

- With *Per Server licensing,* the Client Access Licenses are assigned to a particular server. The maximum number of simultaneous workstation connections that are allowed must equal the number of Client Access Licenses that are assigned to that server.

- With *Per Seat licensing,* a Client Access License is assigned to a particular workstation. Each workstation that connects to SQL Server with either Microsoft-provided client software or third-party software requires a Client Access License. This mode allows an unlimited number of simultaneous workstation connections to multiple servers, without requiring the client to purchase additional licenses for each server.

If you are unsure of which licensing mode to choose, select the Per Server option. The licensing agreement provides a one-time, one-way option to change from Per Server licensing mode to Per Seat licensing mode. For example, if you begin with one server, 30 users, and 30 Client Access Licenses and later install a second server, you can configure the second server with Per Server licensing (and then purchase 30 additional Client Access Licenses). Or you can convert the first server to Per Seat and configure the second server as Per Seat (and purchase no additional Client Access Licenses).

In order for SQL Server 7 Desktop Edition to connect to SQL Server 7 Standard Edition to perform replication or use Data Transformation Services, SQL Server 7 Standard Edition must be installed with Per Seat licensing.

Note Workstation connections and user connections are not the same. A workstation can run several different clients, each using multiple user connections, with one Client Access License.

Installation Path

You can install SQL Server on any local hard drive and in any folder.

Default Installation Path

The default installation path for the program files and data files is C:\Mssql7

Note Some SQL commands (such as BACKUP DATABASE TO DISK...) cannot recognize embedded spaces in folder names. For this reason, use "8.3" style folder names to ensure compatibility.

You can either accept the default installation path for SQL Server or specify another drive or folder for the program files, the data files, or both. The Setup program also installs files in the system folder, the location of which cannot be changed.

Caution Make sure that you have sufficient disk space available on the drive that you specify. If you change the program or data file locations, do not include a space in the name of the new folder. Also note that a Typical installation requires approximately 72 MB of space on the system drive, regardless of the location of the program or data files.

Program Files

The program files folder is the root folder where the Setup program creates folders that contain all of the program files. Program files include the relational database engine, core tools (such as the osql and bcp utilities), upgrade tools, replication objects, and the Microsoft full-text search engine. The size of these files will not increase over time.

Data Files

The data files folder is the root folder in which folders for databases, transaction log files, system log, backup files, and replication data files are created. The Setup program creates database and transaction log files for the master, model, msdb, pubs, Northwind, and tempdb databases in this location. You can specify other locations for data files that are created after installation. These files should be located on a drive that has a sufficient amount of extra space because, unlike program files, data files increase in size over time.

Character Set

During installation, you choose the code page containing the character set that supports the language you use. A code page stores the codes that map to the character set you choose. You choose one character set for all databases on a server. A *character set* is a set of 256 uppercase and lowercase letters, digits, and symbols that SQL Server recognizes in your databases. The first 128 values are the same for all character set choices. The last 128 characters (sometimes called extended characters) differ from set to set and contain language-specific letters and symbols.

Default Character Set

The Setup program selects code page 1252 (ISO Character Set) as the default character set. Every database attached to a specific SQL Server uses the same code page. The following table describes frequently selected character sets.

Character set	Description
Code page 1252 (ISO 8859-1, Latin 1, or ANSI)	This is the default character set. It is compatible with the ANSI characters used by the Windows NT and Windows operating systems. Use this character set if you intend to use Windows NT- and Windows–based clients exclusively or if you must maintain exact compatibility with a SQL Server environment for UNIX or VMS.
Code page 850 (multilingual)	This is a multilingual character set that includes all of the characters used by most languages of European, North American, and South American countries. This character set is a good choice for use in international companies or for use with MS-DOS–based clients that use extended characters.
Code page 437 (U.S. English)	This is the most commonly used character set in the United States, and it includes many characters for graphics that are not usually stored in databases. Unless you have a specific reason to select this character set, choose code page 1252, which provides more compatibility with languages other than U.S. English.

Selecting a Character Set

The code page that you select for SQL Server does not have to match the code page that the Windows NT operating system uses. However, if the data in a server running SQL Server contains extended characters, you must carefully determine the code pages that are used in the database and on the clients. If SQL Server and a client use different code pages and a client also uses extended characters, the potential for translation conflicts exists.

SQL Server recognizes only one character set at a time. When you select a character set, consider the following facts and guidelines:

- Choose a code page that includes the language characters of your database.

- If you want to store data written in multiple languages on the same server, choose the default character set and use Unicode data types when you build your databases.

When you use SQL Server Unicode data types, a column can store any character that the Unicode standard defines, which includes all of the characters that are defined in the various character sets. Unicode data types can support 65,536 different uppercase and lowercase letters, digits, and symbols.

- Use the same character set on both the client and the server unless your databases use only the first 128 characters of a character set.

Caution To change the character set after you have installed SQL Server, you must rebuild all databases.

Sort Order

A *sort order* determines how character data is compared, in what sequence character data is returned from a query, and what characters are considered equal when they are compared. The selection of available sort orders depends on the character set that you choose.

Note Sort order applies only to non-Unicode data. The next topic discusses Unicode collation.

Selecting a Sort Order

The Setup program selects dictionary sort order, case-insensitive as the default. Most users choose the default sort order because selecting a nondefault sort order may affect query result sets, the performance, and the development of clients, as illustrated in the following examples.

- **Effects on query result sets**—If, for example, you choose a case-sensitive sort order and a user performs a query in which lastname='MacDonald', the result set includes only those names that match the case, whereas if you choose a case-insensitive sort order, the result set includes all variations of MacDonald, including Macdonald and macdonald.

- **Effects on performance**—Choosing a sort order that is case-insensitive can improve performance because uppercase and lowercase characters of the same kind do not have to be compared and sorted beyond alphabetization. For example, an uppercase letter *A* is treated the same as a lowercase letter *a*.

- **Effects on development of clients**—Choosing a case-sensitive sort order requires the client to convert characters to the proper case and to reference objects by using the proper case.

You cannot have databases with different sort orders on the same server, and you cannot back up and restore databases among servers that are configured for different sort orders. If you are considering having several SQL Server installations, each with different character sets and sort orders, and you intend to move data among these servers, first consider the consequences. For example, results may sort differently, result sets may differ, and characters may be lost.

Note If you change the sort order after you install SQL Server, you must rebuild all databases. Run sp_helpsort to verify the current sort order.

Unicode Collation

SQL Server 7 supports Unicode and non-Unicode data types for columns in database tables. A Unicode collation acts as a sort order for Unicode data. This is separate from the sort order for non-Unicode data.

A *Unicode collation* consists of one locale and several comparison styles. Locales, usually named after countries or cultural regions, sort characters following the standard in that area. The Unicode collation still provides a sort order for all characters in the Unicode standard, but it gives precedence to the specified locale.

Default Unicode Collation

The Setup program selects general, case-insensitive, width-insensitive, and Kana-insensitive as the default set of options. This default set is based on the character set and sort order that you choose.

Selecting a Unicode Collation

Selecting the same sort order for Unicode and non-Unicode data is generally recommended. You can choose a collation other than the default, but exercise this option with caution. When you choose a different value, migrating data from non-Unicode to Unicode is more difficult, and Unicode and non-Unicode data may sort differently.

Note If you change the Unicode collation after you install SQL Server, you must rebuild all databases.

Network Support

SQL Server uses network libraries to communicate with a specific network protocol and to pass network packets between a client and SQL Server. The server simultaneously listens on multiple network libraries; a client communicates with the server by using a specific network library. This allows different types of clients to use the same server.

Note Selecting the appropriate network support for SQL Server requires a thorough understanding of your Windows NT network topography.

Default Network Libraries

The Setup program selects the Named Pipes, TCP/IP Sockets, and Multiprotocol network libraries as the default for SQL Server when installed on Windows NT. The TCP/IP Sockets and Multiprotocol network libraries are selected as the default for SQL Server when installed on Windows 95 or Windows 98 because these operating systems do not support Named Pipes. The Setup program makes Named Pipes on Windows NT and TCP/IP Sockets on Windows 95 and Windows 98 the default network library for client management tools. The client network library must match one of the network libraries on the SQL Server.

Selecting a Network Library

When you select a network library, consider the following facts:

- Your choice of network libraries requires that the appropriate network protocols be installed on your Windows NT, Windows 95, or Windows 98 computer.
- Windows NT authentication requires either the Named Pipes or the Multiprotocol network library.
- Windows NT encryption requires the Multiprotocol network library.

The following table describes the network libraries supported by SQL Server.

Network library	Description
Named Pipes	Installed by default—allows clients to connect with named pipes over any Microsoft-supplied transport protocol. Not supported by Windows 95 or Windows 98.
TCP/IP Sockets	Installed by default—allows clients to communicate by using standard Windows Sockets across TCP/IP.
Multiprotocol	Installed by default— takes advantage of the Windows NT remote procedure call (RPC) facility. Communicates over Named Pipes, TCP/IP Sockets, NWLink IPX/SPX, and other IPC mechanisms.
NWLink IPX/SPX	Allows Novell SPX clients to connect to SQL Server by using native Novell IPX/SPX.
AppleTalk ADSP	Allows Apple Macintosh–based clients to connect to SQL Server by using native AppleTalk (as opposed to TCP/IP).
Banyan VINES	Supports Banyan VINES Sequenced Packet Protocol (SPP) as the IPC method across the Banyan VINES IP network protocol.

Note To change a network library to SQL Server after installation, use the SQL Server Network Utility.

SQL Server Services Account

Each SQL Server service runs in the security context of an assigned service account. The assigned service account can be a domain user account or the local System account.

The Default SQL Server Services Account

The Setup program selects a domain user account as the default. In general, use the same service account for all SQL Server services.

Using a Domain User Account

If you use a domain user account, the SQL Server services can communicate with remote servers by using trusted connections.

When you select a domain user account, the Setup program grants the right to the domain user to log on as a service on the SQL Server computer.

When you use a domain user account, consider the following facts and guidelines:

- The domain user account that you select must be a member of the Administrators local group on the SQL Server computer.

- Replicating data or multiserver administrative activities assumes that a domain user account is the security context for the SQL Server services.

- If you use SQL Server to send notifications through e-mail, you must use a domain user account.

- If multiple Microsoft BackOffice products, such as Microsoft Exchange Server and SQL Server, are installed on a single computer and the services must communicate with one another, you must use a Windows NT domain user account.

- Use a dedicated domain user account for the SQL Server services account, de-select User Must Change Password At Next Logon, select the Password Never Expires attribute, and allow all logon hours.

- SQL Server often is installed in environments that are composed of one or more Windows NT domains. In these environments, install SQL Server in a domain that has access to all user accounts for all domains.

- Installing SQL Server on a either a Primary Domain Controller (PDC) or Backup Domain Controller (BDC) is generally not recommended, because these computers perform the resource-intensive tasks of maintaining and replicating the network accounts database and performing network logon authentication.

Note If you change the service account after installation, use SQL Server Enterprise Manager to set the service account because it sets the required rights automatically.

Using the Local System Account

The local System account is a built-in account that has the same authority as the Windows NT operating system, but only for local resources. If you choose the local System account, SQL Server services cannot communicate with remote servers using a trusted connection. If you install SQL Server on a computer running Windows NT that is not part of a domain, you can use the local System account. This is not generally recommended; however, it means that you do not need to create a Windows NT account for SQL Server services.

Autostart Services

By default, the Setup program installs the MSSQLServer service (the database engine) to run as an automatically started Windows NT service. The benefit of having this service start automatically is that a system administrator does not have to log on to start it each time Windows NT starts. If you want, you can have the other SQL Server–related services (SQL Server Agent, Microsoft Distributed Transaction Coordinator, and Full Text Search) start automatically too.

Exercise: Granting Administrator Rights to User Accounts

In this exercise, you will log on to your local computer with the local administrator account and add the SQLService domain user account to the Administrators local group. The SQLService domain user account will be used for the SQL Server services account.

Adding the SQLService domain user account to the Administrators local group gives the SQLService domain user account administrator rights on the local computer. This is required in order to install SQL Server on the local computer with the SQLService domain user account for the SQL Server services account.

▶ **To grant local administrator rights to the SQLService domain user account**

1. Log on to your local computer as Administrator or by using another account that is a member of the local Administrators group.

2. Start User Manager for Domains.

3. Add a new user named SQLService.

4. Set the new user password to **password**.

5. Ensure that the User Cannot Change Password and Password Never Expires check boxes are checked and that the User Must Change Password At Next Logon and Account Disabled check boxes are not checked.

6. Click the Groups button.

7. Add SQLService to the Administrators local group. (Administrators must appear in the Member Of list box.) If your computer is part of a Windows NT domain, also add SQLService to the Domain Admins global group.

8. Click OK to close the Group Memberships dialog box, and then click Add to add the SQL Service user. Click Close to close the New User dialog box.

Lesson Summary

Familiarize yourself with the hardware and software requirements of SQL Server 7 before you begin installation. The following options are configured during installation: licensing mode, file locations, character set, sort order, Unicode collation, network support, and SQL Server services accounts.

Lesson 2: Running SQL Server Setup and Testing the Installation

The Setup program runs from the SQL Server CD-ROM or from a shared network folder. Before you can install SQL Server or any component, you must log on to the computer on which you plan to install SQL Server, using an account that is a member of the Administrators local group.

After this lesson, you will be able to

- Identify different types of SQL Server installation
- Install SQL Server and SQL Server management tools using the SQL Server Setup program
- Test the installation of SQL Server

Estimated lesson time: 90 minutes

Types of SQL Server Installation

SQL Server supports three installation types to accommodate different levels of users and different default installation configurations. The following table describes the types of installations offered by the SQL Server Setup program.

Installation type	Description
Typical	Installs SQL Server with default installation options and includes SQL Server management tools and online documentation. A Typical installation does not include full-text search, development tools, and code samples. You can choose the SQL Server services account for all SQL Server services and the destination folder for program and data files.
Compact	Installs SQL Server with default installation options, but without any management tools. You can choose the SQL Server services account for all SQL Server services and the destination folder for program and data files.
Custom	Installs any or all components and presents all server installation options. You can choose components and server installation options. You also can choose the SQL Server services account for all SQL Server services and the destination folder for program and data files.
	Select a Custom installation to install management tools only. This allows you to manage SQL Server from another computer on a network.

The Setup program selects a Typical installation as the default. If you want to change any installation defaults, perform a Custom installation. You can install the management utilities on other computers on your network to make it possible to manage SQL Server without going to the SQL Server computer. To install the management utilities only, perform a Custom installation.

Exercise: Installing SQL Server

In this exercise, you will run the Setup program and install SQL Server and all management tools on your local computer.

▶ **To install SQL Server**

1. Log on to your Windows NT computer as Administrator or another user that is a member of the local Administrators group.

2. Insert the SQL Server version 7 CD-ROM. When the Microsoft SQL Server dialog box appears, click Install SQL Server 7.0 Components.

3. Click Database Server – Standard Edition.

4. Use the information in the following table to complete the installation.

Option	Value
Install method	Local Install - Install to the Local Machine
Name	Your name
Company	Your company name
Serial	Serial number of your copy of SQL Server
Setup type	Custom
Program files	C:\Mssql7
Data files	C:\Mssql7
Components and subcomponents	Accept all defaults
Character set	ISO character set
Sort order	Dictionary order, case-insensitive
Unicode collation	General Unicode, Case-insensitive, Width-insensitive, Kana-insensitive
Network libraries	Named Pipes TCP/IP Sockets Multiprotocol
SQL Server service account	Same account for all services and auto start SQL Server service
Service settings	Domain user account
User name	SQLService
Password	Type **password** (all lowercase)
Domain	STUDYSQL
Licensing mode	Per Server
Number of licenses	50

5. If prompted with the Convert Existing SQL Server Data dialog box, do not select the Yes, Run The SQL Server Upgrade Wizard check box. You can use this wizard after the install if you have data to convert. We will discuss how to upgrade in Chapter 3, "Upgrading to SQL Server 7.0."

Note If you need to install either the program files or the data files in a different location than those suggested below, remember to substitute the locations you selected in subsequent exercises. Even if you install these files in a different location and substitute the correct location for those suggested offered within this book, some of the exercises within this book will not work.

Testing the Installation

Testing to verify proper SQL Server installation involves reviewing the installation results, starting the SQL Server services, and connecting to SQL Server.

Reviewing Installation Results

After you run the Setup program and install SQL Server, it is important to understand what has been installed. The following table summarizes what is typically installed by the SQL Server Setup program. The exact list of what is installed depends on the options selected during installation.

Installed components	Description
SQL Server Services	MSSQLServer SQLServerAgent MS DTC (Microsoft Distributed Transaction Coordinator) Microsoft Search
Management tools	Group of tools used to administer SQL Server.
Databases	master, model, msdb, pubs, Northwind, tempdb
Folders and files	Relational database engine and all tools in C:\Mssql7\Binn, databases in C:\Mssql7\Data, various other files and folders in C:\Mssql7.
Default startup options	A set of default startup options that are written to the Windows NT registry.
Default security mode	Mixed—allows users to connect with Windows NT authentication or SQL Server authentication.
SQL Server sa login account	A built-in SQL Server administrator login account without a password.
SqlAgentCmdExec account	A local Windows NT user account that xp_cmdshell can use when nonadministrators execute commands via xp_cmdshell. By default, the SQL Server Agent service uses this account to execute specific types of jobs that are executed by nonadministrators.

Starting SQL Server Services

After you run the Setup program, you must start the MSSQLServer service to use SQL Server.

Automatically Starting SQL Server

If, during the installation process, you configure SQL Server to start automatically, SQL Server starts each time Windows NT starts.

If you want the SQL Server services to start automatically but you did not choose the Autostart option during installation, you can configure the services to start automatically by using SQL Server Enterprise Manager or Services in Control Panel. Figure 2.1 shows the dialog box you use in SQL Server Enterprise Manager to set the Autostart options.

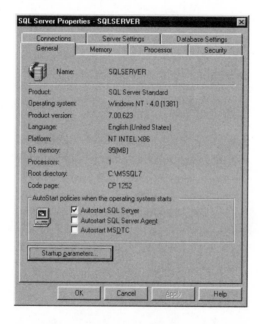

Figure 2.1   The SQL Server Properties dialog box Autostart options

Exercise: Starting the SQL Server Service and the SQL Server Agent Service

In this exercise, you will use the SQL Server Service Manager to test and verify that the MSSQLServer and the SQLServerAgent services are started.

▶ **To verify that the SQL Server service has started and to start the SQL Server Agent service**

1. On the taskbar, double-click the SQL Server Service Manager icon.
2. Verify that the MSSQLServer service is running.

3. Select SQLServerAgent in the Services list box. Click the Start/Continue button to start the SQLServerAgent service.

   Notice that the icon on the taskbar changes when the service starts.

4. Select MSSQLServer in the Services list box.

5. Close SQL Server Service Manager.

   Notice that the SQL Server Service Manager icon remains on the taskbar.

Manually Starting, Pausing, and Stopping a Service

You can start, pause, and stop the SQL Server services manually by using

- SQL Server Service Manager
- SQL Server Enterprise Manager
- Services in Control Panel
- A net command at the command prompt, such as net start mssqlserver, net pause mssqlserver, or net stop SQLServerAgent

Because SQL Server is integrated with Windows NT, you can start, pause, and stop a SQL Server service locally or remotely. Starting, pausing, and stopping SQL Server services have the following effects on SQL Server:

- Starting the MSSQLServer service allows users to establish new connections. You can automate activities and activate alerts after you start the SQLServerAgent service.

- Pausing the MSSQLServer service prevents new connections. Users who are already connected are unaffected. You may want to pause the MSSQLServer service in preparation for server maintenance. Pausing prevents new users from logging on. It also allows enough time for you to send a message that asks current users to log off. Pausing the SQLServerAgent service prevents automatic activities and alerts from occurring.

- Stopping the MSSQLServer service prevents new connections and disconnects current users. Stopping the SQLServerAgent service prevents automatic activities and alerts from occurring.

Note It is recommended that you do not stop the SQL Server service using Services in Control Panel or the net stop command. These methods do not perform checkpoints in each database prior to shutdown, and therefore, using them may increase recovery time the next time that the SQL Server service is started.

Overriding the Default Startup Options

The MSSQLServer service starts with a number of default startup options. You can change these default startup options, or you can start SQL Server using non-default startup options.

To change the default startup options, click the Startup Parameters button on the General tab of the SQL Server Properties dialog box in SQL Server Enterprise Manager. A dialog box appears that allows you to add and remove the startup parameters, as shown in Figure 2.2.

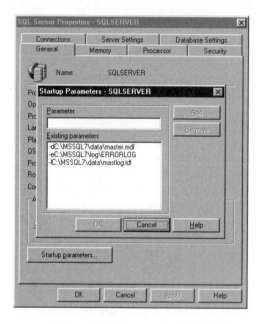

Figure 2.2   The Startup Parameters dialog box

Start SQL Server from the command prompt or from Services in Control Panel to use nondefault startup options.

For example, you may want to start SQL Server in single-user or minimal configuration mode as follows:

- To change server configuration options or recover a damaged database, use single-user mode. To use single-user mode, type sqlservr –m at the command prompt.

- To correct configuration problems that prevent a server from starting, use minimal configuration mode. To use minimal configuration mode, type **sqlservr –f** at the command prompt.

Connecting to SQL Server

Connecting to SQL Server is the final test to verify the SQL Server installation. You can connect to SQL Server using one of the SQL Server graphical administration tools or a command prompt utility.

When you connect to SQL Server, you must use your Windows NT user account or a SQL Server login account. The first time you connect to SQL Server, you must use a Windows NT administrator account or use the SQL Server sa login account. If you connect to SQL Server successfully, you can then configure and use SQL Server.

Practice: Using a Graphical Utility to Connect to SQL Server

To connect to SQL Server, you should use one of the following graphical utilities:

- SQL Server Query Analyzer
- SQL Server Enterprise Manager

Exercise 1: Connecting to a Local SQL Server and Executing a Query

In this exercise, you will use SQL Server Query Analyzer to connect to your SQL Server and execute a query to verify the version of your installation.

▶ **To connect to your local SQL Server and execute a query**

1. Log on to your computer as Administrator or using an account that is a member of the local Administrators group.

2. On the taskbar, click the Start button, point to Programs, point to Microsoft SQL Server 7.0, and then click Query Analyzer.

3. Log on to your SQL Server—for SQL Server, type **SQLServer** (or the computer name of your Windows NT computer if it is not SQLServer). For Connection Information, select Use Windows NT authentication.

    Your account is a member of the Windows NT Administrators local group, which is automatically mapped to the SQL Server sysadmin role.

4. Verify that your database is master. To do this, make sure that master is selected in the DB list box.

5. Type and execute the following query:

    ```
    SELECT @@VERSION
    ```

    @@VERSION is a global system variable that returns current product version information.

    The results pane displays the installed version of SQL Server.

Exercise 2: Verifying Installed Databases

In this exercise, you will execute a query to verify the installed databases.

▶ **To verify the installed databases**

1. Type and execute the following query:

```
SELECT * FROM sysdatabases
```

The results pane displays the names and other information about the installed databases, which include master, model, msdb, Northwind, pubs, and tempdb.

2. On the Query menu, click Results in Grid.

Note that the information is displayed in a grid, which is easier to read than the simple text output.

Exercise 3: Verifying Installed Files

In this exercise, you will verify the installed files.

▶ **To verify the installed files**

1. Open Windows NT Explorer and expand the C:\Mssql7 folder.

2. Open each subfolder and review the installed files.

Note the files in the C:\Mssql7\Binn, C:\Mssql7\Log, and C:\Mssql7\Data folders.

Exercise 4: Using the osql Command-Prompt Utility

The osql utility uses Open Database Connectivity (ODBC) to communicate with SQL Server.

Note In SQL Server 7, osql replaces the SQL Server 6.5 utility called isql. The isql utility, which uses DB-Library to communicate with SQL Server, is still available. DB-Library remains at the SQL Server version 6.5 level of functionality. DB-Library applications such as isql do not support some SQL Server 7 features. For example, they cannot retrieve Unicode ntext data. The osql utility has a user interface modeled on isql and supports the full set of SQL Server 7 features.

▶ **To connect to SQL Server using a command-prompt utility**

1. At a command prompt, type and execute the following command. This command connects to the SQL Server called SQLServer using a trusted connection.

```
osql -E -SSQLServer
```

Note The osql utility and its predecessor, isql, use case-sensitive command-line arguments. For example, the switches –q and –Q have slightly different effects. For a complete list of switches, execute osql -?.

---

2. At the prompt, type the following statements, pressing Enter after each line.

```
SELECT CONVERT(varchar(30), name) FROM sysdatabases
GO
```

You should see a list of databases similar to the one you saw when using SQL Server Query Analyzer, as shown in Figure 2.3.

3. At the prompt, type the following command and press Enter to quit osql.

```
QUIT
```

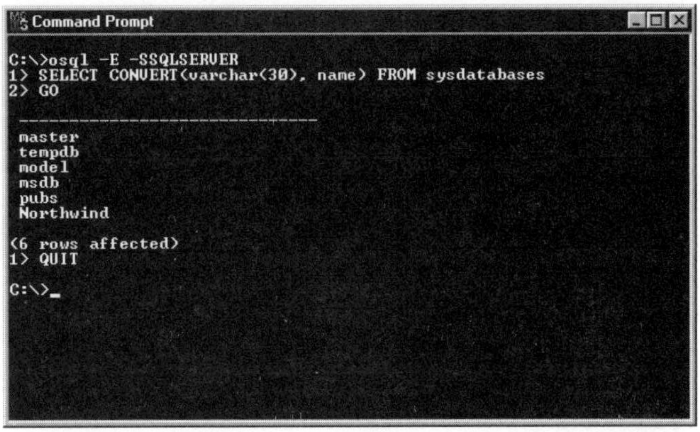

Figure 2.3   Using the osql utility to display a list of databases

Lesson Summary

Three types of installation are available: Typical, Compact, and Custom. The installation types make it possible for users with varying experience to install all or some of the components of SQL Server. After installing SQL Server 7, test the installation by starting and connecting to the server.

Lesson 3: Performing an Unattended Installation

There are three methods for running an unattended installation of SQL Server 7:

- Use the sample unattended installation files included on the CD-ROM
- Generate or create your own custom unattended installation file
- Use Microsoft Systems Management Server (SMS)

After this lesson, you will be able to

- Describe the unattended installation options for SQL Server 7

Estimated lesson time: 30 minutes

Using the Sample Unattended Installation Files

The simplest way to run an unattended setup is to use the batch files and setup initialization scripts provided in the root folder on the SQL Server CD-ROM. To use one of these installations, execute the batch file, which will launch SQL Server Setup using the associated setup initialization script. The following table describes these files.

Batch file	Setup initialization script	Result
Sql70cli.bat	sql70cli.iss	Installs the SQL Server management tools
Sql70ins.bat	sql70ins.iss	Installs a Typical installation of SQL Server, Standard Edition
Sql70cst.bat	sql70cst.iss	Installs a Custom installation of SQL Server, Standard Edition
Deskeins.bat	deskeins.iss	Installs a Typical installation of SQL Server, Desktop Edition
Deskecst.bat	deskecst.iss	Installs a Custom installation of SQL Server, Desktop Edition
Sql70rem.bat		Removes SQL Server

Generating or Creating a Custom Setup Initialization Script File

You can create a setup initialization script file using two methods: running SQL Server Setup interactively or using a text editor to manually create a setup initialization file.

Running SQL Server Setup Interactively

SQL Server Setup can generate an .ISS file without actually installing SQL Server. In the \x86\Setup or \Alpha\Setup directory on the SQL Server CD-ROM, run this program from the command prompt:

```
setupsql.exe k=Rc
```

Running Setupsql.exe with the k=Rc option causes SQL Server Setup to write the Setup.iss file to the \Windows or \WinNT directory while you select setup options, rather than waiting until after the files are copied. When the Setup program prompts you that it is ready to begin copying files, click Cancel to exit without installing SQL Server. When you exit without actually installing SQL Server, the Setup.iss file created with the k=Rc option is incomplete. You must add the [SdStartCopy-0] and [SdFinish-0] sections detailed in SQL Server Books Online.

Using a Text Editor to Manually Create a Setup Initialization File

If you create a setup initialization file manually, the file should be saved with the .ISS filename and be compatible with the Windows initialization file format. See "Creating a Setup Initialization File" in SQL Server Books Online for a complete list of the entries required and their meanings.

Invoking Setup

Once the .ISS file is created, the Setup program is invoked with the following arguments:

- The **-f1** *<initialization_file_path>* argument selects an unattended setup initialization file.
- The -s flag causes the Setup program to run in silent mode with no user interface.

The following syntax is an example of invoking a Setup.

```
start /wait setupsql.exe -f1 C:\ SQL7.iss -SMS -s
```

The start /wait command, together with the -SMS option, returns control to the command prompt only after SQL Server Setup finishes.

Using Microsoft Systems Management Server

You can use Microsoft Systems Management Server (SMS) version 1.2 or later to install Microsoft SQL Server automatically on multiple server computers running Windows NT in your enterprise.

The SQL Server CD-ROM contains a Package Definition Format (PDF) file, Smssql70.pdf, that automates creating a SQL Server package in SMS. The SQL Server package can then be distributed and installed on SMS computers.

Smssql70.pdf includes instructions for running the three setup command files included on the SQL Server CD-ROM. To run a custom command file that you have created, make a copy of Smssql70.pdf and edit it to run your command file.

Lesson Summary

You can run an unattended installation of SQL Server 7 by running the Setup program with a setup initialization script. Standard scripts are supplied on the SQL Server CD-ROM, or you can create your own custom scripts. Alternatively, you can run an unattended installation of SQL Server 7 using SMS.

Review

The following questions are intended to reinforce key information presented in the chapter. If you are unable to answer a question, review the appropriate lesson and then try the question again. Answers to the questions can be found in Appendix A, "Questions and Answers."

1. You are installing several SQL Servers. You want your SQL Server services to connect to network resources with a trusted connection. In what security context should the SQL Server services run? Why?

2. You are installing SQL Server in an environment that has both Windows and Novell clients. You want to use Windows NT authentication. Which network libraries must you install?

3. You installed SQL Server with the default settings. Later, you decide to add a database that requires characters that are not part of the default character set. What must you do to support the new character set?

C H A P T E R   3

Upgrading to SQL Server 7.0

About This Chapter

Microsoft SQL Server 7 provides the ability to upgrade a complete SQL Server 6.*x* installation to SQL Server 7. In this chapter, you will learn how to use the SQL Server Upgrade Wizard and how to perform other tasks associated with cleanly upgrading your existing SQL Servers.

Before You Begin

This chapter provides a theoretical explanation of the upgrade process. There are no prerequisites for completing the lessons in this chapter.

Lesson 1: Introduction to Upgrading SQL Server

As part of your upgrade plan, you should analyze the software requirements and address any upgrade considerations. You must also perform certain tasks to prepare the SQL Server 6.x database for the upgrade process. This lesson describes how to prepare for the upgrade.

After this lesson, you will be able to

- Describe the upgrade process
- Identify and address potential issues before upgrading a database

Estimated lesson time: 15 minutes

The Upgrade Process

The SQL Server Upgrade Wizard automates the process of upgrading SQL Server 6.x databases to SQL Server 7. You can use other tools such as Data Transformation Services or the bcp command-prompt utility to move a production database to SQL Server 7 manually. However, using the SQL Server Upgrade Wizard makes it relatively easy to configure and transfer data, and it accomplishes the upgrade more rapidly than other methods.

Using the SQL Server Upgrade Wizard

The SQL Server Upgrade Wizard can transfer schema, objects, and data as well as logins and database users. It also transfers replication settings, SQL Executive settings (called SQL Server Agent in SQL Server 7), and many SQL Server 6.x configuration options.

The SQL Server Upgrade Wizard does not remove SQL Server 6.x from the computer. After upgrading, you will have two installations of SQL Server and two sets of data. SQL Server 6.x and SQL Server 7 installations are completely separate and independent. You should leave SQL Server 6.x on the computer until you verify the success of the upgrade. Optionally, you can remove SQL Server 6.x devices to save disk space if you use the tape upgrade option.

Switching Between SQL Server 6.x and SQL Server 7

To switch from one version of SQL Server to the other, use the Microsoft SQL Server-Switch application on the Start menu, or run Vswitch.exe in the C:\Mssql7\Binn directory.

Caution Do not switch versions while the Upgrade Wizard is running, as this can cause the upgrade to fail.

Upgrade Considerations

Before running the SQL Server Upgrade Wizard, you should consider these upgrade issues:

Software Requirements

In order to upgrade a SQL Server 6.*x* database, the SQL Server computer must have the following software installed:

- Microsoft Windows NT Server Enterprise Edition 4.0 with Service Pack 4 (SP4) or later, Windows NT Server 4.0 with SP4 or later, or Windows NT Workstation 4.0 with SP4 or later
- SQL Server 6.0 with SP3 or SQL Server 6.5 with SP3 or later
- SQL Server 7

Network Protocols

The SQL Server 6.5 and SQL Server 7 installations must have Named Pipes installed as a network library, even if you are using the tape upgrade option. Both SQL Server 6.*x* and SQL Server 7 must listen on the default pipe, \\.\pipe\sql\query.

SQL Server Versions to Upgrade

You can upgrade only SQL Server 6.*x* databases to SQL Server 7. You cannot upgrade SQL Server 4.2 software or databases directly to SQL Server 7. Instead, you must upgrade the SQL Server 4.2 software and databases to SQL Server 6.5 and then upgrade to SQL Server 7.

Disk Space Requirements

In addition to the hard disk space used by SQL Server 7, you should have free disk space amounting to approximately 1.5 times the space used by the existing SQL Server 6.*x* databases.

You can use the SQL Server Upgrade Wizard to estimate the disk space needed to upgrade the SQL Server 6.*x* server to SQL Server 7. The wizard can estimate the following space requirements:

- Size of SQL Server 7 databases
- Size of SQL Server 7 logs
- Amount of disk space required for the tempdb database in SQL Server 7

Note The space requirement figures that the Upgrade Wizard provides are estimates, not exact sizes.

Replication and Upgrading

When upgrading enterprise servers involved in replication, you must upgrade the Distributor before you upgrade any other servers. You can phase in the conversion of the servers in your replication topology by upgrading the Distributor first and then upgrading other servers as time and resources permit.

Note You cannot use many of the new replication features until you have upgraded all of the servers involved in your replication topology.

Upgrade Tasks

After you install SQL Server 7, and before you use the SQL Server Upgrade Wizard, you must perform the following tasks:

- Run the Database Consistency Checker (DBCC) on all of the SQL Server 6.*x* databases to make sure they are in a consistent state, and then back up all of the SQL Server 6.*x* databases (including the system databases).

- Set the tempdb database in SQL Server 6.*x* to at least 10 MB. The recommended size for the tempdb database when upgrading is 25 MB.

- Create logins in the master database for all database users and ensure that the default database for each login is a database that is being upgraded. The SQL Server Upgrade Wizard examines the master database when determining which database users and objects to import. If the default database for a login is not being upgraded, that login will not be created in SQL Server 7. Objects in a user database cannot be imported if the login for the object owner is not listed as a user for the database.

- Disable any startup stored procedures. The SQL Server Upgrade Wizard starts and stops the SQL Server 6.*x* server during the upgrade process. Stored procedures set to run automatically at startup may cause the upgrade process to hang.

- If you are performing a two-computer upgrade, assign a domain username and password to the MSSQLServer service in your SQL Server 6.*x* and SQL Server 7 installations instead of using the local system account or a local user account. The domain user account should belong to the Administrators group of both of the computers involved in the upgrade. (The local system account is sufficient for a one-computer upgrade.)

- Shut down the server by stopping replication and ensuring that the replication log is empty and by shutting down all applications, including all services that depend on SQL Server.

If you copied your SQL Server 6.*x* databases to a new computer to perform the upgrade, you may need to update the new SQL Server 6.*x* master database as follows:

- Change references from the earlier server name to the current server name in the SQL Server 6.*x* master database.

- Update the device file locations in the SQL Server 6.*x* master database.

- Make sure that all users of the transferred database have logins in the SQL Server 6.*x* master database.

Lesson Summary

SQL Server 7 has many features designed to make it as easy as possible to upgrade from earlier versions. The SQL Server Upgrade Wizard allows you to upgrade from SQL Server 6.*x* with minimum work. The process uses the new SQL Server 7 installation and the old SQL Server 6.*x* installation to copy across all of the old databases and database objects that you select. The process includes the ability to switch back to the old version on the same machine. The upgrade should proceed cleanly if you prepare carefully by checking all of the requirements before you start.

Lesson 2: Using the SQL Server Upgrade Wizard

This lesson describes how to upgrade SQL Server using the SQL Server Upgrade Wizard. When you use the wizard to upgrade from SQL Server 6.x to SQL Server 7, you must

- Decide whether you will use one computer or two to perform the upgrade
- Determine how to transfer the data from SQL Server 6.x to SQL Server 7
- Specify which databases, server configuration, replication settings, SQL Executive settings, and database characteristics to import

Each of these topics is covered in this lesson.

After this lesson, you will be able to

- Upgrade a Microsoft SQL Server 6.x database to SQL Server 7

Estimated lesson time: 30 minutes

Choosing an Upgrade Method

When you upgrade SQL Server 6.x, you must choose whether to upgrade using a single computer or two computers, and then you must select the method of transferring data and objects.

One-Computer Upgrade

You can perform an upgrade on a single computer by using a disk-to-disk named pipe connection or a tape upgrade. When the upgrade is complete, SQL Server 7 immediately takes over as the production server.

For a one-computer upgrade, the same computer is both the import and export server.

Two-Computer Upgrade

You can install SQL Server 7 on one computer and then connect to another computer where SQL Server 6.x is installed. The upgrade takes place using a named pipe connection to transfer data. When the upgrade is complete, SQL Server 7 immediately takes over as the production server.

If you perform a two-computer upgrade, assign a domain user name and password to the MSSQLServer service in your SQL Server 6.x and SQL Server 7 installations instead of using the local system account or a local user account. The domain user account should belong to the Administrators group of both computers. The two computers must both belong to the same domain.

For a two-computer upgrade, the SQL Server 6.x computer is the export server and the SQL Server 7 computer is the import server.

Note If you are upgrading a server used in replication, you must use one computer.

Methods for Transferring Data

SQL Server presents several methods for transferring data from SQL Server 6.*x*
to SQL Server 7. These methods depend on the choice of a one-computer versus
two-computer upgrade and the amount of disk space available on the import server.
Figure 3.1 shows the screen in which you make your choice.

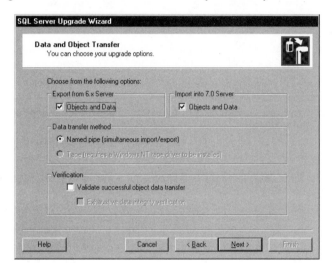

Figure 3.1   Choosing a data and object transfer method

Named Pipes

For a one-computer upgrade, a direct pipeline enables the SQL Server Upgrade
Wizard to transfer data in memory from SQL Server 6.*x* to SQL Server 7. The
named pipe method is the most reliable and provides the best performance. When
performing a single-computer upgrade using Named Pipes, you cannot reuse the
disk space occupied by SQL Server 6.*x* and the SQL Server 6.*x* devices until the
version upgrade process is complete.

Tape

You can use the tape backup option when you want to perform a one-computer
upgrade but the hard disk space is limited. The SQL Server Upgrade Wizard backs
up to tape all of the SQL Server 6.*x* databases you select to upgrade. You also can
use the SQL Server Upgrade to delete all of the SQL Server 6.*x* devices, freeing
disk space before the SQL Server 7 data files are created.

Caution The SQL Server Upgrade Wizard deletes all of the SQL Server 6.*x*
devices, not just the ones that you want to upgrade. You should upgrade all databases if you choose to delete the SQL Server 6.*x* devices.

Selecting Upgrade Options

SQL Server presents several options for upgrading SQL Server 6.*x* databases to SQL Server 7. These options determine what information is imported from the SQL Server 6.*x* installation as well as how the upgrade is performed. Review these options before you run the SQL Server Upgrade Wizard.

Performing Verification

The SQL Server Upgrade Wizard can verify that objects, including schema and stored procedures and data, are transferred correctly.

You can also choose to perform exhaustive data integrity verification. The SQL Server Upgrade Wizard then performs a checksum for each column of each table before and after the upgrade to verify that data values do not change.

Any discrepancies found are reported in the output logs of the SQL Server Upgrade Wizard.

Specifying a Scripting Code Page

The SQL Server Upgrade Wizard requires a scripting code page, used to create the upgrade scripts. Figure 3.2 shows the Code Page Selection screen of the wizard.

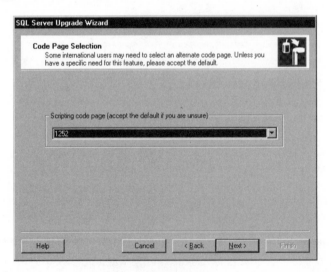

Figure 3.2   Specifying a code page

The default scripting code page is the code page recorded in the master database. If you know that the actual code page is different from the recorded code page, select the actual code page from the list. Most users need only accept the default code page.

If you choose a scripting code page other than the default, it is recommended that you do not upgrade replication settings. If the server is involved in replication, reconfigure the replication settings manually after the upgrade is complete.

Selecting the Databases to Upgrade

You can choose to upgrade some or all of your SQL Server 6.*x* databases. Figure 3.3 shows the screen in which you specify those databases you wish to include or exclude.

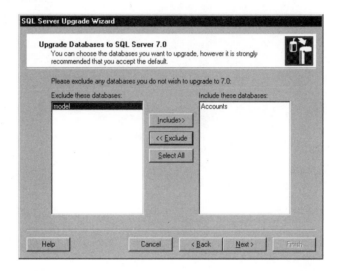

Figure 3.3   Choosing the databases to upgrade

The master, msdb, and distribution system databases, and any sample databases, are not explicitly available for selection. However, you can upgrade the logins and server configuration stored in the master database, the replication settings stored in the distribution database, and the tasks stored in the msdb database by selecting options presented by the wizard.

Note You should upgrade all databases with cross-database dependencies at the same time.

If you run the SQL Server Upgrade Wizard again after you have upgraded the databases, previously updated databases will default to the excluded list. If you want to upgrade a database again, move it to the included list in the wizard. You must delete the database in SQL Server 7 before running the upgrade again.

Choosing a New Database Configuration

The screen shown in Figure 3.4 offers options for creating the SQL Server 7 database and log files. You can have the wizard create the new database automatically, or you can specify a custom configuration.

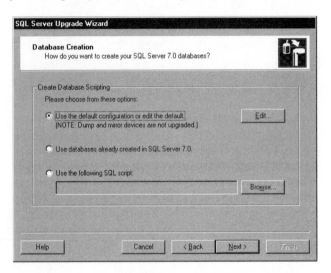

Figure 3.4   Specifying a database configuration

Using the SQL Server Upgrade Wizard (the Default)

The Upgrade Wizard will automatically create new databases, basing the sizes and locations of the data and log files on those of the existing devices. You can view and edit the default database configuration in the Upgrade Wizard. For each database and log file, you can modify the name and file path, the initial size of the file, and the autogrow increment.

Specifying a Custom Configuration

You can specify your own configuration in one of two ways: by using databases and logs that you create in SQL Server 7 before running the Upgrade Wizard, or by using a Transact-SQL script file that you provide. If you provide a script file, it must use the new SQL Server 7 CREATE DATABASE statement syntax. Do not use the script you used to create your databases in SQL Server 6.*x*. If you are not familiar with the new CREATE DATABASE statement, do not use a Transact-SQL script to create the new databases.

Choosing Objects to Transfer

When upgrading system databases, the SQL Server Upgrade Wizard can transfer the server configuration and various service settings, as shown in Figure 3.5.

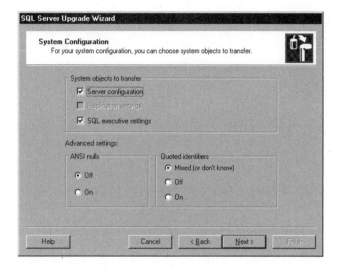

Figure 3.5 Choosing the system objects to transfer and the data characteristics

Server Configuration

When the Server Configuration option is checked, logins and server configuration options relevant to SQL Server 7 are transferred as part of the version upgrade process. The SQL Server 6.x configuration options that are not used in SQL Server 7 are not transferred.

Replication Settings

When the Replication Settings option is checked, all articles, subscriptions, and publications of each selected database, including the distribution database, if any, are transferred and upgraded.

SQL Executive Settings

When the SQL Executive Settings option is checked, all tasks scheduled by SQL Executive are transferred and upgraded so that SQL Server 7 can schedule and run the tasks in SQL Server Agent.

ANSI Nulls

The ANSI Nulls option controls both database default nullability and comparisons against null values. When upgrading SQL Server 6.x to SQL Server 7, you must set the ANSI Nulls option to On or Off.

When the SQL Server Upgrade Wizard creates the SQL Server 7 database tables, the database default nullability determined by the ANSI Nulls option is not an issue. All columns are explicitly qualified as NULL or NOT NULL based on their status in SQL Server 6.x.

The ANSI Nulls option is important with regard to comparisons against null values when the SQL Server Upgrade Wizard creates the SQL Server 7 database objects. With ANSI Nulls On, the comparison operators EQUAL (=) and NOT EQUAL (<>) always return NULL (UNKNOWN) when one of their arguments is NULL. (This is the ANSI SQL-92 standard for handling NULL values.) With ANSI Nulls Off, these operators will return TRUE or FALSE, depending on whether both arguments are NULL.

In SQL Server 6.x, the ANSI Nulls option in objects, such as stored procedures and triggers, is resolved during query execution. In SQL Server 7, the ANSI Nulls option is resolved when the object is created. When upgrading you must choose the ANSI Nulls option that you want for all objects in the databases. The SQL Server Upgrade Wizard then creates all database objects using this setting.

If you have stored procedures in your old database that use SQL Server nullability, set ANSI Nulls to Off. If you have stored procedures in your old database that use ANSI nullability, set ANSI Nulls to On.

Quoted Identifiers

The Quoted Identifiers setting determines what meaning SQL Server gives to double quotation marks (""). When the Quoted Identifiers setting is Off, double quotation marks delimit a character string, just as single quotation marks do. When Quoted Identifiers is On, double quotation marks delimit an identifier, such as a column name. An identifier must be enclosed in double quotation marks, for example, if its name contains characters that are otherwise illegal in an identifier, including spaces and punctuation, or if the name conflicts with a reserved word in Transact-SQL. Regardless of the Quoted Identifiers setting, an identifier can also be delimited by square brackets.

The meaning of the following statement, for example, depends on whether Quoted Identifiers is On or Off:

```
SELECT "x" FROM T
```

If the Quoted Identifiers setting is On, "x" is interpreted to mean the column named x. If it is Off, "x" is the constant string x and is equivalent to the letter *x*.

The Quoted Identifiers setting in the SQL Server Upgrade Wizard corresponds to the SQL Server QUOTED_IDENTIFIER setting. If the previous SELECT statement example were part of a stored procedure created when QUOTED_IDENTIFIER was ON, then "x" would always mean the column named x. Even if the QUOTED-_IDENTIFIER setting was later set to OFF, the stored procedure would act as though it were set to ON and treat "x" as the column named x.

When the SQL Server Upgrade Wizard re-creates database objects in SQL Server 7, the Quoted Identifiers setting determines how all of these objects behave. If all database objects were created in SQL Server 6.*x* with the same QUOTED_IDEN-TIFIER setting, click that setting for Quoted Identifiers, either On or Off. If objects were created in SQL Server 6.*x* with a mix of the two settings, or if you are unsure of the settings used, click Mixed.

With the Mixed option, the SQL Server Upgrade Wizard first converts all objects containing double quotation marks with QUOTED_IDENTIFIER set to ON. The wizard then converts any objects that failed to be created with QUOTED_IDEN-TIFIER set to OFF.

Running the Upgrade

Once you have selected all of the upgrade options, the upgrade process runs. The SQL Server Upgrade Script Interpreter dialog box will keep you informed as each step in the process completes (see Figure 3.6).

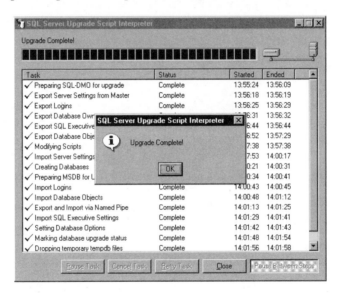

Figure 3.6   Running the upgrade

Lesson Summary

You can perform an upgrade on one or two computers, and you can transfer the data during the upgrade using a named pipes direct transfer or a transfer using tape. Verify the database objects to be transferred before performing the upgrade. In the Upgrade Wizard, you must specify a number of options that determine how objects will be transferred and created.

Lesson 3: After Using the SQL Server Upgrade Wizard

Due to the significant improvements and changes made in SQL Server 7, it is possible that some of the objects in an upgraded database will not be correctly created in SQL Server 7. You should be aware of the changes in SQL Server 7 and should plan to change your databases to use fully supported SQL Server 7 options.

After this lesson, you will be able to

- Troubleshoot a database upgrade
- Set the database compatibility level

Estimated lesson time: 30 minutes

Removing SQL Server 6.5

After upgrading the SQL Server 6.x databases to SQL Server 7, you may want to leave SQL Server 6.x on your computer until you are sure you no longer need it. When ready, you can remove SQL Server 6.x by using the Remove SQL Server 6.x application on the Start menu.

Caution If you need to reinstall SQL Server 6.x, you must first remove SQL Server 7. SQL Server 6.x cannot be installed on a computer alongside an existing SQL Server 7 installation.

Troubleshooting the Upgrade

If you encounter difficulties in upgrading, identify the problem and view the upgrade log files.

Identifying Common Upgrade Problems

You cannot upgrade some objects and settings to SQL Server 7 without modification. If you encounter problems during the upgrade process, check the following:

Objects with Inaccurate or Missing Entries in syscomments

In order to upgrade objects, the text description stored in the syscomments table in SQL Server 6.x must be intact. Objects will not upgrade if

- Text in syscomments has been deleted.
- They were renamed using sp_rename. This system stored procedure does not alter the entry in syscomments for an object.
- They are stored procedures that were created within other stored procedures. There is no entry in syscomments for these stored procedures.

Note Objects created with encrypted text in the syscomments table are upgraded.

A Server Name That Does Not Match the Computer Name

The computer name on which SQL Server runs must match the server name returned by @@SERVERNAME. If the names do not match, the SQL Server Upgrade Wizard may fail. To correct this problem, change the server name returned by @@SERVERNAME to match the computer name, using the sp_dropserver and sp_addserver system stored procedures.

Stored Procedures That Modify and Reference System Tables

Stored procedures that do the following will not upgrade:

- Modify system tables
- Reference system tables or columns that do not exist in SQL Server 7

Restrictions on Creating Tables

During the upgrade process, you may encounter the following problems in upgrading tables and views:

- Tables and views with NULL column names will not upgrade because the wizard cannot script these objects.
- Tables created by the system administrator on behalf of another user who does not have create-table permissions will not upgrade. Because the object owner does not have CREATE permissions, the script to create the object fails.

Viewing the Upgrade Log Files

The SQL Server Upgrade Wizard creates a folder in the C:\Mssql7\Upgrade directory each time it runs. The folder name consists of the server name and the current date and time, in order to distinguish multiple runs of the SQL Server Upgrade Wizard. For example, the name SQLCONV1_092198_151900 indicates that the wizard was run on a SQL Server called SQLCONV1 on 9/21/98 at 15:19.

This folder contains a number of descriptively named log files describing each upgrade step. It contains subfolders for each upgraded database, including the master database. These subfolders contain log files indicating the success or failure of creating objects in the database.

Files with an .OK extension indicate that all instances of that type of object were created successfully. Files with an .ERR extension indicate that at least one instance of that type of object was not created successfully. The error files list each failed object creation statement and the reason the object was not created successfully.

Any log files that indicate a problem are listed at the end of the upgrade, in the SQL Server Upgrade Wizard, for easy access.

Specifying Compatibility Levels

If you are upgrading databases to SQL Server 7, you will probably have objects in the upgraded database that use features that have changed. SQL Server 7 supports different compatibility levels in order to make the transition from previous versions as easy as possible.

What Is a Compatibility Level?

When run with default settings, most SQL Server 6.x applications work unchanged after an upgrade to SQL Server 7 by the SQL Server Upgrade Wizard.

The compatibility level can be set for any SQL Server 7 database, using the sp_dbcmptlevel system stored procedure. The level can be set to 60, 65, or 70, according to the version of SQL Server with which you require compatibility; it defaults to 70 for new databases.

When you upgrade existing systems with existing applications, you can use the database compatibility level settings to retain earlier behaviors if your existing applications depend on those behaviors. Setting a compatibility level gives you time to upgrade applications in a planned, orderly manner, although it is recommended that you update all of your scripts to full SQL Server 7 compatibility when possible. Future versions of SQL Server will not necessarily offer compatibility with versions earlier than SQL Server 7. Many applications are not affected by the changes in behavior.

The effects of the compatibility level settings are generally limited to the behaviors of a small number of Transact-SQL statements that also exist in earlier versions of SQL Server. When the database compatibility level is set to 60 or 65, applications still gain almost all of the benefits of the new performance enhancements of SQL Server 7.

Initial Settings

You can select initial compatibility level settings for user, model, and master databases.

User Databases

The SQL Server Upgrade Wizard sets the compatibility level of upgraded databases to the version number of the export server.

For example, if your server is SQL Server 6.5 and you upgrade to SQL Server 7, the compatibility level for all existing user-defined databases is set to 65. This setting enables existing applications to run with a minimum number of changes after an upgrade.

The model Database

The compatibility level of an upgraded model database is set to 70. If you change this setting, it will propagate to new databases.

The master Database

The compatibility level of an upgraded master database is set to 70. You should not change this setting. If an upgraded stored procedure in the master database requires a SQL Server 6.*x* compatibility level, you must move it out of the master database.

Backward Compatibility Details

If you have been using a previous version of SQL Server, you should be aware of the major feature changes that affect the operation of SQL Server 7. These changes are grouped into four levels:

- **Level 1**—Statements, stored procedures, or other items that have been removed in SQL Server 7. Code or scripts that use these items must be changed before they are used with SQL Server 7.
  Examples: The DISK REINIT and DISK REFIT commands.

- **Level 2**—Changes that cause significantly different behavior in SQL Server 7. Code or scripts that use these items probably need to be changed; new behavior must at least be well understood so that you are not taken by surprise.
  Example: When restoring multiple transaction logs, the last RESTORE statement must specify the WITH RECOVERY option; all other RESTORE statements must specify the WITH NORECOVERY option.

- **Level 3**—Items that are fully supported in SQL Server 7, but for backward compatibility only. Future versions of SQL Server may not support these items, and you should begin using the SQL Server 7 replacement when possible.
  Example: DBCC ROWLOCK enabled Insert Row Locking. Row locking is now automatic and DBCC ROWLOCK is not required.

- **Level 4**—Changes that produce slightly different behavior in SQL Server 7. Example: The SQL-92 syntax for outer joins (LEFT OUTER JOIN and RIGHT OUTER JOIN instead of *= and =*) should be used.

Your upgrade planning should include checking your existing databases and scripts for items that fall into any of these levels and replacing them before or after the upgrade as necessary.

Registering a SQL Server 6.5 Server Using Enterprise Manager

You can register a 6.5 server in SQL Server Enterprise Manager. The 6.5 server can be started and stopped, and selecting the 6.5 server launches the version 6.5 SQL Server Enterprise Manager. The 6.5 SQL Server Enterprise Manager must be installed on the computer. Both versions of Enterprise Manager and the other SQL Server client utilities can be installed on the computer where SQL Server 7 is installed or on any Microsoft Windows 95, Windows 98, or Windows NT computer on a network.

Lesson Summary

One of the most important issues in performing an upgrade is testing the upgrade and reviewing the upgrade log files to ensure that the upgrade correctly transferred your databases. It is possible that you will have to create some objects manually after changing the old scripts for these objects to use new SQL Server 7 syntax. After upgrading, you should begin updating all of your scripts to use SQL Server 7 syntax, even if the objects transfer correctly with the Upgrade Wizard.

You can use the compatibility level to force SQL Server 7 to use SQL Server 6.*x* functionality for certain Transact-SQL statements. Four levels of changes have been defined to help you prioritize the modifications you need to make your code and scripts.

Review

The following questions are intended to reinforce key information presented in the chapter. If you are unable to answer a question, review the appropriate lesson and then try the question again. Answers to the questions can be found in Appendix A, "Questions and Answers."

1. You have a SQL Server 6.5 database running on a Windows NT Server. Both SQL Server and Windows NT Server have Service Pack 2 installed. The size of the tempdb database on SQL Server 6.5 is 8 MB. After installing SQL Server 7 on the same computer, there is 100 MB of free disk space. The size of the SQL Server 6.5 database you want to upgrade is 90 MB. What must you do in order to upgrade this database?

2. During the upgrade process, the SQL Server Upgrade Wizard cannot upgrade a stored procedure in the SQL Server 6.5 user databases. What could cause this failure?

3. You just upgraded a credit card database to SQL Server 7, and you have a client application that contains the following query:

```
SELECT t.title AS cross
FROM titles t
```

You want to use the BACKUP and RESTORE commands as part of maintenance jobs that you create. To allow these commands, you set the database compatibility level to 70. What impact does this setting have on your application?

C H A P T E R   4

System Configuration and Architecture

About This Chapter

Having completed the installation, you are now ready to begin using Microsoft SQL Server. In this chapter, you will learn how to start using some of the client administration utilities and how to configure SQL Server. You will also learn some of the background you will need to create and manage SQL Server databases.

Before You Begin

To complete the lessons in this chapter, you must have

- Installed SQL Server 7. See Chapter 2, "Installation," for installation instructions.
- The ability to log on to SQL Server as an Administrator.

- Installed the Exercise files from the Supplemental Course Materials CD-ROM to your hard disk drive. See the "Getting Started" section in "About This Book" for installation instructions.

Lesson 1: Preparing to Use SQL Server

After you install SQL Server, you should configure SQL Server Enterprise Manager and SQL Server.

After this lesson, you will be able to

- Configure SQL Server Enterprise Manager to work with your server and other SQL Servers
- Configure SQL Server and understand dynamic configuration in SQL Server 7

Estimated lesson time: 45 minutes

Configuring SQL Server Enterprise Manager

To manage a local or remote server with SQL Server Enterprise Manager, you must register the server with SQL Server Enterprise Manager. The local server is registered automatically when you install SQL Server. To manage a remote server with SQL Server Enterprise Manager, you must register the remote server manually.

Registering Servers

Registering a server in Enterprise Manager configures Enterprise Manager to connect to SQL Server; it does not affect the server in any way, and the server has no record of the registration. The SQL Server registration information is maintained in the Microsoft Windows NT registry. SQL Server Enterprise Manager uses this information each time you connect to a registered SQL Server.

You must specify the server name, Windows NT authentication or SQL Server authentication, and a server group. When you register a server, Enterprise Manager attempts to connect to the server; if it cannot connect, a message is displayed and you are asked whether you want to register the server anyway.

Use the Register SQL Server Wizard to register multiple SQL Servers with Enterprise Manager. This allows you to administer all of the servers from one computer. You must be a member of the sysadmin fixed server role in order to administer a server. By default, the Windows NT Administrators local group on the computer on which SQL Server was installed is a member of the sysadmin role. Since members of the Windows NT Domain Admins global group are members of the Administrators local group, domain administrators are able to administer all SQL Servers in a domain.

The default network library that Enterprise Manager uses to connect to a server is Named Pipes. If a remote server is not using Named Pipes (Microsoft Windows 95– or Windows 98–based servers cannot use Named Pipes), use the Client Network Utility to change the network library that you use to connect to the remote SQL Server. This utility can be found in the Microsoft SQL Server 7.0 program group.

Exercise: Verifying and Editing Your Server Registration

In this exercise, you will verify and modify your SQL Server registration in SQL Server Enterprise Manager.

▶ **To verify and edit your SQL Server registration in SQL Server Enterprise Manager**

1. Open SQL Server Enterprise Manager.

2. In the console tree, expand Microsoft SQL Servers, and then expand SQL Server Group.

   Notice that your SQL Server computer is registered automatically.

3. Right-click your server, and then click Edit SQL Server Registration Properties.

   What type of authentication is used by default to connect to your SQL Server?

4. Check the Show System Databases And System Objects option. Click OK.

5. In the console tree, expand your server to verify that you can connect to your SQL Server.

   How can you tell whether your SQL Server is started and whether you are connected to your SQL Server?

Creating Server Groups

When you register a server, you can either place the server in the default SQL Server Group or create new server groups. Groups in Enterprise Manager provide a way to organize servers in a large organization with many servers. They allow you to group servers together in the Enterprise Manager interface. Groups are purely an Enterprise Manager tool; SQL Server does not use server groups, and each server has no record of being part of any group. If you use Enterprise Manager on two different computers, you can create different SQL Server groups on the two computers without affecting the servers in any way. Groups in Enterprise Manager have nothing to do with security.

Accessing Registration Information

Enterprise Manager allows you to maintain private or shared registration information:

- By default, registration information is private, which prevents others from having access to your Enterprise Manager configuration.

- You have the option of specifying that registration information be shared. This allows multiple users to use the same Enterprise Manager configuration on one computer or allows multiple users using different computers to get their Enterprise Manager configuration from a central computer.

To configure private or shared registration information, select Options from the Tools menu in Enterprise Manager. The SQL Server Enterprise Manager Properties dialog box appears, as shown in Figure 4.1.

Figure 4.1   The SQL Server Enterprise Manager Properties dialog box

Exercise: Creating Shared Registration Information

In this exercise, you will create shared registration information using SQL Server Enterprise Manager.

▶ **To create shared registration information**

1. On the Tools menu, click Options.

2. In the SQL Server Enterprise Manager Properties dialog box, uncheck the Store User Independent check box, and then click OK.

3. Expand SQL Server Group.

   Are any servers registered? Why or why not?

4. Right-click SQL Server Group, and then click New SQL Server Registration.

   The Register SQL Server Wizard appears.

5. Click Next.

6. Your server name should be in the Available Servers text box. If it is not, click on your server or (local) in the Available Servers list. Click Add> to add your server to the Added Servers list. Click Next.

7. Click Next again to accept Windows NT authentication as the authentication mode for this registration.

8. Click the Create A New Top-Level SQL Server Group To Add The SQL Server(s) To option and type **Shared Reg Info Group** in the Group Name box. Click Next.

9. Click Finish to register your server.

10. The Register SQL Server Messages dialog box confirms that your server was registered successfully. Click Close.

    Note that two groups are now listed below Microsoft SQL Servers.

11. Expand the Shared Reg Info Group.

    SQL Server Enterprise Manager has successfully registered your server.

12. On the Tools menu, click Options.

13. In the SQL Server Enterprise Manager Properties dialog box, check the Store User Independent check box, and then click OK.

14. The Shared Reg Info Group no longer appears under Microsoft SQL Servers, and your server is once again in the default SQL Server Group.

Exercise: Configuring the SQLServerAgent Service

In this exercise, you will modify the SQL Server properties of your server to start and restart the SQLServerAgent service automatically.

▶ **To configure the SQLServerAgent service to start automatically and to restart automatically**

1. Right-click your server, and then click Properties.

2. Select the Autostart SQL Server Agent check box, and then click OK.

Client Installation

The SQL Server management tools can be installed by themselves in order to manage SQL Server on another networked machine. The procedure to do this is the same as that for installing the complete version of SQL Server. You can install the client utilities by specifically selecting them in the custom installation options screen and leaving the server components unchecked.

If you attempt to install a version of SQL Server that is not valid for a particular operating system (for example, if you try to install the Standard Edition on Windows 98), the Setup program will automatically display the custom installation options screen with the utilities selected.

Once the utilities are installed, you will have to register the SQL Server(s) you want to manage. Remember that the client and server must be using the same network libraries. This is especially important for Windows 95 and Windows 98 machines. SQL Server's default network library is Named Pipes, which is not available in the Windows 95 and Windows 98 environments. After installing, use the Client Network Utility to specify the correct network library.

Configuring SQL Server

The first time you use SQL Server, you should assign the SQL Server sa login account a password and review configuration options.

Assigning the SQL Server sa Login Account Password

When SQL Server is installed, the Setup program does not assign a password for the SQL Server sa login account. You should assign a password to this account to prevent unauthorized users from logging on to SQL Server with administrator privileges. Assign a password, using SQL Server Enterprise Manager or the sp_password system stored procedure.

Dynamic Resource Management

SQL Server manages most SQL Server resources dynamically, based on current system and user requirements. In most cases, SQL Server is able to manage these resources more efficiently than a system administrator can. Manually configuring SQL Server options is not recommended.

However, in some situations, you might need to set server options manually, such as when you want to limit the number of user connections and control the use of memory. You can use SQL Server Enterprise Manager or the sp_configure system stored procedure to configure or view these options. For more information on this topic, search for "Setting user connections" or "Setting memory" in SQL Server Books Online.

Configuring Default ANSI Settings

SQL Server displays certain behavior that is different from the standards specified by ANSI SQL-92. In these cases, you have the option of using the SQL Server behavior or the behavior specified by SQL-92. These options can be specified for a database or for a connection.

To specify the behavior for a database, use SQL Server Enterprise Manager or the sp_dboption system stored procedure to set the ANSI null default, ANSI nulls, quoted identifier, and ANSI warnings database options.

Use the SET command to set ANSI behavior off or on for a single connection. For example, the SET QUOTED_IDENTIFIER command is used to specify whether identifier names can be enclosed in double quotes. Options specified at the connection level override options set for a database. Many of these options are set automatically by the database interface software when a client connects to SQL Server. For example, the SQL Server ODBC driver sets all options to be ANSI compatible whenever it connects.

Troubleshooting SQL Server Installation

If you encounter difficulties in installing or connecting to SQL Server after installation, try to identify the problem by reviewing the Cnfgsvr.out file, viewing log information, and testing network connectivity.

Review the Cnfgsvr.out File

The Cnfgsvr.out file is an output file that is generated by the scripts that run during setup; it records Database Consistency Checker (DBCC) error messages. This text file, which you can view in Notepad, can be found in the C:\Mssql7\ Install folder.

View Log Information

SQL Server and Windows NT log information about the installation and operation of SQL Server. Each time the SQL Server and SQL Server Agent services start, new logs are created. Application events are appended to the Windows NT application event log. The following table describes the different logs you can view.

Log	Description	Location	View by using
Sqlstp.log	Provides information about the installation process of SQL Server	C:\Winnt	Any text editor
Windows NT application event log	Provides information about application-related events in Windows NT		Microsoft Event Viewer
SQL Server error log	Provides information about SQL Server events	C:\Mssql7\Log	SQL Server Enterprise Manager or any text editor
SQL Server Agent error log	Provides information about warnings and errors specific to SQL Server Agent	C:\Mssql7\Log	SQL Server Enterprise Manager or any text editor

Exercise: Viewing the SQL Server Error Log

In this exercise, you will review the entries in the SQL Server error log.

▶ **To view the SQL Server error log**

1. In the console tree of Enterprise Manager, expand your server, expand Management, and then expand SQL Server Logs.

2. Click Current to open the current error log.

3. Scroll through the error log.

   What caused all of the entries in this file?

Exercise: Viewing the Windows NT System and Application Event Logs

In this exercise, you will open the Windows NT system and application event logs and review the entries that relate to the installation and startup of SQL Server.

▶ **To view the Windows NT system and application event logs**

1. On the taskbar, click the Start button, point to Programs, point to Administrative Tools, and then click Event Viewer.

   Does the system log contain any entries that were generated by the installation or startup of SQL Server?

2. On the Log menu, click Application.

   Does the Windows NT application event log contain any entries that were generated by the installation or startup of SQL Server?

Test Network Connections

If a local client can connect to SQL Server but a network client cannot, use the makepipe, readpipe, odbcping, or ping utility to determine the source of the problem.

Some Common Problems

Finding a solution to a problem involves isolating and verifying the symptom. The following table describes solutions to common problems. For more information, search for "Setup troubleshooting" in SQL Server Books Online.

Symptom	Problem	Solution
A SQL Server service does not start.	The SQL Server services cannot access a domain controller.	Reestablish access to a domain controller or reconfigure the SQL Server service to use the Local System account.
"Error 1069: The service did not start due to a logon failure."	The password for the domain user account was changed.	Use Services in the Control Panel to specify the new password for the SQL Server service.
	The SQL Server service account requires the appropriate permissions on the local computer.	Verify that the domain user account has the required local user rights on the SQL Server computer.
The SQL Server service does not start.	SQL Server entries in the Windows NT registry are corrupted.	Run the regrebld utility to rebuild the SQL Server registry entries.
A SQL Server management tool cannot connect to SQL Server.	The SQL Server service has not been started.	Verify that the SQL Server service has started.
"A connection could not be established to [*servername*]."	The client and server network libraries do not match.	Modify the default network library on the client, add a network library to the server, or both.
	You do not have permission to administer the SQL Server computer.	Log on to Windows NT with an account that has permission to administer the SQL Server computer, or connect with a SQL Server login account, such as sa.

Lesson Summary

After you install SQL Server, it is important that you verify the completeness of the installation. SQL Server and Windows NT provide a number of features that allow us to identify possible problems with our installation. Once the setup is complete, SQL Server 7 provides intuitive tools that an administrator can use to modify configuration options.

Lesson 2: Working with SQL Server

The rest of this book describes how you will manage and administer SQL Server. You will use SQL Server Enterprise Manager and SQL Server Query Analyzer for most administrative tasks. This lesson introduces these two important tools.

After this lesson, you will be able to

- Describe SQL Server implementation and administration activities
- Describe how client/server tools are used to administer SQL Server
- Use SQL Server Enterprise Manager
- Use SQL Server Query Analyzer

Estimated lesson time: 60 minutes

SQL Server Activities

SQL Server activities generally fall into one of two categories: implementing a SQL Server database, which is often the job of a developer, and administering a SQL Server database. This section lists some of the tasks involved in each of these categories. The focus of this book is on administering a SQL Server database.

Implementing a SQL Server Database

Implementing a SQL Server database means planning, creating, and maintaining a number of interrelated components.

The nature and complexity of a database application, as well as the process of planning it, can vary greatly. For example, a database can be relatively simple, designed for use by a single person, or it can be large and complex, designed to handle all the banking transactions for hundreds of thousands of clients.

Regardless of the size and complexity of the database, implementing a database usually involves

- Designing the database so that your application uses hardware optimally and allows for future growth, identifying and modeling database objects and application logic, and specifying the types of information for each object and the types of relationships between objects.
- Creating the database and database objects, including tables, data integrity mechanisms, data entry and retrieval objects (often stored procedures), appropriate indexes, and security.
- Designing a database for performance. You want to ensure that the database performs important functions correctly and quickly. In conjunction with correct database design, the correct use of indexes, RAID, and filegroups is essential to achieving good performance.

- Planning deployment, which includes analyzing the workload and recommending an optimal index configuration for your SQL Server database.

- Administering the application after deployment, which includes configuring servers and clients; monitoring server performance; managing jobs, alerts, and operators; managing security; and managing database backup procedures.

This book does not cover these database implementation activities.

Administering a SQL Server Database

Administering a SQL Server database involves

- Installing and configuring SQL Server and establishing network security.

- Upgrading to new versions of SQL Server.

- Building databases, including allocating disk space to the database and the transaction log and the ongoing management of disk space usage.

- Transferring data into and out of databases.

- Planning and implementing a backup and restore strategy.

- Defining and implementing database user and application security.

- Automating jobs for repetitive tasks and alerts for reporting errors.

- Monitoring and tuning databases and the server.

- Setting up replication to publish data to multiple sites.

Client/Server Tools

All of the SQL Server administrative tools are clients. They connect to the SQL Server service (MSSQLServer) just as user applications do. This is always true, whether the administrative tools are running on the SQL Server computer or on another computer on a network. The SQL Server service takes a number of startup parameters. Other than these startup parameters, the only way to interact with the SQL Server service is by making a client connection and sending Transact-SQL commands. None of the tools interact directly with the database files.

The server has to be running for the tools to connect. If the server is not running, most of the administrative tools will show an error message; Enterprise Manager, however, can automatically start the server. When Enterprise Manager connects to the server, it uses the security settings saved in the server registration, so you are not prompted to log on. As you use the graphical interface, Enterprise Manager uses Transact-SQL and the SQL-DMO interface to communicate with the server.

Some database operations require that no other user be using the database when you perform the operation. As far as the server is concerned, each connection is completely independent, so it is possible for tools running on the same computer to interfere with each other. If you have Enterprise Manager and Query Analyzer open at the same time, you have at least two connections to SQL Server (more if you have more than one query window open in Query Analyzer). For example, if Query Analyzer is using a database and you try to perform an exclusive operation on that database with Enterprise Manager, the Query Analyzer connection will prevent the Enterprise Manager connection from gaining exclusive access to the database, and the operation will fail.

We will focus on the Enterprise Manager and the Query Analyzer in this section. Other client utilities available with SQL Server include the SQL Server Client Configuration tool, SQL Server Performance Monitor, SQL Server Profiler, SQL Server Setup, and SQL Server wizards.

SQL Server Enterprise Manager

Enterprise Manager is a server administration and database management client. It is a Microsoft Management Console (MMC) snap-in. MMC is a shared user interface for BackOffice server management that provides a convenient and consistent environment for administrative tools. One or more snap-ins are loaded and configured in MMC to create a console. Enterprise Manager is a preconfigured MMC console. It is possible to configure your own consoles that include other BackOffice or third-party snap-ins. The main parts of the Enterprise Manager window, shown in Figure 4.2, are as follows:

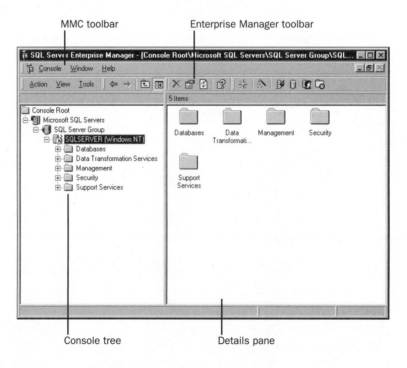

Figure 4.2   The main parts of the Enterprise Manager window

- **MMC toolbar**—This toolbar is not used by Enterprise Manager; you use it to manage consoles if you have other administrative tools open in MMC.
- **Enterprise Manager toolbar**—This toolbar, which is part of the console window, is where you will find the SQL Server Enterprise Manager tools. There are three menus and a number of icons on the toolbar:
    - Action menu: A context-sensitive list of actions for the currently selected item in the console tree.
    - View menu: A list of views that you can select for the details pane. Also allows you to hide or display various windows and window components.
    - Tools menu: A list of administrative tools and wizards that can be launched from Enterprise Manager. Some of these are part of Enterprise Manager; others are separate tools that are provided here for convenience.
- **Console tree**—The console tree presents a hierarchical tree of folders and lists of icons that you use to navigate the administrative components of SQL Server. If there is a + next to the item, you can click the + to expand the detail for that item. Right-click an item for a pop-up menu of operations for that item. Click an item to see the detail for that item in the details pane.
- **Details pane**—This pane displays details for the currently selected item in the console tree. You can view the details as a set of large or small icons, a list of icons, or a detail list, much the same as the file list in Windows Explorer. Figure 4.3 shows a detail list view for a database.

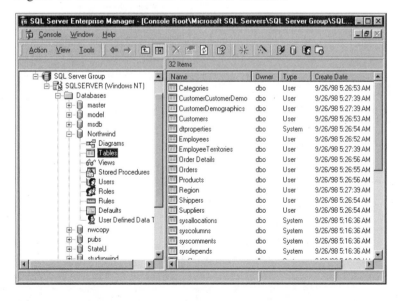

Figure 4.3   The detail list view for a database

For a number of items that you select in the console tree, you can also view a taskpad in the details pane. A *taskpad* may present tasks related to the selected item or a summary report containing useful information and statistics about a SQL Server component. To switch between one of the icon views and the task-pad view, right-click the item in the console tree, point to View, and then click Taskpad. If there is no Taskpad option on the View menu, it means that there is no taskpad for that item. Taskpads are HTML pages, which may have links that you can click in the same way that you click a link on a Web page in your browser. For this reason, when you right-click in a taskpad, you will see the Internet Explorer pop-up menu, not the Enterprise Manager pop-up menu that you see when viewing one of the item views. Figure 4.4 shows the taskpad for a database.

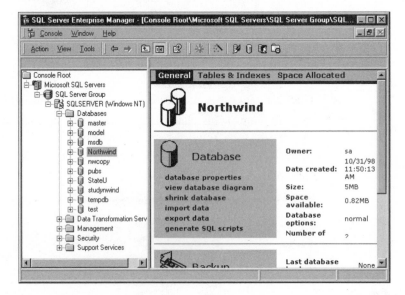

Figure 4.4   The taskpad for a database

You often need to refresh views in Enterprise Manager to see the most up-to-date server information, especially if you execute Transact-SQL commands in Query Analyzer or other tools. Right-click an item in the console tree and click Refresh to refresh that item. If you want to quickly refresh everything, right-click your server and click Disconnect. When you expand your server again, Enterprise Manager makes a new connection to the server and retrieves fresh copies of all items. Note that the presence of a red zigzag line next to the server icon in the console tree indicates that you are connected to the server.

Note In previous versions of SQL Server, Enterprise Manager had a query window in which you could execute interactive queries. Although Enterprise Manager no longer has its own query window, you can now launch Query Analyzer from the Tools menu to execute interactive queries.

Exercise: Using Enterprise Manager

In this exercise you will explore the main features of the Enterprise Manager interface to familiarize yourself with Enterprise Manager in preparation for the exercises in the rest of the book.

▶ **To explore some of the features of the Enterprise Manager interface**

1. Open Enterprise Manager.

2. Expand SQL Server Group, then expand your server.

3. Click your server in the console tree.
   Large icons are listed for the administrative folders on your server.

4. Right-click your server in the console tree, point to View, and click Taskpad. The taskpad for your server is shown. Try clicking on some of the links in the taskpad, and notice that each one takes you to another page that lists links for managing an aspect of SQL Server.

5. Expand your server, expand Databases, and click the Northwind database.

6. Right-click the Northwind database, point to View, and click Taskpad.

7. Review the information about the Northwind database.

8. Click the Tables & Indexes link to see information about the size of the tables and indexes in the Northwind database.

9. Expand Northwind, and click Tables.

10. In the details pane, right-click the Products table, point to Open Table, and click Return All Rows.

    You will see an editable grid, which displays the contents of the Products table. The grid is part of the graphical query builder in Enterprise Manager. You can use the query builder to build and execute queries based on one or many tables.

11. On the Tools menu, click SQL Server Configuration Properties. (You may need to close the table view before accessing the Tools menu.)

12. Click the various tabs in the SQL Server Properties dialog box and review the properties for your server. Do not change any of the default values.

    On the Connections tab, note that the Maximum Concurrent User Connections option is set to 0. This means that SQL Server automatically configures the number of user connections, up to a maximum of 32,767. The Default Connection Options list allows you to configure ANSI defaults for user connections. When a client application connects to SQL Server, data sent between the client and the server can be formatted in a number of ways. These options specify defaults for how data should be formatted. For example, SQL Server can accept or not accept identifiers, such as database or table names, that are enclosed in double quotes (Quoted Identifier). These defaults can be overridden by clients.

On the Memory tab, note that SQL Server is set to dynamically control memory usage.

13. Click Cancel to close the SQL Server Properties dialog box without saving changes.

SQL Server Query Analyzer

SQL Server Query Analyzer is a graphical user interface for designing and testing Transact-SQL statements, batches, and scripts interactively.

Note Query Analyzer replaces the ISQL/w tool found in previous versions of SQL Server.

Query Analyzer provides the following features:

- Free-form text editor for keying in, saving, reusing, and executing Transact-SQL statements and scripts.
- Color coding of Transact-SQL syntax to improve the readability of complex statements.
- Results presented in either a grid or a free-form text window.
- Graphical diagramming of showplan information showing the logical steps built into the execution plan of a Transact-SQL statement. This allows programmers to determine what specific part of a poorly performing query is using a lot of resources. They can then explore changing the query in ways that minimize the resource usage while still returning the desired data.
- Index analysis to analyze a Transact-SQL statement and the tables it references to see if adding additional indexes will improve the performance of a query. (You will learn about graphical showplan output and analysis in Chapter 14, "Monitoring and Maintaining SQL Server.")

The main parts of the Query Analyzer window, shown in Figure 4.5, are as follows:

- **Title bar**—Shows the name of the server, current database, and login for the connection.
- **Current database (DB on the query window toolbar)**—Shows and allows you to change the current database for the connection.
- **Query pane**—Color-coded Transact-SQL editor for entering queries to be sent to SQL Server (executed).
- **Results pane**—Displays the results of executing a query. One or more of the following tabs will be present in the results pane:
    - Messages tab: Shows information and error messages sent back from the server.

- Results tab: Shows results as free-form text. Select Results In Text from the Query menu to show results in this way.

- Results Grid tab: Shows results in a simple scrollable grid. The results grid is not editable. Some queries will cause the server to return more than one result set, in which case there will be more than one Results Grid tab. If the results grid is blank after executing a query, it means that the query did not return a result set. Check the Messages tab for error messages or enter a query that returns a result set. Select Results In Grid from the Query menu to show results in a grid.

- Execution Plan tab: Shows a graphical diagram of the execution plan for the current query. Select Show Execution Plan from the Query menu to show this tab.

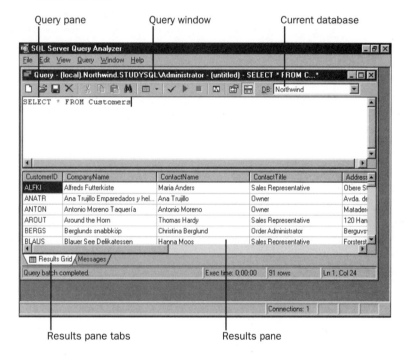

Figure 4.5   The main parts of the Query Analyzer window

You can open multiple query windows in Query Analyzer. This allows you to work in different databases or execute different scripts at the same time. Each window makes its own separate connection to the server (you can use different login credentials for different windows). These connections maintain different settings, and each has its own current database. If you try to perform an exclusive operation on a database from one window while another window is using the database, the operation will fail.

To open a new query window using the login credentials and settings of an existing window, select New Query from the Query menu. To open a new query window using different login credentials and default settings, select Connect from the File menu.

Notice the following when you use Query Analyzer:

- You can type in new queries or open saved queries. When you are finished working with a query, you can save it to a file for reuse.

- Queries can consist of a single statement or multiple statements. Certain statements cannot execute in a query batch with other statements. In such cases, separate the statements with the Transact-SQL batch separator, which is the keyword GO.

- Statements can be typed on a single line or across many lines. Many Transact-SQL statements are too long to fit on a single line. Typing them on multiple lines is recommended as it makes the statement easier to read.

- If no code in the query pane is selected when you execute the query, the entire contents of the query pane are executed. If you select code, just the selected code executes; this makes it easy to test individual statements without opening new windows.

- When you execute a query, Query Analyzer sends the query to SQL Server and then waits for a reply. The query window status bar indicates the status of the query, how long the query has been running, and the number of rows returned by the query (an animated globe also spins on the query toolbar).

- Select Parse from the Query menu to parse a query. Query Analyzer sends the query to the server, and the server parses but does not execute the query. The server returns either a message indicating that the query is correct or an error message.

The following table lists a number of useful keyboard shortcuts you can use in Query Analyzer.

Action	Keyboard shortcut
Execute	Ctrl-E or F5
Find	Ctrl-F
Change selected text to uppercase	Ctrl-Shift-U
Change selected text to lowercase	Ctrl-Shift-L
Results In Text	Ctrl-T
Results In Grid	Ctrl-D
Help using Query Analyzer	F1
Help with a selected Transact-SQL statement	Shift-F1

Exercise: Using Query Analyzer

In this exercise you will use Query Analyzer and explore many of its features.

▶ **To use Query Analyzer**

1. Log on to Windows NT as Administrator or to another account that is a member of the local Administrators group.

2. Open Query Analyzer from the Microsoft SQL Server 7.0 Programs Start menu. Connect to SQL Server using Windows NT authentication.

3. In the query pane, type

```
SELECT @@VERSION
```

4. Click Execute Query on the toolbar. The query returns information in the results pane indicating the version of SQL Server and Windows NT that you are using.

5. In the DB box, select Northwind. In the query pane, type

```
SELECT * FROM Customers
```

6. Click the Execute Query button on the toolbar. The query returns rows of data from the Customers table in the results pane. The output displays as free-form text.

7. On the Query menu, click Results In Grid.

8. Click the Execute Query button on the toolbar. The query returns rows of data from the Customers table in the results pane. The output is displayed in a grid.

9. Click the Messages tab in the results pane. The results pane displays messages that were returned when the query was executed.

10. In the DB box, select pubs. In the query pane, type

```
EXEC sp_help
```

11. Click the Execute Query button on the toolbar. The query returns information about the current database (pubs) in the results pane. There are now two results grids in the results pane, as the sp_help system stored procedure returns both a list of objects and a list of datatypes in the database.

12. On the File menu, click Open. A dialog box warns you that you are going to lose the current contents of the query pane. Click No, as it is not necessary to save the changes in this case.

13. Navigate to and open C:\Sqladmin\Exercise\Ch03\Savedqry.sql.

14. Click the Parse Query button on the toolbar. An error message displays in the results pane, indicating that the query is invalid.

15. Change the INNERJOIN clause on line 12 to INNER JOIN (add a space between INNER and JOIN). The change in the color coding indicates that the clause is now being recognized. Click the Parse Query button on the toolbar again. The message in the results pane now indicates that the query is valid. This does not necessarily mean that the query will execute, just that the syntax of the query is now correct.

16. Click the Execute Query button on the toolbar. The results pane indicates that an error occurred when executing the query. Change the name *Category* on line 11 to *CategoryName*. Click the Execute Query button on the toolbar again. Two results grids and some messages are shown in the results pane.

17. On the File menu, click Save to save the corrected query.

18. Click the New Query button on the toolbar. A second query window opens. This query window opens a separate connection to the SQL Server.

19. In the new query window, in the DB box, select master. This makes the master database the current database for the second query window. The Northwind database is still the current database for the first query window.

20. In the new query window, in the query pane type

```
SELECT * FROM sysdatabases
```

(sysdatabases is a system table that you will learn about in the next section.)

21. Click the Execute Query button on the toolbar. A list of the databases on the server is displayed in the results pane.

Lesson Summary

SQL Server 7 provides a number of client utilities to be used in the administration of a server and the implementation of a database. The Enterprise Manager provides a user-friendly interface with which an administrator can configure a SQL Server and build database objects. The Query Analyzer can be used for a number of tasks, including running queries against database tables, executing stored procedures that retrieve or modify information in a database, and executing system stored procedures that change or retrieve configuration settings.

Lesson 3: SQL Server Databases

An understanding of SQL Server database structure will help you develop and implement your database effectively. This lesson discusses the types of databases found in SQL Server and also describes two types of structural elements: database objects and system tables.

After this lesson, you will be able to

- Describe SQL Server system and user databases
- Understand how database objects are named and referenced in SQL Server
- Describe the purpose of SQL Server system tables
- Define metadata and know how to retrieve it

Estimated lesson time: 30 minutes

Types of Databases

Each SQL Server has two types of databases: system databases and user databases. Structurally there is no difference between system and user databases; both types of databases store data. However, SQL Server recognizes and requires system databases for its own use. System databases store information about SQL Server as a whole. SQL Server uses these databases to operate and manage the system. User databases are databases that users create. One copy of SQL Server can manage one or more user databases. When SQL Server is installed, SQL Server Setup creates four system databases and two sample user databases.

System Databases

The following table describes the system databases.

Database	Description
master	Controls the user databases and operation of SQL Server as a whole by keeping track of information such as login accounts, configurable environment variables, database locations, and system error messages
model	Provides a template, or prototype, for new user databases
tempdb	Provides a storage area for temporary tables and other temporary working storage needs
msdb	Supports SQL Server Agent and provides a storage area for scheduling information and job history
distribution	Stores history and transaction data used in replication

Note The distribution database is installed only when you configure SQL Server for replication activities.

While it is possible to modify and delete data in the system databases, this is not recommended. You should create all user objects in user databases and use system stored procedures only to read and modify data in the system databases.

There is one case in which you can modify a system database directly. If you want certain objects that you create (such as stored procedures, data types, defaults, and rules) to be added to every new user database, you can add these objects to the model database. The contents of the model database are copied into every new database.

User Databases

The pubs and Northwind sample databases are installed when you install SQL Server. These provide useful examples for you to use when learning how to work with SQL Server. They are not required for SQL Server to operate correctly.

Database Objects

A database is a collection of data stored in tables, along with objects that support the storage, retrieval, security, and integrity of this data.

The following table summarizes the SQL Server database objects.

Database object	Description
Table	Stores data as a collection of rows and columns.
Data type	Defines the type of data values allowed for a column or variable. SQL Server provides system-supplied data types. Users can create user-defined data types.
Constraint	Used to define integrity rules for a column or set of columns in a table; the standard mechanism for enforcing data integrity.
Default	Defines a value that is stored in a column if no other value is supplied.
Rule	Defines an expression that is used to check the validity of values that are stored in a column or data type.
Index	A storage structure that provides ordering and fast access for data retrieval and that can enforce data uniqueness.
View	Provides a way to look at data from one or more tables or other views in a database.
Stored procedure	A named collection of Transact-SQL statements or batches that execute together.
Trigger	A special form of a stored procedure that is executed automatically when a user modifies data in a table.

Note In Enterprise Manager, system databases and system objects are hidden by default. You can change the default by editing the server registration information and checking the Show System Databases And System Objects option.

Referring to SQL Server Objects

You can refer to SQL Server objects in several ways. You can specify the full name of the object (its fully qualified name), or you can specify only part of the object's name and have SQL Server determine the rest of the name from the context in which you are working.

Fully Qualified Names

The complete name of a SQL Server object includes four identifiers: the server name, the database name, the owner name, and the object name, in the following format:

```
server.database.owner.object
```

Any name that specifies all four parts is known as a fully qualified name. Each object created in SQL Server must have a unique, fully qualified name. For example, there can be two tables named Orders in the same database only as long as they belong to different owners. In addition, column names must be unique within a table or view.

Partially Specified Names

When referencing an object, you do not always have to specify the server, database, and owner. Leading identifiers can be omitted. Intermediate identifiers can also be omitted as long as their position is indicated by periods. The valid formats of object names are as follows:

```
server.database.owner.object
server.database..object
server..owner.object
server...object
database.owner.object
database..object
owner.object
object
```

When you create an object, SQL Server uses the following defaults if different parts of the name are not specified:

- The server defaults to the local server.
- The database defaults to the current database.
- The owner defaults to the username in the specified database associated with the login ID of the current connection. (Usernames are mapped to login IDs when they are created.)

A user who is a member of a role can explicitly specify the role as the object owner. A user who is a member of the db_owner or db_ddladmin role in the Northwind database can specify the dbo user account as the owner of an object. This practice is recommended.

The following example creates an order_history table in the Northwind database.

```
CREATE TABLE northwind.dbo.order_history
        (
          OrderID INT
        , ProductID int
        , UnitPrice money
        , Quantity int
        , Discount decimal
        )
```

Most object references use three-part names and default to the local server. Four-part names are generally used for distributed queries or remote stored procedure calls.

System Tables

System tables store information, called metadata, about the system and objects in databases. *Metadata* is information about data.

The Database Catalog

Each database (including the master database) contains a collection of system tables that store metadata about that specific database. This collection of system tables is called the database catalog.

The System Catalog

The system catalog, found only in the master database, is a collection of system tables that stores metadata about the entire system and all other databases.

System tables all begin with the *sys* prefix. The following table identifies some frequently used system tables.

System table	Database	Function
sysxlogins	master	Contains one row for each login account that can connect to SQL Server. If you need to access information in sysxlogins, you should do so through the syslogins view.
sysmessages	master	Contains one row for each system error or warning that SQL Server can return.
sysdatabases	master	Contains one row for each database on a SQL Server.
sysusers	All	Contains one row for each Windows NT user, Windows NT group, SQL Server user, or SQL Server role in a database.
sysobjects	All	Contains one row for each object in a database.

Metadata Retrieval

You can query a system table as you would any other table to retrieve information about the system. However, you should not write scripts that directly query the system tables, because if the system tables are changed in future product versions, your scripts may fail or may not provide accurate information.

Caution Writing scripts that directly modify the system tables is strongly discouraged. Changing a system table may make it impossible for SQL Server to operate normally.

When you write applications that retrieve metadata from system tables, you should use system stored procedures, system functions, or system-supplied information schema views. Each of these is described in the sections that follow.

System Stored Procedures

To make it easier for you to gather information about the state of the server and database objects, SQL Server provides a collection of prewritten queries called system stored procedures.

The names of most system stored procedures begin with the *sp_* prefix. The following table describes three commonly used system stored procedures.

System stored procedure	Description
sp_help [*object_name*]	Provides information on the specified database object
sp_helpdb [*database_name*]	Provides information on the specified database
sp_helpindex [*table_name*]	Provides information on the index for the specified table

The following example executes a system stored procedure to get information on the employee table.

```
sp_help employee
```

Many other stored procedures are used to create or modify system information or database objects by modifying the system tables. For example, the system stored procedure sp_addlogin creates a new login account in the master..sysxlogins system table.

As you have seen, there are system stored procedures that modify and query the system tables for you so that you do not have to do so directly.

System Functions

System functions provide a method for querying system tables from within Transact-SQL statements. System functions return specific, single values. The next table describes commonly used system functions and the information they return.

System function	Parameter passed	Results
DB_ID	Database name	Returns the database ID
USER_NAME	User ID	Returns the user's name
COL_LENGTH	Table and column names	Returns the column width
STATS_DATE	Table and index IDs	Returns the date when statistics for the specified index were last updated
DATALENGTH	Expression	Returns the actual length of the value of an expression of any data type

The following example uses a system function in a query to get the user name for user ID 10.

```
SELECT USER_NAME(10)
```

Information Schema Views

Information schema views provide an internal, system table–independent view of the SQL Server metadata. These views conform to the ANSI SQL standard definition for information schema. Information schema views allow applications to work properly even if future product versions change the system tables significantly.

In SQL Server, all information schema views are owned by a predefined information_schema user.

Each information schema view contains metadata for the data objects stored in a particular database. The following table describes commonly used information schema views.

Information schema view	Description
information_schema.tables	List of tables in the database
information_schema.columns	Information on columns defined in the database
information_schema.tables_privileges	Security information for tables in the database

The following example queries an information schema view to get a list of tables in a database.

```
SELECT * FROM information_schema.tables
```

Lesson Summary

The retrieval of metadata—information about objects and their configuration—has been made much easier in SQL Server 7. Information Schema Views, new to this version, provide a means to retrieve valuable information from system tables without writing a query against these tables yourself. SQL Server continues to support the use of system stored procedures, which can be recognized by their *sp_* prefix, to gather valuable information for database objects.

Review

The following questions are intended to reinforce key information presented in the chapter. If you are unable to answer a question, review the appropriate lesson and then try the question again. Answers to the questions can be found in Appendix A, "Questions and Answers."

1. You want to view metadata about objects in a SQL Server database. What methods would you use?

2. What tool can be used to register remote SQL Servers in the Enterprise Manager?

3. Is it possible to have two tables named "Authors" in a database?

4. Which system stored procedure can be used to retrieve information about a particular database?

5. Which system table has a row for each database object?

CHAPTER 5

Database Files

About This Chapter

A Microsoft SQL Server database is a collection of information, tables, and other objects used to facilitate searching, sorting, and recombining data. Databases are stored in primary and secondary data files and use log files to ensure data integrity.

This chapter shows how to create databases and discusses ways to manage them, including advanced management techniques that utilize multiple files and disks. Related topics covered in this chapter are the transaction log, database files and filegroups, and techniques for estimating database size requirements.

Before You Begin

To complete the lessons in this chapter you must have

- Installed SQL Server 7. See Chapter 2, "Installation," for installation instructions.
- The ability to log on to SQL Server as an Administrator.
- Installed the Exercise files from the Supplemental Course Materials CD-ROM to your hard disk drive. See the "Getting Started" section in "About This Book" for installation instructions.

Lesson 1: Introduction to Databases

When you create a database, you set up the data storage structure. This structure includes at least one data file and one transaction log file. Before creating a database, it is important to understand two concepts: how SQL Server 7 stores data and the function of the transaction log file.

After this lesson, you will be able to

- Describe how data is stored in databases and transaction logs

- Evaluate database storage considerations

Estimated lesson time: 15 minutes

How Data Is Stored

An understanding of how SQL Server stores data will give you insight into capacity planning, data integrity, and performance. Figure 5.1 shows how a database allocates space.

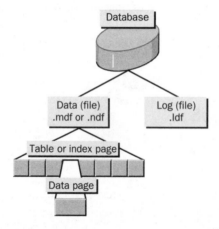

Figure 5.1   Database storage allocation

SQL Server Database Files

SQL Server 7 introduces a new architecture for databases. Database devices, used in previous versions, are no longer needed as storage units for a database. Instead, databases are stored in their own files. The following section introduces these files, which make up a database.

Database File Types

There are three types of database files:

- **Primary data files**—As its name indicates, this file is key. Every database must have one, but only one, primary data file. Primary data filenames usually have an .MDF extension.

- **Secondary data files**—These files can hold all data and objects that are not on the primary data file. Secondary data files are not required. You can choose not to use one, or you can create multiple secondary files. Secondary data filenames usually have an .NDF extension.

- **Log files**—These files hold all of the transaction log information required to recover the database. Every database has at least one log file. Log filenames usually have an .LDF extension.

Database File Considerations

Before creating a database, you must consider a number of issues. To effectively manage resources that the database will use, you must understand how SQL Server stores information. The following list summarizes how SQL Server allocates space to a database and database objects.

- When you create a database, a copy of the *model* database, which includes the system tables, is copied into the database. The minimum size of a database, therefore, is equal to or greater than the size of the model database.

- Data is stored in 8-KB blocks of contiguous disk space. These blocks are called *pages*. A database can store 128 pages per megabyte (MB).

- Rows cannot span pages. The maximum amount of data that can possibly be stored in a single row is 8060 bytes. The maximum amount of space that can be used by all rows on a page is 8094 bytes. Each row has some overhead associated with it, which is why the maximum row length is smaller than the space available on each page to store rows.

Note SQL Server 7 differs significantly from SQL Server 6.5 with regard to data storage. SQL Server 6.5 uses 2-KB pages, thereby limiting a single row to 1962 bytes. Many other capacities have been increased in SQL Server 7; for more information, search for "maximum capacity specifications" in SQL Server Books Online.

- Tables, database objects, and indexes are stored in extents. An *extent* is 8 contiguous pages or 64 KB in size; therefore, a database has 16 extents per megabyte. When as many as eight small objects share an extent, it is called a *mixed extent*. Once a table grows to 8 pages, it uses its own *uniform extent*.

- *Transaction log files* hold all of the information necessary for recovery of the database in case of a system failure. By default, the size of the transaction log is 25 percent of the size of the data files. When planning a database, use this ratio as a guide and adjust it according to the needs of your application.

How the Transaction Log Works

The transaction log records data modifications—INSERT, UPDATE, and DELETE statements—as they are executed.

The logging process, shown in Figure 5.2, occurs as follows:

1. The application sends a data modification.
2. The affected data pages are loaded from the data file into memory (called the *data cache*) if they are not already in the data cache from a previous query.
3. Each data modification statement is recorded as it is made in what is called a write-ahead log. The change is always recorded in the log and written to the log file before that change is made in the database.
4. Once the data pages reside in the data cache and the log pages are recorded on the disk in the transaction log file, the checkpoint process writes all committed transactions to the database on the disk.

A single transaction can include many data modifications. Each transaction starts with a BEGIN TRANSACTION marker. If the application completes all data modifications successfully, the transaction ends with a COMMIT TRANSACTION marker. Such a transaction is referred to as a *committed transaction*.

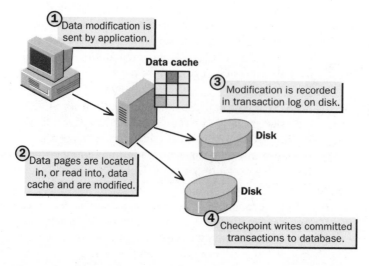

Figure 5.2   How the transaction log works

During normal operation, the checkpoint process routinely checks for committed transactions that have not been written to the data file. The checkpoint process writes the modifications to the data file and checkpoints the transaction to indicate that it has been written to the data file.

If the system fails, the automatic recovery process begins when the SQL Server is restarted. This process uses the transaction log to roll forward (apply the modifications to the data) all committed transactions that have not been checkpointed and roll back (remove) any incomplete transactions.

Transaction logging in SQL Server is not optional. You cannot turn it off, and all normal data modifications must go through the transaction log. For this reason, it is important that the transaction log never become full, as this will prevent data modification in the database. SQL Server does, however, allow two methods of bulk data loading that bypass transaction logging: the bulk copy program (bcp) and the SELECT INTO statement.

Caution Under most circumstances if the hard disk of the computer has a disk-caching controller, you should disable it. Unless a write-caching disk controller is designed specifically for a database, it can seriously harm SQL Server data integrity. Check with your vendor to determine whether the hardware write-caching mechanism of your hard disk is designed for use with a database server.

Lesson Summary

Understanding the structure of a database is crucial to effectively managing resources. The appropriate use of the transaction log can lead to quicker data processing as well as easier data recovery in case of data loss. Understanding how a database uses space allows for better planning and therefore less waste.

Lesson 2: Creating and Dropping Databases

The database is the container that holds all of the database objects, including tables, views, stored procedures, rules, and defaults. As was discussed in the previous lesson, the database may consist of primary and secondary files as well as a transaction log. This lesson describes how to create a database and how to manage an existing one.

After this lesson, you will be able to

- Create a database, specifying size and automatic growth options
- Drop databases that are no longer needed

Estimated lesson time: 45 minutes

Creating Databases

You can create a database using the Database Creation Wizard, SQL Server Enterprise Manager, or the CREATE DATABASE statement. In the course of creating a database you will also create a transaction log for that database.

Using sample exercises, this lesson describes these three procedures step by step and shows you how to specify the name of the database and designate the size and location of the database files. When a new database is created, it is a duplicate of the model database. Any options or settings in the model database are copied to the new database. This lesson also shows you how to drop, or delete, a database.

Caution Information about each database in SQL Server is stored in the sysdatabases system table in the master database. Therefore, you should back up the master database each time you create, modify, or drop a database.

CREATE DATABASE Syntax

Those of you who are familiar with SQL Server 6.5 CREATE DATABASE syntax will notice significant changes in SQL Server 7. For instance, the new version does not use devices, so it is no longer necessary to create a device using the DISK INIT statement. You now specify file information as part of the CREATE DATABASE statement.

```
CREATE DATABASE database_name
[ON
    { [PRIMARY] (NAME = logical_file_name,
        FILENAME = 'os_file_name'
        [, SIZE = size]
        [, MAXSIZE = max_size]
        [, FILEGROWTH = growth_increment] )
    } [,...n]
]
```

```
[LOG ON
    { ( NAME = logical_file_name,
        FILENAME = 'os_file_name'
        [, SIZE = size] )
    } [,...n]
]
[FOR RESTORE]
```

The PRIMARY Option

The PRIMARY option specifies the files in the primary filegroup. The primary filegroup contains all of the database system tables. It also contains all objects not assigned to user-defined filegroups (covered later in this chapter). A database has only one primary data file. The primary data file is the starting point of the database and points to the rest of the files in the database. The recommended file extension for a primary data file is .MDF. If the PRIMARY keyword is not specified, the first file listed in the statement becomes the primary data file.

The FILENAME Option

The FILENAME option specifies the operating system filename and file path. The path in *os_file_name* must specify a folder on a local hard drive of the server on which SQL Server is installed.

Tip If your computer has more than one disk and you are not using Redundant Array of Inexpensive Disks (RAID), place the data file and transaction log file on separate physical disks. This increases performance and can be used, in conjunction with disk mirroring, to decrease the likelihood of data loss in case of media failure.

The SIZE Option

The SIZE option specifies the initial size of each file. You can specify sizes in megabytes using the MB suffix (the default), or in kilobytes using the KB suffix. The minimum value you can assign a file is 512 KB. If a size is not specified for the primary data file, it defaults to the size of the primary data file in the model database. If no log file is specified, a default log file is created that is either 25 percent of the total size of the data files or 512 KB, whichever is larger. If the size is not specified for secondary data files or secondary log files, they default to a size of 1 MB.

The SIZE option sets the minimum size of the file. The file can grow but cannot shrink to less than its designated minimum size. To reduce the minimum size of a file, use the DBCC SHRINKFILE statement.

The MAXSIZE Option

The MAXSIZE option specifies the maximum size to which a file can grow. You can specify sizes in megabytes, using the MB suffix (the default), or in kilobytes using the KB suffix. If no size is specified, the file grows until the disk is full.

The FILEGROWTH Option

The FILEGROWTH option specifies the growth increment of the file. As required, SQL Server will increase a file's size by the amount specified in the FILEGROWTH option. A value of 0 indicates no growth. The value can be specified in megabytes (the default), in kilobytes, or as a percentage (%). A 10 percent default value is assigned if the FILEGROWTH option is not specified. The minimum value that can be assigned is 64 KB, and the specified size is automatically rounded to the nearest 64 KB.

Example: Creating a Database

The following example creates a database called sample, which has a 10-MB primary data file and a 3-MB log file. The primary data file can grow to a maximum of 15 MB in 20 percent increments. In other words, the first time it needed more space, its size would increase by 2 MB. The log file can grow to a maximum of 5 MB in 1-MB increments.

```
CREATE DATABASE sample
ON
   PRIMARY ( NAME=sample_data,
   FILENAME='c:\mssql7\data\sample.mdf',
   SIZE=10MB,
MAXSIZE=15MB,
FILEGROWTH=20%)
LOG ON
   ( NAME=sample_log,
   FILENAME='c:\mssql7\data\sample.ldf',
   SIZE=3MB,
MAXSIZE=5MB,
FILEGROWTH=1MB)
```

Exercise: Creating a Database Using the Create Database Wizard

In this exercise, you will create a database using the Create Database Wizard.

▶ **To create a database using the Create Database Wizard**

1. Log on to your computer as Administrator or another user that is a member of the Administrators local group.

2. Start SQL Server Enterprise Manager.

3. Expand your server group, then expand your server.

4. Click on your server.

5. On the Tools menu, click Wizards. In the Select Wizard window, expand the Database topic, click on Create Database Wizard, and then click OK.

6. Use the information in the following table to create a database with the wizard. For database name, type **sample_wizard**, and when asked to specify a location for the database and log files, type **C:\Mssql7\Data.** Do not create a maintenance plan at this time. Use the wizard defaults for any options not specified in the following table.

File	Initial size	Automatically grow the files	Growth size	Unrestricted file growth
Database	2 MB	Yes	2 MB	Yes
Log	2 MB	Yes	1 MB	Yes

7. Expand the Databases folder, right-click the sample_wizard database, and then click Properties and verify that the database has been created properly.

Exercise: Creating a Database Using SQL Server Enterprise Manager

In this exercise, you will create a database using SQL Server Enterprise Manager.

▶ **To create a database using SQL Server Enterprise Manager**

1. Expand your server group, then expand your server.

2. Right-click Databases, and then click New Database.

3. Type the name **sample_ssem** for the new database.

4. Create the database and log files in the default location: C:\Mssql7\Data. Use the values in the following table to change the properties of the database. You will need to use the General tab to change database properties and the Transaction Log tab to change properties of the transaction log.

File	Initial size	File growth	Maximum file size
Database	2 MB	1 MB	15 MB
Log	1 MB	1 MB	5 MB

5. Click OK to create the new database.

6. Expand the Databases folder, right-click the sample_ssem database, and then click Properties and verify the properties of your new database.

Exercise: Creating a Database Using Transact-SQL Statements

In this exercise, you will use the CREATE DATABASE statement to create a database having the characteristics shown in the following table.

File	Name	Filename	Initial size	File growth	Maximum file size
Database	sample_sql_data	c:\mssql7\data\sample_sql.mdf	2 MB	1 MB	15 MB
Log	sample_sql_log	c:\mssql7\data\sample_sql.ldf	1 MB	1 MB	5 MB

▶   **To create a database using Transact-SQL statements**

1. Open SQL Server Query Analyzer (it can be accessed from the Tools menu of the Enterprise Manager), and log on to the (local) server with Microsoft Windows NT authentication. Your account is a member of the Windows NT Administrators group, which is automatically mapped to the SQL Server sysadmin role.

2. Execute the following CREATE DATABASE statement to create the database. You will find the script for this exercise in C:\Sqladmin\Exercise\Ch05 \Creasmpl.sql. From the Query Analyzer menu, click File, and then select Open. Proceed to the directory referenced above to open Creasmpl.sql.

```
CREATE DATABASE sample_sql
ON
  PRIMARY (NAME=sample_sql_data,
  FILENAME='c:\mssql7\data\sample_sql.mdf',
  SIZE=2MB,
  FILEGROWTH=2MB)
LOG ON
  (NAME=sample_sql_log,
  FILENAME='c:\mssql7\data\sample_sql.ldf',
  SIZE=1MB,
  MAXSIZE=10MB,
  FILEGROWTH=1MB)
```

3. Use sp_helpdb to view the database properties to verify that the database has been created properly.

```
EXEC sp_helpdb sample_sql
```

Dropping a Database

You can drop, or delete, a database by using SQL Server Enterprise Manager or by executing the DROP DATABASE statement. Note that dropping a database means that the database and the disk files used by the database are permanently deleted.

DROP DATABASE Syntax

The syntax for the DROP DATABASE command is as follows:

```
DROP DATABASE database_name [,...n]
```

The following example drops multiple databases using one statement.

```
DROP DATABASE mydb1, mydb2
```

Considerations for Dropping a Database

Before dropping a database, consider the following facts and guidelines:

- With SQL Server Enterprise Manager, you can drop only one database at a time.
- With Transact-SQL, you can drop several databases at once.
- After you drop a database, login IDs for which that particular database was the default database will not have a default database.
- Back up the master database after you drop a database.
- SQL Server does not let you drop master, model, and tempdb databases but does allow you to drop the msdb system database.

Restrictions on Dropping a Database

Due to restrictions, you cannot drop

- A database that is in the process of being restored
- A database that is open for reading or writing by any user
- A database that is publishing any of its tables as part of SQL Server replication

Although SQL Server allows you to drop the msdb system database, you should not drop it if you use, or intend to use, any of the following:

- SQL Server Agent
- Replication
- The SQL Server Web Wizard
- Data Transformation Services (DTS)

Exercise: Deleting a Database Using SQL Server Enterprise Manager

In this exercise, you will use SQL Server Enterprise Manager to delete the sample_wizard database that you created previously.

▶ **To delete a database using SQL Server Enterprise Manager**

1. Expand your server group, then expand your server.

2. Expand Databases, right-click the sample_wizard database, and then click Delete.

3. Verify that the sample_wizard database has been deleted.

Exercise: Deleting a Database Using Transact-SQL Statements

In this exercise, you will use Transact-SQL statements to drop the sample_sql database that you created previously. You will find the script for this exercise in C:\Sqladmin\Exercise\Ch05\Dropdb.sql.

▶ **To delete a database using Transact-SQL statements**

1. Open or switch to SQL Server Query Analyzer.

2. Execute the following DROP DATABASE statement to delete the sample_sql database:

```
DROP DATABASE sample_sql
```

3. Execute the following system stored procedure to generate a list of databases and verify that you have deleted the sample_sql database.

```
EXEC sp_helpdb
```

4. Use SQL Server Enterprise Manager to confirm that the sample_sql database has been deleted.

    If sample_sql is still listed in the Databases folder in SQL Server Enterprise Manager, right-click the Databases folder and click Refresh. The sample_sql database will be removed from the list.

Tip SQL Server Enterprise Manager does not automatically refresh information that has been changed outside of SQL Server Enterprise Manager. To see updated information, use the Refresh option, which is available from the right-click shortcut menu on the various folders.

Lesson Summary

Creating a database can be accomplished by using the Enterprise Manager or a script in the SQL Query Analyzer. One of the most exciting features of SQL Server 7 is the ability to let the database files grow. While this doesn't eliminate the administrator's responsibility for monitoring space usage, it does give much added flexibility in this area.

Lesson 3: Managing Databases

When data modification activity increases or when the size of data increases, the size of the database and log files may need to increase. SQL Server 7 automatically increases the size of database files if the database options are set to do so. You can manually increase or decrease the size of database files by using the ALTER DATABASE, DBCC SHRINKDATABASE, and DBCC SHRINKFILE statements.

You should regularly monitor the size and amount of activity occurring in your transaction log in order to ensure that the transaction log does not run out of space. The SQL Server Performance Monitor provides objects for monitoring the transaction log size and activity.

After this lesson, you will be able to

- Describe options that can be set for a database
- Grow or shrink a database
- Monitor the size of the transaction log
- Grow or shrink database files

Estimated lesson time: 75 minutes

Database Options

After you have created a database, you can view information about the database and change various database options.

Database options determine the characteristics of a database. For example, you can make a database read-only or specify that log entries be removed from the transaction log each time a checkpoint occurs.

Viewing Database Information

You can use SQL Server Enterprise Manager and Transact-SQL to get information about databases.

▶ **To view database information using SQL Server Enterprise Manager**

1. Expand your server group, and then expand your server.
2. Expand Databases, and then click the sample_ssem database.
3. In the details pane, click the Space Allocated tab to view database and transaction log space information.
4. In the Console tree, click the Northwind database.
5. In the details pane, click the Tables & Indexes tab to view table and index space information.

The following table lists commonly used system stored procedures that display information about databases and database options.

System stored procedure	Description
Sp_dboption	Lists all available options.
Sp_helpdb	Reports on all databases on a server. Provides database name, size, owner, ID, creation date, and options.
Sp_helpdb *database_name*	Reports on a specified database only. Provides database name, size, owner, ID, creation date, and options. Additionally, reports details about each data and log file.
Sp_spaceused [*objname*]	Summarizes the storage space used by the current database or by a table in the current database.

Note The size reported by sp_helpdb and sp_spaceused is the total current size of the database including the size of the log files. To determine the size of the data in the database, subtract the size of the log files from the size of the database.

Exercise: Viewing Information About Databases Using Transact SQL Statements

In this exercise, you will use system stored procedures to view information about previously created databases. You will find the script for this exercise in C:\Sqladmin\Exercise\Ch05\Dbinfo.sql.

▶ **To view information about databases using Transact-SQL statements**

1. Open or switch to SQL Server Query Analyzer.

2. Execute the following system stored procedure to generate a list of all databases.

```
EXEC sp_helpdb
```

3. Execute the following system stored procedure to display information about the sample_ssem database.

```
EXEC sp_helpdb sample_ssem
```

4. Execute the following system stored procedure to display information about use of space in the sample_ssem database.

```
USE sample_ssem
EXEC sp_spaceused
```

5. Execute the following system stored procedure to display information about space usage for the authors table in the pubs database.

```
USE pubs
EXEC sp_spaceused authors
```

Setting Database Options

Most database options can be set using SQL Server Enterprise Manager. All database options can be set using the sp_dboption system stored procedure. You can configure database options for only one database at a time. If you want the options applied to future databases, change the model database.

The following table lists some of the more frequently used options:

Database option	Description
dbo use only	Limits use of the database to the database owner only—typically used during development.
read only	Defines a database as read-only—typically used to set security for decision-support databases.
Select into/bulk copy	Allows a database to accept non-logged operations—used during bulk copying of data or when using SELECT INTO to conserve transaction log space.
single user	Restricts database access to one user at a time—used when performing maintenance.
trunc. log on chkpt.	Causes the transaction log to be truncated (committed transactions are removed) every time the checkpoint process occurs—used during development to conserve transaction log space. **Caution: If you set this option, you will need to perform full database backups to ensure recovery in the event of a server or media failure. Since this option negates the usefulness of transaction log backups, it is seldom enabled in a production database.**
autoshrink	Determines whether the database size shrinks automatically.

Exercise: Viewing and Changing Database Options Using Transact-SQL Statements

In this exercise, you will use the sp_dboption system stored procedure to view and change database options. You will find the script for this exercise in C:\Sqladmin \Exercise\Ch05\Dboption.sql. To view and change database options using Transact-SQL statements

1. Switch to SQL Server Query Analyzer (if necessary).

2. Execute the sp_dboption system stored procedure to view a list of database options:

```
EXEC sp_dboption
```

3. Execute the sp_dboption system stored procedure to view a list of database options that are enabled for the sample_ssem database (an empty list is the correct result):

```
EXEC sp_dboption sample_ssem
```

4. Execute the sp_dboption system stored procedure to have the sample_ssem transaction log truncated whenever a checkpoint occurs:

```
EXEC sp_dboption sample_ssem, 'trunc. log on chkpt.', 'true'
```

5. Execute the sp_dboption system stored procedure to verify that the transaction log of the sample_ssem database will be truncated whenever a checkpoint occurs:

```
EXEC sp_dboption sample_ssem
```

Managing Data and Log File Growth

When your database grows, or when data modification activity increases, you may need to expand the size of the data or log files. You can control the size of a database by

- Configuring the data and log files to grow automatically
- Manually increasing the current or maximum size of existing data and log files
- Manually adding secondary data files or log files

Using Automatic File Growth

Using the ALTER DATABASE statement or SQL Server Enterprise Manager, you can opt to have database files expand automatically by a specified amount whenever necessary. The automatic file growth option reduces the administrative tasks involved in database size management and also reduces the possibility of a database running out of space unexpectedly.

This option allows you to specify the initial size, maximum size, and growth increment of each file. If you do not specify a maximum size, a file can continue to grow until it uses all available space on the disk.

The syntax for altering a database is as follows:

```
ALTER DATABASE database
{    ADD FILE <filespec> [TO FILEGROUP filegroup][FOR RESTORE]
    | ADD LOG FILE <filespec>
    | DROP FILE logical_file
    | CREATE FILEGROUP filegroup_name
    | DROP FILEGROUP filegroup
    | MODIFY FILE <filespec>
}
<filespec> ::=
(NAME = 'logical_file_name'
[, FILENAME = 'os_file_name' ]
[, SIZE = size]
[, MAXSIZE = { max_size | UNLIMITED } ]
[, FILEGROWTH = growth_increment] )
```

The MODIFY FILE Option

The MODIFY FILE option allows you to change options for any existing file. In the file specification (filespec) for MODIFY FILE, specify only the name and the option you want to change. You can change only one option at a time; to change more than one option, execute multiple ALTER DATABASE statements. You may not specify the filename.

Expanding Database Files

If an existing file is not configured to grow automatically, you can still increase its size. If you increase the size setting beyond the file's current maximum size without increasing the MAXSIZE statement, the maximum size will be set equal to the new size. A value of 0 for the growth increment (FILEGROWTH) indicates that it does not grow automatically.

The SIZE option sets the minimum size of a file. The file can grow larger but cannot shrink smaller than its designated size. You cannot reduce the file size using the ALTER DATABASE statement. To reduce the minimum size of a file, use the DBCC SHRINKFILE statement.

Adding Secondary Data Files or Log Files

Another way to expand the size of a database is to create secondary data files. The maximum size of a single data file is 32 terabytes, and the maximum size of a single log file is 4 terabytes. It is unlikely that you will need to add files due to insufficient space. Rather, use secondary data files or log files to make use of separate physical disks when you do not use the disk-striping capabilities of RAID systems.

Example: Increasing File Size and Adding a Secondary Data File

The following example increases the current data file size and adds a secondary data file to the sample database.

```
ALTER DATABASE sample
MODIFY FILE ( NAME = 'sample_data',
SIZE = 20MB)
GO
ALTER DATABASE sample
ADD FILE
(NAME = 'sample_data2' ,
FILENAME='c:\mssql7\data\sample2.ndf',
SIZE=10MB ,
MAXSIZE=20MB)
GO
```

Exercise: Modifying a Database Using SQL Server Enterprise Manager

In this exercise, you will add a data file to the sample_ssem database and change the maximum size specification of a data file.

▶ **To modify a database using SQL Server Enterprise Manager**

1. Expand your server group, and then expand your server.

2. Expand Databases, right-click the sample_ssem database, and then click Properties.

3. In the File Name column, click the next empty row and type the filename **sample_ssem_data2**. This is the data file that will contain the additional space. Note that the file location is generated automatically and given the .NDF extension.

4. Change the Space Allocated column value to 2 MB. This is the initial size of the file.

5. To specify that the file should grow by fixed increments, change File Growth to In Megabytes, and change the value to 2.

6. To allow the file to grow as more data space is needed, leave Maximum File Size set to Unrestricted Filegrowth.

7. Click OK to accept your changes and have them applied to the database.

Expanding a Transaction Log

If your transaction log runs out of space, SQL Server cannot record transactions and does not allow changes to your database. When a database grows, or when data modification activity increases, you may need to expand the transaction log.

Monitoring the Log

Monitoring the log helps you determine when it is necessary to expand it. You can monitor the transaction log manually with either SQL Server Enterprise Manager or Microsoft Windows NT Performance Monitor.

SQL Server adds a number of objects and counters to the Windows NT Performance Monitor. Use the Percent Log Used counter of the SQL Server: Database Manager object to monitor the amount of space currently in use in the transaction log of each database. The following table lists the SQL Server: Log Manager object counters you can use to monitor advanced performance statistics for the transaction logs of individual databases.

SQL Server: Log Manager object counter	Displays
Log Bytes Per Flush	Number of bytes in the log buffer when the buffer is flushed
Log Flushes	Number of log flushes
Log Flush Wait Time	Total wait time (in milliseconds)
Log Flush Waits	Number of commits that are waiting on log flush

Expanding the Transaction Log Manually

If the log is not configured to grow automatically, you can still expand the transaction log manually with either SQL Server Enterprise Manager or the ALTER DATABASE statement.

Handling Increased Log Activity

Situations that produce increased transaction log activity include

- Performing a logged bulk data load into a table that has indexes (all inserts, index changes, and extent allocations are logged).

> **Tip** Under certain conditions, it is possible to have non-logged inserts when performing bulk data loads using the bcp utility and the SELECT INTO/bulk copy database option. In this case, if you drop indexes before bulk loading, only extent allocations are logged.

- Transactions that perform many modifications (INSERT, UPDATE, and DELETE statements) to a table within a single transaction. This typically occurs when the statement lacks a WHERE clause, or when the WHERE clause is too general, causing a large number of records to be affected.

- Text or image data in a table being added to or modified using the UPDATE statement. These files are typically large and can cause the transaction log to fill quickly. To avoid this situation, use the WRITETEXT or UPDATETEXT statements. If used correctly, these statements perform non-logged text and image updates to conserve transaction log space.

> **Note** Increased activity can dramatically increase the size of the transaction log. Once increased, space can be freed up quickly by backing up or truncating the log, but it is difficult to reduce the log back to its original size. Log shrinking is a deferred operation that cannot be forced to occur.

Example: Increasing the Log File Size

The following example increases the current log file size for the sample database.

```
ALTER DATABASE sample
MODIFY FILE ( NAME = 'sample_log',
SIZE = 10MB)
GO
```

Exercise: Using Transact-SQL to Increase the Size of the Transaction Log

In this exercise, you will increase the maximum size of the log file to 20 MB for the sample_ssem database. You will find the script for this exercise in C:\Sqladmin\ Exercise\Ch05\Modismpl.sql.

▶ **To increase the maximum size of the transaction log using Transact-SQL statements**

1. Switch to SQL Server Query Analyzer.

2. Execute the following ALTER DATABASE statement to change the maximum size of the sample_ssem database log file to 20 MB:

```
ALTER DATABASE sample_ssem
MODIFY FILE (NAME = 'sample_ssem_log',
MAXSIZE=20MB)
```

3. View the database properties in SQL Server Enterprise Manager or use sp_helpdb to verify that the database has been properly modified.

Note SQL Server Enterprise Manager does not automatically refresh information that has not been changed in SQL Server Enterprise Manager. To keep your information current, use the Refresh option on the various folders often.

Shrinking a Database or a File

When too much space has been allocated, or space is no longer needed, you can either shrink the entire database or shrink specific data files in the database.

There are three ways to shrink a database:

- Remove free space from database files, using the DBCC SHRINKDATABASE statement. When removing free space, you cannot shrink the size of a file below its minimum size (the SIZE specified in the CREATE DATABASE or ALTER DATABASE statements used to create or modify the file).

- Reduce the minimum size of database files, using the DBCC SHRINKFILE statement. You can also use DBCC SHRINKFILE to empty files so that they can be removed with the ALTER DATABASE statement.

- Set the database to shrink automatically.

Shrinking an Entire Database

You can shrink an entire database by using SQL Server Enterprise Manager or by executing the Database Consistency Checker (DBCC) statement, SHRINK-DATABASE. This statement shrinks the size of all data files in the database. Log files are shrunk using a deferred shrink operation, which will occur some time after the log has been backed up or truncated. You cannot force the log files to shrink, even after backing up or truncating the log.

The syntax for the DBCC SHRINKDATABASE command is as follows:

```
DBCC SHRINKDATABASE (database_name [, target_percent]
[, {NOTRUNCATE | TRUNCATEONLY])
```

The target_percent Option

The target_percent option specifies the percentage of free space to be left in the data files after the database has been shrunk. Database files will not shrink below their original size even if this means that the target_percent is not achieved.

Using target_percent, with or without the NOTRUNCATE option, causes used pages to be relocated from the end of the files to the front of the files. The freed space either goes to the operating system (the default) or remains in the file (if NOTRUNCATE is specified). Using the TRUNCATEONLY option causes space at the end of the files to be released to the operating system without moving any pages. The target_percent option is ignored when the TRUNCATEONLY option is used.

The following example sets a target of 25 percent free space for the database, using the statement

```
DBCC SHRINKDATABASE (sample, 25)
```

The following table shows the results when this target is achieved.

Data file	Original size	Current size	Space used	Size after shrinking	Percentage free
Sample_data	20 MB	30 MB	15 MB	20 MB	25 %
Sample_data2	10 MB	15 MB	9 MB	12 MB	25 %
Total	30 MB	45 MB	24 MB	32 MB	25 %

The next table shows the results when the target is not achieved because doing so would require shrinking the files smaller than their original sizes. These results do not show log files, as they would not be affected.

Data file	Original size	Current size	Space used	Size after shrinking	Percentage free
Sample_data	20 MB	30 MB	12 MB	20 MB	40 %
Sample_data2	10 MB	15 MB	3 MB	10 MB	70 %
Total	30 MB	45 MB	15 MB	30 MB	50 %

Exercise: Shrinking a Database

In this exercise, you will use the DBCC SHRINKDATABASE statement to reduce the size of the sample_ssem database so that it contains only 25 percent of the current available space. You will find the script for this exercise in C:\Sqladmin\Exercise\Ch05 \Shrinkdb.sql.

▶ **To shrink a database**

1. Switch to SQL Server Query Analyzer.

2. Execute the following statement to reduce the size of the sample_ssem database to contain only 25 percent free space.

```
DBCC SHRINKDATABASE (sample_ssem, 25)
```

Note You will not see any changes to the database, because the files are still their original size, and shrinking a database will not decrease files below their original size.

Shrinking a Data File in the Database

You can shrink a data file in a database either by using SQL Server Enterprise Manager or by executing the DBCC SHRINKFILE statement (shown in the following example).

```
DBCC SHRINKFILE ({file_name | file_id} [, target_size] [,
{ EMPTYFILE | NOTRUNCATE | TRUNCATEONLY}])
```

These are the only ways to reduce a file to less than its original size.

The target_size Option

The target_size option specifies the size of the data file in megabytes, expressed as an integer. If target_size is not specified, or the target_size is less than the amount of space in use, DBCC SHRINKFILE reduces the size as much as possible.

The EMPTYFILE Option

The EMPTYFILE option migrates all data from the specified file to other files in the same filegroup. Once the file is emptied, SQL Server no longer allows data to be placed in the file. The empty file is dropped using the ALTER DATABASE statement with the REMOVE FILE option.

Example: Shrinking a Data File

This example shrinks the size of the sample_data data file of the sample database to 10 MB:

```
DBCC SHRINKFILE (sample_data, 10)
```

Exercise: Shrinking a Database File

In this exercise, you will use the DBCC SHRINKFILE statement to reduce the size of the secondary database file in the sample_ssem database to 1 MB. You will find the script for this exercise in C:\Sqladmin\Exercise\Ch05\Shrinkfl.sql.

▶ **To shrink a database file**

1. Switch to SQL Server Query Analyzer.

2. Execute the following statement to reduce the size of the sample_ssem_data2 database file to 1 MB. Make sure that you release the freed space to the operating system.

```
USE sample_ssem
DBCC SHRINKFILE (sample_ssem_data2, 1)
```

3. View the database properties to verify that the database file size has been reduced to 1 MB.

Shrinking a Database Automatically

You can also set a database option to recover unused space automatically by setting the database autoshrink option to true. This option can also be changed with SQL Server Enterprise Manager or sp_dboption.

Consider the following guidelines before you shrink a database or a data file:

- The resulting database must be larger than the model database and large enough to hold the existing data.

- Before you shrink a database or a data file, back up both the database and the master database.

- The DBCC SHRINKDATABASE and SHRINKFILE statements execute on a deferred basis, so you may not see the size reduction immediately.

Lesson Summary

When data modification activity increases or when data files grow, the size of the data and log files may need to be expanded. SQL Server 7 provides a way for these files to grow automatically. To manually increase or decrease the size of database files, use the ALTER DATABASE statement and the DBCC SHRINKDATABASE statement.

It is good practice to monitor the activity of your transaction log. The SQL Server Performance Monitor provides an excellent tool to do this.

Lesson 4: Managing Databases on Multiple Disks

If your database implementation uses multiple disks, you may be able to use RAID to increase fault tolerance, achieve better performance, and accommodate database growth more easily.

You can also use named collections of database files (called filegroups) to save data and log files on separate disks in order to simplify administrative tasks, eliminate disk drive contention, and reduce the time it takes to back up critical files.

Note Regardless of the other fault tolerance measures you take to protect your database, remember to back up your files frequently.

After this lesson, you will be able to

- Describe strategies for managing databases on multiple disks
- Create filegroups
- Identify ways to improve database performance using multiple disks

Estimated lesson time: 30 minutes

Leveraging Windows NT Server Fault Tolerance

The *RAID* storage system uses disks that are configured in an array and managed as if they were all one large disk. RAID configurations are not only easy to manage, but also provide increased performance (due to simultaneous disk activity) and reliability (if one disk fails, others keep working). *Fault tolerance* is the ability of the operating system to continue functioning without data loss when part of the system fails. Windows NT supports software implementations of RAID at three levels, 0, 1, and 5. The levels are ranked numerically according to their ability to provide fault tolerance. RAID 0 provides no fault tolerance, whereas RAID 5 provides the best fault tolerance. Windows NT Server implements RAID levels 0, 1, and 5, which can be used with SQL Server.

Using Disk Striping (RAID 0)

Disk striping writes data evenly across multiple disks.

- Microsoft Windows NT Server–based disk striping implements RAID level 0. This is the highest-performance RAID level but offers no fault tolerance.
- If one disk fails, all data on the stripe set is inaccessible.

Using Disk Mirroring (RAID 1)

Disk mirroring protects against media failure by maintaining a fully redundant copy of a partition on another disk.

- Windows NT Server–based disk mirroring is a form of continual backup and implements RAID level 1.

- Windows NT Server–based disk mirroring requires a lot of disk space. Fifty percent of your disk space is redundant.

- Disk mirroring minimizes downtime and other expenses involved in recovering and restoring data.

Note Previous versions of SQL Server supported device mirroring; however, SQL Server 7 does not. Use hardware-based or software-based RAID instead.

Using Disk Striping with Parity (RAID 5)

Disk striping with parity writes data evenly across multiple disks and includes redundant parity data.

- Windows NT Server–based disk striping with parity implements RAID level 5. This RAID level offers excellent performance and fault tolerance.

- You can achieve fault tolerance protection that equals disk mirroring but uses less disk space. All told, the size of one disk in the set is redundant. For example, if you have 5 disks, each 1 GB in size, 1 GB of space would be redundant, making the capacity of the stripe set with parity 4 GB.

- If any one disk fails, lost data is regenerated from the remaining disks of a striped set. In this case, disk striping with parity loses its performance advantage because data recovery takes longer.

- Disk striping with parity requires more system memory (RAM) than disk mirroring.

Note Hardware-based RAID solutions perform better than the software implementation in Windows NT Server, and may support advanced features such as replacing a drive while the system is operating. The main disadvantage of hardware-based solutions is that they are expensive.

Using RAID with SQL Server

The following table lists and compares RAID solutions typically used with SQL Server to show the varying levels of redundancy and fault tolerance.

RAID implementation	Advantages	Disadvantage
Hardware-based RAID level 3 or 5	Has excellent performance Does not compete for processor cycles	Cost
Hardware-based RAID level 1	Has best redundancy Does not compete for processor cycles	Cost
Windows NT–based RAID level 1	Has good redundancy Is low in cost	Uses system processing resources
Windows NT–based RAID level 5	Has excellent read performance Is low in cost	Uses system processing resources

Creating Filegroups

If your hardware setup includes multiple disk drives and you are not using RAID, you can place database files on different disks, as shown in Figure 5.3.

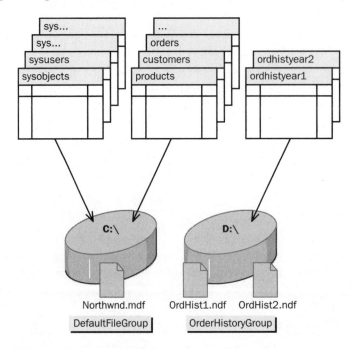

Figure 5.3   Placing database files on different disks

This implementation allows for the building of very large databases that can improve performance because the disks operate simultaneously. To simplify the management of multiple database files, SQL Server provides filegroups. *Filegroups* are named collections of files. Every database has one default filegroup and you can create additional filegroups as needed.

You can assign specific tables, indexes, or the text, ntext, and image data from a table to a specific filegroup. In Figure 5.3, the Ordhist1.ndf and Ordhist2.ndf files are placed on a separate disk to keep files that are heavily queried separate from those that are heavily modified and to reduce disk drive contention.

System administrators can back up and restore individual files or filegroups instead of backing up or restoring an entire database.

Note Log files are not part of a filegroup. Log space is managed separately from data space. Filegroups are used for managing data files only.

Considerations When Using Filegroups

Using filegroups is an advanced database design technique. You must understand your database structure, data, transactions, and queries in order to determine the best way to place tables and indexes in specific filegroups. In many cases, using the striping capabilities of RAID systems provides much of the same performance gain that you might achieve by using filegroups, without the added administrative burden of defining and managing filegroups.

Types of Filegroups

SQL Server offers the following three types of filegroups:

- The *primary filegroup* contains the primary data file and any secondary data files that are not part of another filegroup. All system tables are placed in the primary filegroup. For this reason, it is very important that the primary filegroup does not run out of space.

- *User-defined filegroups*, which are specified using the FILEGROUP keyword in a CREATE DATABASE or an ALTER DATABASE statement.

- The *default filegroup*, which can be any filegroup in the database. Initially the primary filegroup is the default filegroup, but members of the db_owner fixed database role can change the default filegroup at any time. All tables and indexes for which a filegroup was not specified upon creation are placed in the default filegroup.

Sizing the Default Filegroup

It is important to size the primary filegroup correctly. The primary filegroup must be large enough to hold all system tables and, if it remains the default filegroup, large enough to hold any tables not allocated to a user-defined filegroup.

If the primary filegroup runs out of space, new information cannot be added to the system tables. If a user-defined filegroup runs out of space, only the user files that are specifically allocated to that filegroup are affected. The primary filegroup will fill only if the automatic growth option is turned off or if the disk holding the primary filegroup runs out of space. To allow the primary filegroup to grow, turn the automatic growth option back on or free more disk space. For more information on automatic growth, search for "automatic growth" in SQL Server Books Online.

Example: Creating a User-Defined Filegroup

The following example creates a user-defined filegroup in the Northwind database and adds a secondary data file to the user-defined filegroup.

```
ALTER DATABASE northwind
ADD FILEGROUP orderhistorygroup
GO

ALTER DATABASE northwind
ADD FILE
(NAME = 'ordhistyear1',
FILENAME = 'c:\mssql7\data\ordhist1.ndf',
SIZE = 5MB)
TO FILEGROUP orderhistorygroup
GO
```

Viewing Filegroup Information

The following table lists system stored procedures that display information about database files and filegroups.

System stored procedure	Description
sp_helpfile '*logical_file_name*'	Returns the physical names and attributes of all files or a specified file associated with the current database.
sp_helpfilegroup '*filegroup_name*'	Returns the names and attributes of filegroups associated with the current database. If a filegroup name is specified, sp_helpfilegroup returns a list of the files in the group.

Performance Considerations

If you want to achieve the best performance from your database, consider the following guidelines.

Use RAID to Improve Performance or Fault Tolerance

You can use RAID either to gain faster access to data or to increase the safety of your data. Use the appropriate RAID level to achieve the performance gains you want while still maintaining the fault tolerance levels you require.

When you simply want to increase performance, choose RAID disk striping over filegroups.

Eliminate Disk Drive Contention

Place data files and transaction log files on separate physical disks with separate input/output (I/O) controllers so that concurrent writes to the transaction log do not compete with INSERT, UPDATE, or DELETE actions to the database tables.

Appropriate use of filegroups can eliminate disk drive contention. SQL Server 7 uses a proportional space allocation algorithm. For example, if a filegroup has two files, one of which has twice the free space of the other, two pages will be allocated from the file with more empty space for every one page allocated from the other file. This means that every file in a filegroup should have a similar percentage of space used.

Use Filegroups to Simplify Backups

Use filegroups to place database objects on separate disks. This allows you to use individual backup strategies based on how often data is revised. If you have a group of files that change often, you can back up those tables or objects frequently.

Lesson Summary

SQL Server 7 can take advantage of features of Windows NT to more safely and quickly store and retrieve data. In this lesson, you learned how to use Windows NT fault tolerance features to reduce the risk of data loss and eliminate disk drive contention. It is considered best practice to avoid the use of filegroups in SQL Server, instead using RAID for faster access and better protection.

Lesson 5: Capacity Planning

One of the main functions of a system administrator is to allocate, manage, and monitor the space and storage requirements for a database. Estimating the space that a database requires can help you plan your storage layout and determine hardware requirements.

After this lesson, you will be able to

- Estimate the space requirements for a database

Estimated lesson time: 15 minutes

Estimating the Minimum Size of a Database

Figure 5.4 lists a number of factors that you should consider when attempting to determine the space requirements of your database.

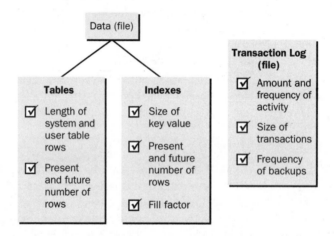

Figure 5.4   Factors to consider when estimating the size of a database

Consider the following when you estimate the amount of space that your database will occupy:

- The size of the model database and the system tables (include projected growth). This is typically not a large percentage of the database size.

- The amount of data in your tables (include projected growth).

- The number of indexes and the size of each, especially the size of the key value, the number of rows, and the fill factor setting.

- The size of the transaction log. Your estimate should take into account factors such as the amount and frequency of modification activity, the size of each transaction, and how often you back up (dump) the log.

Note As a starting point, you should allocate 25 percent of the database size to the transaction log for online transaction processing (OLTP) environments. You can allocate a smaller percentage for databases that are used primarily for queries.

Estimating the Amount of Data in Tables

After you consider the amount of space that is allocated to the model database, you should estimate the minimum amount of data in each table, including projected growth. This can be calculated by determining the total number of rows, the row size, the number of rows that fit on a page, and the total number of pages required for each table in the database.

Estimating the Number of Pages in a Table

To estimate the minimum number of pages required for a table, find out the number of characters for each row and the approximate number of rows that the table will have. Calculate the number of pages, using the following method:

1. Calculate the number of bytes in a row by totaling the number of bytes that each column contains. If one or more columns are defined as variable length— such as a column for names—you can add the column average to the total. Add 9 bytes to the total, as each row has an overhead of 9 bytes.

2. Determine the maximum number of rows contained in each data page. To do this, divide 8094 by the number of bytes in a row. Round the result down to the nearest whole number because SQL Server does not allow a row to cross pages. In practice, it is unlikely that this many rows will actually be stored on a page. SQL Server keeps some free space on each page to allow for a small amount of individual row growth per page when variable-length data is updated to a larger size.

3. Divide the approximate number of rows in the table by the number of rows that are contained in each data page. The result equals the minimum number of pages needed to store your table.

Example: Calculating Table Size

This example calculates the size of a table that has four int columns, three char(30) columns, and one datetime column. The table will have 250,000 rows.

1. Total row size: 4 * 4 bytes (the int columns) + 3 * 30 bytes (the char columns) + 1 * 8 bytes (the datetime column) + 9 bytes (row overhead)= 123 bytes

2. Number of rows per page: 8094 / 123 = 65 rows per page

3. Number of pages in the table: 250,000 / 65 = 3847 pages

4. Size of the table: 3847 * 8 KB = 30,776 KB or about 31 MB

In this example, SQL Server stored 63 rows per page for this table. The total number of pages is 3969, and the table size is 31,752 KB.

Estimating the Amount of Data in Indexes

Estimating index space becomes more difficult when indexes have two types of pages. The first type, called *leaf pages,* holds the indexed key values. The second type forms the binary search tree that speeds indexed search and retrieval.

Index pages can intentionally be left unfilled by specifying a fill factor of less than 100 (percent) when building the index. This increases the number of pages in the index but makes table row inserts and updates faster because fewer new index pages need to be allocated during these operations.

Clustered vs. Nonclustered Indexes

A *clustered index* stores the data rows of a table in the indexed order of the key values of the index. A table can only have one clustered index. A *nonclustered index* is a separate structure that stores a copy of the key values from the table in indexed order and a pointer to each corresponding data row in the table.

Extra space for a clustered index is taken up only by the b-tree index pages because the data rows in the table are the index leaf pages. Also, if a fill factor is specified when building a clustered index, the data pages of the table are filled only to the level specified by the fill factor, making the table larger.

A nonclustered index consists of the b-tree index pages as well as the leaf pages of the index. The leaf pages hold a pointer to and an indexed copy of the key value of each row in the table. If the table has a clustered index, the pointer in a nonclustered index is the clustered index key value. For this reason, you should use small key values for the clustered index of a table that will have nonclustered indexes, or else the nonclustered indexes can become very large.

Index Size Example

The following table shows some examples of the sizes of various indexes added to the table for which the size was calculated in the previous example.

The table first gives the size of an index based on a char(30) key column when there is no clustered index on the table. The size of the same index is then given a second time when there is a clustered index on the table. Finally, the size of the index is given again when the index has a fill factor of 50 percent and there is a clustered index on the table. Note that this index is larger than the table! The clustered index used a char(30) key column—this is not recommended and illustrates the dramatic increase in size of nonclustered indexes if you do use such a large key column for a clustered index.

The same figures are then repeated for an index based in an int key column instead of a char(30) key column.

Reminder: the table has 250,000 rows, and is 3969 pages or 31,752 KB in size.

Key	Clustered on table	Fill factor	Pages	Size
One char(30) column	No	100	1360	10,880 KB
One char(30) column	Yes	100	2296	18,368 KB
One char(30) column	Yes	50	4548	36,384 KB
One int column	No	100	560	4480 KB
One int column	Yes	100	1492	11,936 KB
One int column	Yes	50	2944	23,552 KB

Lesson Summary

There are many factors involved in the estimation of space requirements for a database, including the size of the rows in your tables, the estimated growth of the tables, the number and size of the indexes, and the fill factor for the indexes are some important factors. This lesson gave you the tools to estimate the size requirements of a database, allowing you to manage your resources more effectively.

Review

The following questions are intended to reinforce key information presented in the chapter. If you are unable to answer a question, review the appropriate lesson and then try the question again. Answers to the questions can be found in Appendix A, "Questions and Answers."

1. You are creating a database that you expect will have a high level of INSERT, UPDATE, and DELETE activity. Should you accept the default transaction log size of 25 percent of the total database size? What factors must you consider if the database is going to be used primarily for queries?

2. You are creating a database on multiple disks that will be queried extensively by users. What are some steps that you can take to improve performance and avoid disk contention?

3. During a routine monitoring of the data files and transaction log, you notice that the transaction log is extremely close to being full. What would happen if the log filled? What steps can you take to avoid running out of transaction log space?

CHAPTER 6

Transferring Data

About This Chapter

In this chapter, you will learn how to transfer data and database objects into and out of Microsoft SQL Server databases. SQL Server provides a number of data transfer mechanisms. The bulk of the chapter focuses on one of these—Data Transformation Services (DTS). The others are briefly introduced, with more detail provided in SQL Server Books Online, which can be found in the SQL Server 7 program group.

Before You Begin

To complete the lessons in this chapter, you must have

- Installed SQL Server 7. See Chapter 2, "Installation," for installation instructions.
- The ability to log on to SQL Server as an Administrator.
- Installed the StudyNwind database. See the "Getting Started" section in "About This Book" for StudyNwind database installation instructions.

- Installed the Exercise files from the Supplemental Course Materials CD-ROM to your hard disk drive. See the "Getting Started" section in "About This Book" for installation instructions.

Lesson 1: Introduction to Transferring Data

You can import and export data from SQL Server with several tools and Transact-SQL statements. Additionally, with the programming models and application programming interfaces (APIs) that are available with SQL Server, such as the Data Transformation Services object model, you can write your own programs to import and export data. This lesson provides an overview of the data transfer process and describes the various tools you can use to transfer data in SQL Server 7.

After this lesson, you will be able to

- Describe the rationale for, and the process of, transferring and transforming data
- Describe the tools for transferring data in SQL Server version 7

Estimated lesson time: 45 minutes

Why Transfer Data?

As a system administrator, you must understand how to manage data and transfer it between applications and environments. Almost all environments require some degree of data transfer for one or more of the following reasons:

- To move data to another server or location
- To make a copy of data
- To archive data
- To migrate data

The process of copying data from one environment to another typically involves

- Identifying the data source
- Specifying the data destination
- Manipulating or transforming the data between the source and destination (optional)

Simple importing and exporting of data is the most basic form of data transfer. Even this simple process can transform data—if, for example, you specify a different data type for a column or save a file in another product version or format.

A SQL Server administrator frequently needs to transfer data between heterogeneous environments. For example, you might transfer sales information from an Oracle database to a SQL Server database or transfer data from an online transaction processing system to a data warehouse.

Why Transform Data?

Migrating and transferring data between different environments is a common occurrence that often involves the manipulation or transformation of data. Transforming data can be as simple as mapping transformation data types or as complex as programming data logic to handle data transformations.

During data transformation, missing values can be added and column values summarized, decoded, decomposed, converted, and translated to a common measure or format. The captured data typically is integrated, made consistent, validated, and restructured before it is stored at the destination.

When you transform data, you may want to do one or more of the following:

Change the Format of Data

Transforming data frequently requires changing its format. Suppose, for example, that a value of 1 or 0 is stored in the Active_Customer column in your database, but the data that you want to transfer into your database represents the value as the text 'true' or 'false'. You can convert the 'true' and 'false' values to 1 and 0 values when you transfer the data into your database. Numeric and date formats are frequently changed.

Restructure and Map Data

Restructuring and mapping data frequently involves combining data from multiple data sources, tables, and columns into a single data set at the destination. For example, you can preprocess the data (this is known as data aggregation or summarization) and store the preprocessed data at your destination.

Make Data Consistent

When you import data from another source, you should make sure that the new data is consistent with the existing data. This is sometimes called *data scrubbing*. Data can be inconsistent in several ways:

- The data is consistent, but the representation is not consistent with how you want to store it at the destination. For example, suppose that a credit rating is represented by the values 1, 2, and 3. Making the data consistent may require translating these values to the character string values of 'Good', 'Average', and 'Poor'.

- The data representation is correct, but it is inconsistently represented. For example, a company name may be stored in several ways, such as ABC Corp., ABC, or ABC Corporation. In this instance, you can make the data consistent by requiring that the destination always store the company name as ABC Corporation.

You generally can make your data consistent by translating codes or values to readable strings or by converting mixed values to single values.

Validate Data

When you validate data, you verify the accuracy and correctness of the data that you import. For example, you can require that data meet a specific condition before it can be included with your destination data. Or you can verify that a customer ID already exists at the destination before you transfer additional information for the customer into the destination data.

If you discover any invalid data, try to determine where the fault originated and correct the processes that are contributing to the error. Save invalid data to a log for later examination to determine why it is incorrect.

Tools for Transferring Data in SQL Server

SQL Server provides several tools and Transact-SQL statements for transferring data. The data that you can transfer is typically in the form of tables or files. The method you choose for importing or exporting data depends on a variety of user requirements, including

- The format of the source and destination data
- The location of the source and destination data
- Whether the import or export is a one-time occurrence or an ongoing task
- Whether a command-prompt utility, Transact-SQL statement, or graphical interface is preferred (for ease of use)
- The type of import or export operation

The following table describes the tools that SQL Server provides for transferring data.

Tool	Description	Use
DTS Import Wizard and DTS Export Wizard	Allow users to interactively create DTS packages that can be used to import, export, and transform data.	Transferring data between heterogeneous data sources or transferring all of the objects in a SQL Server 7 database to another SQL Server 7 database.
DTS Designer	Allows experienced database administrators to import, export, and transform data and define complex data workflows.	Transferring homogeneous and heterogeneous data from multiple sources and for setting up complex workflows.
dtsrun utility	A command-prompt utility that allows you to execute existing DTS packages from a command prompt.	Executing a DTS package as part of a batch or scheduled job.
Bulk copy program (bcp utility)	A command-prompt utility that imports and exports native SQL Server data files or ASCII text files.	Importing data into a SQL Server table from a file or exporting data from a SQL Server table to a file.
Transact-SQL statement	SELECT INTO and INSERT SELECT.	Selecting data to add to a table from an existing SQL Server table—SELECT INTO creates a new table, and INSERT SELECT requires an existing table.
	BULK INSERT.	Copying a data file into a database table in a user-specified format. The fastest method of loading large amounts of data into a table.
	BACKUP and RESTORE.	Copying a complete SQL Server database (all data and objects) to another SQL Server.
sp_attach_db	Attaches a database to a server.	Moving or copying a complete SQL Server database (all data and objects) to another SQL Server by copying the database files.
Replication	Maintains duplicate table schema, data, or stored procedure definitions from a source database to a destination database, usually on separate servers.	Maintaining copies of data intermittently on multiple databases (does not guarantee that the data will be consistent at the same point in time). An ongoing process.
Host Data Replicator	Provides replication to and from SQL Server and mainframe databases such as IBM DB2. Runs in conjunction with Microsoft SNA Server, a gateway and application integration platform that is part of BackOffice. Also supports data transformations such as conversion of date and timestamps. Data can replace existing tables or be merged on a row-by-row basis.	Transferring data between SQL Server and mainframe databases such as IBM DB2.

Note DTS is not intended to replace SQL Server replication. Replication uses a store-and-forward database to capture changes in one location and then forward them to multiple destinations. Replication captures changes from relational data sources and normally provides very little data cleansing and transformation capabilities. Using DTS rather than replication requires executing a complete transformation for each destination.

Note The SQL Server Transfer Manager found in previous versions of SQL Server is no longer available. DTS provides all of the functionality formerly provided by the SQL Server Transfer Manager.

Tip To migrate data from SQL Server 6.5 to SQL Server 7, use the SQL Server Upgrade Wizard, as described in Chapter 3, "Upgrading to SQL Server 7.0."

Exercise: Enabling Bulk Copy

In this exercise, you will set the appropriate options in the StudyNwind database to enable fast bulk copy.

Note You will use the StudyNwind database for the first time in this exercise. StudyNwind is a copy of the Northwind sample database that is installed with SQL Server. You must use the C:\Sqladmin\Exercise\Setup\Maknwind.cmd batch file to create the StudyNwind database, as explained in the "Getting Started" section of the "About This Book" material at the front of this book. You can re-create StudyNwind as often as you like by executing the batch file again during the course, so you are free to change the data without worrying about making the database unusable.

▶ **To configure the StudyNwind database for bulk copy**

1. Start SQL Server Enterprise Manager.

2. Expand your server, and expand Databases.

3. Right-click the StudyNwind database icon, and then click Properties.

4. Click the Options tab and verify that the Select Into/Bulk Copy option is checked. If it is not, check it and then click OK.

Exercise: Importing Data with the bcp Utility

In this exercise, you will create a batch file that uses the bcp utility to import more than 1000 records from a tab-delimited text file into the Products table in the StudyNwind database. C:\Sqladmin\Exercise\Ch06\Runbcpa.cmd is a completed batch file for this exercise.

▶   **To import data using the bcp utility**

1. Open Notepad and type the following bcp command:

   bcp StudyNwind..Products in C:\Sqladmin\Exercise\Ch06\Newprods.txt /c /t"," /r\n /e C:\Sqladmin\Exercise\Ch06\Newprods.err /b250 /m50 /SSQLSERVER /Usa

   ---

   Important You must enter the command as a single line (do not insert any hard returns). The command syntax for the bcp utility must include only one line of information. The arguments are case sensitive. Replace the server name with your server name. For more information, search for "bcp utility" in SQL Server Books Online.

   An explanation of the parameters is given in the following table.

Parameter	Value
Database and table	StudyNwind..Products
Data direction	In
Transfer file	C:\Sqladmin\Exercise\Ch06\Newprods.txt
Data: character only	/c
Field terminator: comma	/t","
Row terminator: new line	/r\n
Error file	/e C:\Sqladmin\Exercise\Ch06\Newprods.err
Batch size	/b250
Maximum errors	/m50
Server name (replace SQLSERVER with your server name if your server is not called SQLSERVER)	/SSQLSERVER
Username	/Usa

2. Save the file with the name Runbcp.cmd in the C:\Sqladmin\Exercise\Ch06 folder.

3. From a command prompt, execute the C:\Sqladmin\Exercise\Ch06\Runbcp.cmd file. You are prompted for a password. Enter the password for the sa login and press Enter, or just press Enter if your sa password is blank.

   How many rows were copied?

4. In Notepad, review the output from the C:\Sqladmin\Exercise\Ch06 \Newprods.err error file.

   Did any errors occur?

5. Switch to SQL Server Enterprise Manager.

6. Right-click the StudyNwind database, and then click Properties.

7. In the Properties dialog box, click the Options tab, clear the Select Into/Bulk Copy check box, and then click OK.

Lesson Summary

This lesson provided an overview of the data transfer process and described the various tools you can use to transfer data in SQL 7. You can import and export data from SQL Server with several tools and Transact-SQL statements. Additionally, with the programming models and APIs that are available with SQL Server, such as the DTS object model, you can write your own programs to import and export data.

The method you choose for importing or exporting data depends on a variety of user requirements, including the format of the data, the location of the data, how often the transfer will be occurring, the type of import or export, and finally, ease of use.

Lesson 2: Introduction to Data Transformation Services

Many organizations centralize data to improve corporate decision making. However, this data often is stored in a large variety of formats on a number of different systems. By using DTS, you can import, export, and transform data among multiple homogeneous or heterogeneous sources and destinations using an OLE DB–based architecture. This lesson introduces you to DTS and describes how to create a DTS package.

After this lesson, you will be able to

- Create a DTS package with the DTS Import and DTS Export Wizards

Estimated lesson time: 60 minutes

Overview of DTS

DTS is able to import, export, and transform data between SQL Server and any OLE DB, Open Database Connectivity (ODBC), or text file format. When you use DTS, you can

- Copy table schema and data between database management systems (DBMSs).

- Create custom transformation objects that can be integrated into third-party products.

- Build data warehouses and data marts in SQL Server by importing and transferring data from multiple heterogeneous sources interactively or automatically on a regularly scheduled basis.

- Access applications using third-party OLE DB providers. This allows applications for which an OLE DB provider exists to be used as sources and destinations of data.

DTS can be used with any OLE DB data source and destination; you are not required to use SQL Server 7 for either source or destination. This makes DTS a general-purpose data transfer and transformation tool with a wide range of applications.

Note DTS moves table schema and data only between heterogeneous data sources. Triggers, stored procedures, rules, defaults, constraints, and user-defined data types can be transferred only if the source and destination are both SQL Server 7.

The DTS Process

The process of transferring data is an integral part of all database management systems. DTS provides an extensible Component Object Model (COM)–based architecture that allows customers, independent software vendors (ISVs), and consultants to create new OLE DB data sources and destinations, tasks, and transformations.

With DTS, users create and execute a DTS package, which completely describes all of the work that is performed as part of the transfer and transformation process.

The DTS Package

A DTS package defines one or more data transformation steps. Steps are executed in a coordinated sequence, which you can control. Each step can perform a different type of operation. For example, step 1 might copy and transform data from an OLE DB source to an OLE DB destination by using the DTS Data Pump, step 2 might execute a script, and step 3 might load and execute an external program (.EXE) or even a batch file (.CMD or .BAT). Figure 6.1 illustrates such a DTS package.

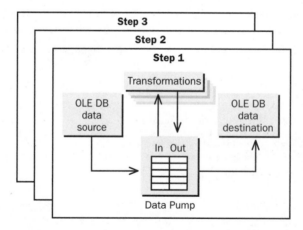

Figure 6.1   An example of a DTS package

DTS packages are self-contained and can be executed from SQL Server Enterprise Manager or by using the dtsrun utility. DTS packages can be stored in the msdb database in SQL Server, linked to the Microsoft Repository, or saved as COM-structured storage files. These options and their implications are described in Lesson 3.

The DTS Data Source and Destination

When you use DTS, the data source and destination can be heterogeneous. Using SQL Server as a data source or destination is not required. DTS may simply be the mechanism that transfers data between two data sources.

DTS uses OLE DB providers to import, export, and transform data. Using OLE DB allows access to a wide variety of data source and destination types. OLE DB is a COM interface–based data access mechanism. It can access any data storage format (databases, spreadsheets, text files, and so on) for which an OLE DB provider is available. An OLE DB provider is a software component that exposes an OLE DB interface. Each OLE DB provider is specific to a particular storage mechanism, such as SQL Server databases, Microsoft Access databases, or Microsoft Excel spreadsheets.

Note OLE DB is an evolutionary extension of ODBC. ODBC is limited to SQL-based relational databases; OLE DB provides access to any data format. OLE DB providers are conceptually the same as ODBC drivers. The OLE DB provider for ODBC makes it possible to use OLE DB applications, such as DTS, with any data source for which you have an ODBC driver.

The following table describes the OLE DB providers available with SQL Server. Other providers are available from third-party vendors.

Data source or data destination	Description
Native OLE DB	Accesses applications such as Microsoft SQL Server, Excel, and Access, as well as workgroup and enterprise databases
ODBC	Accesses Oracle, Access, and DB2 by using the OLE DB provider for ODBC
ASCII text files	Access ASCII fixed-field-length text files and ASCII delimited text files by using the SQL Server DTS Flat File OLE DB provider
Customized	Supports third-party and ISV OLE DB providers

Using DTS steps, it is also possible to create packages that do such things as performing high-speed nonlogged inserts (using bcp or BULK INSERT), transforming and publishing data as HTML, or exporting data to pivot tables in Excel.

The DTS Data Pump

The DTS Data Pump is an OLE DB service provider that provides the infrastructure to import, export, and transform data between heterogeneous data stores. It is a high-speed, in-process COM server that moves and transforms OLE DB rowsets. The DTS Data Pump uses OLE DB because OLE DB provides access to the broadest possible range of relational and nonrelational data stores.

The DTS Data Pump provides the extensible COM-based architecture that allows complex data validations and transformations as the data moves from the source to the destination. The Data Pump exposes the source and destination OLE DB rowsets to scripting languages, such as VBScript, Microsoft JScript, and PerlScript, in a DTS package. This ability allows the expression of complex procedural logic as simple, reusable ActiveX scripts. Scripts can validate, convert, or transform column values as they move from the source through the Data Pump to the destination.

DTS Tools

DTS tools include the DTS Import Wizard, the DTS Export Wizard, DTS Designer, the dtswiz and dtsrun command-prompt utilities, and the Data Transformation Services node in the SQL Server Enterprise Manager console tree.

The DTS Import and DTS Export Wizards

The DTS Import and DTS Export Wizards offer many ways to customize or simplify the method in which data is copied from source to destination. With DTS wizards, you can

- Define DTS packages in an easy-to-use, interactive user interface. The result of using the wizard is a package that you can save and edit directly with DTS Designer if you want to.
- Copy data between heterogeneous data sources.
- Schedule DTS packages for later execution.
- Copy an entire table or the results of a SQL query, such as a query that involves joins of multiple tables or even distributed queries. The Query Builder within the wizard allows users who are inexperienced with the SQL language to build queries interactively.

Tip When copying a table, the DTS wizards by default do not copy indexes, triggers, or constraints. If the table is to be created by the package, you can manually edit the Transact-SQL that is used to create the table and add the statements needed to create indexes, triggers, or constraints.

- Copy all of the objects from one SQL Server 7 database to another.

You can start the DTS Import Wizard and the DTS Export Wizard from SQL Server Enterprise Manager, from the Microsoft SQL Server 7 program group on the Start menu, or by using the dtswiz command-prompt utility.

Note The DTS Import Wizard and the DTS Export Wizard are the same utility. You can move data into or out of SQL Server or any other OLE DB data source using either wizard. The text in the title bar of the utility changes depending on which wizard you select.

Exercise: Importing Data with the DTS Import Wizard

In this exercise, you will import summary data into a new table using the DTS Import Wizard.

▶ **To import data from a SQL query**

1. Right-click your server, point to All Tasks, and then click Import Data. This launches the Data Transformation Services Wizard.

2. Click Next.

   In the following steps, if an option is not specified, accept the default.

3. In Source, select Microsoft OLE DB Provider For SQL Server.

4. In Server, select (local).

5. Select Use Windows NT Authentication.

6. In Database, select StudyNwind. Click Next.

7. In Destination, select Microsoft OLE DB Provider For SQL Server.

8. In Server, select (local).

9. Select Use Windows NT Authentication.

10. In Database, select StudyNwind. Click Next.

11. Select Use A Query To Specify The Data To Transfer. Click Next.

12. In Query Statement, type

    ```
    SELECT ProductName, SUM(o.UnitPrice * Quantity) AS Total
    FROM [Order Details] o
    INNER JOIN Products p ON o.ProductID = p.ProductID
    GROUP BY ProductName
    ```

    If you don't want to type the query, you can click Browse and open C:\Sqladmin\Exercise\Ch06\Query.sql.

13. Click Parse. If you have typed the statement correctly, you see the following confirmation message

    ```
    The SQL statement is valid.
    ```

    Click OK to close the message. Click Next.

14. In the Table(s) list, click the value in the Destination Table column (the default value is Results). Since you are creating a new destination table, you cannot select its name from the drop-down list. Type in the name of the new table: **ProductTotals**.

15. Click the ellipsis button in the Transform column.

16. Check Drop And Recreate Destination Table. Uncheck Nullable for Total under Mappings. Click OK to close the Column Mappings and Transformations dialog box. Click Next.

17. Check only Run Immediately in the When section.

18. Check Save DTS Package and select SQL Server in the Save section. Click Next.

19. In Name, type **StudyNwind Product Totals**. In Description, type **Year to date product totals**.

20. For Server Name, select (local), select Use Windows NT Authentication, and then click Next.

21. Click Finish. The Transferring Data dialog box indicates the progress of the data transfer. An error will occur on the Drop Table ProductTotals Step. This is expected, as the table does not already exist. It will not affect the data transfer.

22. A dialog box indicates when the transfer has completed successfully. Click OK to close the dialog box, and click Done to close the Transferring Data dialog box.

23. Expand your server, expand Data Transformation Services, and click the Local Packages icon. Note that your new DTS package is listed in the details pane.

24. Open SQL Server Query Analyzer.

25. To view the imported results in the ProductTotals table, execute the following Transact-SQL statement.

```
SELECT * FROM StudyNwind..ProductTotals
```

Exercise: Exporting Data with the DTS Export Wizard

In this exercise, you will export data using the DTS Export Wizard and save the DTS package. The DTS package will copy a list of South American customers into a delimited text file.

▶ **To export data by using the DTS Export Wizard**

1. Right-click your server, point to All Tasks, and then click Export Data. This launches the Data Transformation Services Wizard.

2. Click Next.

   In the following steps, if an option is not specified, accept the default.

3. In Source, select Microsoft OLE DB Provider For SQL Server.

4. In Server, select (local).

5. Select Use Windows NT Authentication.

6. In Database, select StudyNwind. Click Next.

7. In Destination, select Text File.

8. In File Name, type **C:\Sqladmin\Exercise\Ch06\Sacust.txt**. Click Next.

9. Select Use A Query To Specify The Data To Transfer. Click Next.

10. Click Query Builder. Click Customers, and then click > to add all columns from the Customers table to the Selected Columns list.

11. In the Selected Columns list, click on Phone and click < to remove it from the list. Do the same for Fax. Click Next.

12. Move Country and CompanyName to the Sorting Order list. (Make sure that Country is above CompanyName.) Click Next.

13. Click Only Rows Meeting Criteria.

14. In the Column drop-down list, select [Customers].[Country]; in the Oper. drop-down list, select =; and in Value/Column, type **'Argentina'** (include the single quotes). On the next line, select OR from the logical operator drop-down list. In the Column drop-down list, select [Customers].[Country]; in the Oper. drop-down, list select =; and in Value/Column, type **'Brazil'** (include the single quotes). Click Next.

15. The query that will return only South American countries has been filled in for you in Query Statement. Click Parse. (If the statement is not valid, return to step 10.) Click Next.

16. For the file format, select Delimited.

17. Set Column Delimiter to Tab. Click Next.

18. Check Run Immediately and Schedule DTS Package For Later Execution in the When section.

19. Click the ellipsis button next to Schedule DTS Package For Later Execution.

20. Click Weekly. Set the Weekly section to Every 1 Week(s) on Mon, Wed, and Fri.

21. In the Daily Frequency section, select Occurs Once At and set the time to 9:00 A.M. Click OK, and then click Next.

22. In Name, type **South American Customers**; in Description, type **South American customer list**.

23. For Server Name, select (local). Select Use Windows NT Authentication. Click Next.

24. Click Finish. The Transferring Data dialog box indicates the progress of the data transfer.

25. A dialog box indicates when the transfer has completed successfully. Click OK to close the dialog box, and click Done to close the Transferring Data dialog box.

26. Open Notepad to review the text file (C:\Sqladmin\Exercise\Ch06\Sacust.txt). The file should contain all of the rows in which customer.country equals Argentina or Brazil. You should see all columns except Phone Or Fax.

Exercise: Reviewing the Job Schedule

In this exercise, you will review the job schedule that was created to execute your DTS package.

▶ **To verify that the schedule was created**

1. To view the schedule that was created, in the Enterprise Manager console tree expand Management and expand the SQL Server Agent icon, and then click Jobs.

2. In the details pane, right-click the job name, South American Customers, and then click Properties. Review the properties of the job that was created by the DTS Wizard. Note that the job step command is not viewable because it is encrypted. Click OK to close the job.

DTS Designer

DTS Designer is a graphical DTS package editor. The work surface includes a toolbar and an extensible tool palette that you can use to add package objects and specify workflow.

When you create a new DTS package from the console tree, the DTS Designer work surface opens in a new Microsoft Management Console (MMC) window. Two tool palettes contain icons for transformation tasks and data connections.

Experienced users can use DTS Designer to integrate, consolidate, and transform data from multiple heterogeneous sources, using complex workflows to simplify the process of building a data warehouse. The next lesson describes data transformations.

Lesson Summary

DTS is a general-purpose data transfer and transformation tool with a wide range of applications. It provides the ability to copy table schema and data between DBMSs, create custom transformation objects, access applications using third-party OLE DB providers, and build data warehouses and data marts in SQL Server. DTS can be used with any OLE DB data source and destination; you are not required to use SQL Server 7 for either source or destination.

DTS tools include the DTS Import Wizard, the DTS Export Wizard, DTS Designer, the dtswiz and dtsrun command-prompt utilities, and the Data Transformation Services node in the SQL Server Enterprise Manager console tree.

Lesson 3: Transforming Data with DTS

Transforming data with DTS involves planning and designing the transformation and creating and executing a DTS package. This lesson takes you through this process.

After this lesson, you will be able to

- Describe the design and planning steps taken before using DTS
- Describe the data transformation process used by DTS
- Use DTS Designer to create, edit, and save complex data transformations

Estimated lesson time: 105 minutes

Restructuring and Mapping Data

Data transformation involves formatting and modifying data that is extracted from the data source into merged or derived values that are more useful at the destination. New values can easily be calculated from one or more columns in the source rowset, and a single source column can be decomposed into multiple destination columns.

Mapping Data Types

DTS allows you to specify the attributes of the destination columns and to indicate how the source columns are mapped to the destination columns. Transformation flags specify whether data of one type in the source can be converted to another type in the destination. For example, you can allow data type promotion, such as converting 16-bit integers to 32-bit integers, or data type demotion, such as converting 32-bit integers to 16-bit integers (data may be lost in this case). You can also require an exact match between source and destination data types.

Each database defines its own data types as well as its column and object naming conventions. DTS attempts to define the best possible data type matches between a source and destination. However, you can override DTS mappings and specify different destination data type, size, precision, and scale properties.

Merging and Separating Data

You can merge and separate data in several ways:

At the File Level

You can combine information from multiple sources and place it into a single table, or you can take information from a single source and place it into multiple tables. Heterogeneous joins are an example of combining multiple sources into a single result set that is saved at the destination.

At the Column Level

You can combine information from multiple columns and place it into a single column, or you can take information from a single column and place it into multiple columns. For example, you can summarize monthly sales totals for each product, or you can decompose a phone number that is stored in one column in order to store the area code in one column and the phone number in another.

Defining Transformation Steps

A DTS package is composed of one or more steps, which you can define. A step defines a unit of work that is performed as part of the transformation process. A step can

- Execute a SQL statement.
- Move and transform homogeneous or heterogeneous data from an OLE DB source to an OLE DB destination, using the DTS Data Pump.
- Execute a JScript, PerlScript, or VBScript script. These scripts can perform any operation that their scripting language supports, allowing the implementation of any complex procedural logic that is required. ActiveX scripts can also access and manipulate data by using ActiveX Data Objects (ADO) or any other COM Automation components.
- Launch an external program.
- Retrieve and execute other DTS packages.

For example, you can create a DTS package that summarizes sales information for each product for a given month. The DTS package drops (if the table already exists) and creates the table on the destination, gets data from the source connection (OLE DB), processes the transformation (summarization), and finally sends the data to the destination connection (OLE DB).

Creating a DTS Package

When you use DTS to transfer and transform data, you create DTS packages that describe all of the work to be performed as part of the transformation process. You can create the DTS package interactively, using the DTS wizards or DTS Designer, or programmatically, using a language that supports OLE Automation, such as Microsoft Visual Basic.

Saving a DTS Package

Saving the DTS package allows you to modify it, reuse it, or schedule it for later execution. If you do not save the DTS package, it executes immediately. You must save the DTS package if you want to schedule it for later execution.

You can save a DTS package that you create in one of three ways:

- **To SQL Server**—Packages saved to SQL Server are referred to as Local packages and are stored in the msdb database. Local packages are the most efficient and are available to other SQL Servers. They are listed in the Local Packages node under Data Transformation Services in the console tree.

- **To Microsoft Repository**—The Microsoft Repository is a database that stores descriptive information about software components and their relationships. It consists of a set of published COM interfaces and information models that define database schema and data transformations through shared metadata.

  Saving a DTS package in the Microsoft Repository makes package metadata reusable and available to other applications. Using the Microsoft Repository also enables you to track data lineage at the package and row level of a table, which allows you to determine the source of each piece of data and the transformations that are applied to it.

  When you save a package to the Microsoft Repository, the package is stored in the msdb database, but package metadata can be imported into the repository. Packages stored in this way are listed in the Repository Packages node under Data Transformation Services in the console tree. After you import the package metadata into the repository, you can view it using the Metadata Browser in the Metadata node under Data Transformation Services in the console tree.

- **To a File**—Saving a DTS package in a COM-structured storage file makes it easy to distribute the DTS package using e-mail or network file servers. DTS packages saved as files do not appear in the SQL Server Enterprise Manager console tree. To open a package file for editing, right-click Data Transformation Services in the console tree, point to All Tasks, and click Open Package.

Implementing Package Security

You can encrypt DTS packages that are saved to SQL Server or to COM-structured storage files in order to protect sensitive user names and password information. When a DTS package is encrypted, all of its collections and properties are encrypted, except for the package name, description, ID, version, and creation date.

DTS packages provide two levels of security: owner password and operator password.

Owner Password

The owner password level of security provides complete access to all collections and properties. By default, DTS packages without owner passwords are not encrypted and can be read by any user with access to the package.

Operator Password

The operator password level of security allows a user to execute but not edit or view the package definition. If an operator password is specified, an owner password must be supplied.

Defining Workflows

With DTS, you can define a workflow that controls the execution sequence of each step. Control of flow logic and conditional processing is achieved using precedence constraints. DTS tasks can also be prioritized. This section discusses using DTS Designer to edit and customize packages.

Steps, Tasks, and Precedence Constraints

Workflows control the flow of execution for the package. A package is made up of data connections (sources and destinations) and tasks that are performed using those connections. The action of executing a task is controlled by a step. A step can be subject to one or more precedence constraints. A step with no precedence constraints executes immediately. If a step has precedence constraints, it cannot execute until all of its precedence constraints have been satisfied.

In DTS Designer, steps are represented by task icons and a solid Data Transformation arrow between two data connection icons. Precedence constraints are represented by dashed blue (Completion), green (Success), or red (Failure) arrows. An arrow points to the step that is subject to the precedence constraint; this is called the *destination step*. If the destination step is a data transformation, the arrow points to the source data connection of the step. An arrow points from the step that must be completed to satisfy the precedence constraint; this is called the *source step*. If the source step is a data transformation, the arrow points from the destination data connection of the step.

To make your DTS Designer diagrams easier to read, you can add the same connection to the diagram more than once. When you do so, specify it as an existing connection. If a connection is involved in more than one transformation, it is recommended that you add the connection once for each transformation. If you do not, the diagram will have a single data connection icon with a large number of arrows (both data transformations and precedence constraints) pointing to and from it.

Note The terms *source* and *destination* are used to refer to both data connections and steps in DTS Designer. When working with a source or a destination, always make sure that you know whether it is a source or destination connection or a source or destination step.

In addition, arrows are used to represent both precedence constraints and data transformations in DTS Designer. When working with an arrow in a DTS diagram, make sure that you know whether it is a constraint or a Data Transformation arrow.

Steps are defined using the Workflow Properties dialog box. To open this dialog box, right-click on the destination step (either the task icon or the Data Transformation arrow if the step is a data transformation step). Then select Workflow

Properties (you may need to point to Workflow to get to the Workflow Properties option) from the context menu. You can also open the Workflow Properties dialog box by right-clicking a precedence constraint arrow, but this is not recommended, as it is confusing and does not allow access to the General tab.

The Precedence tab of the Workflow Properties dialog box allows you to add precedence constraints to or remove them from the step. The order of precedence constraints in the list is not important. You can also add precedence constraints from the Workflow menu or from the toolbar in DTS Designer, but this is not recommended, as it is easy to confuse the destination and source steps using this method. The General tab of the Workflow Properties dialog box allows you to set workflow properties such as task priority and transaction management for the task of the destination step.

Precedence Constraint Types

The type of precedence constraint you select determines the requirement for executing a step:

- Success indicates that the source step must complete successfully before the destination step executes.
- Failure indicates that the source step must complete with an indication of failure before the destination step executes.
- Completion indicates that the source step must simply complete (with failure or success) before the destination step executes.

Precedence constraints create a finish-start relationship between the step being executed (the source step) and the step that will be executed (the destination step). Given two steps A and B, a precedence constraint says

```
Step B cannot start until step A finishes
```

not

```
If step A finishes, step B will start
```

This is important when multiple steps are involved, as a step may have many precedence constraints that all must be satisfied before it can execute.

Controlling Step Execution

Under the control of precedence constraints, steps execute in sequence, in parallel, or in a combination of these:

- Some steps must execute in a certain sequence.

  For example, data can be loaded into a table (step B) only after the table has been successfully created (step A).

- Multiple steps can execute in parallel to improve performance.

  For example, a package can load data from Oracle and DB2 into separate tables simultaneously.

- Steps can use a combination of sequential and parallel execution.

  For example, a package can load data from several different heterogeneous files into a set of tables. The loading of data can be done in parallel, but only after the creation of the tables.

Figure 6.2 shows a package with six steps that demonstrate a combination of parallel and sequential execution. Steps A, B, and C have no precedence constraints and execute immediately. Step D waits for step A to complete successfully before executing. Step E waits for step D to complete with a failure before executing. Step F waits for step C to complete (regardless of success or failure) before executing. Steps A, D, and E execute sequentially. Steps C and F execute sequentially. Steps A (and its sequential steps), B, and C (and its sequential step) execute in parallel.

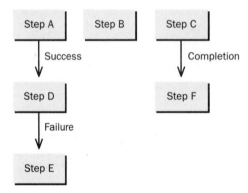

Figure 6.2   A package with steps that execute both in parallel and sequentially

Figure 6.3 shows how one step can have multiple precedence constraints. In this case, step C can execute only when both step A and step B have successfully completed.

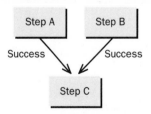

Figure 6.3   A step with multiple precedence constraints

Conditional Processing

Conditional processing using basic IF-THEN-ELSE logic allows a DTS package to respond to run-time conditions that vary. To implement conditional processing, use a combination of steps with Success and Failure precedence constraints, as shown in Figure 6.4. In the figure, step B executes only if step A completes successfully. Step C will execute if step A fails. Step C would typically send a notification such as an e-mail message or would take corrective action that is in turn the condition for another precedence constraint that then allows the original step to be repeated.

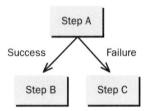

Figure 6.4   Conditional processing using precedence constraints

Specifying Task Priority

You can specify the priority of tasks. By default, each thread within the DTS package executes at the same priority as the DTS package. However, if some operations are more time-critical than others, you can assign an execution priority to each step. You can specify each step to execute at Idle, Normal, or High priority.

Exercise: Creating a Package with DTS Designer

In this exercise, you will create a package using DTS Designer. The package will transfer some of the columns from the Products table in an Access database to a new table in a SQL Server database. The package will use a custom data transformation to look up and then convert data values from the Access table to new values in the SQL Server table. You will use an ActiveX script to convert the values.

▶ **Using DTS Designer to create a package**

1. Right-click Data Transformation Services in the console tree, and then click New Package.

2. On the Data tool palette, click the Microsoft Access icon.

3. In New Connection, type **Access Connection**.

4. In File Name, type **C:\Sqladmin\Exercise\Ch06\Nwind.mdb**. Click OK to add the Microsoft Access data connection.

5. On the Data tool palette, click the Microsoft OLE DB Provider For SQL Server icon.

6. In New Connection, type **SQL Server Connection**.

7. In Database, select StudyNwind. Click OK to add the SQL Server data connection.

8. On the Task tool palette, click the Execute SQL Task icon.

9. In Description, type **Drop ProductsCopy**. In Existing Connection, select SQL Server Connection.

10. In SQL Statement, type

```
DROP TABLE StudyNwind..ProductsCopy
```

11. Click Parse Query to confirm that you have typed the statement correctly. Click OK to close the dialog boxes and save the task.

12. On the Task tool palette, click the Execute SQL Task icon.

13. In Description, type **Create ProductsCopy**. In Existing Connection, select SQL Server Connection.

14. In SQL Statement, type

```
CREATE TABLE StudyNwind..ProductsCopy (
    ProductID int NOT NULL ,
    ProductName nvarchar (40) NOT NULL ,
    QuantityPerUnit nvarchar (20) NULL ,
    UnitPrice money NULL ,
    IsAnimal char (3) NULL
)
```

15. Click Parse Query to confirm that you have typed the statement correctly. Click OK to close the dialog boxes and save the task.

16. Click Package on the menu and click Save. In Package Name, type **Copy Access Products to SQL Server**.

17. The defaults in the Save DTS Package dialog box will save the package to SQL Server. Click OK to save the package.

18. On the taskbar, click Execute. This tests the package to see that the connections and tasks are working and also creates the table, which needs to be on the server when you add the data transformation. The first step will indicate that an error occurred; this is normal since the table cannot be dropped the first time the package is executed.

19. On the DTS Designer work surface, click Access Connection. Then hold down the Ctrl key and click SQL Server Connection.

20. Click Workflow on the menu, and click Add Transform. A Data Transformation arrow pointing from the Access connection to the SQL Server connection is added to the work surface.

21. Right-click the Data Transformation arrow and click Properties.

22. In Description, type **Copy data from Access to SQL Server**.

23. In Table Name, select Products. Click the Destination tab.

24. In Table Name, select [StudyNwind].[dbo].[ProductsCopy].

25. Click the Advanced tab. Click the Lookups button.

26. Click Add. In the Name column, type **myLookup**. In the Connection column, select Access Connection, then click the ellipsis button in the Query column.

27. Type the following query in the code pane of the query builder:

```
SELECT CategoryName
FROM Categories
WHERE (CategoryID = ?)
```

28. Click OK to close the query builder, then click OK to close the Data Transformation Lookups dialog box and save the data lookup for your transformation.

29. Click the Transformations tab.

30. Click the line pointing from SupplierID to QuantityPerUnit, and click Delete. Click the line pointing from CategoryID to UnitPrice, and click Delete. Click the line pointing from QuantityPerUnit to IsAnimal, and click Delete.

31. Click QuantityPerUnit in the Source Table and Destination Table columns, and then click New. Click UnitPrice in the Source Table and Destination Table columns, and then click New.

32. Click CategoryID in the Source Table column and IsAnimal in the Destination Table column. In New Transformation, select ActiveX Script, and then click New.

33. Replace the default code in Script by typing the following VBScript:

```
Function Main()
Select Case _
 DTSLookups("myLookup").Execute(DTSSource("CategoryID").Value)
Case "Dairy Products", "Meat/Products", "Seafood"
    DTSDestination("IsAnimal") = "Yes"
Case Else
    DTSDestination("IsAnimal") = "No"
End Select
Main = DTSTransformStat_OK
End Function
```

34. Click OK to save the transformation script.

Tip To edit individual column transformations, you need to right-click on the lines pointing from the Source Table list to the Destination Table list.

---

35. Click OK to close the Data Transformation Properties dialog box and save your changes to the data transformation.

36. Right-click Create ProductsCopy on the work surface. Point to Workflow and click Workflow Properties.

37. In the Workflow Properties dialog box, click New to add a precedence constraint for the Create ProductsCopy step.

38. In the Source Step column, select Drop ProductsCopy. In the Precedence column, select Completion. Note that you cannot change the Destination Step, because you are editing the precedence constraints for Create ProductsCopy, which is the destination step. Click OK to close the Workflow Properties dialog box and save the precedence constraints for Create ProductsCopy.

39. Now you will add a precedence constraint for the data transformation step. Unlike the Create ProductsCopy step, which is represented by its icon, the data transformation step is represented by the arrow connecting the two data connections.

40. Right-click the Data Transformation arrow (the arrow from Access Connection to SQL Server Connection) on the work surface. Click Workflow Properties.

41. In the Workflow Properties dialog box, click New to add a precedence constraint for the data transformation step.

42. In the Source Step column, select Drop ProductsCopy. In the Precedence column, select Completion. Note that you cannot change the Destination Step, because you are editing the precedence constraints for Create ProductsCopy, which is the destination step. Click OK to close the Workflow Properties dialog box and save the precedence constraints for Create ProductsCopy.

43. On the Package menu, click Save. Close the DTS Designer dialog box.

Exercise: Executing the New Package

In this exercise you will execute the package you have just created and then view the data in the new table.

▶ **To execute the new package and verify its results**

1. In the console tree, expand Data Transformation Services, and click Local Packages.

2. Right-click Copy Access Products to SQL Server in the details pane, and click Execute Package.

3. The Executing DTS Package dialog box appears and indicates the progress of each of the steps as the package executes.

4. Click OK, and click Done to close the dialog boxes.

5. In the console tree, expand Databases, expand StudyNwind, and then click Tables.

6. In the details pane, right-click ProductsCopy (if you do not see this table, refresh your Enterprise Manager view), point to Open Table, and click Return All Rows. A grid displays the table that was created by the DTS package. Note the values in the IsAnimal column that were set by the ActiveX script and the lookup.

Executing and Scheduling a DTS Package

Each DTS package is self-contained after you create it. A package is a complete description of all of the work to be performed as part of the transformation process. This section describes how to execute and schedule a DTS package that you have created.

Executing a DTS Package

After you save a DTS package, you can retrieve and execute it, using SQL Server Enterprise Manager or the dtsrun command-prompt utility.

The example given here shows the dtsrun command-prompt utility being used to execute a DTS package that creates and populates a summary table in the StudyNwind database on the SQL Server named SQLSERVER. The /U option specifies the sa login. If the specified login has a password, it must be specified with the /P option. Note that the name of the package is enclosed in double quotes; this is necessary if the name contains spaces. Remember that the DTS package is a complete description of all of the work to be performed as part of the transformation process.

```
dtsrun /SSQLSERVER /Usa /N"StudyNwind Product Totals"
```

Scheduling a DTS Package

You can schedule a saved DTS package for execution at a specific time, such as daily at midnight, or at recurring intervals, such as on the first or last day of the month or weekly on Sunday at 6 A.M.

You can schedule a DTS package for execution in the following ways:

- By using the DTS Import or DTS Export Wizards when you save the DTS package to the SQL Server msdb database.

- By using SQL Server Enterprise Manager to create a SQL Server job that executes the DTS package by running the dtsrun command-prompt utility. Do this manually for packages saved as files. For Local packages and repository packages, right-click the package and select Schedule Package from the context menu.

Exercise: Transferring a Database

In this exercise, you will use the DTS Import Wizard to create a copy of the entire Northwind database.

▶ **Transferring an entire database using DTS**

1. Click on your server in the console tree in SQL Server Enterprise Manager.

2. Click the Tools menu, and then click Wizards.

3. In the Select Wizard dialog box, expand Data Transformation Services. Double-click DTS Import Wizard. Click Next.

4. In the Choose a Data Source dialog box, for Database select Northwind. Click Next.

5. In the Choose a Destination dialog box, for Database select <new>. A Create Database dialog box appears.

6. In Name, type **NwindTransfer**. Click OK to close the Create Database dialog box and create the new empty database. Click Next.

7. Click Transfer Objects And Data Between SQL Server 7.0 Databases. Click Next.

8. Review the default options in the Select Objects to Transfer dialog box. These options will make an exact copy of Northwind in NwindTransfer.

9. In Script File Directory, type **C:\Mssql7\Transfer**. Click Next.

10. Click Next again. You want to run the transfer immediately without saving it.

11. Click Finish. The Transferring Data dialog box shows the progress of the transfer. The transfer may take a few minutes.

12. When the transfer is complete, the Transferring Data dialog box indicates whether the transfer was successful. If there are errors in the transfer, they will be recorded in files with a .LOG extension in the Script file directory (C:\Mssql7\Transfer in this exercise). Click Done.

13. In the console tree, right-click Databases and click Refresh.

14. In the console tree, expand Databases, and then expand NwindTransfer. Click Tables, Views, and Stored Procedures in the console tree and note that all of the objects from the Northwind database have been copied to the NwindTransfer database and are displayed in the details pane.

15. In the console tree, click Tables. In the details pane, right-click Customers, point to Open Table, and click Return All Rows. The query grid displays the data from the Customers table, showing that all of the data from the Northwind database has been copied to the NwindTransfer database. Close the query grid.

16. Right-click NwindTransfer in the console tree, and click Delete. Click Yes to delete the NwindTransfer database, as you will not need it again.

Lesson Summary

A DTS package is composed of one or more steps, which you can define. A step is a unit of work with many possible actions. It can perform a number of actions, including but not limited to executing SQL statements and launching external programs.

With DTS you can control the execution sequence of each step. Precedence constraints and conditional processing allow you to prioritize steps.

Lesson 4: Linked Servers

SQL Server allows you to create links to OLE DB data sources called linked servers. This section explores the creation of linked servers and their use in queries.

After this lesson, you will be able to

- Add a linked server
- Execute a distributed query

Estimated lesson time: 50 minutes

Introduction to Linked Servers

SQL Server allows you to create links to OLE DB data sources called linked servers. This allows SQL Server clients to perform fully distributed queries and transactions. After linking to an OLE DB data source, you can

- Reference rowsets from the OLE DB data sources as tables in Transact-SQL statements sent to SQL Server. This means that client software does not need to use many different dialects of the SQL language and can access many different servers through a single connection to SQL Server.

- Reference multiple linked servers and perform either update or read operations against each individual linked server. A single distributed query can perform read operations against some linked servers and update operations against other linked servers. The types of queries executed against linked servers depend on the level of support for transactions present in the OLE DB providers.

Figure 6.5 illustrates how linked servers work.

Adding Linked Servers

A linked server definition specifies an OLE DB provider and an OLE DB data source.

An OLE DB provider is a dynamic-link library (DLL) that manages and interacts with a specific data source. An OLE DB data source is any data store accessible through OLE DB. Although data sources queried through linked server definitions are usually database servers (such as SQL Server or Oracle), OLE DB providers exist for a wide variety of files and file formats, including file-based databases (such as Microsoft Access and Microsoft Visual FoxPro), text files, spreadsheet data, and the results of full-text content searches. The following table shows examples of the most common OLE DB providers and data sources for SQL Server.

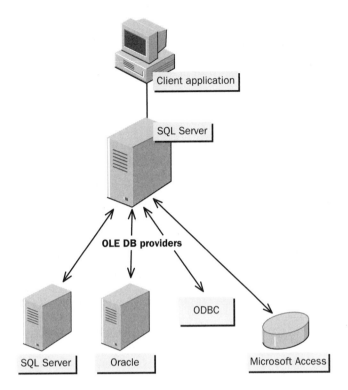

Figure 6.5   How linked servers work

OLE DB provider	OLE DB data source
Microsoft OLE DB Provider for SQL Server	SQL Server database, such as pubs or Northwind
Microsoft OLE DB Provider for Jet	Pathname of .MDB database file
Microsoft OLE DB Provider for ODBC	ODBC data source name (pointing to a particular database)
Microsoft OLE DB Provider for Oracle	SQL*Net alias that points to an Oracle database
Microsoft OLE DB Provider for Indexing Service	Content files on which property searches or full-text searches can be run

Note Linked server support has been tested with the Microsoft OLE DB Provider for SQL Server, Microsoft OLE DB Provider for Jet, Microsoft OLE DB Provider for Oracle, Microsoft OLE DB Provider for Indexing Service, and Microsoft OLE DB Provider for ODBC. However, SQL Server distributed queries are designed to work with any OLE DB provider that implements the requisite OLE DB interfaces.

For a data source to return data through a linked server, the OLE DB provider (DLL) for that data source must be present on the same server as SQL Server.

When setting up a linked server, register the connection information and data source information with SQL Server. After registration is accomplished, the data source can always be referred to with a single logical name.

You can create or delete a linked server definition with system stored procedures or through SQL Server Enterprise Manager.

For a table of the different parameter values that you need to specify when creating a linked server, see sp_addlinkedserver in SQL Server Books Online.

Security Considerations for Linked Servers

When you execute a query against a linked server, SQL Server must provide a login name and password to the linked server on behalf of the user executing the query.

The login name and password provided to the linked server can be specified explicitly by adding a mapped login for the linked server. If many users need to use the linked server, it may not be practical to added mapped logins for each user. If a mapped login has not been created for a user who is trying to use a linked server, one of the following can occur:

- The user is denied access.
- The user is mapped to a single login specified for all users that do not have a mapped login.
- SQL Server provides no login or password. This works for data sources that do not enforce security.
- SQL Server provides the user's SQL Server login credentials. This requires that the user have the same login name and password on the linked server, and it is called *impersonation*.

When creating mapped logins for users, you can either specify a login name and password to be used on the linked server or specify that the user be impersonated on the linked server. Login mappings are stored on SQL Server, which passes the relevant login information to the linked server whenever necessary.

By specifying that users without login mappings must be denied access, you can control access to other data sources at the SQL Server level or provide access control to data sources that do not provide their own security. For example, you could place a Microsoft Access database file on a Windows NT drive and use NTFS permissions to disallow access to all users. Only users that have SQL Server logins would gain access to the Access database as a linked server.

System Stored Procedures for Working with Linked Servers

SQL Server provides system-stored procedures for working with linked servers. For example, the sp_addlinkedserver system stored procedure is used to create a linked server definition, and the sp_linkedservers system stored procedure is used to view information about linked servers. The following table provides a list of system stored procedures that can be used for working with linked servers.

System stored procedure	Purpose
sp_addlinkedserver	Create a linked server definition
sp_linkedservers	View information about linked servers
sp_dropserver	Delete a linked server definition
sp_addlinkedsrvlogin	Add a linked server login mapping
sp_droplinkedsrvlogin	Delete a linked server login mapping

Executing a Distributed Query

When executing a distributed query against a linked server, include a fully qualified, four-part table name for each data source to be queried. This four-part name should be in the form

```
linked_server_name.catalog.schema.object_name
```

On SQL Server, *catalog* refers to the database name, and *schema* refers to the table owner. The following example shows a query that retrieves data from linked SQL Server and Oracle databases:

```
SELECT emp.EmloyeeID, ord.OrderID, ord.Discount
FROM SQLServer1.Northwind.dbo.Employees emp INNER JOIN
OracleSvr.Catalog1.SchemaX.Orders ord
ON ord.EmployeeID = emp.EmployeeID
WHERE ord.Discount > 0
```

▶ **To configure a Microsoft Access linked server**

1. In the console tree, expand your server, expand Security, and then right-click Linked Servers. Click New Linked Server.

2. In Linked Server, enter the name LINKEDJET for the new linked server.

3. Under Server Type, click Other Data Source.

4. For Provider Name, select Microsoft Jet 4.0 OLE DB Provider from the list of providers.

5. In Data Source, type the path to the linked server Microsoft Jet database— **C:\Sqladmin\Exercise\Ch06\Nwind.mdb**.

6. On the Security tab, click They Will Be Mapped To and type **Admin** in Remote User. This step maps all SQL Server logins to the login Admin, which is the default user name for Access databases that do not have security enabled.

7. Click OK to close the Linked Server Properties dialog box and add the new linked server.

8. In the console tree, expand LINKEDJET, and then click Tables. In the details pane you see a list of the tables from the Access Nwind.mdb file.

9. Switch to or open Query Analyzer. Select Northwind in the DB list box.

10. In the query pane, type and execute the following query:

```
SELECT ProductName, CategoryName, DATALENGTH(ProductName)
FROM LINKEDJET...Products Prd JOIN Categories Cat
ON Prd.CategoryID = Cat.CategoryID
```

This query retrieves data from the Category table in the SQL Server Northwind database and joins it to data retrieved from the Products table in the Access Nwind.mdb database file.

The JOIN syntax of this query is valid in Transact-SQL but will not work in Microsoft Access (INNER JOIN would have to be specified). The query uses the Transact-SQL DATALENGTH function, which is not available in Microsoft Access. The DATALENGTH function returns the length of the data in the specified column. The value returned is twice the number of characters in the column because the data is stored using two-byte-per-character Unicode characters.

Lesson Summary

A linked server allows access to distributed, heterogeneous queries against OLE DB data sources. For example, information can be accessed from an Oracle or Access database by using a SQL Server connection. SQL Server provides system-stored procedures to create and view information about linked servers. Once the linked server is created, a query can be run that uses both SQL Server tables and other OLE DB data sources.

Review

The following questions are intended to reinforce key information presented in the chapter. If you are unable to answer a question, review the appropriate lesson and then try the question again. Answers to the questions can be found in Appendix A, "Questions and Answers."

1. You want to create a DTS package using a basic query. What tool is most appropriate?

2. You want to be certain that a DTS package is secure so that no one can copy it or view sensitive information. What can you do to secure this DTS package?

3. You plan to upgrade the hardware that currently runs SQL Server 7. The new hardware will be faster. Which tool would you select to transfer the database and all of its objects to the new hardware?

4. You are required to recommend a solution for an organization that has an existing Oracle database and a new SQL Server database. The applications using the SQL Server database need access to a table on the Oracle server. Which of the following would provide the best solution and why?

    A. Set up SQL Server replication to replicate the table from Oracle to SQL Server.

    B. Create a DTS package and schedule it to transfer the contents of the table from Oracle to SQL Server once every hour.

    C. Add the Oracle database as a linked server on SQL Server.

    D. Install the Oracle and SQL Server client software on every user's computer and access the Oracle table directly from the application.

CHAPTER 7

Web Publishing and Full-Text Indexing

About This Chapter

Database data is commonly published to Internet and intranet Web pages. In this chapter, you will learn how to automatically generate Web pages from your Microsoft SQL Server databases.

Full-text indexing and searching in SQL Server 7 give you the ability to perform complex linguistic searches that are not normally possible on text or character data in a relational database. This chapter also shows you how to set up full-text indexing and introduces you to full-text searches.

Before You Begin

To complete the lessons in this chapter, you must have

- Installed SQL Server 7. See Chapter 2, "Installation," for installation instructions.

- The ability to log on to SQL Server as an Administrator.

- Installed the StudyNwind database. See the "Getting Started" section in "About This Book" for StudyNwind database installation instructions.

- Installed the Exercise files from the Supplemental Course Materials CD-ROM to your hard disk drive. See the "Getting Started" section in "About This Book" for installation instructions.

Lesson 1: Publishing Database Data to Web Pages

You can generate Hypertext Markup Language (HTML) Web pages from SQL Server table data with the SQL Server Web Assistant Wizard. The wizard provides a user interface to the sp_makewebtask system stored procedure, which creates Web Assistant jobs. This lesson provides an overview of Web publishing and describes how to use Web Assistant to create and update Web pages.

After this lesson, you will be able to

- Create a Web page with SQL Server Web Assistant Wizard
- Use Web publishing system stored procedures
- Schedule a Web Assistant job to be executed at regular intervals
- Have a Web Assistant job update a Web page whenever data changes

Estimated lesson time: 90 minutes

How Web Publishing Works

You can generate HTML Web pages from SQL Server using the SQL Server Web Assistant. Using the Web Assistant, you can create Web Assistant jobs that publish and format information from a database. These jobs are executed on demand or automatically (see Figure 7.1).

When a Web Assistant job is created with the Web Assistant Wizard or the sp_makewebtask system stored procedure, a number of objects may be created. For all Web Assistant jobs,

- A row is added to a system table in the msdb system database. This entry records the name of the Web Assistant job and the location of the HTML file that will be generated by the job.

- A stored procedure with the same name as the job is created in the database that is specified when the job is created. This stored procedure contains the Transact-SQL query for the job. When the job is executed, the stored procedure is executed and an HTML Web page containing the query results is generated.

If a Web Assistant job is created for one-time execution, the entry in msdb and the stored procedure are deleted immediately after the job has been executed.

A Web Assistant job can be executed manually at any time using SQL Server Enterprise Manager or the sp_runwebtask system stored procedure. For Web Assistant jobs that are to execute automatically, one of the following occurs when the job is created:

- For scheduled Web Assistant jobs, a SQL Server Agent job with the same name as the Web Assistant job is created.

- For each Web Assistant job that is to execute when data changes, three triggers are created. These are named after the Web Assistant job, with a number appended to each to make the names unique.

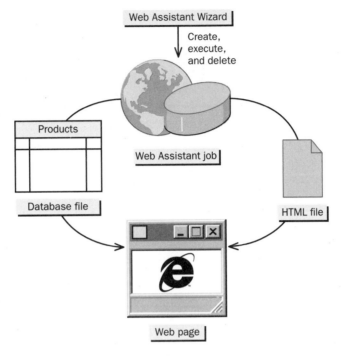

Figure 7.1 Creating a Web page with SQL Server Web publishing

Specifying Web Page Characteristics

Web Assistant jobs produce HTML documents that contain the result set(s) of a query. When you use Web Assistant Wizard to define a Web Assistant job and the Web page that it will generate, you must supply query, update timing, file location, and formatting information.

Specifying the Query

Web Assistant Wizard allows you to select the data that is displayed in the Web page by

- Specifying a single table and selecting columns from that table
- Entering a query directly as text
- Specifying an existing stored procedure that returns one or more result sets

Automating Web Page Updates

The following table describes the scheduling options that you can use when you create a Web Assistant job.

Scheduling option	Description
Only one time when I complete this wizard	Immediate one-time execution. After execution, the Web Assistant job is deleted.
On demand	Optionally runs immediately, and the Web Assistant job is saved so that it can be run later.
Only one time at	The job runs once at a specific date and time.
At regularly scheduled intervals	The job runs at regular intervals that you specify.
When the SQL Server data changes	The job runs when underlying SQL Server data changes.

Scheduled Web Page Updates

When you schedule a Web Assistant job, a SQL Server Agent job is created to execute it, as shown in Figure 7.2.

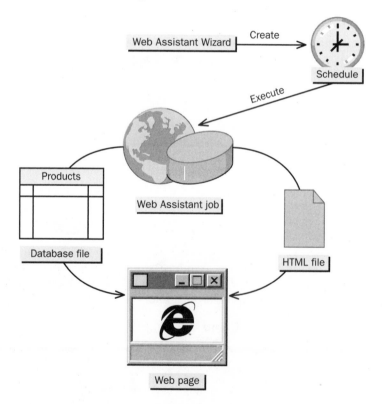

Figure 7.2   Scheduling Web page updates

Do not confuse these two kinds of jobs; you will learn more about creating SQL Server Agent jobs in Chapter 13, "Automating Administrative Tasks." SQL Server Agent must be running for scheduled jobs to run.

It is the SQL Server Agent job that is scheduled, not the Web Assistant job. When the SQL Server Agent job runs on schedule, it in turn executes the Web Assistant job, using the sp_runwebtask system stored procedure. The SQL Server Agent job is created by the sp_makewebtask system stored procedure.

To change the schedule for a scheduled Web Assistant job, you need to edit the schedule of the SQL Server Agent job; you cannot edit a Web Assistant job. If you delete the Web Assistant job with SQL Server Enterprise Manager or the sp_dropwebtask system stored procedure, the SQL Server Agent job is automatically deleted as well.

Triggered Web Page Updates

When you create a Web Assistant job that updates the Web page whenever data changes, three triggers are added to the table that contains the target data (see Figure 7.3). These triggers fire when data is inserted into, updated in, or deleted from the table. The Web Assistant job can query a different table than the one in which the triggers are defined.

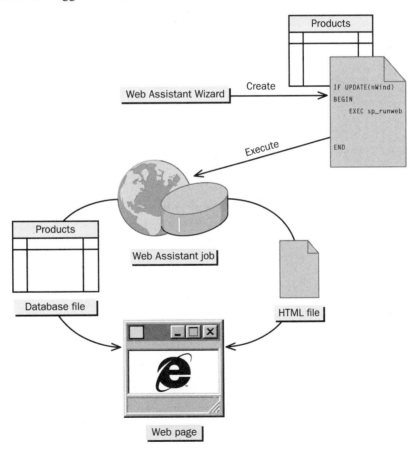

Figure 7.3 Triggered Web page updates

The triggers execute the Web Assistant job by using the sp_runwebtask system stored procedure. If you delete the Web Assistant job with SQL Server Enterprise Manager or the sp_dropwebtask system stored procedure, the triggers are automatically removed from the table.

Setting the Output File Location

Web Assistant Wizard allows you to specify the output filename and path for a Web page. This can be on the local computer or a remote one. The folder you specify must already exist.

Caution The default is the C:\Mssql7\Html folder. It is recommended that you use another folder, as the default folder stores files that are used by SQL Server Enterprise Manager. If you store your files in this folder and then later delete some of the SQL Server Enterprise Manager files by mistake, SQL Server Enterprise Manager will not work correctly.

Specifying Format Options

If you do not use an HTML template file (described in the section "Using an HTML Template File" later in this chapter), Web Assistant Wizard allows you to specify the following options for the HTML file that is generated:

- Text for the title of the Web page
- Text and point size of the title of the table that contains the query results
- Whether to include a time and date stamp
- Whether to include column headers and borders for the table that contains the query results
- Font characteristics for the table that contains the query results
- Whether one or more hyperlinks should be included in the page
- A limit for the total number of rows that a query returns and for the number of rows displayed on each page

Web Assistant Wizard provides defaults for options that you do not specify.

After a Web page is generated, you can edit it manually and add other HTML tags to enhance the formatting and presentation of the data. Do not do this for pages that are regenerated when data is updated or according to a schedule, as your changes will be overwritten the first time the page is regenerated. If you wish to be able to customize the look of pages, it is recommended that you use a template file.

Exercise: Creating a Static Web Page

In this exercise, you will start the SQL Server Web Assistant Wizard from within SQL Server Enterprise Manager to create a static Web page.

▶ **To create a Web page using the Web Assistant Wizard**

1. Open SQL Server Enterprise Manager and click your server.

2. On the Tools menu, click Wizards.

3. Expand Management, and then double-click Web Assistant Wizard.

4. Create an HTML page with the information in the following table. Accept the defaults for any options that are not listed.

Option	Value
Database	StudyNwind
What do you want to name this Web Assistant job?	Current_stock
What data do you want to publish to the table on the Web page?	Data from the Transact-SQL statement I specify
Transact-SQL Query	SELECT ProductName, UnitsInStock FROM Products ORDER BY ProductName
When should the Web Assistant update the Web page?	Only one time when I complete this wizard
Where do you want to publish the Web page?	C:\Sqladmin\Exercise\Ch07\Instock.htm
Do you want Web Assistant to help you format the layout of the Web page?	Yes, help me format the Web page
What do you want to title the Web page?	Northwind Traders Current Stock
What do you want to title the HTML table that contains the data?	Inventory of Items
Write Transact-SQL to File	C:\Temp\Instock.sql

Exercise: Viewing the Web Page

In this exercise, you will view the Web page and the source HTML created by the Web Assistant job.

▶ **To view the created Web page**

1. Open Internet Explorer.

2. Open the C:\Sqladmin\Exercise\Ch07\Instock.htm file and view the Web page.

3. On the View menu, click Source, and then review the HTML.

Exercise: Viewing the Transact-SQL Script

In this exercise, you will view the Transact-SQL script that the Web Assistant Wizard generated.

▶ **To view the generated Transact-SQL script**

1. Open SQL Server Query Analyzer and log on to the (local) server with Microsoft Windows NT authentication.

2. Open the C:\Temp\Instock.sql file and review the contents.

   Note that the Web Assistant Wizard generates a single call to the sp_makeweb-task system stored procedure, supplying parameter values according to your choices on the wizard screens.

   What is the meaning of the @whentype = 1 parameter?

Using an HTML Template File

You can use an HTML template file to format a Web page. A template provides the layout for a Web page that you create. With a template, you can specify precisely how to display database data. When the Web page is generated, the results from the query are merged with the HTML template file.

Specifying an HTML Template File

Create the template file as you would any standard HTML file. HTML template files usually have a .TPL extension.

Formatting an HTML Template File

In order to specify where the query results are to be displayed, the file must contain one of the following:

- A single <%insert_data_here%> tag at the place where you want SQL Server to merge the result of the query into the document. The result of the query is inserted as a single HTML table.

- A block starting with the <%begindetail%> tag and ending with the <%end-detail%> tag. Between these tags, specify a complete row layout, with one <%insert_data_here%> tag for each column in the query. Typically these tags would be placed within <TR></TR> and <TD></TD> tags to format the results in an HTML table.

When the Web Assistant job is executed, the results of the query will be inserted into the positions indicated by the special tags; the rest of the HTML template file will be left as is. Therefore, you have complete control over the output from the Web Assistant.

The following example shows the contents of a simple template file that can be used with a Web Assistant job to create a Web page that lists the products sold by Northwind Traders and the prices for each product. The following table explains the meaning of the HTML tags in the template. Everything in the template is standard HTML except for the <%begindetail%>, <%enddetail%>, and <%insert_data_here%> tags.

```
<HTML>
<HEAD>
<TITLE>Northwind Traders Price List</TITLE>
</HEAD>
<BODY>
<H1>Items For Sale</H1>
<HR>
<P>
<TABLE BORDER>
<TR><TH><I>Product Name</I></TH><TH>Price</TH></TR>
<%begindetail%>
<TR>
<TD><I><%insert_data_here%></I></TD>
<TD ALIGN=RIGHT><B>$<%insert_data_here%></B></TD>
</TR>
<%enddetail%>
</TABLE>
<P>
<A HREF = "http://www.microsoft.com">Microsoft</A>
<P>
</BODY>
</HTML>
```

HTML tags	Contents contained within tags translate to
<HTML> </HTML>	The entire HTML document
<HEAD> </HEAD>	Header of the document
<TITLE> </TITLE>	Title (usually displayed in the title bar of the browser)
<BODY> </BODY>	Body of the document
<H1> </H1>	Header—first level
<HR>	Horizontal rule
<P>	Paragraph marker
<TABLE BORDER> </TABLE>	Table structure with borders
<TR> </TR>	Table row
<TH> </TH>	Table column heading
<TD> </TD>	Table data

(continued)

HTML tags	Contents contained within tags translate to
<TD ALIGN=RIGHT> </TD>	Table data, right aligned
<I> </I>	Italic text
<B> </B>	Bold text
<%begindetail%> <%enddetail%>	The result set format for an entire row
<%insert_data_here%>	Data from a single column that is returned from a Transact-SQL query
<A HREF> </A>	URL hyperlink

Exercise: Examining a Template File

In this exercise, you will examine a template file that you will later use to create a Web page.

▶ **To review a template file**

1. Open Notepad.

2. Open C:\Sqladmin\Exercise\Ch07\Pricelst.tpl and review the contents.

   Note the location of the <%insert_data_here%> tags.

Exercise: Creating and Executing a Web Assistant Job

In this exercise, you will execute a Transact-SQL script that generates a Web page based on an HTML template.

▶ **To create and execute a Web Assistant job with the sp_makewebtask system stored procedure**

1. Switch to SQL Server Query Analyzer, open C:\Sqladmin\Exercise\Ch07\Pricelst.sql, and review its contents.

   Notice the value of each parameter, the name of the output file, and the reference to the C:\Sqladmin\Exercise\Ch07\Pricelst.tpl template file.

2. Execute the script.

Exercise: Viewing the Web Page

In this exercise, you will view the Web page and the source HTML.

▶ **To view the generated Web page**

1. Switch to Internet Explorer.

2. Open the C:\Sqladmin\Exercise\Ch07\Pricelst.htm file and view the Web page.

3. On the View menu, click Source, and then review the HTML.

Managing Web Assistant Jobs

You can use SQL Server Enterprise Manager or system stored procedures to manage Web Assistant jobs.

Viewing Web Assistant Jobs

To view Web Assistant jobs in SQL Server Enterprise Manager, expand Management in the console tree and then click Web Publishing. You cannot list all Web Assistant jobs using Transact-SQL.

Executing a Web Assistant Job

To execute a Web Assistant job in SQL Server Enterprise Manager, in the console tree expand Management, click Web Publishing, right-click the job in the details pane, and click Start Web Assistant Job.

You can also execute a Web Assistant job with the sp_runwebtask system stored procedure, as follows:

```
sp_runwebtask [[@procname =] 'procname '][,[@outputfile = ]
 'outputfile']
```

Replace *procname* with the name of the Web Assistant job to run and *outputfile* with the name of the HTML file to create. The *procname* parameter is so called because the stored procedure in the database is executed when the job runs. You can specify either parameter or both parameters. The parameter(s) you specify must exactly match the parameters specified when the Web Assistant job was created.

The example given here runs a Web Assistant job by using an @outputfile parameter of 'C:\Web\Myfile.html' and a @procname parameter of 'My Web Assistant Job'.

```
sp_runwebtask @procname = 'My Web Assistant Job', @outputfile =
 'C:\Web\Myfile.'
```

Deleting a Web Assistant Job

To delete a Web Assistant job in SQL Server Enterprise Manager, in the console tree expand Management, click Web Publishing, right-click the job in the details pane, and click Delete.

You can also delete a Web Assistant job with the sp_dropwebtask system stored procedure, as follows:

```
sp_dropwebtask [[@procname =] 'procname '] [,[@outputfile = ]
 'outputfile']
```

The *procname* parameter is so called because the stored procedure in the database is deleted when the job is deleted.

This example deletes a Web Assistant job named MYHTML that has an output file of C:\Web\Myfile.html.

```
sp_dropwebtask 'MYHTML', 'C:\Web\Myfile.html'
```

Note When you execute sp_runwebtask or sp_dropwebtask, you must be using same database that was specified in the SQL Server Web Assistant Wizard or with the dbname parameter of the sp_makewebtask system stored procedure when the Web Assistant job was created.

Exercise: Creating a Web Assistant Job That Updates a Web Page When Data Changes

In this exercise, you will use the SQL Server Web Assistant Wizard to create a Web Assistant job that is triggered to update a Web page whenever data changes in the database.

▶ **To create a Web Assistant job that will update a Web page whenever specified data changes**

Use the SQL Server Web Assistant Wizard to create an HTML page based on the options in the following table. Accept the defaults for any options that are not listed.

Option	Value
Database	StudyNwind
What do you want to name this Web Assistant job?	Web_trigger
What data do you want to publish to the table on the Web page?	Data from tables and columns that I select
What table and columns do you want to publish to the Web page?	Products table; ProductName, UnitsInStock, UnitPrice columns
Which rows from the table do you want to publish to the Web page?	Only those rows that meet the following criteria
Column	[Products].UnitsInStock
Operator	<
Value	3
When should the Web Assistant update the Web page?	When the SQL Server data changes

Option	Value
Generate a Web page when the wizard is completed.	Checked
What table and columns should Web Assistant monitor?	Products table; UnitsInStock column
Where do you want to publish the Web page?	C:\Sqladmin\Exercise\Ch07\ Lowstock.htm
Do you want Web Assistant to help you format the layout of the Web page?	Yes, help me format the Web page
What do you want to title the Web page?	Northwind Traders Low Stock
What do you want to title the HTML table that contains the data?	Low Stock List
Write Transact-SQL to File	C:\Temp\Invtrig.sql

Exercise: Viewing the Generated Script

In this exercise, you will view the Transact-SQL script that the SQL Server Web Assistant Wizard generated. This script executes sp_makewebtask with parameters that cause it to create both the Web Assistant job and the triggers that execute the job to update the page when data in the UnitsInStock column changes.

▶ **To view the generated Transact-SQL script**

1. Switch to SQL Server Query Analyzer.

2. Open the C:\Temp\Invtrig.sql file and review its contents.

   What is the meaning of the parameters @whentype = 10 and @datachg = N'TABLE = Products COLUMN = UnitsInStock'?

Exercise: Viewing the Job

In this exercise, you will use SQL Server Enterprise Manager to view the Web Assistant job created previously.

▶ **To view the Web_Trigger job**

1. In the console tree, expand Management, and then click Web Publishing.

2. In the details pane, right-click the Web_Trigger job, and then click Properties.

3. In the Web_Trigger Properties dialog box, review the properties of the job.

4. Click Cancel to close the dialog box.

Exercise: Viewing the Trigger

In this exercise, you will use SQL Server Enterprise Manager to examine the trigger that the SQL Server Web Assistant Wizard created.

▶ **To view the trigger**

1. In the console tree, expand Databases, expand the StudyNwind database, and then click Tables.

2. In the details pane, right-click the Products table, point to All Tasks, and then click Manage Triggers.

3. Examine all triggers on the Products table by selecting the various triggers in the Name drop-down list.

   What triggers exist?

Exercise: Viewing the Web Page

In this exercise, you will view the Web page and the source HTML.

▶ **To view the generated Web page**

1. Switch to Internet Explorer.

2. Open the C:\Sqladmin\Exercise\Ch07\Lowstock.htm file and view the Web page.

3. On the View menu, click Source, and then review the HTML.

Exercise: Testing the Trigger

In this exercise, you will insert new information into the Products table, which will cause the INSERT trigger to fire. This will execute the Web Assistant job, which will update the Low Stock Web page.

▶ **To test the trigger**

1. Open SQL Server Query Analyzer, and log on to the (local) server with Microsoft Windows NT authentication.

2. Type the following statements:

```
USE StudyNwind
UPDATE Products SET UnitsInStock = (UnitsInStock - 38)
WHERE ProductName = 'Chai'
```

   Changing the value of the UnitsInStock column initiates the trigger that creates a new version of the Web page.

3. Switch to Internet Explorer, and then refresh and view the C:\Sqladmin\ Exercise\Ch07\Lowstock.htm file. The product Chai will have been added to the table on the Web page.

Lesson Summary

The SQL Server Web Assistant allows you to generate Hypertext Markup Language (HTML) Web pages from SQL Server table data. The wizard provides a user interface to the sp_makewebtask system stored procedure, which creates Web Assistant jobs. SQL Server uses triggers to automatically update the Web pages when changes have been made to the data.

Lesson 2: Full-Text Indexing and Searching

SQL Server 7 allows users to issue full-text queries against plain character-based data in SQL Server tables, including searching for words and phrases and multiple forms of a word or phrase. This lesson describes how to use the full-text search capabilities of SQL Server.

After this lesson, you will be able to

- Describe the Microsoft Search service
- Set up full-text indexing on tables in a database
- Populate a full-text catalog
- Perform basic full-text searches

Estimated lesson time: 75 minutes

Introduction to Full-Text Searching

In earlier versions of SQL Server, the ability to query text data was very limited. Beginning with SQL Server 7, you can query character-based data in tables by using full-text searches. The component of SQL Server 7 that performs full-text querying is the Microsoft Search service.

Microsoft Search Service

The Microsoft Search service is a full-text indexing and search engine. The same engine is used with Internet Information Server, where it is called Index Server. The service can be installed only when SQL Server is installed on Windows NT Server. (It cannot be installed on Windows NT Workstation, Windows 95, or Windows 98.)

Installation

You can install Full-Text Search during the initial install of SQL Server if you perform a Custom Install. If you did not install it during your SQL Server installation, you can install Full-Text Search by running SQL Server Setup. Full-Text Search is not installed when the default installation is chosen. In the Select Components dialog box, clear all components and then check Full-Text Search. If you do not clear all components (including Server Components) before you check Full-Text Search, other components may be installed.

Indexing

The Microsoft Search service operates separately from SQL Server. It doesn't store information in SQL Server databases, tables, or indexes. It simply communicates with SQL Server to perform indexing and searching.

A full-text index and a standard SQL Server index are very different. Full-text indexes are stored in files in a folder structure in the file system, called a catalog. By default, these folders are created under C:\Mssql7\Ftdata. A single catalog can be used for one or more indexes in the same database, but databases cannot share catalogs. You can create many catalogs for a single database.

The Microsoft Search service accepts a request to populate the full-text index of a given table into a full-text catalog after the table is set up for full-text indexing. It processes some or all of the rows in a table and extracts key words from the columns specified for full-text searching. These words are stored in an index in the catalog.

Querying

The Microsoft Search service processes full-text search queries received from the MSSQLServer service. It provides advanced search capabilities such as proximity and linguistic searches in multiple languages.

Full-Text Search with SQL Server 7

Earlier versions of SQL Server support only basic character searches against columns in a database:

- Searches for a character value equal to, less than, or greater than a character constant
- Searches for a character value containing a specific string or a wildcard string

In SQL Server 7, the Microsoft Search service enables SQL Server to support complex searches on character or text data in a database or in files outside any database.

Storing Text Data

You can store text data inside or outside the database. The bulk of an organization's text data is usually stored in files of various types, external to any database. You can store from 4 KB to 2 GB of text in a single SQL Server database field with the char, varchar, text, ntext, nchar, or nvarchar data type. This text data, as well as the text data in word processor documents, spreadsheets, and other documents, can all be indexed and searched with the Microsoft Search service.

Querying Text Data

The principal design requirement for full-text indexing and querying is the presence of a single-column unique index on all tables that are registered for full-text search. A full-text index associates words with the unique index key value of each row in SQL Server tables.

When SQL Server receives a query that requires a full-text search, it passes the search criteria to Microsoft Search, which processes the search and returns the key value and a ranking value for each row that contains matches. The MSSQLServer service uses this information to construct the query result set.

Eliminating Noise Words

To prevent the full-text index from becoming bloated with words that do not help the search, extraneous words (known as noise words) such as "a," "and," "is," and "the" are ignored. For example, specifying the phrase "the products ordered during these summer months" is the same as specifying the phrase "products ordered during summer months."

Noise-word lists for many languages are provided and are available in the C:\Mssql7\ Ftdata\Sqlserver\Config folder, which is created when you install Full-Text Search on your server.

Administrators can use any text editor to modify the contents of these lists. For example, system administrators at high-tech companies might add the word "computer" to their noise-word list. Modifications to the list have an effect only when the full-text indexes are next populated.

Introduction to Creating Full-Text Indexes

Full-text support for SQL Server 7 data involves two features: the ability to issue queries against character data, and the creation and maintenance of the underlying indexes that facilitate these queries.

When you work with full-text indexes, you must remember the following:

- Full-text indexes are stored in the file system but are administered through the database.
- There is only one full-text index per table.
- The addition of data to full-text indexes, known as population, must be requested through either a schedule or a specific request.
- One or more full-text indexes within the same database are gathered together into a full-text catalog.
- It can be beneficial to create separate catalogs for large tables in a database. When you populate full-text indexes, a complete catalog is populated, so creating separate catalogs reduces the amount of data that must be populated at one time.

Maintaining Full-Text Indexes

Before you can implement a full-text search in a given database, you must ensure that the full-text search indexes are populated regularly.

Populating Full-Text Indexes

You can update a full-text index by using one of the following methods:

Full Population

A full population refreshes the full-text catalog indexes for all rows in a table regardless of whether the index entries have changed since the last population. This is typically used when a catalog is first populated.

Incremental Population

An incremental population refreshes the full-text catalog indexes for rows that have changed since the last population. An incremental population automatically results in a full population in the following cases:

- A table without a timestamp column is enabled for full-text indexing
- New columns have been enabled for full-text processing since the last population
- The table schema have been modified in some way since the last population

Updating Full-Text Indexes

Unlike standard relational database indexes, full-text indexes are not modified instantly when values in full-text-enabled columns are updated, when rows are added to full-text-registered tables, or when rows are deleted from full-text-enabled tables. You must start the population process manually or schedule it to occur at regular intervals. Full-text indexes are populated asynchronously because

- It typically requires significantly more time to update a full-text index than it does to update a standard index
- Full-text searches are usually less precise than standard searches, so the need for a dynamically synchronized index is not as great

Deactivating Full-Text Indexes

You can deactivate the full-text index for a table so that it no longer participates in the population of the full-text catalog. The full-text index metadata remains, and you can reactivate the table.

After you deactivate a full-text index for a particular table, the existing full-text index remains in place until the next full population. This index is not used because SQL Server blocks queries on deactivated tables.

If you reactivate the table and do not repopulate the index, the old index is still available for queries against any remaining (but not new) full-text-enabled columns. Data from deleted columns is matched in queries that specify a search of all full-text columns (*).

You must use the sp_fulltext_table system stored procedure to deactivate the full-text index for a table.

Setting Up Full-Text Search

Before you can issue full-text queries, you must make sure that the Microsoft Search service is running, and you must create full-text indexes on the tables that will be queried.

Starting Microsoft Search Service

You can start and stop the Microsoft Search service in one of the following ways:

- Use the context menu of the Full-Text Search object in SQL Server Enterprise Manager.
- Use SQL Server Service Manager and select Microsoft Search.
- Execute net start mssearch (or net stop mssearch) from a command prompt.

Creating Full-Text Indexes

You can set up and administer full-text features in SQL Server by using the Full-Text Indexing Wizard and the context menus in SQL Server Enterprise Manager, or by using system stored procedures.

Important If you have a database selected in the console tree when you run the wizard, you will be able to work only with that database in the wizard. If you want to be able to select any database while in the wizard, you must run the wizard with your server selected in the console tree.

The following table lists the system stored procedures that are used to set up full-text indexing.

Stored procedure	Function
sp_fulltext_database	Initializes full-text indexing or removes all full-text catalogs from the current database.
sp_fulltext_catalog	Creates or drops a full-text catalog and starts or stops the indexing action for a catalog.
	You can create multiple full-text catalogs for each database.
sp_fulltext_table	Marks or unmarks a table for full-text indexing.
sp_fulltext_column	Specifies whether a particular column of a table participates in full-text indexing.
sp_fulltext_service	Changes Microsoft Search service (full-text search) properties and cleans up a full-text catalog on a server.

Getting Information About Full-Text Search

You can get information about full-text search indexes and catalogs by using full-text search system stored procedures and SQL Server Enterprise Manager.

Using System Stored Procedures to Get Information About Indexes

You can use the system stored procedures in the following table to obtain information about full-text indexes.

Stored procedure	Function
sp_help_fulltext_catalogs	Returns the ID, name, root directory, status, and number of full-text indexed tables for a specified full-text catalog
sp_help_fulltext_tables	Returns a list of tables that are enabled for full-text indexing
sp_help_fulltext_columns	Returns a list of columns that are enabled for full-text indexing

Using SQL Server Enterprise Manager to Get Information About Catalogs

You can get information about full-text search catalogs in a database by clicking the Full-Text Catalogs object in any database in the console tree and then double-clicking on a catalog in the details pane. The Full-Text Catalog Properties dialog box indicates the following information about the catalog:

- Name, location, and physical name
- Status—the current population status of the catalog
- Item count—the total number of full-text indexed items in the catalog

- Catalog size, in MB
- Unique word count—the total number of unique words in the catalog (this excludes noise words, as they are removed before the index is created)
- Last population date—the date and time that the catalog was last populated

Exercise: Adding Full-Text Search to a Table

In this exercise, you will add full-text search capability to the Employees table in the StudyNwind database, using the Full-Text Indexing Wizard.

▶ **To set up full-text search using the Full-Text Indexing Wizard**

1. Open SQL Server Enterprise Manager.

2. In the console tree, expand Databases, expand StudyNwind, and then click Tables.

3. In the details pane, right-click the Employees table, point to Full-Text Index Table, and then click Define Full-Text Indexing On A Table.

4. Use the information in the following table to complete the wizard. Accept the defaults for any options that are not specified.

Option	Value
Select a unique index	PK_Employees
Added columns	Notes
Create a new catalog?	Checked
New catalog – Name	Emp_catalog
Select or Create Population Schedules (Optional)	No

The final dialog box of the wizard confirms that the full-text index for the Employees table has been defined but not populated. You will populate the full-text index in the next exercise.

5. Open SQL Server Query Analyzer, and log on to the (local) server with Microsoft Windows NT authentication.

6. Execute the following system stored procedure and confirm that full-text indexing is enabled for the Employees table:

```
USE StudyNwind
EXEC sp_help_fulltext_tables
```

You will need to scroll the output in the results pane to the right in order to see all of the information about full-text indexing for the Employees table.

Exercise: Populating a Full-Text Index

In this exercise, you will view catalog information and populate the full-text index for the Emp_Catalog catalog, enabling it for full-text searching.

▶ **To create a full-text index**

1. Switch to SQL Server Enterprise Manager.

2. In the console tree, click Full-Text Catalogs below the StudyNwind database.

3. In the details pane, right-click Emp_Catalog, and then click Properties. View the information about the catalog. Note that the population status is currently idle and that the item count is currently 0. Click Cancel to close the Properties dialog box.

4. Right-click Emp_Catalog, point to Start Population, and then click Full Population to populate the full-text index.

5. Right-click Emp_Catalog, and then click Properties. View the information about the catalog. If you open the Properties dialog box quickly enough, the population status may show that a full population is in progress. Click Refresh until the status is idle. The item count is now 10, and there are 178 unique words in the catalog (your values may vary). Click Cancel to close the Properties dialog box.

Writing Full-Text Queries

With a full-text query, you can perform advanced searches of text data in tables enabled for full-text searches. Unlike the LIKE operator, which is used to search for character patterns, full-text searches operate on combinations of words and phrases. Full-text searches also weigh query terms and report how well a match scored or ranked against the original search term.

Using Transact-SQL Predicates and Functions

You can use the following Transact-SQL predicates and row-set value functions to write full-text queries:

- Use the CONTAINS and FREETEXT predicates in any search condition (including a WHERE clause) of a SELECT statement.

- Use the CONTAINSTABLE and FREETEXTTABLE functions in the FROM clause of a SELECT statement.

Although the Transact-SQL statement used to specify the full-text search condition is the same for both the predicates and the functions, there are major differences in the way they are used. When you work with these Transact-SQL components, consider the following facts and guidelines:

- CONTAINS and FREETEXT both return a TRUE or FALSE value, so they are typically specified in the WHERE clause of a SELECT statement.

- CONTAINS and FREETEXT can be used only to specify selection criteria, which SQL Server uses to determine the membership of the result set.

- CONTAINSTABLE and FREETEXTTABLE both return a table of zero, one, or more rows based on the selection criteria, so they must always be specified in the FROM clause.

- The table returned by CONTAINSTABLE and FREETEXTTABLE has a column named KEY that contains full-text key values and a column named RANK that contains values between 0 and 1000.

   The values in the KEY column are the unique key values of the rows that match the selection criteria specified in the full-text search condition.

   The values in the RANK column are used to rank the rows returned according to how well they meet the selection criteria.

- CONTAINS and CONTAINSTABLE are used to search for precise or "fuzzy" (less precise) matches to single words and phrases, words within a certain distance of one another, or weighted matches.

- FREETEXT and FREETEXTTABLE match the meaning but not the exact wording of the text in the specified free-text string.

```
CONTAINS({column | *}, '<contains_search_condition>' )
FREETEXT({column | * }, 'freetext_string')
CONTAINSTABLE(table, {column | *}, '<contains_search_condition>')
FREETEXTTABLE(table, {column | *}, 'freetext_string')
```

Replace *column* with the name of the full-text indexed column to search, or specify * to indicate that all full-text indexed columns should be searched. Replace *table* with the name of the table to be searched.

The following query returns the plant_id, common_name, and price for all rows in which the phrase "English Thyme" is present in any of the full-text-enabled columns.

```
SELECT plant_id, common_name, price
FROM plants
WHERE CONTAINS( *, ' "English Thyme" ' )
```

The following query returns rows in which the full-text indexed description column contains text such as "Jean LeDuc has always loved ice hockey" or "Jean Leduc on Ice—Hockey at Its Best."

```
SELECT article_id
FROM hockey_articles
WHERE CONTAINS(description, ' "Jean LeDuc"
AND "ice hockey" ' )
```

The following example uses a FREETEXT predicate against a column named description.

```
SELECT * FROM news_table WHERE
FREETEXT(description, ' "The Fulton County Grand Jury said Friday
 an investigation of Atlanta's recent primary election produced no
 evidence that any irregularities took place." ')
```

Here the rows containing text in the description column that matches words, phrases, and meaning within the specified free text will be returned.

Exercise: Writing and Executing Full-Text Queries

In this exercise, you will write and execute full-text queries with SELECT statements that use the CONTAINS and FREETEXT predicates.

▶ **To write and execute full-text queries**

1. Open or switch to SQL Server Query Analyzer.

2. Type and execute three SELECT statements that select the lastname, title, hiredate, and notes columns from the employees table. Use three different search terms on the employees.notes column, as given in the following SELECT statements:

```
USE StudyNwind
SELECT lastname, title, hiredate, notes
FROM employees
WHERE CONTAINS(notes, '"sales management"')
```

```
USE StudyNwind
SELECT lastname, title, hiredate, notes
FROM employees
WHERE CONTAINS(notes, '"sales" AND "management"')
```

```
USE StudyNwind
SELECT lastname, title, hiredate, notes
FROM employees
WHERE CONTAINS(notes, '"sales" NEAR "management"')
```

3. Write a SELECT statement with the CONTAINS predicate that selects the lastname, title, hiredate, and notes columns from the employees table when the employees.notes column contains any form of the word *graduate*.

```
USE StudyNwind
SELECT lastname, title, hiredate, notes
FROM employees
WHERE CONTAINS(notes, 'FORMSOF(INFLECTIONAL, "graduate")')
```

4. Write a SELECT statement with the FREETEXT predicate that selects the lastname, title, hiredate, and notes columns from the employees table when the employees.notes column contains the words *cold* and *toast*.

```
USE StudyNwind
SELECT lastname, title, hiredate, notes FROM Employees
WHERE FREETEXT(notes, 'cold toast')
```

Lesson Summary

Earlier versions of SQL Server support only basic character searches against columns in a database. SQL Server 7, however, supports full-text queries.

Full-text queries can perform advanced searches of text data in tables enabled for full-text searches. With a full-text query, you can search for combinations of words and phrases. Full-text searches also weigh query terms and report how well a match scored or ranked against the original search term.

Review

The following questions are intended to reinforce key information presented in the chapter. If you are unable to answer a question, review the appropriate lesson and then try the question again. Answers to the questions can be found in Appendix A, "Questions and Answers."

1. When the season changes, the supplier sets different prices on certain items. How can you use Web Assistant Wizard to republish the price list in order to reflect these changes?

2. Does the Web Publishing Wizard create dynamic Web pages for which users can specify variable parameter values and see real-time data?

3. You have created a Web Assistant job and scheduled it to update your HTML Web pages weekly. If you receive a new price list from the marketing department and update the database with the new information, do you have to wait until the Web Assistant job executes on schedule, or can you execute the job immediately to update the Web pages?

4. The marketing department at your firm has been entering a large amount of free-text information about customers into the customer database for many months. The marketing manager says that her staff is struggling to create reports based on customer profiles. Can you suggest a way to make it possible to create more effective queries of this information?

5. When trying to define full-text indexing on a table using SQL Server Enterprise Manager, you find that all of the full-text indexing menus are grayed (not available). What would cause this?

C H A P T E R   8

Backup and Restore Overview and Strategy

About This Chapter

This chapter presents an overview of the Microsoft SQL Server backup and restore processes and discusses issues that you should consider when planning a backup and restore strategy for a SQL Server database. Chapters 9 and 10 describe how to actually back up and restore databases.

Before You Begin

There are no prerequisites for this chapter.

Lesson 1: Backup Overview

Data loss and data corruption are major concerns for any database administrator. SQL Server provides a sophisticated backup mechanism that makes it possible to minimize and even eliminate data loss and data corruption. This lesson introduces the SQL Server backup process and the types of backup plans that can be implemented. You should carefully analyze the data protection requirements of your organization and produce a backup strategy that meets these requirements.

After this lesson, you will be able to

- Describe the SQL Server online backup mechanism
- Determine the appropriate times to perform backups

Estimated lesson time: 45 minutes

Preventing Data Loss

The need to prevent data loss is one of the most critical issues that system administrators encounter. You can minimize data loss by having a backup strategy and performing regular backups.

Have a Backup Strategy

You must have a backup strategy to minimize data loss and recover lost data. You can lose data as a result of hardware or software failures or due to any of the following mishaps:

- Accidental or malicious use of the DELETE statement
- Accidental or malicious use of the UPDATE statement—for example, not using a WHERE clause with the UPDATE statement (all rows are updated rather than a single row in a particular table)
- Destructive viruses
- Natural disasters, such as fire, flood, and earthquakes
- Theft

If you have an appropriate backup strategy, you can restore data with minimal cost to production time and minimize the chance of permanent data loss. Think of a backup strategy as an insurance policy. Your backup strategy should put your system back to where it was before a problem occurred. As with an insurance policy, ask yourself, "How much am I willing to pay, and how much loss is acceptable to me?"

The costs associated with a backup strategy include the amount of time spent designing, implementing, automating, and testing the backup procedure. Although you cannot prevent data loss completely, you should design your backup strategy to minimize the extent of the damage. When you plan your backup strategy, consider the acceptable amount of time that the system can be down, as well as the acceptable amount of data loss (if any) in case of a system failure.

Back Up Regularly

How frequently you back up your database depends on the amount of data that you are willing to lose and the volume of database activity. When you back up user databases, consider the following facts and guidelines:

- You should back up your database frequently if your system is in an online transaction processing (OLTP) environment.

- You can back up your database less frequently if your system has little activity or is used primarily for decision support.

- You should try to schedule backups when SQL Server is not in the process of being heavily updated.

- You can back up different databases and parts of databases independently; this means that you can design your databases to support more regular backups of frequently modified data.

Using Backup and Restore for Other Purposes

Backing up and restoring databases is useful for other purposes, such as moving or copying a database from one server to another. By backing up a database on one computer and restoring it to another, you can quickly and easily copy a database.

SQL Server Backup

SQL Server allows you to perform a number of different types of backups. This section describes the types of backups you can perform and gives an overview of the backup process.

Note Previous versions of SQL Server used the terms *dump* for backup and *load* for restore. You will still see these terms in some documentation and Transact-SQL statements—for example, sp_addumpdevice.

Complete Database Backups

When you perform a complete backup of a database, SQL Server backs up

- The schema and file structure
- The data
- Portions of the transaction log files

  The portion of the transaction log that is backed up contains database activities occurring since the start of the backup process.

A complete database backup records all active data pages from the database. Unused pages are not backed up, so the backup will usually be smaller than the database. SQL Server records the specifications of the original database files. This type of backup is used to re-create all files of a database in their original locations, complete with objects and data, when you restore a database.

Transaction Log Backups

In a transaction log backup, only the transaction log is backed up. Transaction log backups record the transactions that have modified a database since the last complete database, differential database, or transaction log backup.

After the transaction log is backed up, the inactive portion of the transaction log is truncated (removed); this frees up space in the transaction log so that it does not become full. Transaction log backups cannot be used if nonlogged transactions are performed on the database (that is, if the trunc. log on chkpt. database option is true). Transaction log backups cannot be restored without a previous database backup.

Differential Database Backups

Differential database backups record the data pages that have changed since the last complete database backup, making a differential backup smaller than a database backup. Differential backups allow you to make less-frequent database backups. They cannot be restored without a previous complete database backup. If you need to restore a database, you must restore both the most recent complete database backup and the most recent differential database backup.

Understanding Complete, Transaction Log, and Differential Backups

To understand the differences among complete, transaction log, and differential backups, think of a manual in a three-ring binder. You can store a copy of the manual or changes to the manual in a number of ways:

- You could keep a copy of the entire manual in the binder; this represents a complete database backup.

- You could keep a list of all changes made to the manual—for example, you could make a note to replace all occurrences of the phrase "raises an alert" with the phrase "fires an alert." You would then go through the entire manual looking for the phrase "raises an alert," scratching it out, and writing in the phrase "fires an alert." This is similar to applying a transaction log backup to a database.

- You could keep copies of replacement pages representing all changes to the manual as of a given date. You would then remove the old pages from the binder and replace them with the new ones. This is similar to restoring a differential database backup.

File or Filegroup Backups

File or filegroup backups are a specialized form of database backup in which only certain individual files or filegroups from a database are backed up. This is usually done when there is not enough time to perform a database backup. To make use of file and filegroup backups, transaction log backups must be created as well.

Performing and Storing Backups

You can back up databases by executing Transact-SQL statements or by using SQL Server Enterprise Manager. When planning a backup strategy, assign someone the responsibility of performing the backups and checking that the backup process is completing correctly. Also consider where your backups will be stored.

Who Performs Backups

Members of the following roles have permission to back up a database:

- Members of the sysadmin fixed server role can back up all databases on the server.
- Members of the db_owner fixed database role for a database can back up that database.
- Members of the db_backupoperator fixed database role for a database can back up that database.

Additional roles can be created and granted permission to back up one or more databases.

Where to Store Backups

SQL Server can back up to hard disk files, tapes, or named pipe devices. To determine which method of storing backups is right for you, consider the following:

- Disk files (local or network) are the most common medium for storing backups. Once a database has been backed up to a disk file, the disk file can in turn be backed up to tape as part of the regular file system backup. In case of media failure, the disk files will have to be restored from tape and then the database restored in SQL Server from the disk files.

Important If you want to back up to a network disk file, you must use the Transact-SQL BACKUP command. You cannot perform the backup using SQL Server Enterprise Manager.

- When you back up to a tape, the tape drive must be attached locally to SQL Server. If you back up to tape, backups can be stored at another location.
- SQL Server provides the ability to back up to a named pipe to allow users to take advantage of the backup and restore features of third-party software packages.

The SQL Server Online Backup Process

When SQL Server backs up an online database (one that is actively being utilized by clients), it performs the following steps:

1. Issues a checkpoint on the database and records the log sequence number (LSN) of the oldest active transaction log record.
2. Writes all pages to the backup medium by reading the disks directly (bypassing the data cache).
3. Writes all transaction log records from the LSN captured in step 1 through the end of the log.

Activities That Are Restricted During Backup

You can back up a database while the database is online and active. However, a few operations, listed here, cannot take place during the backup process:

- Creating or deleting database files
- Creating indexes
- Performing non-logged operations
- Shrinking a database

Note Automatic database growth cannot occur during a backup operation.

If you attempt to start a backup operation when one of these operations is in progress, the backup operation aborts. If a backup operation is already in progress and one of these operations is attempted, the operation fails and the backup operation continues.

If the Transaction Log Becomes Full

If you do not perform regular transaction log backups, the transaction log will eventually become full; either it will grow to its MAXSIZE or the disk will run out of space, preventing further automatic growth. When this happens, SQL Server will prevent further database modifications until you clear the transaction log. If you do not plan to use transaction log backups as part of your backup strategy, do one of the following:

- Clear the transaction log regularly, using the BACKUP LOG statement with the WITH TRUNCATE_ONLY option.

Caution If you use the WITH TRUNCATE_ONLY option with the BACKUP LOG statement, you cannot restore from the backup, as the backup is not written to a backup device.

- Set the trunc. log on chkpt. database option to true.

  When you use this option, the transaction log is truncated automatically whenever a checkpoint occurs. The transaction log does not contain the changes that were made to the database since the last database backup.

Caution If you set the trunc. log on chkpt. option to true, you cannot use transaction log backups as part of your backup strategy, since the log will not contain all of the transactions.

When to Back Up Databases

Your decision as to when and how often you back up your database depends on your particular business environment. There are also times when you may need to perform unscheduled backups. For instance, after loading data or performing database maintenance, you may need to back up a specific user database or the system databases.

Backing Up System Databases

System databases store important data about SQL Server and all user databases. Therefore, you should back up system databases regularly, as well as before performing actions that modify them.

The master database contains system information and high-level information about all databases on a SQL Server. If the master database becomes damaged, SQL Server may fail to start, and user databases may be unavailable. In this case, the master database has to be restored from a backup before user databases can be restored or referenced.

Note Without a current backup of the master database, you must completely rebuild all of the system databases with the Rebuild Master (rebuildm) utility. This utility program rebuilds all system databases as a unit.

When you execute certain statements or system stored procedures, SQL Server modifies the master database. Therefore, back up the master database after using any of the following:

- The CREATE DATABASE, ALTER DATABASE, and DROP DATABASE statements, which create, alter, and remove databases. Automatic file growth does not affect the master database. Adding or removing files or filegroups does affect it.

- The sp_addlogin, sp_addremotelogin, sp_droplogin, sp_dropremotelogin, sp_grantlogin, and sp_password system stored procedures, which work with logins and other operations related to login security. Operations related to database security, such as adding roles or assigning database permissions, do not affect the master database.

- The sp_addserver, sp_addlinkedserver, and sp_dropserver system stored procedures, which add or drop servers.

- The sp_addumpdevice and sp_dropdevice system stored procedures, which add and remove backup devices.

- The sp_renamedb system stored procedure, which renames a database.

- The sp_dboption, sp_configure, and sp_serveroption system stored procedures, which change serverwide or database configuration options.

You should also back up the master database after using SQL Server Enterprise Manager to perform any of the operations just listed.

Tip It is recommended that user objects not be created in the master database. Otherwise, it needs to be backed up more frequently. Additionally, user objects compete with the system objects for space.

Note Transaction log backups and differential backups cannot be performed on the master database. The master database needs to be restored in a single operation, so only complete database backups of this database are allowed.

The msdb Database

Back up the msdb database after modifying information about jobs, alerts, and operators that are used by SQL Server Agent. If you do not have a current backup of the msdb database, you must rebuild all of the system databases if a system failure occurs and then re-create each job, alert, and operator.

Tip It is recommended that user objects not be created in the msdb database. Otherwise, it needs to be backed up more frequently. Additionally, user objects compete with the system objects for space.

The model Database

Back up the model database if you modify it to include the default configuration for all new user databases. If the master or msdb databases are rebuilt, the model database is also rebuilt, and therefore changes are lost. You can restore a backup of your customized model database in case of a system failure.

Note User objects created in the model database are added to every new database. Therefore, you should not add user objects to the model database unless you intend for them to be created in every new database.

The tempdb Database

SQL Server does not allow the tempdb database to be backed up, as it contains only temporary data that will never need to be restored.

Backing Up User Databases

You should plan to back up user databases regularly. You should also perform a backup after a database or index is created and when certain nonlogged operations are executed.

After Creating Databases

Back up a database after it has been created or loaded with data. Without a complete database backup, you cannot restore transaction log or differential database backups, because you must have a baseline for these backups.

After Creating Indexes

The transaction log records only the fact that an index was created, not the actual data page modifications. Therefore, although you are not required to do so, you should perform a backup of the database after creating indexes on large tables.

Backing up a database after an index is created ensures that the database backup device contains the data and the index structures. This will save you time during the restore process if a database is lost.

If you back up only the transaction log after an index is created, SQL Server must rebuild the index when you restore that transaction log. For large tables, the amount of time required to do this may be longer than the time it takes to restore a database backup.

After Clearing the Transaction Log

You should perform a complete backup of a database after clearing the transaction log with the BACKUP LOG WITH TRUNCATE_ONLY statement. After this statement executes, the transaction log no longer contains a record of database activity and cannot be used to recover changes to the database.

After Performing Nonlogged Operations

Operations that are not recorded to the transaction log are called nonlogged operations; they are usually used to prevent the transaction log from filling rapidly and to enhance performance during large operations.

You cannot recover changes made by the following nonlogged operations:

- Use of the WRITETEXT or UPDATETEXT statements. These statements modify data in text columns. By default, due to the size of text modifications, this activity is not recorded in the transaction log. Note that you can specify the WITH LOG option to have these activities logged normally.

- Use of the SELECT INTO statement when the trunc. log on chkpt. database option is set to true.

- Fast bulk copy using the bcp command-line utility when the trunc. log on chkpt. database option is set to true.

You should make a backup of a database after performing a nonlogged operation because the transaction log has no record of the data that has been added to or modified in the database.

Lesson Summary

An appropriate backup strategy will allow you to both restore data with minimal cost to production time and minimize the chance of permanent data loss. SQL Server backups can be performed by using Transact-SQL or the SQL Server Enterprise Manager.

There are three types of backups: complete, differential, and transaction log. When deciding which to use and how often to use them, consider your business environment. At times you will need to perform unscheduled backups because of activities that modify the system databases or nonlogged operations.

Lesson 2: Backup Strategy

In Lesson 1, you learned about the SQL Server backup process. In this lesson, you will learn how to apply this process to develop a reliable backup strategy that is appropriate for the requirements of your organization. This lesson presents samples of various backup strategies that will help you to develop your own strategy.

After this lesson, you will be able to

- Design an appropriate backup strategy

Estimated lesson time: 30 minutes

Planning a Backup Strategy

There are two overall backup and restore strategies, each with its own strengths and weaknesses:

- Backing up only the database. With this strategy, the entire database is backed up regularly. In case of failure, you will lose all committed transactions that occurred after your most recent database backup.

  The primary advantage of using only database backups is simplicity. Backing up is a single operation, normally scheduled at regular intervals. Should a restore be necessary, it can be accomplished easily in one step.

- Backing up the database and the transaction log. With this strategy, the entire database is backed up less frequently; the transaction log is backed up frequently between database backups. In case of failure, you will be able to recover all backed-up transactions and possibly even committed (complete) transactions that occurred since the last transaction log backup. Only uncommitted (incomplete) transactions will be lost.

  Transaction log backups provide the information necessary to redo changes made after a database backup was performed. They make it possible to back up large production databases at short intervals, as well as to restore a database up to a specific point in time.

Caution Recovery of the active transaction log will be possible only if the transaction log and primary data files are undamaged. For this reason, consider placing the transaction log and primary data files on fault-tolerant disks.

Both of these strategies can be augmented by the use of differential database backups to increase the speed of the backup and restore processes.

Finally, it is possible to perform database backups of individual files or filegroups, segmenting a database backup into smaller backup procedures that can be completed in less time. This may be necessary for very large, busy databases.

The Database Backup Strategy

When using the database backup strategy, you back up the entire database every time a backup is performed. Figure 8.1 illustrates this backup strategy. Database size and frequency of data modification determine the time and resources involved in implementing a database backup strategy.

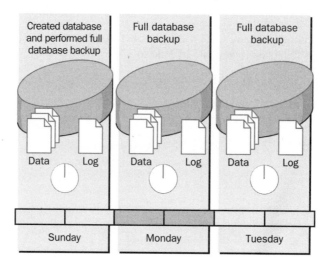

Figure 8.1   The database backup strategy

Use database backups if

- The database is small. The amount of time required to back up a small database is reasonable.

- The database has few data modifications or is read-only. If the database fails between backups, data modified since the last backup will be lost, so up-to-the-minute recovery and point-in-time recovery will not be possible.

- You are willing to accept the loss of changed data if the database fails between backups and must be restored.

Consider the following example of a backup plan and the steps you would take to restore your database. Assume the following:

- The database contains 10 megabytes (MB) of data.

- The database backup process takes a few minutes to complete.

- The database is used mostly for decision support and is modified very little each day.

- The possibility of losing a day's worth of changes to the database is acceptable. These changes can be re-created easily.

- The system administrator does not want to monitor the log size or perform any maintenance on the transaction log.

- The trunc. log on chkpt. database option is set to true, to ensure that the transaction log does not become full. The transaction log does not hold a record of changes to the database over time and cannot be used to restore the database in case of a system failure.

- A database backup is done each day at 6:00 P.M.

- The database becomes corrupted at 10:00 A.M.

To recover the database, you would restore the database backup from the previous night at 6:00 P.M., overwriting the corrupted version of the database.

The limitation of this approach is that all data modifications that were made since the last database backup at 6:00 P.M. are lost.

Note You may be able to recover changes since the backup of the previous night if the transaction log and the primary data file are not damaged (using the BACKUP LOG statement with the NO_TRUNCATE option). However, if the potential data loss is too great, you should consider implementing a backup strategy that includes periodic transaction log backups.

The Database and Transaction Log Backup Strategy

When using a strategy that combines database backups and transaction log backups, you make complete database backups at less frequent regular intervals. Between database backups, the transaction log is backed up, so that you have a record of all database activities that occurred between database backups. This common backup strategy is illustrated in Figure 8.2.

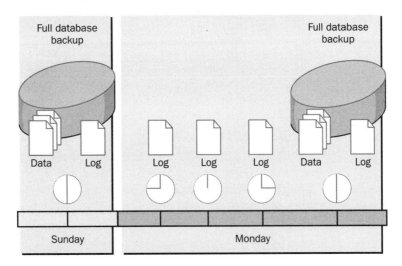

Figure 8.2   The database and transaction log backup strategy

Restoring a database that has been backed up using a database and transaction log strategy involves two steps. First you must restore the most recent complete database backup. Then you apply all of the transaction log backups that were created since the most recent complete database backup.

Use this backup strategy when you cannot afford to lose changes since the most recent database backup or when you need to be able to restore data to a specific point in time.

Consider the following example of a backup plan and the steps you would take to restore your database. Assume the following:

- The database and transaction logs are stored in separate files on separate physical media.

- A database backup is done each night at 6:00 P.M.

- Transaction log backups are performed each day at 9:00 A.M., 12:00 noon, and 3:00 P.M.

- The physical medium that contains the secondary data file(s) is damaged at 1:30 P.M.

You would go through the following steps to recover the database:

1. Back up the transaction log, using the WITH NO_TRUNCATE option. (This is possible only if the transaction log and the primary data files are available.)

2. Restore the database backup that was created the previous night at 6:00 P.M.

3. Apply all transaction logs that were created that day (9:00 A.M. and 12:00 noon).

4. Apply the transaction log backup that was created at the beginning of the restore process (if one was created).

   Applying the transaction log created at the beginning of the restore brings the database back to the state it was in when it was damaged. If you are not able to make a backup of the transaction log before starting the restore, you will be able to restore the database to the state it was in at 12:00 noon.

The Differential Backup Strategy

Figure 8.3 illustrates the differential backup strategy. Use this strategy to augment either a database backup strategy or a database and transaction log backup strategy. Differential backups consist only of the portions of the database that have changed since the last database backup.

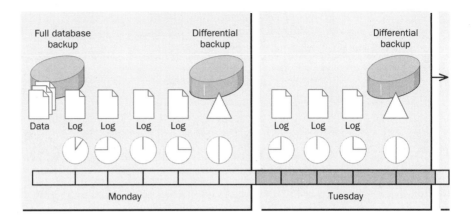

Figure 8.3 The differential backup strategy

Recovery using a differential backup requires that you restore the most recent complete database backup and the most recent differential backup. If transaction log backups are also made, only those created since the most recent differential backup need to be applied to fully recover the database. Use this strategy to reduce recovery time if the database becomes damaged.

For example, rather than applying many transaction logs, you would use the most recent differential backup to restore data that has changed since the last complete database backup and then apply only the transaction log backups taken since that differential backup.

Consider the following example of a backup plan and the steps that you would take to restore your database. Assume the following:

- A database backup is performed once a week. The last database backup was made on Sunday at 1:00 A.M.

- A differential backup is performed at the end of each business day. A differential backup was performed on both Monday and Tuesday at 6:00 P.M.

- Transaction log backups are performed every hour during the business day (8:00 A.M. to 5:00 P.M.). A transaction log backup was performed on Wednesday at 8:00 A.M. and again at 9:00 A.M.

- The database becomes corrupted on Wednesday at 9:30 A.M.

You would go through the following steps to recover the database:

1. Back up the transaction log, using the WITH NO_TRUNCATE option. (This is possible only if the transaction log and the primary data file are available.)

2. Restore the database backup that was created on Sunday at 1:00 A.M.

3. Restore the differential backup that was created on Tuesday at 6:00 P.M. This backup is the latest differential backup and contains all of the data that has changed since the complete database backup on Sunday at 1:00 A.M.

4. Apply the transaction log backups that were created on Wednesday at 8:00 A.M. and 9:00 A.M.

5. Apply the transaction log backup that was created at the beginning of the restore process (if one was created).

The application of the last transaction log backup brings the database back to where it was at the time it was damaged. If you are not able to make a backup of the transaction log before starting the restore, then you will be able to restore the database to the state it was in at 9:00 A.M. on Wednesday.

The Database File or Filegroup Backup Strategy

Figure 8.4 illustrates the database file backup strategy. The database filegroup strategy works similarly, except that it works with filegroups rather than individual files. When you implement a database file or filegroup backup strategy, you must back up the transaction log as part of the strategy.

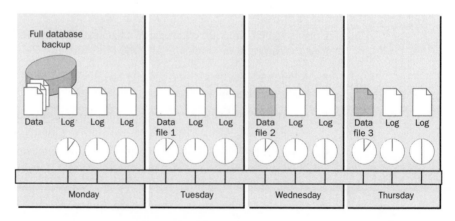

Figure 8.4   The database file backup strategy

Use this strategy for very large databases that are partitioned among multiple files. When combined with regular transaction log backups, this technique makes it possible to perform backups when time is limited.

For example, if you have only one hour to perform a database backup that would normally take four hours, you could create the database using four data files, back up only one file each night, and still ensure data consistency. Transaction log backups could be performed at short intervals during the day.

Consider the following example of a backup plan and the steps you would take to restore your database. Assume the following:

- The data in a database is divided among data files File1, File2, and File3.
- A database backup is performed every week. A complete database backup is performed on Monday at 1:00 A.M.
- Selected files are backed up on a rotating basis each day at 1:00 A.M.
  - File1 is backed up on Tuesday and Friday at 1:00 A.M.
  - File2 is backed up on Wednesday and Saturday at 1:00 A.M.
  - File3 is backed up on Thursday and Sunday at 1:00 A.M.
- Transaction log backups are performed hourly between database backups.
- On Thursday at 8:00 A.M., the physical medium of File2 becomes damaged.

You would go through the following steps to recover the database:

1. Back up the transaction log, using the WITH NO_TRUNCATE option. (This is possible only if the transaction log and the primary data file are available.)
2. Restore the backup of File2 that was created on Wednesday at 1:00 A.M.
3. Apply the transaction log backups made since Wednesday at 1:00 A.M. (2:00 A.M. Wednesday through 7:00 A.M. Thursday).
4. Apply the transaction log backup that was created at the beginning of the restore process (if one was created).

The performance that is gained by using this strategy results from the fact that only transaction log events that affect data stored in the failed file need to be applied. In this example, only transactions for File2 made after 1:00 A.M. on Wednesday are applied. If File1 had failed, transaction log backups made after 1:00 A.M. on Tuesday would have been applied. If File3 had failed, transaction log backups made after 1:00 A.M. on Thursday would have been applied.

Performance Considerations

Consider some of the issues that affect the performance of SQL Server when you back up databases:

- Backing up to multiple physical devices is generally faster than using a single physical device. SQL Server takes advantage of multiple backup devices by writing the data to each backup device in parallel.

- The time needed to back up a database depends on the speed of the physical device. Tape drives are generally slower than disk devices.

- You should minimize concurrent activity when you back up a database. Concurrent activity on SQL Server may affect the time it takes to back up your database.

Lesson Summary

There are two approaches administrators can take when planning a backup strategy. They can back up only the database at frequent intervals, or they can back up the database and the transaction logs. The first strategy allows a simple restore of the database in case of data loss but can result in data being lost during the interval between backups. The second strategy may involve more work when restoring data but often can bring your database back to the state it was in before the loss.

Review

The following questions are intended to reinforce key information presented in the chapter. If you are unable to answer a question, review the appropriate lesson and then try the question again. Answers to the questions can be found in Appendix A, "Questions and Answers."

1. Your database consists of 5 gigabytes (GB) of data and is stored in one database file. This database is used as an order-taking system for a mail-order catalog company. Operators take orders 24 hours a day. The company typically receives about 2000 orders each day. Describe an appropriate backup plan for this database.

2. Your database contains image data that is gathered from a weather satellite and is continually being updated. The database is 700 GB. Each table exists in a separate filegroup in the database. If you were to perform a database backup, the process would take about 20 hours. How can you minimize the amount of time that is spent performing backups each day and still ensure good data recoverability in case of a system failure?

C H A P T E R   9

Backing Up Databases

About This Chapter

In this chapter, you will learn about the media that you can use when creating Microsoft SQL Server backups and how to perform backups using SQL Server Enterprise Manager or the Transact-SQL BACKUP statement.

Before You Begin

To complete the lessons in this chapter, you must have

- Installed SQL Server 7 on your computer. Installation procedures are covered in Chapter 2, "Installation." The exercises assume that you are working on a Microsoft Windows NT Server configured as a domain controller, although you can complete the exercises using SQL Server installed on Windows NT Workstation or on a standalone Windows NT Server. You can also complete all of the exercises for this chapter on SQL Server installed on Microsoft Windows 95 or Windows 98.

- Installed the StudyNwind database. See the "Getting Started" section in "About This Book" for StudyNwind database installation instructions.

- Installed the Exercise files from the Supplemental Course Materials CD-ROM to your hard disk drive. See the "Getting Started" section in "About This Book" for installation instructions.

- Experience using the SQL Server Enterprise Manager and SQL Server Query Analyzer.

Lesson 1: Backup Devices

An important part of an administrator's strategy for backup and recovery of data is the type of device that will hold the backed-up data—the backup device. A backup device is used by SQL Server to back up databases, transaction logs, and data files. Backup devices include disk, tape, and named pipe devices.

After this lesson, you will be able to

- Create named backup devices
- Describe temporary backup devices
- Describe striped backups

Estimated lesson time: 45 minutes

Overview of Backup Devices

Backup devices always have a physical name that refers to the name used by the operating system to access the device. They can also have a logical name stored in the system tables. Devices that have a logical name are called logical, permanent, or named backup devices. Devices that do not have a logical name are called physical, or temporary, backup devices. There is no difference in the devices themselves, only in whether you can use a logical name to refer to the device. When backing up or restoring data, you can use physical or logical names.

Note The term *backup file* is sometimes used instead of *backup device*. *Backup device* is preferred because backups can be made to tapes and named pipes as well as to disk files. When you see the term *backup file*, it will usually be referring specifically to a disk backup device, which is stored as a file in the file system of the SQL Server computer or on a shared network drive.

Creating Named Backup Devices

If you want to use a logical name for a backup device, you must create the named backup device before using it. When using the device for backups and restores, you then reference the device by its logical name only.

Why Create Named Backup Devices?

Named backup devices are simpler to use than physical devices because they have shorter names. SQL Server Enterprise Manager lists only named backup devices in the console tree. (You can use physical names for backup devices elsewhere in SQL Server Enterprise Manager when necessary.) You can create named backup devices with SQL Server Enterprise Manager or by executing the sp_addumpdevice system stored procedure.

Using the sp_addumpdevice System Stored Procedure

Execute the sp_addumpdevice system stored procedure to create a named backup device on disk or tape, or to direct data to a named pipe. When you create named backup devices, consider the following facts:

- The device is not physically created until it is used. For example, if you look in the C:\Mssql7\Backup folder after creating a new device with a physical name of C:\Mssql7\Backup\Mydev.bak, you will not see a file called Mydev.bak. Only after you make the first backup to the new device will Mydev.bak be present in the folder.

- SQL Server creates logical and physical names in the sysdevices system table of the master database.

- You must specify the logical and physical names of the backup device.

- If you want to create a backup device that uses a network disk file, you must specify the network disk file location. The location can use a UNC path name or a mapped drive letter.

When you create a backup device with SQL Server Enterprise Manager, SQL Server executes the sp_addumpdevice system stored procedure for you.

The syntax for the sp_addumpdevice statement is as follows:

```
sp_addumpdevice [@devtype = ] 'device_type',
[@logicalname = ] 'logical_name',
[@physicalname = ] 'physical_name'
```

where *device_type* is {DISK | TAPE | PIPE}.

The following example creates a backup device on a local disk using the sp_addumpdevice statement.

```
USE master
EXEC sp_addumpdevice 'disk', 'mybackupfile',
 'C:\Mssql7\Backup\Mybackupfile.bak'
```

The following example uses the sp_addumpdevice statement to create a backup device on a network disk.

```
USE master
EXEC sp_addumpdevice 'disk', 'mynetworkbackup',
 '\\servername\sharename\path\mynetworkbackup.bak'
```

The next example creates a named backup device on a tape with the logical name mytape1 and the physical name \\.\tape0, using the sp_addumpdevice statement.

```
USE master
EXEC sp_addumpdevice 'tape', 'mytape1', '\\.\tape0'
```

Exercise: Creating Backup Devices with SQL Server Enterprise Manager

In this exercise, you will use SQL Server Enterprise Manager to create two named backup devices.

▶ **To create backup devices with SQL Server Enterprise Manager**

1. Log on to your computer as Administrator or another account that is a member of the Administrators local group.

2. Start SQL Server Enterprise Manager.

3. In the console tree, expand Management, right-click Backup, and then click New Backup Device.

4. Use the information in the following table to create two new named backup devices.

Name	Filename
NwA	C:\Mssql7\Backup\Nwa.bak
Nwlog	C:\Mssql7\Backup\Nwlog.bak

5. Close SQL Server Enterprise Manager.

Exercise: Creating Backup Devices with Transact-SQL

In this exercise, you will create two new named backup devices with the sp_addumpdevice system stored procedure. You will find the script for this exercise in C:\Sqladmin\Exercise\Ch09\ Makedev2.sql.

▶ **To create a permanent backup device with Transact-SQL**

1. Open SQL Server Query Analyzer and log on to the (local) server with Windows NT authentication. Your Administrator account is a member of the Windows NT Administrators group, which is automatically mapped to the SQL Server sysadmin role.

2. Write and execute a Transact-SQL statement to create two named backup devices based on the information in the following table.

Device type	Logical name	Physical name
Disk	NwstripeA	C:\Mssql7\Backup\NwstripeA.bak
Disk	NwstripeB	C:\Mssql7\Backup\NwstripeB.bak

Deleting Named Backup Devices

You can delete named backup devices using SQL Server Enterprise Manager or the sp_dropdevice system stored procedure. If you use SQL Server Enterprise Manager to delete a named backup device and the device is a disk, the backup device's file will not be removed from the disk. You must remove the file manually from C:\Mssql7\Backup (or the location it was created in, if not the default location). If you use sp_dropdevice to delete a named backup device and the device is a disk, you can specify the DELFILE option to have sp_dropdevice delete the file, as conveyed in the following example.

```
USE master
EXEC sp_dropdevice 'mybackupfile', DELFILE
```

Creating Temporary Backup Devices

While it is preferable to create a named backup device and use a logical name to reference it, you can also reference a backup device with its physical name only.

Why Create Temporary Backup Devices?

If you do not plan to reuse a backup device, you can use a temporary backup device. This makes it unnecessary to use the sp_addumpdevice system stored procedure to add the device before using it. For example, if you are performing a one-time-only backup of a database or are testing the backup operation that you plan to automate, you may want to use a temporary backup device.

Creating a Named Backup Device from a Temporary Backup Device

When specifying the location for a named backup device in SQL Server Enterprise Manager or as the physical name parameter of the sp_addumpdevice system stored procedure, you can specify an existing temporary backup device location. The temporary backup device then becomes a named backup device that can be referenced by its logical name and managed in SQL Server Enterprise Manager. If you try to add a device that is already a named backup device, the operation will fail.

Initializing a Device

SQL Server initializes a backup device the first time it is used. For named backup devices, the device is initialized with the physical name that was specified when the device was created. For temporary backup devices, the device is initialized with the physical name specified in the BACKUP statement.

If you create a temporary backup device, you must

- Specify a media type (DISK, TAPE, or PIPE).
- Specify the complete path and filename for disk and tape devices. If you want to use a network disk file, you must specify a network disk file location, using a UNC pathname or a mapped drive letter.
- Specify the name of the pipe for named pipe devices.

The partial syntax for the BACKUP DATABASE statement is as follows:

```
BACKUP DATABASE database_name
TO { backup_device_name|
    {DISK | TAPE | PIPE} ='temp_backup_file' [, …n]
```

The following example uses a named backup device to back up the Northwind database.

```
USE master
BACKUP DATABASE northwind TO mybackupfile
```

The example that follows uses a temporary backup device on a disk to back up the Northwind database.

```
USE master
BACKUP DATABASE northwind TO DISK = 'C:\Temp\Mynwind.bak'
```

Using Multiple Backup Devices to Store Backups

SQL Server can write to multiple backup devices at the same time (in parallel). When you have multiple backup devices, data is striped across all devices that are used to create the backup. These devices store a striped backup set. A *backup set* is a result of a single backup operation on one or more devices. Figure 9.1 shows how backups can be made to multiple backup devices and how the parts of a single backup across the devices together make up a backup set.

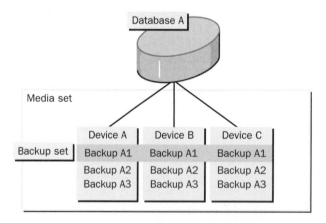

Figure 9.1   Using multiple devices to store backups

Storing Backups on Multiple Backup Devices

Backing up to multiple devices decreases the total time required to back up a database. For example, if a backup operation that uses one tape drive normally takes four hours to complete, you can add a second tape drive and possibly reduce the length of the backup operation to only two hours.

When you use multiple devices to store your backups, consider the following facts:

- All devices that are used in a multiple backup operation must be of the same media type (disk or tape).

- Devices that are used in a multiple backup operation do not need to be the same size or operate at the same speed.

- You can use a combination of named and physical devices together.

- When restoring from a multiple-device backup, it is not necessary to use the same number of devices as was used to create the backup.

Media Sets

A *media set* is a collection of backup devices used to contain one or more backup sets. A media set can be a single backup device. If the backup devices in a multi-device media set are disk drives, then each backup device is a single file. If the backup devices in a multidevice media set are tape drives, then each backup device is made up of one or more tapes, together called a *media family*. The first tape in a media family is called the *initial media*; other tapes are called *continuation media*.

When using media sets,

- Tapes used as part of a media set for a multiple-device backup can be used only by SQL Server.

- If you define a number of backup devices as members of a media set, you must always use the backup devices together.

- You cannot use only one member of the media set for a backup operation unless you reformat the backup device.

- If you reformat one member of a media set, the data contained in the other members of the media set is invalid and unusable.

If a striped backup set was created on two backup devices, those two backup devices are now part of a media set. All subsequent backup operations that involve this media set must use these same two backup devices. You can append additional striped backup sets to this media set by using these two backup devices. However, if you want to use one of these backup devices on its own to back up another database or as part of another media set, you must reformat the backup device.

Lesson Summary

One of the first steps in planning a successful backup strategy is deciding on the medium. Will the backup be to disk, tape, or named pipe devices? Once the type of device is selected, the backup process can be made more efficient by using striped devices.

SQL Server can write to multiple backup devices at the same time (in parallel). When you have multiple backup devices, data is striped across all devices that are used to create the backup. These devices store a striped backup set. A *backup set* is a result of a single backup operation on one or more devices.

Lesson 2: Performing Backups

Once the backup strategy is in place and the medium for the backup devices is decided on, you are ready to perform the actual backups. Backups can be performed using the SQL Server Enterprise Manager or Transact-SQL.

After this lesson, you will be able to

- Perform a database backup
- Perform a transaction log backup
- Perform a differential backup
- Perform a file or filegroup backup

Estimated lesson time: 90 minutes

Using the BACKUP Statement

You can perform backup operations with SQL Server Enterprise Manager, the Backup Wizard, or Transact-SQL. You should be familiar with certain backup options whenever you use any of the SQL Server backup methods.

The syntax for the BACKUP DATABASE statement with options is as follows:

```
BACKUP DATABASE {database_name | @database_name_var}
TO <backup_device> [, ...n]
[WITH
    [[, ] FORMAT]
    [[,] {INIT | NOINIT}]
    [[, ] RESTART]
    [[,] MEDIANAME = {media_name | @media_name_variable}]
]
```

Note The BACKUP statement replaces the DUMP statement found in previous versions of SQL Server. DUMP is still supported but for backward compatibility only. You should use the BACKUP statement.

Using the MEDIANAME Option

You can use the MEDIANAME option of the BACKUP statement or the Media Name option in SQL Server Enterprise Manager to specify the name of the media set for the backup. If specified for a new backup device or a backup device that is being formatted, this name will be written to the media header. If specified for subsequent backups, SQL Server will check that the name specified matches the name on the media and will cause the backup to fail if the names do not match, preventing accidental use of the incorrect media.

When you use multiple devices to back up a database, the media set name is also used to associate the backup devices with one another. It can be used to check that the correct media are used together for subsequent backups.

Names can have up to 128 characters if specified with the MEDIANAME option of the BACKUP statement and up to 64 characters if specified with the Media Name option in SQL Server Enterprise Manager.

Using the INIT or NOINIT Option

When you back up a database, you can overwrite existing data on the backup device or append the backup set after existing data on the backup device.

Use the NOINIT option to append a backup set to an existing backup device. This is the default.

If you use the INIT option, SQL Server writes the backup set at the beginning of the device, overwriting any existing data on the backup media but retaining the media header.

The backup operation fails and data is not overwritten if

- The EXPIREDATE option was specified for backup sets on the backup device and the backup sets on the backup device have not yet expired.

- The *media_name* parameter that you specified in the MEDIANAME option does not match the media name of the backup device.

- You attempt to overwrite one member of a previously named media set. SQL Server detects that the device is a member of a media set and that overwriting its contents would make the whole set unusable.

Using the FORMAT Option

You use the FORMAT option to overwrite the contents of a backup device and split up a media set. When you use the FORMAT option

- A new media header is written on all devices that are used for this backup operation.

- SQL Server overwrites both the existing media header and the contents of the backup device.

Use the FORMAT option carefully. Formatting only one backup device of a media set renders the entire media set unusable. The media name of the media is not checked when using the FORMAT option, making it possible to change the media name of an existing device. This is another reason to use the FORMAT option with caution; you will not be warned if you are accidentally using the wrong media.

Using the RESTART Option

If you want SQL Server to restart an interrupted backup operation from the point of interruption, use the RESTART option. You must restart the backup process manually by executing the original BACKUP statement with the RESTART option.

Backing Up to a Tape Device

Tapes are a convenient medium for backups because they are inexpensive, provide a large amount of storage, and can be stored off-site for data safety and security.

When you back up to a tape, the tape drive must be attached locally to SQL Server.

Recording Backup Information on the Tape Label

When you back up to a tape, SQL Server records the following backup information on the tape label:

- Database name
- Time
- Date
- Type of backup

Storing SQL Server and Non–SQL Server Backups

SQL Server uses a standard backup format called Microsoft Tape Format to write backups to tape. Consequently, both SQL Server and non–SQL Server data can be stored on the same tape.

This does not mean that SQL Server can use backups written to a tape by another application. It simply means that SQL Server backups can exist on the same tape as backups written by other applications that use the MTF format. For example, you could perform a SQL Server backup to disk and then use Windows NT Backup to back up the disk files to tape. To restore the files, you would have to use Windows NT Backup to restore the files to disk, and then use SQL Server to restore the SQL Server backup from the disk backup device; you cannot restore the Windows NT backup directly from the tape with SQL Server.

Specifying Tape Options

When you back up to a tape, you can use options that are specific to this backup medium. This section describes these tape-specific options.

The UNLOAD Option

SQL Server automatically rewinds and unloads the tape from the tape drive after the backup is complete. The UNLOAD option is the SQL Server default and remains set until you select the NOUNLOAD option.

The NOUNLOAD Option

Use the NOUNLOAD option if you do not want SQL Server to rewind and unload the tape from the tape drive automatically after a backup. The NOUNLOAD option remains set until you select UNLOAD.

The BLOCKSIZE Option

Use the BLOCKSIZE option to change the physical block size in bytes if you are overwriting a tape with the FORMAT or SKIP and INIT options. When you back up to a tape, SQL Server selects an appropriate block size. You can override this selection by using the BLOCKSIZE option.

The FORMAT Option

Use the FORMAT option to write a header on all of the volumes (disk files or tapes) that are used for a backup. SQL Server overwrites all headers and backups on the media. The header includes information that is found in the MEDIANAME and MEDIADESCRIPTION options.

When you use the FORMAT option to back up to a tape device, the INIT and SKIP options are implied, and therefore you do not need to specify these options.

Use this option with caution, as the new backup will overwrite the media without checking the existing header and password (if any) on the media. If the media are part of an existing media set that has been used for a striped backup set, that backup set will be unusable.

The SKIP Option

Use the SKIP option to skip headers. This option causes SQL Server to ignore any existing ANSI tape labels on the tape device. The ANSI label of a tape can provide warning information about the expiration date of the tape, as well as enforce write permissions.

The NOSKIP Option

Use the NOSKIP option if you want SQL Server to read ANSI tape labels. This is the SQL Server default.

Performing a Complete Database Backup

A complete database backup serves as your baseline in case of a system failure. When you perform a complete database backup, SQL Server backs up everything in the database, including any portions of the transaction log needed to ensure data consistency when the backup is restored.

The following example creates a named backup device with the logical name nwndbac and performs a complete database backup.

```
USE master
EXEC sp_addumpdevice 'disk', 'nwndbac',
'C:\mssql7\backup\nwndbac.bak'
BACKUP DATABASE northwind TO nwndbac
```

The example that follows performs a complete database backup to the nwndbac device and overwrites any previous backups on that device.

```
BACKUP DATABASE northwind TO nwndbac WITH INIT
```

The next example appends a complete database backup to the nwndbac device. Any previous backups on the device are left intact.

```
BACKUP DATABASE northwind TO nwndbac WITH NOINIT
```

The following example performs a complete database backup to a temporary backup device.

```
BACKUP DATABASE northwind TO
DISK = 'D:\Temp\Mytempbackup.bak'
```

Exercise: Clearing Options Set for the StudyNwind Database

Before proceeding with exercises in which you will perform database backups, in this exercise you will clear any database options that are set for the StudyNwind database.

▶   **To clear the database options**

1. Open SQL Server Enterprise Manager.

2. In the console tree, expand the Databases folder.

3. Right-click the StudyNwind database icon, and then click Properties.

4. On the Options tab, clear any selected options.

5. Click OK.

Exercise: Using SQL Server
Enterprise Manager to Back Up the StudyNwind Database

In this exercise, you will perform a complete database backup of the StudyNwind database to the nwA backup device.

▶ **To back up a database with SQL Server Enterprise Manager**

1. Switch to SQL Server Enterprise Manager.

2. In the console tree, expand Databases, right-click the StudyNwind database, point to All Tasks, and then click Backup Database.

3. In the SQL Server Backup dialog box, click the General tab if it is not already selected.

4. Ensure that StudyNwind is selected in Database.

5. In Name, type the backup set name **StudyNwindFull**.

6. In Description, type the description **First backup of StudyNwind**.

7. Under Backup, click Database - Complete.

8. Under Destination, Disk should be selected. If you do not have a tape drive connected to the computer, Disk and Tape will both be grayed and Disk will be selected; this is correct.

9. Under Destination, click Add to add the nwA backup device.

10. In the Choose Backup Destination dialog box, click Backup Device and select nwA from the drop-down list of devices. (If nwA is not in the list, you may already have added it as a destination or you may not yet have created it.)

11. Click OK to close the dialog box and add nwA to the Backup To list.

12. If there are any other devices in the Backup To list, highlight them and click Remove to remove them.

13. Under Overwrite, click the Overwrite Existing Media option to overwrite any existing backups on the backup device.

14. Click the Options tab.

15. Check the Verify Backup Upon Completion option, and make sure none of the other options are checked.

16. Click OK to perform the backup.

Exercise: Using Transact-SQL to Append a Backup to the nwA Device

In this exercise, you will write and execute a Transact-SQL statement to perform another complete database backup of the StudyNwind database and append the backup to the nwA backup device. You will find the script for this exercise in C:\Sqladmin\Exercise\Ch09\Append.sql.

▶ **To append a subsequent backup to a backup device with Transact-SQL**

1. Switch to SQL Server Query Analyzer.

2. Write and execute a Transact-SQL statement that backs up the StudyNwind database and appends the backup to the nwA backup device. Use the options shown in the following table.

Option	Value
Database name	StudyNwind
Backup device	nwA
Append, overwrite, or initialize	Append (WITH NOINIT)
Name	StudyNwindFull2
Description	The second full backup of StudyNwind

Exercise: Viewing the Contents of the Backup Device

In this exercise, you will use SQL Server Enterprise Manager to view the contents of the nwA backup device to ensure that it contains two complete database backups.

▶ **To view the contents of the backup device**

1. Switch to SQL Server Enterprise Manager.

2. In the console tree, expand Management, and click Backup.

3. In the details pane, right-click the nwA backup device, and then click Properties.

4. Click View Contents.

5. Confirm that the backup device contains two complete database backups.

6. Use Windows NT Explorer to view the C:\Mssql7\Backup folder. Note the size of the nwA.bak file, which is the backup device containing two database backup sets.

Exercise: Using Transact-SQL to Overwrite the Backup

In this exercise, you will write and execute a Transact-SQL statement to back up the StudyNwind database and overwrite any existing backups on the nwA backup device. You will find the script for this exercise in C:\Sqladmin\Exercise\Ch09\ Overwrit.sql.

▶ **To overwrite an existing backup with Transact-SQL**

1. Switch to SQL Server Query Analyzer.

2. Write and execute a Transact-SQL statement to back up the StudyNwind database onto the nwA backup device. To do so, use the options shown in the following table.

Option	Value
Database name	StudyNwind
Backup device	NwA
Append, overwrite, or initialize	Overwrite (WITH INIT)
Name	StudyNwindFull3
Description	The third full backup of StudyNwind; overwrites the others

3. Use SQL Server Enterprise Manager, as you did in the previous exercise, to view the contents of nwA and confirm that the other backups were overwritten.

Exercise: Backing Up the StudyNwind Database to Multiple Backup Devices

In this exercise, you will use SQL Server Enterprise Manager to perform a complete database backup of the StudyNwind database onto two existing backup devices: nwstripeA and nwstripeB. You will also overwrite any existing data, including header information.

▶ **To back up one database to multiple backup devices**

1. Switch to SQL Server Enterprise Manager.

2. In the console tree, expand Databases, right-click the StudyNwind database, point to All Tasks, and then click Backup Database.

3. In the SQL Server Backup dialog box, click the General tab if it is not already selected.

4. Ensure that StudyNwind is selected in Database.

5. In Name, type the backup set name **StudyNwind Striped**.

6. In Description, type the description **A parallel backup of StudyNwind**.

7. Under Backup, click Database - Complete.

8. Under Destination, Disk should be selected. If you do not have a tape drive connected to the computer, Disk and Tape will both be grayed and Disk will be selected; this is correct.

9. Under Destination, click Add to add nwstripeA.

10. In the Choose Backup Destination dialog box, click Backup Device and select nwstripeA from the drop-down list of devices. (If nwstripeA is not in the list, you may already have added it as a destination or you may not yet have created it.)

11. Click OK to close the dialog box and add nwstripeA to the Backup To list.

12. Repeat steps 9, 10, and 11 for the nwstripeB device.

13. If nwA or any other devices appear in the Backup To list, highlight them and click Remove to remove them.

14. Under Overwrite, click the Overwrite Existing Media option to overwrite any existing backups on the backup device.

15. Click the Options tab.

16. Check the Initialize And Label Media option, and make sure that no other options are checked.

17. Type **nwstripe** for the Media Set Name.

18. Type **Striped backup of StudyNwind** for the Media Set Description.

19. Click OK to perform the backup.

Exercise: Viewing the Contents of the Backup Devices

In this exercise, you will use SQL Server Enterprise Manager to view the contents of the nwstripeA and nwstripeB backup devices to ensure that they contain a striped database backup.

▶ **To view the contents of multiple backup devices**

1. Switch to SQL Server Enterprise Manager.

2. In the console tree, expand Management, and then click Backup.

3. In the details pane, right-click the nwstripeA backup device, and then click Properties.

4. Click View Contents.

5. Confirm that the backup device contains a database backup.

6. Note the media name and the media sequence of the media.

7. Repeat steps 3 through 6 for nwstripeB.

   Note that both devices are part of the nwstripe media set but that each device contains a different family from the media set. For these disk devices, the media number is always 1; for tape devices, each tape in a family will have a different number.

8. Use Windows NT Explorer to view the C:\Mssql7\Backup folder. Note the size of the nwstripeA.bak and nwstripeB.bak files, which are the backup devices that each contain part of the striped database backup set.

Exercise: Backing Up the StudyNwind Database to a Temporary Device

In this exercise, you will write and execute a single Transact-SQL statement to back up the StudyNwind database to a new backup device. You will find the script for this exercise in C:\Sqladmin\Exercise\Ch09\Bactonew.sql.

▶ **To back up a database and create a temporary backup device**

1. Switch to SQL Server Query Analyzer.

2. Write and execute a single Transact-SQL statement that backs up the StudyNwind database to a new backup device. Use the options shown in the following table.

Option	Value
Database name	StudyNwind
File location	C:\Mssql7\Backup\Mynewbackup.bak
Append, overwrite, or initialize	Initialize (WITH FORMAT)
Name	MyNewBackup
Description	New backup device, not recorded as a named backup device

3. Start Microsoft Windows NT Explorer.

4. Expand the C:\Mssql7\Backup folder and examine Mynewbackup.bak to confirm that this backup device was created and populated.

Performing a Transaction Log Backup

You back up transaction logs to record modifications to the database since the last database or transaction log backup. Do not back up a transaction log unless you have performed a complete database backup at least once, because transaction logs cannot be restored without a corresponding database backup.

How SQL Server Backs Up the Transaction Log

When you back up the transaction log, SQL Server does the following:

- Backs up the transaction log from the point at which the last successful backup ended to the end of the current transaction log.

- Truncates the transaction log up to the beginning of the active portion of the transaction log. The active portion of the transaction log starts at the earlier of the most recent checkpoint or the oldest open transaction and continues to the end of the transaction log.

The syntax for the BACKUP LOG statement is as follows:.

```
BACKUP LOG {database_name | @database_name_var}
TO <backup_device> [, …n]
[WITH
    [[,] {INIT | NOINIT}]
    [[,] [NAME = {backup_set_name | @backup_set_name_var}]
]
```

Note The BACKUP LOG statement replaces the DUMP TRANsaction statement found in previous versions of SQL Server. DUMP TRANsaction is still supported but for backward compatibility only. You should use the BACKUP LOG statement.

The following example creates a named backup device and backs up the transaction log of the Northwind database.

```
USE master
EXEC sp_addumpdevice 'disk', 'nwndbaclog',
    'c:\mssql7\backup\nwndbaclog.bak'
BACKUP LOG northwind TO nwndbaclog
```

Exercise: Using SQL Server Enterprise Manager to Back Up the StudyNwind Transaction Log

In this exercise, you will use SQL Server Enterprise Manager to back up the transaction log for the StudyNwind database onto the nwlog backup device.

▶ **To back up a transaction log with SQL Server Enterprise Manager**

1. Switch to SQL Server Enterprise Manager.
2. In the console tree, expand Databases, right-click the StudyNwind database, point to All Tasks, and then click Backup Database.
3. In the SQL Server Backup dialog box, click the General tab if it is not already selected.
4. Ensure that StudyNwind is selected in Database.
5. In Name, type the backup set name **StudyNwindLog**.
6. In Description, type **Transaction log backup of StudyNwind**.
7. Under Backup, click Transaction Log.
8. Under Destination, Disk should be selected. If you do not have a tape drive connected to the computer, Disk and Tape will both be grayed and Disk will be selected; this is correct.
9. Under Destination, click Add to add the nwlog backup device.

10. In the Choose Backup Destination dialog box, click Backup Device and select nwlog from the drop-down list of devices. (If nwlog is not in the list, you may already have added it as a destination or you may not yet have created it.)

11. Click OK to close the dialog box and add nwlog to the Backup To list.

12. If there are any other devices in the Backup To list, highlight them and click Remove to remove them.

13. Under Overwrite, click the Overwrite Existing Media option to overwrite any existing backups on the backup device.

14. Click OK to perform the backup.

15. After the backup completes, view the contents of the nwlog backup device with SQL Server Enterprise Manager under Management, Backup.

Exercise: Using Transact-SQL to Append a Transaction Log Backup

In this exercise, you will write and execute a Transact-SQL statement to append a second backup of the transaction log to the nwlog backup device. You will find the script for this exercise in C:\Sqladmin\Exercise\Ch09\Appendlg.sql.

▶ **To back up a transaction log with Transact-SQL statements**

1. Switch to SQL Server Query Analyzer.

2. Write and execute a Transact-SQL statement to append a second backup of the transaction log to the nwlog backup device. Use the options shown in the following table.

Option	Value
Database name	StudyNwind
Backup device	nwlog
Append, overwrite, or initialize	Append (WITH NOINIT)

Clearing the Transaction Log

You can use the BACKUP LOG statement with either the TRUNCATE_ONLY option or the NO_LOG option to clear the transaction log. You should back up the transaction log regularly to keep it at a reasonable size. If the transaction log becomes full, users cannot update the database. You must then truncate the transaction log to free up space.

Using the TRUNCATE_ONLY or NO_LOG Option

To truncate the transaction log when it has become full or clear the transaction log without keeping a backup copy of the data, use the BACKUP LOG statement with the TRUNCATE_ONLY or NO_LOG option. SQL Server removes the inactive part of the log without making a backup copy of it. This frees space in the transaction log file. Note the following regarding the use of these options:

- You can clear the transaction log before you perform a complete database backup. Doing so may result in a smaller complete database backup.

- Once you have cleared the transaction log, you can no longer recover the changes that were recorded in it. You should always execute the BACKUP DATABASE statement immediately after truncating the transaction log using one of these options.

- Using these options breaks the transaction log backup sequence. You must perform a database backup before performing further normal transaction log backups.

- You cannot use both the TRUNCATE_ONLY option and the NO_LOG option in the same statement.

- The TRUNCATE_ONLY and NO_LOG options are synonymous. In previous versions of SQL Server, they had different functions.

- The transaction log file will not become smaller after truncation. Space is freed within the file so that database modifications are again possible, but the file itself stays the same size.

- To reduce the size of the transaction log file, use the DBCC SHRINK-DATABASE statement. Remember that this is a deferred operation and the transaction log file will become smaller only when a certain amount of activity has occurred in the database.

The syntax for the BACKUP LOG statement is as follows:

```
BACKUP LOG {database_name | @database_name_var}
TO <backup_device> [, ...n]
[WITH {TRUNCATE_ONLY | NO_LOG }]
```

The following example uses the BACKUP LOG statement to remove the inactive portion of a transaction log without making a backup copy.

```
BACKUP LOG northwind WITH TRUNCATE_ONLY
```

Exercise: Using Transact-SQL to Clear the Transaction Log

In this exercise, you will write and execute a Transact-SQL statement to clear the transaction log of the StudyNwind database. Assume that the log has become full. After you clear the transaction log, you must back up the database. You will find the script for this exercise in C:\Sqladmin\Exercise\Ch09\Clearlog.sql.

▶ **To clear a transaction log without making a backup copy**

1. Write and execute a Transact-SQL statement to clear the transaction log of all committed transactions.

2. Write and execute a Transact-SQL statement to back up the database to the nwA backup device.

Setting the trunc. log on chkpt. Option

You can set the trunc. log on chkpt. option to true to have SQL Server automatically truncate the transaction log when a checkpoint occurs. Use this option when you want to prevent the transaction log from becoming full, such as when you are working with a test database or if you are using a backup strategy that involves database backups only.

If you set the trunc. log on chkpt. option to true, you cannot back up the transaction log and use it to help restore the database in the event of a system failure. The transaction log no longer stores the changes that have been made to the database since the last database backup.

Using the NO_TRUNCATE Option

If secondary data files that are not part of the primary filegroup are damaged or lost, you should back up the database with the NO_TRUNCATE option. Using this option backs up all recent database activity from the transaction log.

If NO_TRUNCATE is specified, SQL Server does the following:

- Backs up the transaction log even if the database is inaccessible
- Does not purge the transaction log of committed transactions
- Allows you to recover data up to the time when the system failed

When you restore the database, you can restore the database backup and apply the transaction log backup created with the NO_TRUNCATE option to recover data.

Important You can use the NO_TRUNCATE option only if the database's primary data and transaction log files are intact. If you intend to use this option, you should create a secondary file in another filegroup and make this the default filegroup. This will keep the primary data file small and free of user objects. You should also place the primary data and transaction log files on mirrored disks so that they will still be available even if one disk fails.

The following example uses the WITH NO_TRUNCATE clause to back up the transaction log without truncating the inactive part of the log.

```
USE master
EXEC sp_addumpdevice 'disk', 'nwndnotrunclog',
    'c:\mssql7\backup\nwndnotrunclog.bak'
BACKUP LOG northwind TO nwndnotrunclog WITH NO_TRUNCATE
```

Performing a Differential Backup

You should perform a differential backup to minimize the backup and restore time for frequently modified databases. Perform a differential backup only if you have performed a complete database backup.

In a differential backup, SQL Server backs up the parts of the database that have changed since the last complete database backup. Note that subsequent differential backups continue to back up all changes since the last complete backup; differential backups are not incremental.

When performing a differential backup, SQL Server backs up extents rather than individual pages (for a review of extents, see Chapter 5, "Database Files"). An extent is backed up when the LSN on any page in the extent is greater than the LSN of the last complete database backup.

When you perform a differential backup, consider the following facts and guidelines:

- If a certain row in the database has been modified several times since the last complete database backup, the differential backup contains only the last set of values for that row. This is different from a transaction log backup, which contains a history of all changes to that row.

- A differential backup minimizes the time required to back up a database because the backup sets are smaller than in complete backups and you do not have to apply a series of transaction logs.

- You should establish a naming convention for backup devices that contain differential backups to distinguish them from devices that contain complete database backups.

The syntax for the BACKUP DATABASE statement is as follows:

```
BACKUP DATABASE {database_name | @database_name_var}
TO <backup_device> [, …n]
[WITH
    [[,] DIFFERENTIAL]
]
```

The following example creates a differential backup on a temporary backup device.

```
BACKUP DATABASE northwind TO
DISK = 'D:\Mydata\Mydiffbackup.bak'
WITH DIFFERENTIAL
```

Exercise: Using SQL Server Enterprise Manager to Perform a Differential Backup of the StudyNwind Database

In this exercise, you will perform a differential backup of the StudyNwind database and append the differential backup to the nwdiff.bak backup device. You will find the script for this exercise in C:\Sqladmin\Exercise\Ch09\Diffbac.sql.

▶ **To perform a differential backup with SQL Server Enterprise Manager**

1. Switch to SQL Server Enterprise Manager.

2. In the console tree, expand Databases, right-click the StudyNwind database, point to All Tasks, and then click Backup Database.

3. In the SQL Server Backup dialog box, click the General tab if it is not already selected.

4. Ensure that StudyNwind is selected in Database.

5. In Name, type the backup set name **StudyNwindDiff**.

6. In Description, type the description **Differential backup of StudyNwind**.

7. Under Backup, click Database - Differential.

8. Under Destination, Disk should be selected. If you do not have a tape drive connected to the computer, Disk and Tape will both be grayed and Disk will be selected; this is correct.

9. Under Destination, click Add to add the backup device.

10. In the Choose Backup Destination dialog box, click File Name and type **C:\mssql7\backup\nwdiff.bak** as the filename.

11. Click OK to close the dialog box and add the device to the Backup To list.

12. If there are any other devices in the Backup To list, highlight them and click Remove to remove them.

13. Under Overwrite, click the Overwrite Existing Media option to overwrite any existing backups on the backup device.

14. Click OK to perform the backup.

15. After the backup operation completes, use Windows NT Explorer to confirm that the new backup device is now in the C:\Mssql7\Backup folder.

Performing Data File or Filegroup Backups

Perform data file or filegroup backups on very large databases (VLDB) or when it is not feasible to make a complete database backup due to time constraints.

Filegroups contain one or more data files. When SQL Server backs up files or filegroups, it does the following:

- Backs up only the data files that you specify with the FILE or FILEGROUP option.
- Allows you to back up specific data files instead of the entire database.

When you perform data file or filegroup backups,

- You must specify the logical file or filegroup names.
- You must perform transaction log backups in order to make restored files consistent with the rest of the database. For this reason, file or filegroup backups are not possible if the trunc. log on chkpt. database option is set to true.
- You should establish a plan to back up each file or filegroup in a database on a rotating basis. This is necessary to ensure that all data files or filegroups are backed up regularly.
- You do not need to create different file or filegroup backups on different backup devices, although you may want to create different named backup devices to make it easier to manage file and filegroup backups.

The syntax for making filegroup backups with the BACKUP DATABASE statement is as follows:

```
BACKUP DATABASE database_name
    [<file_or_filegroup> [, …n]] TO <backup_device> [, …n]]
```

where *<file_or_filegroup>* is

```
{FILE = logical_file_name
|
FILEGROUP = logical_filegroup_name
}
```

The following example performs a backup of the Orders2 file, followed by a transaction log backup. The phoneorders database has three data files: Orders1, Orders2, and Orders3. The transaction log is stored in the Orderlog file. These backup devices already exist: Orderbackup1, Orderbackup2, Orderbackup3, and Orderbackuplog.

```
BACKUP DATABASE phoneorders
FILE = orders2 TO orderbackup2
BACKUP LOG phoneorders to orderbackuplog
```

If an index has been created on a table in a filegroup, the entire filegroup must be backed up. Files in the filegroup cannot be backed up individually. Furthermore, if indexes are created on filegroups other than the filegroup in which their base tables exist, the filegroups must all be backed up together. This can cause the need to back up multiple filegroups together, so you should plan your index and backup requirements carefully when designing your indexes and filegroups. (See Figure 9.2.)

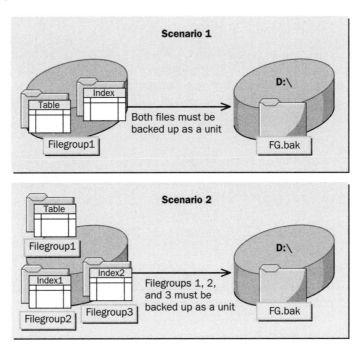

Figure 9.2 Scenarios illustrating filegroup backup restrictions

Lesson Summary

Backup operations can be performed with SQL Server Enterprise Manager, the Backup Wizard, or Transact-SQL. You should be familiar with certain backup options whenever you use any of the SQL Server backup methods.

A complete database backup serves as your baseline in case of a system failure. When you perform a complete database backup, SQL Server backs up everything in the database, including any portions of the transaction log needed to ensure data consistency when the backup is restored.

A differential backup minimizes the backup and restore time for frequently modified databases. Perform a differential backup only if you have performed a complete database backup previously.

Review

The following questions are intended to reinforce key information presented in the chapter. If you are unable to answer a question, review the appropriate lesson and then try the question again. Answers to the questions can be found in Appendix A, "Questions and Answers."

1. You have a database for which you generally perform only database backups. The transaction log exists on a separate physical disk from the secondary data files. It is allowed to accumulate changes but is periodically cleared. The disk that contains the secondary data files is damaged. After you replace the disk, what can you do to minimize data loss?

2. What are the advantages and disadvantages of using differential backups as part of your backup strategy?

C H A P T E R   1 0

Restoring Databases

About This Chapter

This chapter will teach you how to restore backups in case of database or server failure. You will learn about the Microsoft SQL Server recovery process and how to restore user and system databases, back up the transaction log in case of a database failure, rebuild the system databases, and implement a standby SQL Server.

Before You Begin

To complete the lessons in this chapter, you must have

- Installed SQL Server 7. See Chapter 2, "Installation," for installation instructions.

- The ability to log on to SQL Server as an Administrator.

- Installed the Exercise files from the Supplemental Course Materials CD-ROM to your hard disk drive. See the "Getting Started" section in "About This Book" for installation instructions.

Lesson 1: The SQL Server Recovery and Restore Processes

SQL Server has both a manual and automatic recovery and restore process. The automatic recovery process occurs when you restart SQL Server after a database failure or shutdown. It attempts to ensure the consistency of data. Manual recovery is necessary after restoring a database, in order to put the database in a consistent state by recovering the restored transaction log.

For a video demonstration that covers SQL Server transactions, run the Trans.htm file from the \Media folder on the Supplemental Course Materials CD-ROM.

After this lesson, you will be able to

- Describe the SQL Server recovery process
- Describe the activities that take place during a SQL Server restore

Estimated lesson time: 15 minutes

Database Recovery

During SQL Server operation, a database exists in two places: most of the data pages are on disk in the primary and secondary data files, and some pages are in memory, in the data cache. All database modifications are recorded in the transaction log as they occur, as part of a transaction. Once a modification has been recorded in the transaction log, the pages in the data cache are modified. The following details regarding transactions are pertinent to the recovery process:

- If a transaction is busy modifying pages in the data cache (an uncommitted transaction), the pages being modified reflect an inconsistent state in the database. Pages modified by a transaction are not written to disk until after the transaction is complete (committed), thus guaranteeing the consistency of the data file pages. If the transaction is canceled (rolled back), the changes to the pages in the data cache will be undone.

- If the transaction that modified pages in the data cache is complete (a committed transaction), the pages are considered part of the consistent state of the database, and they will be written to disk by the next checkpoint process. The checkpoint process will then mark the transaction in the transaction log to indicate that it has been applied to the data file pages.

When the server stops, expectedly or unexpectedly, there may be committed transactions in the transaction log that have not yet been checkpointed. There may also be uncommitted transactions in the transaction log; these transactions can never be committed, as the server has stopped. The recovery process deals with these committed and uncommitted transactions that occurred after the last checkpoint.

The SQL Server recovery process is an internal mechanism that ensures that your database is consistent by examining the transaction log and taking appropriate actions. The recovery process runs automatically when SQL Server is started, and it can be initiated manually during restore operations. The process is as follows:

1. SQL Server examines the transaction log, beginning at the last checkpoint. A checkpoint is like a bookmark, marking the point up to which all data changes have been written to the database.

2. If committed transactions are found, they have not yet been written to the database (otherwise, they would not be after the last checkpoint). SQL Server rolls these transactions forward, applying their changes to the database.

3. If the transaction log contains any uncommitted transactions, SQL Server rolls them back (removes them). The fact that the recovery process is taking place means that these uncommitted transactions can never be committed, so they must not be written to the database.

Note Although it may seem that changes are not seen by connected users until after a checkpoint takes place, this is not the case. The changes are available in the data cache immediately after a transaction is committed. Connected users always get data directly from the data cache, so they will see the committed changes even if they have not yet been written to disk.

Automatic Recovery

When your system is restarted after a failure or shutdown, SQL Server begins the automatic recovery process to ensure data consistency. You do not have to start this process manually—it occurs automatically.

Manual Recovery

The recovery process can optionally be initiated as part of the restore process. The manual recovery process is similar to the automatic recovery process that occurs when SQL Server is restarted.

Manual recovery is necessary after restoring a database, in order to put the database in a consistent state by recovering the restored transaction log. Manual recovery must be performed only once when restoring a database. If you have transaction log backups to restore as well as the database backup, perform the manual recovery after restoring the database backup and all of the transaction log backups. If you are restoring only a database backup, perform the manual recovery after the database restore; this is necessary because a database backup includes a copy of the transaction log at the time of the database backup.

SQL Server Activities During the Restore Process

When you restore a database, SQL Server automatically performs certain actions to ensure that your database is restored quickly and with minimal impact on production activities.

Safety Check

SQL Server performs a safety check when you execute the RESTORE DATABASE statement. This internal mechanism prevents you from accidentally overwriting an existing database with a backup of a different database or with incomplete information.

SQL Server does not restore the database in the following situations:

- If you are trying to restore a database using a new name, and a database with that name already exists on the server.
- If the set of database files on the server is different from the set of database files contained in the backup set.
- If not all of the backup devices needed to restore a database or filegroup are supplied. SQL Server generates an error message specifying which backup devices must be restored as a unit (in one restore operation).

For example, if you attempt to restore a backup of the Northwind database to a database named Accounting, and Accounting already exists on the server, SQL Server will prevent the restore from occurring. If you intend to restore a backup of Northwind and overwrite the data in Accounting, you can override the safety check with the REPLACE option of the RESTORE statement.

Database Re-creation

When you restore a database from a complete database backup, SQL Server re-creates the original database files and places them in the locations that were recorded when the backup was made. All database objects are re-created automatically. You do not need to rebuild the database schema before you restore the database.

Note In previous versions of SQL Server, it was necessary to re-create a device and a database before restoring from backup. This is not necessary with SQL Server 7.

Lesson Summary

The SQL Server recovery process is an internal mechanism that ensures that your database is consistent by examining the transaction log and taking appropriate actions. The recovery process runs automatically when SQL Server is started and can be initiated manually during restore operations.

Lesson 2: The RESTORE Statement

The RESTORE statement retrieves information about a backup set or backup device before you restore a database, file, or transaction log. This lesson describes how to use the RESTORE statement and its options.

After this lesson, you will be able to

- Use the RESTORE statement to get information about a backup set or backup device before you restore a database, file, or transaction log
- Describe the purpose of various important RESTORE statement options

Estimated lesson time: 30 minutes

Preparing to Restore a Database

You should verify backups before restoring them. Do this to confirm that you are restoring the intended data and objects and that the backup contains valid information. This section explains how to verify backups and describes other tasks you should perform to ensure a smooth restore process.

Verifying Backups

Before you perform a restore, you must ensure that the backup device is valid and contains the expected backup set(s). You can use SQL Server Enterprise Manager to view the property sheet for each backup device. For more detailed information about the backups, you can execute the Transact-SQL statements described in the sections that follow.

The RESTORE HEADERONLY Statement

Use the RESTORE HEADERONLY statement to obtain a list of header information for all backup sets on a backup device.

When you execute the RESTORE HEADERONLY statement, the information you receive includes

- The backup set name and description
- The backup method: 1 = complete database, 2 = transaction log, 4 = file, and 5 = differential database
- The position of the backup set on the device; this is needed for the FILE option of the RESTORE statement
- The type of backup medium: 5 or 105 = tape, and 2 or 102 = disk
- The date and time that the backup was performed
- The size of the backup

The RESTORE FILELISTONLY Statement

Use the RESTORE FILELISTONLY statement to obtain information about the original database or transaction log files that are contained in a backup set. Executing this statement can help you avoid restoring the wrong backup files.

When you execute the RESTORE FILELISTONLY statement, SQL Server returns the following information:

- The logical name(s) of the data and transaction log file(s)
- The physical name(s) of the data and transaction log file(s)
- The type of file, such as a data (D) or a transaction log (L) file
- The filegroup membership
- The backup set size, in megabytes (MB)
- The maximum allowed file size, in MB

The RESTORE LABELONLY Statement

Use the RESTORE LABELONLY statement to obtain information about the backup medium that holds a backup device. This is useful if you are using multiple backup devices in a media set.

The RESTORE VERIFYONLY Statement

Use the RESTORE VERIFYONLY statement to verify that a backup set is complete and that all backup devices are readable. SQL Server does not verify the structure of the data contained in the backup.

Other Tasks to Perform Before Restoring Backups

Before you restore backups, you should restrict access to the database, back up the transaction log, and switch to the master database, as described in the sections that follow.

Set the dbo use only Database Option

A member of the sysadmin or db_owner role should set the dbo use only database option to true before restoring the database. This setting restricts access to the database so that users cannot interfere with the restore. You can set the dbo use only database option in the following ways:

- Using the database property sheet in SQL Server Enterprise Manager
- Using the sp_dboption system stored procedure and setting the dbo use only database option to true, as follows:

```
EXEC sp_dboption database_name, 'dbo use only', true
```

Back Up the Transaction Log

Database consistency is ensured if you back up the transaction log before you perform any restore operations. The following are some considerations regarding the transaction log backup:

- The transaction log backup is used to recover the database as the last step in the restore process.

- If you do not back up the transaction log before you restore a backup, you lose data modifications that occurred between the last transaction log backup and the time when the database was taken offline.

- In some cases it may not be possible to back up the transaction log before beginning the restore—for example, if the trunc. log on chkpt. database option is set to true, or if you have used the BACKUP LOG statement with the TRUNCATE_ONLY or NO_LOG option since the last complete database backup.

Switch to the master Database

If you are using SQL Server Query Analyzer or executing a script from the command prompt to restore backups, you should execute the following command before beginning to restore the database:

```
USE master
```

This ensures that you are not using the database that you are trying to restore.

Using the RESTORE Statement

You can use the RESTORE statement or SQL Server Enterprise Manager to perform restore operations. The RESTORE statement has various options that allow you to specify how the backup should be restored. Each of these options has a counterpart in SQL Server Enterprise Manager. This section describes the RESTORE statement and the various restore options.

The syntax for the RESTORE database statement is as follows:

```
RESTORE DATABASE database_name __
[FROM <backup_device> [, ... n]]
[WITH
    [[,] FILE = file_number]
    [[,] MOVE 'logical_file_name' TO operating_system_file_name']
    [[,] REPLACE]
    [[,] {NORECOVERY | RECOVERY | STANDBY = undo_file_name}]]
```

where <backup_device> is

```
{{backup_device_name | @backup_device_name_var}      |
{DISK | TAPE | PIPE} = {'temp_backup_device' |
 @temp_backup_device_var}
}
```

> **Note** The RESTORE statement replaces the LOAD statement found in previous versions of SQL Server. LOAD is still supported for backward compatibility only. You should use the RESTORE statement.

The following example restores the Northwind database from a named backup device.

```
USE master
RESTORE DATABASE northwind
FROM nwindbac
```

The RECOVERY Option

In SQL Server Enterprise Manager, the RECOVERY option corresponds to specifying Leave Database Operational. No Additional Transaction Logs Can Be Restored for the Recovery Completion State on the Options tab of the Restore Database dialog box.

Use this option to return the database to a consistent state when restoring

- The last transaction log backup
- A complete database backup without transaction log backups
- A differential database backup without transaction log backups

This option causes SQL Server to roll back any uncommitted transactions and roll forward any committed transactions that were restored from the backup. The database is available for use after the recovery process is complete.

> **Note** Do not use the RECOVERY option if you have additional transaction logs or differential backups that must be restored, because this option indicates that you are restoring the final backup and brings the database back online.

The NORECOVERY Option

In SQL Server Enterprise Manager, the NORECOVERY option corresponds to specifying Leave Database Nonoperational, But Able To Restore Additional Transaction Logs for the Recovery Completion State on the Options tab of the Restore Database dialog box.

Use this option when you have multiple backups to restore. Keep the following in mind:

- Specify the NORECOVERY option for all backups *except* the last backup to be restored.
- When this option is specified, SQL Server neither rolls back any uncommitted transactions in the transaction log nor rolls forward any committed transactions.
- The database is unavailable for use until the database is recovered.

The FILE Option

In SQL Server Enterprise Manager, the FILE option is specified by checking Restore for one or more backup sets in the restore list on the General tab of the Restore Database dialog box.

Use this option to select specific backups from a backup device that contains multiple backups. You must specify a file number that corresponds to the order in which the backup sets exist within the backup device. The position column of the output from the RESTORE HEADERONLY statement gives the file number of each backup.

The MOVE TO Option

In SQL Server Enterprise Manager, the MOVE TO option is specified by changing the Restore As name for one or more files in the Restore Database Files As list on the Options tab of the Restore Database dialog box.

Use this option to specify where to restore data or log files if you are restoring the files to a different location, such as a different disk drive or server or a standby SQL Server.

You are required to specify the existing logical name and the new location for the file(s) in the backup that you wish to move. Use the RESTORE FILELISTONLY statement to determine the existing logical filenames if these are not known.

Tip You can copy the files from a database to a different location or SQL Server and use either the sp_attach_db or the sp_attach_single_file_db system stored procedure to bring the database online from its new location or on the new server.

The REPLACE Option

In SQL Server Enterprise Manager, the REPLACE option is specified by checking Force Restore Over Existing Database on the Options tab of the Restore Database dialog box.

Use the REPLACE option only if you want to replace an existing database with data from a backup of a different database.

By default, SQL Server performs a safety check that ensures that an existing database is *not* replaced if

- You are specifying a new name for the database being restored and a database with that name already exists on the target server.
- The set of files in the database is different from the files contained in the backup set. SQL Server ignores differences in file size.

When you specify the REPLACE option, no checks are performed, and SQL Server will overwrite the existing database, if one exists.

Lesson Summary

You can use the RESTORE statement or SQL Server Enterprise Manager to perform restore operations. The RESTORE statement has various options that allow you to specify how the backup should be restored. Each of these options has a counterpart in SQL Server Enterprise Manager.

Lesson 3: Performing a Database Restore

This lesson explains how to restore backups of various types. Before undertaking any type of restore operation, you should make sure that you have a valid backup set and that you have all devices that contain the backup set.

After this lesson, you will be able to

- Restore backups from different backup types

Estimated lesson time: 90 minutes

Restoring from a Complete Database Backup

When you restore a database from a complete database backup, SQL Server re-creates the database and all of its associated files and then places them in their original locations. All database objects are re-created automatically. You do not need to rebuild the database schema before you restore the database.

You will typically restore from a complete database backup when

- The physical disk containing the database is damaged
- The entire database is damaged, corrupted, or deleted
- An identical copy of the database is being restored to a different SQL Server, such as a standby SQL Server

Specifying a Recovery Option

The RECOVERY option initiates the recovery process so that your database is returned to a consistent state. Use the following guidelines in choosing the RECOVERY or NORECOVERY option:

- If you use a complete database backup strategy and do not have any transaction log or differential backups, specify the RECOVERY option.
- If any transaction log or differential backups exist, specify the NORECOVERY option to postpone the recovery process until the last backup is restored.

The following example assumes that a complete backup exists on the nwindbac named backup device and that two backup sets are appended to that device. The Northwind database is completely replaced by the second backup set on the nwindbac named backup device. Finally, the recovery process returns the database to a consistent state (rolls forward committed changes and rolls back uncommitted activities).

```
USE master
RESTORE DATABASE northwind
FROM nwindbac
WITH FILE = 2,    RECOVERY
```

Exercise: Creating the nwcopy Database

In this exercise, you will restore the nwcopy database from a backup. You will use this database in the other exercises in this chapter to practice restoring databases.

▶ **To create the nwcopy database**

1. Log on to your computer as Administrator or as another user that is a member of the local Administrators group.

2. Copy the C:\Sqladmin\Exercise\Ch10\Nwc1.bak file to C:\Mssql7\Backup on your local hard disk drive.

3. Open SQL Server Query Analyzer and log on to the (local) server with Microsoft Windows NT authentication. Your account is a member of the Windows NT Administrators group, which is automatically mapped to the SQL Server sysadmin role.

4. Open and execute the C:\Sqladmin\Exercise\Ch10\Setupnwc.sql script.

   This script restores the nwcopy database, which is used in the other exercises in this chapter.

Exercise: Modifying the nwcopy Database

In this exercise, you will execute a script that adds a row to the Products table. You will then write and execute a query that returns the new row.

▶ **To modify the nwcopy database**

1. Open a query window, open C:\Sqladmin\Exercise\Ch10\Addprod.sql, review its contents, and then execute it.

   This script adds the new product Maple Flavor Pancake Mix to the Products table.

2. Review the results to confirm that the new row was added.

Exercise: Backing Up the nwcopy Database

In this exercise, you will execute a script that backs up the nwcopy database to a single backup device.

► **To back up the nwcopy database**

Open C:\Sqladmin\Exercise\Ch10\Makeback.sql, review its contents, and then execute it.

This script backs up the nwcopy database to a single backup device. This backup device has a logical name of nwc2 and a physical name of C:\Mssql7\Backup\Nwc2.bak.

Exercise: Simulating Database Damage

In this exercise, you will execute a script that damages the database by updating all rows in the Products table. You will then write and execute a query to confirm that, due to the erroneous update, the product Maple Flavor Pancake Mix no longer appears in the Products table.

► **To simulate accidental data modification**

1. Open a query window, open C:\Sqladmin\Exercise\Ch10\Dataloss.sql, review its contents, and then execute it.

   This script damages the database by updating all rows in the Products table.

2. Review the result to confirm that the product Maple Flavor Pancake Mix can no longer be found in the Products table, as its name has been incorrectly changed.

3. Close the query window.

Exercise: Using SQL Server Enterprise Manager to Restore the nwcopy Database

In this exercise, you will use SQL Server Enterprise Manager to restrict access to the nwcopy database, restore from a complete database backup, and then allow access to the database after the restore process is complete.

Important You must close the query window or select another database in the query window in order to complete this exercise. The restore operation requires that no users use the database during the restore. Check that no other query windows are using the nwcopy database.

▶ **To restore the nwcopy database from a full database backup**

1. Open SQL Server Enterprise Manager.

2. In the console tree, expand the Databases folder.

3. In the console tree, right-click the nwcopy database icon, and then click Properties.

4. On the Options tab, check the Single User and DBO Use Only options to restrict access to the database during the restore process.

5. Click OK to close the dialog box and save your changes to the database options.

6. In the console tree, right-click the nwcopy database icon, point to All Tasks, and then click Restore Database.

7. In the Restore Database dialog box, review the automatic selections:

   ▪ On the General tab, Database is selected for Restore. This allows a complete database backup and any associated differential or transaction log backups to be restored.

   ▪ The First Backup To Restore option is set to the last complete backup of the nwcopy database. You can change this selection to restore from older backups when necessary. The backup history listed here reflects entries in the msdb database. If the backup set has since been overwritten, you will not be able to restore it.

   ▪ In the list of backup sets, the backup set you made previously, called nwcopy-Complete, with a filename of C:\Mssql7\Backup\Nwc2.bak, is checked.

8. On the Options tab, check Leave Database Operational. No Additional Transaction Logs Can Be Restored, as you have no transaction log backups to restore. This corresponds to the RECOVERY option of the RESTORE statement.

9. Click OK to perform the restore.

Exercise: Confirming Data Recovery

In this exercise, you will write and execute a query that returns the Maple Flavor Pancake Mix product and another that lists all of the products in the Products table.

▶ **To confirm that data was recovered**

Open a query window, open C:\Sqladmin\Exercise\Ch10\ChkRest.sql, review its contents, and then execute it.

Restoring from a Differential Backup

When you restore a database from a differential database backup, the following occur:

- Only the parts of the database that have changed since the last complete database backup are restored.

- The database is returned to the exact condition that it was in when the differential backup was performed.

The restore often takes less time than it does to apply a series of transaction logs representing the same database activity.

When you restore from a differential backup, consider the following facts and guidelines:

- The syntax for restoring a differential backup is the same as for restoring a complete database backup. The backup device specified with the FROM clause and the file number specified with the FILE option must simply refer to a differential backup rather than a complete backup.

- You must restore a complete database backup, specifying the NORECOVERY option, before you can restore a differential backup.

- Specify the NORECOVERY option when restoring a differential database backup if there are transaction logs to be restored; otherwise, specify the RECOVERY option.

The following example restores a differential backup without recovering the database. The nwindbacdiff device contains a differential backup. Specifying the NORECOVERY option allows you to restore transaction logs. The RECOVERY option will be specified for the last transaction log restore.

```
USE master
RESTORE DATABASE northwind
FROM nwindbacdiff
WITH NORECOVERY
```

Restoring from a Transaction Log Backup

When you restore from a transaction log backup, SQL Server reapplies changes to the database that are recorded in the transaction log.

You will typically restore transaction logs as a means of applying changes made to the database since the last complete database or differential backup. In addition, you can restore transaction logs to recover a database up to a specific point in time.

Considerations for Restoring Transaction Logs

Although restoring a differential backup may speed up the restore process, you may have to restore additional transaction log backups that were created after a differential backup, to ensure data consistency.

Before you restore any transaction logs, you first must restore the complete database backup, specifying the NORECOVERY option. When you have multiple transaction logs to apply, specify the NORECOVERY option for all transaction logs except the last one. This causes SQL Server to suspend the recovery process until the last transaction log is restored.

The syntax for the RESTORE LOG statement is as follows:

```
RESTORE LOG {database_name | @database_name_var}
[FROM <backup_device> [, …n]]
[WITH
    [[,] {NORECOVERY | RECOVERY | STANDBY = undo_file_name}]
    [[,] STOPAT = {date_time | @date_time_var}]
```

Note The RESTORE LOG statement replaces the LOAD TRANsaction statement found in previous versions of SQL Server. LOAD TRANsaction is still supported for backward compatibility only. You should use the RESTORE LOG statement.

The following example assumes that a complete database backup exists on the backup device named nwindbac and that two transaction log backups exist on the backup device named nwindbaclog. Three separate restore operations are performed to ensure database consistency.

1. The first step restores from a complete database backup without recovering the database.

```
USE master
RESTORE DATABASE northwind
FROM nwindbac
WITH NORECOVERY
```

2. The second step restores the first transaction log without recovering the database. The progress of the restore process is displayed.

```
USE master
RESTORE LOG northwind
FROM nwindbaclog
WITH FILE = 1,
    STATS,
    NORECOVERY
```

3. The third step restores the second transaction log. The RECOVERY option returns the Northwind database to a consistent state, rolling forward any committed transactions and rolling back any uncommitted transactions:

```
USE master
RESTORE LOG northwind
FROM nwindbaclog
WITH FILE = 2,
    RECOVERY
```

Restoring to a Specific Point in Time

When you restore transaction logs, you can restore to a specific point in time by using the STOPAT option. The following are some guidelines for using this option:

- Use the STOPAT option to recover a database to the state it was in at the exact moment before data corruption or some other event occurred.

  For example, if you know that a malicious update to a database occurred at 11:00 A.M., you can restore the changes in the transaction log through 10:59 A.M. and not apply any changes that occurred after that point.

- You must specify the date and time at which to stop loading a backup onto the database. SQL Server restores all of the transaction log records that were written to the database *before* the specified point in time.

Note The STOPAT option can be specified only when restoring transaction log backups; it cannot be used with complete or differential database backups, which are taken as a snapshot of a database at a particular time. Transaction logs record individual changes over time; transaction log backups can therefore be used to restore changes up to a particular time.

The following example assumes that a complete database backup was made to the nwindbac named backup device at 8:00 P.M. on January 2, 1998. In addition, two transaction log backups were made at 10:00 A.M. and 1:00 P.M. on January 3, 1998, to the nwindbaclog named backup device. Only changes that occurred before 11:00 A.M. on January 3, 1998, must be restored. Three separate restore operations are performed to ensure database consistency:

1. The first step restores a database from a complete database backup without recovering the database.

```
USE master
RESTORE DATABASE northwind
FROM nwindbac
WITH NORECOVERY
```

2. The second step restores the first transaction log without recovering the database.

```
USE master
RESTORE LOG northwind
FROM nwindbaclog
WITH FILE = 1,
    NORECOVERY
```

3. The third step restores the second transaction log, applies changes that occurred before 11:00 A.M. on January 3, 1998, and recovers the database.

```
USE master
RESTORE LOG northwind
FROM nwindbaclog
WITH FILE = 2,
    RECOVERY,
    STOPAT = 'January 3, 1998 11:00 AM'
```

Restoring from a File or Filegroup Backup

You can restore from a file or filegroup backup to reduce the time required to restore part of a very large database. Restore from a file or filegroup when a particular file was accidentally deleted or damaged.

When you restore from a file or filegroup, consider the following:

- SQL Server requires you to restore the filegroup backups as a unit if a table and its associated indexes exist on two different filegroups.

- SQL Server allows you to restore an individual database file from a complete database backup or from an individual file backup.

- You must apply all transaction logs that were created since the backup from which the file was restored, in order to bring the restored file or filegroup into a state that is consistent with the rest of the database. For this reason, the RECOVERY option is not allowed when restoring a file or filegroup. If you have not done a transaction log backup since making the backup from which you are attempting to restore a file or filegroup, the file or filegroup restore operation will terminate with an error. If the primary data file and the transaction log file are intact, you can make a transaction log backup, using the NO_TRUNCATE option, before restoring the file or filegroup. SQL Server applies only those transactions that affect the restored file.

The syntax for the RESTORE DATABASE statement is as follows:

```
RESTORE DATABASE {database_name | @database_name_var}
    <file_or_filegroup> [, ...m]
[FROM <backup_device> [, ...n]]
```

where *<file_or_filegroup>* is

```
{FILE = logical_file_name | FILEGROUP = logical_filegroup_name}
```

The following example assumes that a database exists in three files: Nwind1, Nwind2, and Nwind3. The Nwind2 database file contains a single table and its related indexes. The Nwind2 database file was backed up onto the Nwind2bac backup device. One transaction log backup was performed after the Nwind2 file was last backed up. Nwind2 must be restored because the physical medium is damaged. The restore consists of two steps to ensure database consistency:

1. The first step restores the backup of the Nwind2 database file without rolling forward any committed transactions or rolling back any uncommitted transactions.

```
USE master
RESTORE DATABASE northwind
    FILE = Nwind2
FROM Nwind2bac
WITH NORECOVERY
```

2. The second step restores the transaction log backup. The RECOVERY option returns the Northwind database to a consistent state, rolling forward any committed transactions and rolling back any uncommitted transactions:

```
USE master
RESTORE LOG northwind
FROM nwindbaclog
WITH RECOVERY
```

Practice: Restoring a Database

In this practice, you will first perform a number of data modifications and backups of the nwcopy database. Then you will simulate a media failure and restore the database from your backups.

Exercise 1: Backing Up the nwcopy Database

In this exercise, you will execute a script that makes a complete database backup of the nwcopy database to the nwc3 named backup device. This backup is the baseline for the restore operation later.

▶ **To perform a full database backup of the nwcopy database**

Open a query window, open C:\Sqladmin\Exercise\Ch10\Compback.sql, review its contents, and then execute it. This script backs up the nwcopy database to the nwc3 named backup device.

Exercise 2: Modifying the nwcopy
Database and Backing Up the Transaction Log

In this exercise, you will execute a script that adds a customer to the Customers table and confirms that the customer was added. Then you will execute another script that backs up the transaction log to the nwchange named backup device.

▶ **To modify the nwcopy database and back up the transaction log**

1. Open a query window, open C:\Sqladmin\Exercise\Ch10\Addcust1.sql, review its contents, and then execute it.

   This script adds the Health Food Store as a customer to the Customers table and queries the table to return the new customer.

2. Open a query window, open C:\Sqladmin\Exercise\Ch10\Logback1.sql, review its contents, and then execute it.

   This script backs up the transaction log of the nwcopy database to the nwchange named backup device.

Exercise 3: Modifying the nwcopy
Database and Performing a Differential Backup

In this exercise, you will execute a script that adds another customer to the Customers table and returns that customer to confirm that the customer was added. You will then execute another script that performs a differential backup and appends it to the nwchange named backup device.

▶ **To modify the nwcopy database and perform a differential backup**

1. Open a query window, open C:\Sqladmin\Exercise\Ch10\Addcust2.sql, review its contents, and then execute it.

   This script adds the Volcano Coffee Company to the Customers table and queries the table to return the new customer.

2. Open a query window, open C:\Sqladmin\Exercise\Ch10\Diffback.sql, review its contents, and then execute it.

   This script performs a differential backup to capture all changes since the last complete database backup. The differential backup is appended to the nwchange named backup device.

Exercise 4: Modifying the nwcopy Database

In this exercise, you will execute a script that adds a third customer to the nwcopy database and confirms that the customer was added.

▶ **To modify the nwcopy database**

Open a query window, open C:\Sqladmin\Exercise\Ch10\Addcust3.sql, review its contents, and then execute it. This script adds The Wine Cellar as a customer to the Customers table and queries the table to return the new customer.

Note The remaining exercises simulate a media failure and recovery from the failure. At this stage you have backups of all modifications except the addition of the third customer. You will simulate the media failure before backing up that modification, demonstrating SQL Server's ability to back up transactions after a media failure.

Exercise 5: Simulating Database Damage

In this exercise, you will simulate damage to the medium that stores the nwcopy database.

▶ **To simulate damage to the database**

1. Switch to SQL Server Enterprise Manager, and then exit.

2. Open SQL Server Service Manager, and then stop the SQL Server service.

3. Use Windows NT Explorer to rename the secondary data file for the nwcopy database from C:\Mssql7\Data\Nwcopy_data2.ndf to Nwcopy_data2.bad. Be careful not to change the primary data file, C:\Mssql7\Data\Nwcopy_data.mdf, or the transaction log file, C:\Mssql7\Data\Nwcopy_log.ldf.

4. Restart the SQL Server service.

5. Open SQL Server Enterprise Manager.

6. In the console tree, expand the Databases folder, and then click the nwcopy database icon.

7. If the details pane shows database object icons, right-click the nwcopy database icon, point to View, and then click Taskpad.

8. SQL Server displays an error message stating that an error occurred while trying to access the database information.

9. Open Windows NT Event Viewer and examine the contents of the Application Log.

   You should find an information message stating that there was a device activation error for the C:\Mssql7\Data\Nwcopy_data2.ndf file.

   What should you do to restore and recover the nwcopy database?

Exercise 6: Performing a Transaction Log Backup of the nwcopy Database

In this exercise, you will execute a script that performs a transaction log backup after the simulated failure of the nwcopy database. The backup is appended to the nwchange named backup device.

Note Backup of the transaction log after failure is possible only if the primary data and the transaction log files are intact.

▶ **To perform a transaction log backup after secondary data file failure**

1. Open a query window.

2. Open C:\Sqladmin\Exercise\Ch10\Logback2.sql, review its contents, and then execute it.

   This script uses the NO_TRUNCATE option to back up the transaction log of the nwcopy database when the database is not available.

Exercise 7: Examining the nwcopy Backups

In this exercise, you will use SQL Server Enterprise Manager to examine the contents and creation date of all nwcopy database backups.

▶ **To examine available backups**

1. Switch to SQL Server Enterprise Manager

2. In the console tree, expand the Management folder, and then click Backup.

3. In the details pane, right-click the nwc3 device, and then click Properties.

4. Click View Contents to examine the contents of the nwc3 device. Notice the type, description, and date and time of the backup set on the device.

   What does the nwc3 device contain?

5. Click Close to close the Backup Media Contents dialog box. Click Cancel to close the Backup Device Properties dialog box.

6. Repeat steps 3, 4, and 5 to examine the contents of the nwchange device. Notice the type, description, and date and time of each backup set on the device.

   What does the nwchange device contain?

Exercise 8: Reviewing the Restore Strategy

In this exercise, you will review the restore strategy suggested by SQL Server Enterprise Manager and determine whether it is appropriate.

▶ **To review the suggested restore strategy**

1. In the console tree, right-click the nwcopy database icon, point to All Tasks, and then click Restore Database.

2. The Restore Database dialog box appears. Verify that the nwcopy database is selected in the Restore As Database list.

   Notice that four backup sets are listed. SQL Server automatically selects the most recent complete database backup and the corresponding differential and/ or transaction log backup sets that should be restored to return the database to a consistent state. Three out of four backups are selected (full database, differential, and one transaction log).

   Do you agree that the selected backups should be restored?

   Why is the first transaction log backup not selected?

3. Click Cancel to close the Restore Database dialog box.

In Exercises 9, 10, and 11, instead of simply restoring the full database as suggested by SQL Server Enterprise Manager, you will restore the different backup sets individually. This is done so that you can see and understand the effect of each restore.

Exercise 9: Restoring the Complete and Differential Backups

In this exercise, you will use SQL Server Enterprise Manager to restore the complete database and differential backups and allow access to the database after the restore process is complete.

▶ **To restore the complete and differential database backups**

1. Open SQL Server Enterprise Manager.

2. In the console tree, expand the Databases folder.

3. In the console tree, right-click the nwcopy database icon, point to All Tasks, and then click Restore Database.

4. In the Restore Database dialog box, review the automatic selections:

   - On the General tab, Database is selected for Restore. This allows a complete database backup and any associated differential or transaction log backups to be restored.

   - In the Restore list, you should see the four backups you made. The first (complete), third (differential), and fourth (transaction log) backups are checked. To restore only the complete and differential database backup sets, uncheck the third checked backup set (nwcopy-Log2) to deselect it.

5. On the Options tab, click Leave Database Read-Only And Able To Restore Additional Transaction Logs, as you will restore the transaction log backups later. This corresponds to the RESTORE statement STANDBY option.

6. Check both Prompt Before Restoring Each Backup and Force Restore Over Existing Database.

7. Click OK to restore the complete database backup.

8. Click OK to restore the differential database backup.

Exercise 10: Examining the Contents of the Database

In this exercise you will execute a script that lists the new customers in the Customers table in order to evaluate the restore process.

▶ **To examine the contents of the database**

1. Open a query window, open C:\Sqladmin\Exercise\Ch10\Listcust.sql, review its contents, and then execute it.

   This script determines whether the three new customers that were previously added to the Customers table were recovered.

   Have all three new customers been recovered?

2. Close the query window.

Important You must close the query window or select another database in this and any other open query windows in order to complete Exercise 11 in this Lesson. The restore operation requires that no users be using the database.

Exercise 11: Restoring the Transaction Log Backup

In this exercise, you will use SQL Server Enterprise Manager to restore the transaction log and then allow access to the database after the restore process is complete.

▶ **To restore the transaction log backup**

1. Switch to SQL Server Enterprise Manager.

2. Expand the Databases folder.

3. In the console tree, right-click the nwcopy database icon, point to All Tasks, and then click Restore Database.

4. In the Restore Database dialog box, on the General tab, click the From Device option in the Restore section.

5. Click the Select Devices button.

6. In the Choose Restore Devices dialog box, click Disk for the Restore From option if it is not selected.

7. Click Add to add the backup device to the Restore From list.

8. In the Choose Restore Destination dialog box, click Backup Device.

9. In the Backup Device drop-down list, select nwchange. Click OK to accept the nwchange device.

10. If there are any devices other than nwchange in the Restore From list, highlight them and click Remove to remove them.

11. Click OK to accept nwchange as the device from which to restore.

12. Click the View Contents button to select a backup set from the nwchange device.

13. Check the check box next to the nwcopy-Log2 backup set. This is the transaction log backup taken after the simulated database failure. Click OK to accept the selected backup set. Note that the Backup number is now set to 3; this corresponds to selecting the third backup set with the FILE option of the RESTORE statement.

14. Click the Restore Backup Set option and the Transaction Log option if they are not selected.

15. On the Options tab, click Leave Database Operational. No Additional Transaction Logs Can Be Restored, as you have no more transaction log backups to restore. This corresponds to the RECOVERY option of the RESTORE statement.

16. Click OK to perform the restore.

17. Switch to SQL Server Query Analyzer. Open a query window, open C:\Sqladmin\Exercise\Ch10\Listcust.sql, and execute it. All three new customer records are now present, indicating a successful restore of transactions backed up after a simulated database failure.

Lesson Summary

When restoring databases, you should obtain information about the backups that you plan to restore. Make sure that the files are valid and contain all of the backups that are required to restore the database to a consistent state. Use the NORECOVERY option if you have additional backups that must be restored. Use the RECOVERY option on the last backup to return the database to a consistent state.

Lesson 4: Using a Standby SQL Server

If your business environment requires that the production server always be accessible, you may want to consider using a standby SQL Server. This lesson describes how to set up and use a standby SQL Server as well as how to restore the production server once the problem has been resolved. This lesson also introduces the use of clustering in the Enterprise Edition of SQL Server.

After this lesson, you will be able to

- Set up a standby SQL Server computer and restore a production server

Estimated lesson time: 30 minutes

Setting Up a Standby SQL Server

If you determine that a standby SQL Server is appropriate for your business environment, you must decide on its purpose and then create and maintain it.

Note In previous versions of SQL Server, a standby server was implemented by setting the no chkpt. on recovery option to true for databases on the standby server. This database option is no longer supported in SQL Server 7. The RECOVERY, NORECOVERY, and STANDBY options of the RESTORE statement now provide this functionality.

The Purpose of a Standby SQL Server

A standby SQL Server is a second server that mirrors the production server. You can use a standby SQL Server to replace a production server in case of a failure or to provide a read-only copy of one or more databases for decision support applications. In addition, a standby server can be used to validate database integrity by running the Database Consistency Checker (DBCC) without increasing the load on the primary server.

Initial Creation

Create a standby SQL Server by backing up the databases and transaction logs on the production server and then restoring them to another SQL Server, using the STANDBY option with the RESTORE statement.

When you restore backups to a standby SQL Server, consider the following facts and guidelines:

- If the standby SQL Server is a duplicate of a production server, a copy of each database, including system databases, on the production server is restored to the standby SQL Server.

- Use the MOVE_TO option to specify a new location for the database on the standby SQL Server if the location is different from the location on the primary server. For example, data files might be located in C:\Mssql7 on the primary server and in D:\Standby on the standby server.

- You must specify the NORECOVERY or STANDBY option when restoring a backup to a standby server.

  Do not recover the database until you replace the production server with the standby SQL Server.

Tip An alternative to restoring the databases when initially creating them on the standby server is to copy database files from one server to another and then attach them to the standby server by using either the sp_attach_db or sp_attach_single_file_db system stored procedure.

The syntax for the RESTORE statement is as follows:

```
RESTORE {DATABASE | LOG}{database_name | @database_name_var}
FROM <backup_device> [, …n]
    [[,] MOVE 'logical_file_name' TO 'operating_system_file_name']
    [WITH NORECOVERY | RECOVERY | STANDBY = undo_file_name}]
]
```

The STANDBY Option

The STANDBY option specifies the name of an undo file. This file contains the information used to define the state of the database before transactions in an unknown state are rolled back. This allows the database to be available for read-only operations before a recovery has been performed to fully recover the database.

Be aware of the following when specifying the undo file.

- If the file specified by *undo_file_name* does not exist, SQL Server creates it.

- The same *undo_file_name* can be used for each transaction log restore operation; SQL Server will delete and re-create it as necessary.

- If the *undo_file_name* exists, SQL Server overwrites the file unless the file contains current undo information for another database.

- The size of the *undo_file_name* is limited to the disk space available where the file resides.

The following example restores a database backup and a transaction log backup to a standby server. The database on the standby server is available in read-only mode, and additional transaction logs can be applied. This example assumes that the standby server and production server use the same locations for the database files.

```
USE MASTER
RESTORE DATABASE nwcopy FROM nwcomplete
WITH STANDBY = 'c:\mssql7\standby\nwundo.ldf'

RESTORE LOG nwcopy FROM nwlogbackup
WITH STANDBY = 'c:\mssql7\standby\nwundo.ldf'
```

Maintenance

To maintain the standby SQL Server, you must regularly restore all additional transaction log backups to it. Restoring transaction logs ensures that the standby SQL Server is consistent with the production server. Consider the following facts and guidelines when you maintain a standby SQL Server:

- Perform regular transaction log backups on the production server.
- Each time a transaction log backup is performed on the production server, restore it to the standby SQL Server.
- Specify the NORECOVERY option when restoring backups to the standby server if you do not want the standby server to be available until it is brought online.
- If you want the database to be available for read-only activity, you must specify the STANDBY option and supply a filename to contain the undo information.
- If the standby SQL Server is used as a read-only database, change the dbo use only option to false in order to make the database available to users.

Using the Standby SQL Server as a Read-Only Server

The standby SQL Server can function as a read-only copy of the production server, reducing the amount of activity on the production server. Using the standby SQL Server in this way has the following additional advantages:

- Users can access data for decision support queries in the time period between restore processes of each transaction log.
- You can execute DBCC statements (for example, DBCC CHECKDB) to check the validity of the database.
- Successfully restoring and validating each backup confirms the reliability of your backups.

Using the Standby SQL Server to Troubleshoot Data Corruption

Another use for a standby SQL Server is to determine the point at which a database became corrupted. You can use the STANDBY option to review the contents of the database for corruption or bad data as each transaction log backup is applied.

The following steps illustrate how to troubleshoot data corruption:

1. Apply a transaction log to a standby SQL Server by using the STANDBY option.

2. Check the consistency and examine the contents of the database before you apply the next transaction log by executing DBCC statements to check for corruption and using queries to check for bad data.

3. Continue applying the series of transaction logs and examining the contents of the database after each restore (steps 1 and 2) until you identify the cause of the problem and the time at which the problem occurred.

4. Restore the database and transaction logs on the production server by using point-in-time recovery to recover the database to the moment before the problem occurred.

5. Reset the standby SQL Server so that it reflects the state of the database on the production server.

Replacing a Production Server with a Standby SQL Server

You will typically use a standby SQL Server as a replacement for a production server to minimize down time. Follow these steps to bring a standby SQL Server on line to replace a production server:

1. Back up the transaction log from the production server. If possible, use the BACKUP LOG statement with the NO_TRUNCATE option for each database to back up any committed transactions since the last transaction log backup.

2. Take the production server off the network.

3. Change the computer name of the standby SQL Server to the name of the production server.

4. Restore the final transaction log to the standby SQL Server and specify the RECOVERY option. SQL Server recovers the database and allows users to read and write transactions to the database.

   If the standby SQL Server has been used as a read-only server and you do not have additional transaction logs to restore, perform a manual recovery on the standby SQL Server by executing the RESTORE DATABASE WITH RECOVERY statement. At this point, the standby SQL Server is recognized as the production server.

Restoring the Production Server

You will typically restore the production server after the problem is resolved. To restore the production server, you must perform the following steps:

1. Perform complete database and transaction log (if needed) backups of the standby SQL Server to capture all changes. When you replaced the production server with the standby SQL Server, the standby SQL Server recorded changes in its copy of the database and transaction log.

2. Restore the standby SQL Server database and transaction logs to the production server.

3. Take the standby SQL Server off line.

4. Bring the production server on line.

5. Perform a complete database backup of all databases on the production server.

6. Restore the backups to the standby SQL Server, but do not recover the database. Use the STANDBY option, if appropriate. This ensures that the standby SQL Server is a duplicate of the production server and allows additional transaction logs to be restored.

Using Clustering

Clustering describes using multiple Windows NT Servers to provide increased reliability and capacity. Clustering is available in the Enterprise Edition of SQL Server running on Windows NT Enterprise Edition. In a clustered installation of SQL Server, clients connect to a *virtual server,* instead of connecting to an actual Windows NT Server as is done with a typical installation of SQL Server. Virtual servers appear externally to be regular Windows NT Servers when they are in fact a group of servers working together. The servers in a cluster monitor each other's status. If an application failure is due to a server failure, another server takes over. This process is known as *failing over,* or *failover.*

In a mission-critical environment where high availability of SQL Server databases is required and a Windows NT Server Enterprise Edition cluster is available, the Enterprise Edition of SQL Server installed with failover support provides the most scalable and reliable solution. For more information about clustering, see SQL Server Books Online and search for "Configuring SQL Server failover support."

Lesson Summary

You can use a standby SQL Server to replace a production server in case of a failure or to provide a read-only copy of one or more databases for decision support applications. In addition, a standby server can be used to validate database integrity by running the Database Consistency Checker (DBCC) without increasing the load on the primary server. The Enterprise Edition of SQL Server can be run on a Windows NT Server Enterprise Edition cluster.

Lesson 5: Restoring System Databases

If the media that contain the system databases are damaged, you may have to rebuild the system databases. This lesson describes how to do this, as well as how to restore system databases and attach user databases once the system databases are rebuilt.

If the SQL Server service can be started, you can use the RESTORE DATABASE statement or SQL Server Enterprise Manager to restore the system databases from a valid backup.

After this lesson, you will be able to

- Rebuild the system databases
- Restore damaged system databases
- Attach user databases

Estimated lesson time: 15 minutes

Rebuilding System Databases

If the master database is damaged and you cannot start SQL Server, perform the following steps:

1. Rebuild the system databases with the rebuildm.exe command-prompt utility stored in C:\Mssql7\Binn.
2. Restart the SQL Server service.
3. Restore backups of the system databases, as described in the next section.

Caution Rebuilding the system databases overwrites the existing master, model, and msdb databases.

Restoring System Databases

After you have rebuilt the system databases and started SQL Server, you should perform the following steps:

1. Restore the master database from a backup, if one exists.

   If a valid backup of the master database does not exist, use SQL Server Enterprise Manager or execute scripts to re-create the information stored in the master database. Create serverwide objects such as logins. It is not necessary to create databases; these can be restored or attached as described in the next section.

2. Restore the msdb database from a backup, if one exists.

   You must restore the msdb database when you rebuild the master database. When you run the rebuildm utility, the msdb database is re-created. Therefore, all scheduling information is lost.

3. Restore the model database from a backup, if one exists. You must restore the model database when you rebuild the master database. When you run the rebuildm utility, the model database is re-created. Therefore, any changes to the model database are lost.

Attaching or Restoring User Databases

You either attach or restore user databases, depending on whether the master database was rebuilt.

If the master database was restored from a valid backup, it will contain references to each user database. If the databases are not damaged, no further action is needed. If the databases are damaged, restore them from backups.

If the master database was rebuilt and a valid backup was not applied, you must do one of the following:

- If the database files are not available, restore the user databases from a backup.

- If the database files are available, attach them to the server, using either the sp_attach_db or sp_attach_single_file_db system stored procedure.

  Attaching existing database files updates the master database to correctly reference a user database. This is faster and easier than restoring from a backup and can be done without using a database backup. Backups are still necessary if the database files are damaged.

The following example attaches the Northwind database to the master database.

```
USE master
EXEC sp_attach_single_file_db @dbname = 'northwind',
@physname = 'C:\Mssql7\Data\Northwind.mdf'
```

Lesson Summary

In this section you learned how to rebuild the system databases in the event that they are damaged. The rebuildm.exe utility allows you to rebuild the system databases in case of failure. Once you run this utility, you can then restore the databases from valid backups.

Review

The following questions are intended to reinforce key information presented in the chapter. If you are unable to answer a question, review the appropriate lesson and then try the question again. Answers to the questions can be found in Appendix A, "Questions and Answers."

1. What is the automatic recovery process, and when is it initiated?

2. What steps should you take before you restore a database?

3. You have a complete database backup and several transaction log backups. Your database is spread among four files. The disk on which the third file resides fails. What should you do to restore and recover the database?

4. You have a complete database backup and several transaction log backups. A malicious update to the database occurs at 9:21 A.M. The time is now 9:30 A.M. What should you do to restore and recover the database to a consistent state?

5. In the scenario presented in question 4, will any changes be lost due to the restore process?

6. You have set up a standby SQL Server that functions as a read-only server. What must you do to replace the production server with this standby SQL Server?

CHAPTER 11

Logins, User Accounts, and User Roles

About This Chapter

Before a user can access data in a Microsoft SQL Server database, three levels of access are verified:

- The user's access to SQL Server is authenticated against a login account. This authentication can be performed by Microsoft Windows NT or by SQL Server.
- The user's access to a particular database is determined by the login account's defined database user account or role membership.
- The user's access to objects or tasks within a database is determined by permissions that have been granted to the user's account or role.

In this chapter, you will learn how to create and manage logins, users, and roles. You will also learn about the important difference between logins that are authenticated by Windows NT and those that are authenticated by SQL Server.

Before You Begin

To complete the lessons in this chapter, you must have

- Experience using the SQL Server Enterprise Manager and SQL Server Query Analyzer.

- Knowledge of Windows NT Server user accounts, groups, Windows NT User Manager for Domains, and .CMD (or .BAT) files. This chapter refers to Windows NT User Manager for Domains, although your Windows NT–based computer may display Windows NT User Manager. Both utilities work the same for the purposes of this chapter.

You must also have done the following:

- Installed the Exercise files from the Supplemental Course Materials CD-ROM to your hard disk drive. See the "Getting Started" section in "About This Book" for installation instructions.
- Configured your Windows NT–based computer to allow the group Everyone to log on locally. (You can do this with the User Manager For Domains User Rights option under the Policies menu.) This allows you to log on as various users and test different security configurations in the exercises.
- Installed SQL Server version 7. See Chapter 2, "Installation," for installation instructions.

Important The exercises in this chapter assume that you are working on a Windows NT Server configured as a domain controller, although you can complete the exercises using SQL Server installed under Windows NT Workstation or on a standalone Windows NT Server. You cannot complete all of the exercises for this chapter on SQL Server installed under Microsoft Windows 95 or Windows 98.

- Created the users and the groups (local groups will suffice for this exercise, but you should create global groups if you are using an Windows NT Server installed as a domain controller) listed in the following table, in your Windows NT domain. You can create these using the Windows NT User Manager for Domains, or you can run the batch file makeusrs.cmd located in the C:\Sqladmin\Exercise\Setup folder.

Windows NT group	Members	Password
Customer_mgmt	Carl	password
	Cathy	password
Domain Users	Carl	password
	Cathy	password
	Paul	password
	Max	password

- Installed the StudyNwind database. See the "Getting Started" section in "About This Book" for StudyNwind database installation instructions.

Lesson 1: Adding Login Accounts

To use a database on SQL Server, a user first connects to the server, using a login account. A login account can be

- The user's Windows NT user account or the account of any group of which the user is a member
- A SQL Server login account that you create
- A default SQL Server login account

Logins are stored in the master database syslogins system table.

After this lesson, you will be able to

- Describe default login accounts
- Grant Windows NT users and groups access to SQL Server
- Describe and create SQL Server logins

Estimated lesson time: 30 minutes

Default Databases

When a login is added to SQL Server, it often is assigned a default database. Assigning a default database to a login account sets the default context for actions that the user takes; it does not give the user access to the database. As with any database, to gain access to the assigned default database, the user must be granted access, be a member of a Windows NT group that has been granted access, or be a member of a SQL Server role that has been granted access. If the default guest user account exists in the database, it can be used to gain access to the assigned default database. If you do not assign a default database, the default database will be the master database.

Default Login Accounts

SQL Server has two default login accounts: sa and BUILTIN\Administrators.

System administrator (sa) is a special SQL Server login that has all rights on the SQL Server and in all databases.

BUILTIN\Administrators is provided as the default Windows NT login account for all Windows NT administrators. It has all rights on the SQL Server and in all databases.

Granting a Windows NT Account Access to SQL Server

If a user connects to SQL Server using a Windows NT–authenticated login, that user is represented by her own Windows NT user account and the accounts of all Windows NT groups of which she is a member. You can use SQL Server Enterprise Manager or the sp_grantlogin system stored procedure to allow a Windows NT user or group account to connect to SQL Server. Only system or security administrators can grant access to Windows NT users or groups.

Exercise: Using SQL Server Enterprise Manager to Grant Access Rights

In this exercise, you will use SQL Server Enterprise Manager to grant SQL Server access to existing Windows NT user and group accounts. Use the data from the following table when performing the exercise.

Name	Default database
STUDYSQL\Paul	StudyNwind
STUDYSQL\Customer_mgmt	StudyNwind

▶ **To grant a Windows NT user or group access to SQL Server**

Repeat the following steps for each login:

1. Expand your server group and then expand your server in SQL Server Enterprise Manager.
2. Expand Security, right-click Logins, and then click New Login.
3. Click Windows NT Authentication.
4. Select the domain where the accounts reside.
5. Enter the Microsoft Windows NT account name to add after the domain name in the Name field.
6. Select StudyNwind as the default database; leave the default language as is.
7. Click OK to create the login.

   (For a script that adds the users in this table, see C:\Sqladmin\Exercise\Ch11\ Ntlogin.sql. To add the users with this script instead of using SQL Server Enterprise Manager and the following instructions, open the script file in SQL Server Query Analyzer and execute it.)

Using sp_grantlogin to Add a Windows NT Login to SQL Server

The syntax for the sp_grantlogin statement is as follows:

```
sp_grantlogin 'login'
```

The following example uses the sp_grant_login procedure to add the Windows NT user Paul as a SQL Server login.

```
sp_grantlogin 'STUDYSQL\Paul'
```

The *login* parameter is the name of the Windows NT user or group to be added. The Windows NT user or group must be qualified with a Windows NT domain name. The limit for combined domain and user or group names is 128 characters.

Consider the following facts and guidelines about adding Windows NT logins to SQL Server:

- Because SQL Server has a single login for a Windows NT group, no changes to SQL Server are required when membership in a Windows NT group changes. This prevents orphaned objects (objects that are owned by a user who no longer exists in SQL Server), as long as you do not drop the group.

- Deleting a Windows NT group or user from the NT domain in User Manager for Domains does not drop that group or user from SQL Server. This prevents orphaned objects (objects whose owners have been deleted from SQL Server).

- When you remove Windows NT users or groups, you should first remove them from Windows NT in order to disallow network access. Then use sp_changeobjectowner to change the owner of objects owned by the account you wish to drop. Finally, remove the login from SQL Server.

- Add a login account for a Windows NT group account if every member of the group will be connecting to the SQL Server.

- Add a login account for a Windows NT user account only if the user is not a member of a group that can be granted permission collectively.

- Although users log on to SQL Server as members of Windows NT groups, SQL Server still knows the identities of the users. The SUSER_SNAME function returns users' domain and login names when users are members of a Windows NT group.

The following table lists other system stored procedures that you can use for managing Windows NT login accounts.

System stored procedure	Description
sp_revokelogin	Removes the login entries for a Windows NT user or group from SQL Server
sp_denylogin	Prevents a Windows NT user or group from connecting to SQL Server

Note Users can change their own passwords at any time by using the sp_password system stored procedure. System administrators can change any user's password using SQL Server Enterprise Manager or by using sp_password with NULL as the old password.

Adding a SQL Server Login

You can use SQL Server Enterprise Manager or the sp_addlogin system stored procedure to create a SQL Server login. Only system or security administrators can create SQL Server logins.

Exercise: Adding a SQL Server Login
Using SQL Server Enterprise Manager

In this exercise, you will use SQL Server Enterprise Manager to add three SQL Server login accounts. Use the data from the following table when creating the logins. (For a script that adds the users listed in the following table, see C:\Sqladmin\Exercise\Ch11\Sqllogin.sql. To add the users with this script instead of using SQL Server Enterprise Manager and the following instructions, open the script file in SQL Server Query Analyzer and execute it.)

Name	Password	Default database
Carl	Password	StudyNwind
Cathy	Password	StudyNwind
Umberto	Password	StudyNwind

▶ **To use SQL Server Enterprise Manager to add SQL Server login accounts**

Repeat the following steps for each login:

1. Expand your server group and then expand your server in SQL Server Enterprise Manager.

2. Expand Security, right-click Logins, and then click New Login.

3. Enter the name of the new SQL Server login.

4. Click SQL Server Authentication.

5. Enter the password.

6. Select StudyNwind as the default database; leave the default language as is.

7. Click OK to create the login.

Note If you receive an error message stating, "The login <name> has not been granted access to the default database and therefore will not be able to gain access to the default database. Continue?," click OK. You will grant access to this database later in this chapter.

Using sp_addlogin to Add SQL Server Logins

The syntax for the sp_addlogin statement is as follows:

```
sp_addlogin 'login' [, 'password' [, 'database']]
```

The following example creates the login Carl with the password *password* in the StudyNwind database.

```
sp_addlogin 'Carl' , 'password' , 'StudyNwind'
```

The sp_addlogin system stored procedure adds a record to the syslogins table of the master database. After sp_addlogin is executed, the user can log on to SQL Server with that account.

SQL Server logins and passwords can contain up to 128 characters, including letters, symbols, and digits. However, logins cannot

- Contain a backslash character (\) other than the one required to delimit the domain name of a Windows NT login
- Be a reserved login account—for example, sa or public—or an existing login account
- Be NULL or an empty string (' ')

Lesson Summary

In this lesson you learned that when users connect to SQL Server they use a login account, which can be their Windows NT user or group account or a login account added directly to SQL Server. Windows NT accounts must be granted access to the SQL Server.

Lesson 2: How Login Accounts Are Authenticated When Users Connect

Microsoft SQL Server version 7 supports two authentication modes, Windows NT Authentication Mode and Mixed Mode. This lesson describes the process of authentication in each mode and the steps that you must take in implementing authentication.

Note Windows NT Authentication Mode was called Integrated Security in SQL Server version 6.5. Standard Security supported in SQL Server 6.5 is no longer available.

After this lesson, you will be able to

- Describe how users are authenticated when connecting to SQL Server
- Understand and choose between Windows NT Authentication Mode and Mixed Mode security
- Implement your chosen authentication mode

Estimated lesson time: 30 minutes

Authentication Processing

In any secure computer environment, users must be identified and validated. This process is known as authentication.

Authentication is similar to using a cash card at an ATM. Your card identifies you as an account holder at the bank. You then enter your PIN to prove that you are the rightful owner of the card.

Each SQL Server user is identified by a SQL Server login account, a Windows NT user account, or by membership in a Windows NT group. These are all known in SQL Server as logins. Validation that the user is allowed to use the login is performed either by SQL Server or by Windows NT.

How SQL Server Processes Logins That Windows NT Authenticates

The following steps (shown in Figure 11.1) describe how SQL Server processes logins that Windows NT authenticates:

1. When a user connects to a Windows NT Server, she enters her username and password.

2. The user's Windows NT security attributes are established and validated through a sophisticated password encryption mechanism.

3. When connecting, the client opens a trusted connection, and Windows NT–based facilities are used to pass the user's security attributes to SQL Server. SQL Server does not need to revalidate the password, because Windows NT has already validated it.

4. SQL Server checks the user's Windows NT security attributes to see if a Windows NT user account or a Windows NT group account defined there matches an entry in the SQL Server syslogins system table.

5. If one is found, the connection is accepted. The user's login account is the account that matched a syslogins entry—the Windows NT user account or one of the group accounts to which the user belongs.

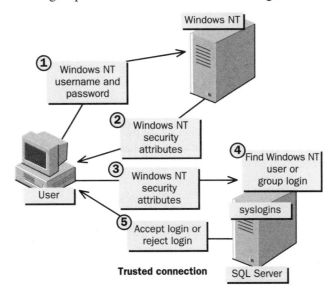

Figure 11.1 Windows NT authentication login steps

Windows NT user and group account names are not actually listed in the security attributes; rather, a unique identifier represents each account. These unique identifiers are known as SIDs (Security Identifiers). SQL Server stores the SIDs of Windows NT users and groups that are granted access to the SQL Server in the syslogins table. These are compared to the SIDs listed in the user's security attributes. For this reason, SQL Server will not recognize users or groups that you have dropped and re-created in Windows NT. You must drop the group from SQL Server and add it again, because SQL Server uses the Windows NT SID to identify the group.

Note the following with respect to Windows NT authentication:

- If multiple SQL Server computers participate in a domain or a group of trusted domains, logging on to a single network domain is sufficient to enable access to all SQL Servers.

- Most of the graphical tools do not require that you enter a username and password when using NT authentication. The SQL Server command-line utilities support options that allow you to connect using a trusted connection.

- SQL Server running under Windows 95 or Windows 98 does not support Windows NT authentication mode.

How SQL Server Processes Logins That It Authenticates

The following steps (shown in Figure 11.2) describe how SQL Server processes logins that it authenticates:

1. When connecting, the client opens a nontrusted connection and passes a SQL Server login account and password.

2. SQL Server verifies that a login exists in the syslogins table and that the specified password matches the previously recorded password.

3. If SQL Server finds that the login and password are correct, the user is connected. If SQL Server does not have a matching login account or if the password is incorrect, authentication fails and the connection is refused.

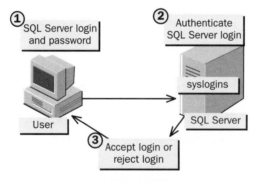

Nontrusted connection

Figure 11.2   SQL Server login authentication steps

Choosing an Authentication Mode

In Windows NT Authentication Mode, SQL Server accepts only logins authenticated by Windows NT. In Mixed Mode, SQL Server accepts both Windows NT–authenticated logins and logins that it authenticates. There is no mode that accepts only SQL Server–authenticated logins.

The security needs of your server and network environments will determine the authentication mode that you use for your SQL Server. You can use SQL Server Enterprise Manager to set the authentication mode of your server.

Advantages of Windows NT Authentication Mode

Use Windows NT Authentication Mode in network environments in which all clients support trusted connections. Windows NT authentication offers several advantages over SQL Server authentication, including

- Providing more features, such as secure validation and encryption of passwords, auditing, password expiration, minimum password length, and account lockout after an invalid password
- Enabling you to add groups of users to SQL Server by adding a single login account
- Enabling users to connect to SQL Server quickly, without having to enter another login account and password

Advantages of Mixed Mode

Use Mixed Mode to connect non-trusted or Internet clients only. Mixed Mode, and the SQL Server authentication mechanism in particular, offers the following advantages:

- Mixed Mode enables non–Windows NT clients, Internet clients, and mixed client groups to connect to SQL Server.
- SQL Server authentication allows you to add another layer of security over Windows NT.

Steps in Implementing One of the Authentication Modes

Perform the following tasks from a system administration account to implement your chosen authentication mode. For Windows NT Authentication Mode, perform steps 1 through 5; for Mixed Mode, perform steps 1 through 6.

1. Use the SQL Server Network Utility (found under Microsoft SQL Server 7.0 on the Start menu) to verify that a protocol that supports trusted connections (Multi-Protocol, Named Pipes, or TCP/IP Sockets) is in place for clients that will use Windows NT authentication (see Figure 11.3).

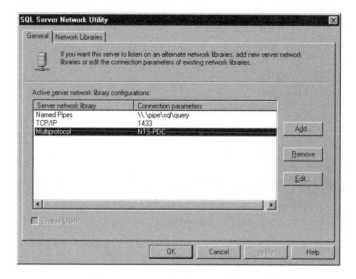

Figure 11.3   The SQL Server Network Utility

2. Right-click your server in the SQL Server Enterprise Manager and select Properties to open the SQL Server Properties dialog box. Select the Security tab (see Figure 11.4). Set the login security mode of SQL Server to SQL Server And Windows NT (Mixed Mode) or to Windows NT Only (Windows NT Authentication Mode).

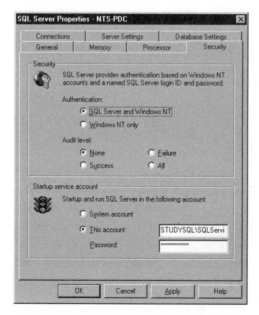

Figure 11.4   SQL Server properties and security

3. Stop and then restart the MSSQLServer service for the security option to take effect.

4. Create the Windows NT groups and users that are authorized to connect to SQL Server over trusted connections. If you do not have permission to administer Windows NT groups and users, have a Windows NT administrator perform this task for you.

5. Use SQL Server Enterprise Manager or sp_grantlogin to grant Windows NT groups and users access to SQL Server.

6. To allow access to the server for those users who are not connecting to the server over trusted connections, use SQL Server Enterprise Manager or sp_addlogin to create a SQL Server login for each user.

▶ **To verify which authentication mode is being used**

1. Right click on your server in the SQL Server Enterprise Manager, and select Properties from the context menu.

2. Click on the Security tab.

3. Confirm that the Authentication is set to the authentication mode you set in step 2 of the preceding list of steps.

Lesson Summary

In this lesson you learned about the two authentication modes supported by SQL Server: Windows NT Authentication Mode and Mixed Mode. You can now describe the process of authentication in each mode and the steps that you must take to implement authentication. The two modes allow you maximum flexibility in choosing the best security architecture for your organization.

Lesson 3: Granting Access to Databases

After a user is connected to SQL Server, she needs to be given access to one or more databases. A user gains access to databases based on user accounts or roles created and managed separately in each database. Although you can create a login for an individual user, normally you will create logins for Windows NT groups, allowing all members of the group access to the database.

If a user is connected to SQL Server using a Windows NT–authenticated login, that user is represented by her own Windows NT user account as well as the accounts of all Windows NT groups of which she is a member. The user can therefore gain access to a database if database access has been granted to any of these accounts.

If a user is connected to SQL Server using a SQL Server–authenticated login, the user is represented by the SQL Server login only. The user can therefore gain access to a database only if database access has been granted to this login.

After this lesson, you will be able to

- Grant database access to Windows NT user and group accounts and SQL Server logins
- Describe the two default database user accounts
- Assign logins to fixed server roles
- Assign security accounts to fixed database roles
- Create and assign security accounts to user-defined database roles

Estimated lesson time: 60 minutes

Granting Database Access to Logins

To access a database, a *login* (which can be any of the following: a Windows NT user or group account that has been granted access to SQL Server [see Figure 11.5], a SQL Server login [see Figure 11.6], or one of the default SQL Server logins) uses either an assigned database user account or one of the default database user accounts. User accounts can be assigned to Windows NT users, Windows NT groups, or SQL Server logins.

To assign a user account to a login, you can use SQL Server Enterprise Manager or execute the sp_grantdbaccess system stored procedure. Only database owners and database access administrators can assign a user account to a login. An entry is added to the sysusers table in the database to which access is granted.

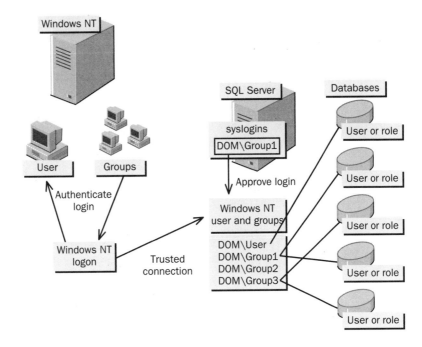

Figure 11.5   Login authentication and database access using Windows NT–
authenticated logins

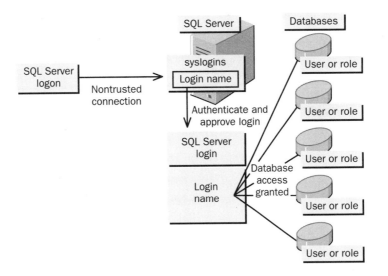

Figure 11.6   Login authentication and database access using SQL Server–
authenticated logins

Exercise: Granting Database Access with SQL Server Enterprise Manager

In this exercise, you will grant some of the logins you created earlier in this chapter access to the StudyNwind database. Two methods are provided to give you practice using different parts of SQL Server Enterprise Manager.

▶ **To grant database access with SQL Server Enterprise Manager**

Perform the following steps for the logins Carl and Cathy, which were created in the Exercise, "Adding a SQL Server Login Using SQL Server Enterprise Manager" in Lesson 1 of this chapter.

1. In SQL Server Enterprise Manager, expand your server.
2. Expand Security, and then click Logins.
3. In the details pane, right-click the login to modify, and then click Properties.
4. On the Database Access tab, check the box next to StudyNwind.
5. Click OK to close the SQL Server Login Properties dialog box and assign database access to the login.

Perform the following steps for the logins STUDYSQL\Paul and STUDYSQL\Customer_mgmt created in an earlier exercise.

1. In SQL Server Enterprise Manager, expand your server.
2. Expand Databases, and then expand the StudyNwind database.
3. Right-click Users, and then click New Database User.
4. Under Login Name, click the login name.
5. Click OK to close the Database User Properties — New User dialog box and assign database access to the login.

Granting Database Access with sp_grantdbaccess

The syntax for the sp_grantdbaccess statement is as follows:

```
sp_grantdbaccess 'login' [,'name_in_db']
```

The following example uses the sp_grantdbaccess statement to give the logins Carl and Paul access to the database.

```
sp_grantdbaccess 'Carl'
sp_grantdbaccess 'STUDYSQL\Paul'
```

Important For scripts that provide examples of assigning the logins from the previous exercise, see C:\Sqladmin\Exercise\Ch11\Sqllogin.sql and C:\Sqladmin\Exercise\Ch11\Ntlogin.sql. These scripts can be reviewed and executed in the Query Analyzer.

The *login* parameter is the name of the login for the new account in the database. It can be any Windows NT user, Windows NT group, or SQL Server login.

The *name_in_db* parameter is an optional name for the account in the database.

Tip It is possible to use the sp_grantdbaccess system stored procedure to grant access to a Windows NT user or group that has not been added as a login. This is not possible in SQL Server Enterprise Manager. Granting access in this way allows a user to connect to the SQL Server using one Windows NT account and then to be granted access to a database based on another account. Remember that every user is represented by her own Windows NT user account as well as the accounts of all Windows NT groups of which she is a member.

The following table lists other system stored procedures that you can use for managing database access.

System stored procedure	Description
sp_revokedbaccess	Removes a security account from the current database
sp_change_users_login	Changes the relationship between a SQL Server login and a SQL Server user in the current database

Default User Accounts

Each database within SQL Server also has two default user accounts: dbo and guest.

The Database Owner (dbo) Account

The sa login account and members of the System Administrators (sysadmin) role are mapped to a special user account inside all databases called dbo. Any object that a system administrator creates automatically belongs to dbo. The dbo user cannot be dropped.

The guest User Account

The guest user account allows logins without user accounts access to a database. Logins assume the identity of the guest user account when both of the following conditions are met:

- The login has access to SQL Server but does not have access to the database through its own user account.
- The database contains a guest user account.

Permissions can be applied to the guest user account as if it were any other user account. You can drop and add the guest user to any database except the master and tempdb databases. By default, the guest user account is not given any permissions, but it is a member of the public role. You should therefore be careful when assigning permissions to the public role; drop the guest user account if necessary.

Assigning Logins to Roles

Roles provide a means of assembling users into a single unit to which permissions can be applied.

Note Roles replace the SQL Server 6.5 concepts of aliases and groups.

SQL Server provides predefined fixed server and database roles for common administrative functions so that you can easily grant a selection of administrative permissions to a particular user.

You can also create your own database roles to represent work that a class of employees in your organization performs. As employees rotate into certain positions, you simply add them as members of the role; as they rotate out of the positions, remove them from the role. You do not have to grant and revoke permissions repeatedly as employees commence or leave various positions. If the function of a position changes, it is easy to change the permissions for the role and have the changes applied automatically to all members of the role.

Fixed Server Roles

The fixed server roles provided by SQL Server are listed in the following table.

Fixed server role	Description
Sysadmin	Can perform any activity in SQL Server
Serveradmin	Can configure serverwide settings
Setupadmin	Can install replication and manage extended procedures
Securityadmin	Can manage server logins
Processadmin	Can manage processes running in SQL Server
Dbcreator	Can create and alter databases
Diskadmin	Can manage disk files

The permissions of the sysadmin fixed server role span all of the other fixed server roles. The sysadmin role is the equivalent of the sa login.

Fixed server roles provide groupings of administrative privileges at the server level. They are managed independently of user databases and are stored in the master..syslogins system table. It is not possible to add new server roles.

Assigning a Login Account to a Fixed Server Role

You can use SQL Server Enterprise Manager or the sp_addsrvrolemember system stored procedure to add a login account as a member of a fixed server role. Only members of the fixed server roles can add a login account as a member of a fixed server role.

▶ **To use SQL Server Enterprise Manager
to assign a login to a fixed server role**

1. Expand your server group, then expand your server.

2. Expand Security, and click Server Roles.

3. In the details pane, right-click the role Security Administrators, and then click Properties.

4. On the General tab, click Add.

5. Click the login to add: STUDYSQL\Paul.

6. Click OK twice to close the dialog boxes and assign STUDYSQL\Paul to the Security Administrators fixed server role.

Using sp_addsrvrolemember to Assign a Login to a Fixed Server Role

The syntax for the sp_addsrvrolemeber statement is as follows:

```
sp_addsrvrolemember 'login', 'role'
```

The following example adds the login Paul to the securityadmin role.

```
sp_addsrvrolemember 'STUDYSQL\Paul', 'securityadmin'
```

Note For a script that adds a login to a fixed server role, see C:\Sqladmin\Exercise\ Ch11\Ntlogin.sql. You can review and execute this script in the Query Analyzer.

When you add a login to a server role, the corresponding row for the login in the syslogins table is updated to indicate that the login is a member of the role. The login then has the permissions that are associated with the server role.

Consider the following facts about assigning login accounts to fixed server roles:

- Fixed server roles cannot be added, modified, or removed.

- Any member of a fixed server role can add other login accounts to that role.

- You can add a Windows NT user or group to a role, even if the user or group has not yet been added as a login. The user or group will be added as a login automatically when you execute sp_addsrvrolemember.

- The sp_addsrvrolemember system stored procedure cannot be executed within a user-defined transaction.

Use the sp_dropsrvrolemember system stored procedure to remove a member from a fixed server role.

Fixed Database Roles

The fixed database roles provided by SQL Server are listed in the following table.

Fixed database role	Description
db_owner	Can perform the activities of all database roles, as well as other maintenance and configuration activities in the database
db_accessadmin	Can add or remove Windows NT groups, Windows NT users, and SQL Server users in the database
db_datareader	Can see any data from all user tables in the database
db_datawriter	Can add, change, or delete data from all user tables in the database
db_ddladmin	Can add, modify, or drop objects in the database
db_securityadmin	Can manage roles and members of SQL Server database roles, and can manage statement and object permissions in the database
db_backupoperator	Can back up the database
db_denydatareader	Cannot see any data in the database, but can make schema changes
db_denydatawriter	Cannot change any data in the database

The permissions of the db_owner fixed database role span all of the other fixed database roles.

Fixed database roles provide groupings of administrative privileges at the database level. Fixed database roles are stored in the sysusers system table of each database.

The public Role

A special database role to which every database user belongs, the public role

- Maintains all default permissions for users in a database
- Cannot have users, groups, or roles assigned to it because users, groups, and roles already belong by default
- Is contained in every database, including master, msdb, tempdb, model, and all user databases
- Cannot be dropped

Without being granted any specific permissions, a user possesses the permissions that are granted to the public role and can

- Execute statements that do not require permissions, such as the PRINT statement
- View system table information and execute certain system stored procedures to retrieve information from the master database and user databases to which she has access
- Gain access to any database with a guest account

Note In the pubs and Northwind databases, the public role has been granted all permissions. Security is set this way only because these are sample databases; you should never grant all permissions to the public role in production databases.

Assigning a Security Account to a Fixed Database Role

Use SQL Server Enterprise Manager or the sp_addrolemember system stored procedure to add a security account as a member of a fixed database role. Only members of the db_owner role can execute the sp_addrolemember system stored procedure.

▶ **To use SQL Server Enterprise Manager to assign security accounts to a fixed database role**

1. Expand your server group, and then expand your server.
2. Expand Databases, and then expand the StudyNwind database.
3. Click Users.
4. In the details pane, right-click Cathy, and then click Properties.
5. Under Database Role Membership, click db_datareader and db_datawriter. (Make sure the boxes next to the roles are checked.)
6. Click OK to close the dialog box and add Cathy to the db_datareader and db_datawriter fixed database roles.
7. In the console tree, click Roles.
8. In the details pane, right-click the role db_datareader, and then click Properties.
9. Under User, click Add.
10. Select Carl to add.
11. Click OK twice to close the dialog boxes and add Carl to the db_datareader fixed database role.

Using sp_addrolemember to Assign Security Accounts to a Fixed Database Role

The syntax for the sp_addrolemember statement is as follows:

```
sp_addrolemember 'role', 'security_account'
```

The following example adds the user Carl to the db_datareader role.

```
sp_addrolemember 'Carl', 'db_datareader'
```

Note For a script containing examples of adding users to fixed database roles, see C:\Sqladmin\Exercise\Ch11\Sqllogin.sql. You can review and execute this script using the Query Analyzer.

Consider the following facts when you assign security accounts to a fixed database role:

- Fixed database roles cannot be added, modified, or removed.
- Any member of a fixed database role can add other login accounts to that role.

Use the sp_droprolemember system stored procedure to drop a security account from a role.

User-Defined Database Roles

Creating a user-defined database role allows you to create a group of users with a set of common permissions. Add a user-defined role to the database

- When a group of people needs to perform a specified set of activities in SQL Server and no applicable Windows NT group exists
- If you do not have permissions to manage Windows NT user accounts
- When you are using Mixed Mode authentication

For example, a company may form a new Charity Event committee that includes employees from different departments at several different levels. These employees need access to a special project table in the database. A Windows NT group does not exist that includes only these employees, and there is no other reason to create one in Windows NT. You could create a user-defined role, CharityEvent, for this project and then add individual Windows NT user accounts to the role. When permissions are applied, the individual user accounts in the role gain access to the project table.

Creating a User-Defined Database Role

Use SQL Server Enterprise Manager or the sp_addrole system stored procedure to create a new database role. An entry is added to the sysusers table of the current database for each user-defined role. Only members of the db_securityadmin or db_owner roles can execute sp_addrole.

Using sp_addrole to Create a User-Defined Database Role

The syntax for the sp_addrole stored procedure is as follows:

```
sp_addrole 'role', 'owner'
```

The following example uses the sp_addrole stored procedure to create the Cust_mgmt role.

```
sp_addrole 'Cust_mgmt'
```

The *owner* parameter must be a user or role in the current database and defaults to dbo.

Consider the following facts and guidelines when you create a database role:

- The sp_addrole system stored procedure adds a new SQL Server role to the current database.

- When you apply permissions to the role, each member of the role gains the effects of the permission as if the permission were applied directly to the member's own account.

Assigning a Security Account to a User-Defined Database Role

After you add a role, use SQL Server Enterprise Manager or the sp_addrolemember system stored procedure to add users or roles as members of the role. Only members of the db_owner fixed database role or a role owner can execute sp_addrolemember to add a member to a user-defined database role.

▶ **To use SQL Server Enterprise Manager to create a user-defined database role and assign a security account to the role**

1. Expand your server group, and then expand your server.

2. Expand Databases, and then expand the StudyNwind database.

3. Right-click Roles, and then click New Database Role.

4. Type the name of the new role: **Cust_mgmt**.

5. Click Add to add members to the standard role.

6. Select Carl and Cathy.

7. Click OK twice to close the dialog boxes and add the new user-defined role and its members.

Using sp_addrolemember to Assign a Security Account to a User-Defined Database Role

The syntax for the sp_addrolemember stored procedure is as follows.

```
sp_addrolemember 'role', 'security_account'
```

The following example uses the sp_addrolemember to add Carl to the Cust_mgmt role.

```
sp_addrolemember 'Cust_mgmt', 'Carl'
```

Note For a script that has an example of adding a user-defined database role and assigning users to the role, see C:\Sqladmin\Exercise\Ch11\Sqllogin.sql. You can review and execute this script using the Query Analyzer.

Consider the following facts when you assign security accounts to a user-defined database role:

- When you use the sp_addrolemember system stored procedure to add a security account to a role, any permissions applied to the role are applied to the new member.

- You can add a SQL Server role as a member of another SQL Server role, but you cannot create recursive roles. Therefore, role A cannot be added as a member of role B if role B is already a member of role A. Furthermore, role A cannot be added as a member of role C if role B is already a member of role A and role C is already a member of role B.

- Nesting roles multiple times can decrease system performance.

The following table lists additional system stored procedures that you can use for managing database roles.

System stored procedure	Description
sp_droprole	Drops a SQL Server role from the current database
sp_droprolemember	Drops a security account from a SQL Server role

Exercise: Testing the Accounts You Have Created

In this exercise, you will test the various accounts that you have created to get a better understanding of each of the different types of login, user, and role.

▶ **To test the logins, users, and roles that you have created and assigned**

1. Start SQL Server Query Analyzer and, by using SQL Server authentication, connect as Carl with the password **password**.

   To what database are you connected, and why?

2. Execute a query to retrieve data from the Products table. For example,

   ```
   SELECT productname FROM Products
   ```

   Did you receive any results? Why or why not?

3. Execute a query to change data in the Products table. For example:

```
UPDATE Products
    SET productname = 'Tofu, unsalted'
    WHERE productname = 'Tofu'
```

Was the update successful? Why or why not?

4. Select Connect from the File menu and open a new connection logged on as Cathy. What happens if you perform steps 2 and 3 logged on as Cathy?

5. Log off from Windows NT and log on again as STUDYSQL\Carl with the password **password**.

6. Start SQL Server Query Analyzer and connect with Windows NT authentication.

   Notice that you cannot provide a login name or password when you connect to SQL Server with Windows NT authentication and that your user name is displayed in the title bar of the query window.

   How did Carl connect to the database when his Windows NT login was not authorized to use SQL Server?

7. Log off from Windows NT and log on again as STUDYSQL\Max with the password **password**.

8. Start SQL Server Query Analyzer and connect with Windows NT authentication.

   What happens and why?

Lesson Summary

In this lesson you learned that a user needs to be given access to databases based on user accounts or roles created and managed separately in each relevant database. Although you can create a user account for an individual user, normally you will create user accounts for Windows NT groups, giving all the members of the group access to the database.

A user connected to SQL Server using a Windows NT–authenticated login is represented by her own Windows NT user account and the accounts of all Windows NT groups of which she is a member. This means that the user can gain access to a database if database access has been granted to any of these accounts.

A user connected to SQL Server using a SQL Server–authenticated login is represented by the SQL Server login only. This means that the user can gain access to a database only if database access has been granted to this login.

Review

The following questions are intended to reinforce key information presented in the chapter. If you are unable to answer a question, review the appropriate lesson and then try the question again. Answers to the questions can be found in Appendix A, "Questions and Answers."

1. What can users do after they have been authenticated if their logins do not have permissions in any database?

2. What type of authentication mode would you implement in an environment that contains users who connect from both UNIX and Windows NT? Why?

C H A P T E R   1 2

Permissions and Security Planning

About This Chapter

Logins grant access to SQL Server. Users and roles grant access to a database. This is analogous to using your cash card and PIN to gain access to an ATM. Before you can withdraw cash from your account, the bank will check to see that you have sufficient funds and that you are not trying to withdraw more than a daily limit. In the same way, every time you attempt to execute statements or use objects in the database, SQL Server will check that you have permission to perform these operations.

Permissions are granted to or revoked from users and roles in the database. It is important to plan the permissions that you grant to each user or role. Remember that a user of a database may be an individual user or a Microsoft Windows NT group. Each database has its own independent permissions system. This chapter covers Permissions and how to use them to secure your databases.

Before You Begin

To complete the lessons in this chapter, you must have

- Experience using SQL Server Enterprise Manager and SQL Server Query Analyzer.

- Knowledge of Windows NT Server user accounts, groups, Windows NT User Manager for Domains, and .CMD (or .BAT) files. This chapter refers to Windows NT User Manager for Domains, although your Windows NT–based computer may display Windows NT User Manager. Both utilities work the same for the purposes of this chapter.

You must also have done the following:

- Installed the Exercise files from the Supplemental Course Materials CD-ROM to your hard disk drive. See the "Getting Started" section in "About This Book" for installation instructions.

- Configured your Windows NT–based computer to allow the group Everyone to log on locally. This allows you to log on as various users and test different security configurations in the exercises.

- Installed SQL Server version 7. See Chapter 2, "Installation," for installation instructions.

Important The exercises in this chapter assume that you are working on a Windows NT Server configured as a domain controller, although you can complete the exercises using SQL Server installed on a Windows NT Workstation or on a standalone Windows NT Server. You cannot complete all of the exercises for this chapter on SQL Server installed under Microsoft Windows 95 or Windows 98.

- Created the users and the group listed in the "Before You Begin" section in Chapter 11, "Logins, User Accounts, and User Roles," in your Windows NT domain. If you did not do this in Chapter 11, you can create these users and groups by using the Windows NT User Manager for Domains, or you can run the batch file makeusrs.cmd located in the C:\Sqladmin\Exercise\Setup folder.

- Installed the StudyNwind database. See the "Getting Started" section in "About This Book" for StudyNwind database installation instructions.

- Completed the exercises in Chapter 11 to set up the users and roles needed in the exercises in this chapter. If you have not done this, run the Ch12.cmd batch file in the C:\Sqladmin\Exercise\Setup folder.

Lesson 1: Types of Permissions

To allow a user to access or create objects in SQL Server, that user must be granted permissions on the object. High-level users can be given permissions that allow them to develop objects in the database. Users can also be given permissions that allow them to access objects, such as the ability to select from a table. This lesson discusses the types of permissions in SQL Server.

After this lesson, you will be able to

- Describe the three different types of permissions in SQL Server

Estimated lesson time: 15 minutes

The Three Types of Permissions

There are three types of permissions in SQL Server: statement, object, and implied. The following table summarizes the SQL Server permissions, grouping them by type, and indicates which database or object the permission applies to.

Permission type	Permission	Applies to
Statement	CREATE DATABASE	The master database
	CREATE DEFAULT	All databases
	CREATE PROCEDURE	All databases
	CREATE RULE	All databases
	CREATE TABLE	All databases
	CREATE VIEW	All databases
	BACKUP DATABASE	All databases
	BACKUP LOG	All databases
Object	SELECT	Tables, views, and columns
	INSERT	Tables and views
	DELETE	Tables and views
	UPDATE	Tables, views, and columns
	REFERENCES (DRI in SQL Server Enterprise Manager)	Tables and columns
	EXECUTE	Stored procedures
Implied	Fixed role	Depends on role
	Object owner	The owned object

Statement Permissions

Activities that involve creating a database or items in a database require a class of permissions called statement permissions. These permissions give users the privilege of issuing certain Transact-SQL statements. Statement permissions, such as CREATE DATABASE, are applied to the statement itself, rather than to a specific item that is defined in the database. Only members of the sysadmin, db_owner, or db_securityadmin roles can grant statement permissions.

Object Permissions

Activities that involve working with data or executing procedures require a class of permissions known as object permissions.

Table and View Permissions

Object permissions for tables and views control users' abilities to gain access to data using the SELECT, INSERT, UPDATE, and DELETE statements against the table or view. Object permissions are therefore called SELECT, INSERT, UPDATE, and DELETE.

Using a WHERE clause in an UPDATE statement requires both SELECT and UPDATE permissions.

The REFERENCES Permission

Another object permission called REFERENCES applies to tables. When a user adds a row to a table or changes data in a table with a FOREIGN KEY constraint, SQL Server must validate the data in the table that is referenced in the FOREIGN KEY constraint. If the user does not have SELECT permissions on the referenced table, the REFERENCES permission for the table must be granted to the user.

In SQL Server Enterprise Manager, the REFERENCES permission is referred to as DRI (Declarative Referential Integrity).

Column Permissions

SELECT, UPDATE, and REFERENCES permissions can be applied selectively to individual columns. This means that rather than giving a user or role access to an entire table, you can grant access to certain columns of the table only. To work with column permissions, you must use Transact-SQL. SQL Server Enterprise Manager does not allow you to grant, revoke, or deny column permissions.

Tip It is recommended that you use views rather than column permissions. Views are easier to manage and give better performance than using column permissions.

Stored Procedure Permissions

The EXECUTE permission is the only object permission for a stored procedure. This permission allows a user to execute the stored procedure.

Implied Permissions

Members of fixed roles and owners of database objects can perform certain activities apart from those governed by normal statement and object permissions. Permissions to perform these activities are called implied, predefined, or implicit permissions.

Fixed Role Permissions

Fixed roles have implied administrative permissions. For example, a user who is added as a member of the sysadmin role automatically inherits full permissions to do or read anything in a SQL Server installation. The sysadmin role has permissions that cannot be changed, as well as implied permissions that cannot be applied to other user accounts, such as the ability to configure the SQL Server installation.

Object Owner Permissions

Object owners also have implied permissions that allow them to perform all activities on objects that they own. For example, a user who is a table owner, or a member of a group that is designated as the table owner, can perform any activity that is related to the table. The user can view, add, or delete data, alter the table definition, and control the permissions that allow other users to work with the table.

Tip It usually not a good idea to grant individual user accounts the ability to create objects. It adds a layer of complexity to your security model that is difficult to manage. A better idea is to use the implied permissions of roles such as db_owner and sysadmin so that all objects are owned by the same role.

Lesson Summary

Statement permissions are permissions to perform activities that involve creating a database or items in a database. Object permissions are permissions to perform activities that involve working with data or executing procedures. Members of fixed roles and owners of database objects can perform certain activities apart from those governed by normal statement and object permissions. Permissions to perform these activities are called implied, predefined, or implicit permissions.

Lesson 2: Assigning Permissions to Users and Roles

This lesson explores how to grant and deny permissions to users and roles as well as how to revoke permissions. You will explore how role and user permissions interact with each other and how being assigned to more than one role can affect a user's permissions.

After this lesson, you will be able to

- Grant permissions to users and roles
- Deny permissions to users and roles
- Revoke permissions from users and roles

Estimated lesson time: 75 minutes

Permission States

Permissions for a user or role can be in one of three states: granted, denied, or revoked. Permissions are stored as entries in the sysprotects system table. If a permission is granted or denied, an entry is recorded in the sysprotects table. If a permission has not been granted or denied, or if it has been revoked after being granted or denied, there is no entry for that permission in the sysprotects system table. Note that a permission is in the revoked state if it has never been granted or denied; it does not have to be revoked with the REVOKE statement. The following table summarizes the three states of a permission.

Permission state	State of entry in sysprotects table	Effect
GRANT	Positive	Can perform action, can be overridden by role membership
DENY	Negative	Cannot perform action, cannot be overridden by role membership
REVOKE	None	Cannot perform action, can be overridden by role membership

Granted permissions are cumulative—users can perform all of the actions that they have been granted individually or as a result of Windows NT group membership, as well as all of the actions granted to any roles to which they belong. Role hierarchies mean that users can get permissions indirectly by being members of a role that is in turn a member of another role to which permissions have been granted.

The DENY statement prevents users from performing actions. It overrides a permission, whether the permission was granted to a user directly or to a role to which the user belongs.

Users have permission to perform an action only if both of the following are true:

- They have been granted the permission directly or they belong to a role that has directly or indirectly been granted the permission.

- The permission has not been denied to the user directly or to any of the roles of which the user is a member.

Figure 12.1 shows an example of a user who is a member of a Windows NT group (NT group A) and a database role (role C). NT group A is a member of role A, and role C is a member of role B. The figure shows how the user accumulates permissions directly from NT group A and role C and indirectly from role A and role B. Notice that the DELETE permission is revoked from role C, but this does not prevent members of role C from getting the DELETE permission from role B.

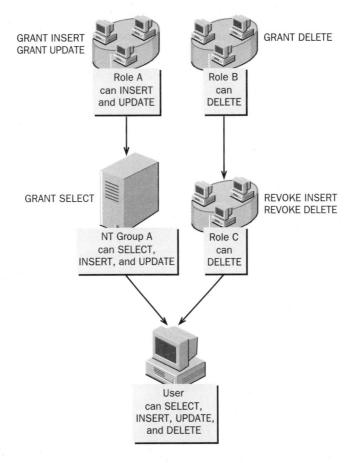

Figure 12.1 How granted and revoked permissions interact

Figure 12.2 shows the same roles, NT group, and user as Figure 12.1. Notice that the DELETE permission is denied to role C; this prevents members of role C from getting the permission from role B.

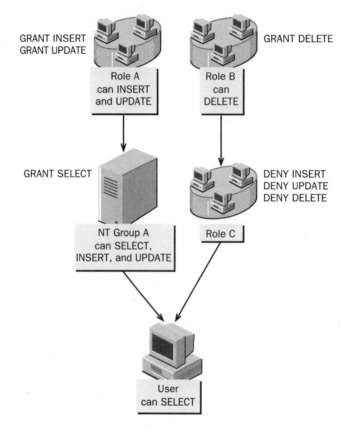

Figure 12.2 How granted and denied permissions interact

Each of the following tables shows a further example of accumulated permissions.

Account	Permission assigned	Result
Role A	GRANT SELECT	Members of role A have SELECT permission.
Role B, member of role A	GRANT INSERT	Members of role B have SELECT permissions (because role B is a member of role A) and INSERT permission.
User A, member of role B	DENY INSERT	User A has SELECT permission because it is a member of role A. User A does not have INSERT permission because INSERT has been denied to this user.
Role A	DENY SELECT	Members of role A do not have SELECT permission.

Account	Permission assigned	Result
Role B, member of role A	GRANT SELECT	Members of role B do not have SELECT permission because role B is a member of role A, which denies the SELECT permission.
User A, member of role B	GRANT INSERT	User A has INSERT permission only.
Role A	GRANT SELECT	Members of role A have SELECT permission.
Role B, member of role A	REVOKE SELECT	Members of role B have SELECT permission because they still get it from role A.
User A, member of role B	GRANT INSERT	User A has SELECT permissions (because the user is a member of role B) and INSERT permissions.

Granting Permissions

You grant permissions to security accounts to allow them to perform activities or work with data in a database.

Consider the following facts when you grant permissions:

- You can grant permissions in the current database only.

- The right to grant permissions defaults to members of the sysadmin, db_owner, and db_securityadmin roles and to object owners.

- The CREATE DATABASE statement permission can be granted only to users and roles in the master database. This is because records are added to system tables in the master database when you create a new database.

Use SQL Server Enterprise Manager or the GRANT statement to grant permissions. The syntax for the GRANT statement for statement permissions is as follows:

```
GRANT {ALL | statement [,…n]}
TO security_account[,…n]
```

The syntax for the GRANT statement for object permissions is as follows:

```
GRANT {ALL [PRIVILEGES] | permission[,…n]}
    {
        [(column[,…n])] ON {table | view}
        | ON {table | view}[(column[,…n])]
        | ON {stored_procedure | extended_procedure}
    }
TO security_account[,…n]
[WITH GRANT OPTION]
[AS {group | role}]
```

When used to assign statement permissions, the ALL argument specifies that all statement permissions are granted. When used to assign object permissions, the ALL argument specifies that all object permissions that apply to the specified object are granted. Only the system administrator and database owner can use the ALL argument.

Note Windows NT usernames must be enclosed in brackets when they are referenced in a statement—for example, [STUDYSQL\Paul].

Example 1

In this example, SELECT permissions are given to the orders role, and additional permissions are given to a few users. These users (Eva, Ivan, and David) then have all permissions on the Products table because they are also members of the orders role. (Do not try to perform these examples on your SQL Server. You will perform practical exercises using roles later in the chapter.)

```
USE Northwind
GRANT SELECT
ON Products
TO orders
GO

GRANT INSERT, UPDATE, DELETE
ON Products
TO Eva, Ivan, David
GO
```

Figure 12.3 shows how the Object Properties dialog box looks after the permissions in this example have been assigned.

Example 2

This example demonstrates how to grant CREATE DATABASE permissions.

```
USE master
GRANT CREATE DATABASE
TO Eva, Ivan, [STUDYSQL\Paul]
```

Figure 12.4 shows how the Permissions tab of the Master Properties dialog box looks after the permission in this example has been assigned.

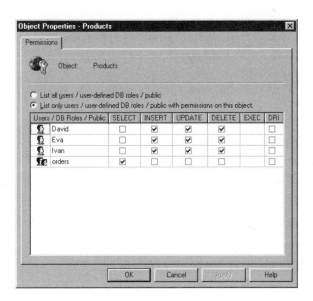

Figure 12.3 The Object Properties dialog box for the Products table after permissions have been granted

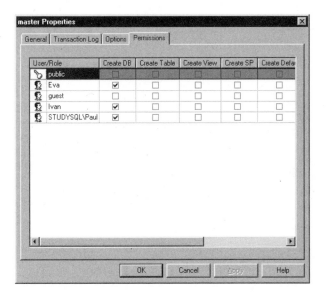

Figure 12.4 The Permissions tab of the Master Properties dialog box after CREATE DATABASE permission has been granted

Example 3

This example demonstrates how to grant CREATE TABLE permissions.

```
USE Northwind
GRANT CREATE TABLE
TO Eva, Ivan, [STUDYSQL\Paul]
```

Figure 12.5 shows the Permissions tab of the Northwind Properties dialog box after the permission in this example has been assigned.

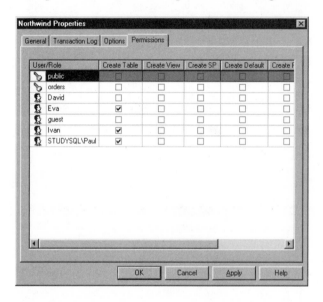

Figure 12.5   The Permissions tab of the Northwind Properties dialog box after CREATE TABLE permission has been granted

Exercise: Granting Statement Permissions

In this exercise, you will grant statement permissions. You will allow the user Cathy to create views and stored procedures. You will find the script for this exercise in C:\Sqladmin\Exercise\Ch12\StGrant.sql.

▶ **To grant statement permissions**

1. Log on to Windows NT as Administrator or another account that is a member of the local Administrators group.

2. Start SQL Server Query Analyzer, and connect with Microsoft Windows NT authentication.

   You are connected as a member of the System Administrators (sysadmin) role.

3. Execute the following statements to allow Cathy to create views and stored procedures.

```
USE StudyNwind
GRANT CREATE VIEW, CREATE PROCEDURE
TO Cathy
```

4. From SQL Server Enterprise Manager, verify the permissions granted to Cathy. You can see these permissions by right-clicking the StudyNwind database and selecting Properties. In the Properties dialog box, select the Permissions tab.

Exercise: Testing the Statement Permissions

In this exercise, you will test the statement permissions assigned to Cathy in the previous exercise. You will find the script for this exercise in C:\Sqladmin\ Exercise\Ch12\TestStat.sql.

▶ **To test the statement permissions**

1. Open a new query window and connect with SQL Server authentication as Cathy with the password **password**.

2. Execute the following SQL statements to create a view:

```
USE StudyNwind
GO
CREATE VIEW test_view as
SELECT firstname, lastname
FROM Employees
```

Were you able to create the view?

3. Execute a CREATE TABLE statement:

```
USE StudyNwind
CREATE TABLE testtable
(column1 INT NOT NULL,
column2 CHAR(10) NOT NULL)
```

Did the statement execute successfully? Why or why not?

Exercise: Granting Object Permissions

In this exercise, you will grant object permissions. Use the information in the following table to complete this exercise. You will find the script for this exercise in C:\Sqladmin\Exercise\Ch12\ObjGrant.sql.

Role	Object	Permissions to assign
Public	Categories table	GRANT ALL
Public	Products table	GRANT ALL

▶ **To grant object permissions**

1. Switch to SQL Server Query Analyzer, and close all query windows.

2. Open a new query window, and connect with Windows NT authentication.

   You are connected as a member of the System Administrators (sysadmin) role.

3. Execute the following Transact-SQL statements to implement the permissions listed in the preceding table:

```
USE StudyNwind
GRANT ALL ON Categories TO public
GRANT ALL ON Products TO public
```

4. Verify the permissions that have been granted in SQL Server Enterprise Manager. To see these permissions, right-click the Categories or Products table in the Enterprise Manager and select Properties. In the Properties dialog box, click the Permissions button.

Exercise: Testing the Object Permissions

In this exercise, you will log on as different users to test the permissions of users and roles. You will find the script for this exercise in C:\Sqladmin\Exercise\Ch12\TestObj.sql.

▶ **To test the object permissions**

1. Switch to SQL Server Query Analyzer, and close all query windows.

2. Open a new query window and, using SQL Server authentication, connect as Carl with the password **password**.

   Remember that Carl is a member of the Cust_Mgmt and db_datareader roles.

3. Execute each of the following Transact-SQL statements to test permissions for Carl:

```
USE StudyNwind
SELECT * FROM Customers
SELECT * FROM Categories
SELECT * FROM Products
SELECT * FROM Orders
```

Which tables can Carl query? Which tables is he not able to query? Why?

4. Open a new query window and, by using SQL Server authentication, connect as Umberto with the password **password**.

5. Execute each of the following Transact-SQL statements to test permissions for Umberto:

```
USE StudyNwind
SELECT * FROM Customers
SELECT * FROM Categories
SELECT * FROM Products
SELECT * FROM Orders
```

Which tables can Umberto query? Which tables is he not able to query? Why?

Denying Permissions

You occasionally may want to limit the permissions of a certain user or role by denying permissions to that security account. Denying permissions on a security account does the following:

- Negates the permissions that were previously granted to the user or role
- Deactivates permissions that are inherited from another role
- Ensures that a user or role does not inherit permissions from any other role in the future

Consider the following facts when you deny permissions:

- You can deny permissions in the current database only.
- Permission to deny permissions defaults to members of the sysadmin, db_owner, and db_securityadmin roles and to object owners.

Use SQL Server Enterprise Manager or the DENY statement to deny permissions. The syntax for the DENY statement for statement permissions is as follows:

```
DENY {ALL | statement[,…n]}
TO security_account[,…n]
```

The syntax for the DENY statement for object permissions is as follows:

```
DENY {ALL [PRIVILEGES] | permission[,…n]}
    {
        [(column[,…n])] ON { table | view}
        | ON {table | view} [( column[,…n])]
        | {procedure | extended_procedure}
    }
TO security_account
```

Example 4

In this example, SELECT permissions are granted to the orders role. SELECT, INSERT, and UPDATE permissions are then denied for a few users that are members of the role. These users (Eva, Ivan, and David) cannot have these forms of access to the Products table, even though the SELECT permission was granted to the orders role.

```
USE Northwind
GO

GRANT SELECT
ON Products
TO orders
GO

DENY SELECT, INSERT, UPDATE
ON Products
TO Eva, Ivan, David
```

Figure 12.6 shows the Properties dialog box for the Products table after the permissions in this example have been assigned.

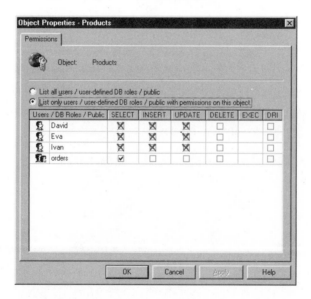

Figure 12.6   The Object Properties dialog box for the Products table after permissions have been denied

Example 5

This example denies users Eva, Ivan, and STUDYSQL\Paul the ability to create databases.

```
USE master
DENY CREATE DATABASE
TO Eva, Ivan, [STUDYSQL\Paul]
```

Figure 12.7 shows the Permissions tab of the Master Properties dialog box after the permission in this example has been assigned.

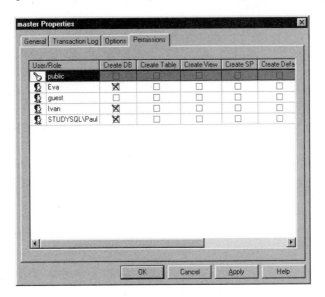

Figure 12.7   The Permissions tab of the Master Properties dialog box after CREATE DATABASE permission has been denied

Example 6

This example denies users Eva, Ivan, and STUDYSQL\Paul the ability to create tables.

```
USE Northwind
DENY CREATE TABLE
TO Eva, Ivan, [STUDYSQL\Paul]
```

Figure 12.8 shows the Permissions tab of the Northwind Properties dialog box after the permission in this example has been assigned.

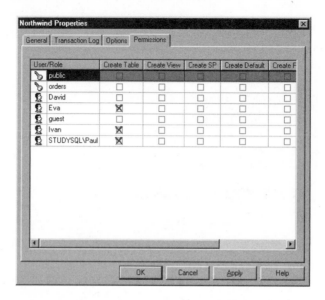

Figure 12.8   The Permissions tab of the Northwind Properties dialog box after CREATE TABLE permission has been denied

Exercise: Denying Object Permissions

In this exercise, you will deny object permissions. Use the information in the following table to complete this exercise. You will find the script for this exercise in C:\Sqladmin\Exercise\Ch12\ObjDeny.sql.

Role	Object	Permissions to assign
Cust_Mgmt	Customers table	DENY ALL
Public	Categories table	DENY ALL

▶   **To deny object permissions**

1. Switch to SQL Server Query Analyzer, and close all query windows.

2. Open a new query window, and connect with Windows NT authentication.

    You are connected as a member of the System Administrators (sysadmin) role.

3. Execute the following Transact-SQL statements to implement the permissions that are listed in the preceding table:

```
USE StudyNwind
DENY ALL ON Customers TO Cust_Mgmt
DENY ALL ON Categories TO public
```

4. Verify the permissions that have been granted in SQL Server Enterprise Manager. To see these permissions, right-click the Customers or Categories table in the Enterprise Manager and select Properties. In the Properties dialog box, click the Permissions button.

Exercise: Testing the Object Permissions

In this exercise, you will log on as different users to test the permissions of users and roles. You will find the script for this exercise in C:\SqladminExercise\Ch12\ TestObj.sql.

▶ **To test the object permissions**

1. Switch to SQL Server Query Analyzer, and close all query windows.

2. Open a new query window and, using SQL Server authentication, connect as Carl with the password **password**.

   Remember that Carl is a member of the Cust_Mgmt and db_datareader roles.

3. Execute each of the following Transact-SQL statements to test permissions for Carl:

```
USE StudyNwind
SELECT * FROM Customers
SELECT * FROM Categories
SELECT * FROM Products
SELECT * FROM Orders
```

   Which tables can Carl query? Which tables is he not able to query? Why?

4. Open a new query window and, by using SQL Server authentication, connect as Umberto with the password **password**.

5. Execute each of the following Transact-SQL statements to test permissions for Umberto:

```
USE StudyNwind
SELECT * FROM Customers
SELECT * FROM Categories
SELECT * FROM Products
SELECT * FROM Orders
```

   Which tables can Umberto query? Which tables is he not able to query? Why?

Revoking Granted and Denied Permissions

You can deactivate a granted or denied permission by revoking it. Revoking is similar to denying permissions in that both actions remove a granted permission. The difference is that while revoking a permission removes a granted permission, it does not prevent the user or role from inheriting that permission in the future.

You can also remove a previously denied permission by revoking the DENY statement for the permission.

Consider the following facts when you revoke permissions:

- You can revoke permissions in the current database only.
- Revoking a permission removes the entries in the sysprotects system table that were created by granting and denying the permission.
- Permission to revoke permissions defaults to members of the sysadmin, db_owner, and db_securityadmin roles and to object owners.

You can use SQL Server Enterprise Manager or the REVOKE statement to remove a previously granted or denied permission.

The syntax for the REVOKE statement for statement permissions is as follows:

```
REVOKE {ALL | statement[,…n]}
FROM security_account[,…n]
```

The syntax for the REVOKE statement for object permissions is as follows:

```
REVOKE [GRANT OPTION FOR]
{ALL [PRIVILEGES] | permission[,…n]}
    {
        {[(column[,…n])] ON {table | view}
        | {procedure | extended_procedure}
    }
FROM security_account[,…n]
[AS {group | role}]
```

Example 7

This example revokes multiple statement permissions from multiple users.

```
USE Northwind
REVOKE SELECT, INSERT, UPDATE
```

```
ON Products
FROM Eva, Ivan
```

Figure 12.9 shows the Products Object Properties dialog box after the permissions in this example have been assigned.

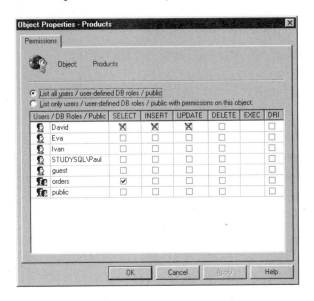

Figure 12.9   The Object Properties dialog box for the Products table after permissions have been revoked

Example 8

This example revokes the CREATE TABLE permissions granted to the user Eva. It removes the permissions that allowed Eva to create a table through her user account; however, she still can create tables if CREATE TABLE permissions have been granted to any roles of which she is a member.

```
USE Northwind
REVOKE CREATE TABLE FROM Eva
```

Figure 12.10 shows the Permissions tab of the Northwind Properties dialog box after the permission in this example has been assigned.

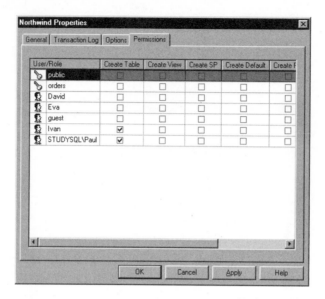

Figure 12.10 The Permissions tab of the Northwind Properties dialog box after CREATE TABLE permission has been revoked

When a Revoke Is Not a Revoke

Because a revoke will remove previously granted or denied permissions, the result of a revoke may be that an account no longer has permissions, or it may be that an account now has permissions. For this reason, you must carefully consider the result of revoking or denying permissions. The following example illustrates this somewhat confusing behavior. Assume that User is a member of role A.

1. Permission is granted to role A—User has permissions based on membership in role A.

2. Permission is denied to User—User has no permissions. The deny for User overrides the grant from role A.

3. Permission is revoked from User—User *has* permissions because the *denied* permission is revoked and User now goes back to having permission based on membership in role A.

4. Permission is revoked from role A—User has *no* permissions because the *granted* permission is revoked from the role from which User was getting permissions.

Exercise: Revoking Object Permissions

In this exercise, you will revoke object permissions. Use the information in the following table to complete this exercise. You will find the script for this exercise in C:\Sqladmin\Exercise\Ch12\ObjRevk.sql.

Role	Object	Permissions to assign
Cust_Mgmt	Customers table	REVOKE ALL
Public	Categories table	REVOKE ALL
Public	Products table	REVOKE ALL

▶ **To revoke object permissions**

1. Switch to SQL Server Query Analyzer, and close all query windows.
2. Open a new query window, and connect with Windows NT authentication.

   You are connected as a member of the System Administrators (sysadmin) role.
3. Execute the following Transact-SQL statements to implement the permissions that are listed in the table:

```
USE StudyNwind
REVOKE ALL ON Customers FROM Cust_Mgmt
REVOKE ALL ON Categories FROM public
REVOKE ALL ON Products FROM public
```

Exercise: Testing the Object Permissions

In this exercise, you will log on as different users to test the permissions of users and roles. You will find the script for this exercise in C:\Sqladmin\Exercise\Ch12\TestObj.sql.

▶ **To test the object permissions**

1. Switch to SQL Server Query Analyzer, and close all query windows.
2. Open a new query window and, using SQL Server authentication, connect as Carl with the password **password**.

   Remember that Carl is a member of the Cust_Mgmt and db_datareader roles.

3. Execute each of the following Transact-SQL statements to test permissions for Carl:

```
USE StudyNwind
SELECT * FROM Customers
SELECT * FROM Categories
SELECT * FROM Products
SELECT * FROM Orders
```

Which tables can Carl query? Which tables is he not able to query? Why?

4. Open a new query window and, by using SQL Server authentication, connect as Umberto with the password **password**.

5. Execute each of the following Transact-SQL statements to test permissions for Umberto:

```
USE StudyNwind
SELECT * FROM Customers
SELECT * FROM Categories
SELECT * FROM Products
SELECT * FROM Orders
```

Which tables can Umberto query? Which tables is he not able to query? Why?

Lesson Summary

Permissions can be granted, revoked, and denied at the user or role level. Permissions granted specifically to a user must be revoked specifically from that user. The DENY statement overrides all other statements.

Lesson 3: Planning Security

This lesson looks at creating a plan to allow appropriate user access to resources. It also discusses default logins and roles and their use in this plan.

After this lesson, you will be able to

- Describe the goals of security planning
- Describe five common considerations when creating a security plan

Estimated lesson time: 15minutes

Goals in Creating a Security Plan

The goals in creating a security plan are as follows:

- List all of the items and activities in the database that must be controlled through security.
- Identify the individuals and groups in the company.
- Cross-reference the two lists to identify which users can see what data and perform what activities in the database.

This lesson introduces five common considerations that can help you create your security plan.

Determine the Use of Default Logins

In creating a security plan, you need to determine how or whether you will use the sa or BUILTIN\Administrators logins.

The sa Login

Although sa is a built-in administrator login, it should not be used routinely. Instead, system administrators should be members of the sysadmin fixed server role and should log on with their own logins. The sa login cannot be dropped or disabled. Log on as sa if you inadvertently remove all members of sysadmin.

Tip When SQL Server is installed, the sa login is not assigned a password. It is recommended that you change the password immediately to prevent unauthorized access to SQL Server with the sa login. Store the password in a safe place!

The BUILTIN\Administrators Login

The local Windows NT group Administrators is automatically mapped to the SQL Server BUILTIN\Administrators login. By default, BUILTIN\Administrators is a member of the sysadmin role.

If you do not want all Windows NT administrators in your organization to have complete access to your SQL Server, you can remove the BUILTIN\Administrators login or remove the login from the sysadmin role. You can replace the login and assign permissions to it if you later decide that you do want to use it.

Another method of limiting the BUILTIN\Administrators login is to remove the Domain Admins global group from the local Administrators group in Windows NT.

Determine public Role Permissions

The public role is a special database role to which every database user belongs. It controls the permissions that all users have by default in each database. You should carefully consider which permissions the public role will have in each database; by default, the public role has no permissions.

Determine the Function of the guest User Account

The guest user account allows a login without a user account to gain access to a database. You should decide whether your databases will have a guest account and, if so, what permissions the guest account should have in your databases. New databases do not have a user called guest. If you wish to enable the guest user in a database, you must add it to the database using SQL Server Enterprise Manager or sp_grantdbaccess. When you add a user called guest to a database with SQL Server Enterprise Manager, you do not have to specify a login name because the guest user is a special user not associated with a login. When you add a user called guest to a database with sp_grantdbaccess, you must specify guest as the login name and as the name in the database.

Map Logins to User Accounts and Roles

Before assigning logins to a database, decide whether you will use user accounts or roles to apply permissions. In general, the following mappings are recommended:

- If members of a Windows NT group are the only ones who perform a series of tasks, create a user account for the group and apply permissions to it.
- If more than one login will perform a group of tasks, create a role and assign the login to the role.
- If a login will perform common administrative tasks, map the login to the appropriate fixed server or database role.

Create Objects with Owner dbo

It is very important to determine which users and roles can create objects in a database. In general, it is recommended that only the sysadmin, db_owner, and db_ddladmin fixed database roles be permitted to create database objects.

It is further recommended that all objects be defined with the dbo user specified as the object owner. Defining objects with dbo as the owner enables any user in the database to refer to the object without including the owner name. Any object created from the sysadmin role has dbo as the owner. From any other role, always specify the dbo user as the owner name when you create the object; otherwise, the object will be created with your user name as the object owner.

Changing Object Owners

If objects were not created with the dbo user as the object owner, you can change the object owner with the sp_changeobjectowner system stored procedure as follows:

```
sp_changeobjectowner [@objname =] 'object' ,[@newowner =] 'owner'
```

Consider the following facts about changing database object owners:

- Only members of the db_owner and db_ddladmin fixed database roles and members of the securityadmin server role can change database object owners.

- Scripts and batch files that included the old owner name in references to the object need to be updated manually. SQL Server cannot perform this update automatically.

Lesson Summary

A security plan looks at the items and activities in a database and the individuals and groups in the company. It cross-references the two, determining who needs access to resources. When creating a security plan, it is important to look at built-in logins, such as sa, and roles, such as db_owner, and decide how they will be used.

Lesson 4: Managing Application Security

You have learned how to control access to a database using login authentication and permissions. You may also wish to secure access to databases at the application level. SQL Server provides views, stored procedures, and application roles to support application-level security.

After this lesson, you will be able to

- Describe the use of views and stored procedures to provide application-level security

- Describe the use of application roles to provide application-level security

Estimated lesson time: 60 minutes

Managing Security with Views and Stored Procedures

Views and stored procedures provide a secondary method of giving users access to data and the ability to perform activities in a database. They allow you to set up security with SQL Server objects that are created for an application.

Views and stored procedures enable you to manage the permissions for the view or stored procedure only, rather than the permissions for the objects to which they refer. They also shield users from changes to the underlying tables.

Using Views to Simplify Security

You can use views to prevent users from knowing that there are certain columns to which they do not have access in a table.

Tip You could also restrict access to certain columns using column permissions. However, views are easier to manage and give better performance.

Grant permissions on a view to users without granting permissions on the underlying tables. The users can then use the view despite having no access to the underlying tables, thus protecting the underlying tables.

For example, the Salary column in a table contains confidential employee information, but the rest of the columns contain information to which users must have access. You can define a view that includes all of the columns in the table with the exception of the Salary column. As long as the table and the view have the same owner, granting SELECT permissions on the view allows users to view nonconfidential columns without permissions to the table itself.

Example 1

This example creates a view that retrieves employee information from the Employees table but excludes a column with confidential data. Figure 12.11 shows how the view is used to permit an end user to see only some of the information in the underlying table. The end user has no permissions to use the underlying table.

```
CREATE VIEW Employee_View
AS
SELECT EmpID, FirstName, LastName, DOB
FROM Employees
```

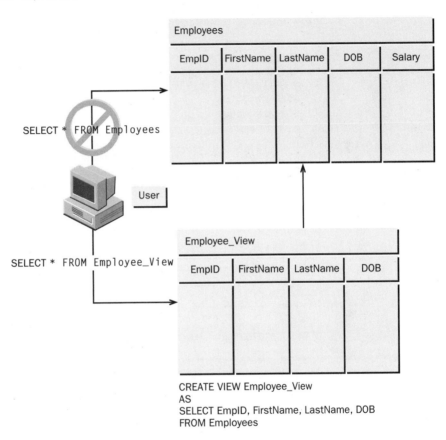

CREATE VIEW Employee_View
AS
SELECT EmpID, FirstName, LastName, DOB
FROM Employees

Figure 12.11   Using a view to prevent users from seeing all of the columns in a table

Using Stored Procedures to Simplify Security

Grant users permissions to execute a stored procedure without granting them access to the tables that are read or modified. Then only applications that are written to execute the stored procedure will be able to gain access to the data.

In an archiving scenario, data that is older than a specified interval is copied into an archive table and then deleted from the primary table. Permissions can be used to prevent users from deleting rows from the primary table directly or from inserting rows into the archive table. You can create a stored procedure to ensure that both activities are performed together, and then you can grant permissions to users to execute the stored procedure.

Example 2

This example creates a stored procedure that can be used to insert a row into the Employees table. Figure 12.12 shows a user who has permission to execute a stored procedure to insert data into a table. The user does not have permission to insert data directly into the table.

```
CREATE PROCEDURE Insert_Emp
    @EmpID int,
    @FirstName varchar(30),
    @LastName varchar(30),
    @DOB datetime,
    @Salary money
AS
INSERT Employees
VALUES (@EmpID, @FirstName, @LastName, @DOB, @Salary)
```

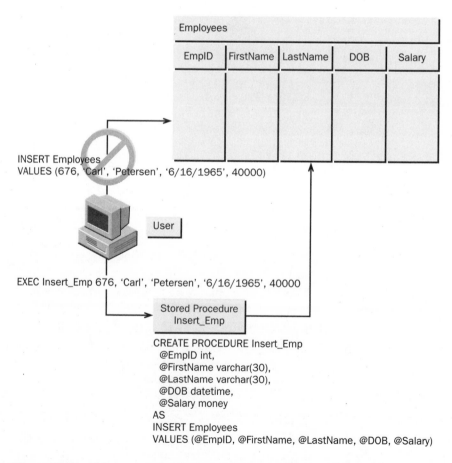

Figure 12.12   Using a stored procedure to insert a row into a table

The following query executes the stored procedure.

```
EXEC Insert_Emp 676, 'Carl', 'Petersen', '6/16/1965', 40000
```

Exercise: Using a View or Stored Procedure to Implement Permissions

In this exercise, you will create a view called Employee_View and a stored procedure called Employee_Proc. You then will grant the public role permissions on Employee_View and Employee_Proc. You will find the script for this exercise in C:\Sqladmin\Exercise\Ch12\CrVwSP.sql.

▶ **To use a view or stored procedure to implement permissions**

1. Switch to SQL Server Query Analyzer, close all query windows, and log on with Microsoft Windows NT authentication.

    You should be connected as a member of the sysadmin role.

2. Execute the following statement to create a view on the Employees table that includes only the FirstName, LastName, and Title columns:

    ```
    USE StudyNwind
    GO
    CREATE VIEW Employee_View AS
    SELECT FirstName, LastName, Title
    FROM Employees
    ```

3. Execute the following statement to create a stored procedure that queries the FirstName, LastName, and Title columns of the Employees table:

    ```
    USE StudyNwind
    GO
    CREATE PROCEDURE Employee_Proc AS
    SELECT FirstName, LastName, Title
    FROM Employees
    ```

4. Execute the following statements to allow the public role to select from Employee_View and to execute Employee_Proc:

    ```
    USE StudyNwind
    GRANT SELECT ON Employee_View TO public
    GRANT EXEC ON Employee_Proc TO public
    ```

Exercise: Testing Permissions on the View and Stored Procedure

In this exercise, you will query data from the Employee_View view and execute the Employee_Proc stored procedure. You will then attempt to query the Employees table directly. You will find the script for this exercise in C:\Sqladmin\Exercise\Ch12\TstVwSP.sql.

▶ **To test the permissions on the view and stored procedure**

1. Switch to SQL Server Query Analyzer, and close all query windows.

2. Open a new query window and, using SQL Server authentication, connect as Umberto with the password **password**.

   Umberto does not belong to any database or server roles and has no specific permissions other than those that are associated with the public role.

3. Execute the following statement to query the Employee_View view:

   ```
   SELECT * FROM Employee_View
   ```

   Were you able to query the view? Why or why not?

4. Execute the Employee_Proc stored procedure:

   ```
   EXEC Employee_Proc
   ```

   Were you able to execute the stored procedure? Why or why not?

5. Execute the following statement to query the Employees table:

   ```
   SELECT * FROM Employees
   ```

   Were you able to query the table? Why or why not?

Managing Security with Application Roles

Application roles allow you to enforce security for a particular application. By using application roles, you can ensure that users gain access to data through specific applications only.

Figure 12.13 shows how you might want order entry clerks to be able to update the Orders table when they use the order entry application. You do not want the clerks to be able to gain access to the tables from another product, such as Microsoft Excel. In this situation, you could create an application role for the order entry application.

Application roles differ from other roles. The following lists the fundamental differences between application roles and other roles:

- Application roles have no members—a user uses an application that activates an application role. The role then controls all database access for the user's connection. The user thus gains permissions when using the application. This avoids the need to grant permissions to users directly.

- Application roles require a password to be activated.

- To protect the security of the application role password, you may want to use a simple encrypted key. You could also use an extended stored procedure to store the password at the server so that it is not transmitted across the network.

- An activated application role overrides the user's other permissions in the database. SQL Server temporarily ignores all permissions that are applied to the user account or to other roles to which the user belongs.

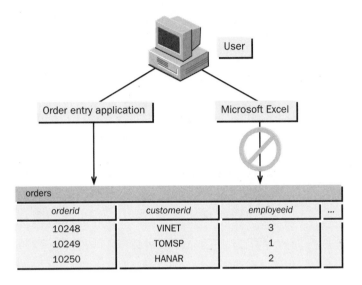

Figure 12.13   Using application roles to control application access

Creating Application Roles

Use SQL Server Enterprise Manager or the sp_addapprole system stored procedure to create a new application role. Only members of the db_owner, db_securityadmin, and sysadmin roles can execute the sp_addapprole system stored procedure. The syntax for the sp_addapprole system stored procedure in this case is as follows:

```
sp_addapprole [@rolename =] 'role', [@password =] 'password'
```

Consider the following facts when you create new application roles:

- The sp_addapprole system stored procedure adds a security account for the new role by adding a record to the sysusers table in the current database.

- The *password* value is the password that is required to activate the role, and it is stored in encrypted form.

Example 3

This example adds the new application role SalesApp to the current database with the password hg_7532LR.

```
EXEC sp_addapprole SalesApp, hg_7532LR
```

Exercise: Defining an Application Role

In this exercise, you will define an application role called Order_Entry in the StudyNwind database, using SQL Server Enterprise Manager. This process is very similar to creating a database role, with the exception that you do not define any members.

▶ **To define an application role**

1. Log on to your computer as Administrator or another account that is a member of the local Administrators group.
2. Start SQL Server Enterprise Manager.
3. Expand your server group, and then expand your server.
4. Expand Databases, and then expand the StudyNwind database.
5. Right-click Roles, and then click New Database Role.
6. Type **Order_Entry** for the name of the new role.
7. Click Application Role, and type **password** for the password.
8. Click OK to close the dialog box and create the new role.

Managing Application Role Permissions

Use SQL Server Enterprise Manager or the GRANT, DENY, and REVOKE statements in Transact-SQL to manage application role permissions.

Example 4

This example grants SELECT permissions for the Products table to the SalesApp application role.

```
GRANT SELECT
ON Products
TO SalesApp
```

Exercise: Assigning Permissions to an Application Role

In this exercise, you will assign permissions to the Order_Entry application role. The following table lists the permissions that must be assigned to Order_Entry.

Table	Permissions
Categories	SELECT
Customers	SELECT, INSERT, UPDATE
Order Details	SELECT, INSERT, UPDATE
Orders	SELECT, INSERT, UPDATE
Products	SELECT

► **To assign permissions to an application role**

1. Using SQL Server Enterprise Manager, select the Roles folder in the StudyNwind database.

2. Right-click the Order_Entry application role, and then click Properties.

3. Click Permissions.

4. In the list of objects, check each of the permissions shown in the table at the beginning of the exercise.

5. Click OK twice to close the dialog boxes and accept the permission assignments you have made.

Activating Application Roles

After a client connects to SQL Server with any login account, the client application must execute the sp_setapprole system stored procedure to activate the permissions that are associated with an application role. The sp_setapprole stored procedure can be executed by direct Transact-SQL statements only; it cannot be executed within another stored procedure or from within a user-defined transaction.

The syntax for the sp_setapprole procedure is as follows:

```
sp_setapprole [@rolename =] 'name' ,
[@password =] {Encrypt N 'password'} | 'password'
[,[@encrypt =] 'encrypt_style']
```

Consider the following facts when you activate application roles:

- The current application must provide the password.

- The scope of an application role is the current database only; if users change to another database, they are allowed to perform activities based on the permissions in that database.

- After an application role is activated with the sp_setapprole system stored procedure, the role cannot be deactivated in the current database until the user disconnects from SQL Server.

Example 5

This example activates the SalesApp application role with a password of hg_7532LR.

```
EXEC sp_setapprole 'SalesApp',' hg_7532LR'
```

Example 6

The following example shows how to set an application role from a Microsoft Visual Basic application that uses ActiveX Data Objects (ADO).

```
' Set up a connection
Dim cnADO As ADODB.Connection
Dim strConnect As String

Set cnADO = New ADODB.Connection
strConnect = "driver={SQL Server};" _
 & "uid=Carl;pwd=password;server=sqlserver;database=StudyNwind"
cnADO.Provider = "MSDASQL"
cnADO.ConnectionString = strConnect
cnADO.CursorLocation = adUseNone
cnADO.Open

' Carl is connected using permissions assigned to his account
' or any roles or Windows NT groups to which he belongs


' Initialize variables for the application role
Dim cmADO As ADODB.Command
Dim pmADO As ADODB.Parameter
Dim strRoleName AS String
Dim strRolePass AS String

Set cmADO = New ADODB.Command

' Set values for the role name and password
strRoleName = "SalesApp"
strRolePass = "hg_7532LR"

' Define the command and type (stored procedure)
With cmADO
    .CommandText = "sp_setapprole"
    .CommandType = adCmdStoredProc
End With

' Set up parameters for role name and password
Set pmADO = cmADO.CreateParameter("rolename", _
 adVarChar, adParamInput, Len(strRoleName), strRoleName)
cmADO.Parameters.Append pmADO
Set pmADO = cmADO.CreateParameter("password", _
 adVarChar, adParamInput, Len(strRolePass), strRolePass)
cmADO.Parameters.Append pmADO

' Execute the command to activate the application role
cmADO.ActiveConnection = cnADO
cmADO.Execute

' Now the application role is active for this connection
' and Carl has only the permissions assigned to the
' application role SalesApp
```

Exercise: Activating an Application Role

In this exercise, you will use SQL Server Query Analyzer to log on as a user and activate the Order_Entry application role. You will find the script for this exercise in C:\Sqladmin\Exercise\Ch12\ActApp.sql.

▶ **To activate an application role**

1. Open SQL Server Query Analyzer and, by using SQL Server authentication, connect as Carl with the password **password**.

2. Execute the sp_setapprole system stored procedure to activate the role:

```
EXEC sp_setapprole 'Order_Entry', 'password'
```

3. Execute SELECT statements to query the Employees and Customers tables.

```
SELECT * FROM Employees
SELECT * FROM Customers
```

   What permissions does Carl have after the Order_Entry application role is activated?

   How long will the Order_Entry role be activated for Carl?

4. Close the query window to end the session. This will deactivate the Order_Entry role for Carl.

The following table lists additional system stored procedures that you can use for managing application roles.

System stored procedure	Description
sp_dropapprole	Drops an application role from the current database
sp_approlepassword	Changes the password for an application role

Lesson Summary

SQL Server provides views, stored procedures, and application roles to support application-level security. You can use views to limit columns or rows accessed by users. Stored procedures can be used to access data. Users needing access to the data can be given access only to the stored procedure. An application role is a role that has no members—a user uses an application that activates an application role. The role then controls all database access for the user's connection. The user thus gains permissions when using the application. This avoids the need to grant permissions to users directly.

Review

The following questions are intended to reinforce key information presented in the chapter. If you are unable to answer a question, review the appropriate lesson and then try the question again. Answers to the questions can be found in Appendix A, "Questions and Answers."

1. When should you assign permissions to a login account directly?

2. When should you avoid using the sa login?

3. If permissions to update a table are granted to a user, but the permissions were denied to a role in which the user has membership, does the security account retain permissions to update the table?

CHAPTER 13

Automating Administrative Tasks

About This Chapter

Much of the work involved with running Microsoft SQL Server is repetitive maintenance and responding to the ongoing demands of the server. SQL Server 7 provides advanced tools for automatically performing this work, alerting you to problems as they occur and responding automatically to problems. This chapter explains how these tools are implemented and teaches you how to use them.

Before You Begin

To complete the lessons in this chapter, you must have

- Installed SQL Server 7. See Chapter 2, "Installation," for installation instructions.

- The ability to log on to SQL Server as an Administrator.

- Installed the Exercise files from the Supplemental Course Materials CD-ROM to your hard disk drive. See the "Getting Started" section in "About This Book" for installation instructions.

- Installed the StudyNwind database. See the "Getting Started" section in "About This Book" for StudyNwind database installation instructions.

Lesson 1: Introduction to SQL Server Automated Administration

SQL Server provides many options for automating routine administrative tasks. This lesson discusses the benefits of automating administration, the SQL Server components that enable automated administration, and how to prepare your server for automated administration.

After this lesson, you will be able to

- Explain how the components of SQL Server automated administration interact
- Explain how jobs and alerts are processed
- Configure SQL Server Agent to use a MAPI client to send e-mail messages

Estimated lesson time: 75 minutes

Reasons to Automate

Automating routine maintenance tasks on your local server or in a multiserver environment allows you to spend time on other database administrative functions that lack predictable responses. Another benefit of automated administration is the ability to configure your server to recognize and respond to potential problems.

Performing Regularly Scheduled Tasks

You perform several maintenance and administrative tasks routinely on SQL Server, such as

- Backing up databases
- Transferring data
- Maintaining indexes

You can automate these tasks to occur on a regular schedule. For example, you can define index maintenance tasks to occur on the first Sunday of every month.

Recognizing and Responding to Potential Problems

SQL Server allows you to be proactive and prepare for potential problems by

- Responding to SQL Server errors. You can define a job to correct a given problem. For example, error number 9002 indicates that the transaction log is full. You can define a job that, when error number 9002 is raised, executes a Transact-SQL statement to back up and truncate the transaction log.

- Defining performance conditions that monitor potential problems. For example, you can define SQL Server Agent to detect when locks are blocking users from modifying data and automatically notify a system administrator that a particular user is causing the locks that are blocking the data.

Before you automate tasks, it is important to consider the fundamentals of preparing for and performing SQL Server automated administration.

For a video demonstration that covers automating administration tasks, run the Auto.htm file located in the \Media folder on the Supplemental Course Materials CD-ROM.

Components of SQL Server Automated Administration

Components of SQL Server automated administration include the SQL Server SQLServerAgent and MSSQLServer services and the Microsoft Windows NT EventLog service. As Figure 13.1 illustrates, these services work together to allow automated administration. The term *administrative task* refers generically to activities that system administrators or database owners perform.

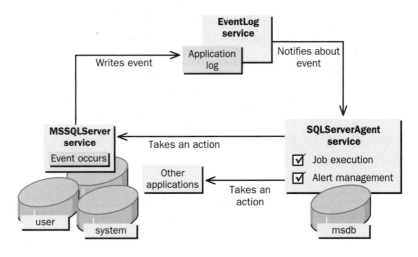

Figure 13.1   Components of SQL Server automated administration

Note SQL Server Agent was called SQL Server Executive in previous versions of SQL Server.

The SQLServerAgent Service

When the SQLServerAgent service starts, it registers with the EventLog service and connects to the MSSQLServer service. This allows the EventLog service to notify the SQL Server Agent when events are written to the Windows NT application log. The SQLServerAgent service then reads the Windows NT application log to determine whether the event was generated by SQL Server and if so to determine whether there is a defined action to be taken in response to the event.

The SQLServerAgent service communicates with the MSSQLServer service to take action when an event occurs. Actions include executing jobs or firing alerts. These actions are defined in the msdb database. SQL Server Agent can also execute other applications.

The EventLog Service

The MSSQLServer service writes events to the Windows NT application log. An event is anything that happens within the system or application that requires attention. Events are written to the EventLog service by SQL Server when

- SQL Server errors with severity levels between 19 and 25 occur
- Error messages have been defined to be written to the Windows NT application log with the sp_addmessage or sp_altermessage system stored procedures
- The RAISERROR WITH LOG statement is executed
- The xp_logevent extended stored procedure is executed

Note Windows 95 and Windows 98 do not support services. When you run SQL Server on Windows 95 or Windows 98, SQL Server Profiler is used to monitor logged events and forward them to SQL Server Agent.

Processing Jobs and Alerts

Jobs and alerts are defined separately and can be executed or fired independently. A job is a maintenance or administrative task that consists of one or more steps. Jobs execute according to their defined schedules or in response to an alert. You can automate the process of recognizing and responding to potential problems by creating alerts. Alerts fire when SQL Server Agent is notified about events by the EventLog service or when SQL Server Agent receives performance data from the MSSQLServer service. Figure 13.2 illustrates how SQL Server processes jobs and alerts.

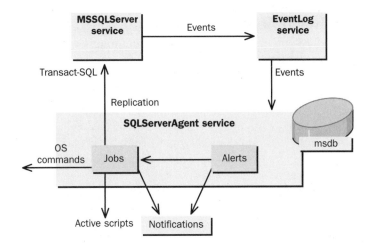

Figure 13.2   Processing jobs and alerts

Note Jobs were called tasks in previous versions of SQL Server.

Defining an Alert That Executes a Job

You will typically create an alert to notify an operator when an error occurs in a database or to execute a job in response to the fired alert. For example, you can create an alert that fires if a transaction log backup fails due to a tape device error. The alert executes a job that performs the backup to a disk device and notifies an operator.

Defining a Job That Executes Regularly

You can create a job that executes on a regular schedule and notifies an operator when it completes. For example, you can define a job to transfer data from another database into the Northwind database once a month. The job definition may include several steps: backing up the transaction log, transferring the data, and then backing up the database.

Other things you can define a job to do include

- Deleting itself when it completes, if it is a one-time action
- Notifying operators if any of the job steps fail to execute
- Writing the success or failure of the job to the Windows NT application log

Defining an Alert That May Fire While a Job Is Executing

Jobs and alerts complement one another because an alert may fire in response to an error that has occurred because a job step failed. The alert can in turn execute a job to correct the problem.

Preparing to Automate

Before you begin creating jobs and defining alerts, you should ensure that SQL Server Agent is running and has been set up properly. If you plan to notify operators by e-mail or pager, you should also configure a SQL Server Agent mail profile.

Ensure That SQL Server Agent Is Running

SQL Server Agent is a Windows NT service that must be running in order to execute jobs automatically and fire defined alerts. You should set up the SQLServerAgent service to start automatically whenever you start Windows NT.

Use an Appropriate SQL Server Agent User Account

When SQL Server is installed, a user account is specified in the startup properties of the SQLServerAgent service. SQL Server Agent can use either the local System account or a domain user account.

Using the local System account for SQL Server Agent allows the service access to the local computer only. A domain user account is required for SQL Server Agent to have permission to

- Communicate with most e-mail systems to send or receive e-mail
- Access resources across the network
- Perform SQL Server replication
- Execute multiserver administrative jobs

Configure a SQL Server Agent Mail Profile

If you plan to send notifications to operators using e-mail or pagers, you must

- Have a MAPI-1-compliant e-mail client
- Configure a mail profile for SQL Server Agent to use to establish a mail session with your messaging server

SQL Server Agent requires a profile in order to start a mail session and send notification by e-mail or pager. A SQL Server Agent mail session is started every time the SQLServerAgent service is started. You can create the profile with a mail client, such as Microsoft Outlook, that is installed locally on the SQL Server computer.

If Microsoft Exchange Server is used, a mail profile must be configured for the domain user account that SQL Server Agent uses.

For pager notifications, SQL Server Agent sends e-mail to your messaging server. On the messaging server, you must have third-party pager-to-e-mail software and/or hardware that converts the inbound e-mail into pager messages.

Sharing a Profile with SQL Mail

SQL Server uses two separate mail sessions:

- The MSSQLServer service uses a mail session that is referred to as SQL Mail.

  SQL Server uses this mail session when your database applications execute the xp_sendmail extended stored procedure to send a message or query result set to a recipient or when they execute the sp_processmail system stored procedure to process incoming mail.

- The SQLServerAgent service uses a mail session that is exclusive to SQL Server Agent activities.

If the SQLServerAgent and MSSQLServer services use the same Windows NT domain user account, by default they will use the same mail profile for SQL Server Agent and SQL Mail mail sessions. This allows both services to share a common mailbox.

Creating Separate Profiles

You can configure separate mailboxes for SQL Server and SQL Server Agent by creating separate mail profiles. There are two ways to accomplish this:

- Use separate domain user accounts for each service. This requires you to configure a mail profile for each user account.

- Use the same domain user account for each service and create multiple mail profiles.

Practice: Configuring Mail Profiles

In this practice, you will use Windows Messaging to configure the Microsoft Mail service and create profiles for the SQLService user account to enable SQL Server Agent and SQL Mail to send and receive messages. You will then create a profile for your administrative user account, to send and receive messages with Windows Messaging. Finally, you will use SQL Server Enterprise Manager to configure SQL Server Agent to use the mail profile that is configured for the SQLService user account. You will configure SQL Mail in Lesson 2.

Exercise 1: Configuring a Workgroup Postoffice and Adding Mailboxes

In this exercise you will configure a workgroup postoffice and add mailboxes to the newly created postoffice.

▶ **To configure a workgroup postoffice and add mailboxes to the postoffice**

1. Log on to your computer as Administrator.

2. Open Control Panel. If there is an icon for Microsoft Mail Postoffice, go to step 7.

3. Open Add/Remove Programs in the Control Panel.

4. On the Windows NT Setup tab, check Windows Messaging in the Components list.

5. Click OK to close the Add/Remove Programs dialog box. Follow the prompts to install Windows Messaging.

6. You may have to close and reopen Control Panel or select Refresh from the View menu before you see the Microsoft Mail Postoffice icon.

7. Double-click Microsoft Mail Postoffice in the Control Panel.

8. Select the Create A New Workgroup Postoffice radio button, and click Next.

9. Type **C:** in Postoffice Location, and click Next. Click Next again to confirm the new postoffice location.

10. Type **Admin** in Name and Mailbox. Click OK, and then click OK again.

11. Double-click Microsoft Mail Postoffice in the Control Panel.

12. Select the Administer An Existing Workgroup Postoffice option, and click Next. Click Next again to accept the postoffice location.

13. Type **Admin** in the Mailbox field and **password** in the Password field. Click Next.

14. In the Postoffice Manager, click Add User to add a new user to the workgroup postoffice.

15. Type **SQLAgent** in Name and Mailbox. Click OK.

16. Click Add User to add another new user to the workgroup postoffice.

17. Type **SQLMail** in Name and Mailbox. Click OK.

18. Click Close to close the Postoffice Manager.

Exercise 2: Configuring Profiles for the SQLService Account

In this exercise, you will configure profiles for the user account, SQLService.

▶   **To configure profiles for the SQLService account**

1. Log on to your computer with a user name of **SQLService** and a password of **password**, in the STUDYSQL domain.

2. Double-click Inbox on the desktop. Under Use The Following Information Services, check Microsoft Mail. Ensure that no other services are checked. Click Next. Click Next to confirm the postoffice path of C:\Wgpo0000.

3. In the list of mailbox names, select SQLAgent. Click Next.

4. Type **password** in Password, and click Next.

5. Click Next to accept the personal address book location.

6. Click Next to accept the personal folders location.

7. Click Next if you are prompted to do so to indicate that the Inbox should not be added to the Startup group.

8. Click Finish to complete the creation of the new profile and open the Inbox.

9. Close the Inbox – Windows Messaging application. (The application may be called Inbox – Microsoft Exchange.)

   You have now added a profile for SQL Server Agent to use. Next you will change the default name of this profile and add a profile for SQL Mail.

10. Double-click Mail in the Control Panel. (This icon may be labeled Mail And Fax.)

11. Click Show Profiles. One profile, called Windows Messaging Settings, is shown. Highlight Windows Messaging Settings, and click Copy. (If there is no profile called Windows Messaging Settings, copy the profile called MS Exchange Settings or the currently active profile.)

12. Type **SQLServerAgent Profile** in New Profile Name, and click OK.

13. Highlight SQLServerAgent Profile, and click Copy.

14. Type **SQLMail Profile** in New Profile Name, and click OK.

15. Highlight SQLMail Profile, and click Properties.

16. Highlight Microsoft Mail, and click Properties.

17. On the Logon tab, change the name in the Enter The Name Of Your Mailbox field to **SQLMail**. Click OK to close the Microsoft Mail dialog box, and then click OK to close the SQLMail Profile Properties dialog box.

18. Click Close to close the Mail dialog box.

19. Log off of Windows NT.

Exercise 3: Configuring a Profile for the Administrator Account

In this exercise, you will configure a profile for the Administrator user account.

▶ **To configure a profile for the Administrator account**

1. Log on to your computer as Administrator.

2. Double-click Inbox on the desktop. Under Use The Following Information Services, check Microsoft Mail. Ensure that no other services are checked. Click Next. Click Next to confirm the postoffice path of C:\Wgpo0000.

3. In the list of mailbox names, select Admin. Click Next.

4. Type **password** in Password, and click Next.

5. Click Next to accept the personal address book location.

6. Click Next to accept the personal folders location.

7. Click Next if you are prompted to do so to indicate that the Inbox should not be added to the Startup group.

8. Click Finish to complete the creation of the new profile, and open the Inbox.

9. On the Tools menu, click Services.

10. Highlight Microsoft Mail in the list of information services, and then click Properties.

11. On the Delivery tab of the Microsoft Mail dialog box, change the Check For New Mail Every option to 1 minute. Click OK twice to close the dialog boxes.

12. Leave the Inbox open, as you will begin receiving messages in the exercises that follow.

Exercise 4: Configuring SQL Server Agent to Use the Profile

In this exercise, you will use SQL Server Enterprise Manager to configure SQL Server Agent to start a mail session that uses the SQLServerAgent Profile profile.

▶   **To configure SQL Server Agent to use the mail profile**

1. In SQL Server Enterprise Manager, expand your server, and then expand Management.

2. In the console tree, right-click SQL Server Agent, and then click Properties.

3. In the Mail Profile drop-down list, select SQLServerAgent Profile.

4. Click Test.

   A message appears, indicating that the test was successful. Click OK to close the message.

5. Click OK to close the SQL Server Agent Properties dialog box.

   A message appears asking you if you want to restart SQL Server Agent so that the changes you have made will take effect. Click Yes. Click OK when the service has restarted.

6. In the console tree, right-click SQL Server Agent, and then click Display Error Log.

7. In the Type drop-down list, select All Types.

8. Verify that a mail session was established when SQL Server Agent was started.

Lesson Summary

Automating administration saves time and reduces errors that occur when a database administrator forgets to perform a task or is unavailable. SQL Server uses the SQLServerAgent service and the Windows NT application log to enable automated administration. If you intend to make full use of automated administration, you must ensure that the SQLServerAgent service is running, configure an account for the SQLServerAgent, and configure a SQL Server Agent mail profile.

Lesson 2: Automating Routine Maintenance Tasks

When you automate routine maintenance tasks, you typically use SQL Server Enterprise Manager to create operators and jobs. You can also use the Create Job Wizard, execute system stored procedures, or write your own administrative application using SQL-DMO. This lesson describes how to create operators, create and schedule jobs, and configure SQL Mail to send and receive e-mail messages.

After this lesson, you will be able to

- Create operators to notify when a job completes or when an alert is fired
- Understand the different types of job steps supported by SQL Server
- Create and schedule jobs
- Configure SQL Mail to send and receive e-mail messages

Estimated lesson time: 90 minutes

Creating Operators to Notify

When a job completes, you have several notification options. You can write to the Windows NT application log, delete the job, or notify an operator by pager, e-mail, or a net send command.

To define new operators, you can use SQL Server Enterprise Manager or execute the sp_add_operator system stored procedure. The operator definitions are stored in the msdb..sysoperators system table. When you create operators, consider the following facts and guidelines:

- You can use a group e-mail alias to notify more than one individual to respond to potential problems.
- You should test each notification method used to notify the operator to ensure that the operator is able to receive messages.
- You should specify an on-duty schedule for each operator to be notified by pager. If a job that is defined to notify an operator by pager conflicts with the operator's on-duty schedule, the notification fails.
- Use a Windows NT net send command to send messages to network operators. (This is not supported in Windows 95 and Windows 98.)

Troubleshooting Operator Notifications

For each operator, the date and time of the most recent attempts to send each type of notification (e-mail, pager, and net send command) are logged.

If an operator is not receiving notifications, you should

- Ensure that the operator is available to receive notifications
- Review the most recent notification attempts to determine the date and time of the last notification
- Test individual notification methods outside of SQL Server by verifying that you can send e-mail messages, page an operator, or successfully execute a net send command

Exercise: Creating an Operator

In this exercise, you will create an operator, send a message, and verify that the message was received.

▶ **To create an operator**

1. In the console tree, expand Management, and then expand SQL Server Agent.
2. Right-click Operators, and then click New Operator.
3. On the General tab, in Name, type the name **Admin**.
4. In Email Name, type the operator's mailbox address, **Admin**. (Or click the ellipsis button and add Admin from the address book.)
5. In Net Send Address, type the computer name **SQLServer** (or the name of your computer if it is not SQLServer).
6. Click Test for both e-mail and the net send command. Click OK to close the resulting dialog boxes, and finally, click OK to close the New Operator Properties dialog box and add the new operator.
7. Check the Inbox to see that the test message was received from SQL Server Agent.

Tip If the message has not yet arrived, click Deliver Now on the Tools menu to check for new messages. Do this to check for new messages immediately whenever you are expecting a new message; otherwise, the message will take a little while to arrive.

Creating Jobs

To define a new job, you can use SQL Server Enterprise Manager or execute the sp_add_job system stored procedure. You can also use the Create Job Wizard. The job definition is stored in the msdb..sysjobs system table. This table is maintained in cache to improve performance. When you define jobs, you should

- Ensure that a job is enabled. Jobs are enabled by default. If a job is disabled, it cannot execute as scheduled. However, a disabled job can be executed when an alert fires or when a user starts the job in SQL Server Enterprise Manager.

- Specify the owner who is responsible for performing the job. By default, the owner is the Windows NT or SQL Server user login account creating the job.

- Define whether the job executes on a local server or on multiple remote servers.

- Create job categories to help you organize, filter, and manage many jobs. For example, you can create job categories that correspond to the departments in your company. Categories are particularly useful when automating jobs in a multiserver environment.

Exercise: Defining a Job with the Create Job Wizard

In this exercise, you will use the Create Job Wizard to define a job that backs up the StudyNwind transaction log every day at 5:00 P.M.

▶ **To use the Create Job Wizard**

1. In the console tree, click your server.

2. On the SQL Server Enterprise Manager Tools menu, click Wizards.

3. Expand Management, and then double-click Create Job Wizard.

4. Use the information in the following table to create a job that is scheduled to back up the StudyNwind database transaction log daily at 5:00 P.M. Accept the defaults for any options that are not listed.

Option	Value
Job command type	Transact-SQL command
Database name	StudyNwind
Transact-SQL statement	BACKUP LOG StudyNwind TO DISK = 'C:\Mssql7\Backup\Nwindlog.bak'
Schedule	On a recurring basis: Daily, Every 1 day, Occurs once at 5:00 P.M.
Notifications	E-mail Admin and Net send Admin
Job name	StudyNwind Log Backup

Exercise: Executing the Job Manually

In this exercise, you will verify that your job was created successfully and that notifications were sent.

▶ **To execute the job manually**

1. Verify that the trunc. log on chkpt. database option of the StudyNwind database is false.

2. In SQL Server Enterprise Manager, expand Management, and then expand SQL Server Agent.

3. In the console tree, click the Jobs icon to display all defined jobs in the details pane.

4. In the details pane, right-click the StudyNwind Log Backup job, and then click Start Job. This executes the job manually.

Note that a message appeared on your screen from a net send command.

5. In the details pane, right-click the StudyNwind Log Backup job, and then click View Job History to verify that the job completed successfully.

What information is displayed in the job history when Show Step Details is selected? What information is displayed when this option is cleared?

6. Switch to the Inbox to verify that you received an e-mail message.

Defining Job Steps

When you create a job, you must define the individual steps that make up that job. You can use SQL Server Enterprise Manager or execute the sp_add_jobstep system stored procedure to define each job step. The job step definitions are stored in the msdb..sysjobsteps system table.

Job steps can be Transact-SQL statements, replication tasks, operating system commands, or Active Scripts. Each job step can be only one type. Different types of job steps can be combined in the same job.

Using Transact-SQL Statements

Job steps execute Transact-SQL statements most often. For example, Transact-SQL statements can be used to back up the database and transaction log, update index statistics, and verify database integrity.

When you define job steps to execute Transact-SQL statements, stored procedures, or extended stored procedures, consider the following facts and guidelines:

- You should include required variables and parameters in the job step.

- You can send the result set of a job step to an output file. Output files are often used in troubleshooting to capture any error messages that may have occurred while the statement was executing. You cannot use an output file from one job step as input into a succeeding step.

Specifying Database User Context to Execute Job Steps

SQL Server Agent executes Transact-SQL job steps if the job owner or the database user defined to execute the job step has appropriate permissions.

SQL Server Agent calls the SETUSER statement to set the job owner's database user context for Transact-SQL job steps when

- The job is owned by a SQL Server login account that is not a member of the sysadmin role

- A member of the sysadmin role owns the job, but the individual Transact-SQL step has been defined to execute under another database user context

- The job is owned by a Windows NT user account that is not a member of the sysadmin role

The SETUSER statement goes to the Primary Domain Controller (PDC) or Backup Domain Controller (BDC) to determine the group membership of the job or job step account. SQL Server then determines the associated SQL Server database permissions.

Using Operating System Commands

In addition to executing Transact-SQL statements, you can define job steps to execute a program or operating system command. The .EXE, .BAT, .CMD, and .COM extensions identify these programs. When you define a job step that is an operating system command, you should

- Identify a process exit code to indicate that the command was successful.

- Include the full path to the executable program in the Command text box when you start an operating system command. The path is required to help SQL Server Agent find the program source.

Using Active Scripting Languages

Many companies have developed business applications with Active Scripting languages, such as Microsoft Visual Basic, Scripting Edition (VBScript), or JavaScript. Creating a job to execute these scripts provides developers with the added benefit of scheduling jobs and notifying operators.

Permissions Required to Execute Operating System or Active Scripting Job Steps

By default, all job owners are allowed to execute job steps that contain operating system commands or Active Script. Jobs owned by login accounts that are members of the sysadmin role execute job steps in the security context of the SQL-ServerAgent service account. Jobs owned by login accounts that are not members of the sysadmin role execute in the security context of the SQLAgentCmdExec Windows NT user account. This account is created as a local user account, with no administrative privileges, when SQL Server is installed. The account is added as a member of the Users and Domain Users groups.

A user who has no operating system privileges but who has permissions to add a job can create a job that can execute operating system commands or Active Script, with the operating system privileges of the SQLAgentCmdExec account.

You can specify that only members of the sysadmin role have the ability to execute operating system and Active Scripting job steps by modifying the SQL Server Agent properties. Figure 13.3 shows the Job System tab of the SQL Server Agent Properties dialog box with this option checked.

Figure 13.3   Defining job step privileges for the sysadmin role

Determining Action Flow Logic for Each Job Step

When creating jobs, you can specify actions that will be taken if a failure occurs during job execution. You can accomplish this by determining the action that should be taken upon the success or failure of each job step:

- By default, SQL Server advances to the next job step upon success and stops upon failure of a job step. However, job steps can go to any step defined in the job upon success or failure.

- You can specify the number of times that SQL Server should attempt to retry execution of a job step if the step fails. You can also specify the retry intervals (in minutes).

    For example, if the job step requires a connection to a remote server, you could define several retry attempts in case the connection fails.

Figure 13.4 shows an example of logic flow between job steps.

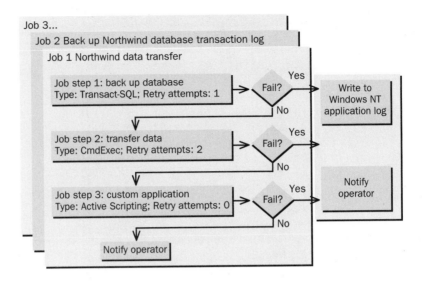

Figure 13.4   Example of logic flow between job steps

Scheduling Jobs

A job is executed by SQL Server Agent based on one or more predefined schedules or by a user on demand. You can use SQL Server Enterprise Manager or execute the sp_add_jobschedule system stored procedure to define each job schedule. The job schedules are stored in the msdb..sysjobschedules system table.

A job can be executed by SQL Server Agent as scheduled only when the job and the schedule are enabled.

Jobs can be scheduled to occur

- At a specific time (one time only)
- On a recurring basis (daily, weekly, or monthly)

Jobs can also be scheduled to start automatically when

- SQL Server Agent is started
- The CPU is idle

You can define and enable the idle CPU condition for your server in the SQL Server Agent Properties dialog box, as shown in Figure 13.5. The default condition occurs when the average CPU usage remains below 10 percent for 600 seconds.

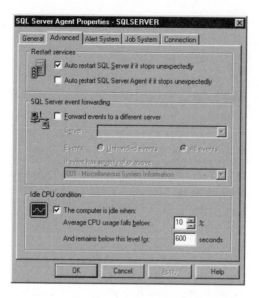

Figure 13.5   The Advanced tab of the SQL Server Agent Properties dialog box, showing the Idle CPU Condition options

Multiple Schedules

A job can have multiple schedules. For example, a job to back up a database transaction log could be scheduled to execute every two hours during peak business hours, Monday through Friday, and every four hours during nonpeak hours. Figure 13.6 shows an example of a job with multiple schedules.

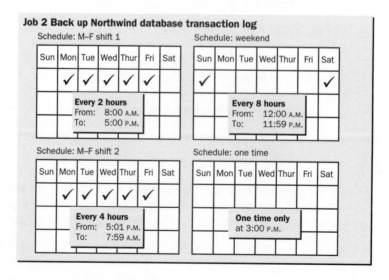

Figure 13.6   Example of a job with multiple schedules

Reviewing and Configuring Job History

SQL Server Agent captures job and job step execution status and stores the information in the msdb..sysjobhistory system table. You can view history information for individual jobs, as well as configure the size of the job history table, with SQL Server Enterprise Manager.

Reviewing an Individual Job History

If a job fails, you can view the job history to obtain information about each job step, the cause for the failure, and solutions to resolve the problem. Specifically, the job history records

- The date and time that the job step occurred
- Whether the job step failed or succeeded
- The operator who was notified and the notification method
- The duration of the job step
- Errors or messages

If SQL Server shuts down while a Transact-SQL statement is executing, the job history contains information about the job step that was in progress when the shutdown occurred.

Configuring the Size of the Job History Log

The history of SQL Server Agent job executions is stored in the sysjobhistory system table. On the Job System tab of the SQL Server Agent Properties dialog box, you can configure the maximum size of the job history log. The size is specified as the number of rows in the sysjobhistory system table.

Without any defined limits for job history growth, the sysjobhistory table will grow. Depending on the autogrowth settings for the msdb database, the database will then either become full or grow to take up an increasing amount of disk space.

When you configure the size of the job history log, consider the following facts:

- By default, the maximum size of the job history log is set at 1000 rows.
- By default, the maximum job history for individual jobs is set at 100 rows.
- Rows will be removed from the sysjobhistory system table in a first-in, first-out (FIFO) manner when the limits are reached.

Note It is important to check the job step history for failed jobs, as the most accurate description of the reason for the failure will usually be recorded there.

Exercise: Creating a Job with Multiple Job Steps

In this exercise, you will create a job that transfers a data file into the Products table in the StudyNwind database and then backs up the database after the data transfer successfully completes.

▶ **To create a job with multiple job steps**

1. In SQL Server Enterprise Manager, expand Management, and then expand SQL Server Agent.

2. Right-click Jobs, and then click New Job.

3. In the New Job Properties dialog box, on the General tab, type the name **StudyNwind Monthly Data Transfer** in Name. Leave the other options on the General tab as they are.

4. Use the information in the following tables to add two new steps on the Steps tab. Leave options that are not listed as they are.

Option	Tab	Value
Step name	General	Copy new product data
Type	General	Operating System Command (CmdExec)
Command	General	C:\Sqladmin\Exercise\Ch13\Transfer.cmd
On success action	Advanced	Go to the next step
Retry attempts	Advanced	1
Retry interval (minutes)	Advanced	1
On failure action	Advanced	Quit the job reporting failure
Output file	Advanced	C:\Temp\Prodcopy.txt
Output file option	Advanced	Overwrite

Option	Tab	Value
Step name	General	Backup StudyNwind DB
Type	General	Transact-SQL Script (TSQL)
Database	General	StudyNwind
Command	General	BACKUP DATABASE StudyNwind TO DISK = 'C:\Mssql7\Backup\Nwind.bak' WITH INIT
On success action	Advanced	Go to the next step
Retry attempts	Advanced	1
Retry interval (minutes)	Advanced	1
On failure action	Advanced	Quit the job reporting failure
Output file	Advanced	C:\Temp\Prodcopy.txt
Output file option	Advanced	Append

5. Use the information in the next table to create a new schedule on the Schedules tab. Leave options that are not listed as they are.

Option	Value
Name	First day of the month
Schedule Type	Recurring, Monthly, Day 1 of every 1 month. Occurs once at 1:00 A.M.

6. On the Notifications tab, check E-mail Operator and Net Send, and type **Admin** as the address for each.

7. Click OK to close the New Job Properties dialog box and add the new job.

Exercise: Simulating a Job Step Failure

In this exercise, you will rename the data transfer file to simulate a failure that causes the first job step to fail.

▶ **To simulate a failure and verify that a job step failed**

1. Open Windows NT Explorer.

2. Rename the file C:\Sqladmin\Exercise\ch13\Prods.txt to C:\Sqladmin\Exercise\Ch13\Prods.sav.

3. Switch to SQL Server Enterprise Manager.

4. Right-click the StudyNwind Monthly Data Transfer job, and then click Start Job. The Start Job dialog box allows you to start a job at any step. Click Start to have the job execute starting with the first step.

5. You will have to wait for about a minute before a message appears on your screen from a net send command. This is because the job was set to retry once if it fails. The notification is sent only if the retry also fails.

6. In the details pane, right-click the StudyNwind Monthly Data Transfer job, and then click View Job History to verify that the job did not complete successfully. The job will appear in the history only after the retry, but the initial failure will be seen immediately if the Show Step Details option is checked.

   What do you notice in the history?

   You will correct the error and execute the job again in Lesson 4 of this chapter.

Note If the error message in step 1 is "The system cannot find the path specified," the command in step 1 is incorrect. In this case, edit the step and make sure that the path in the command is correct (it should be C:\Sqladmin\Exercise\Ch13\Transfer.cmd).

---

7. Open the Windows NT application log to confirm that the job failure was logged.

   What information is displayed in the log?

8. Switch to Inbox to confirm that you received an e-mail message notifying you that the job failed.

9. Open Notepad, and then open C:\Temp\Prodcopy.txt.

   What information is displayed in the output file?

Practice: Configuring SQL Mail

In the following exercises, you will configure the SQL Mail service to see how you can have SQL Server send e-mail messages. You can use this capability to send your own e-mail notifications and results from Transact-SQL scripts and stored procedures.

Exercise 1: Starting the SQL Mail Session

In this exercise, you will verify that SQL Mail is not running. You will then specify a mail profile name for SQL Mail and start it.

▶ **To start the SQL Mail session**

1. Switch to SQL Server Enterprise Manager.

2. Expand Support Services. Note that SQL Mail is not running.

3. Right-click SQL Mail, and then click Start.

   Did a SQL Mail session start successfully?

4. Review the messages in the current log in SQL Server Logs in the Management folder in the console tree.

   What was the source of the error messages associated with SQL Mail?

5. Return to the Support Services folder. Right-click SQL Mail, and then click Properties.

6. In the Profile Name, select SQLMail Profile, and then click Test. A message confirms that a MAPI session was started using the profile. Click OK to close the dialog box.

   You have now configured SQL Mail and SQL Server Agent to use different profiles. This allows them to use separate mailboxes in your messaging system. They can both be configured to use the same profile if you want them to share the same mailbox.

7. Right-click SQL Mail, and then click Start.

   Did the SQL Mail session start successfully?

Exercise 2: Sending a Query Result Using SQL Mail

In this exercise, you will execute the xp_sendmail extended stored procedure to send the result set of a query to yourself to verify that the SQL Mail session works as expected.

▶ **To send a query result using SQL Mail**

1. Open SQL Server Query Analyzer, and log on to the (local) server with Microsoft Windows NT authentication. Your Administrator account is a member of the Windows NT Administrators group, which is automatically mapped to the SQL Server sysadmin role.

2. Open C:\Sqladmin\Exercise\Ch13\Sqlmail.sql, and review its contents.

3. Execute the script. You should see a message in the results pane indicating that the message was sent.

4. Switch to Inbox and open the new message.

   What was the query result?

Lesson Summary

Jobs allow you to automate administrative tasks. You can execute jobs on demand or according to a schedule, and a job can generate an e-mail message, a Windows NT pop-up message, or a pager message when it succeeds or fails. To use the messaging features, you need to configure operators to receive one of the message types. Jobs provide full multistep capabilities and the ability to control the flow of jobs steps. SQL Server maintains a history of job executions, with messaging indicating success or failure of each job step.

Lesson 3: Creating Alerts

SQL Server allows you to respond to potential problems by creating alerts to respond to SQL Server errors, user-defined errors, or SQL Server performance conditions. You can also create a fail-safe operator in the event that a pager notification fails to contact an operator. This lesson describes how to perform these tasks.

After this lesson, you will be able to

- Create alerts to respond to SQL Server 7 errors

- Use SQL Server performance condition alerts to notify a system or database administrator (also known as an operator) of potential problems before they occur

- Configure SQL Server event forwarding

- Assign a fail-safe operator

Estimated lesson time: 90 minutes

Using Alerts to Respond to Potential Problems

Alerts respond to SQL Server or user-defined errors (events) that have been written to the Windows NT application log. SQL Server errors are raised in response to predefined problems, such as insufficient user permissions to modify a table or the transaction log becoming full. To raise user-defined messages, the database application (typically a stored procedure or trigger) must call the RAISERROR statement.

Exercise: Creating an Alert with the Create Alert Wizard

In this exercise, you will use the Create Alert Wizard to create an alert that is defined to send e-mail and net send notifications when an error with severity level 17 occurs.

▶   **To create an alert by using the Create Alert Wizard**

1. Open SQL Server Enterprise Manager, and expand your server.

2. On the Tools menu, click Wizards.

3. Expand Management, and then double-click Create Alert Wizard.

4. Create an alert using the information in the following table. Accept defaults for any items that are not listed.

Option	Value
For any error of severity	017—Insufficient Resources
Database name	(All Databases)
Job to execute	(No job)
Notify operator(s)	Admin—E-mail and Net send
Include error message text in	E-mail and Net send
Alert notification message to send to operator	My first alert
Alert name	Severity level 17 errors

5. In the console tree, expand Management, expand SQL Server Agent, and then click the Alerts icon.

6. In the details pane, verify that the alert named Severity Level 17 Errors was created.

7. Right-click the alert, and then click Properties to review the alert definition.

   What additional responses to the alert can be defined that were not included as part of the wizard?

Creating Alerts to Respond to SQL Server Errors

You can create alerts that fire in response to specific SQL Server errors or that fire in response to all errors of a specific severity level.

Tip SQL Server has a number of predefined demonstration alerts. Since there are no operators assigned to these alerts, they do nothing. You should assign operators to these alerts and give them names that are more meaningful or replace them with alerts of your own.

Defining Alerts Based on SQL Server Error Numbers

You can use SQL Server Enterprise Manager, the Create Alert Wizard, or the sp_add_alert system stored procedure to define a new alert. The alert definition is stored in the msdb..sysalerts system table. This table is maintained in cache to improve performance. When you define an alert for a SQL Server error number, consider the following facts and guidelines:

- Alerts fire only for errors that are written to the Windows NT application log.

- You can define alerts based on SQL Server system or user-defined error numbers that are stored in the master..sysmessages system table.

- You can define more than one alert for a SQL Server error number. However, each alert must be limited to a specific database or must apply to all databases.

  For example, to respond to error number 9002 in both the payroll and customer databases, you could create two separate alerts. Alternatively, you could create one alert to respond to error number 9002 in all databases.

- When you create an alert that applies to all databases, ensure that the error message provides a sufficiently detailed explanation, typically giving the database name in the message. If the message does not give a detailed explanation, create separate alerts for each database.

- You can make the alert more specific or selective by specifying text that must be contained in the error message for the alert to fire.

  For example, if you create an alert for error 18456, the error message includes the name of a user who fails to log on. You could specify the text "Login failed for user 'sa'" so that the alert occurs only when someone is trying to log on as sa.

Defining Alerts Based on Error Severity Levels

The following table provides a summary of the SQL Server error severity levels.

Severity level	Description	Can be corrected by	Written to NT application log
0 – 10	Informational messages; these are not errors	N/A	Optional
11 – 16	User errors	User	Optional
17	Insufficient resource errors	Administrator, possibly database owner	Optional
18	Nonfatal internal error	Administrator	Optional
19	Nonconfigurable resource error	Administrator	Yes
20 – 25	Fatal errors	Administrator	Yes

When you define an alert for an error severity level as a condition, consider the following facts and guidelines:

- SQL Server errors with severity levels 19 through 25 are automatically written to the Windows NT application log.

- Severity levels 20 through 25 are fatal errors, meaning that the code in which the error occurs is terminated and the user is disconnected. You should always define an operator to be notified when these SQL Server errors occur.

- You can create an alert to be fired when an error of a specific severity level occurs on all databases or on a particular database.

- You can make the alert more specific or selective by specifying text that must be contained in the error message. For example, you can create an alert to notify you when a severity level 17 error that includes the string "log" in the error message occurs in any database.

- To ensure that notifications for severe errors are received, it is recommended that you configure alerts for severe errors to send notifications to groups rather than to individual users.

Creating Alerts Based on User-Defined Error Messages

You can create alerts based on user-defined (customized) error messages. These can be defined for individual database applications, allowing you to define sophisticated solutions to avoid potential problems before they occur.

For example, you could create a user-defined error message to be raised from an update trigger on an inventory table. When a column in the inventory table is updated, indicating that inventory levels have fallen below 25 percent for a particular product, the trigger will raise your user-defined error. You could then define an alert for the error message that executes a job to reorder inventory and sends an e-mail message to the purchasing agent.

Before creating an alert for a user-defined error message, you must first create the error message. The programmer must raise the error from the database application, using the RAISERROR statement; SQL Server will not raise the error.

Creating an Error Message

To create user-defined error messages, you can use SQL Server Enterprise Manager or the sp_addmessage system stored procedure. When you create user-defined error messages, consider the following facts:

- The numbers assigned to user-defined error messages must be greater than 50000. Error numbers less than 50000 are reserved for predefined SQL Server errors.

- Error messages can include parameters to report specific details such as a database or user name.

- SQL Server error messages are displayed in the language that is selected during Setup. If you administer a multiple-language SQL Server environment, you can create user-defined messages for other languages.

- You must write the error message to the Windows NT application log if you plan to fire an alert on the message.

Example of an Alert Based on a User-Defined Error Message

An account manager wants to be notified by e-mail any time a customer is removed from the database. She also wants to know the name of the employee who deleted the customer in the event that subsequent action is necessary.

The following steps give the sequence of events that occur in this scenario when the alert fires. Figure 13.7 illustrates the scenario.

1. Eva Corets, a customer service representative, removes customer van Dam from the customers table. The removecustomer stored procedure is executed, which raises error number 50099.
2. The error (event) is written to the Windows NT application log.
3. SQL Server Agent is notified that an event has occurred and then reads the Windows NT application log.
4. SQL Server Agent compares the error to defined alerts in the msdb..sysalerts system table.
5. SQL Server Agent processes the alert that was found for the 50099 error. Notifications defined in the msdb..sysnotifications system table are sent to operators based on details defined in the msdb..sysoperators system table.

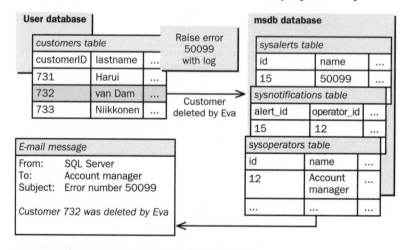

Figure 13.7   Example of an alert based on a user-defined error message

Exercise: Creating a User-Defined Error Message

In this exercise, you will use SQL Server Enterprise Manager to create a user-defined error message that occurs when the number of stock units for a particular product reaches the reorder level.

▶ **To create a user-defined error message**

1. Right-click your server, click All Tasks, and then click Manage SQL Server Messages.

2. In the Manage Server Messages dialog box, click the Messages tab.

Note The Messages tab of the Manage SQL Server Messages dialog box will always be empty when you display it. If you want to see messages, you must first enter search criteria on the Search tab and click Find. This will populate the Messages tab with a list of messages that match your search criteria. For this exercise, you are adding a message, so it is not necessary to enter search criteria.

---

3. Click New.

4. Note that the error number 50001 has been generated for your new error message. Do not change this number; it is required to be 50001 in a later exercise.

5. In the New SQL Server Message dialog box, in the Severity list, click Severity Level 009 – User Defined.

6. In the Message text box, type the following event message:
   The units in stock for %s has reached %d. Please reorder.

7. Check the Always Write To Windows NT Eventlog option to write the event message to the Windows NT application log.

8. Click OK to close the dialog box and add your new error message.

9. Click OK to close the Manage SQL Server Messages dialog box.

Exercise: Creating an Alert for the User-Defined Error Message

In this exercise, you will create an alert that sends an e-mail message to the warehouse manager when your new user-defined error message occurs.

▶ **To create an alert for the user-defined error message**

1. Expand your server, expand Management, expand SQL Server Agent, right-click Alerts, and then click New Alert.

2. In the New Alert Properties dialog box, in the Name box, type **Reorder Inventory**.

3. Click Error Number and type **50001** in the error number field, the error number of your user-defined error message.

   Note that as you type, the message next to Error Number changes from (Not a valid error number) to the error message when the error number is found in the sysmessages table.

   You can search for errors by message text, error number, or severity by clicking browse (…) to open the Manage SQL Server Messages dialog box.

4. In the Database Name list, click StudyNwind to restrict the alert to a specific database.

5. Click the Response tab.

6. Check E-mail and Net Send for the operator Admin.

7. Click OK to close the dialog box and add the new alert.

8. Verify that the alert was created. The Reorder Inventory alert should appear in the details pane.

Exercise: Raising the User-Defined Error Message

In this exercise, you will use SQL Server Query Analyzer to execute a stored procedure in the StudyNwind database that will raise error 50001 to test that the Reorder Inventory alert works as expected.

▶ **To raise a user-defined error message**

1. Open SQL Server Query Analyzer and log on to the (local) server with Microsoft Windows NT authentication. Your account is a member of the Windows NT Administrators group, which is automatically mapped to the SQL Server sysadmin role.

2. Execute the reorder stored procedure by supplying any valid product ID value. For example,

```
USE StudyNwind
EXEC reorder @prodid = 2
```

Did you receive the defined notifications in response to the alert?

Configuring Event Forwarding

You can configure SQL Server Agent to forward unhandled event messages or all event messages to another SQL Server. You can specify that only events above a certain severity level be forwarded. The other SQL Server handles the events based on its own alert definitions. The name of the server on which the error occurred will be reported in the alert notification.

In a multiserver environment, this means that you need to define alerts on only one server. You may want to forward events to a server that has less traffic than other servers.

For example, you can configure errors with severity levels of 18 or above to be forwarded to the Accounting server, as shown in Figure 13.8. If an error occurs on your server with severity level 19, the event is automatically forwarded to the Accounting server to address the problem.

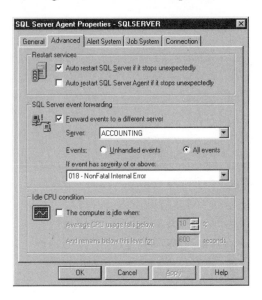

Figure 13.8   The Advanced tab of the SQL Server Agent Properties dialog box, showing the SQL Server Event Forwarding options

Important Event forwarding is available only when SQL Server is installed on Windows NT, not Windows 95 or Windows 98.

Responding to Performance Condition Alerts

You can create alerts to respond to SQL Server performance conditions defined by the objects and counters used in Windows NT Performance Monitor. An alert is fired when the monitored value exceeds, equals, or falls below a defined limit. Such alerts allow you to proactively avert problems and keep your server and databases running smoothly.

For example, you can create a performance condition alert to be fired when the transaction log in the Northwind database has exceeded 75 percent of its capacity. Figure 13.9 illustrates such an alert.

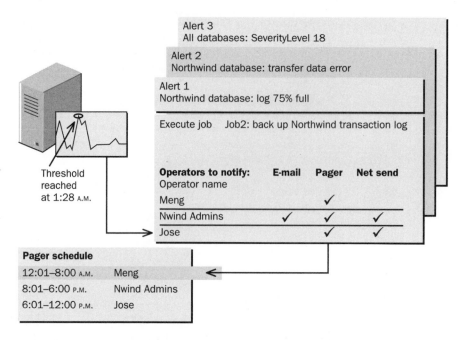

Figure 13.9   Example of an alert based on a performance condition

You can create SQL Server performance condition alerts based on most of the SQL Server Performance Monitor objects. Examples of the measures on which you can base alerts include

- The memory buffers used by SQL Server, such as free memory and the buffer cache hit ratio
- The number of index searches or the number of pages that are allocated to indexes and data
- The amount of SQL Server cache used to store objects such as stored procedures, triggers, and query plans
- The amount of free log space available or the number of active transactions in the database
- Lock time-outs and deadlocks
- Custom stored procedures or any Transact-SQL statements that return a value to be monitored

Windows NT Performance Monitor does not need to be running on your SQL Server for you to use performance condition alerts.

Note Previous versions of SQL Server required Windows NT Performance Monitor to be running in order to use performance-based alerts. A utility called sqlalrtr had to be executed from Windows NT Performance Monitor to report performance alerts. This is not necessary in SQL Server 7.

Practice: Creating a Performance Condition Alert

In these exercises, you will execute a script that creates a multistep job to back up the StudyNwind transaction log. Next, you will use SQL Server Enterprise Manager to create a performance condition alert based on the Percent Log Used counter that notifies you and executes the backup job when the StudyNwind database transaction log has reached 60 percent capacity. Finally, you will verify that the condition alert works as expected.

Exercise 1: Creating a Job to Back Up the Transaction Log

In this exercise, you will execute a script that creates a multistep job to back up the StudyNwind transaction log.

▶ **To execute a script that creates a job to back up the StudyNwind transaction log**

1. Switch to SQL Server Query Analyzer, and open a new query window.

2. Open C:\Sqladmin\Exercise\Ch13\Makejob.sql, and then execute it.

   This script creates a multistep job called Backup StudyNwind Log Alert that will back up the StudyNwind transaction log. Job steps also include contingencies to truncate the transaction log and back up the database if the BACKUP LOG statement fails.

   Note As this script is executing, you will receive warning messages that non-existent steps are referenced. This is normal behavior. When each job step is created, actions to take upon success or failure are specified. The first few job steps reference steps that have not yet been created.

   ---

3. Switch to SQL Server Enterprise Manager, expand your server, and then expand Management. Right-click SQL Server Agent, and click Refresh.

4. Expand SQL Server Agent, and then click Jobs. The Backup StudyNwind Log Alert job should appear in the details pane.

5. Double-click the Backup StudyNwind Log Alert job to review the job properties.

Exercise 2: Creating a Performance Condition Alert for the StudyNwind Transaction Log

In this exercise, you will create a performance condition alert that fires when the Percent Log Used counter rises above 60 percent for the StudyNwind database.

▶ **To create a performance condition alert**

1. Open SQL Server Enterprise Manager.

2. Expand Management, and then expand SQL Server Agent. Right-click Alerts and click New Alert.

3. Type **StudyNwind Log 60% Full** in Name.

4. In Type, select SQL Server Performance Condition Alert.

5. Use the values in the following table to create the Performance alert condition definition.

Option	Value
Object	SQLServer:Databases
Counter	Percent Log Used
Instance	StudyNwind
Alert if counter	rises above
Value	60

6. Click the Response tab and define the response to the alert with the information in the following table. Accept the defaults for any items that are not listed.

Option	Value
Execute job	Backup StudyNwind Log Alert
Operators to notify	Admin by E-mail and Net send
Delay between responses	0 minutes, 0 seconds

7. Click OK to close the dialog box and add the new alert.

Exercise 3: Testing the Performance Condition Alert

In this exercise, you will review and execute a script that generates activity in the StudyNwind database to fill the transaction log. Then you will verify that SQL Server Agent raised the alert and executed the job as defined.

▶ **To test the performance condition alert**

1. In Windows NT Explorer, find and double-click the C:\Sqladmin\Exercise\Ch13\ Watchlog.pmc file. This opens the Windows NT Performance Monitor and displays two counters. The counters show the size of the StudyNwind transaction log (green) and the percentage of the transaction log currently in use (red). The scale for the size of the transaction log is ×100 KB. The Percent Log Used counter always shows the amount of space used in the transaction log as a percentage of the current size of the transaction log, so the percentage will drop if the log grows. The percentage is not determined by size settings for the log such as maximum size, only by the current size.

2. Switch to SQL Server Query Analyzer, open C:\Sqladmin\Exercise\Ch13\ Fulltlog.sql, review its contents, and then execute it.

   This script simply generates activity in the StudyNwind database that fills the transaction log.

3. Switch to Performance Monitor; you will see the transaction log filling up and possibly see the transaction log size grow.

4. When the alert is raised, you will receive a net send message. Shortly after the alert message, you will receive another net send message indicating that the transaction log has been backed up; the percentage of the transaction log in use will then drop. Allow the alert to fire two or three times, and then stop the execution of the script.

Important Do not allow the script to run for too long, or the transaction log backup file will grow very large.

---

5. Open Inbox to confirm that you received an e-mail message notifying you of an error.

6. Switch to SQL Server Enterprise Manager.

7. Review the job history for the Backup StudyNwind Log Alert job.

   The job history should display the most recent date and time that the job was executed successfully.

8. Review the alert history of StudyNwind Log 60% Full by right-clicking the alert and selecting Properties. The history can be found at the bottom of the General tab. It should show the most recent date and time that the alert was raised.

Assigning a Fail-Safe Operator

You can assign a fail-safe operator to respond to an alert when pager notifications to defined operators fail. For example, if an operator is off-duty when an alert fires, the fail-safe operator will be contacted.

A fail-safe operator is notified when

- The operator(s) assigned to the alert cannot be paged
- SQL Server Agent cannot access the system tables in msdb

When you assign a fail-safe operator, consider the following facts:

- The fail-safe operator information is cached. Therefore, even if SQL Server Agent stops unexpectedly, the fail-safe operator can still be notified.
- You can have only one fail-safe operator.
- For safety reasons, you cannot delete an operator that has been designated as the fail-safe operator. You must either designate a new fail-safe operator or remove the fail-safe operator assignment and then delete the operator.

Lesson Summary

Alerts make it possible to create automated responses to errors and other conditions on SQL Server. Alerts can be created based on error numbers, error severity levels, user-defined error messages, and performance conditions. In a large environment, multiple SQL Servers can forward events for processing on a single server, centralizing the administration of the alert responses. It is important that somebody always be notified when certain alerts occur; you can configure a fail-safe operator that can be notified if the normal operators cannot be notified.

Lesson 4: Troubleshooting SQL Server Automated Administration

If your automated jobs, alerts, or notifications are not working properly, use the guidelines found in this lesson to isolate and solve the problem.

After this lesson, you will be able to

- Troubleshoot potential problems when jobs or alerts do not execute as anticipated

Estimated lesson time: 30 minutes

Automated Administration Troubleshooting Checklist

Each of the following items is discussed in turn in the sections that follow.

- Verify that SQL Server Agent has been started.
- Verify that the job, schedule, alert, or operator is enabled.
- Ensure that the SQLAgentCmdExec account is correctly configured.
- Review error logs.
- Review job history.
- Verify that the mail client is working properly.

Verify That SQL Server Agent Has Been Started

If SQL Server Agent has stopped for any reason, it is not able to execute jobs or fire alerts.

You should consider having the SQLServerAgent service start automatically whenever the Windows NT Server is started.

The SQLServerAgent Monitor provides self-checking for SQL Server Agent. If the SQLServerAgent service stops unexpectedly, SQLServerAgent Monitor can attempt to restart the service. Enable SQLServerAgent Monitor through SQL Server Enterprise Manager as shown in Figure 13.10, or by running the xp_sqlagent_monitor extended stored procedure. When SQL Server Agent Monitor restarts the SQL Server service, an error is written to the Windows NT application log, making it possible to configure an alert to fire when the service is restarted.

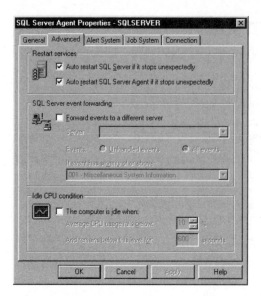

Figure 13.10 The Advanced tab of the SQL Server Agent Properties dialog box, showing the Restart Services options

Verify That the Job, Schedule, Alert, or Operator Is Enabled

If jobs are not executing as scheduled, alerts are not being fired, or operators are not receiving notifications, verify that the job, schedule, alert, or operator is enabled.

The fact that a job, schedule, alert, or operator is disabled is not recorded in the SQL Server Agent error log or the job history.

Ensure That the SQLAgentCmdExec Account Is Correctly Configured

An operating system command or Active Scripting job step in a job owned by a user who is not a member of the sysadmin role cannot execute under the following conditions:

- If the SQLAgentCmdExec account has been improperly installed
- If the SQLAgentCmdExec account has been removed
- If changes to the SQLAgentCmdExec account password have been made outside of the SQL Server Agent Properties dialog box
- If SQL Server Agent has been set to allow only members of sysadmin to execute CmdExec and Active Scripting job steps

Note If a job step fails for this reason, you will probably not see an entry in the SQL Server Agent Error Log. The error will be recorded in the job step history.

Review Error Logs

Reviewing error messages in the Windows NT application log and the SQL Server Agent and SQL Server error logs may help you troubleshoot the source of your problem.

The Windows NT Application Log

If the maximum size of the Windows NT application log is too small or is defined to be overwritten frequently, events may not exist for SQL Server to process. To avoid losing event information about SQL Server, increase the maximum log size for the Windows NT application log. Use Windows NT Event Viewer to check that events are being recorded for SQL Server. SQL Server Agent fires alerts only for events that are recorded in the Windows NT application log.

The SQL Server Agent Error Log

SQL Server Agent errors are recorded in the SQL Server Agent error log. By default, all SQL Server Agent errors and warnings are recorded in the error log. You can also record execution trace messages when troubleshooting specific problems; this can cause the log to become large, however, so it should not be enabled during normal operation. Note the following:

- Each time SQL Server Agent is stopped and restarted, a new error log is created.

- You can view the current error log with SQL Server Enterprise Manager or any text editor. Up to nine previous versions of the error log are saved in the C:\Mssql7\Log directory.

- You can define an error message pop-up recipient to be sent a net send command when errors are logged into the SQL Server Agent error log.

The SQL Server Error Log

You should also review the SQL Server error log. By comparing the dates and times for events in the SQL Server error log, the SQL Server Agent error log, and the Windows NT application log, you can narrow down the list of probable causes of problems.

Review Job History

After you review the SQL Server Agent error log, you also may want to review history information on an alert, an operator, or a job. The date and time of the single most recent action is recorded for alerts and operators. Full job history is captured in the msdb database.

The maximum amount of job history information can be resized. Having a full sysjobhistory system table can cause alerts and jobs to fail. If you must keep large amounts of job history information, you should expand the msdb database to a size that is sufficient to accommodate the growth.

Tip Some job errors are not written in the SQL Server Agent error log but do get written in the job history, so you should check the job history even if the SQL Server Agent error log shows no error.

Exercise: Correcting a Problem

In this exercise, you will rename the data transfer file to correct the simulated failure from a previous exercise.

▶ **To correct a problem and verify that a job works**

1. Open Windows NT Explorer.

2. Rename the C:\Sqladmin\Exercise\Ch13\Prods.sav file to C:\Sqladmin\Exercise\Ch13\Prods.txt

3. Switch to SQL Server Enterprise Manager.

4. Right-click the StudyNwind Monthly Data Transfer job, and then click Start Job. The Start Job dialog box allows you to start a job at any step. Click Start to have the job execute starting with the first step.

5. In the details pane, right-click the StudyNwind Monthly Data Transfer job, and then click View Job History. Verify that the job completed successfully.

6. Open Notepad, and then open C:\Temp\Prodcopy.txt.

   What information is displayed in the output file?

Verify That the Mail Client Is Working Properly

If e-mail or pager notifications are not working, verify that the mail client is working properly. To do so, log on to the mail client, using the SQL Server Agent domain user account, and send an e-mail or pager notification to an operator.

Troubleshooting Alerts

Because SQL Server Agent both depends on and monitors SQL Server events, it can become caught in an endless loop, firing the same alert repeatedly. This generally occurs when SQL Server runs out of an essential global resource and an alert has been defined on this event.

A looping condition occurs when SQL Server Agent fires an alert that attempts to execute a job. Executing the job in turn causes the same error that originally fired the alert. This causes the job to be executed again, and so on.

Signs that looping alerts may be occurring are that the Windows NT application log rapidly fills with the same error, the CPU use is unusually high, or the number of alert responses is high.

Under these conditions, the delay increases between when the event appears in the Windows NT application log and when SQL Server Agent responds to that event. This causes a backlog of alerts.

Resolving Looping Alerts

When looping alerts occur, resolve the error condition and clear the backlog of events from the Windows NT application log. You can do this in one of the following ways:

- Use Windows NT Event Viewer to clear the Windows NT application log. If you do this, all events, including those not generated by SQL Server, are cleared. You should try to resolve the alert backlog by other means if you do not want to lose your current Windows NT application log.

- SQL Server Agent processes an alert only once within a defined period of time. This time defaults to one minute, so SQL Server Agent will process the same alert only once every minute, no matter how many times the error on which the alert is based occurs. Use the Delay Between Responses option for each alert to set this time. A longer delay reduces the number of alerts that can fire due to any one condition and will decrease the number of alerts fired when looping alerts are occurring.

Tip The default delay between responses is 0 for alerts added with the Create Alert Wizard or the sp_add_alert system stored procedure. In most cases, it is recommended that you change this to 1 minute after using the wizard to create alerts.

- To prevent recurring alerts on specific error numbers from consuming all of your resources, you can define them as non-alert-generating.

  To create an error that is non-alert-generating, you must modify the Windows NT registry. The result of this modification is that SQL Server Agent will not fire the alert when the error occurs.

  Use this solution as a last resort only. Refer to SQL Server Books Online for information on how to configure non-alert-generating errors.

Lesson Summary

Most problems with automated administration are caused by accounts or services that are configured incorrectly or by services that are not running. When errors occur, you can check the SQL Server and SQL Server Agent error logs as well as the job histories to determine the source of the problem. Planning your alerts carefully will prevent looping alerts from occurring.

Lesson 5: Establishing a Multiserver Environment

This lesson describes how to establish a multiserver environment and automate administrative tasks within this environment. The multiserver administration model consists of a master server (MSX) and one or more target servers (TSX). Target servers do not need to be registered in SQL Server Enterprise Manager to set up multiserver administration, although it will make setup easier if they are.

After this lesson, you will be able to

- Automate administrative tasks within a multiserver environment

Estimated lesson time: 20 minutes

Grouping Multiple Servers

Having a multiserver administration configuration allows you to

- Group multiple servers into logical functioning business units
- Manage multiple servers from one location

For example, if a subset of your customer database is maintained at each branch office, you can create a job at the corporate headquarters to back up the customer databases in each branch office.

Important Multiserver administration requires SQL Server version 7 on all servers. Your servers cannot use older versions of SQL Server.

Defining a Master Server

A master server loosely manages all of the servers that have enlisted into it. The master server should be defined on a computer running Windows NT Server because of the higher connection load that it requires.

Use SQL Server Enterprise Manager or the Make MSX Wizard to define the master server. There are system stored procedures for managing a multiserver environment, but it is recommended that you use SQL Server Enterprise Manager. For details on using the system stored procedures, see SQL Server Books Online.

Consider the following facts and guidelines about master servers:

- When you define a master server, you also enlist at least one target server. This inserts a row into the systargetservers system table on the master server. The existence of rows in this table designates the master server.

- The wizard creates an MSXOperator on the master server and on each target server.

- The master server usually represents a primary department or business unit server. In smaller organizations, one master server can serve the entire company.

- You should designate the master server as the event forwarding server.

  If the master server is not performing database production functions, the load of managing events that are forwarded from target servers will not affect database application performance.

Defining Target Servers

You can use SQL Server Enterprise Manager or execute the sp_msx_enlist system stored procedure to define target servers. You can also use the Make Target Server Wizard. The target server definition is stored in the msdb..systargetservers system table. A target server

- Is assigned to only one master server

- Must either reside in the same Windows NT domain as the master server or reside in a trusted Windows NT domain

- Cannot be a member of another master server until it defects from its current master server

Automating Jobs in a Multiserver Environment

You can create jobs on the master server to occur at a target server. SQL Server goes through the following steps to process jobs in a multiserver environment:

1. The master server posts jobs for the target servers in the msdb..sysdownloadlist system table.

2. The target servers periodically connect to the master server to determine whether any new or updated jobs have been posted for the target server to download. If a job exists, the target server downloads the job information.

3. The target server uploads the outcome status for any multiserver jobs that have completed since the last download and disconnects from the master server.

Figure 13.11 illustrates this process.

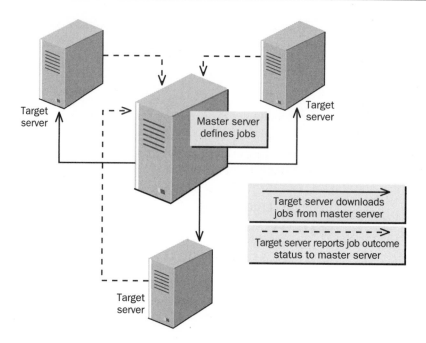

Figure 13.11   Job processing in a multiserver environment

Modifying Multiserver Job Definitions

The master server stores the master copy of job definitions and schedules. When you make any changes to jobs in a multiserver environment, consider the following facts and guidelines:

- Job definitions cannot be modified at the target servers.
- Any changes to the job must be made on the master server.
- SQL Server Enterprise Manager automatically posts the necessary instructions to the download list.

Reviewing Job History

The master server records the job outcome information from the target servers in the msdb..sysjobservers system table. This is in addition to the normal job history information recorded in the msdb..sysjobhistory system table of each local target server.

Lesson Summary

Multiserver administration makes it possible to centrally administer many SQL Servers with minimum effort. Set up a master server with target servers, and you have to create jobs only once for all of the servers in your organization. Job histories of jobs created on the master server are available on the master server, making it possible to manage and monitor all jobs centrally.

Review

The following questions are intended to reinforce key information presented in the chapter. If you are unable to answer a question, review the appropriate lesson and then try the question again. Answers to the questions can be found in Appendix A, "Questions and Answers."

1. You want to back up the transaction log of your production database every hour during peak business hours (8:00 A.M. to 6:00 P.M.) and every three hours during nonpeak hours (6:00 P.M. to 8:00 A.M.). What is the most efficient method for automating these tasks?

2. The customer account manager has asked to be notified whenever a customer's credit limit is changed (increased or decreased). In addition, she wants the name of the customer representative who updated the customer's account, as well as any remarks about why the change was made. How would you accomplish this task?

3. Your new database application is now in production, and you want to execute tests to review its performance. Specifically, you want to know whether the lock wait time is over 20 seconds. How can you be notified automatically when this event occurs?

CHAPTER 14

Monitoring and Maintaining SQL Server

About This Chapter

In Chapter 13, "Automating Administrative Tasks," you learn how to configure alerts to notify you when problems occur in SQL Server. Ideally those problems should never occur. In this chapter, you will learn how to monitor SQL Server to find out when things are not performing normally and thereby take steps to rectify the problem before alerts fire.

This chapter also introduces the Database Maintenance Plan Wizard, which you can use to automatically create all of the jobs and tasks that should be part of your database maintenance plan.

Before You Begin

To complete the lessons in this chapter you must have

- Installed SQL Server 7. See Chapter 2, "Installation," for installation instructions.

- The ability to log on to SQL Server as an Administrator.

- Installed the StudyNwind database. See the "Getting Started" section in "About This Book" for StudyNwind database installation instructions.

- Installed the Exercise files from the Supplemental Course Materials CD-ROM to your hard disk drive. See the "Getting Started" section in "About This Book" for installation instructions.

Lesson 1: Why Monitor SQL Server?

You should monitor SQL Server to determine whether it is performing optimally and, if it is not, to identify the factors that are adversely affecting performance. This lesson discusses the reasons for monitoring SQL Server performance, lists the factors that affect performance, and describes how to establish a baseline so that you will be able to detect system bottlenecks.

After this lesson, you will be able to

- Explain why monitoring Microsoft SQL Server 7 is important
- Describe factors that affect SQL Server performance

Estimated lesson time: 25 minutes

Reasons to Monitor SQL Server

Monitoring enables you to determine whether a server is performing optimally and, if it is not, to isolate the cause. The primary reasons for monitoring server performance and database activity are to determine the cause of poor system performance, examine total system throughput, and examine the consistency of database data.

Determine the Cause of Poor Performance

Optimal performance delivers minimum response time and maximum overall throughput on SQL Server. Performance varies according to the specific environment and depends on hardware configuration, software settings, and how individuals and applications use SQL Server. Monitoring makes it possible to determine which of these factors is causing less than optimum response time or overall throughput.

Response time is the length of time it takes for SQL Server to return the first row of the result set. Response time is usually referred to as the perceived time, as this is how the user receives visual affirmation that a query is being processed.

Examine the Throughput of All Processing for All Users

Throughput measures the number of queries that can be handled by the server during a given time period, along with the number and size of the rows that are returned to the client.

As the number of users or level of user activity increases, additional queries and processes compete for limited system resources. This competition for resources can cause response time to increase and overall throughput to decrease.

Examine the Consistency of Data

Database structures, such as actual data pages and indexes, can become damaged over time. You can use Database Consistency Checker (DBCC) statements to check the logical and physical consistency of a database.

Factors That Affect Performance

Factors that affect performance can be grouped into six general categories: server hardware, operating system, network, SQL Server, database application, and client application.

Note The system administrator may not have control over all of these areas, but each area can be assessed to determine where the greatest performance impact occurs. The factors over which the administrator does have control can then be tuned.

Factors Involving Server Hardware

The factors that can affect the performance of the server include

- **Processors**—the number of processors, as well as their speed, influences performance.
- **Disk I/O**—the number of disks, as well as their speed and the number and type of controllers, affects performance.
- **Memory**—sufficient RAM is crucial for all server processes.

Factors Involving the Operating System

The factors that can affect the performance of the operating system include

- **Concurrent Windows NT services and activities**—concurrent services or activities compete for the same resources as SQL Server.
- **Paging files**—the size, number, and location of paging files can have a major impact on system performance. For best performance, the server should have enough RAM to ensure that paging files are infrequently used.
- **Disk management**—various RAID levels can have a positive or negative impact on performance.

Factors Involving the Network

Network connection speed and activity—concurrent network activity, bandwidth, and data transfer rate—affect performance.

Factors Involving SQL Server

SQL Server factors that affect performance include

- **Configuration**—many critical settings are managed dynamically by SQL Server, including memory management and user connections. Unless you have reason to change these settings, you should allow SQL Server to manage the resources dynamically.

- **Locking**—contention for database resources can block processes and adversely affect SQL Server performance.

- **Logging**—writing a large amount of information to the transaction log can affect performance.

- **Concurrent SQL Server activities**—maintenance activities, such as backing up and restoring databases, executing DBCC operations, and building indexes, use resources and can slow overall SQL Server performance.

Factors Involving Database Application

Database application factors that affect performance include

- **Logical and physical design**—the level of normalization of the database can affect query performance.

- **Transaction control**—the level of transaction control that an application uses can determine the number and duration of locks (longer-running transactions hold locks for longer), which affects overall throughput.

- **Conflicts**—repeated conflicts (attempts to access data that is locked by another process) can slow down an application.

- **Queries**—how queries are written and whether they are encapsulated in stored procedures can affect their execution time. Queries that are encapsulated in stored procedures generally perform better than ad hoc queries.

Factors Involving Client Application

Client application factors that can affect performance include

- **User requirements**—the number of concurrent users and connection and dis-connection strategies affect the way SQL Server uses memory.

- **Transaction control**—minimizing locking conflicts generally improves performance.

- **Client response to locking conflicts**—how the client deals with resubmitting queries and data modification statements when a collision occurs can affect performance.

- **Cursors**—the kind of cursor, as well as how much data is retrieved and where data is cached, affect both use and response time.

Detecting Performance Bottlenecks

A *bottleneck* is any component or activity that limits performance. Every system has bottlenecks, but one of the objectives of monitoring your server is to locate bottlenecks that lower performance below expectations.

Decide What to Examine

Look first at the system-level issues to determine the source of a bottleneck before you examine client-level and query-level issues. For example, system-level bottlenecks that are caused by disk and memory use can affect how the entire application performs, including individual queries. Resolving issues such as disk thrashing before you examine the performance of a particular query is useful.

Know the Acceptable Range

As with any troubleshooting technique, knowing the acceptable range of performance helps identify problem areas. Low numbers can be as meaningful as high numbers. If a number is lower or higher than expected, it may indicate that a problem exists. Sometimes a problem in one area negatively affects or disguises problems in another area. For example,

- A component may prevent the load from reaching another component.
- Network congestion may prevent client requests from reaching the server.
- Clients may have bottlenecks that prevent them from accessing the server.

Discover the actual limits by simulating a workload on SQL Server while you monitor the system by using the tools described in this chapter.

Establish a Performance Baseline

Monitor your system over time to establish a performance baseline. Record measurements to determine the peak hours of database activity, production query or batch command response times, and the time required to back up or restore the database. After you have established a baseline, you can compare the actual performance of your server against the baseline to determine which areas require further investigation.

Configuring a Query Governor

It is possible to submit queries to SQL Server that consume too much of the available server resources and negatively affect performance. This can be due to

- Queries without WHERE clauses
- Queries with too few join clauses, otherwise known as Cartesian Products or Cartesian Joins
- Queries that access databases that do not have referential integrity
- Queries or stored procedures that legitimately attempt to perform too much work

In order to prevent one long-running query from monopolizing resources and threatening the overall health and performance of the server, system administrators can configure a query governor.

SQL Server refuses to execute any query that has an estimated execution duration, in seconds, that exceeds the value specified by the query governor cost limit. Specifying 0 for this option allows all queries to run, regardless of their estimated duration.

If you use sp_configure or SQL Server Enterprise Manager to change the value of the query governor cost limit, the change is serverwide. Figure 14.1 shows the query governor setting on the Server Settings tab of the SQL Server Properties dialog box in SQL Server Enterprise Manager. Use the SET QUERY_GOVERNOR_COST_LIMIT statement to change the query governor setting for individual connections.

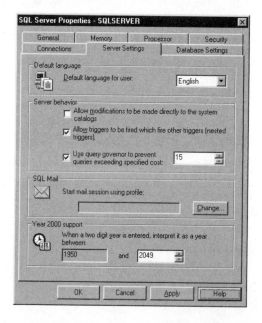

Figure 14.1   The query governor setting in the SQL Server Properties dialog box

Lesson Summary

Monitoring SQL Server lets you determine the cause of poor performance, examine the actual processing throughput for all users, and examine the consistency of the data in your databases. Many factors affect SQL Server performance, so you should never consider individual factors in isolation. Understanding and monitoring the factors that affect SQL Server performance make it possible to detect performance bottlenecks and tune your hardware and software to overcome them.

Lesson 2: Tools for Monitoring SQL Server

SQL Server includes several tools for monitoring the performance of your server. This lesson presents these tools and shows the different kinds of monitoring possible with SQL Server. You will learn how to monitor your SQL Server using the SQL Server Performance Monitor (Windows NT Performance Monitor), Transact-SQL statements, SQL Server Profiler, SQL Server Query Analyzer, and Current Activity in SQL Server Enterprise Manager.

After this lesson, you will be able to

- Describe what you can monitor in SQL Server
- Monitor hardware performance with Microsoft Windows NT Performance Monitor
- Use Transact-SQL tools to monitor performance
- Monitor SQL Server activity with SQL Server Profiler
- Enable the query history and view the last 100 SQL Server events in SQL Server Profiler
- Examine specific query performance in SQL Server Query Analyzer
- Examine process and lock Current Activity information in SQL Server Enterprise Manager

Estimated lesson time: 90 minutes

Common Monitoring Tasks

SQL Server provides several tools that you can use to examine different aspects of performance. These tools show varying degrees of detail to help you isolate problem areas. Your goal should be to determine the factor that is having the greatest negative impact on performance.

This limiting factor, also called a bottleneck, could be outside the realm of SQL Server—such as a hardware problem—or within the SQL Server data files, such as whether tables require specific indexes to produce faster queries. Often, isolating the bottleneck involves several iterations of this monitoring process.

System-Level Monitoring

As you evaluate your system, first look at the highest level to ensure that you have sufficient hardware to handle the requirements of the tasks you need to perform. For this level of monitoring, use

- Windows NT Event Viewer
- SQL Server Performance Monitor

SQL Server–Specific Monitoring

Next, monitor the SQL Server–specific areas. Look at the SQL Server activity and the consistency of the data.

SQL Server Activity

Monitor the amount of locking and contention, user connections, and tempdb use. For this level of monitoring, use

- SQL Server Profiler
- Current Activity in SQL Server Enterprise Manager
- System stored procedures
- Transact-SQL statements

Consistency of Data

To ensure that the internal data structures are correct, use DBCC statements.

Specific Query Performance

Finally, examine specific queries to evaluate their performance. Items to review include index usage, CPU time for a query, and actual I/O. For this detailed level of monitoring, use

- SQL Server Profiler
- SQL Server Query Analyzer
- The Index Query Wizard

Using the Windows NT Event Viewer

You can use the Windows NT Event Viewer to identify events that may be causing performance bottlenecks. This information can help you determine which events or areas of performance you want to examine further.

The Windows NT Event Viewer allows you to look at the event logs listed in the following table. Events that interrupt or hinder system performance are written to these logs. Some log messages that you might watch for include notification that a log file is full, that a file is bad, or that an application error (raised as part of a stored procedure) has occurred.

The Windows NT application log also captures informational messages about events, including startup, recovery, shutdown, and alerts. To help you locate pertinent information, you can filter the error messages by type.

All SQL Server messages are also logged to the SQL Server error log, which you can view in SQL Server Enterprise Manager.

Type	Description
Windows NT application log	Records events logged by applications, such as SQL Server. For example, a database application might record a file error in the application log.
Windows NT system log	Records events that the Windows NT system components log. For example, the failure of a driver or other system component to load during startup is recorded in the system log.
Windows NT security log	Records security events. For example, attempts to log on to the system are recorded here.

Using SQL Server Performance Monitor

When you want to track activity information and performance statistics for your server, use SQL Server Performance Monitor. You can use SQL Server Performance Monitor to log performance over time or to observe server activity as it happens.

SQL Server–Specific Counters in Windows NT Performance Monitor

SQL Server Performance Monitor is actually the Windows NT Performance Monitor. A number of Performance Monitor objects and counters for monitoring SQL Server–specific metrics are added at installation. The Performance Monitor item within the Microsoft SQL Server 7 program group simply launches Windows NT Performance Monitor, using a predefined set of these counters that are saved in the Sqlctrs.pmc file. This set of counters is a small subset of the available counters. There are 16 objects and more than 100 counters available. You can change the counters and save the Sqlctrs.pmc file or create your own .PMC files to launch Performance Monitor with your own predefined sets of counters.

As with all performance monitoring tools, you should expect some performance overhead when you monitor SQL Server with SQL Server Performance Monitor. The fewer counters you monitor at any time, the lower the overhead of using Performance Monitor.

Note The Performance Monitor is not available for SQL Server running on Microsoft Windows 95 or Windows 98. Clients running on Windows 95 or Windows 98 cannot monitor Performance Monitor counters on a Windows NT–based SQL Server.

Appropriate Security

If the server is using Windows NT authentication, only a member of the System Administrators (sysadmin) role can use SQL Server Performance Monitor.

Counters to Monitor

Standard Windows NT counters and the SQL Server counters provide valuable information about the performance of SQL Server.

Predefined Counters

When you start SQL Server Performance Monitor, it monitors a predefined set of SQL Server counters, defined in the Sqlctrs.pmc file. This file is loaded automatically when you start SQL Server Performance Monitor. The predefined counters and a brief description of each are given in the following table.

Object/Counter	Description
SQLServer:Buffer Manager/ Buffer Cache Hit Ratio	Percentage of pages that were found in the buffer cache without having to incur a read from disk.
SQLServer:General Statistics/ User Connections	Number of users connected to the server.
SQLServer:Memory Manager/ Total Server Memory (KB)	Total amount of dynamic memory that the server is currently using.
SQLServer:SQL Statistics/ SQL Compilations/sec	Total SQL compilations (including recompilations) per second.
SQLServer:Buffer Manager/ Page Reads/sec	Number of physical database page reads issued per second.
SQLServer:Buffer Manager/ Page Writes/sec	Number of physical database page writes issued per second.

SQL Server Counters

The following table contains additional SQL Server counters that are useful in monitoring the server.

Object/Counter	Description
SQLServer:Buffer Manager/ Free Buffers	Number of free buffers available.
SQLServer:Databases/ Active Transactions	Number of active transactions for a given database.
SQLServer:Databases/ Percent Log Used	Percentage of log space in use for a given database.
SQLServer:Access Methods/ Full Scans/sec	Number of unrestricted full scans per second. These can be either base table or full index scans.
SQLServer:Access Methods/ Index Searches/sec	Number of index searches per second. These are used to start range scans, fetch single index records, and reposition nodes in an index.
SQLServer:Locks/ Number of Deadlocks/sec	Number of lock requests per second that resulted in a deadlock.

Windows NT Counters

The following table describes some of the more important Windows NT counters to monitor.

Object/Counter	Description
Memory/Pages/sec	Number of pages read from or written to the page file per second to resolve memory references to pages that were not in memory at the time of the reference. An increase in this figure may indicate a RAM shortage.
Memory/Page Faults/sec	Number of page faults per second. An increase in this figure may indicate a RAM shortage.
Process/Page Faults/sec (sqlservr instance)	Number of page faults caused by SQL Server per second. An increase in this figure indicates that SQL Server is not getting enough RAM.
Processor/% Processor Time	Percentage of elapsed time the CPU was busy (non-idle time).
Process/% Processor Time (sqlservr instance)	Percentage of elapsed time the CPU was busy with SQL Server work.
PhysicalDisk/% Disk Time	Percentage of elapsed time the disk was busy with read/write activity.
PhysicalDisk/Avg. Disk Queue Length	Number of system requests waiting for disk access. Should not be more than 1.5 to 2 per physical disk.

Important In order to use the counters of the PhysicalDisk object, you must enable them using the Windows NT diskperf command. These counters are disabled by default, as monitoring disk activity can cause increased disk access times. See the Windows NT documentation for more information.

User-Defined Counters

You can also create up to ten user-defined counters. The SQLServer:User Settable object provides the Query counter, which has 10 instances: User counter 1 through 10. You can provide values for these counters by calling the system stored procedures sp_user_counter1 through sp_user_counter10 and passing them the value you wish to monitor. A counter can monitor information that is returned by a SQL statement or by any operation that returns a value, such as the execution of a stored procedure.

Practice: Monitoring SQL Server Activity with SQL Server Performance Monitor

In this practice, you will set up your system to monitor SQL Server activity with the SQL Server Performance Monitor.

Exercise 1: Setting Up Stress Files

▶ **In this exercise, you will set up stress files. To set up the stress files**

1. Create a new folder called C:\Monitor.

2. Copy the files from C:\Sqladmin\Exercise\Ch14\Monitor to the new folder.

Exercise 2: Creating the nwcopy Database

In this exercise, you will restore a backup of the nwcopy database to add it to your server.

▶ **To create the nwcopy database**

1. Log on to your computer as Administrator or another account that is a member of the Administrators local group.

2. Copy the C:\Sqladmin\Exercise\Ch10\Nwc1.bak file to C:\Mssql7\Backup on your local hard disk.

3. Open SQL Server Query Analyzer and log on to the (local) server with Microsoft Windows NT authentication. Your account is a member of the Windows NT Administrators group, which is automatically mapped to the SQL Server sysadmin role.

4. Open C:\Sqladmin\Exercise\Ch14\Setupnwc.sql, and then review and execute it.

   This script restores the nwcopy database that is used in the exercises that follow.

Exercise 3: Configuring the Windows NT Performance Monitor

In this exercise, you will add Performance Monitor counters to monitor SQL Server activity.

▶ **To configure Windows NT Performance Monitor**

1. Start Windows NT Performance Monitor.

2. Open the C:\Sqladmin\Exercise\Ch14\Monlab.pmc file and skip the rest of this exercise, or continue with step 3 to add the counters yourself.

3. On the toolbar, click Add Counter (+). The Add To Chart dialog box appears.

4. Add counters using the information in the following table. Click Add after each counter is configured. Click Done when you have added all of the counters.

Object	Counter	Instance
SQLServer:Buffer Manager	Buffer Cache Hit Ratio	
SQLServer:SQL Statistics	Batch Requests/sec	
SQLServer:Access Methods	Full Scans/sec	
SQLServer:Access Methods	Index Searches/sec	
SQLServer:Databases	Percent Log Used	Nwcopy
SQLServer:Memory Manager	Lock Blocks	

Exercise 4: Simulating Server Activity

In this exercise, you will execute a batch file to simulate server activity. This batch file creates several command-prompt sessions that interact with SQL Server.

▶ **To simulate server activity**

1. Stop and restart SQL Server.

2. At a command prompt, change to the C:\Monitor folder, and execute the Monitor.bat batch file. This file opens seven command-prompt windows.

3. Switch to the SQL Server Performance Monitor window.

   Watch the Chart window while the monitoring batch files execute. What trends do you notice?

Exercise 5: Adding Counters to the Chart

In this exercise, you will add counters to the chart in order to observe the response of various counters.

▶ **To add counters to the chart**

1. On the toolbar, click Add Counter (+). The Add To Chart dialog box appears.

2 Add counters, using the information in the following table. Click Add after each counter is configured. Click Done when you have added all of the counters.

Object	Counter	Instance
Memory	Page Faults/sec	
Memory	Pages/sec	
Process	% Processor Time	sqlservr
Process	Page Faults/sec	sqlservr

3. Watch the Chart window while the monitoring batch files continue to execute. (Press Ctrl-H to highlight the currently selected counter.)

   What trends do you notice?

4. Close each command-prompt window. The Windows NT Performance Monitor counters should reflect the lack of activity on the server.

5. Exit Windows NT Performance Monitor.

Using Transact-SQL to Monitor SQL Server

In addition to the graphical tools, you can use several Transact-SQL statements to monitor SQL Server.

System Stored Procedures

Use the system stored procedures in the following table to see real-time information or statistics about your database or server.

System stored procedure	Reports information on
sp_who	Current SQL Server users and processes
sp_lock	Active locks
sp_spaceused	The amount of disk space used by a table or by the entire database
sp_helpdb	Databases and their objects
sp_monitor	Overall SQL Server statistics
sp_helpindex	Indexes on a table

Functions

The next table lists some of the functions that you can use to obtain specific statistics or information. See SQL Server Books Online for many more functions.

Note In previous versions of SQL Server, functions that had names beginning with @@ were called global variables. Global variables in SQL Server 7 refer to variables that can be referenced by multiple Data Transformation Services tasks.

Function	Purpose
@@CONNECTIONS	Returns the number of connections or attempted connections since SQL Server was last started.
@@CPU_BUSY	Returns the time in milliseconds that the CPU has spent doing work since SQL Server was last started.
@@IO_BUSY	Returns the time in milliseconds that SQL Server has spent doing input and output operations since it was last started.
@@IDLE	Returns the time in milliseconds that SQL Server has been idle since it was last started.

Function	Purpose
@@TOTAL_ERRORS	Returns the number of disk read/write errors encountered by SQL Server since it was last started.
@@PACKET_ERRORS	Returns the number of network packet errors that have occurred on SQL Server connections since it was last started.

Transact-SQL SET Statements

The Transact-SQL programming language provides several SET statements that alter the current session handling of specific information. The following table lists some of the Transact-SQL SET statements you can use to show statistics or display a text-based query execution plan.

SET statement	Purpose
SET STATISTICS IO	Causes SQL Server to display information regarding the amount of disk activity generated by Transact-SQL statements.
SET STATISTICS TIME	Causes SQL Server to display the number of milliseconds required to parse, compile, and execute each statement.
SET SHOWPLAN_TEXT	Causes SQL Server not to execute Transact-SQL statements. Instead, SQL Server returns detailed information about how the statements are executed.

DBCC Statements

You can use DBCC statements to check performance and activity, as well as the logical and physical consistency of a database.

Some DBCC statements that you might use to monitor performance are listed in the following table.

DBCC statement	Reports information on
SQLPERF(LOGSPACE)	Transaction log space usage in all databases
OPENTRAN	The oldest active transaction in a specified database
SHOW_STATISTICS	The selectivity of an index, which provides the basis for determining whether an index is useful to the optimizer
SHOW_CONTIG	Fragmentation of data and indexes of a table
CHECKDB	The allocation and structural integrity of all objects in a database
CHECKFILEGROUP	The allocation and structural integrity of all tables in a filegroup
CHECKALLOC	The allocation and use of all pages in a database
CHECKTABLE	The integrity of the data, index, text, ntext, and image pages for a table

Note In previous versions of SQL Server, the DBCC MEMUSAGE, DBCC SQLPERF, and DBCC PERFMON statements were used to show various SQL Server performance statistics. These DBCC statements are still available but are no longer documented. In SQL Server 7, use the Performance Monitor to monitor instead.

Trace Flags

You can use trace flags to set specific server characteristics, but you also can use them to diagnose performance issues and debug queries and system stored procedures. You set the trace flags with the DBCC TRACEON statement and disable traces with the DBCC TRACEOFF statement.

The following table lists some of the trace flags you can use to monitor your server.

Trace flag	Description
325	Prints information about the cost of using a nonclustered index or a sort to process an ORDER BY clause.
326	Prints information about the estimated and actual cost of sorts.
330	Enables full output when you use the SET SHOWPLAN option, which gives detailed information about joins.
1204	Returns the type of locks that are participating in a deadlock and the current statement that is affected.
1205	Returns more detailed information about the statement being executed at the time of a deadlock.
1704	Prints information when a temporary table is created or dropped.
3604	Sends trace output to the client—used only when setting trace flags with the DBCC TRACEON and DBCC TRACEOFF statements.
3605	Sends trace output to the error log. If you start SQL Server from the command prompt, the output also appears on the screen.
8501	Performs detailed logging that describes all Microsoft Distributed Transaction Coordinator (MS DTC)–related context and state changes.

Note For many of the trace flags, the extra output is seen only by starting SQL Server from the command prompt or by sending the trace flag output to the error log by turning on trace flag 3605.

Use trace flags with care. You can get unpredictable results if you use undocumented trace flags. The use of trace flags is generally not supported by Microsoft.

Using SQL Server Profiler

SQL Server Profiler provides you with the ability to monitor server and database activity, including login, user, and application activity. You can also capture the data to a table, file, or SQL script for later analysis.

Note In previous versions of SQL Server, Profiler was called SQL Trace. SQL Server Profiler can read trace files saved in SQL Trace.

Monitoring Current Server Activity

To use SQL Server Profiler, first decide what you want to monitor, and then choose criteria to monitor. Traces can be public—available to all users of the computer—or private, available only to the user who defined the trace.

You can capture information about a wide assortment of events and then filter and group the information meaningfully so that only significant data is captured. Some events that you might want to monitor include

- Poorly performing queries
- Queries that cause table scans
- Activities of individual users or applications
- Deadlock problems
- Login attempts, failures, connections, and disconnections
- Logical disk reads and physical writes
- CPU use at the statement level
- Error severity levels
- Wait time for all post-execution events

Capturing Real-Time Results

You can monitor the results of server activity and see commands being processed at the server in real time.

Capturing Data to a File

Saving trace information allows you to

- Replay the activity against a server
- Analyze and perform additional filtering of the event activity
- Provide a load file for use with the Index Tuning Wizard
- Step through and execute SQL batches and stored procedures to debug an application

Using the Index Tuning Wizard

The Index Tuning Wizard allows you to select and create an optimal set of indexes and statistics for a SQL Server database without requiring an expert understanding of the structure of the database, the workload, or the internals of SQL Server. You can launch the Index Tuning Wizard from SQL Server Profiler or SQL Server Enterprise Manager.

To build a recommendation of the optimal set of indexes that should be in place, the wizard requires a workload. A workload consists of a SQL script or a SQL Server Profiler trace.

Exercise: Configuring SQL Server Profiler

You suspect that users are submitting queries that take a long time to execute and that unauthorized users are trying to gain access to your SQL Server. In this exercise, you will create a trace to detect long-running queries and events, record query activity, and organize the output by duration.

► **To configure SQL Server Profiler**

1. Start SQL Server Profiler.

2. On the File menu, select New, then click Trace to create a new trace. Use the information in the following table to set options on the General tab of the Trace Properties dialog box.

Option	Value
Trace Name	LongQueries
Trace Type	Private
SQL Server	SQLServer (or your server name if different)
Capture To File	Checked C:\Sqladmin\Exercise\Ch14\Monitor\LongQueries.trc

3. On the Events tab, define the trace to monitor the events in the next table. (To add an event to the Selected Events list, expand the event category in the Available events lists, select the required event, and click Add>>.)

Event category	Selected events
TSQL	RPC:Completed
TSQL	SQL:BatchCompleted
Sessions	Connect
Sessions	Disconnect
Sessions	ExistingConnection
Misc.	Login Failed

4. Click the Data Columns tab.

5. Use the Add>> and <<Remove buttons to move the data column names between the Unselected Data and Selected Data lists so that you have the data column names listed in the following table in the Selected Data list.

   Use the Up and Down buttons to order the data columns in the Selected Data list. In particular, ensure that Duration is the only data column in the Groups category. This will cause the trace output to be grouped by event duration.

Data column	Category
Duration	Groups
Event Class	Columns
Text	Columns
Application Name	Columns
NT User Name	Columns
CPU	Columns
Reads	Columns
Writes	Columns
Integer Data	Columns

6. Click OK to start the trace.

Exercise: Detecting Login Attempts

In this exercise, you will monitor an unauthorized login attempt. To do this, you will attempt to log on with an invalid account, and then you will review the SQL Server Profiler.

▶ **To detect login attempts**

1. Start SQL Server Query Analyzer.

2. Try to connect to SQL Server with SQL Server authentication, the login account Maria, and no password.

3. Try to connect to SQL Server with SQL Server authentication, the sa login account, and an incorrect password.

4. Switch to the SQL Server Profiler window.

5. Expand the node labeled Duration = 0.

   What information is recorded?

6. Connect to SQL Server with the sa login account and a correct password.

7. Switch to the SQL Server Profiler window, and expand all nodes on the tree.

   What information is recorded?

Exercise: Editing the Current Trace

In this exercise, you will edit the current trace by setting up a filter to show only events longer than 100 milliseconds in duration.

▶ **To edit the current trace**

1. Stop the active trace.
2. On the Edit menu, click Clear Trace Window.
3. On the main window toolbar, click Edit Trace Properties.
4. On the Events tab, remove the LoginFailed event from the trace.
5. Click the Filters tab.
6. In the Trace Event Criteria list, click Duration.
7. Type **100** in Minimum. This filters out all events that have a duration of less than 100 milliseconds.
8. Start the trace.

Exercise: Detecting Long-Running Queries

In this exercise, you will use the current trace to detect the longest-running queries in a batch of SQL statements.

▶ **To detect long-running queries**

1. Open a command-prompt window.
2. Simulate server activity by executing the C:\Sqladmin\Exercise\Ch14\ Monitor\LongQry.bat batch file. This executes several queries on tables in the nwcopy database.
3. Switch to SQL Server Profiler.
4. Expand Duration for each event, and examine the events with long run times.

   What events are included?
5. Locate the SELECT statement with the longest duration.
6. Expand SQL:BatchCompleted to see the text of the query.

   What is the query text?
7. Stop the trace and close SQL Server Profiler.

Using the Query History

The query history is a trace of the last 100 events in SQL Server, which uses the extended stored procedures of the SQL Server Profiler. You can use the query history to troubleshoot serious SQL Server failures and when reporting failures to your primary support provider.

Enabling the query history has little impact on SQL Server performance.

Determine the Cause of a Disaster

The 100 most recent events are automatically recorded in the Blackbox.trc trace file in the C:\Mssql7\Log folder if an exception of severity 17 or higher occurs. By using the information in the query history trace file, you can step through the events just prior to a server crash and examine the ones that resulted in errors.

Activate Query History with xp_trace_setqueryhistory

To enable the query history, execute the xp_trace_setqueryhistory extended stored procedure. The syntax for this procedure is as follows:

```
EXECUTE xp_trace_setqueryhistory (0 | 1)
```

This example enables the query history.

```
EXECUTE xp_trace_setqueryhistory 1
```

Write to Disk with xp_trace_flushqueryhistory

To write the current contents of the query history to a trace file, execute the xp_trace_flushqueryhistory extended stored procedure. The syntax for this procedure is as follows:

```
EXECUTE xp_trace_flushqueryhistory 'filename'
```

This example writes the query history to a file called C:\Mssql7\Log\Qhist.trc.

```
EXECUTE xp_trace_flushqueryhistory 'c:\mssql7\log\qhist.trc'
```

View the File with SQL Server Profiler

You can use SQL Server Profiler to open the Blackbox.trc or trace files saved with xp_trace_flushqueryhistory. The trace file displays detailed information about the 100 events that occurred immediately prior to the file being saved, including the event class, Transact-SQL text that was executed, the client that is responsible for the event, the user, and the server name. It also shows any relevant error messages. SQL Server does not have to be running to view the file in SQL Server Profiler.

Exercise: Starting the Query History

In this exercise, you will use a system stored procedure to start the query history and capture recent SQL Server activity.

▶ **To start the query history**

1. Open SQL Server Query Analyzer and connect with Windows NT authentication.

2. Ensure that master is selected in the DB list box. If master is not the current database, the following step will fail.

3. Type and execute the following Transact-SQL statement:

```
EXEC xp_trace_setqueryhistory 1
```

Exercise: Simulating User Activity and Flushing the Query History

In this exercise, you will execute a batch file that simulates user activity and then shuts down the server.

▶ **To simulate user activity and flush the query history**

1. In SQL Server Query Analyzer, open the C:\Sqladmin\Exercise\Ch14\ Activity.sql script file. Execute the script to generate activity on the server.

2. Type and execute the following Transact-SQL statement to flush the query history to a file:

```
EXEC xp_trace_flushqueryhistory 'C:\Sqladmin\Exercise\Ch14\QryHist.trc'
```

3. Type and execute the following Transact-SQL statement to stop the query history:

```
EXEC xp_trace_setqueryhistory 0
```

Exercise: Viewing the Contents of the Trace File

In this exercise, you will use SQL Server Profiler to examine the contents of the query history trace file.

▶ **To view the contents of the QryHist.trc file**

1. In SQL Server Profiler, on the File menu, point to Open and then click Trace File. Navigate to the C:\Sqladmin\Exercise\Ch14\QryHist.trc trace file and open it. The file may take a while to open.

2. Examine the trace.

Using SQL Server Query Analyzer

You can use SQL Server Query Analyzer as a monitoring tool to collect information on a specific query.

Displaying a Graphical Plan of Execution

When you select Show Execution Plan on the Query menu in SQL Server Query Analyzer, the analyzer visually displays the plan of execution in the Execution Plan tab of the results pane when you execute a command batch, as shown in Figure 14.2. You can also use Display Estimated Execution Plan on the Query menu to see an estimation of the query plan without actually executing the command batch. Each icon in the plan represents a step in the query process. The execution plan provides detailed information, including

- Which indexes are used
- The types of access methods (such as table scans) that are performed
- Approximate or actual I/O work
- The estimated or actual CPU time required to complete the query

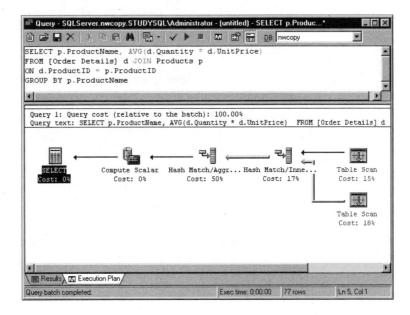

Figure 14.2 The graphical execution plan in SQL Server Query Analyzer

Using the Index Analysis Tool

SQL Server Query Analyzer provides a utility to recommend indexes for a particular query. The Index Analysis tool suggests indexes that will optimize a query and generates the Transact-SQL statements required to create the indexes. Select Perform Index Analysis from the Query menu to run the Index Analysis tool.

Exercise: Generating Performance Statistics and an Execution Plan

In this exercise, you will use SQL Server Query Analyzer to generate performance statistics as well as an execution plan for a long-running query.

▶ **To execute a query and generate an execution plan and statistics**

1. Open SQL Server Query Analyzer and connect to SQL Server with Windows NT authentication.

2. In the DB list box, click nwcopy.

3. Type the following query, which was previously identified as a long-running query, into the query window:

```
SELECT e.lastname, p.productname, avg(d.quantity * d.unitprice)
FROM employees e JOIN orders o ON e.employeeID = o.employeeid
JOIN [order details] d ON o.orderid = d.orderid
JOIN products p ON d.productid = p.productid
GROUP BY e.lastname, p.productname
```

4. On the Query menu, click Show Execution Plan. This enables the graphical query output, which you will see when you execute the query later.

5. On the Query menu, click Current Connection Options.

6. Check the Show Stats Time option and the Show Stats I/O option. Click OK to close the dialog box and save your changes.

7. Execute the query.

8. Scroll to the end of the query result set on the Results tab, and record the count of logical reads for each table.

9. Click the Execution Plan tab to display the graphical execution plan for this query. Note that statistics about each step are given if you move your mouse pointer over the step icons. The Table Scan steps may show a message stating that statistics are missing for the table. This is correct because the tables in nwcopy do not have indexes or statistics created for them.

   Were table scans used to process this query? What can be done to improve performance?

10. Open another query window, and make sure that nwcopy is selected in the DB list box.

11. Execute the following queries:

    ```
    EXEC sp_helpindex Employees
    EXEC sp_helpindex Orders
    EXEC sp_helpindex [Order Details]
    EXEC sp_helpindex Products
    ```

    What indexes exist on the Employees, Orders, Order Details, and Products tables?

Using Current Activity in SQL Server Enterprise Manager

Current Activity in SQL Server Enterprise Manager displays

- Information about current user connections and locks
- The process number, status, locks, and last TSQL command for active users
- Information about objects that are locked and the kinds of locks that are present

SQL Server Processes

Current Activity in SQL Server Enterprise Manager displays information about current processes. There are a number of system processes, as well as one process for each user connection. Many of the processes will be inactive, awaiting a command. The information displayed includes

- Process ID
- Username

- Current database
- Client application name
- CPU utilization
- Physical I/O utilization
- Memory utilization
- Login time
- Time of last command batch run
- Client network library
- Client network address
- Process ID of any process blocking this process
- Process ID of any process being blocked by this process

Locks

Current Activity in SQL Server Enterprise Manager also displays information about locks acquired and held on objects by processes. Two views of locking are available:

- Locks/Process ID lists locks by process ID. This view highlights processes that are blocked by or are blocking other processes.
- Locks/Object lists locks by object.

To prevent simultaneous transactions from interfering with one another (concurrency control), SQL Server places locks on the relevant tables or data pages. The type of lock depends on the type and size of operation being performed.

Exclusive locks are applied for the UPDATE, INSERT, and DELETE data modification operations. Exclusive locks are always held until the end of the transaction, blocking additional users from reading or modifying the data. Shared locks are applied for read operations, allowing other users to read but not modify the data. Shared locks are usually held only for the duration of the read operation; however, the HOLDLOCK keyword holds the shared lock until the end of the transaction.

Blocking

A transaction waiting for a lock on an object is said to be blocked. SQL Server transactions do not time out when they are blocked unless you specify a value for the LOCK_TIMEOUT setting. Blocking is normal and is necessary to prevent transactions from overwriting one another. Do not confuse blocking with deadlock. Optimizing applications and database design to minimize blocking is one of the ways to ensure good overall system performance.

Deadlock

A deadlock occurs when two users (or sessions) have locks on separate objects and each user wants a lock on the other's object. Each user waits for the other to release its lock, but because they are waiting for each other, they will wait indefinitely. Meanwhile, other users cannot lock either of the objects involved in the deadlock, and system performance degrades.

Figure 14.3 shows two transactions involved in a deadlock. Transaction 1 has a lock on Table A and is waiting to obtain a lock on Table B. Transaction 2 has a lock on Table B and is waiting to obtain a lock on Table A.

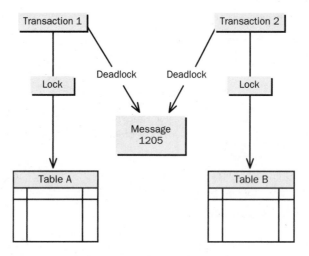

Figure 14.3   Two deadlocked transactions

SQL Server detects deadlocks and selects one of the transactions as a victim. It rolls back the deadlock victim's transaction, notifies the user's application (by returning error message number 1205), cancels the user's current request, and then allows the other transaction to continue.

Managing Processes and Locks

In addition to viewing information about selected processes, you can use Current Activity in SQL Server Enterprise Manager to send a message to a selected user or to terminate a selected process.

Practice: Managing Locks

In these exercises, you will open three query windows in SQL Server Query Analyzer, called connection 1, 2, and 3. You will then use the BEGIN TRANSACTION and ROLLBACK TRANSACTION statements to control how an UPDATE statement is processed on the member table. You will use system stored procedures and Current Activity in SQL Server Enterprise Manager to monitor the connections.

Exercise 1: Viewing Locking Information

In this exercise, you will use Current Activity to view locking information.

▶ **To view locking information**

1. Open SQL Server Query Analyzer (connection 1), and select nwcopy in the DB list box.

2. Execute the following system stored procedures, using connection 1, and review the output:

```
EXEC sp_who
EXEC sp_lock
```

3. Do not close the connection 1 query window in SQL Server Query Analyzer; you will continue to use it in the next exercise.

4. Start SQL Server Enterprise Manager. Expand your server, expand Management, and then expand Current Activity.

5. Explore the Current Activity information by clicking Process Info, expanding Locks/Process ID, and clicking on a few processes and then expanding Locks/Object and clicking a few objects.

Note The information under Current Activity is not updated dynamically. To see updated information, you must periodically right-click Current Activity and then click Refresh.

Exercise 2: Holding Locks on Server Resources

In this exercise, you will execute SQL statements that obtain and hold locks on server resources. You will use system stored procedures, as well as SQL Server Enterprise Manager, to examine locking information. You will continue to use the connection 1 query window from the previous exercise and open a second query window called connection 2.

▶ **To hold locks on the server**

1. Open a new query using SQL Server Query Analyzer (connection 2), and ensure that nwcopy is selected in the DB list.

2. Open C:\Sqladmin\Exercise\Ch14\Lock.sql, using connection 2, and review its contents.

   Notice that a transaction is started with the BEGIN TRAN statement, but a corresponding COMMIT TRAN or ROLLBACK TRAN statement to complete the transaction does not exist. The absence of these statements keeps the transactions open and the associated locks active so that you can view locking information.

3. Execute C:\Sqladmin\Exercise\Ch14\Lock.sql, using connection 2, and review the results.

   Record the server process ID (spid) for this connection.

4. Switch to connection 1, execute the sp_lock system stored procedure, and then review the lock information.

   Using the spid recorded in step 3, identify what locks were granted to the transaction that was issued by connection 2.

5. Switch to SQL Server Enterprise Manager, refresh Current Activity, and review the locking information.

Exercise 3: Detecting Lock Blocking

In this exercise, you will create and observe a blocking situation in which one query must wait while another query uses a resource. You will continue to use the connection 1 and 2 query windows from the previous exercise and open a third query window called connection 3.

▶ **To detect lock blocking**

1. Open a new query window using SQL Server Query Analyzer (connection 3), and ensure that nwcopy is selected in the DB list box.

2. Open and execute C:\Sqladmin\Exercise\Ch14\Lock.sql, using connection 3.

   Does the query complete?

3. Switch to connection 1 and execute the sp_lock system stored procedure.

   Is the spid for connection 3 waiting for any resources? (Look for WAIT in the Status column.)

4. Switch to SQL Server Enterprise Manager, refresh Current Activity, and review the locking information. In particular, note the information under Locks/ Process ID.

   Why can't connection 3 complete the query?

5. Switch to connection 2 in the Query Analyzer.

6. Type **ROLLBACK TRAN** on a new line in the query pane, and highlight it. Now execute the statement. (Only the highlighted ROLLBACK TRAN statement is executed.)

7. Switch to connection 1 and execute the sp_lock system stored procedure.

   You will see that the locks that were acquired by the transaction in connection 2 have now been released and connection 3 is no longer waiting.

8. Switch to connection 3 and complete the transaction by executing a ROLL-BACK TRAN statement.

9. Switch to SQL Server Enterprise Manager, refresh Current Activity, and review the locking information. Confirm that the exclusive and intent locks have been released.

10. Close all SQL Server Query Analyzer connections.

Lesson Summary

SQL Server includes several tools for monitoring the performance of your server. The tools allow you to monitor the SQL Server computer, the overall SQL Server performance, and individual queries and database objects. The primary tools are the SQL Server Performance Monitor (Windows NT Performance Monitor), Transact-SQL statements, SQL Server Profiler, SQL Server Query Analyzer, and Current Activity in SQL Server Enterprise Manager.

Lesson 3: Maintaining SQL Server

To maintain your database, you should perform several tasks, either manually or automatically. These tasks form the core of a database maintenance plan. They include

- Updating information about data optimization
- Verifying the integrity of data
- Performing backups
- Creating reports and a maintenance history of the database

If you choose to have these tasks performed automatically, you can set up and schedule your database maintenance plan with the Database Maintenance Plan Wizard.

This lesson gives details on each task you should consider for your database maintenance plan and takes you through the process of automating your plan.

After this lesson, you will be able to

- Develop a database maintenance plan
- Use the Database Maintenance Plan Wizard to implement a database maintenance plan

Estimated lesson time: 40 minutes

Developing a Database Maintenance Plan

Several tasks can help you maintain your database. The most important tasks, which should be performed for all SQL Server databases, are updating data optimization information, verifying data integrity, performing backups, and keeping a history of maintenance activities. These tasks should be performed on a regular basis. How often you run these tasks depends on the level of database activity and the size of your database. See Chapter 13, "Automating Administrative Tasks," for more information about creating scheduled SQL Server jobs to perform these tasks automatically.

Update Information About Data Optimization

As data and index pages fill up, updating requires more time, and pages can become fragmented. Reorganizing your data and index pages can improve performance.

Maintain Indexes Using the fillfactor Option

You can specify the percentage of available free space (fillfactor) in your index and data pages. This enhances performance: if space is available in existing pages when performing inserts and updates, SQL Server does not have to split pages and allocate new pages. The fillfactor percentage is used when the index is first created and whenever the index is rebuilt. You can specify a percentage or allow SQL Server to select the optimal value automatically.

Update Statistics That Are Used by the Query Optimizer

You should run UPDATE STATISTICS on tables that are being modified. This updates the information about the key value distribution for one or more indexes in a table, which the query optimizer uses to generate optimal query plans.

Remove Unused Space from the Database Files

You can execute DBCC SHRINKDATABASE to recover any unused disk space in the database tables. You can also enable the autoshrink option on databases.

Verify the Integrity of Data

Data integrity tests detect inconsistency in the database caused by hardware or software errors.

Perform Internal Data Integrity Tests

Execute DBCC CHECKALLOC to check the allocation of data and index pages for each table within the extent structures of the database.

Perform Database Integrity Tests

Execute DBCC CHECKDB to check the allocation and structural integrity of the objects in the database. Execute DBCC CHECKTABLE to check the integrity of the data, index, text, and index pages for a table. If DBCC finds an error, you can specify that it repair the error automatically.

DBCC CHECKDB performs all of the checks performed by DBCC CHECKALLOC and DBCC CHECKTABLE on each table in the database. If you run DBCC CHECKDB regularly, it is not necessary to run DBCC CHECKALLOC and DBCC CHECKTABLE as well. If time is limited, you can use DBCC CHECK-ALLOC and DBCC CHECKTABLE to perform smaller checks at different times rather than running a full DBCC CHECKDB at once. If DBCC CHECKDB reports only allocation errors, you can use DBCC CHECKALLOC to repair the errors. The safest option is to run DBCC CHECKDB with the repair option; this repairs all errors, including allocation errors. While DBCC CHECKDB is running, it is not possible to create, alter, or drop tables.

Note Previous versions of SQL Server had a DBCC NEWALLOC statement. This is supported in SQL Server 7 for backward compatibility only; you should use DBCC CHECKALLOC instead.

Perform Backups

Perform backups on a regular basis to protect against data loss. You should back up the transaction log to capture changes to the database between full database backups.

Maintain a Maintenance History

Maintain a history of the maintenance tasks. This history should include what actions were performed, as well as the results of any corrective actions.

Automating the Database Maintenance Plan Tasks

You can use either the Database Maintenance Plan Wizard or the sqlmaint utility to automate your database maintenance plan so that it runs on a regularly scheduled basis.

The Database Maintenance Plan Wizard

The Database Maintenance Plan Wizard helps you set up the core maintenance tasks that are necessary to ensure that your database performs well, is regularly backed up in the event of a system failure, and is checked for inconsistencies. When you run the wizard, you will specify the following:

Databases That the Plan Maintains

You can define a single maintenance plan for all databases or plans for one or more databases.

Data Optimization Information

You can have the wizard reorganize data and index pages, update the index statistics to ensure that the query optimizer has current information regarding the spread of data in the tables, and compress data files by removing empty database pages.

Data Verification Tests

You can have the wizard perform internal consistency checks of the data and data pages within the database to ensure that a system or rare software problem has not damaged data. You can specify whether indexes should be included in the checks and whether the wizard should attempt to repair minor problems that it finds.

Frequency and Destination of Backups

You can schedule database and transaction log backups and keep backup files for a specified time.

Location of History Files

The results that the maintenance tasks generate can be written as a report to a text file, saved in history tables, or sent in an e-mail message to an operator.

The sqlmaint Utility

Use the sqlmaint utility to execute DBCC statements, dump a database and transaction logs, update statistics, and rebuild indexes. The sqlmaint utility is a command-prompt utility that performs functions similar to those handled by the Database Maintenance Plan Wizard.

Exercise: Using the Database Maintenance Plan Wizard to Create a Database Maintenance Plan

In this exercise, you will create a maintenance plan using the Database Maintenance Plan Wizard.

▶ **To create a database maintenance plan that consists of multiple jobs by using the Database Maintenance Plan Wizard**

1. Switch to SQL Server Enterprise Manager.

2. On the Tools menu, click Wizards.

3. Expand Management, click Database Maintenance Plan Wizard, and then click OK to run the wizard. Click Next on the first screen of the wizard.

4. Click These Databases, and then check only StudyNwind in the Databases list. Click Next.

5. Check the Update Statistics Used By Query Optimizer option. Set the value of the Sample option to 10% of the database.

6. Check the Remove Unused Space From Database Files option. Set the value of the When It Grows Beyond option to 5 MB. Set the value of the Amount Of Free Space To Remain After Shrink option to 15% of free space.

7. Click Change to open the Edit Recurring Job Schedule dialog box. In Occurs, click Monthly. In Monthly, set the value to Day 1 Of Every 3 Month(s).

8. Click OK to close the Edit Recurring Job Schedule dialog box. Click Next.

9. Check the Check Database Integrity option.

10. Click Change to open the Edit Recurring Job Schedule dialog box. In Occurs, click Monthly. In Monthly, set the value to The 1st Saturday Of Every 1 Month(s).

11. Click OK to close the Edit Recurring Job Schedule dialog box. Click Next.

12. Check the Back Up The Database As Part Of The Database Plan option.

13. Click Change to open the Edit Recurring Job Schedule dialog box. In Occurs, click Weekly. In Weekly, set the value to Every 1 Week(s) On Sunday. In Daily Frequency, set the value to Occurs Once At 11:00 P.M.

14. Click OK to close the Edit Recurring Job Schedule dialog box. Click Next.

15. Check and set the Remove Files Older Than 2 Week(s) option.

16. Click Next.

17. Check the option Backup The Transaction Log As Part Of The Maintenance Plan.

18. Click Change to open the Edit Recurring Job Schedule dialog box. In Occurs, click Weekly. In Weekly, set the value to Every 1 Week(s) On Monday, Wednesday And Friday. In Daily Frequency, set the value to Occurs Once At 11:00 P.M.

19. Click OK to close the Edit Recurring Job Schedule dialog box. Click Next.

20. Check and set the option Remove Files Older Than 1 Week(s).

21. Click Next.

22. Check the option Write Report To A Text File In Directory.

23. Click Next.

24. Check Write History To The msdb.dbo.sysdbmaintplan_history Table On The Local Server.

25. Check the option Limit Rows In The Table To. Set the value to 1000 rows for this plan.

26. Click Next.

27. In Plan Name, type **StudyNwind Maintenance Plan**.

28. Click Finish to create the new plan. Click OK to close the confirmation that your maintenance plan has been created.

29. In the console tree, expand Management, then click the Database Maintenance Plans icon.

30. In the details pane, right-click StudyNwind Maintenance Plan, and then click Properties. Review your new plan, noting that the wizard has created a plan with all of the settings that you selected.

31. Click Cancel to close the Database Maintenance Plan dialog box. If you are prompted to save changes, click No.

32. In the console tree, expand SQL Server Agent, and then click the Jobs icon. Verify that four jobs were created successfully for StudyNwind Maintenance Plan.

33. In the details pane, right-click Integrity Checks Job For DB Maintenance Plan 'StudyNwind Maintenance Plan', and click Start to manually start the Integrity Check Job.

34. Review the job history to verify that the job was executed successfully.

Lesson Summary

It is important to regularly perform various maintenance tasks on your databases. Regular maintenance includes keeping table and index statistics up to date, performing database consistency checks, making backups, and organizing database space allocation. You can automate maintenance by creating your own jobs or by creating a database maintenance plan using the Database Maintenance Plan Wizard.

Review

The following questions are intended to reinforce key information presented in the chapter. If you are unable to answer a question, review the appropriate lesson and then try the question again. Answers to the questions can be found in Appendix A, "Questions and Answers."

1. Users complain that the server slows down considerably every day at 2:00 P.M. How can you find out what is causing this delay?

2. You want to find out the locks that are being held on a specific SQL Server table. What tools would you use?

3. You want to see a query plan and the statistics for a specific query in SQL Server Query Analyzer. What steps must you take?

CHAPTER   15

Introducing Replication

About This Chapter

This is the first chapter of three that deal with SQL Server replication. In this chapter, you will learn about the concepts and terminology associated with replication. In Chapter 16, "Planning and Setting Up Replication," you will learn how to plan and implement replication; and in Chapter 17, "Managing Replication," you will learn how to maintain replication and replicate data with non-SQL Server databases.

Before You Begin

There are no prerequisites for this chapter.

Lesson 1: Introduction to Distributed Data

This lesson starts with a description of the distributed data environment and addresses factors in deciding how to distribute data. It then summarizes the various methods of distributing data.

After this lesson, you will be able to

- List the various methods for distributing data
- Describe the characteristics of Microsoft SQL Server version 7 replication

Estimated lesson time: 20 minutes

The Need for Distributed Data

A *distributed data environment* is one that can include multiple copies of the same information on multiple servers. For example, in an international company using a sales tracking application, data originates in one country and is distributed to servers in other countries to make querying more efficient.

If a distributed data environment evolves, rather than being created intentionally, it may become necessary to implement a solution that makes it more manageable. For example, during the early development of a company, different divisions typically have their own independent servers, which may run different database management systems. The challenge is to make the data more accessible to the whole company.

When you create a distributed data environment, you design a solution that

- Brings the data closer to the user
- Allows sites to operate independently (autonomously)
- Separates online transaction processing (OLTP) from read-intensive applications, such as data marts and data warehousing
- Can reduce conflicts
- Because data can be distributed throughout the network, the information is made available to many users, and conflicts are reduced during user requests.

Considerations for Distributing Data

Two principal strategies exist for implementing distributed data: distributed transactions and replication. With both strategies, it is possible to keep multiple copies of data current. It also is possible to design a distributed environment that includes aspects of each strategy. Figure 15.1 compares the major differences between replication and distributed transactions; these differences are described in the sections that follow.

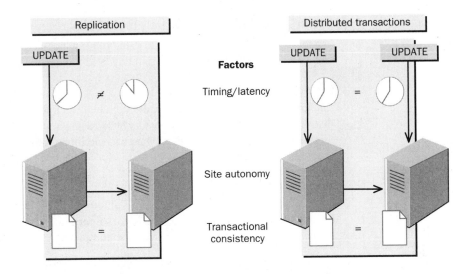

Figure 15.1 Comparing replication with distributed transactions

Distributed Transactions

Distributed transactions guarantee that all copies of your data are consistent all the time. This is usually based on the two-phase commit protocol. Each server that is included in a distributed transaction must be online and able to complete its part of the transaction. The distributed transactions method is less scalable than replication because the failure of a transaction at one site means failure at all sites. You should use this approach only when data must be synchronized at all times.

Distributed transactions are typically used for, but not limited to, applications that make simultaneous updates to data in more than one database. For example, distributed transactions might be used in an invoicing application that adds an invoice to a branch invoicing database and updates a central stock database, which records stock levels at a warehouse used by all branches.

Replication

With replication, recent copies of data are duplicated and distributed from a source database to a destination database, usually on a separate server. Autonomous sites are supported, allowing more scalability because sites can be online intermittently. Databases participating in replication can be located on a large server servicing hundreds of users but can also be located on a single user's computer, making replication useful for a wide variety of applications.

Replication is typically used for, but not limited to, data that is duplicated from one database to another. For example, replication might be used for a product catalog that is maintained at a central office and replicated to branch offices.

Factors in Deciding How to Distribute Data

When you decide how to distribute data, you must consider such factors as latency, site autonomy, transactional consistency, and database update conflicts.

Latency

Latency is the time delay that occurs between the updates to two or more sets of distributed data. You need to consider what degree of latency is acceptable for your database application. Distributed transactions require near-zero latency, while replication may cause or allow latency of a few seconds to a number of days.

Site Autonomy

Site autonomy refers to the degree to which sites can operate independently. Distributed transactions require that sites be permanently connected, whereas some forms of replication can allow sites to be completely disconnected for long periods.

Transactional Consistency

A *transaction* is a series of data modifications that must be completed entirely or not at all. Distributed transactions enforce complete, immediate transactional consistency. Some forms of replication maintain transactional consistency, although there is a delay from the initial update; other forms of replication do not guarantee transactional consistency.

Database Update Conflicts

If data is being updated at different sites, conflicts can occur. Distributed transactions give the same degree of multi-user consistency for multiple sites as a single server. Some forms of replication prevent conflicts by allowing data to be updated at only one site. Alternatively, you can design your application so that each participating site works with data that is strictly segregated, or partitioned, from other sites. For example, you might design your order entry system so that a given sales representative has a unique territory code, preventing orders from conflicting with those of other sales representatives.

Note The term *immediate guaranteed consistency* replaces the term *tight consistency* used in SQL Server 6.x. The term *latent guaranteed consistency* replaces the term *loose consistency* used in SQL Server 6.x.

Methods of Distributing Data with SQL Server

As illustrated in Figure 15.2, the different methods of distributing data provide varying degrees of transactional latency and autonomy. It is important to select the method that best suits your particular business needs and environment.

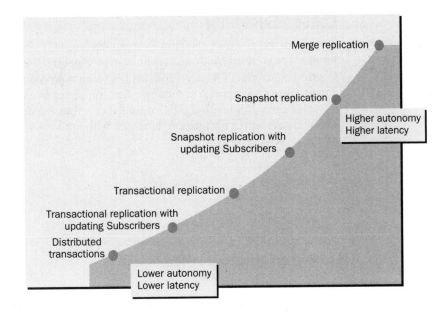

Figure 15.2 Comparison of methods for distributing data

Distributed Transactions

Using distributed transactions guarantees that all sites have the same data at the same time. Microsoft Distributed Transaction Coordinator (MS DTC) facilitates distributed transactions in SQL Server by using a protocol known as two-phase commit to guarantee that a transaction completes at all participating sites at the same time.

Replication

Various types of replication exist for distributing data in SQL Server. They are summarized here and presented in detail in Lesson 3.

- **Transactional replication**—Only changed data is distributed. The sequence of transactions is maintained. Conflicts do not arise, because there is only one location where data is changed.

- **Snapshot replication**—A picture of the entire current data (changed and unchanged) at a source server replaces data at a destination server on a periodic basis or on demand.

- **Merge replication**—Multiple sites make changes to data independently of one another. The changes are periodically merged together at the source server. Conflicts can occur (and be resolved), so this type does not guarantee transactional consistency.

Lesson Summary

Data is commonly distributed in an organization. SQL Server provides support for distributed transactions and replication to support these distributed data needs. Distributed transactions are implemented using a protocol known as two-phase commit that guarantees that a transaction completes at all participating sites at the same time. Replication duplicates and distributes recent copies of data from a source database to a destination database. With replication, distribution of changed data may be delayed.

Lesson 2: Introduction to SQL Server Replication

This lesson describes the publisher-subscriber metaphor, which is the SQL Server model for defining the source and destination of replicated data and the sets of data that will be replicated. It also discusses different types of data filtering.

Before you continue with the lesson, run the Rep.htm video demonstration located in the \Media folder on the Supplemental Course Materials CD-ROM that accompanies this book. This demonstration provides an overview of the SQL Server replication process.

After this lesson, you will be able to

- Explain the publisher-subscriber metaphor, including articles, publications, and subscriptions
- Explain the process of filtering data for replication

Estimated lesson time: 30 minutes

The Publisher-Subscriber Metaphor

Replication uses a publisher-subscriber metaphor for distributing data. In a replication environment, a Publisher sends data and a Subscriber receives data.

A single SQL Server can act as a Publisher, a Distributor, a Subscriber, or any combination of the three for one or more databases at the same time. Figure 15.3 illustrates the Publisher-Distributor-Subscriber relationship.

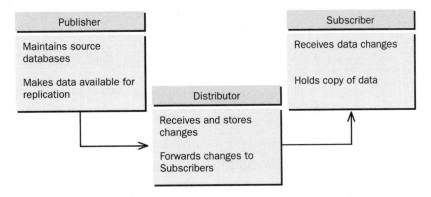

Figure 15.3   The Publisher-Distributor-Subscriber relationship

Publisher

A Publisher is a SQL Server that maintains a source database, makes published data from that database available for replication, and sends changes to the published data to the Distributor.

Subscriber

A Subscriber is a SQL Server that holds a copy of the replicated data and receives updates to this data. It is possible to allow the data on a Subscriber to be changed, and a Subscriber can, in turn, be a Publisher to other Subscribers.

Distributor

The Distributor receives a copy of all changes to the published data, stores the changes, and then makes them available to the appropriate Subscribers. A special system database called the *distribution database* and a folder called the *distribution working folder* are created on the Distributor for storing this data and replication configuration information. By default, the distribution folder is C:\Mssql7\ Repldata, but this can be changed and other folders can be created. Storing the replicated data in this way makes it possible to forward data to Subscribers at short or long intervals and allows for Subscribers that are not always connected. The Distributor can send changes to Subscribers, or Subscribers can fetch changes from the Distributor.

Although the Publisher and the Distributor can be on the same computer, it is more typical in larger or more active sites to locate the Distributor on its own server. If the Distributor is located on another computer, a complete, separately licensed SQL Server installation is required on that computer. It is also possible for one distribution server to support multiple publication servers.

Note The most important concept in replication is that *every replicated data element has only one Publisher*. None of the SQL Server replication options uses a so-called "multiple master" model. This does not mean that data can be modified only on a single server. You will learn how to allow subscribed data to be changed, and even published, but in doing so no data element will have more than one Publisher.

Publications and Articles

In keeping with the publisher-subscriber metaphor, the terms *publication* and *article* are used to refer to data that is published.

Publications

A *publication* is a collection of articles. The following facts apply to a publication:

- A publication is the basis of a subscription. A subscription to a publication includes all articles in the publication, and Subscribers subscribe to publications, not to articles. A publication will typically include all of the data necessary to support a particular application or operation, so that a Subscriber will not have to subscribe to many publications in order to support the application or operation.

- One or more publications can be created in a database.

- A publication cannot span databases. All of the data in a publication must come from the same database.

Articles

An *article* is the basic unit of replication and represents a single data element that is replicated. Subscribers subscribe to publications, not articles. An article can be

- An entire table. When using snapshot replication, the table schema, including triggers, as well as the data can be replicated.
- Certain columns from a table, by using a vertical filter.
- Certain rows from a table, by using a horizontal filter.
- Certain rows and columns from a table, by using a vertical and a horizontal filter.
- A stored procedure definition. When using snapshot replication, the entire stored procedure is replicated.
- The execution of a stored procedure. When using transactional replication, a record of the execution of a stored procedure, rather than the data changes that resulted from the execution of the stored procedure can be replicated. This can dramatically reduce the amount of data that must be sent to the Subscriber(s).

Important In previous versions of SQL Server, you could subscribe to an article as well as to a publication. For backward compatibility, SQL Server 7 supports subscriptions to articles, but you cannot create them in Enterprise Manager, and it is recommended that you replace them with subscriptions to publications.

Filtering Data

It is possible to publish a subset of a table as an article. This is known as filtering data. Filtering data helps to avoid replication conflicts when multiple sites are allowed to update data. You can filter tables vertically, horizontally, or both vertically and horizontally. Each instance of a filtered table is a separate article. Figure 15.4 shows examples of vertical and horizontal filtering.

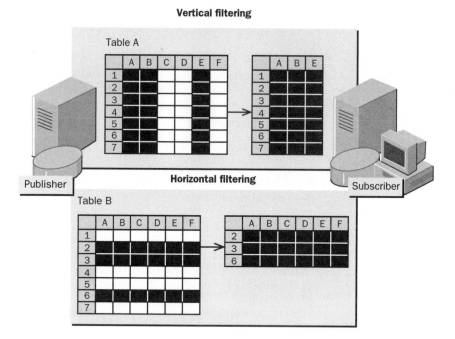

Figure 15.4   Vertical and horizontal filtering

Vertical Filtering

As shown in the upper half of Figure 15.4, a vertical filter contains a subset of the columns in a table. The Subscriber receives only the replicated columns. For example, you might use a vertical filter to publish all but the Salary column from the Employee table. Vertical filtering is similar to specifying only certain columns from a table in a SELECT statement.

Merge replication (described in Lesson 3) does not support vertical filtering.

Horizontal Filtering

As shown in the lower half of Figure 15.4, a horizontal filter contains a subset of the rows in a table. The Subscriber receives only the subset of rows. For example, you can publish order records by region to each region. Horizontal filtering is similar to specifying a WHERE clause in a SELECT statement.

Additional Ways to Create Data Subsets

An alternative to filtering is to create separate tables. This can be more efficient than filtering, preventing conflicts and simplifying the logical view of the data. For example, instead of storing the sales data from multiple branches in a single table at a head office, you could create a separate table for each branch. The disadvantages to creating separate tables are that applications must deal with the separate tables and that administration can be more complex because, if the table structure changes, tables on different servers may have to be altered.

Creating separate tables that use the same schema but contain different rows is usually called *partitioning*. Creating separate tables containing different columns is less common.

Partitioning Rows

Partitioning rows (horizontal partitioning) involves physically defining a horizontal subset of data as a separate table. For example, you can partition a customer table into separate tables for each region.

Partitioning Columns

Partitioning columns (vertical partitioning) involves physically defining a vertical subset of data as a separate table. For example, you can vertically partition an employee table by placing the name, title, and office number columns in one table and other confidential information, such as birth date and salary information, in another table.

Subscriptions

The configuration that defines how a database on a Subscriber will receive a publication from a Publisher is referred to as a *subscription*.

Two kinds of subscriptions are possible. The type of subscription determines how subscriptions are created and administered and how data is replicated. There can be many subscriptions of both types to a single publication, as shown in Figure 15.5.

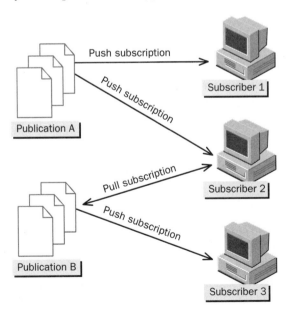

Figure 15.5 Push vs. pull subscriptions

Note In previous versions of SQL Server, the subscription types affected only how subscriptions were administered.

Push Subscriptions

You can set up subscriptions while creating or administering publications on the Publisher. This is known as a *push subscription*. Push subscriptions centralize subscription administration in the following ways:

- A push subscription is defined at the Publisher.
- Many Subscribers can be set up at once for each publication.

With a push subscription, the Distributor propagates the changes to a Subscriber without a request from the Subscriber to do so. Typically, push subscriptions are used in applications that must send changes to Subscribers as soon as they occur. Push subscriptions are best for applications that require higher security and near-real-time updates, and where the higher processor overhead at the Distributor does not affect performance.

For push subscriptions, the replication agents that replicate data to the Subscriber run at the Distributor or the Publisher.

Pull Subscriptions

You can also set up a subscription while administering a Subscriber. This is known as a *pull subscription*. The following are distinguishing characteristics of a pull subscription:

- The Subscriber initiates a pull subscription.
- The publication must be enabled to allow pull subscriptions.
- Only SQL Server Subscribers fully support pull subscriptions.
- The system administrator or database owner of the Subscriber decides which publications are received and when to receive them.

Pull subscriptions are best for applications that need lower security, need more Subscriber autonomy (such as mobile users), and need to support a high number of Subscribers (such as Subscribers that use the Internet).

Two kinds of pull subscriptions are available. Standard pull subscriptions are registered on the Publisher. Anonymous pull subscriptions are set up entirely on the Subscriber; no information about the subscription is stored on the Publisher. Anonymous subscriptions are ideal for Subscribers that connect via the Internet. Internet-based Subscribers can connect using the FTP protocol.

For pull subscriptions, the replication agents that replicate data to the Subscriber run at the Subscriber.

Tip This discussion of subscriptions states that creation and administration of subscriptions is performed on the Publisher for push subscriptions and on the Subscriber for pull subscriptions. This does not mean that these tasks must be performed physically at these servers. You can register a Publisher and a Subscriber in SQL Server Enterprise Manager running on a client computer, and then manage both push and pull subscriptions simply by selecting the relevant server.

Lesson Summary

SQL Server replication uses a publisher-subscriber metaphor. Data identified for replication is distributed from a Publisher server through a distribution server to a Subscriber server. Data marked for replication, called a publication, can be filtered horizontally and vertically. A subscription configures a Subscriber to receive data from a Publisher. Subscriptions can be configured from the Publisher (a push subscription) or from the Subscriber (a pull subscription).

Lesson 3: SQL Server Replication Types

This lesson describes the three types of replication provided by SQL Server: snapshot, transactional, and merge replication. The different characteristics of the three types are suited to different application and distributed data needs. While the replication process is based on the Publisher-Subscriber metaphor for each type, they each use the replication agents and server resources differently.

A replication type applies to a single publication. It is possible to use multiple types of replication within the same database. The processes that implement the replication types are called agents; these are discussed at the end of this lesson.

After this lesson, you will be able to

- Explain the SQL Server replication types
- Describe SQL Server replication agents

Estimated lesson time: 35 minutes

Snapshot Replication

Snapshot replication is the periodic bulk transfer of an entire publication to Subscribers. It is the easiest type of replication to set up and maintain. Figure 15.6 illustrates snapshot replication.

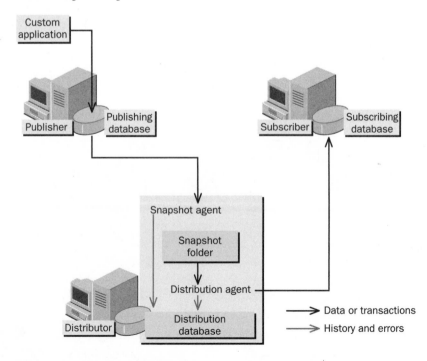

Figure 15.6   Snapshot replication

The characteristics of snapshot replication are as follows:

- It has a high degree of latency, because data is refreshed only periodically.
- It has a high degree of site autonomy.
- Replicated tables do not require primary keys.
- It is not suitable for very large publications.
- It has low processor overhead because there is no continuous monitoring.

The Snapshot Replication Process

In snapshot replication, the Snapshot Agent reads the publication database and creates snapshot files in the distribution working folder (the Snapshot folder) on the Distributor. SQL Server stores status information in the distribution database but does not store data.

The Distribution Agent, running on the Distributor for push subscriptions and on the Subscriber for pull subscriptions, applies snapshots of data from the distribution working folder to the Subscriber.

Transactional Replication

In *transactional replication*, incremental changes at the Publisher are replicated to the Subscriber. Characteristics of transactional replication include the following:

- Replication typically takes place with minimal latency (seconds).
- It has a lower degree of site autonomy, especially if low latency is required.
- Replicated tables require primary keys.
- It is suitable for any size publication.
- It involves continuous monitoring of transactions (insertions, updates, and deletions) in tables that are marked for replication.

   Only committed transactions are replicated to Subscribers, and they are guaranteed to be applied in the same order as they occurred on the Publisher.

Note You cannot create transactional publications on the Desktop Edition of SQL Server. You can subscribe to transactional publications from another server, and you can create and subscribe to snapshot and merge publications using the Desktop Edition.

The Transactional Replication Process

Figure 15.7 illustrates the transactional replication process. This process starts with a snapshot replication. The Distribution Agent uses the files that are copied by the Snapshot Agent to set up transactional replication on the Subscriber.

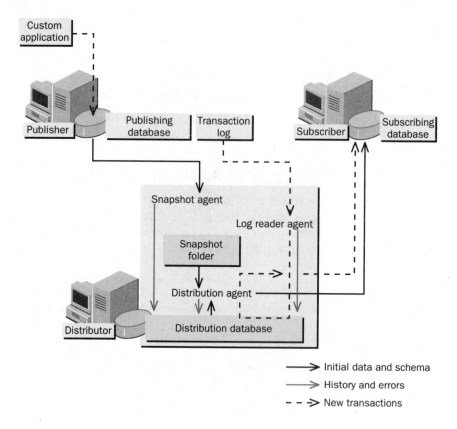

Figure 15.7   Transactional replication

Transactional replication then uses the Log Reader Agent to read the transaction log on the Publisher periodically and store the information in the distribution database. The Distribution Agent, running on the Distributor for push subscriptions and on the Subscriber for pull subscriptions, applies changes to Subscribers.

The Immediate Updating Subscribers Option

Both snapshot and transactional replication require that replicated data not be modified on the Subscribers. This is because data flows in one direction, from the Publisher to the Subscribers. Modifications made on a Subscriber will never be reflected on the Publisher or on the other Subscribers.

In environments that require data to be updated at many sites, you can partition tables so that different partitions of the same table can be published by different sites. Each site is then the Publisher for part of the replicated table and a Subscriber to the other portions of the table.

SQL Server 7 also introduces a new way of allowing data to be updated at Subscribers, called the Immediate Updating Subscribers Option. This option combines transactional or snapshot replication with the two-phase commit protocol managed by MS DTC. Data can be modified on Subscribers as long as the modifications can be applied to the Publisher at the same time, using the two-phase commit protocol.

Figure 15.8 shows how changes made at the Subscriber are applied simultaneously on the Publisher using MS DTC. The rest of the replication process is the same as snapshot or transactional replication.

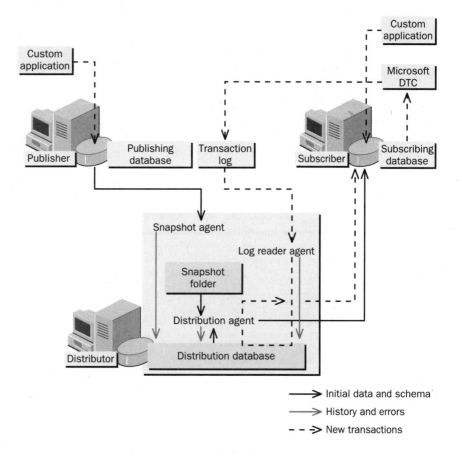

Figure 15.8   Replication under the Immediate Updating Subscribers option

Note that this option enables an update on the Subscriber to immediately update the Publisher only. The other Subscribers receive the update by regular replication. An update made on the Publisher is not immediately applied to a Subscriber—that would no longer be replication; instead, it would be a distributed transaction.

Using this option requires a well-connected, reliable network between the Publisher and the Subscriber.

Because the modification is made on both the Publisher and the Subscriber,

- The user connected to the Subscriber can continue working without interruption, as the change does not need to be replicated from the Publisher.
- The change is guaranteed to be replicated to all other Subscribers.

If you use this option with snapshot replication, you will need to partition the published data. This is because an Immediate Updating Subscriber cannot modify rows that have changed on the Publisher until those rows have been replicated to the Subscriber. The update on the Subscriber fails if the row being modified is different on the Publisher and the Subscriber. This will occur if the data has been changed directly on the Publisher or if another Immediate Updating Subscriber has changed the row. This is less likely to happen if you are using transactional replication because changes are replicated almost immediately. With snapshot replication, changes are not replicated often, so you will have to partition the data to ensure that two Subscribers or a Subscriber and the Publisher do not both update the same data.

Merge Replication

Merge replication allows sites to make autonomous changes to replicated data. Later, changes from all sites are merged, either periodically or on demand. An automatic customizable mechanism is used to resolve conflicts that occur when changes are merged.

Characteristics of merge replication include the following:

- Its latency can be high or low.
- It has a high degree of site autonomy.
- Replicated tables have a unique identifier column added to guarantee row uniqueness across all copies.
- It is suitable for any size publication.
- Triggers in the tables published for merge replication mark rows that are changed so that they can be replicated.
- It does not guarantee transactional consistency, but it does guarantee that all sites converge to the same result set.
- It does not support vertical filtering.

Merge replication can be useful for data that is filtered or partitioned according to your business practices, such as data that is structured so that sales representatives can update only the records of customers in their own territories. It is particularly suited to "self-partitioning" applications where conflicts are not expected.

The Merge Replication Process

As shown in Figure 15.9, merge replication, starts with a snapshot replication. The Merge Agent uses the files that are copied by the Snapshot Agent to set up merge replication on the Subscriber.

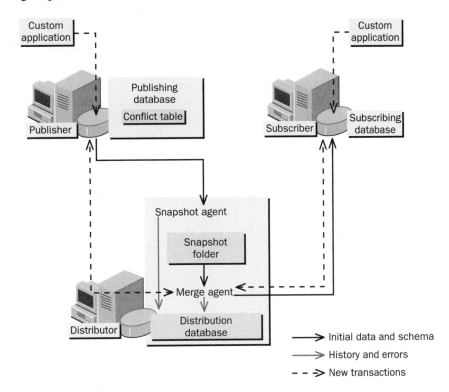

Figure 15.9   Merge replication

For a push subscription, the Merge Agent runs on the Distributor. For a pull subscription, the Merge Agent runs on the Subscriber. In merge replication, SQL Server stores status information on the distribution database but does not store data.

The Merge Agent takes changes from the Publisher and applies them to the Subscribers. It then takes changes from all Subscribers, applies them to the Publisher, and resolves any update conflicts.

Considerations for Using Merge Replication

Merge replication makes changes to the schema to prevent or resolve conflicts.

Changes to the Schema

For merge replication to work, SQL Server makes three important changes to the schema of the published database:

- It identifies a unique column for each row in the table being replicated. This column must use the uniqueidentifier datatype and have the ROWGUIDCOL property. If there is no such column, one will be added. This allows the row to be uniquely identified across multiple copies of the table.

- It adds several system tables to support data tracking, efficient synchronization, and conflict detection, resolution, and reporting.

- It creates triggers on tables at the Publisher and Subscriber that track changes to the data in each row or, optionally, each column. These triggers capture changes that are made to the table and record these changes in merge system tables.

  Because SQL Server supports multiple triggers of the same type on the base table, merge replication triggers do not interfere with the application-defined triggers; that is, both application-defined and merge replication triggers can coexist.

Note Support for multiple triggers of the same type is new in SQL Server 7; previous versions of SQL Server did not support this feature.

Conflict Resolution

Because merge replication allows independent updates, conflicts can occur. These are addressed by using priority-based conflict resolution:

- The Merge Agent tracks every update to a row.

  The history of changes to a row is known as the lineage of the row. When the Merge Agent is merging changes and encounters a row that might have multiple changes, it examines the lineage to determine whether a conflict exists. Conflict detection can be at the row or column level.

- The Merge Agent evaluates both the arriving and current data values, and any conflicts between new and old values are automatically resolved based on assigned priorities.

- All sites ultimately end up with the same data values, but not necessarily the ones they would have arrived at had all updates been made at one site.

Note SQL Server supports stored procedure or COM-based custom conflict resolvers.

SQL Server Replication Agents

SQL Server has several agents that implement the various types of replication. Each agent is a separate process that is usually run by SQL Server Agent. Publications and subscriptions have named agents associated with them. A named agent is really a SQL Agent job that configures one of the replication agents to process the data for a specific publication or subscription. Replication agent jobs have a category of REPL-*<agentname>*.

The Snapshot Agent

The publication and subscription data must be synchronized before replication is possible. The Snapshot Agent is used for initial synchronization of all types of publications and for ongoing replication of snapshot publications. This agent prepares the schema and data from publications and stores these in files on the Distributor.

The Snapshot Agent runs on the Distributor and moves data from the Publisher to the Distributor.

The Distribution Agent

The Distribution Agent applies snapshot and transaction replication data from the Distributor to Subscribers for snapshot and transactional publications. For push subscriptions, it runs on the Distributor; for pull subscriptions, it runs on the Subscribers. The Distribution Agent is not used in merge replication.

The Log Reader Agent

The Log Reader Agent copies transactions that are marked for replication from the transaction log on the Publisher to the distribution database.

The Log Reader Agent runs on the Distributor and moves data from the Publisher to the Distributor.

The Merge Agent

The Merge Agent merges data changes from multiple sites that have taken place since the initial snapshot was created. It moves data in both directions between Publishers and Subscribers. The Merge Agent runs on the Distributor for push subscriptions and on the Subscriber for pull subscriptions. It is not used for snapshot or transactional replication.

Note Custom subscriber applications can be developed based on the Distribution Agent or the Merge Agent, using the SQL Distribution Control and the SQL Merge Control. These are ActiveX controls supplied with SQL Server 7.

Lesson Summary

SQL Server provides three types of replication: snapshot, transactional, and merge replication. SQL Server uses four programs called agents to implement replication: the Snapshot Agent, the Distribution Agent, the Log Reader Agent, and the Merge Agent. The replication process is based on the publisher-subscriber metaphor, but each type uses the replication agents and server resources differently.

Snapshot replication is suited to data that does not change regularly. Snapshot replication occurs infrequently, and a large amount of data is replicated when replication occurs. Data can be changed only at the Publisher.

Transactional replication is suited to data that changes regularly. This type of replication can occur frequently, and a relatively small amount of data is replicated when replication occurs. Unless transactional replication is used in conjunction with distributed transactions, data can be changed only at the Publisher.

Merge replication is suited to data that changes regularly. Merge replication can occur frequently, and a relatively small amount of data is replicated when replication occurs. Data can be changed at the Publisher or at the Subscribers. A conflict resolution mechanism resolves conflicting changes made at more than one server.

Lesson 4: Physical Replication Models

This lesson presents the physical replication models used in SQL Server, drawing a connection between the replication types (snapshot, transactional, and merge) and the physically implemented replication models. The lesson concludes with examples of each of these models.

After this lesson, you will be able to

▪ Describe the physical replication models used in SQL Server

Estimated lesson time: 25 minutes

Overview of the Replication Models

The basic physical replication models shown in Figure 15.10 illustrate how the server replication roles can be implemented in replication. Each of these models is discussed in turn in this section.

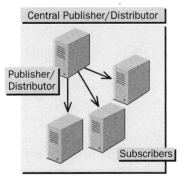

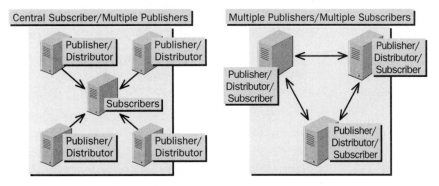

Figure 15.10   Physical replication models

The Central Publisher/Distributor Model

In the central Publisher/Distributor model (the SQL Server default), one or two servers are defined as the Publisher/Distributor. The Publisher/Distributor publishes and distributes data to any number of servers that are set up as Subscribers.

The Publisher and the Distributor can reside on one server or on separate servers. In either case, the publication server is the primary owner or source of all replicated data. Typically, the distribution server stores data before the data is replicated to the subscribing servers. Data that is received at subscription sites is intended to be read-only. Administrators must ensure that only the SELECT permission is allowed on Subscriber tables.

If the Publisher and the Distributor are established on separate servers, this model offloads much of the replication work from the Publisher to the Distributor.

The Central Subscriber/Multiple Publishers Model

In the central Subscriber/multiple Publishers model, multiple Publishers replicate data to a single Subscriber. This model addresses the need for consolidating data at a centralized site and providing the local sites with local data only. Because multiple Publishers are writing to the same subscription table, it is important to ensure that all data has a unique local owner so that another Publisher does not overwrite it. You can accomplish this by filtering the data horizontally.

The Multiple Publishers/Multiple Subscribers Model

In the multiple Publishers/multiple Subscribers model, multiple publication servers and multiple subscription servers each potentially play a dual role. This model is the closest implementation to fully distributed data processing. You must be careful when you design both the schema and update types to ensure that an adequate level of data consistency exists at all sites. Horizontal filtering or partitioning will be necessary to achieve this.

Combining Replication Models and Types

For each publication, you can use any of the replication models with any of the replication types. The following statements are facts about the interaction between the replication model and the replication type:

- The replication model is the physical implementation of your replication design. You will spend most of your development time in designing your replication model.

- The replication type (snapshot, transactional, or merge) provides the functionality that details how to maintain replicated data. This will be determined by the latency, consistency, and site autonomy requirements of your environment.

- Any of the replication models can use any of the replication types. You typically select the model and the type at the same time; one does not determine the other.

A single database can have many publications with different replication types. For example, in your company database, you might have a publication for inventory information that uses transactional replication with the Immediate Updating Subscribers option. Another publication that contains a customer list could use merge replication so that all sites can update it.

An Example of the Central Publisher/Remote Distributor Model

The example in this section features a sales analysis system used by a corporate headquarters and regional sales offices.

The Current Process

Currently, sales personnel in European regional sales offices are required to forecast sales prior to the end of each month. One of the primary tools that they use is a sales analysis system that exists at the corporate headquarters in New York. The regional sales offices have reliable, high-speed network connections to London. They can connect to the New York headquarters only via dialup Internet connections, however. For this reason, sales data at the regional offices is often unavailable.

The Business Issue

Regional sales offices cannot accurately forecast sales because they do not have consistent access to current sales data. Cost prohibits installing high-speed network connections between all of the regional offices and New York.

The Proposed Replication Model

Implementing a central Publisher model with snapshot replication can make the sales information available to Subscribers in each region. Publications can be created that horizontally filter data so that each region receives sales data for its customers only. This reduces the amount of data that each Subscriber receives.

A remote Distributor can take advantage of a high-speed network connection between New York and London. The Distributor then sends filtered subscriptions to the regional Subscribers in the Rome, Paris, and Dublin offices. Network connections between New York and the Subscriber locations are unnecessary. London would also be a Subscriber for its own data. Figure 15.11 illustrates this proposed solution.

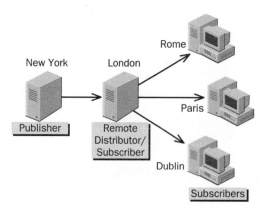

Figure 15.11   Example of a central Publisher/remote Distributor

With this solution, users in each region can query their regional SQL Servers for sales data rather than use the SQL Server at corporate headquarters. The subscribed data cannot be, and doesn't need to be, updated. The snapshot can be scheduled to take place daily, weekly, or at some other appropriate interval.

A variation of this solution would be to configure London as a Publishing Subscriber. It would subscribe to the data from New York and then publish the data to the other European offices. This would be a good approach if all of the regional offices were receiving all of the data and not only their own filtered data.

An Example of the Central Subscriber/Multiple Publishers Model

The example in this section features an automobile parts manufacturer with four regional warehouses across the country.

The Current Process

Currently, inventory levels fall below reorder levels and are not noticed until the warehouse is unable to fill a customer order completely. All warehouses manage their own inventories. When the quantity for a part falls below the inventory reorder point, the inventory control manager at the warehouse places an order with the factory. This procedure requires manual monitoring and order placing by each warehouse.

The Business Issue

No centralized inventory monitoring exists at the factory.

The Proposed Replication Model

Implementing a central Subscriber/multiple Publishers model that uses transactional replication to roll up the inventory information from all of the regional sites to a main inventory database at the central factory site can solve this problem. Inventory can be reordered automatically when established reorder points are reached for individual parts in each warehouse.

Because the ID number for the parts is the same in all regions, adding a separate region code column (reg_code) uniquely identifies data from the regions when the data is rolled up at the central site. The region code column is used as part of a composite primary key (the reg_code and id columns) to uniquely identify the parts from each region. Figure 15.12 illustrates this solution.

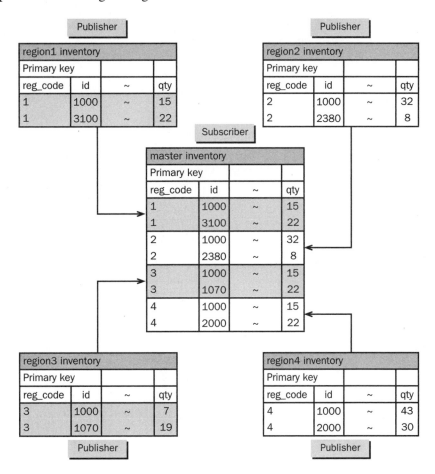

Figure 15.12 Example of a central Subscriber with multiple Publishers

With this solution, data does not need to be updated at the factory; each warehouse updates only the rows that it publishes.

An Example of the Multiple Publishers/Multiple Subscribers Model

A pastry company has three shops in different parts of the city. Each shop has a server that publishes its own orders table and subscribes to the orders tables that the other shops publish.

The Current Process

Currently, each shop runs out of certain ingredients on a regular basis. When one shop runs out of a necessary ingredient, it must contact one or both of the other shops to find out whether the ingredient is in stock and then separately arrange to have it ordered.

The Business Issue

Because it is impossible to know the inventory of the other shops until the last minute, situations arise in which all shops are out of the same ingredient at the same time.

The Proposed Replication Model

Implementing a multiple Publishers/multiple Subscribers model that uses transactional replication enables each shop to know immediately if the inventory of the other shops can solve a given problem. Shortages can be anticipated so that each store is able to fill its orders.

As shown in Figure 15.13, shops A, B, and C each have a copy of the orders table. Each shop is both a Publisher and a Subscriber—the server at each shop publishes some rows from the orders table to the other two shops and subscribes to the rows of the orders table published by the other two shops.

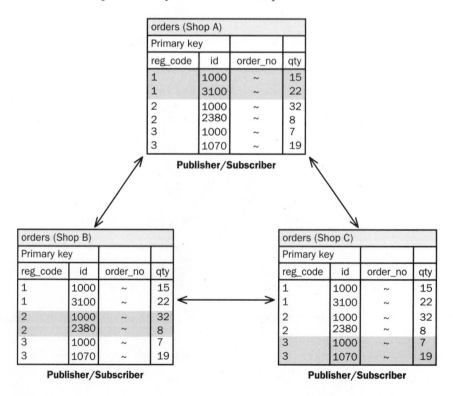

Figure 15.13   Example of multiple Publishers with multiple Subscribers

Each shop has responsibility for only a portion of the data. The orders table is horizontally filtered by area. For example, shop A is responsible for updating the data in area 1. For this scenario to work with transactional replication, each shop can update the data in its area only.

Lesson Summary

You can use many different physical models when you implement replication. The primary models are the central Publisher/Distributor model, the central Subscriber/ multiple Publishers model, and the multiple Publishers/multiple Subscribers model. These models can be mixed or combined. When implementing replication, you can also choose whether to place the Publisher and the Distributor on the same computer or on different computers.

Review

The following questions are intended to reinforce key information presented in the chapter. If you are unable to answer a question, review the appropriate lesson and then try the question again. Answers to the questions can be found in Appendix A, "Questions and Answers."

1. Your company has been experiencing contention problems. This occurs when the sales and marketing departments run their daily reports while the order-processing department is processing orders. Your company has decided to implement some form of data replication. To choose the appropriate method for making copies of the company data, which features and characteristics should you consider?

2. Your company, a large, international manufacturer with many vendors around the world, has decided to distribute data by using replication. You are currently in the planning and design phase of your replication strategy. Your goal is to receive all of the sales information from the vendors at the company headquarters on a daily basis. Because most of your vendors are remote, you are concerned about the high long-distance costs. Which replication model or models would you implement? Why?

CHAPTER 16

Planning and Setting Up Replication

About This Chapter

In this chapter, you will learn about planning a replication implementation and performing a number of replication tasks, including setting up servers, creating publications, and setting up subscriptions.

Before You Begin

To complete the lessons in this chapter, you must have

- Completed and understood the material in Chapter 15 "Introducing Replication."
- Installed Microsoft SQL Server 7. See Chapter 2, "Installation," for installation instructions.
- Installed the StudyNwind database. See the "Getting Started" section in "About This Book" for StudyNwind database installation instructions.
- The ability to log on to SQL Server as an Administrator.

- Installed the Exercise files from the Supplemental Course Materials CD-ROM to your hard disk drive. See the "Getting Started" section in "About This Book" for installation instructions.

Lesson 1: Planning Replication

Good planning is the key to successful replication implementation. Setting up a replication scenario can be complex. The graphical tools make the physical implementation easy, but the design of the scenario warrants the same level of attention that the development of your original database schema did. You must have a working model before you can implement replication successfully.

This lesson begins with a conceptual consideration of business issues. It then addresses the details of physically implementing a replication solution. The lesson concludes with a discussion of data definition issues in replication.

After this lesson, you will be able to

- Address issues in planning a Microsoft SQL Server version 7 replication scenario

Estimated lesson time: 30 minutes

Design Considerations

Designing the implementation of replication is similar to designing a database: you must plan the logical design before attempting the physical implementation. This section considers the questions you should address.

What Data Will You Publish?

When distributing data, your subscribing servers often require only a subset of data from the database. It is important to replicate only necessary data to reduce disk space use, processing time, and network input/output (I/O).

Think about how you should group articles. Will you publish subsets of data—such as by group, by site, or by region? If you have a central Subscriber/multiple Publisher scenario, perhaps each site should publish all of its tables, and the central location should subscribe to each publication.

If you disseminate data, you must do one of the following:

- Create one publication for global data to which all sites will subscribe and one publication for partitioned data for each Subscriber
- Create one publication for each Subscriber that contains both the global data and the partitioned data

---

Important You are able to make changes to publications, such as adding new articles, but you have to remove all subscriptions to the publication before you do so. You must then re-create the subscriptions after making the changes. This is one of the reasons why you should plan carefully before adding all of your publications and subscriptions.

Who Receives the Data?

Which servers will subscribe to the data? What characteristics do the destination servers have? Are they known, or are they off line? If sites must have update capabilities, you need to address how to resolve conflicts or have high-quality connections to those sites to make the Immediate Updating Subscribers option feasible.

How Often Must Data Be Replicated?

How will replication be accomplished—on a schedule or on demand?

If your application requirements allow latency, you can schedule infrequent updates. For example, if a site uses data for summary reporting or trend reporting on sales activity for the current year, the data need not be 100 percent current. A marketing department (decision support) is a good example of a site that would not require the most current information; once a week or once a month might be adequate.

What Are the Network Characteristics?

Use the following network considerations to help you choose the type of replication that best suits your network:

- Are all nodes in the network always available, or are they available only at periodic intervals?

  If they are not always available, consider using a type of replication that supports higher latency.

- Is the network fast?

  If not, you may want to use filtering to minimize the quantity of data that is sent across the network. Be sure to note whether slow links exist that could be bypassed by having a remote distribution server.

- What is the network capacity?

  If the capacity is low, consider using remote Distributors. Determine the time of day that has the greatest activity level. This is important if offline Subscribers will connect during peak usage periods. Schedule accordingly.

- How reliable is the network?

  If failures are common, it is not wise to use a replication plan that includes distributed transactions, as these cannot be completed when the servers involved in the distributed transaction are not connected.

Determining a Replication Solution

Preliminary planning of the physical implementation of the logical design includes addressing the questions in this section.

What Is Your Replication Topology?

What replication topology will you implement? Establishing the server roles lays the physical framework for implementing replication. The decisions to be made are as follows:

- Select the physical replication model.
- Determine whether the Distributor will be local or remote.
- Determine whether the distribution database will be shared. If you have multiple Publishers that share a Distributor, will each use its own distribution database, or will they all share a distribution database on the Distributor?

What Type of Replication Will You Use?

You can select snapshot, transactional, or merge replication. For more information on these replication types, see Chapter 15, "Introducing Replication."

Who Initiates Replication Activities?

Push subscriptions use Distributor resources, and pull subscriptions use Subscriber resources.

How Many Subscribers Will There Be?

Estimating the number of Subscribers will help to determine the load on the distribution server.

What Are Your Space Requirements?

The following factors affect transaction log sizes for all databases that are involved in replication, as well as the size of the distribution database and working folder on the Distributor:

- The amount of activity in the published databases
- The number of publications and articles
- Replication frequency
- Replication latency
- Type of replication

Data Definition Issues

Replication data must be defined with specific characteristics because some characteristics cannot be replicated or are altered when replication takes place. This section discusses the issues involved in data definition.

Using Data Types

The following table lists the data types that affect replication.

Data type	Impact
Timestamp	Indicates the sequence of SQL Server activity on a row. Despite the name, timestamp values are not related to date or time; they are database-wide, unique numbers that are intended only to indicate whether a row has changed. The values do not usually have any relevance on the Subscriber, so the timestamp column can be filtered out. If replicated, a timestamp column is replicated to the Subscriber as a binary(8) data type. If you are using the Immediate Updating Subscribers option, a timestamp column is required; one will be added to a table if it does not already exist. Timestamp columns must be removed from merge publications because it is not possible for timestamp column values to ever converge across all sites.
Uniqueidentifier	A globally unique identifier (GUID) created by setting the default for the column to the NEWID() function. In tables published for merge replication, a uniqueidentifier column is required; one will be added to a table if it does not already exist.
User-defined	Cannot be replicated unless the user-defined data type already exists in the Subscriber database.

Tip For consistent query results on data that is replicated between servers, it is recommended that each server that participates in replication use the same character set and sort order. This is not required, but this practice ensures that query processing behavior is consistent across all servers.

Using an IDENTITY Property

During replication, the value of the column with an IDENTITY property is replicated, but the property itself is not replicated. At initial snapshot, identity columns are not created with the IDENTITY property. This means that values on the Subscriber will always match those on the Publisher.

To partition the data at each site, you can set up an identity column again on the Subscriber. Be sure that you

- Use appropriate seed values and CHECK constraints to avoid conflicts
- Combine the identity column with another column that uniquely identifies data that is modified on the Subscriber

Using the NOT FOR REPLICATION Option

The NOT FOR REPLICATION option allows you to disable certain features—such as the IDENTITY property, CHECK constraints, and triggers—for data replicated to a Subscriber. When users modify data on the Subscriber, these features operate normally.

A good use of this option is with the multiple Publishers/multiple Subscribers model. For example, you may have a CHECK constraint that verifies that a location is within a particular sales region, ensuring that sales representatives cannot enter orders for customers who are not within their regions. Adding the NOT FOR REPLICATION option to the CHECK constraint allows the data from other regions to be replicated even though it will contain invalid locations.

Set this option when you define a column with an IDENTITY property or a CHECK constraint or when you create triggers.

Configuring Network Security Access

Before you begin implementing a replication scenario, you should ensure that you have met certain basic requirements. This section describes the tasks you need to perform.

Establish Trust Relationships Among Domains

If servers that participate in replication reside within separate Microsoft Windows NT Server domains, you must establish trust relationships between those domains. For information on establishing trust relationships, see Windows NT Server Help.

Verify the Windows NT Domain User Account for SQL Server Agent

By default, replication uses the Windows NT domain user account that SQL Server Agent uses. It is advisable to use the same SQL Server Agent domain user account for all servers that are participating in replication.

Verify that you have a domain user account with administrative privileges in Windows NT for SQL Server Agent. The account should be a member of the Windows NT local Administrators group.

Note The Windows NT account that you use for SQL Server Agent cannot be the Local System or a local user account, because neither account allows access to the network. You can use a SQL Server login account rather than a Windows NT account.

Lesson Summary

Before you implement replication, you must consider all of the replication types and physical models and design a replication solution that matches your environment. Certain data types and table attributes require special attention when designing your replication solution. The first step in implementing a replication solution is to ensure that you have configured your SQL Server security for network access.

Lesson 2: Preparing the Servers

Setting up replication involves a number of different steps. This lesson describes each of the different parts of the configuration process.

First you must set up a Distributor and a Publisher; they are both set up during the same process. After these are set up, you can define publications and subscriptions.

When you use SQL Server Enterprise Manager to configure replication, you will often be configuring more than one part at the same time. For example, it is possible to create a publication using the Create Publication Wizard before you have set up the server as a Publisher. This does not mean that you do not have to set up the Publisher; rather, the wizard goes ahead and sets up the server as a Publisher for you.

After this lesson, you will be able to

- Identify the tasks that must be performed to configure SQL Server for replication
- Set up and configure a distribution server
- Set up publication and subscription servers

Estimated lesson time: 115 minutes

Setting Up a Distributor

You must set up the Distributor before you create dependent Publishers. System administrator permissions are necessary to create a Distributor.

Prepare servers using the Configure Publishing and Distribution Wizard in SQL Server Enterprise Manager. All servers that participate in the replication scenario must be registered in SQL Server Enterprise Manager.

The following topics give more information about some of the options that you will specify when enabling the Distributor.

Configure the Distribution Database

The distribution database, a store-and-forward database that holds all transactions that are waiting to be distributed to Subscribers, is installed automatically when you set up a Distributor.

You also have options to

- Specify an existing remote distribution server or create a new distribution database on a server that has been configured as a Distributor

- Define one or more distribution databases, each of which can support one or more publications
- Specify the location of the distribution database data and log files

Ensure the Accessibility of the Distribution Working Folder

During various stages of the different replication processes, the Snapshot Agent creates files that are used by the Distribution Agent or the Merge Agent. These files are created in the distribution working folder. You must ensure that the distribution working folder is available to these replication agents when necessary.

By default, the distribution working folder is created in C:\Mssql7\Repldata and is accessed by other servers on the default Windows NT administrative share (C$) as \\*computer_name*\C$\Mssql7\Repldata. You can create your own custom share if you prefer not to use the default administrative share and update the configuration to use it. The share must be accessible to the SQL Server Agent service account or to the replication agents' account if you configure another account for the replication agents.

Important On Windows 95 and Windows 98 computers configured as Distributors, you will need to create a share because the C$ share is not created by default, as it is on Windows NT. If you want to use the default Publisher configuration, create a share called C$ in the root of the C: drive and make it accessible to the SQL Server Agent service account or to the replication agents' account.

Ensure Sufficient Memory

You also must ensure adequate memory for the distribution server, especially if the Distributor and the Publisher are located on the same computer. Base the memory requirement on the anticipated amount of data and the number of Subscribers; it is a good idea to allocate generous resources to the Distributor.

Configuring a Distributor

After you have enabled the Distributor, you can open the Publisher and Distributor Properties dialog box to configure the Distributor.

Note To open the Publisher and Distributor Properties dialog box, run the Configure Publishing and Distribution Wizard or select Tools/Replication/Configure Publishers, Subscribers And Distribution. This menu selection is grayed if you have not selected a server and is called Tools/Replication/Configure Publishing And Subscribers if you have not enabled the Distributor.

In the Publisher and Distributor Properties dialog box, you can perform the following Distributor-related tasks:

- Create and configure distribution databases. For each distribution database, you can specify the name and file specifications and set the retention properties for history and transaction records.
- Set the password to be used when Publishers connect.
- Configure agent profiles for agents associated with the Distributor.
- Specify the Publishers that will be allowed to use this server as their (remote) distribution server. When you add a Publisher, you specify which distribution database (if there is more than one) the Publisher must use. Changing the distribution database that a Publisher uses involves disabling the Publisher, dropping all publications and subscriptions, and then enabling the publishing server as a new Publisher with a different distribution database.

Other options in the Publisher and Distributor Properties dialog box allow you to configure the Publisher.

Ensuring Sufficient Space

Ensure that you have enough storage space for the distribution working folder and the distribution database:

- For snapshot and merge replication, data is stored in the distribution working folder; the distribution database tracks only status.
- For transactional replication, the distribution database must be able to store replicated information for all publishing and subscribing servers. Because the distribution database contains all transactions that are waiting to be distributed, the database can grow large.

Regardless of the type of replication you use, you should consider the following factors to determine the size of the distribution database:

- The total number of tables that are published
- The number of columns and text and image data types in an article
- The length of articles
- The maximum retention time for transactions and history

  Transaction information is retained at the Distributor until it is applied to all Subscribers. If some Subscribers are offline, the database may grow large until the Subscribers are able to connect and retrieve their transactions.

For transactional replication, consider these additional factors:

- The number of INSERT and UPDATE statements, because each contains data
- The estimated transaction rate
- The average transaction size

Deleting a Distribution Database

It is possible to delete a distribution database without disabling the Distributor by first disabling all Publishers that use that particular distribution database.

Use Caution when Uninstalling a Distributor

You can uninstall a Distributor by using the Disable Publishing and Distribution Wizard. This completely removes the replication components from the server. If you do this and you later want to use replication again, you will have to reconfigure replication from the start. The effects of uninstalling a Distributor are as follows:

- All distribution databases on that server are deleted.
- All Publishers that use the Distributor are disabled. All publications on those servers are deleted.
- All subscriptions to the publications are deleted (although subscribed data on the Subscribers is not deleted).

Setting Up a Publisher

A server will often be configured as both a Publisher and a Distributor. You use the same dialog box for managing both Publisher and Distributor properties. If you are managing more than one server in SQL Server Enterprise Manager, make sure that you have the correct server selected before you open the Publisher and Distributor Properties dialog box. After you configure the Distributor, you can set the following options for the Publisher with the Publisher and Distributor Properties dialog box:

- Specify the databases that will publish data using transactional or merge replication.
- Enable Subscribers and set Subscriber security and default scheduling options.
- Manage the publication access list of logins that are able to access the Publisher in order to set up pull and immediate-updating subscriptions. Individual publications can have their own custom list of accounts.

You will learn how to create publications in Lesson 3 of this chapter.

Note If you use a remote Distributor, make sure that the Snapshot Agent that runs at the Distributor can access the Publisher as well as the distribution working folder for replication. It is easiest to use the same SQL Server Agent domain user account on both the Publisher and the Distributor.

Setting Up a Subscriber

There are two types of Subscribers: *registered Subscribers* and *anonymous Subscribers*. For registered Subscribers, information about each Subscriber is stored at the Publisher, and performance information about each Subscriber is kept at the Distributor. The Publisher and the Distributor do not store detailed information about an anonymous Subscriber.

If you will have a large number of Subscribers, or you don't want the overhead of maintaining extra information, you can allow anonymous subscriptions to a publication. This can be especially useful if you want to allow Subscribers to connect using the Internet.

Setting up a registered Subscriber involves enabling the Subscriber at the Publisher and creating either a push or a pull subscription. Anonymous Subscribers do not have to be enabled at the Publisher, and anonymous subscriptions can only be pulled from the Subscriber.

Enabling and Configuring a Subscriber

Enabling a Subscriber at the Publisher involves

- Adding the Subscriber to the list of Subscribers in the Publisher and Distributor Properties dialog box
- Configuring the security settings and default agent schedules for the Subscriber
- Verifying that you have a valid account to access the Distributor and the distribution working folder

  If you pull subscriptions from a remote Distributor, you must also make sure that the Distribution Agent or Merge Agent that runs at the Subscriber can access the distribution working folder.

You will learn how to create subscriptions in Lesson 4 of this chapter.

Disabling a Subscriber

You can disable a Subscriber at the Publisher. When you do so, subscriptions to all publications are automatically deleted. However, the administrator of the Subscriber has responsibility for deleting the subscription database or any of its objects.

Note The only time you need to do anything on the Subscriber is when you pull subscriptions. You do not need to set up the Subscriber before pulling subscriptions.

Agent Profiles

There are a number of settings that you can configure for each replication agent, such as replication batch sizes, time-outs, and polling intervals. Because each publication and subscription has one or more agents associated with it, there may be a large number of agents to configure.

Different subscriptions may require different settings; for example, a subscription that is performed across a slow link may need a longer time-out and a less frequent polling interval than a subscription across a fast network link.

To make administration simpler, agent settings are stored in profiles. You can configure each agent to use a default profile or create custom profiles for individual agents.

Practice: Replication Exercises

In the replication exercises, your server will be the Publisher, Distributor, and Subscriber. You will create publications in the StudyNwind database (representing the Publisher) and subscriptions in other databases or tables (representing the Subscribers).

You will learn more about publishing and subscribing in Lessons 3 and 4. These exercises give you an opportunity to enable replication on your server and see replication at work for the first time. Replication uses many dialog boxes and processes, so do not expect to see or understand them all right away. You may find it useful to refer back to the lesson text as you perform the exercises.

Exercise 1: Enabling Publishing and Distribution and Creating a Publication

In this exercise, you will create a new publication of the Products table in the StudyNwind database. In doing so, you will automatically enable publishing and distribution.

▶ **To enable publishing and distribution and create a publication**

1. In the console tree of SQL Server Enterprise Manager, click your server.

2. On the Tools menu, point to Replication and then click Create And Manage Publications.

3. In the Create And Manage Publications dialog box, click StudyNwind, and then click Create Publication.

4. Use the Create Publication Wizard and the information in the following table to create your publication. Accept defaults for options not specified.

Option	Value
Distributor	Your server
Publication type	Transactional publication
Allow Immediate-Updating Subscriptions	No
Subscriber Types	All Subscribers will be servers running SQL Server
Articles for publication	Check dbo.Products, click the ellipsis to set the Article name and the Destination table name
Article name	ReplProducts_Article
Destination table name	ReplProducts Click OK to return to the wizard
Publication name	StudyNwind_Products_Publication
No, create a publication without data filters and with the following properties	Selected

5. If you are prompted to have the SQL Server Agent start automatically, click Yes. You will see a dialog box that informs you that the Replication Monitor has been added to the console tree. Click Close. You will learn about the Replication Monitor in Chapter 17, "Managing Replication."

6. After the publication has been created, click Close to close the Create and Manage Publications dialog box.

7. On the Tools menu, point to Replication and then click Configure Publishers, Subscribers And Distribution.

8. In the Publisher and Distributor Properties dialog box, on the Distributor tab, select Distribution in Databases, and then click Properties.

9. In the Store The Transactions, At Least option, type **24** to have the distributor store the transactions for at least 24 hours.

10. Click OK twice to close the Distribution Properties and the Publisher And Distributor Properties dialog boxes.

11. In the console tree, expand your server, and then expand Replication Monitor.

12. If prompted, click Yes to turn polling on. Click OK to save the refresh and rate settings.

13. Expand Publishers, expand your server, and then click StudyNwind_Products_ Publication:StudyNwind. The status of the Snapshot and Log Reader Agents for your new publication is shown in the details pane.

Exercise 2: Creating a New Database

In this exercise, you will create a new database that will be used to create a pull subscription in the next exercise.

▶ **To create a new database**

1. In the console tree, right-click Databases, and then click New Database.

2. In Name, type **PullSubs**, and then click OK to close the Database Properties dialog box and create the new database.

Exercise 3: Creating a Subscription

In this exercise, you will create a subscription to pull the publication that you published in a previous exercise.

▶ **To create a subscription**

1. Click your server. On the Tools menu, point to Replication, and then click Pull Subscription To 'SQLSERVER' (or your server name if different).

2. Select PullSubs, and then click Pull New Subscription.

3. Use the Pull Subscription Wizard and the information in the following table to pull StudyNwind_Products_Publication from the Publisher.

Option	Value
Choose Publication	Expand your server, then select StudyNwind_ Products_Publication: StudyNwind
Destination Database	PullSubs
Initialize Subscription	Yes, initialize the schema and data at the Subscriber
Distribution Agent Schedule	Continuously
Start Required Services	SQLServerAgent (on SQLSERVER)

4. When you have completed all of the steps in the wizard, close the Pull Subscription dialog box.

5. After the subscription has been created, in the console tree, expand your server, expand Management, expand SQL Server Agent, and then click Jobs.

The job called SQLSERVER-StudyNwind-StudyNwind_Products_Pub-SQLSERVER-PullSubs- 0, with a category of REPL-Distribution, is the job that starts the Distribution Agent for your new subscription.

Which server's system resources will this job consume? Would a push subscription change the resources being used?

6. In the console tree, expand Replication Monitor, expand Agents, and then click Distribution Agents. The agent listed in the details pane is the Distribution Agent for your new subscription being monitored by the Replication Monitor. Note that the Last Action for the agent says, "The initial snapshot for article 'ReplProducts_Article' is not yet available." This is because the Snapshot Agent has not yet been run. It is scheduled to run, by default only, at 11:30 P.M. each day. In the next exercise, you will start the Snapshot Agent manually.

Exercise 4: Running the Snapshot Agent

In this exercise, you will start the Snapshot Agent to create a snapshot of the data and schema of the publication. Once the snapshot has been created, the Distribution Agent will use it to create the ReplProducts table and populate it in the PullSubs database.

▶ **To run the Snapshot Agent**

1. In the console tree, expand Replication Monitor, expand Publishers, expand your server, and then click StudyNwind_Products_Publication:StudyNwind.

2. In the details pane, right-click Snapshot, and then click Start.

3. Wait for the Status column to say, "Succeeded," indicating that the Snapshot Agent has generated a snapshot successfully.

4. Right-click Snapshot, and then click Agent History. In the history list, there will be a single entry indicating the successful generation of a snapshot of 1 article.

5. Click Session Details. Review the list of actions that were performed when the snapshot was generated. Click Close twice to close both the Snapshot and Agent History dialog boxes.

6. Use Windows Explorer to review the folders and files that were created below C:\Mssql7\Repldata\Unc. Note the ReplProducts_Article.bcp, ReplProducts_Article.idx, and ReplProducts_Article.sch files that the Snapshot Agent created and that were referenced in the session details you reviewed in the previous step.

7. With Notepad, open the ReplProducts_Article.sch file and review the script that was generated. This script contains the table schema creation statements.

8. With Notepad, open the ReplProducts_Article.idx file and review the script that was generated. This script contains index creation statements.

9. Switch to SQL Server Enterprise Manager. In the console tree, expand Replication Monitor, expand Agents, and then click Distribution Agents.

   View the agent history and action messages by right-clicking the agent in the details pane and selecting Agent History. The Distribution will say that there are no replicated transactions available because no new transactions have occurred since it replicated the snapshot.

10. Open SQL Server Query Analyzer. Verify that the article was published to the ReplProducts table by executing the following statement:

```
USE PullSubs
SELECT * FROM ReplProducts
```

Exercise 5: Exploring Changes Due to Replication

In this exercise, you will use SQL Server Enterprise Manager to see some of the changes that are made to a server when replication is enabled.

▶ **To explore some of the changes after replication is enabled**

1. Right-click your server in the console tree, and click Disconnect. Many of the steps in this exercise require data to be refreshed in SQL Server Enterprise Manager; by disconnecting before you begin, you force all of the information to be refreshed.

2. In the console tree, expand your server, and then expand Databases. Note that the distribution database has been added to the list of databases.

   If distribution (and other system databases such as master) is not listed, right-click on your server and click Edit SQL Server Registration properties. On the property sheet, make sure that the Show System Databases And System Objects option is checked.

   You must neither delete the distribution database nor add objects to or remove objects from the distribution database. It is used to store replication information and replication data from the Publisher that is to be sent to or retrieved by the Subscribers.

3. Notice that the StudyNwind database icon has a hand below it, indicating that it has been published. Expand the StudyNwind database. A node called Publications has been added.

4. Expand Publications, and then click StudyNwind_Products_Publication. In the details pane, all subscriptions to the selected publication are listed.

5. Expand the PullSubs database. Notice that a node called Pull Subscriptions has been added.

6. Click Pull Subscriptions. In the details pane, the subscription to StudyNwind_Products_Publication is listed.

7. In the details pane, right-click the subscription and then click Properties. Review the properties of your pull subscription.

8. Click Cancel to close the Pull Subscription Properties dialog box.

Exercise 6: Updating the Published Article

In this exercise, you will update the Products table (on the Publisher) and verify that the updated information is replicated to the Subscriber.

▶ **To update the published article**

1. In SQL Server Query Analyzer, type and execute the following:

```
USE StudyNwind
SELECT * FROM Products WHERE ProductID = 1
```

2. Review the result set. Make a note of the ReorderLevel for the product (it should be 10).

3. Switch to SQL Server Enterprise Manager, and then expand Replication Monitor. Expand Agents, and then click Log Reader Agents. You must now switch to SQL Server Query Analyzer and type and execute the following script. Immediately after executing the script, switch back to SQL Server Enterprise Manager and watch the Status of the Log Reader Agent.

```
USE StudyNwind
UPDATE Products SET ReorderLevel = 20 WHERE ProductID = 1
SELECT * FROM Products
```

Within a few moments, the Status of the Log Reader Agent entry should change to Running, and the Last Action should indicate that 1 transaction with 1 command was delivered.

4. In the console tree, click Distribution Agents. Within a few moments, the Status of the Distribution Agent entry should change to Running, and the Last Action should indicate that 1 transaction with 1 command was delivered.

5. In the console tree, click Log Reader Agents. Right-click SQLSERVER (or your server name, if different), and then click Agent History. Click Session Details to see the details for the current session. You may still see the action indicating that 1 transaction with 1 command was delivered; otherwise, the action will now indicate that no replicated transactions are available. The detail above the action messages includes various statistics for the current session for the Log Reader Agent.

6. In the console tree, click Distribution Agents. Right-click the publication in the details pane, and then click Agent History. Click Session Details to see the details for the current session. You may still see the action indicating that 1

transaction with 1 command was delivered; otherwise, the action will now indicate that no replicated transactions are available. The detail above the action messages includes various statistics for the current session for the Distribution Agent.

7. If you wish to see the agents running again, execute the query from step 3 with a different reorder level. You must use a different reorder level or the Distribution Agent will not run, because the Log Reader will detect that no data has actually changed.

8. Switch to SQL Server Query Analyzer. Execute the following statement to view the reorder level in the ReplProducts table in the PullSubs database and verify that the data was replicated:

```
USE PullSubs
SELECT * FROM Products WHERE ProductID = 1
```

Lesson Summary

When you implement replication, at least one SQL Server becomes a distribution server, and the distribution database is created on this server. Some special considerations are necessary for the distribution server, such as configuring the distribution database, making the distribution share accessible to other SQL Servers, and possibly adding extra memory. Replication agents are enabled on the relevant servers as you create publications and subscriptions. To simplify the configuration of these agents, they can all use common agent configuration profiles.

Lesson 3: Publishing

This lesson discusses publishing tasks, as well as aspects of publishing that are specific to each replication type. Initial synchronization is necessary whenever a new Subscriber subscribes to a publication.

After this lesson, you will be able to

- Create publications
- Configure initial synchronization

Estimated lesson time: 50 minutes

Creating Publications

After you have configured your servers, you can create publications. You will use the Create Publication Wizard to create new publications. SQL Server Enterprise Manager provides several ways to launch the wizard: with the Tools/Wizards menu, with the Tools/Replication/Create and Manage Publications menu, from the console tree, or from the Replicate Data taskpad. You can create one or more publications from each user database on a Publisher.

Defining a Publication

A publication contains one or more articles. When you create a publication, you can specify

- Whether the publication is a snapshot, transactional, or merge publication.
- Whether all Subscribers will be SQL Servers.
- Snapshot requirements, such as when to schedule the Snapshot Agent or whether to maintain a publication snapshot at the Distributor.
- The tables or stored procedures that will be the articles in the publication. You can also set options such as filters on these articles.
- Whether to allow anonymous or updating Subscribers or pull subscriptions.
- Publications that share an agent. The default is that each publication has its own agent.

Note You cannot create transactional publications on the Desktop Edition of SQL Server. Using the Desktop Edition, you can subscribe to transactional publications on another server and you can create and subscribe to snapshot and merge publications.

Important To maintain referential integrity between published tables, include all tables that are involved in the relationship within one publication. This guarantees that transactions are applied at the same time and that integrity is maintained.

Important You can add new articles and change a number of other publication properties after creating the publication, but you have to remove all Subscribers before making changes. For this reason, you should carefully plan your publications before adding Subscribers.

Specifying Articles

As shown in Figure 16.1, the Specify Articles screen of the Create Publication Wizard lists the tables and, for snapshot and transactional publications, the stored procedures in the database. To publish a table or stored procedure, check it in the list. To change the properties of an article, click the ellipsis button (…) next to the article.

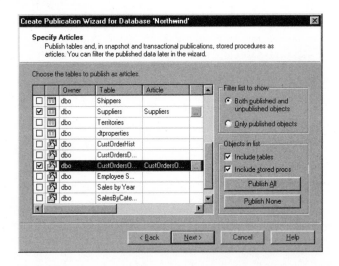

Figure 16.1   The Specify Articles screen in the Create Publication Wizard

Tables published as articles in merge publications cannot have a timestamp column. If a table has a timestamp column, it will have a clock icon in place of the check box in the list of tables in the Create Publication Wizard, as shown in Figure 16.2. If you need to publish the table using merge replication, drop the timestamp column, using the ALTER TABLE statement, before you create the publication.

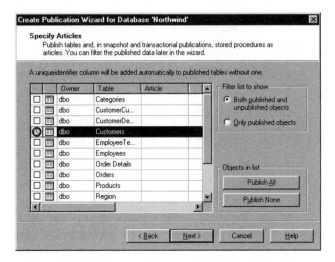

Figure 16.2   The Specify Articles screen, showing a table with a timestamp column

Creating Filters

You can define an article that is a subset of a table by creating filters or scripts that specify the columns or rows to be included. You can define a subset of data vertically, horizontally, or as a combination of the two:

- To create a vertical filter, select only the columns that you want to replicate. Merge replication does not allow vertical filters. The replicated columns must contain the primary key, unless you are using snapshot replication.

- To create a horizontal filter, use a WHERE clause to restrict the set of rows to be replicated.

Merge replication supports dynamic filters that allow each Subscriber to receive different replicated data from the same publication.

Using the Immediate Updating Subscribers Option

Setting the Immediate Updating Subscribers option when you create a publication allows a Subscriber to update a copy of the local data, provided that the changes can automatically be reflected on the Publisher by using a distributed transaction. The Publisher then sends changes to all other Subscribers. This option is not available for merge replication.

You must include a timestamp column in tables that will be updated. When a user attempts to update a row on the Subscriber, SQL Server uses the timestamp column to determine whether any updates have been made at the Publisher. If no timestamp column exists in the table, the Create Publication Wizard will add one.

Publishing Considerations

This section describes several publishing considerations and restrictions in SQL Server 7.

Publishing Restrictions

Certain restrictions exist on replication publishing in SQL Server:

- Publications cannot span databases; each publication can contain articles from only one database.
- It is not possible to replicate the model, tempdb, msdb, master, or distribution databases, because these are system databases.
- A table should have a primary key to identify a row and ensure entity integrity, except in snapshot replication.

Limited Support for Nonlogged Operations

Limited support exists for nonlogged operations on text, ntext, and image data types, as the following table indicates. Changes made to columns with these data types are not logged if the changes are made using the WRITETEXT or UPDATETEXT operations. Do not use these operations if you want changes to be replicated in all cases.

Type of replication	Support for nonlogged changes
Snapshot	Changes are detected and replicated
Transactional	Log Reader Agent does not detect changes
Merge	Triggers do not detect changes

Due to the potentially large size of this data, the max text repl size server configuration option specifies the maximum size of text and image data change that may be replicated. The default is 64 KB.

Ensuring Unique Identities in Merge Replication

It is essential to uniquely identify rows in merge replication. A table published for merge replication must have a column that uses the uniqueidentifier data type and the ROWGUIDCOL property. Globally unique values can be generated for the column by setting its default to the NEWID function. When SQL Server finds a column with this property, it automatically uses the column as the row identifier for the replicated table.

If there is no column with the ROWGUIDCOL property, SQL Server adds one to the base table.

Columns with the uniqueidentifier data type hold a 128-bit globally unique identifier (GUID) that is generated by the NEWID function. These values are guaranteed to be globally unique, so no two rows will ever have the same GUID. Here is an example of a GUID:

```
6F9619FF-8B86-D011-B42D-00C04FC964FF
```

Initial Synchronization

Before a new Subscriber can receive a publication, the source and destination tables should contain the same schema and data. The synchronization process that accomplishes this is called the initial snapshot, and the Publisher initiates the process.

All articles within a publication are synchronized initially as a single logical unit. This helps to maintain integrity relationships that originate from the underlying tables.

The Snapshot Agent creates different scripts depending on the type of replication. The scripts are stored in the distribution working folder, and the status of the synchronization jobs are stored in the distribution database. The different scripts contain

- Schema definitions
- The bulk copy program (bcp) output file(s) of the data to be replicated
- Index definitions
- Additional script files for merge replication

The synchronization process uses the bcp utility in either native (SQL Server) or character format. Native format is smaller and faster but cannot be used by non–SQL Server Subscribers. When creating the publication, you can specify whether all Subscribers will be SQL Servers. This determines which bcp format will be used. You can modify the format later by editing the publication properties.

Synchronization Frequency

For new Subscribers only, you can schedule when the initial synchronization files are created. After initial synchronization, a Subscriber does not have to be reinitialized unless a problem occurs.

You have the option to bypass the initial synchronization. This is useful when you have employed other means to do an initial synchronization or when you want a slightly different schema at your Publisher than at your Subscriber. For example, if you are publishing a 20-GB database, you can perform the synchronization manually using a tape backup and restore, meaning that the 20 GB of data will not have to be transferred across the network between the Publisher and the Subscriber. However, if you elect to bypass the initial synchronization, you must complete the step manually. Depending on the type of replication you are using, this can include performing such tasks as adding timestamp and unique-identifier columns.

Editing Publication Properties

To edit the properties of a publication, select Tools/Replication/Create And Manage Publications, navigate to the publication, and click Properties & Subscriptions. Alternatively, navigate to the publication in the console tree in the Publications node below the published database, right-click the publication, and select Properties. This opens the publication Properties dialog box, which allows you to define the following:

- Articles and filters
- Subscription properties
- Subscription options:
    - Whether to allow pull and anonymous subscriptions
    - Whether to allow snapshot downloads using FTP
    - Whether to report merge conflicts at the Publisher (centralized conflict reporting) or at the Subscribers (decentralized conflict reporting)
- The publication access list
- Service and agent status
- Scripts that are used to create and delete the publication

Important Before making changes to the properties of a publication, it is necessary to remove all subscriptions to the publication. Do this from the Subscriptions tab of the publication Properties dialog box. After removing all Subscribers, you must close the publication Properties dialog box and either reopen it (as prompted) or refresh your console tree view (right-click your server and click Refresh) and then reopen the publication Properties dialog box to make your changes.

Agents Created for a Publication

When you create a publication, one or more agents are created to support it, as shown in the following table. You can see information about these agents in the Replication Monitor after creating a publication.

Type of replication	Agents created
Snapshot	Snapshot Agent for initial synchronization and ongoing replication
Transactional	Snapshot Agent for initial synchronization and Log Reader Agent for ongoing replication
Merge	Snapshot Agent for initial synchronization

Exercise: Creating a Merge Publication

In this exercise, you will create a merge publication.

▶ **To create a merge publication on the Publisher**

1. In the console tree, click your server.

2. On the Tools menu, point to Replication, and then click Create And Manage Publications.

3. Verify that StudyNwind is selected, and then click Create Publication.

   Note that this time the Create Publishing Wizard does not prompt you for the information needed to enable publishing and distribution; rather, you immediately begin defining the new publication.

4. Use the information in the next table to create a new publication.

Option	Value
No, I will define the articles and properties	Selected
Publication Type	Merge publication
All Subscribers will be servers running SQL Server	Selected
Specify articles	Check dbo.Customers, dbo. Employees, dbo.Order Details, dbo.Orders, dbo.Products and dbo.Shippers
When prompted to add an indexed uniqueidentifier column	Click OK
Publication name	StudyNwind_Merge_Publication
No, create a publication without data filters and with the following properties	Selected

Note that you are warned that the published data references data not being published. This is intentional for the exercise. When publishing live data, you should be careful to include all data that will be needed on the Subscribers. The Create Publication Wizard makes this easier for you by issuing this warning.

5. Expand Replication Monitor, expand Publishers, and expand your server. If StudyNwind_Merge_Publication is not listed, right-click your server name and then click Refresh.

6. Click the StudyNwind_Merge_Publication.

7. In the details pane, right-click the Snapshot Agent and click Start. The agent will run for a few minutes, generating the initial snapshot of the new publication. Wait until the Last Action column in the details pane displays the following message: "A snapshot of 6 articles was generated."

Exercise: Reviewing the Snapshot Agent Job History

In this exercise, you will open the Replication Monitor and review the history of the creation of the snapshot files.

▶ **To review the Snapshot Agent job history**

1. When the snapshot is complete, in the details pane, right-click Snapshot, and then click Agent History.

2. Click Session Details.

   Review the session details associated with the creation of the snapshot.

3. Open Windows Explorer, and review the directories and files that were created under the C:\Mssql7\Repldata\Unc folder.

   Notice that these are the same files that the Agent History indicated were created.

Lesson Summary

All data that is to be replicated must be defined as part of a publication on the Publisher. Each table or stored procedure that is to be replicated is defined as an article in a publication. Subscribers subscribe to an entire publication. When you create a new publication, a snapshot is created for the publication. This snapshot is used to perform an initial synchronization when Subscribers subscribe to the publication. You can specify various properties for publications, such as whether Subscribers will be able to create anonymous subscriptions and whether FTP can be used to download the initial snapshot.

Lesson 4: Subscribing

This lesson describes how to create a subscription, specify subscription characteristics, and specify how often to refresh data on the Subscriber with data from the Publisher.

After this lesson, you will be able to

- Set up subscriptions

Estimated lesson time: 50 minutes

Setting Up Push and Pull Subscriptions

The characteristics of a subscription are determined by the type of publication to which it subscribes and whether it is a push or a pull subscription. Each type of publication supports either a push or a pull subscription. Use the Push Subscription Wizard and the Pull Subscription Wizard to create subscriptions.

Depending on the publication and subscription types, to create a subscription, you may need to do the following:

- Specify the login credentials for the Subscriber agent if using a pull subscription
- Select the publication
- Select an existing subscription database or create a new one at the Subscriber
- Select one of the initial synchronization methods
- Specify a schedule for ongoing replication
- For subscriptions to merge publications, specify a subscription priority to be used when resolving conflicts during replication
- For subscriptions to publications that are enabled for anonymous subscription, specify whether the subscription must be anonymous

Push Subscriptions

You define a push subscription centrally at the Publisher. Push subscriptions are useful with centralized administration and are set up at the Publisher.

The type of subscription controls the execution of the agents that you use to manage replication. For snapshot and transactional replication, the Distribution Agent runs at the Distributor; for merge replication, the Merge Agent runs at the Distributor.

Pull Subscriptions

You define a pull subscription at each Subscriber. With pull subscriptions, Subscribers decide what to subscribe to and when to subscribe, which offloads administration and processing from the Publisher and the Distributor. Anonymous subscriptions offload even more of the work than regular pull subscriptions and are particularly suited to Internet subscriptions.

For snapshot and transactional replication, the Distribution Agent runs at the Subscriber; for merge replication, the Merge Agent runs at the Subscriber. For pull subscriptions, you can configure the initial synchronization to use FTP to transfer data.

Using the Immediate Updating Subscribers Option

For each subscription to a publication that has the option enabled, you can choose to use the Immediate Updating Subscribers Option. If this option is used, both the Publisher and the Subscriber must be running the Microsoft Distributed Transaction Coordinator (MS DTC).

Triggers are created in the table(s) on the Immediate Updating Subscriber to perform the two-phase commit update on the Publisher.

The next two sections discuss some restrictions to using this option.

Data Type Update Restrictions

When you are using the Immediate Updating Subscribers option, the Subscriber

- Cannot update timestamp, identity, text, or image data type values
- Cannot insert into a table that has a timestamp or identity column unless the table has a unique index

Row Identity Update Restrictions

When you are using the Immediate Updating Subscribers option, the Subscriber cannot update the unique index or primary key, because these are used to identify the row.

Note If you drop a subscription and want to continue to modify a table at the subscribing site, you must drop triggers on the replicated table at the Subscriber manually.

Editing Subscription Properties

To view the properties of a push subscription on the Publisher, open the Properties dialog box for the publication. On the Subscriptions tab, select the subscription and click Properties. There are no editable properties for a push subscription.

To edit the properties of a pull subscription on the Subscriber, select Tools/ Replication/Pull Subscription to '*servername*', navigate to the subscription, and click Properties. Alternatively, navigate to the subscription in the console tree in the Pull Subscriptions node below the subscribing database, right-click the subscription, and select Properties. This opens the Pull Subscription Properties dialog box, which allows you to

- Set Distribution Agent properties
- Enable the Windows Synchronization Agent for the subscription
- Configure security settings for the Subscriber to access the Publisher
- Enable and configure the subscription to use FTP to download the initial snapshot

Agents Created for a Subscription

When you create a publication, one or more agents are created to support the publication, as shown in the following table. You can see information about these agents in the Replication Monitor after creating a subscription.

Type of replication	Type of subscription	Agents created
Snapshot	Push	Distribution Agent at the Distributor
	Pull	Distribution Agent at the Subscriber
Transactional	Push	Distribution Agent at the Distributor
	Pull	Distribution Agent at the Subscriber
Merge	Push	Merge Agent at the Distributor
	Pull	Merge Agent at the Subscriber

Publications in the same database that are not set up for immediate synchronization use the same Distribution Agent for all subscriptions of the same type, push or pull, in a single database on a Subscriber. When the same Distribution Agent is used for multiple publications, the agent is referred to as a shared Distribution Agent. In the Replication Monitor under Distribution Agents, shared Distribution Agents are listed as <Multiple Publications> in the Publication column.

Exercise: Creating a Push Subscription

In this exercise, you will push the articles (to the Subscriber) that were published (on the Publisher) in Lesson 3 of this chapter.

► **To create a push subscription to a publication**

1. In SQL Server Enterprise Manager, click your server.

2. On the Tools menu, point to Replication, and then click Push Subscriptions To Others.

3. Expand StudyNwind, click StudyNwind_Merge_Publication, and then click Push New Subscription.

4. Use the information in the following table to create the push subscription.

Option	Value
Choose Subscribers	Select your server.
Subscription database(s)	nwrepl
	Click Browse Databases. Click Create New, type **nwrepl** in Name, and click OK to create the new database.
When should the Merge Agent update the subscription?	Using the following schedule: Click Change and set the schedule to Daily, Every 1 day, Occurs every 2 minutes.
Yes, initialize the schema and data at the Subscriber	Selected
Start the Merge Agent to initialize the subscription immediately.	Checked
Use the following priority to resolve the conflict	25.00

5. After the subscription is created, in the console tree of SQL Server Enterprise Manager, expand your server, expand Replication Monitor, expand Agents, and then click Merge Agents.

   It will take a few minutes for the Merge Agent to complete the initialization of the new subscription.

6. In the details pane, *after* the Status column indicates that the Merge Agent has succeeded, right-click StudyNwind_Merge_Publication, and then click Agent History. In the history list, select the oldest entry (this is the entry for the subscription initialization and should have about 38 actions). If there are other entries, they represent the Merge Agent running every 2 minutes according to

the schedule you created for the subscription. Click Session Details. Review the history of the Merge Agent.

Whose system resources does this Merge Agent consume? Would a pull subscription change the resources that are used?

Exercise: Updating the Source Table on the Publisher

In this exercise, you will update the Customers table (on the Publisher) and verify that the updated information replicates to the Subscriber.

▶ **To update the source table on the Publisher**

1. Switch to SQL Server Query Analyzer.

2. Type and execute the following script:

```
USE StudyNwind
SELECT * FROM Customers
```

3. Review the result set. Notice the first row, with the value Maria Anders in the ContactName column.

4. Type and execute the following script:

```
USE StudyNwind
UPDATE Customers
SET ContactName = 'Maria Anders-Smith'
WHERE CustomerID = 'ALFKI'
SELECT * FROM Customers
```

How long will it take for this update to be replicated?

5. Type and execute the following script to verify that the update has been replicated to the nwrepl database:

```
USE nwrepl
SELECT * FROM Customers
```

6. In SQL Server Enterprise Manager, expand Replication Monitor, expand Agents, and then click Merge Agents.

7. In the details pane, right-click StudyNwind_Merge_Publication, and then click Agent History.

8. Click the session that indicates that data changes were merged, and then click Session Details.

Review the actions that were taken during the session.

Exercise: Updating Simultaneously from a Publisher and a Subscriber

In this exercise, you will update the Customers table on the Publisher and the Subscriber with conflicting information and then review the results.

▶ **To update simultaneously on a Publisher and a Subscriber**

1. Switch to SQL Server Query Analyzer. Open two query windows.

2. Type the following script in the first query window, but do not execute the script:

```
USE StudyNwind
UPDATE Customers
SET ContactName = 'Maria Anders-Smyth'
WHERE CustomerID = 'ALFKI'
SELECT * FROM Customers
```

3. Type the following script in the second query window, but do not execute the script:

```
USE nwrepl
UPDATE Customers
SET ContactName = 'Maria Anders-Smythe'
WHERE CustomerID = 'ALFKI'
SELECT * FROM Customers
```

4. Execute the statements in the two query windows one after the other, as closely together as possible.

5. Switch to SQL Server Enterprise Manager.

6. In the Merge Agent details pane, verify that the update has been replicated and that there was one conflict. This will take up to two minutes.

7. Switch to SQL Server Query Analyzer and execute the following query in each of the query windows:

```
SELECT * FROM Customers
```

Which update was applied? Was it the update made on the Publisher server (in the StudyNwind database) or on the Subscriber server (in the nwrepl database)?

Exercise: Resolving the Conflict

In this exercise, you will resolve the conflict, using the Microsoft Replication Conflict Viewer.

▶ **To resolve the conflict**

1. In the console tree, expand Databases, then right-click the StudyNwind database, point to All Tasks, and click View Replication Conflicts.

The Microsoft Replication Conflict Viewer appears, indicating a conflict in the Customers table of the StudyNwind database.

2. Click View.

3. Click Overwrite with revised data.

4. In the ContactName box, type **Maria Anders**, and then click Resolve.

5. Click Close.

6. Switch to SQL Server Query Analyzer and execute the following query in both of the query windows:

```
SELECT * FROM Customers
```

Was the revised data applied to both servers?

Important To perform conflict resolution at the Subscribers, you have to enable the decentralized conflict-reporting option for the publication before adding Subscribers to the publication. If you do this, you have to resolve each conflict at the losing Subscriber, so you may not always be able to perform conflict resolution at the same server.

Lesson Summary

After creating publications on the Publisher, you can create two kinds of subscriptions to these publications. Push subscriptions are created and managed on the Publisher. Pull subscriptions are created and managed on the Subscribers. The Distribution Agent for push subscriptions runs on the Distributor, and the Distribution Agent for push subscriptions runs on the Subscriber.

SQL Server 7 introduces Immediate Updating Subscribers, which allow updates to be made to subscribed data on a Subscriber. The updates made on a Subscriber are applied immediately on the Publisher, using a distributed transaction managed by MS DTC.

Review

The following questions are intended to reinforce key information presented in the chapter. If you are unable to answer a question, review the appropriate lesson and then try the question again. Answers to the questions can be found in Appendix A, "Questions and Answers."

1. You are trying to configure replication between two servers. Both servers appear to be set up correctly, but replication does not work. What do you think is the problem? What should you do to fix it?

2. When you set up the distribution server, what should you consider when estimating the appropriate size of the distribution database?

3. Your company has decided to use SQL Server replication. The publication server runs an intensive application and does not have the capacity to manage any replication overhead. You will have a large number of Subscribers. Some Subscribers may be offline periodically, and all Subscribers must have the ability to update data. Which model and method of replication would best address these requirements? Why?

CHAPTER 17

Managing Replication

About This Chapter

In this final chapter on replication, you will learn how to monitor the replication agents and use various tools in Microsoft SQL Server to troubleshoot replication problems. You will also learn how to publish data to non–SQL Server Subscribers, replicate data from non–SQL Server databases, and make a publication available for subscription on the Internet.

Before You Begin

To complete the lessons in this chapter, you must have

- Installed SQL Server 7. See Chapter 2, "Installation," for installation instructions.
- The ability to log on to SQL Server as an Administrator.
- Completed the exercises in Chapter 16, "Planning and Setting Up Replication."
- Installed the StudyNwind database. See the "Getting Started" section in "About This Book" for StudyNwind database installation instructions.
- Installed the Exercise files from the Supplemental Course Materials CD-ROM to your hard disk drive. See the "Getting Started" section in "About This Book" for installation instructions.

- Switched the license mode of the SQL Server version 7.0 evaluation software by stepping through the following procedure:
  1. Open License Manager from the Administrative Tools program group.
  2. Select the Products View tab and double-click on MS SQL Server 7.0.

3. Select the Server Browser tab, choose SQLSERVER, and click Edit.

4. Select MS SQL Server 7.0 and click Edit.

5. Select the Per Seat mode, click Yes to acknowledge the change, and click OK.

6. Agree to the license agreement and click OK twice to return to the License Manager main dialog box.

7. Close License Manager.

Lesson 1: Monitoring and Troubleshooting Replication

It is important to monitor all aspects of the replication process, from overseeing changes that are made to a publication to verifying the replicated changes on the Subscriber. SQL Server tools that are designed for this purpose are the most efficient means of monitoring replication, but it is also possible to use system stored procedures and to retrieve information from system tables.

After this lesson, you will be able to

- Monitor and troubleshoot SQL Server 7 replication using tools, system stored procedures, and system tables
- Generate a replication script

Estimated lesson time: 60 minutes

Using SQL Server Replication Monitor

SQL Server Replication Monitor is a component of SQL Server Enterprise Manager that is added to the console tree on the Distributor when the Distributor is enabled. It is designed for viewing the status of replication agents and for troubleshooting potential replication problems.

You can use SQL Server Replication Monitor to

- View a list of Publishers, publications, and subscriptions to the publications supported by the Distributor
- View the real-time status of scheduled replication agents
- Display current execution data for a replication agent to obtain a running total of transactions, statements, inserts, and updates that have been processed
- Configure replication agent profiles and properties
- Set up and monitor alerts that are related to replication events
- View replication agent histories

Note Although the Distribution and Merge Agents run on the Subscriber for pull subscriptions, the Replication Monitor is not available on the Subscriber. The status of the agents running on the Subscriber is monitored in the Replication Monitor running on the Distributor to which the Subscriber agents connect.

Maintaining Replication

When you manage replication, you will need to address certain maintenance issues, including space management and backup strategies.

Space Management

Space management requires that you

- Monitor the size of the distribution database to ensure that enough space exists to store the replication jobs. This involves the following:
    - Determining the retention period for the replication history and replicated transactions
    - Setting up Distributor properties to control the retention period
- Monitor Miscellaneous Agents.

    History tables and replicated transactions consume database storage space. Several replication agents clear these tables periodically. Ensure that the agents listed in the following table are running.

Miscellaneous agent	Description
Agent history clean up: distribution	Removes replication agent history records from the distribution database
Distribution clean up: distribution	Removes replicated transactions from the distribution database
Expired subscription clean up	Detects and removes inactive subscriptions from published databases
Reinitialize subscriptions having data validation failures	Reinitializes (performs another initial synchronization of) all subscriptions that have failed due to data validation failure
Replication agents checkup	Detects replication agents that are not actively logging history

Backup Strategies

It is important to back up the distribution database, because if it is lost you must re-create all publications and subscriptions. By default, the trunc. log on chkpt. option is enabled when the distribution database is created. If you choose to perform transaction log backups on the distribution database, you must first disable this option. Plan and implement backup strategies by

- Monitoring any issues with the distribution database that will affect the Publisher. For example, if the distribution database runs out of space, transactions that are waiting to be published cannot be removed from the transaction log on the Publisher.

- Preparing recovery and resynchronization plans in the event that a Publisher, Distributor, or Subscriber fails.

Due to the large number of different possible replication configurations, detailed backup and restore strategies are not presented in this book. SQL Server Books Online has matrixes that present strategies for each possible configuration.

Using Replication Scripts

A replication script provides many benefits, including the following:

- It can save time if many servers must be configured identically. You can execute the script instead of performing installation steps repeatedly with SQL Server Enterprise Manager.

- It provides a recovery mechanism. For example, if a Publisher or Distributor fails, you can execute the script to reinstall replication after the server hardware is replaced.

- It allows you to track different versions of your replication environment by periodically creating and storing scripts in a source code control system.

- It allows you to customize an existing replication environment.

Creating and Executing Replication Scripts

To create replication scripts, select Tools/Replication/Generate Replication Scripts in SQL Server Enterprise Manager. Figure 17.1 shows the resulting dialog box. A script automatically has the name of the server that was used when replication was defined. To execute a script on another server, change server names in the script as appropriate.

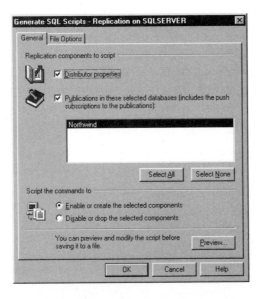

Figure 17.1   The Generate SQL Scripts – Replication dialog box

Exercise: Generating a Replication Script

In this exercise, you will generate a script, preview it, and then save it to disk.

▶   **To generate a script**

1. In the console tree of SQL Server Enterprise Manager, click your server.
2. On the Tools menu, point to Replication, and then click Generate Replication Scripts.
3. Review the available options.
4. Click Preview.
5. Review the script that was generated.
6. Click Save As. Save the script to C:\Sqladmin\Exercise\Ch17\Replication.sql.
7. Click OK to acknowledge that the script was saved.
8. Click Close and Cancel to close the Generate Script dialog boxes.

Monitoring SQL Server Replication Performance

You can use the Replication Monitor in SQL Server Enterprise Manager, Microsoft Windows NT Performance Monitor, and system stored procedures to monitor replication performance. You can obtain information on delivered transactions, undelivered transactions, rates of delivery, and latency.

Using Windows NT Performance Monitor

Replication counters that graphically display replication details are useful for retrieving information about replication. You can use the counters described in this section in Windows NT Performance Monitor.

SQLServer:Replication Agents

The counter for the SQLServer:Replication Agents object has an instance for each type of replication agent.

Counter	Description
Running	The number of replication agents, of the specified type, currently running

SQLServer:Replication Dist.

The SQLServer:Replication Dist. object has counters for monitoring instances of the Distribution Agent.

Counter	Description
Dist:Delivery Latency	The current amount of time, in milliseconds, that elapses between when transactions are delivered to the Distributor and when they are applied at the Subscriber

Counter	Description
Dist:Delivered Commands/sec	The number of commands per second delivered to the Subscriber
Dist:Delivered Transactions/sec	The number of transactions per second delivered to the Subscriber

SQLServer:Replication Logreader

The SQLServer:Replication Logreader object has counters for monitoring instances of the Log Reader Agent.

Counter	Description
Logreader:Delivery Latency	The current amount of time, in milliseconds, that elapses between when transactions are applied at the Publisher and when they are delivered to the Distributor
Logreader:Delivered Commands/sec	The number of commands per second delivered to the Distributor
Logreader:Delivered Transactions/sec	The number of transactions per second delivered to the Distributor

SQLServer:Replication Merge

The SQLServer:Replication Merge object has counters for monitoring instances of the Merge Agent.

Counter	Description
Uploaded Changes/sec	The number of rows per second merged from the Subscriber to the Publisher
Downloaded Changes/sec	The number of rows per second merged from the Publisher to the Subscriber
Conflicts/sec	The number of conflicts per second occurring during the merge process

SQLServer:Replication Snapshot

The SQLServer:Replication Snapshot object has counters for monitoring instances of the Snapshot Agent.

Counter	Description
Snapshot:Delivered Commands/sec	The number of commands per second delivered to the Distributor
Snapshot:Delivered Transactions/sec	The number of transactions per second delivered to the Distributor

Using System Stored Procedures

You can retrieve information about replication using system stored procedures. This method allows you to reference replication information that may be used in triggers, user-defined stored procedures, or scripts. Some of these system stored procedures are listed in the following table.

To retrieve information on	Use
Servers	sp_helpserver
	sp_helpremotelogin
Databases	sp_helpdb
	sp_helpdistributor
	sp_helppublication
	sp_helpsubscription
	sp_helpsubscriberinfo
Replication activity	sp_replcmds
	sp_repltrans
	sp_replcounters

Viewing Replication Agent Histories

History tables contain information for all replication agents. You should regularly view replication histories to identify any tasks that fail and the reasons for the failures. Message detail provides an indicator of the issues—for example, connectivity problems, permission restrictions, and log-full errors.

Viewing Selected Replication Agent Histories

With the Agent History in SQL Server Replication Monitor, you can view replication information from the history tables for one or more sessions of a selected agent. Agent History allows you to filter the list of sessions to show

- All sessions
- Sessions in a specified time frame, such as the last 24 hours, the last two days, or the last seven days
- Sessions with errors

Using System Tables

The history tables in the distribution database track replication job activity for all replication agents. Instead of viewing the agent histories in the Replication Monitor, you can query the tables directly in the distribution database. These history tables (one for each agent) are

- MSsnapshot_history
- MSlogreader_history

- MSdistribution_history
- MSmerge_history

Troubleshooting Replication

Many difficulties in replication processing involve connectivity and security. Before these can be addressed, you must determine which servers are involved in a replication problem by observing the processing order of the replication agents. Troubleshooting and resolution should focus on the access to each of the servers and to the databases that are involved in the replication scenario.

Check the Error Logs

Several error logs can assist you in troubleshooting replication problems: SQL Server Error Log, SQL Server Agent Error Log, and Windows NT Event Viewer. You also can use SQL Server Profiler to troubleshoot replication.

Configure and Monitor Replication Alerts

Replication alerts are standard SQL Server alerts, configured to respond to conditions caused by the replication process. In SQL Server Enterprise Manager, you can configure all of the replication alerts under Alerts in SQL Server Agent or under Replication Alerts in the Replication Monitor. You must add new replication alerts under Replication Alerts in the Replication Monitor; otherwise they will show up only in SQL Server Agent. If you use the sp_add_alert system stored procedure to add a replication alert, you must specify the category 'Replication' with the @category_name argument if you want the new alert to be listed under Replication Alerts in the Replication Monitor.

A number of predefined replication alerts are created when you enable publishing and distribution. In order to use any of these alerts, you must enable it and add one or more operators to be notified when it fires. As for standard SQL Server Agent alerts, you can specify a job to be executed when the alert fires. The following predefined replication alerts are created for you:

- Replication: Agent custom shutdown
- Replication: Agent failure
- Replication: Agent retry
- Replication: Agent success
- Replication: Expired subscription dropped
- Replication: Subscriber has failed data validation
- Replication: Subscriber has passed data validation
- Replication: Subscriber reinitialized after validation failure

Verify SQL Server Services

Replication agents run under the user context of the SQLServerAgent service. If you have difficulty with the MSSQLServer service or the SQLServerAgent service, verify that

- MSSQLServer and SQLServerAgent services are running.

- The service account and password are properly configured for the SQLServer-Agent service. It is recommended that all participants in the replication process use the same Windows NT domain account for the SQLServerAgent service.

- Multidomain environments have service accounts that are trusted across domains.

Test the Connectivity

By default, SQL Server replication uses the same Windows NT domain user account that SQL Server Agent uses. If you experience a problem with connectivity, test the connectivity as follows:

- For a push subscription,

  - Log on to the Distributor with the same Windows NT account that the SQLServerAgent service uses on the Distributor.

  - From the Distributor, use SQL Server Query Analyzer, choose Windows NT Authentication Mode, and connect to the Subscriber.

- For a pull subscription,

  - Log on to the Subscriber with the same Windows NT account that SQL Server Agent uses on the Subscriber.

  - From the Subscriber, use SQL Server Query Analyzer, choose Windows NT Authentication Mode, and connect to the Distributor.

If you cannot connect using either of these methods, the problem is with security rather than replication.

Connectivity to Microsoft Windows 95 and Windows 98 Servers

On Windows NT–based SQL Servers that need to replicate data from a Windows 95–based or Windows 98–based SQL Server, use the SQL Server Client Network Utility to define an alias for the Windows 95 or Windows 98 server that uses the TCP/IP or Multiprotocol network library. This is necessary because Windows NT–based SQL Servers use the Named Pipes client network library by default, and Windows 95–based and Windows 98–based SQL Servers do not support incoming Named Pipes connections.

Check the Replication Agent Schedules

If replication is not occurring as expected, you may simply have to wait for the agents to start as scheduled, or you can manually start the agents to initiate the replication process.

Consider the following transactional replication scenario. After creating a publication and a subscription, the tables corresponding to the publication articles are not being created and populated on the Subscriber. You have checked the security and the connectivity between the Publisher, the Distributor, and the Subscriber, and they are working correctly.

The most likely cause for the replication not occurring in this case is that the initial synchronization has not taken place. This is probably because the Snapshot Agent has not run to generate the initial snapshot that the Distribution Agent needs in order to perform the initial synchronization. Depending on how the initial snapshot was scheduled when the publication was created, the initial snapshot may be created later or on demand. You need either to wait for the snapshot to be created or to start the Snapshot Agent for the publication manually before the initial synchronization will occur. After the initial synchronization is complete, regular transactional replication will begin.

Exercise: Modifying the History Retention Properties on the Distributor

In this exercise, you will modify the length of time that the Distributor retains transaction records in the distribution database. You will also modify the length of time that the Distributor retains replication performance history.

▶   **To modify the history retention properties of the Distributor**

1. In the console tree of SQL Server Enterprise Manager, click your server. On the Tools menu, point to Replication, and then click Configure Publishing, Subscribers, And Distribution.

2. Click Properties to modify the properties of the distribution database.

3. Increase the maximum length of time that the Distributor stores transaction records to 96 hours.

4. Increase the length of time that the Distributor stores replication performance history to 72 hours.

5. Click OK to close the Distribution Properties dialog box.

6. Click OK to close the Publisher And Distributor Properties dialog box.

Exercise: Reviewing the Properties of the Miscellaneous Agents

In this exercise, you will review the properties of the Miscellaneous Agents.

▶ **To review the properties of the Miscellaneous Agents**

1. In the console tree, expand Replication Monitor, expand Agents, and then click Miscellaneous Agents.

2. For each of the agents in the details pane, perform steps 3, 4, and 5 to see some of the properties of each agent.

3. Right-click the agent, and then click Agent Properties.

   What is the function of this agent and how often does it run?

4. On the Steps tab, click Edit, and then review the Command box.

5. Click Cancel, and then click Cancel again to close the agent dialog boxes.

Lesson Summary

It is important to make backups of the distribution database if you are using replication because most of the replication configuration information is stored in the distribution database. SQL Server provides many tools for monitoring and checking replication. You can use the Replication Monitor in SQL Server Enterprise Manager, the Windows NT Performance Monitor, system stored procedures, agent histories, and replication alerts to monitor the status and performance of replication on your servers. Most problems with replication are caused by connectivity or security problems between the servers.

Lesson 2: Replicating in Heterogeneous Environments

With SQL Server, it is possible to replicate data *to* heterogeneous Subscribers by using Open Database Connectivity (ODBC) and OLE DB. It is also possible to replicate data *from* sources other than SQL Server. In this lesson you will learn how to configure replication in these heterogeneous environments and also how to make publications available for subscription on the Internet.

After this lesson, you will be able to

- Describe how to replicate to and from heterogeneous databases
- Publish to Internet Subscribers

Estimated lesson time: 45 minutes

Replicating Data with ODBC

SQL Server supports replication to heterogeneous databases (databases that are not running on SQL Server) on Windows NT, Windows 95, and Windows 98. You can also replicate to other platforms, provided you have the appropriate ODBC or OLE DB driver and necessary communication software.

Data Sources Other Than SQL Server

Heterogeneous databases that are supported by SQL Server replication include

- Microsoft Access databases
- Oracle databases
- IBM DB2/MVS and IBM DB2/AS400
- Other databases that comply with SQL Server ODBC subscriber requirements

Replicating from a SQL Server 6.5 Publisher/Distributor to a SQL Server 7 Subscriber

To perform replication from a SQL Server 6.5 Publisher/Distributor to a SQL Server 7 Subscriber, you must perform one of these actions to ensure that the SQL Server 7 Subscriber behaves in a backward-compatible fashion:

- Add the SQL Server Authentication login, repl_publisher, with no password at the SQL Server 7 Subscriber.
- Run the SQL Server 7 Subscriber server using trace flag -T3685.

ODBC Driver Requirements

SQL Server comes with Microsoft ODBC drivers for Oracle, Access, and the IBM data protocol Distributed Relational Database Architecture (DRDA). Drivers for other ODBC subscriber types must conform to SQL Server replication requirements for generic ODBC subscribers. The ODBC driver must

- Allow updates
- Conform to ODBC Level 1
- Support transactions
- Support the Transact-SQL data definition language (DDL) statements
- Be 32-bit and thread-safe

Publishing Data to Heterogeneous Subscribers

You can publish data to heterogeneous Subscribers by using replication wizards in SQL Server Enterprise Manager.

Creating a Subscription

You can create a push subscription from the Publisher to the heterogeneous Subscriber by using the Push Subscription Wizard. Creating a heterogeneous pull subscription is possible by programming the replication ActiveX control.

Restrictions Involving Heterogeneous Subscriber Types

The following table lists the restrictions that apply to replication with heterogeneous Subscriber types that use ODBC.

Restriction	Explanation
Data types	SQL Server data types are mapped to the closest data type on the target database.
Snapshots	Snapshots must use the bcp character format, not the native SQL Server format.
Using the publication option to truncate the destination table before synchronization	Heterogeneous subscriptions to publications that have this option selected are not supported.
Batched statements	Batched statements are not supported to ODBC subscribers.
ODBC configuration issues	The ODBC data source name (DSN) must conform to SQL Server naming conventions. The quoted identifier setting on the target server, as reported by the ODBC driver, is used.

Using System Stored Procedures

The following table lists the system stored procedures that support replication to ODBC subscribers.

System stored procedure	Description
sp_enumdsn	Returns a list of ODBC and OLE DB data sources available to the SQL Server
sp_dsninfo	Retrieves ODBC or OLE DB data source information from the Distributor associated with the current server, including whether the data source can be a Subscriber

Replicating from Heterogeneous Databases

SQL Server enables third-party replication products to become Publishers within the SQL Server replication framework. This allows these applications to leverage a full set of the replication features provided by SQL Server 7. Figure 17.2 illustrates how a third-party product can be used in a SQL Server replication framework. A SQL Server Publisher and a third-party Publisher are both using the same remote Distributor, and the Subscriber has subscribed to publications on both of the Publishers.

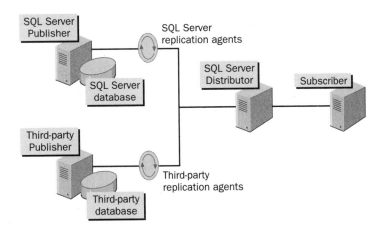

Figure 17.2   Replication from heterogeneous databases

To integrate heterogeneous data sources with SQL Server replication, a developer can create a SQL-DMO program written in Microsoft Visual Basic, C, or C++ that defines a publication and its articles and subscriptions. A second program using the Replication Distributor Interface must be written in C or C++; this program stores the replication transactions in the Distributor. After the publication, articles, and subscriptions are created and the transactions are stored in the Distributor, the transactions are forwarded by the SQL Server Distribution Agent and can be monitored using the Replication Monitor in SQL Server Enterprise Manager.

Exercise: Enabling a Microsoft Access Jet 4 Subscriber

In this exercise, you will enable a new Microsoft Access Jet 4 Subscriber. You will specify a Jet database that does not exist; it will be created automatically when a subscription is initialized in a later exercise.

▶ **To enable a Microsoft Access Jet 4 Subscriber**

1. In the console tree, click your server.

2. On the Tools menu, point to Replication, and then click Configuring Publishing, Subscribers, And Distribution.

3. On the Subscribers tab, click New Subscriber.

4. Select Microsoft Jet 4.0 database (Microsoft Access). Click OK.

5. Click Add to register a Jet database as a new linked server.

6. In Linked Server Name, type **REPLICATION**.

7. In Database File And Path Name, type **C:\Sqladmin\Exercise\Ch17\Repl.mdb**. Click OK.

8. In the list of linked servers, select the REPLICATION entry.

9. In Login Name, type **Admin,** and then click OK.

10. Click OK to close the Publisher And Distributor Properties dialog box.

Exercise: Creating a Publication and a Heterogeneous Push Subscription

In this exercise, you will create a publication and a heterogeneous push subscription.

▶ **To create a publication and a heterogeneous push subscription**

1. In the console tree, click your server.

2. On the Tools menu, point to Replication and click Create And Manage Publications.

3. Click StudyNwind and then click Create Publication.

4. Use the Create Publication Wizard and the information in the following table to create your publication. Accept defaults for options not specified.

Option	Value
No, I will define the articles and properties	Selected
Publication Type	Snapshot publication
No, do not allow immediate-updating subscriptions	Selected
One or more Subscribers will not be a server running SQL Server	Selected
Specify articles	Check dbo.Customers
If prompted to add an indexed uniqueidentifier column	Click OK
Publication name	StudyNwind_Access_Publication
No, create a publication without data filters and with the following properties	Selected

5. When the wizard has created the new publication, in the Create and Manage Publications dialog box, select the StudyNwind_Access_Publication listed below the StudyNwind database, and click Push New Subscription.

6. Use the information in the next table to create the push subscription.

Option	Value
Choose Subscribers	Select REPLICATION (Microsoft Jet 4.0)
When should the Distribution Agent update the subscription?	Using the following schedule: Occurs every 1 day(s), every 1 hour(s) between 12:00:00 A.M. and 11:59:00 P.M.
Yes, initialize the schema and data at the Subscriber	Selected
Start the Snapshot Agent to begin the initialization process immediately	Checked

7. Close the dialog boxes to return to SQL Server Enterprise Manager.

Exercise: Running the Distribution Agent for the New Subscription

In this exercise, you will manually run the Distribution Agent for the new hetero-geneous subscription and verify that the Jet database was created.

▶ **To run the Distribution Agent for the new subscription**

1. In the console tree, expand Replication Monitor, and then expand Agents and click Distribution Agents.

2. In the details pane, right-click the entry that has a value of REPLICATION:DSN in the Subscription column, and then click Start.

3. Wait for the Status and Last Action columns to indicate that the agent has successfully applied the snapshot to the Subscriber.

4. In Windows Explorer, navigate to the C:\Sqladmin\Exercise\Ch17 folder. Note that a new Jet database file called Repl.mdb is now present in the folder. The file is a new Jet 4 database, which you cannot open in Microsoft Access 97. If you push a subscription to an existing Jet database, created in Microsoft Access 97, you will be able to use the file in Microsoft Access 97, as you normally would.

5. Switch to SQL Server Query Analyzer and execute the following query to confirm that the data from the Customers table has been replicated to the Jet 4 database:

```
SELECT * FROM [REPLICATION]...Customers
```

Making a Publication Available on the Internet

You can use the TCP/IP network library to connect servers on the Internet. For pull and anonymous subscriptions, you can use File Transfer Protocol (FTP) to transfer snapshots from the Distributor to the Subscriber.

Consider the following requirements when you want to make publications avail-able on the Internet:

- Push subscriptions cannot use FTP to transfer snapshots.

- Use FTP only when applying a snapshot to a Subscriber; all other replication data exchanges must occur using a network library connection.

- If you are using a firewall, ensure that the Publisher and the Distributor are both on the same side of the firewall.

- Make sure that the Publisher and the Distributor have a direct network con-nection with each other and are not connected by the Internet alone.

- Enable the TCP/IP protocol on each Subscriber where the Distribution Agent and Merge Agent execute and on the computers to which these agents connect.

- Ensure that the Distributor is installed on the same server as Microsoft Internet Information Server (IIS).

- Set the FTP home directory on IIS to the distribution working folder. The default is *computer_name*\C$\Mssql7\Repldata.

  Ensure that this working folder is available to Subscribers.

- Configure the FTP address and login details using the Pull Subscription Properties dialog box.

Lesson Summary

SQL Server supports replication with non–SQL Server databases. A SQL Server Publisher can publish data to any ODBC or OLE DB Subscriber. Third-party vendors can create agents that allow their databases to be Publishers and to publish data into the SQL Server replication environment. You can control replication using the replication ActiveX control from within applications you write. You can allow Subscribers to receive snapshots on the Internet by enabling a publication to use FTP.

Review

The following questions are intended to reinforce key information presented in the chapter. If you are unable to answer a question, review the appropriate lesson and then try the question again. Answers to the questions can be found in Appendix A, "Questions and Answers."

1. How can you determine the number of transactions that are marked for replication in the transaction log, waiting to be read by the Distribution Agent?

2. What would you check first if all of your publications on a server stopped working?

3. You are finished setting up replication. You make changes to data in a publication, but the changes are not replicating to the Subscriber. How would you determine which replication agent is failing?

APPENDIX A

Questions and Answers

Page 1

Chapter 1
Overview of SQL Server

Review Questions

Page 29

1. You have an existing application that uses SQL Server and Windows 95 and Windows NT Workstation client computers. Another department that uses a Novell network wants access to the database. Is this possible?

   Yes. You would install the appropriate Net-Library for Novell IPX/SPX on SQL Server and on the client computers on the Novell network.

2. You want to develop a SQL Server application using ADO or OLE DB. What are some of the factors to consider?

   ADO is easier to implement and is usually more appropriate for business application development. OLE DB provides more control over application behavior and better performance but is more difficult to implement.

Page 30

Chapter 2
Installation

Review Questions

Page 53

1. You are installing several SQL Servers. You want your SQL Server services to connect to network resources with a trusted connection. In what security context should the SQL Server services run? Why?

   The SQL Server services must run in the context of a Windows NT domain user account in order to use a trusted connection. The local system account cannot establish a trusted connection with any resources on a remote computer.

2. You are installing SQL Server in an environment that has both Windows and Novell clients. You want to use Windows NT authentication. Which network libraries must you install?

   NWLink IPX/SPX and Multiprotocol.

3. You installed SQL Server with the default settings. Later, you decide to add a database that requires characters that are not part of the default character set. What must you do to support the new character set?

Your first option is to install a separate SQL Server to support this new character set. The character set in the installed SQL Server is used for all databases on the existing server. You cannot have different character sets for different databases.

Another option is to use Unicode data types for this new database on the existing server to support the characters that are not part of the default character set.

Page 55

Chapter 3
Upgrading to SQL Server 7

Review Questions

Page 73

1. You have a SQL Server 6.5 database running on a Windows NT Server. Both SQL Server and Windows NT Server have Service Pack 2 installed. The size of the tempdb database on SQL Server 6.5 is 8 MB. After installing SQL Server 7 on the same computer, there is 100 MB of free disk space. The size of the SQL Server 6.5 database you want to upgrade is 90 MB. What must you do in order to upgrade this database?

First, install SQL Server 6.5 Service Pack 3 or later. Set the size of the SQL Server 6.5 tempdb database to at least 10 MB. Because there is limited disk space available, you should use a tape upgrade to transfer the data from SQL Server 6.5 to SQL Server 7 and delete the SQL Server 6.5 devices when you use the SQL Server Upgrade Wizard. Because the original devices will be deleted during the upgrade, you should back up all of the SQL Server 6.5 databases before starting the upgrade process.

2. During the upgrade process, the SQL Server Upgrade Wizard cannot upgrade a stored procedure in the SQL Server 6.5 user databases. What could cause this failure?

It is possible that the stored procedure directly modifies a system table or references a system table or a column in a system table that does not exist in SQL Server 7. It is also possible that the object owner is not listed as a user of the database you want to update. SQL Server cannot re-create the stored procedure if the login for the object owner is missing.

3. You just upgraded a credit card database to SQL Server 7, and you have a client application that contains the following query:

```
SELECT t.title AS cross
FROM titles t
```

You want to use the BACKUP and RESTORE commands as part of maintenance jobs that you create. To allow these commands, you set the database compatibility level to 70. What impact does this setting have on your application?

You can issue BACKUP and RESTORE statements because SQL Server 7 supports these commands. However, the query in your application no longer executes correctly, because it uses the word *cross* as a column alias. The word *cross* is a reserved word for SQL Server 7. You must rewrite the query before setting the compatibility level to 70.

Page 75
Chapter 4
System Configuration and Architecture

Page 77
▶ **To verify and edit your SQL Server registration in SQL Server Enterprise Manager**

3. Right-click your server, and then click Edit SQL Server Registration Properties.

What type of authentication is used by default to connect to your SQL Server?

Windows NT authentication.

5. In the console tree, expand your server to verify that you can connect to your SQL Server.

How can you tell whether your SQL Server is started and whether you are connected to your SQL Server?

The green arrowhead on the SQL Server icon indicates that your SQL Server is started. The vertical red zigzag line indicates that you are connected to your SQL Server.

Page 78
▶ **To create shared registration information**

3. Expand SQL Server Group.

Are any servers registered? Why or why not?

No servers are registered. When the Store User Independent check box is cleared, the shared registration information is displayed. Until you create shared registration information, there is no shared information.

Page 82
▶ **To view the SQL Server error log**

3. Scroll through the error log.

What caused all of the entries in this file?

Starting SQL Server caused all of the entries. There are entries for the server starting and for each of the databases being opened and started.

Page 82   ▶   **To view the Windows NT system and application event logs**

1. On the taskbar, click the Start button, point to Programs, point to Administrative Tools, and then click Event Viewer.

   Does the system log contain any entries that were generated by the installation or startup of SQL Server?

   If the installation of SQL Server was successful, the Windows NT system log contains no entries for SQL Server.

2. On the Log menu, click Application.

   Does the Windows NT application event log contain any entries that were generated by the installation or startup of SQL Server?

   The Windows NT application event log contains numerous entries associated with the startup of SQL Server and SQL Server Agent. These entries relate to the entries in the SQL Server and SQL Server Agent error logs.

Review Questions

Page 101

1. You want to view metadata about objects in a SQL Server database. What methods would you use?

   You could query the information schema views, execute system stored procedures, or use system functions. You also could query the system tables directly, but this is not advised because they may change in later product versions.

2. What tool can be used to register remote SQL Servers in the Enterprise Manager?

   The Register SQL Server Wizard.

3. Is it possible to have two tables named "Authors" in a database?

   Yes; however, a table name is actually a combination of the owner name, the database name, and the table name. As long as the two tables are owned by two different users the names are considered unique. For example, pubs.dbo.Authors and pubs.carl.Authors are two different tables. The object name of each table is Authors, but the full name of each table is different. While this scenario is possible, it is not a recommended practice because you cannot reference either table by the table name Authors. Instead, you would always have to use at least the object name and the owner name, so the tables would have to be referenced as dbo.Authors and carl.Authors in all queries that use them.

4. Which system stored procedure can be used to retrieve information about a particular database?

   Sp_helpdb *<database_name>*.

5. Which system table has a row for each database object?

   The sysobjects table.

Page 103

Chapter 5
Database Files

Review Questions

Page 136

1. You are creating a database that you expect will have a high level of INSERT, UPDATE, and DELETE activity. Should you accept the default transaction log size of 25 percent of the total database size? What factors must you consider if the database is going to be used primarily for queries?

   For a heavily updated database, you should either increase the size of the transaction log manually or specify enough free disk space for the log to grow automatically. Databases that are used primarily for queries typically do not require a very substantial transaction log. You might want to reduce the log size to 10 percent of the total database size.

2. You are creating a database on multiple disks that will be queried extensively by users. What are some steps that you can take to improve performance and avoid disk contention?

   You could use disk striping (RAID), to increase performance.

   A second strategy would be to use filegroups to improve performance. In particular, place the transaction log files on a separate disk from the data files to avoid disk contention as SQL Server queries the database and records actions in the log. Also, filegroups could be used to separate a portion of the data files that require frequent backups because they are frequently modified.

3. During a routine monitoring of the data files and transaction log, you notice that the transaction log is extremely close to being full. What would happen if the log filled? What steps can you take to avoid running out of transaction log space?

   If the transaction log fills, you are unable to modify the data in the database until the log is archived or expanded. To prevent a full transaction log, monitor the log space regularly, expand the log whenever necessary, set the log to grow automatically, and set an alarm to notify you when the available log space falls below a specified level. Scheduling or performing frequent transaction log dumps is the best way to reclaim available space in the transaction log.

Page 137

Chapter 6
Transferring Data

Page 143

▶ **To import data using the bcp utility**

3. From a command prompt, execute the C:\Sqladmin\Exercise\Ch06\Runbcp.cmd file. You are prompted for a password. Enter the password for the sa login and press Enter, or just press Enter if your sa password is blank.

   How many rows were copied?

   1341.

4. In Notepad, review the output from the C:\Sqladmin\Exercise\Ch06\Newprods.err error file.

Did any errors occur?

Yes. Two errors were intentionally introduced into the Newprods.txt file on rows 26 and 27.

Review Questions

Page 171

1. You want to create a DTS package using a basic query. What tool is most appropriate?

   Use the DTS Import and DTS Export Wizards for creating simple transformations.

2. You want to be certain that a DTS package is secure so that no one can copy it or view sensitive information. What can you do to secure this DTS package?

   You can assign an owner password to the package when it is created so that no one can view or edit it. Someone can still execute the package. If you want to require a password when the package is executed, add an operator password.

3. You plan to upgrade the hardware that currently runs SQL Server 7. The new hardware will be faster. Which tool would you select to transfer the database and all of its objects to the new hardware?

   You could select the DTS Import Wizard, BACKUP and RESTORE, or copy and attach the database files. Each of these methods allows you to transfer all data and objects to the new hardware. The DTS Import Wizard allows you to perform the transfer in a single operation.

4. You are required to recommend a solution for an organization that has an existing Oracle database and a new SQL Server database. The applications using the SQL Server database need access to a table on the Oracle server. Which of the following would provide the best solution and why?

   A. Set up SQL Server replication to replicate the table from Oracle to SQL Server.

   B. Create a DTS package and schedule it to transfer the contents of the table from Oracle to SQL Server once every hour.

   C. Add the Oracle database as a linked server on SQL Server.

   D. Install the Oracle and SQL Server client software on every user's computer and access the Oracle table directly from the application.

   Option C, adding a linked server, would work well in this scenario. Users do not need to have the Oracle client software installed on their computers, but applications can use Transact-SQL to access the table in the Oracle database directly via the linked server.

Page 173 **Chapter 7**
Web Publishing and Full-Text Indexing

Page 180 ▶ **To view the generated Transact-SQL script**

2. Open the C:\Temp\Instock.sql file and review the contents.

Note that the Web Assistant Wizard generates a single call to the sp_makeweb-task system stored procedure, supplying parameter values according to your choices on the wizard screens.

What is the meaning of the @whentype = 1 parameter?

This parameter specifies that the Web page is generated upon completion of the wizard and that no Web Assistant job is saved for later execution. Actually, a job is created and then immediately deleted. This corresponds to the "Only one time when I complete this wizard" choice in the wizard.

Page 185 ▶ **To view the generated Transact-SQL script**

2. Open the C:\Temp\Invtrig.sql file and review its contents.

What is the meaning of the parameters @whentype = 10 and @datachg = N'TABLE = Products COLUMN = UnitsInStock'?

These parameters specify that the Web Assistant job and the necessary triggers should be created to update the Web page when data in the Products.UnitsInStock column changes.

Page 186 ▶ **To view the trigger**

3. Examine all triggers on the Products table by selecting the various triggers in the Name drop-down list.

What triggers exist?

There are three triggers named Web_Trigger_x, one each for INSERT, UPDATE, and DELETE. These triggers use the sp_runwebtask system stored procedure to execute the Web Assistant job, named Web_Trigger, when the data in the Products.UnitsInStock column changes.

Review Questions

Page 199 1. When the season changes, the supplier sets different prices on certain items. How can you use Web Assistant Wizard to republish the price list in order to reflect these changes?

Create a Web task to regenerate a Web page by using a trigger that determines when the underlying data tables have changed.

2. Does the Web Publishing Wizard create dynamic Web pages for which users can specify variable parameter values and see real-time data?

No. For creating dynamic Web applications, you must create Web pages that execute code on the Web server to query the database. You can do this with Active Server Pages or the Internet Database Connector running on Microsoft Internet Information Server.

3. You have created a Web Assistant job and scheduled it to update your HTML Web pages weekly. If you receive a new price list from the marketing department and update the database with the new information, do you have to wait until the Web Assistant job executes on schedule, or can you execute the job immediately to update the Web pages?

You can update the Web pages immediately using SQL Server Enterprise Manager or the sp_runwebtask system stored procedure.

4. The marketing department at your firm has been entering a large amount of free-text information about customers into the customer database for many months. The marketing manager says that her staff is struggling to create reports based on customer profiles. Can you suggest a way to make it possible to create more effective queries of this information?

Create full-text indexes on the free-text data in the customer database. This will allow full-text queries on words, phrases, and derived words in all of the customer data.

5. When trying to define full-text indexing on a table using SQL Server Enterprise Manager, you find that all of the full-text indexing menus are grayed (not available). What would cause this?

The Microsoft Search service is not started. Start the service and the menus will become available.

Page 201

Chapter 8
Backup and Restore Overview and Strategy

Review Questions

Page 219

1. Your database consists of 5 gigabytes (GB) of data and is stored in one database file. This database is used as an order-taking system for a mail-order catalog company. Operators take orders 24 hours a day. The company typically receives about 2000 orders each day. Describe an appropriate backup plan for this database.

SQL Server backups can occur while the database is online. However, avoid scheduling backups during times of high database activity.

Because the database exists in a single database file, you cannot back up individual parts of the database. You must back up the entire database as a single unit.

Consider a backup plan that includes database and transaction log backups. You may want to add differential backups, which shorten the backup and restore time.

2. Your database contains image data that is gathered from a weather satellite and is continually being updated. The database is 700 GB. Each table exists in a separate filegroup in the database. If you were to perform a database backup, the process would take about 20 hours. How can you minimize the amount of time that is spent performing backups each day and still ensure good data recoverability in case of a system failure?

Use a backup plan that starts with one database backup. A database backup will be done infrequently. Perform a backup of one of the database files each day on a rotating basis. Perform differential backups in addition to transaction log backups to minimize recovery time.

Page 221

Chapter 9
Backing Up Databases

Review Questions

Page 246

1. You have a database for which you generally perform only database backups. The transaction log exists on a separate physical disk from the secondary data files. It is allowed to accumulate changes but is periodically cleared. The disk that contains the secondary data files is damaged. After you replace the disk, what can you do to minimize data loss?

Try to back up the undamaged transaction log by using the NO_TRUNCATE option. This captures some of the activity since the last database backup. After you restore the database, apply the transaction log backup and recover the database.

2. What are the advantages and disadvantages of using differential backups as part of your backup strategy?

Differential backups save time in the restore process. You can recover a database by restoring the database backup and the latest differential backup only. It is not necessary to apply all of the transaction logs or previous differential backups in order to bring the database to a consistent state.

A disadvantage of differential backups is that because differential backups do not capture intermediate changes to the database, you cannot use them to recover data from a specific point in time. You must use transaction log backups to perform point-in-time recovery.

Page 247   ## Chapter 10
                   ## Restoring Databases

Page 267   ▶   **To simulate damage to the database**

9. Open Windows NT Event Viewer and examine the contents of the Application
   Log.

   You should find an information message stating that there was a device activation error for the C:\Mssql7\Data\Nwcopy_data2.ndf file.

   What should you do to restore and recover the nwcopy database?

   **If possible, back up the transaction log of the damaged database, using
   the NO_TRUNCATE option to capture the latest activity in the log.
   Determine which backups are available and usable. Restore the complete
   database backup. Restore the latest differential backup. (This will include
   the changes in the first transaction log backup.) And restore the last set
   of transaction log backups, and recover the database.**

Page 268   ▶   **To examine available backups**

4. Click View Contents to examine the contents of the nwc3 device. Notice the
   type, description, and date and time of the backup set on the device.

   What does the nwc3 device contain?

   **The nwc3 device contains a full database backup. The date and time reflect
   the fact that it was created before the backups on the nwchange device.**

6. Repeat steps 3, 4, and 5 to examine the contents of the nwchange device. Notice the type, description, and date and time of each backup set on the device.

   What does the nwchange device contain?

   **The nwchange device contains two transaction log backups, as well as a
   differential backup. The time stamps show that a transaction log backup
   was created first, followed by a differential backup and then another
   transaction log backup.**

Page 269   ▶   **To review the suggested restore strategy**

2. The Restore Database dialog box appears. Verify that the nwcopy database is
   selected in the Restore As Database list.

   Notice that four backup sets are listed. SQL Server automatically selects the
   most recent complete database backup and the corresponding differential and/
   or transaction log backup sets that should be restored to return the database to
   a consistent state. Three out of four backups are selected (full database, differential, and one transaction log).

   Do you agree that the selected backups should be restored?

   Yes.

Why is the first transaction log backup not selected?

The changes recorded in this transaction log backup are reflected in the differential backup and therefore do not need to be restored from the transaction log backup.

Page 270 ▶ **To examine the contents of the database**

1. Open a query window, open C:\Sqladmin\Exercise\Ch10\Listcust.sql, review its contents, and then execute it.

   This script determines whether the three new customers that were previously added to the Customers table were recovered.

   Have all three new customers been recovered?

   No, only the rows for Health Food Store and Volcano Coffee Company are in the database. Both of these rows were recorded in the differential backup. The row for The Wine Cellar was recorded in the transaction log backup, taken after the database failure. This backup set was not restored.

Review Questions

Page 279

1. What is the automatic recovery process, and when is it initiated?

   Automatic recovery occurs whenever SQL Server is restarted. It rolls transactions backward or forward to maintain database integrity after a system failure.

2. What steps should you take before you restore a database?

   Set the database to dbo use only. If the transaction log files and the primary data file are available, back up the transaction log so that it can be applied at the completion of the restore operation.

3. You have a complete database backup and several transaction log backups. Your database is spread among four files. The disk on which the third file resides fails. What should you do to restore and recover the database?

   Set the database to dbo use only. If possible, back up the transaction log so that it can be applied at the completion of the restore operation. Replace or fix the disk. Restore the third backup file with the complete backup as the source. Restore all of the transaction log backups, specifying the NORECOVERY option for all but the last one. Restore the last transaction log backup with the RECOVERY option specified.

4. You have a complete database backup and several transaction log backups. A malicious update to the database occurs at 9:21 A.M. The time is now 9:30 A.M. What should you do to restore and recover the database to a consistent state?

   Set the database to dbo use only. Back up the transaction log. Restore the database, specifying the REPLACE and NORECOVERY options. Apply all but the last transaction log with the NORECOVERY option. Apply the last transaction log, specifying RECOVERY, STOPAT = 'month, xx, year, time', where time is 9:20 A.M.

5. In the scenario presented in question 4, will any changes be lost due to the restore process?

If any activity occurred between 9:20 and 9:21 A.M., these changes are lost.

6. You have set up a standby SQL Server that functions as a read-only server. What must you do to replace the production server with this standby SQL Server?

If possible, back up the transaction log of the production server without truncating it. Take the production server off line, and change the name of the standby SQL Server to that of the production server. Restore all available transaction logs to the standby SQL Server, and recover the database.

Page 281

Chapter 11
Logins, User Accounts, and User Roles

Page 304   ▶   **To test the logins, users, and roles that you have created and assigned**

1. Start SQL Server Query Analyzer and, by using SQL Server authentication, connect as Carl with the password **password**.

To what database are you connected, and why?

You are connected to StudyNwind because it was specified as the default database when you created the account.

2. Execute a query to retrieve data from the Products table. For example,

```
SELECT productname FROM Products
```

Did you receive any results? Why or why not?

You did receive results. Carl is a member of the db_datareader database role. All members of this role are allowed to query data in all tables in the database.

3. Execute a query to change data in the Products table. For example:

```
UPDATE Products
    SET productname = 'Tofu, unsalted'
    WHERE productname = 'Tofu'
```

Was the update successful? Why or why not?

The update was not successful. Carl is not a member of a role that has permission to update data in StudyNwind.

4. Select Connect from the File menu and open a new connection logged on as Cathy. What happens if you perform steps 2 and 3 logged on as Cathy?

Because Cathy is a member of the db_datareader and db_datawriter database roles, she is able to query and update the data. All members of these roles are allowed to query and modify data in the StudyNwind database.

6. Start SQL Server Query Analyzer and connect with Windows NT authentication.

Notice that you cannot provide a login name or password when you connect to SQL Server with Windows NT authentication and that your user name is displayed in the title bar of the query window.

How did Carl connect to the database when his Windows NT login was not authorized to use SQL Server?

Carl is a member of the STUDYSQL\Customer_mgmt group in Windows NT, which has been authorized to use SQL Server.

8. Start SQL Server Query Analyzer and connect with Windows NT authentication.

What happens and why?

Max is denied access to SQL Server. He is a valid Windows NT user, but he has not been authorized to use SQL Server and does not belong to a Windows NT group that has been authorized to access SQL Server.

Review Questions

Page 306

1. What can users do after they have been authenticated if their logins do not have permissions in any database?

They can connect to the server and query some system tables but cannot gain access to any user databases.

2. What type of authentication mode would you implement in an environment that contains users who connect from both UNIX and Windows NT? Why?

Mixed Mode because the UNIX connections are not trusted.

Page 307

Chapter 12
Permissions and Security Planning

Page 319

▶ **To test the statement permissions**

2. Execute the following SQL statements to create a view:

```
USE StudyNwind
GO
CREATE VIEW test_view as
SELECT firstname, lastname
FROM Employees
```

Were you able to create the view?

Yes, because permissions have been granted to Cathy to create views.

3. Execute a CREATE TABLE statement:

```
USE StudyNwind
CREATE TABLE testtable
(column1 INT NOT NULL,
column2 CHAR(10) NOT NULL)
```

Did the statement execute successfully? Why or why not?

The CREATE TABLE statement failed because Cathy does not have statement permissions that allow her to execute it.

Page 320 ▶ **To test the object permissions**

3. Execute each of the following Transact-SQL statements to test permissions for Carl:

```
USE StudyNwind
SELECT * FROM Customers
SELECT * FROM Categories
SELECT * FROM Products
SELECT * FROM Orders
```

Which tables can Carl query? Which tables is he not able to query? Why?

He can query all of the tables because he is a member of the db_datareader fixed database role.

5. Execute each of the following Transact-SQL statements to test permissions for Umberto:

```
USE StudyNwind
SELECT * FROM Customers
SELECT * FROM Categories
SELECT * FROM Products
SELECT * FROM Orders
```

Which tables can Umberto query? Which tables is he not able to query? Why?

He can query only the Categories and Products tables. He can query these tables because permissions have been granted to the public role. He cannot query any other tables, because permissions have not been given to the public role, his own account, or any roles or groups to which he belongs (they are in the revoked state).

Page 325 ▶ **To test the object permissions**

3. Execute each of the following Transact-SQL statements to test permissions for Carl:

```
USE StudyNwind
SELECT * FROM Customers
SELECT * FROM Categories
```

```
SELECT * FROM Products
SELECT * FROM Orders
```

Which tables can Carl query? Which tables is he not able to query? Why?

He can no longer query the Customers table because he is a member of the Cust_Mgmt role, which has been denied permissions, overriding the db_datareader permissions. He can no longer query the Categories table because the public role has been denied permissions, overriding the db_datareader permissions. He can still query the Products and Orders tables because he is a member of the db_datareader fixed database role.

5. Execute each of the following Transact-SQL statements to test permissions for Umberto:

```
USE StudyNwind
SELECT * FROM Customers
SELECT * FROM Categories
SELECT * FROM Products
SELECT * FROM Orders
```

Which tables can Umberto query? Which tables is he not able to query? Why?

He can no longer query the Categories table because permissions have been denied to the public role. He cannot query the Customers or Orders tables because permissions have not been given to the public role, his own account, or any roles or groups to which he belongs (they are in the re-voked state). He can query the Products table because permissions have been granted to the public role.

Page 329 ▶ **To test the object permissions**

3. Execute each of the following Transact-SQL statements to test permissions for Carl:

```
USE StudyNwind
SELECT * FROM Customers
SELECT * FROM Categories
SELECT * FROM Products
SELECT * FROM Orders
```

Which tables can Carl query? Which tables is he not able to query? Why?

He can again query the Customers table because the deny to the Cust_Mgmt role has been revoked, allowing him to have the db_datareader permissions. He can again query the Categories table because the deny to the public role has been revoked, allowing him to have the db_datareader permissions. He can still query the Products and Orders tables because he is a member of the db_datareader fixed database role.

5. Execute each of the following Transact-SQL statements to test permissions for Umberto:

```
USE StudyNwind
SELECT * FROM Customers
SELECT * FROM Categories
SELECT * FROM Products
SELECT * FROM Orders
```

Which tables can Umberto query? Which tables is he not able to query? Why?

He can no longer query the Products table because permissions have been revoked from the public role and permissions have not been given to the public role, his own account, or any roles or groups to which he belongs (they are in the revoked state). He still cannot query the Categories table. Although permissions are no longer denied to the public role, permissions have not been given to the public role, his own account, or any roles or groups to which he belongs (they are in the revoked state). He still cannot query the Customers or Orders tables because permissions have not been given to the public role, his own account, or any roles or groups to which he belongs (they are in the revoked state).

Page 338   ▶   **To test the permissions on the view and stored procedure**

3. Execute the following statement to query the Employee_View view:

```
SELECT * FROM Employee_View
```

Were you able to query the view? Why or why not?

Yes, you can query the view, even though Umberto does not have permissions on the underlying table. This is because the table and the view have the same owner.

4. Execute the Employee_Proc stored procedure:

```
EXEC Employee_Proc
```

Were you able to execute the stored procedure? Why or why not?

Yes, you can execute the stored procedure, even though Umberto does not have permissions on the underlying table. This is because the table and the stored procedure have the same owner.

5. Execute the following statement to query the Employees table:

```
SELECT * FROM Employees
```

Were you able to query the table? Why or why not?

No. Umberto has permissions that allow him to use only the Employee_ View view and the Employee_Proc stored procedure because those permissions have been granted to the public role. SELECT privileges have not been granted to the public role for Employees.

Page 343 ▶ **To activate an application role**

3. Execute SELECT statements to query the Employees and Customers tables.

```
SELECT * FROM Employees
SELECT * FROM Customers
```

What permissions does Carl have after the Order_Entry application role is activated?

Carl has only the permissions that are associated with the Order_Entry role. An application role is exclusive; any other permissions that Carl has directly or in other roles of which he is a member will be ignored (except fixed server roles). For example, Carl can query the Employees table through his membership in the db_datareader role, but these permissions are ignored after an application role is activated.

How long will the Order_Entry role be activated for Carl?

The Order_Entry application role remains active until the session (connection) is closed or until the user changes to another database.

Review Questions

Page 344

1. When should you assign permissions to a login account directly?

When that login account maps to a Windows NT group that requires common permissions.

2. When should you avoid using the sa login?

At all times. Use the sa login only for installing SQL Server and for recovery in the event that the members of the sysadmin role are dropped inadvertently.

3. If permissions to update a table are granted to a user, but the permissions were denied to a role in which the user has membership, does the security account retain permissions to update the table?

No. Denial of permissions to the role supersedes granting of permissions to the security account.

Page 345   **Chapter 13**
                        Automating Administrative Tasks

Page 357   ▶   **To execute the job manually**

5. In the details pane, right-click the StudyNwind Log Backup job, and then click View Job History to verify that the job completed successfully.

What information is displayed in the job history when Show Step Details is selected? What information is displayed when this option is cleared?

Show step details provides information (error messages and notifications) on each job step and the outcome. When the option is not checked, only the outcome is displayed.

Page 365   ▶   **To simulate a failure and verify that a job step failed**

6. In the details pane, right-click the StudyNwind Monthly Data Transfer job, and then click View Job History to verify that the job did not complete successfully. The job will appear in the history only after the retry, but the initial failure will be seen immediately if the Show Step Details option is checked.

What do you notice in the history?

After the first step failed, it executed again according to the retry interval. The error message from step 1 is "Unable to open BCP host data-file."

7. Open the Windows NT application log to confirm that the job failure was logged.

What information is displayed in the log?

SQL Server Agent is the event source. The event category is Job Engine. The description includes the name of the job, who invoked the job, the job failure message, and the step number of the last step to run.

9. Open Notepad, and then open C:\Temp\Prodcopy.txt.

What information is displayed in the output file?

The command-prompt output, including the SQLState error number, native error number, and error message "Unable to open BCP host data-file."

Page 366   ▶   **To start the SQL Mail session**

3. Right-click SQL Mail, and then click Start.

Did a SQL Mail session start successfully?

No. An error was received indicating that it failed to start.

4. Review the messages in the current log in SQL Server Logs in the Management folder in the console tree.

What was the source of the error messages associated with SQL Mail?

ODS reported a MAPI login failure.

7. Right-click SQL Mail, and then click Start.

Did the SQL Mail session start successfully?

Yes.

Page 367 ▶ **To send a query result using SQL Mail**

4. Switch to Inbox and open the new message.

What was the query result?

Product Total of 77.

Page 368 ▶ **To create an alert by using the Create Alert Wizard**

7. Right-click the alert, and then click Properties to review the alert definition.

What additional responses to the alert can be defined that were not included as part of the wizard?

Execute a job, notify additional operators, specify additional notification message to send to operator, and delay between responses.

Page 374 ▶ **To raise a user-defined error message**

2. Execute the reorder stored procedure by supplying any valid product ID value. For example,

```
USE StudyNwind
EXEC reorder @prodid = 2
```

Did you receive the defined notifications in response to the alert?

Yes. A net send command message and e-mail message were received.

Page 384 ▶ **To correct a problem and verify that a job works**

6. Open Notepad, and then open C:\Temp\Prodcopy.txt.

What information is displayed in the output file?

The command prompt output from the successful BCP, stating that five rows were copied.

Review Questions

Page 389

1. You want to back up the transaction log of your production database every hour during peak business hours (8:00 A.M. to 6:00 P.M.) and every three hours during nonpeak hours (6:00 P.M. to 8:00 A.M.). What is the most efficient method for automating these tasks?

Create one job to back up the transaction log, and specify two schedules.

2. The customer account manager has asked to be notified whenever a customer's credit limit is changed (increased or decreased). In addition, she wants the name of the customer representative who updated the customer's account, as well as any remarks about why the change was made. How would you accomplish this task?

The first step is to create a custom error message that specifies the customer account name, credit limit, remarks (assuming that the column already exists in the database), and the name of the customer representative who made the update.

The next step is to modify the stored procedure or trigger that changes customer credit limits to raise the custom error with the RAISERROR statement.

Then you would create the customer account manager as an operator.

Finally, you would create an alert on the custom error message that sends an e-mail message to the customer account manager when the alert is fired.

3. Your new database application is now in production, and you want to execute tests to review its performance. Specifically, you want to know whether the lock wait time is over 20 seconds. How can you be notified automatically when this event occurs?

Create a performance condition alert on the Lock Wait Time (ms) counter of the SQLServer:Locks object.

Page 391   ## Chapter 14
Monitoring and Maintaining SQL Server

Page 403   ▶ **To simulate server activity**

3. Switch to the SQL Server Performance Monitor window.

Watch the Chart window while the monitoring batch files execute. What trends do you notice?

Observations will vary. The cache-hit ratio may rise almost immediately and remain high. Index searches and full scans are taking place. The number of batch requests will rise and then stabilize. The Percent Log Used and Total Transactions counters will rise.

Page 403   ▶ **To add counters to the chart**

3. Watch the Chart window while the monitoring batch files continue to execute. (Press Ctrl-H to highlight the currently selected counter.)

What trends do you notice?

Observations will vary. The Memory/Page Faults/sec counter remains high, while the Memory/Pages/sec counter remains low. Windows NT is paging, but much of the data is already in main memory (on a standby list) and does not need to be brought in from disk. The Process/Page Faults/sec/SQL Server counter is low, indicating that SQL Server is performing some paging. The Process/%Processor Time/SQL Server counter indicates that SQL Server is using only a portion of the total processor time.

Page 409   ▶   **To detect login attempts**

5. Expand the node labeled Duration = 0.

What information is recorded?

You should see the failed login attempts for Maria and sa.

7. Switch to the SQL Server Profiler window, and expand all nodes on the tree.

What information is recorded?

You should see all of the events associated with making a connection from SQL Server Query Analyzer. Notice that SQL Server Query Analyzer submits several queries as part of the startup process. It uses the information that it requests to establish the session and populate the user interface. For example, the query "select name from master..sysdatabases order by name" is used to populate the DB drop-down box in SQL Server Query Analyzer.

Page 410   ▶   **To detect long-running queries**

4. Expand Duration for each event, and examine the events with long run times.

What events are included?

You should see disconnect events, as well as the execution of several queries. The queries include system stored procedures (sp_help), as well as some complex queries that use tables from the nwcopy database.

6. Expand SQL:BatchCompleted to see the text of the query.

What is the query text?

Answers may vary; however, the following query will be among the worst performers:

```
SELECT e.lastname, p.productname, avg(d.quantity * d.unitprice)
FROM employees e JOIN orders o ON e.employeeID = o.employeeid
JOIN [order details] d ON o.orderid = d.orderid
JOIN products p ON d.productid = p.productid
GROUP BY e.lastname, p.productname
```

Page 413 ▶ **To execute a query and generate an execution plan and statistics**

    9. Click the Execution Plan tab to display the graphical execution plan for this query. Note that statistics about each step are given if you move your mouse pointer over the step icons. The Table Scan steps may show a message stating that statistics are missing for the table. This is correct because the tables in nwcopy do not have indexes or statistics created for them.

    Were table scans used to process this query? What can be done to improve performance?

    This query requires several table scans in order to join the Products, Order Details, Employees, and Orders tables. Creating appropriate indexes will likely improve the performance of this query.

    11. Execute the following queries:

```
EXEC sp_helpindex Employees
EXEC sp_helpindex Orders
EXEC sp_helpindex [Order Details]
EXEC sp_helpindex Products
```

    What indexes exist on the Employees, Orders, Order Details, and Products tables?

    None; the nwcopy database has no indexes.

Page 417 ▶ **To hold locks on the server**

    4. Switch to connection 1, execute the sp_lock system stored procedure, and then review the lock information.

    Using the spid recorded in step 3, identify what locks were granted to the transaction that was issued by connection 2.

    Locks that are held should include the following: a shared database lock (Type – DB, Mode – S), an intent page lock (Type - PAG, Mode - IX), and an exclusive row lock (Type - RID, Mode - X).

Page 418 ▶ **To detect lock blocking**

    2. Open and execute C:\Sqladmin\Exercise\Ch14\Lock.sql, using connection 3.

    Does the query complete?

    No, the query is waiting.

    3. Switch to connection 1 and execute the sp_lock system stored procedure.

    Is the spid for connection 3 waiting for any resources? (Look for WAIT in the Status column.)

    Yes, it is waiting for a lock to be granted on the row to be updated.

4. Switch to SQL Server Enterprise Manager, refresh Current Activity, and review the locking information. In particular, note the information under Locks/ Process ID.

Why can't connection 3 complete the query?

The row to be updated is exclusively locked by connection 2. Both the sp_lock procedure and the Current Activity window show that the spid for connection 3 is waiting for the row lock to be released.

Review Questions

Page 426

1. Users complain that the server slows down considerably every day at 2:00 P.M. How can you find out what is causing this delay?

First, determine whether the problem is due to a load on the system as a whole or on SQL Server alone. To do this, use SQL Server Performance Monitor to compare the resource use of Windows NT with that of SQL Server.

If the problem is due to SQL Server activity, create a trace by using SQL Server Profiler to record the activity that occurs around 2:00 P.M. every day. This trace should look at events that might increase the load on the server, such as user connections, Transact-SQL statements, stored procedures, or use of the tempdb database. Consider grouping this information by duration and by application or user.

With this information, you can determine which events are placing the greatest load on the system.

2. You want to find out the locks that are being held on a specific SQL Server table. What tools would you use?

On a table level, you can use SQL Server Profiler, the sp_lock and sp_who system stored procedures, and Current Activity in SQL Server Enterprise Manager.

3. You want to see a query plan and the statistics for a specific query in SQL Server Query Analyzer. What steps must you take?

First, generate the estimated execution plan for the query. This does not actually execute the query. Statistical information cannot be generated unless the query is executed. You then must execute the query with statistics turned on. You can show the execution plan when you execute the query to see the actual execution plan.

Page 427

Chapter 15
Introducing Replication

Review Questions

Page 456

1. Your company has been experiencing contention problems. This occurs when the sales and marketing departments run their daily reports while the order-processing department is processing orders. Your company has decided to implement some form of data replication. To choose the appropriate method for making copies of the company data, which features and characteristics should you consider?

   At a minimum, you should consider transactional consistency, latency, site autonomy, security, existing data sources, data update frequency, performance, administration, and whether to allow updating Subscribers.

2. Your company, a large, international manufacturer with many vendors around the world, has decided to distribute data by using replication. You are currently in the planning and design phase of your replication strategy. Your goal is to receive all of the sales information from the vendors at the company headquarters on a daily basis. Because most of your vendors are remote, you are concerned about the high long-distance costs. Which replication model or models would you implement? Why?

   The best way to address these requirements would be to combine two of the replication models. You could have a Central Subscriber in each region that would collect all of the daily sales information for the region. The regional Central Subscribers could then publish the data to company headquarters at night. By using a single Central Subscriber/Publisher in each region, you minimize the long-distance communication costs.

Page 457

Chapter 16
Planning and Setting Up Replication

Page 470

▶ **To create a subscription**

5. After the subscription has been created, in the console tree, expand your server, expand Management, expand SQL Server Agent, and then click Jobs.

   The job called SQLSERVER-StudyNwind-StudyNwind_Products_Pub-SQLSERVER-PullSubs- 0, with a category of REPL-Distribution, is the job that starts the Distribution Agent for your new subscription.

   Which server's system resources will this job consume? Would a push subscription change the resources being used?

   This job will consume the system resources of the Subscriber. If a push subscription were used, the system resources of the Distributor would be used. For the purposes of this exercise, the Subscriber and the Distributor are on the same computer, but normally they would be on different computers.

Page 486   ▶   **To create a push subscription to a publication**

6. In the details pane, *after* the Status column indicates that the Merge Agent has succeeded, right-click StudyNwind_Merge_Publication, and then click Agent History. In the history list, select the oldest entry (this is the entry for the subscription initialization and should have about 38 actions). If there are other entries, they represent the Merge Agent running every 2 minutes according to the schedule you created for the subscription. Click Session Details. Review the history of the Merge Agent.

Whose system resources does this Merge Agent consume? Would a pull subscription change the resources that are used?

This Merge Agent consumes the system resources of the Distributor. A pull subscription would use the system resources of the Subscriber. For the purposes of this exercise, the Subscriber and the Distributor are on the same computer, but normally they would be on different computers.

Page 487   ▶   **To update the source table on the Publisher**

4. Type and execute the following script:

```
USE StudyNwind
UPDATE Customers
SET ContactName = 'Maria Anders-Smith'
WHERE CustomerID = 'ALFKI'
SELECT * FROM Customers
```

How long will it take for this update to be replicated?

It will take up to two minutes for these updates to be replicated, based on the schedule that was set in the previous exercise.

Page 488   ▶   **To update simultaneously on a Publisher and a Subscriber**

7. Switch to SQL Server Query Analyzer and execute the following query in each of the query windows:

```
SELECT * FROM Customers
```

Which update was applied? Was it the update made on the Publisher server (in the StudyNwind database) or on the Subscriber server (in the nwrepl database)?

The update made on the Publisher server was applied. Updates made at the Publisher will always "win" over conflicting updates made at Subscribers. Which Subscriber will win when conflicting updates are made at different Subscribers depends on Subscriber priorities or custom resolvers.

Page 488   ▶   **To resolve the conflict**

6. Switch to SQL Server Query Analyzer and execute the following query in both of the query windows:

```
SELECT * FROM Customers
```

Was the revised data applied to both servers?

Yes.

Review Questions

Page 490   1. You are trying to configure replication between two servers. Both servers appear to be set up correctly, but replication does not work. What do you think is the problem? What should you do to fix it?

First make sure that the network between the two servers is running. Then check the account that SQL Server is using for replication (the default is SQL Server Agent). Make sure that this account has access to the other server. Finally, check that the schedule for the various agents is correct, and possibly start the initial synchronization manually.

2. When you set up the distribution server, what should you consider when estimating the appropriate size of the distribution database?

The number of Publishers, publications, and Subscribers; the amount of data that will be changing; the frequency of data changes; the type of replication that is used; the latency; and whether Subscribers are anonymous.

3. Your company has decided to use SQL Server replication. The publication server runs an intensive application and does not have the capacity to manage any replication overhead. You will have a large number of Subscribers. Some Subscribers may be offline periodically, and all Subscribers must have the ability to update data. Which model and method of replication would best address these requirements? Why?

The best model and method would be a single Publisher using a remote Distributor (on a separate computer) that allows read-only Subscribers and Subscribers with the Immediate Updating Subscribers option. For offline Subscribers, you should allow read-only Subscribers or merge replication. For online Subscribers, you would enable the Immediate Updating Subscribers option. Using this option will add some extra processing on the Publisher, however.

Page 491

Chapter 17
Managing Replication

Page 502   ▶   **To review the properties of the Miscellaneous Agents**

3. Right-click the agent, and then click Agent Properties.

What is the function of this agent, and how often does it run?

Agent	Function	Schedule
Agent history cleanup: distribution	Removes replication agent history from the distribution database	Every 10 minutes
Distribution cleanup: distribution	Removes replicated trans-actions from the distribution database	Every 10 minutes
Expired subscription cleanup	Detects and removes expired subscriptions from published databases	Daily at 1:00 A.M.
Reinitialize subscriptions having data validation failures	Reinitializes all subscriptions that have data validation failures	On demand, or in response to an alert
Replication agents checkup	Detects replication agents that are not actively logging history	Every 10 minutes

Review Questions

Page 510

1. How can you determine the number of transactions that are marked for repli-cation in the transaction log, waiting to be read by the Distribution Agent?

Use SQL Server Performance Monitor and view the Repl. Pending Xacts counter of the SQLServer:Databases object.

2. What would you check first if all of your publications on a server stopped working?

Check the SQLServerAgent service to make sure that it is running and configured properly. Also check the distribution database and the SQL Server Agent logs.

3. You are finished setting up replication. You make changes to data in a publi-cation, but the changes are not replicating to the Subscriber. How would you determine which replication agent is failing?

View the agent histories and check each agent to determine whether it was successful.

A P P E N D I X   B

Database Schemata

The schemata provided in this appendix represent the major databases that are referenced throughout this training kit.

The Northwind Database and the StudyNwind Database Schema

Figure B.1 is a schema diagram for the Northwind database and the StudyNwind database. (The StudyNwind database is a relative duplication of the Northwind database.) The diagram was generated in the SQL Server Enterprise Manager. The schema shows the tables in the Northwind and StudyNwind databases. The columns in each table and the relationships between the tables are shown. Use the schema diagram to understand the structure of the databases when you are working with them in the examples and exercises in this training kit or whenever you use these sample databases.

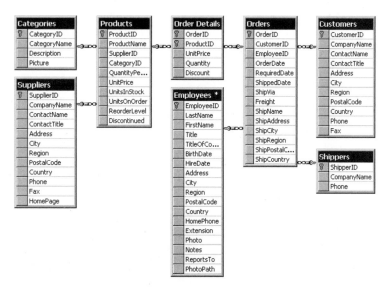

Figure B.1 Schema diagram for the Northwind and StudyNwind databases

The pubs Database Schema

Figure B.2 is a schema diagram for the pubs database. The diagram was generated in the SQL Server Enterprise Manager. The schema shows the tables in the pubs database. The columns in each table and the relationships between the tables are shown. Use the schema diagram to understand the structure of the pubs database when you are working with it in the examples and exercises in this training kit or whenever you use this sample database.

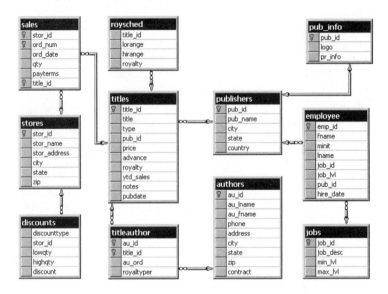

Figure B.2   Schema diagram for the pubs database

Glossary

A

active statement An SQL statement that has been executed but whose result set has not yet been canceled or fully processed. When using default result sets, Microsoft SQL Server supports only one active statement at a time on a connection. ODBC and OLE DB–based applications support multiple active statements on a SQL Server connection when using application programming interface (API) server cursors.

add-in A custom extension, written in any language that supports the component object model (COM), usually Microsoft Visual Basic, that interacts with the OLAP Manager and provides specific functionality. Add-ins are registered with the online analytical processing (OLAP) Add-In Manager. They are called by the OLAP Add-In Manager in response to user actions in the user interface.

ad hoc connector name A connector name used for infrequent queries against OLE DB data sources that are not defined as linked servers. The OpenRowset function in the FROM clause of a query, which allows all connection information for an external server and data source to be issued every time the data must be accessed, provides the properties and parameters necessary to access specific data.

ADO MD *See* Microsoft ActiveX Data Objects (Multidimensional) (ADO MD).

aggregate functions Functions that calculate summary values, such as averages and sums, from the values in a particular column and return a single value for each set of rows to which the function applies. The aggregate functions are AVG, COUNT, COUNT(*), MAX, MIN, SUM, STDEV, STDEVP, VAR, and VARP. Aggregate functions can be applied either to all rows in a table, to a subset of table rows specified by a WHERE clause, or to one or more groups of table rows specified by the GROUP BY clause.

aggregate query A query that summarizes information from multiple rows by including an aggregate function such as SUM or AVG. Aggregate queries that use the GROUP BY clause can also display subtotal information by creating groups of rows that have data in common.

aggregation A table or structure containing precalculated data for a cube. Aggregations support rapid and efficient querying of a multidimensional database. *See* precalculate.

aggregation prefix A string that is combined with a system-defined ID to create a unique name for a partition's aggregation table. A default string is generated based on the name of the partition and the name of its parent cube, but a user-defined string of up to 21 characters can be specified to replace the automatically generated string.

alert A user-defined response to a SQL Server event. Alerts can either execute a defined task or send an e-mail and/or pager message to a specified operator.

alias In structured query language, an alternate name for a table or column in expressions that is often used to shorten the name for subsequent reference in code, prevent possible ambiguous references, or provide a more descriptive name in query output. In SQL Server 6.5, a database username shared by several login IDs. In SQL Server 7, aliases have been replaced by roles.

All level The optional highest level of a dimension, named "(All)" by default. The All level contains a single member that is the summary of all members of the immediately subordinate level.

allocation page *See* Global Allocation Map (GAM).

allocation unit *See* Global Allocation Map (GAM).

American National Standards Institute (ANSI) An organization of American industry and business groups that develops trade and communication standards for the United States. Through membership in the International Organization for Standardization (ISO) and the International Electrotechnical Commission (IEC), ANSI coordinates American standards with corresponding international standards. ANSI published the ANSI SQL-92 standard in conjunction with the ISO/IEC SQL-92 standard.

ancestor A member in a superior level in a dimension hierarchy that is related through lineage to the current member within the dimension hierarchy. For example, in a Time dimension containing the levels Quarter, Month, Day, Qtr1 is an ancestor of January 1. *See* child; descendant; parent; sibling.

anonymous subscription A pull subscription that allows a server known to the Publisher only for the duration of the connection to receive a subscription to a publication. Anonymous subscriptions require less overhead than standard pull subscriptions because information about them is not stored at the Publisher or the Distributor.

ANSI *See* American National Standards Institute (ANSI).

ANSI SQL-92 *See* SQL-92.

ANSI to OEM conversion Conversion behavior when you connect to a server, controlled by an operating system option, AutoANSItoOEM. If ON (the default), conversion occurs in these cases:

- ANSI clients to original equipment manufacturer (OEM) servers (Microsoft Windows and Microsoft Windows NT)

- OEM clients to ANSI servers (Windows NT)

  The DB-Library Automatic ANSI to OEM option converts characters from OEM to ANSI when communicating with SQL Server, and from ANSI to OEM when communicating from SQL Server to the client. You can set Automatic ANSI to OEM by using the SQL Server Client Network Utility.

API *See* application programming interface (API).

API server cursor A server cursor built to support the cursor functions of an application programming interface (API), such as ODBC, OLE DB, ADO, and DB-Library. An application does not usually request a server cursor directly; it calls the cursor functions of the

API. The SQL Server interface for that API implements a server cursor if that is the best way to support the requested cursor functionality.

application log A Windows NT file that records events. It can be viewed only by using Windows NT Event Viewer. When SQL Server is configured to use the Windows NT application log, each SQL Server session writes new events to that log. (Unlike the SQL Server error log, a new application log is not created each time you start SQL Server.)

application programming interface (API) A set of routines available in an application, such as DB-Library, for use by software programmers when designing an application interface.

application role A SQL Server role created to support the security needs of an application. Such a role is activated by a password and the use of the sp_setapprole system stored procedure.

argument A switch supported by a function that allows you to specify a particular behavior. Sometimes called an option or a parameter.

article The basic unit of replication. An article contains data originating from a table or stored procedure marked for replication. One or more articles are contained within a publication.

attribute A qualifier of an entity or a relation describing its character quantity, quality, degree, or extent. In database design, tables represent entities and columns represent attributes of those entities. For example, the title column represents an attribute of the entity titles.

authentication The operation that identifies the user and verifies the permission to connect with SQL Server.

authorization The operation that verifies the permissions and access rights granted to a user.

automated server restart If SQL Agent detects that the SQL Server service has stopped unexpectedly, it will automatically attempt to restart SQL Server. This automated restart behavior can be adjusted by modifying properties in the SQL Server Agent Properties sheet.

automatic recovery Recovery that occurs every time SQL Server is restarted. Automatic recovery protects your database if there is a system failure. In each database, the automatic recovery mechanism checks the transaction log. If the log has committed transactions that have not been written to the database, it performs those transactions again. This action is known as rolling forward. If the log has uncommitted transactions that have not been written to the database, it removes those transactions from the log. This action is known as rolling back.

automatic synchronization Synchronization that is accomplished automatically by SQL Server when a server initially subscribes to a publication. A snapshot of the table data and schema are written to files for transfer to the Subscriber. The table schema and data are transferred by the distribution agent. No operator intervention is required.

auto-start options The Setup program can configure the SQL Server and SQL Agent services to run as an automatically started service. For each service, this choice is called the autostart option.

axis A set of tuples. Each tuple is a vector of members. A set of axes defines the coordinates of a multidimensional dataset. For more information about axes, see your OLE DB documentation. *See also* slice; tuple.

B

B-tree Balanced tree. This term describes SQL Server index structures.

back end A term applied to the database server level where processing, data storage, and data retrieval occur.

back up To create a copy of a database, transaction log, file, or filegroup in a database on another device or file. A backup is made to tape, named pipe, or hard disk. Backups are made using either SQL Server Enterprise Manager or the BACKUP statement.

backup device A tape, disk file, or named pipe used in a backup or restore operation.

backup domain controller (BDC) In a Windows NT domain, a server that receives a copy of the domain's security database from the primary domain controller (PDC) and shares the user login authentication load.

backup file A file that stores a full or partial database, transaction log, or file and/or filegroup backup.

backup media The disk, tape, or named pipe used to store the backup set.

backup set The output of a single backup operation.

base data type Any system-supplied data type—for example, char, varchar, binary, and varbinary—from which user-defined data types are made.

base object *See* underlying object.

base table A table from which a view is derived. Also called an underlying table. A view can have one or more base tables or base views.

batch A set of SQL statements submitted together and executed as a group. A script is often a series of batches submitted one after the other. A batch, as a whole, is compiled only one time and is terminated by an end-of-batch signal (such as the GO command in SQL Server utilities).

bcp *See* bulk copy program (bcp).

bcp files Files that have been exported from SQL Server through bcp. Though not required, native bcp files usually have a .BCP extension, and character bcp files customarily have a .TXT extension. During replication synchronization, the .SCH and .BCP files are a synchronization set that represents a snapshot in time of an article.

bcp utility *See* bulk copy program (bcp)

binary data type A data type storing hexadecimal numbers. The binary data type can contain 0 bytes, but when specified, n must be a value from 1 through 8000. Storage size is n regardless of the actual length of the entry.

binding In SQL application programming interfaces (APIs), associating a result set column with a program variable so that data is moved automatically into or out of a program variable when a row is fetched or updated. In Transact-SQL, associating rules or defaults with table columns by using sp_bindrule or sp_bindefault.

bit data type A data type that holds a value of either 1 or 0. Integer values other than 1 or 0 are accepted but interpreted as 1. The storage size is 1 byte. Multiple bit data types in a table can be collected into bytes. Use bit for true/false or yes/no data.

BLOB (binary large object) A type of data column containing binary data such as graphics, sound, or compiled code. This is a general term for text or image data type. BLOBs are not stored in the table rows themselves, but in separate pages referenced by a pointer in the row.

blocks A series of statements enclosed by BEGIN and END. Blocks define which set of statements will be affected by control-of-flow language such as IF or WHILE. You can nest BEGIN...END blocks within other BEGIN... END blocks.

Books Online *See* SQL Server Books Online.

Boolean expression An expression that returns a true or false value. For example, comparing the value 1 to the value 5 returns a false value (1=5). WHERE clauses are boolean expressions.

broken ownership chain *See* ownership chain.

browse mode A function that lets you scan database rows and update their values one row at a time. Several browse mode functions return information that an application can use to examine the structure of a complicated ad hoc query.

buffer cache The pool of buffer pages into which data pages are read.

built-in functions A group of functions provided by SQL Server and grouped as follows:

- System functions, most of which return information from system tables

- String functions, for manipulating values, such as char, varchar, binary, and varbinary

- Text and image functions, for manipulating text and image values

- Mathematical functions, for trigonometry, geometry, and other number handling

- Date and time functions, for manipulating datetime and smalldatetime values

- Two conversion functions, CONVERT and CAST, for converting expressions from one data type to another and for formatting dates in a variety of styles

bulk copy program (bcp) A command-line utility that copies SQL Server data to or from an operating system file in a user-specified format.

BULK INSERT A Transact-SQL command for importing external data into SQL Server tables.

business rules An organizational standard operating procedure that requires that certain policies be followed to ensure that a business is run correctly. Business rules ensure that the database maintains its accuracy with business policies. SQL Server can use defaults, rules, triggers, and stored procedures to ensure that data adheres to business rules.

C

cache A buffer used to hold data during input/output (I/O) transfers between disk and random access memory (RAM). *See also* buffer cache.

cached pages Pages that are held in cache. One page is 8 KB of data.

calculated member A member of a dimension whose value is calculated at run time using an expression. Calculated member values may be derived from other members' values. A calculated member is any member that is not an input member. For example, a calculated member Profit can be determined by subtracting the value of the member Costs from the value of the member Sales. *See also* Calculated Member Builder; input member.

Calculated Member Builder A dialog box in the OLAP Manager used to create calculated members. You can pick parent members and members from a list. In addition, you can construct calculated value expressions using the cube data and analytical functions provided. *See also* calculated member.

call-level interface (CLI) The interface supported by ODBC for use by an application.

candidate key A unique identifier for a row within a database table. A candidate, or surrogate, key can be made up of one or more columns. In a normalized database, every table must have at least one candidate key, in which case it is considered the primary key for a table automatically. However, it is possible for a table to have more than one candidate key, in which case one of them must be designated as the primary key. Any candidate key that is not the primary key is called the alternate key.

capture The process of recording and storing information during the monitoring process.

Cartesian product All of the possible combinations of the rows from each of the tables involved in a join operation. The number of rows in a Cartesian product of two tables, for example, is equal to the number of rows in the first table multiplied by the number of rows in the second table. Cartesian products almost never provide useful information. Queries using the CROSS JOIN clause or queries without enough JOIN clauses create Cartesian products.

cascading delete A delete operation that deletes all related database rows or columns. Cascading deletes are typically implemented using triggers or stored procedures.

cascading update An update operation that updates all related database rows or columns. Cascading updates are typically implemented using triggers or stored procedures.

catalog (database) *See* database catalog.

catalog (full-text) Full-text indexes are contained in full-text catalogs. Each database can use one or more full-text catalogs. Full-text catalogs and indexes are not stored in the database to which they belong. The catalogs and indexes are managed separately by the Microsoft Search service.

catalog (system) *See* system catalog.

cell In a relational database, the addressable attribute of a row and column. In a cube, the set of properties, including a value, specified by the intersection when one member is selected from each dimension. *See also* coordinate.

change script A text file that contains SQL statements for all changes made to a database, in the order in which they were made, during an editing session. Each change script is saved in a separate text file with an .SQL extension. Change scripts can be applied back to the database later, using a tool such as isql.

character *See* char(*n*) data type.

character format Data stored in a bulk copy data file using text characters.

character set A set that determines the types of characters that SQL Server recognizes in the char, varchar, and text data types. A character set is a set of 256 letters, digits, and symbols specific to a country or a language. The printable characters of the first 128 values are the same for all character sets. The last 128 characters, sometimes referred to as extended characters, are unique to each character set. A character set is related to, but separate from, Unicode characters. A character set is also referred to as a code page.

char(*n*) data type A character data type that holds a maximum of 8000 characters. Storage size is *n* regardless of the actual length of the entry. The SQL-92 synonym for char is character.

CHECK constraints Constraints that specify data values that are acceptable in a column. You can apply CHECK constraints to multiple columns, and you can apply multiple CHECK constraints to a single column. When a table is dropped, CHECK constraints are also dropped.

checkpoint The point at which all changed data pages from the buffer cache are written to disk.

child In OLAP Services, a member in the next lower level in a hierarchy that is directly related to the current member. For example, in a Time dimension containing the levels Quarter, Month, and Day, January is a child of Qtr1. In referential integrity, the term "child" is sometimes used to describe the "many" table in a parent/child, or one-to-many, relationship. *See also* ancestor; descendant; parent; sibling.

CLI *See* call-level interface (CLI).

client A front-end application that uses the services provided by a server. The computer that hosts the application is referred to as the client computer. SQL Server client software enables computers to connect to a computer running SQL Server over a network.

client application In OLAP Services, an application that retrieves data from an OLAP server and performs local analysis and presentation of data from relational or multidimensional databases. Client applications connect to the OLAP server through the PivotTable Service component. *See also* PivotTable Service. In client/server computing, *see also* client.

client cursor A cursor implemented on the client. The entire result set is first transferred to the client, and the client application programming interface (API) software implements the cursor functionality from this cached result set. Client cursors typically do not support all types of cursors, only static and forward-only cursors.

client/server computing A system of computing in which two or more computers share processing across a network. The server computer manages a shared resource, such as a database, and responds to requests from clients for use of this resource. The client computer interacts with a user and makes requests for use of a shared resource. Client/server computing separates the functions of an application into two parts: a front-end component and a back-end component. The client presents and manipulates data on the workstation; the server stores, retrieves, and protects data.

clustered index An index in which the logical or indexed order of the key values is the same as the physical stored order of the corresponding rows that exist in a table.

clustering The use of multiple computers to provide increased reliability, capacity, and management capabilities.

code page *See* character set.

collection (COM) A group of objects of the same type contained within a parent object. For instance, in SQL-DMO, the Database object exposes a Tables collection. *See also* SQL-DMF.

column In a SQL database table, the area, sometimes called a field, in each row that stores the data about an attribute of the object modeled by the table (for example, the ContactName column in the Customers table of the Northwind database). Individual columns are characterized by their maximum length and the type of data that can be placed in them. A column contains an individual data item within a row.

column-level constraint A restriction used to enforce data integrity on a column. SQL Server provides these types of constraints: CHECK, DEFAULT, FOREIGN KEY REFERENCE, PRIMARY KEY, and UNIQUE. *See also* table-level constraint.

COM *See* component object model (COM).

commit A statement used to complete a transaction begun with a BEGIN TRAN statement, which guarantees that either all or none of the transaction's modifications are made a permanent part of the database. A COMMIT statement also frees resources, such as locks, used by the transaction. *See also* roll back.

common key A key created to make explicit a logical relationship between two tables in a database. *See also* foreign key (FK); primary key (PK).

complex relationship A relationship among more than two entities, subsets, dependencies, or relations.

component object model (COM) The programming model on which several SQL Server and database application programming interfaces (APIs), such as SQL-DMO, OLE DB, and ADO, are based.

composite index An index that uses more than one column in a table to index data.

composite key A key composed of two or more columns. A drawback of composite keys is that they require more complex joins when two or more tables are joined.

COM-structured storage file A component object model (COM) compound file consisting of a root storage object containing at least one stream object representing its native data, along with one or more storage objects corresponding to its linked and embedded objects. The root storage object maps to a filename in whatever file system it happens to reside.

concatenation Combining two or more character strings or expressions into a single character string or expression, or combining two or more binary strings or expressions into a single binary string or expression.

concurrency A process that allows multiple users to access and change shared data at the same time. SQL Server uses locking to allow multiple users to access and change shared data at the same time without conflicting with one another.

concurrency control The control of concurrent access. SQL Server uses locking to allow multiple users to access and change shared data at the same time without conflicting with one another.

concurrent access Occurs when more than one user accesses and updates shared data at the same time.

connection A successful login to a computer running SQL Server. A connection occurs through an interprocess communication mechanism such as named pipes between the client application and SQL Server.

connectivity The ability of different classes of computers to communicate with one another.

console tree In Microsoft Management Console, the left-hand panel is known as the console tree. Highlighting objects in the console tree

will determine which details are shown in the details pane, which is the right-hand panel. *See also* details pane.

console utility The console command-prompt utility displays backup and restore messages when backing up to or restoring from tape dump devices, and is used by the person responsible for backing up and restoring a database.

constant Any constant or literal string, built-in function, or mathematical expression. The value cannot include the names of any columns or other database objects.

constant expression An expression that contains only constant values (it does not include the names of any columns or other database objects). You can use any constant, built-in function, mathematical expression, or global variable. The default value must be compatible with the data type of the column.

constant value *See* constant.

constraint A property that can be placed on a column or set of columns in a table. SQL Server provides these constraints: CHECK, DEFAULT, FOREIGN KEY, REFERENCE, PRIMARY KEY, and UNIQUE.

continuation media The media inserted when the initial medium becomes full, allowing continuation of the backup operation.

control-break report A report whose summary values are controlled by user-defined groupings or breaks.

control file *See* master database.

controlled access protocols Protocols that control the access that Subscribers have to a publication by marking the publication as either unrestricted or restricted.

- Unrestricted publications are visible to and can be subscribed to by any Subscriber known to the Publisher.

- Restricted publications are visible only to those Subscribers authorized for access. Servers not authorized for access cannot subscribe to the publication; they cannot even view it. As a result, users setting up subscriptions at servers not authorized for access will not even know of a restricted publication. At those servers, it will not appear in any list.

control-of-flow language Transact-SQL keywords that control the flow of execution of SQL statements, statement blocks, and stored procedures. IF and WHILE are examples of control-of-flow language.

conversion function *See* type conversion function.

coordinate An element (member or tuple) of an axis. The intersection of a set of coordinates determines a cell. *See also* cell.

correlated subquery A repeating subquery. Many queries can be evaluated by executing the subquery once and substituting the resulting value or values into the WHERE clause of the outer query. In queries that include a correlated subquery, the subquery depends on the outer query for its values. This means that the subquery is executed repeatedly, one time for each row that is selected by the outer query.

covering index A nonclustered index that contains all of the columns required to satisfy a query, in both the selection list and the WHERE clause.

CPU busy A SQL Server statistic that reports the time, in milliseconds, that the central processing unit (CPU) spent on SQL Server work. CPU busy is reported as part of the sp_monitor output.

creation script A script that contains CREATE statements. In SQL Enterprise Manager and replication, an option that adds object-creation statements to a script.

cube A subset of data, usually constructed from a data warehouse, that is organized and summarized into a multidimensional structure defined by a set of dimensions and measures. A cube's data is stored in one or more partitions.

Cube editor A tool in the OLAP Manager that you can use to create new cubes or edit existing ones.

cube file *See* local cube.

cursor A database object used by applications to manipulate data by rows instead of by sets. Using cursors, multiple operations can be performed row by row against a result set with or without returning to the original table. In other words, cursors conceptually return a result set based on tables within the database(s). For example, a cursor can be generated to include a list of all user-defined table names within a database. After the cursor has been opened, movement (fetching) through the result set can include multiple operations against each table by passing each table name as a variable. Cursors are powerful when combined with stored procedures and the EXECUTE statement (to build strings dynamically). Cursors are a powerful component of the SQL Server application programming interfaces (APIs).

cursor library A part of the ODBC and DB-Library application programming interfaces (APIs) that implements client cursors. A cursor library is not commonly used in current systems; server cursors are used instead.

D

data The coded representation of information for use in a computer. Data has attributes, such as type and length.

database A collection of information, tables, and other objects organized and presented to serve a specific purpose, such as facilitate searching, sorting, and recombining data. Databases are stored in files.

database catalog The set of system tables in a database that describes the database contents. *See also* system catalog.

Database Consistency Checker (DBCC) A statement used to check the logical and physical consistency of a database, check memory usage, decrease the size of a database, check performance statistics, and so on. Database Consistency Checker (DBCC) ensures the physical and logical consistency of a database and can repair certain database errors.

database diagram A graphical representation of any portion of a database schema. A schema is a description of a database to the database management system (DBMS), generated using the data definition language (DDL) provided

by the DBMS. A database diagram can be either a whole or a partial picture of the structure of a database; it includes objects for tables, the columns they contain, and the relationship between them.

database file A file in which a database is stored. One database can be stored in several files.

database language The language used for accessing, querying, updating, and managing data in relational database systems. SQL is a widely used database language. With SQL, you can retrieve data from a database, create databases and database objects, add data, modify existing data, and perform other complex functions. Many of these capabilities are implemented by using one of three types of SQL statements: data definition language (DDL), data manipulation language (DML), and data control language (DCL). The Microsoft SQL Server implementation of SQL is called Transact-SQL.

database management system (DBMS) A repository for the collection of computerized data files that enables users to perform a variety of operations on those files, including retrieving, appending, editing, updating, and generating reports.

database name A name given to a database. Database names must be unique within a server and conform to the rules for identifiers. They can be up to 128 characters.

database object One of the components of a database: a table, index, trigger, view, key, constraint, default, rule, user-defined data type, or stored procedure.

database object owner A user who creates a database object (table, index, view, trigger, or stored procedure) and is automatically granted all permissions on it. The middle section of a fully qualified object name identifies the database object owners. For example, northwind.**dbo**.customers.

database owner A member of the database administrator role of a database. There is only one database owner, although multiple people can be assigned the role of db_owner. The owner is usually the database creator and has full permissions in that database and determines the access and capabilities provided to other users.

database query *See* query.

database script A collection of statements used to create database objects. Transact-SQL scripts are saved as text files, usually ending with .SQL.

database verification utility *See* Database Consistency Checker (DBCC).

data block *See* page.

data cache *See* buffer cache.

data control language (DCL) The subset of SQL statements used to control permissions on database objects. Permissions are controlled using the GRANT and REVOKE statements. *See also* data definition language (DDL); data manipulation language (DML).

data definition The process of setting up databases and creating database objects, such as tables, indexes, constraints, defaults, rules, procedures, triggers, and views.

data definition language (DDL) The subset of SQL statements used for modeling the structure (rather than the contents) of a database or a cube. The DDL gives you the ability to create, modify, and remove databases and database objects.

data-definition query A SQL-specific query that contains data definition language (DDL) statements. These are statements that allow you to create or alter objects (such as tables, indexes, views, and so on) in the database.

data dictionary A system table containing descriptions of database objects and how they are structured.

data dictionary view *See* system tables.

data explosion The exponential growth in size of a multidimensional structure, such as a cube, because of the storage of precalculated data.

data file A file that contains data such as tables, rows, and stored procedures. Databases can span multiple data files. *See* log file.

data integrity The accuracy and reliability of data. Data integrity is important in both single-user and multiuser environments. In multiuser environments, where data is shared, both the potential for and the cost of data corruption are high. In large-scale relational database management system (RDBMS) environments, data integrity is a primary concern.

data lineage A mechanism for recording information to determine the source of any piece of data, and the transformations applied to that data using Data Transformation Services (DTS). Data lineage can be tracked at the package and row levels of a table and provides a complete audit trail for information stored in a data warehouse. Data lineage is available only for packages stored in Microsoft Repository.

data manipulation language (DML) The subset of SQL statements used to retrieve and manipulate data—for example, SELECT, INSERT, UPDATE, and DELETE.

data mart A subset of the contents of a data warehouse, stored within its database. A data mart tends to contain data focused at the department level, or on a specific business area. It is frequently implemented to manage the volume and scope of data. *See also* data warehouse.

data migration The process of extracting data from operational systems to a data warehouse with minimal effect on the source systems, and the transformation of the source data into a format consistent with the design and requirements of the data warehouse. *See also* data transformation; data warehouse.

data model *See* relational data model.

data modification Adding, deleting, or changing information in a database by using the INSERT, DELETE, and UPDATE Transact-SQL statements.

data pump An OLE DB service provider that provides the infrastructure to import, export, and transform data between heterogeneous data stores using Data Transformation Services (DTS).

dataset In general, a collection of related information made up of separate elements that can be treated as a unit. In OLE DB for OLAP, the set of multidimensional data that is the result of executing a multidimensional expression (MDX) statement. For more information about datasets, see your OLE DB documentation.

data scrubbing The process of making data consistent, either manually, or automatically using programs. For example, a database with inconsistent data might contain customer addresses that have the State column set to "WA" for one customer but "Washington" for another. Data scrubbing is performed prior to or during the transfer of data to a data warehouse. *See also* data transformation.

data sharing The ability to share individual pieces of data transparently from a database across different applications.

data source The source of data for an object such as a cube or a dimension. Also, the specification of the information necessary to access source data. Sometimes refers to a DataSource object. *See also* data source name (DSN).

data source name (DSN) The name assigned to an ODBC data source. Applications can use data source names (DSNs) to request a connection to a system ODBC data source, which specifies the computer name and (optionally) the database to which the DSN maps. A DSN can also refer to an OLE DB connection.

data synchronization *See* synchronization.

data transfer The process of copying data to or from a computer running SQL Server.

data transformation A set of operations applied to source data before it can be stored in the destination, using Data Transformation Services (DTS). For example, DTS allows new values to be calculated from one or more source columns, or a single column to be broken into multiple values to be stored in separate destination columns. Data transformation is often associated with the process of copying data into a data warehouse.

Data Transformation Services (DTS) A SQL Server component used to import, export, and transform data from different data sources.

data type An attribute that specifies what type of information can be stored in a column or variable. System-supplied data types are provided by SQL Server; user-defined data types can also be created. *See also* base data type.

data type conversion functions Functions that transform expressions from one data type into another. The CAST and CONVERT functions provide this capability.

data warehouse A database specifically structured for query and analysis. A data warehouse typically contains data representing the business history of an organization. Data in a data warehouse is usually less detailed and longer lived than data from an OLTP system. For example, a data warehouse may store daily order totals by customer over the past 5 years, whereas an OLTP system would store every order processed but retain those records for only a few months.

date and time functions Functions used to display information about dates and times. They manipulate datetime and smalldatetime values, including arithmetic.

datetime data type A SQL Server system data type. A datetime data type is stored in 8 bytes of two 4-byte integers: 4 bytes for the number of days before or after the base date of January 1, 1900, and 4 bytes for the number of milliseconds after midnight.

DBCC *See* Database Consistency Checker (DBCC).

DBCS (Double-Byte Character Set) A character set that uses 1 or 2 bytes to represent a character, allowing more than 256 characters to be represented. Double Byte Character Set (DBCS) character sets are typically used in environments that use ideographic writing systems, such as Japanese, Korean, and Chinese. *See also* Unicode.

DB-Library A series of high-level language (including C) libraries that provide the application programming interface (API) for the client in a client/server system. DB-Library sends requests from a client to a server. DB-Library allows the developer to incorporate Transact-SQL statements into an application to retrieve and update data in a SQL Server database.

DBMS *See* database management system (DBMS).

DBO *See* database owner.

DCL *See* data control language (DCL).

DDL *See* data definition language (DDL).

deadlock A situation in which two users, each having a lock on one piece of data, attempt to acquire a lock on the other's piece. Each user waits for the other to release the lock. SQL Server detects deadlocks and terminates one user's process. *See also* livelock.

decision support Database applications optimized for performance in data queries that do not change data. Decision support typically requires read-only access to data.

Decision Support Objects (DSO) The Microsoft SQL Server OLAP Services server object model. Decision Support Objects (DSO) are used to create applications that define and manage cubes and other objects. DSOs can also be used to extend the functionality of the OLAP Manager or to automate the ongoing maintenance of your system.

declarative referential integrity (DRI) The SQL Server built-in capacity that checks the data integrity of a specific related table. Implemented using PRIMARY, UNIQUE and FOREIGN KEY (REFERENCES) constraints.

default A value inserted into a column automatically if the user does not enter one. In a relational database management system, every data element (a particular column in a particular row) must contain a value, even if that value is NULL. Because some columns do not accept null values, another value must be entered, either by the user or by SQL Server. In general computing terms, the behavior exhibited by a statement or a component unless overridden by the user.

default database The database the user is connected to immediately after logging on to SQL Server.

default language The language (for example, French, German, or English) used to communicate with the server. After the default language is set, the user is logged on automatically using that language.

default result set The default mode SQL Server uses to return a result set back to a client. Rows are sent to the client in the order they are placed in the result set, and the application must process the rows in this order. After executing a SQL statement on a connection, the application cannot do anything on the connection other than retrieve the rows in the result set until all of the rows have been retrieved. The only other action that an application can perform before the end of the result set is to cancel the remainder of the result set. This is the fastest method to get rows from SQL Server to the client.

delete query A query that removes rows from one or more tables.

delimiter The character used for separating elements in a list.

denormalization *See* denormalize.

denormalize To introduce redundancy into a table in order to incorporate data from a related table. The related table can then be eliminated. Denormalization can improve efficiency and performance by reducing complexity in a data warehouse schema. Denormalization is also sometimes used in OLTP databases to optimize certain operations. *See also* star schema.

density The relative percentage of a multidimensional structure's cells that contain data. OLAP Services stores only cells that contain data. A dense cube requires more storage than a sparse cube of identical structure design. *See also* data explosion; sparsity.

deny To remove a permission from a user account and prevent the account from gaining permission through membership in groups or roles within the permission.

dependencies The views and procedures that depend on the specified table or view.

descendant A member in a dimension hierarchy that is related to a member of a higher level within the same dimension. For example, in a Time dimension containing the levels Year, Quarter, Month, and Day, January is a descendant of 1997. *See also* ancestor; child; parent; sibling.

destination database *See* subscription database.

destination server *See* Subscriber.

destination table The subscribing table created as a replica of a published table. A destination table in a subscription database is synchronized with and contains data derived from the published table in a publication database.

details pane In SQL Server Enterprise Manager, which opens with Microsoft Management Console, the left-hand panel is known as the console tree. Highlighting objects in the console tree will determine which details are shown in the details pane, which is the right-hand panel. *See also* console tree.

device In general computing, a hardware component—for example, a hard drive or tape backup unit. In SQL Server 6.5, devices are operating system files that contain databases. In SQL Server 7, devices are not used to store databases. Backups are stored in devices. *See also* file.

differential database backup A database backup that records only pages that have changed in the database since the last full database backup. A differential backup is smaller and faster to restore than a full backup and has minimal effect on performance.

dimension A structural attribute of a cube, which is an organized hierarchy of categories (levels) that describe data in the fact table. These categories typically describe a similar set of members upon which the user wants to base an analysis. For example, a geography dimension might include levels for Country, Region, State or Province, and City. *See also* level; measure.

dimension editor A tool in the OLAP Manager that you can use to create, examine, and edit a dimension and its levels. It offers two views: Schema, which examines and edits the dimension table structure, and Browse, which checks dimension data.

dimension hierarchy One of the hierarchies of a dimension. *See also* hierarchy.

dimension table A table in a data warehouse whose entries describe data in a fact table. Dimension tables present business entities.

direct response mode The default mode in which SQL Server statistics are gathered separately from the SQL Server Statistics display. Data is available immediately to SQL Server Performance Monitor; however, the statistics displayed are one period behind the statistics retrieved.

dirty pages Cached pages that have been modified since the last checkpoint.

dirty read Reads that contain uncommitted data. For example, transaction 1 changes a row. Transaction 2 reads the changed row before transaction 1 commits the change. If transaction 1 rolls back the change, transaction 2 reads a row that is considered to have never existed.

disk mirroring The process that protects against media failure by maintaining a fully redundant copy of a partition on another disk. It is recommended that you use a redundant array of independent disks (RAID) for disk mirroring.

distribute To move transactions or snapshots of data from the Publisher to Subscribers, where they are applied to the destination tables in the subscription databases.

distributed database A database implemented on a network in which the component partitions are distributed over various nodes of the network. Depending on the specific update and retrieval traffic, distributing the database can enhance overall performance significantly.

Distributed Management Objects (DMO) SQL Distributed Management Objects (SQL-DMO) are 32-bit component object model (COM) objects for the Windows 95, Windows 98, and Windows NT operating systems. SQL-DMO objects are OLE Automation compatible. The SQL-DMO object model includes objects, properties, methods, and collections used to write programs to administer multiple SQL Servers distributed across a network. SQL-DMO programs can range from simple Visual Basic scripts to complex Visual C++ applications.

distributed processing Data processing in which some or all of the processing, storage, and control functions, in addition to input/output functions, are situated in different places and connected by transmission facilities. The transparent access of both applications and data by programs and users is an important goal of distributed processing systems.

distributed query A single query that accesses data from heterogeneous data sources.

Distribution Agent The replication component that moves the transactions and snapshot jobs held in distribution database tables to Subscribers.

distribution database A store-and-forward database that holds all transactions waiting to be distributed to Subscribers. The distribution database receives transactions sent to it from the Publisher by the Log Reader Agent and holds them until the Distribution Agent moves them to the Subscribers.

distribution process In replication, the process that moves transactions from the distribution database tables to subscription servers, where they are applied to the destination tables in the destination databases.

Distributor The server containing the distribution database. The Distributor receives all changes to published data, stores the changes in its distribution database, and transmits them to Subscribers. The Distributor may or may not be the same computer as the Publisher. *See also* local Distributor; remote Distributor.

DLL *See* dynamic link library (DLL).

DML *See* data manipulation language (DML).

DMO *See* Distributed Management Objects (DMO).

domain In Windows NT security, a collection of computers grouped for viewing and administrative purposes that share a common security database.

domain integrity Integrity that enforces valid entries for a given column. Domain integrity is enforced by restricting the type (through data types), the format (through CHECK constraints and rules), or the range of possible values (through REFERENCE and CHECK constraints, and rules).

DRI *See* declarative referential integrity (DRI).

drill down/drill up A technique for navigating through levels of data ranging from the most summarized (up) to the most detailed (down). For example, to view the details of sales data by year, a user can drill down to display sales data by quarter, and drill down further to display data by month.

DSO *See* Decision Support Objects (DSO).

DTS *See* Data Transformation Services (DTS).

dump *See* back up.

dump file *See* backup file.

dynamic backup A backup performed while the database is active.

dynamic cursor A cursor that can reflect data modifications made to the underlying data while the cursor is open. Updates, deletes, and inserts made by users are reflected in the dynamic cursor.

dynamic link library (DLL) An executable routine containing a specific set of functions stored in a .DLL file and loaded on demand when needed by the program that calls it.

dynamic locking The process used by SQL Server to determine the most cost-effective locks to use at any one time.

dynamic recovery The process that detects and/or attempts to correct software failure or loss of data integrity within a relational database management system (RDBMS).

dynamic SQL statements In Embedded SQL for C, a SQL statement built and executed at run time.

E

element The location where a row and a column meet in a table. Element is synonymous with field.

enabling The process of allowing full-text querying to occur on the current database. Execute sp_fulltext_database with action set to enable.

encrypted trigger A trigger created with an optional encryption parameter that encrypts the definition text and cannot be decrypted. Encryption makes the information indecipherable to protect it from unauthorized viewing or use.

encryption A method for keeping sensitive information confidential by changing data into an unreadable form.

entity A real-world object, referred to by a noun (person, place, thing, or idea)—for example, titles, authors, and publishers.

entity integrity Integrity that defines a row as a unique entity for a particular table and ensures that the column cannot contain duplicate values. It usually enforces the primary key of a table (through indexes, UNIQUE constraints, or PRIMARY KEY constraints).

equijoin A join in which the values in the columns being joined are compared for equality, and all columns are included in the results.

error log A log file that records information from SQL Server. You can view the error log by using SQL Server Enterprise Manager or any text editor. Each time SQL Server is started, it retains the previous logs and creates a new log.

error state number A number that provides information about the context of an error. Valid error state numbers are from 1 through 127. An error state number identifies the source of the error (if the error can be issued from more than one source).

escape character A character used to indicate that another character in an expression is meant literally and not as an operator.

event log A file that contains both SQL Server error messages and messages for all activities on the computer.

exclusive lock A lock that prevents any other transaction from acquiring a lock on a resource until the original lock on the resource is released at the end of the transaction. An exclusive lock is always applied during an update operation (INSERT, UPDATE, or DELETE).

explicit transaction A group of SQL statements enclosed in the transaction delimiters BEGIN TRANSACTION and COMMIT TRANSACTION, and optionally one of the following statements:

- BEGIN DISTRIBUTED TRANSACTION
- BEGIN TRANSACTION
- COMMIT TRANSACTION
- COMMIT WORK
- ROLLBACK TRANSACTION
- ROLLBACK WORK
- SAVE TRANSACTION

export file *See* bcp files.

expression A column name, function, variable, subquery, or any combination of column names, constants, and functions connected by an operator or operators in a subquery.

extended relational analysis A systematic database design process. The database is designed by modeling entities into tables, relationships into columns or tables, and attributes into columns.

extended stored procedure   A SQL Server–provided procedure that dynamically loads and executes a function within a dynamic link library (DLL) in a manner similar to a stored procedure. Actions outside of SQL Server can be triggered and external information returned to SQL Server. Return status codes and output parameters (identical to their counterparts in regular stored procedures) are also supported.

extent   The space allocated upon creation of a SQL Server object, such as a table or index. In SQL Server, an extent is eight contiguous pages.

extent lock   A lock held on a group of eight database pages while they are being allocated or freed. Extent locks are set while a CREATE or DROP statement is running or while an INSERT or UPDATE statement that requires new data or index pages is running.

F

fact   A row in a fact table in a data warehouse. A fact contains one or more numeric values that measure a data event such as a sales transaction.

fact table   A central table in a data warehouse that contains numerical measures and keys relating facts to a dimension table. Fact tables contain data that describes a specific event within a business, such as a bank transaction or product sale. *See also* data warehouse; dimension table; snowflake schema; star join; star schema.

FAT file system   A method for managing disk storage. A file allocation table (FAT) file system is used by an operating system to keep track of the status of various segments of disk space used for file storage. *See also* Windows NT File System (NTFS).

fatal error   An error message with a severity level of 19 or higher. Contact your primary support provider when these errors occur.

Federal Information Processing Standard (FIPS)   Standards that apply to computer systems purchased by the United States government. Each Federal Information Processing Standard (FIPS) standard is defined by the National Institute of Standards and Technology (NIST). The current standard for SQL products is FIPS 127-2, which is based on the ANSI SQL-92 standard. ANSI SQL-92 is aligned with ISO/IEC SQL-92.

fetch   An operation that retrieves a row or block of rows from a cursor. Forward-only cursors support a FETCH NEXT statement only. Scrollable cursors support FETCH NEXT as well as FETCH FIRST, FETCH LAST, FETCH PRIOR, FETCH RELATIVE(n), and FETCH ABSOLUTE(n). FETCH RELATIVE(n) fetches the row n rows from the current position in the cursor. FETCH ABSOLUTE(n) fetches the nth row in the cursor. Transact-SQL batches, stored procedures, and triggers use the FETCH statement to fetch from Transact-SQL cursors. Applications use application programming interface (API) functions, such as the ODBC SQLFetch and SQLFetchScroll functions.

field   A single item of information contained within a row. A field is more commonly called a column in a SQL database.

field length The maximum number of characters needed to represent data in a bulk copy character format data file.

field terminator One or many characters marking the end of a field or row, separating one field or row in the data file from the next.

file A file in which a database is stored. One database can be stored in several files. SQL Server uses three types of files: data files (which store data), log files (which store transaction logs), and backup files (which store backups of a database).

filegroup A named collection of one or more database files that forms a single unit of allocation and administration. Filegroups enable the creation of objects in a specific place—for example, placing a heavily accessed table on a very fast drive. They also provide the ability to back up specific objects.

file storage type A storage type that describes how data is stored in a bulk copy data file.

file system The portion of an operating system that translates file-operations requests from an application into low-level, sector-oriented tasks that can be understood by the drivers that control the disk drives. SQL Server is usually installed on disk drives formatted for the Windows NT file system (NTFS) or file allocation table (FAT) file systems. It can be installed on a compressed NTFS volume, but at a performance cost.

fill factor An option used when creating an index to reserve free space on each page of the index. This option accommodates future expansion of table data and reduces the potential for page splits. It is a percentage from 0 through 100 that specifies how much of the data pages should be filled after the index is created.

filter A set of criteria applied to records to show a subset of the records or to sort the records.

filtering To designate selected rows or columns of a table for replication as an article. *See also* horizontal filtering; partitioning; vertical filtering.

FIPS *See* Federal Information Processing Standard (FIPS).

firehose cursors Obsolete term for default result sets. *See also* default result set.

fixed database role A predefined role defined at the database level and existing in each database.

fixed server role A predefined role defined at the server level and existing outside individual databases.

FK *See* foreign key (FK).

float data type A data type that holds positive or negative floating-point numbers. SQL Server float data types are float, double precision, and float(n) .

foreign key (FK) The column or combination of columns whose values match the primary key (PK) or unique key in the same or another table. A foreign key does not have to be unique. A foreign key is often in a many-to-one relationship with a primary key. Foreign key values should be copies of the primary key values; no value in the foreign key except NULL should ever exist unless the same value exists in the primary key. A foreign key may be NULL; if any part of a composite foreign key is NULL, the entire foreign key must be NULL.

FOREIGN KEY constraint When a FOREIGN KEY constraint is placed on a column, any inserted data must equal the value of the referenced PRIMARY KEY or UNIQUE constraint. FOREIGN KEY constraints enforce referential integrity by preventing the deletion of parent rows that have related rows in the child table and the insertion of child rows that have no related record in the parent table. *See also* child; parent.

forwarding server A server running SQL Server that receives designated events.

forward-only cursor A cursor that cannot be scrolled; rows can be read only in sequence from the first row to the last row.

fragmentation A condition that occurs when data modifications are made. You can reduce fragmentation and improve read-ahead performance by dropping and re-creating a clustered index. DBCC DBREINDEX, which can rebuild all of the indexes for a table in one statement, is often used to defragment tables.

front end Software used to access a database or capture input data.

full outer join A type of outer join in which all rows in all joined tables are included, whether they are matched or not.

full-text catalog A catalog that stores a database's full-text index.

full-text index The portion of a full-text catalog that stores all of the full-text words and their locations for a given table.

full-text query As a SELECT statement, a query that searches for words, phrases, or multiple forms of a word or phrase in the character-based columns (of char, varchar, text, ntext, nchar, or nvarchar data types). The SELECT statement returns those rows meeting the search criteria.

full-text service The SQL Server component that performs the full-text querying.

function A set of instructions that operates as a single logical unit, can be called by name, accepts input parameters, and returns information. In programming languages such as C, a function is a named subroutine of a program that encapsulates some logic. The function can be called by name, using parameters to pass data into the function and retrieve data produced by the function. In Transact-SQL, a function is a unit of syntax consisting of a keyword and, usually, a set of parameters. There are several categories of Transact-SQL functions: string, math, system, niladic, text and image, date, aggregate, and conversion functions.

G

gateway A network software product that allows computers or networks running dissimilar protocols to communicate, providing transparent access to a variety of foreign database management systems (DBMSs). A gateway moves specific database connectivity and conversion processing from individual client computers to a single server computer. Communication is enabled by translating up one protocol stack and down the other. Gateways usually operate at the session layer.

gateway server A network server on which a gateway application resides.

Global Allocation Map (GAM) Pages that record what extents have been allocated. Each GAM covers 64,000 extents, or nearly 4 GB of data. The GAM has one bit for each extent in the interval it covers. If the bit is 1, the extent is free; if the bit is 0, the extent is allocated.

global group A Windows NT group containing user accounts from the Windows NT Server domain in which it is created. Global groups cannot contain other groups or users from other domains and cannot be created on a computer running Windows NT Workstation.

global variable In SQL Server 7, a variable that can be referenced by multiple Data Transformation Services (DTS) tasks. In earlier versions of SQL Server, the term referred to the Transact-SQL system functions whose names start with two at signs (@@).

grant To apply a permission to a user account, allowing the account to perform an activity or work with data.

granularity The degree of specificity of information contained in a data element. A fact table that has fine granularity contains many discrete facts, such as individual sales transactions. A table that has coarse granularity stores facts that are summaries of individual elements, such as sales totals per day.

graphical showplan An option of SQL Server Query Analyzer and SQL Server Enterprise Manager that shows the execution plan for a query. *See also* showplan.

group An administrative unit within Windows NT that contains Windows NT users or other groups.

guest A special user account in each database for logins without a database user account. Guests can be removed from a database.

H

hash join A sophisticated join algorithm that builds an interim structure to derive result sets. *See also* nested loops joins.

heterogeneous data Any non-SQL Server data. Heterogeneous data can be accessed in place through OLE DB, Linked Servers, ODBC, and the OPENROWSET and OPENQUERY commands. Heterogeneous data can be imported through Data Transformation Services (DTS), bcp, and the BULK INSERT command, among others.

hierarchy An arrangement of members of a dimension into levels based on parent-child relationships, such as Year, Quarter, Month, and Day or Country, Region, State or Province, and City. Members in a hierarchy are arranged from more general to more specific.

HOLAP (hybrid OLAP) A storage mode that uses a combination of multidimensional data structures and relational database tables to store multidimensional data. OLAP Services stores aggregations for a hybrid OLAP (HOLAP) partition in a multidimensional structure and facts in a relational database. *See also* MOLAP (multidimensional OLAP); ROLAP (relational OLAP).

homogeneous data Data that comes from one or more SQL Server databases.

horizontal filtering To create an article that replicates only selected rows from the base table. Subscribers receive only the subset of horizontally filtered data. You can use horizontal filtering to partition your base table horizontally. *See also* horizontal partitioning; vertical filtering.

horizontal partitioning To segment a single table into multiple tables based on selected rows. Each of the multiple tables has the same columns but fewer rows. *See also* horizontal filtering; vertical partitioning.

hybrid OLAP *See* HOLAP (hybrid OLAP).

I

identifier The name of a database object. An identifier can be from 1 through 128 characters. The first character must be a letter, underscore (_), at sign (@), or number sign (#). An identifier beginning with # denotes a temporary table. An identifier beginning with @ denotes a variable. Embedded spaces are not allowed.

identity column A column in a table that uses the identity property for a system-generated, monotonically increasing number.

identity property A property that enables columns to contain system-generated values that uniquely identify each row within a table. When inserting values into a table that has an identity column, SQL Server generates the next identifier automatically based on the last used identity value (incremented by adding rows) and the increment value specified during column creation.

idle time The time, in milliseconds, that SQL Server has been idle.

IEC *See* International Electrotechnical Commission (IEC).

image data type A SQL Server system data type of variable length that can hold from 0 through 2,147,483,647 bytes of binary data. The image data type cannot be used for variables. Conversions and calculations of hexadecimal numbers stored as binary can be unreliable.

immediate consistency A replication model that guarantees that all copies are identical to the original. It is implemented using Microsoft Distributed Transaction Coordinator (MS DTC), and it requires a high-speed, well-connected local area network (LAN). It reduces database availability and is less scalable in its implementation than latent consistency.

immediate transactional consistency A level of transaction consistency in which all participating sites are guaranteed to have the same data values at the same time, and the data is in a state that could have been achieved if all of the work had been done at one site. *See also* latent transactional consistency; no guaranteed consistency.

implicit transaction A transaction in which each single SQL statement is considered an atomic unit.

implied permission Permission to perform an activity specific to a role. Implied permissions cannot be granted, revoked, or denied.

incremental update The set of operations that either adds new members to an existing cube or dimension, or adds new data to a partition. One of three processing options for a cube or partition. One of two processing options for a dimension. *See also* process; refresh data.

index In a relational database, a database object that provides fast access to data in the rows of a table, based on key values. Indexes provide quick access to data and can enforce uniqueness on the rows in a table. SQL Server supports clustered and nonclustered indexes.

index intersection A technique that allows the query processor to evaluate multiple indexes from a table, construct a hash table from those multiple indexes, and use the hash table to reduce I/O. The resulting hash table essentially becomes a covering index and provides the same I/O performance benefits that covering indexes do.

index ORing An execution strategy that consists of looking up rows of a single table using several indexes, followed by producing the result (by combining the partial results).

Usually corresponds to an OR in the WHERE *<search_conditions>*. For example, WHERE R.a = 6 OR R.b = 7 with indexes on columns R.a and R.b.

index page A database page containing index filters.

initial media The first medium in each media family.

initial snapshot The process that ensures that publication and destination tables contain the same schema and data before a Subscriber receives replicated transactions from a Publisher. This process is performed by the Snapshot Agent and Distribution Agent. *See also* synchronization.

initial synchronization *See* synchronization.

inner join A join in which records from two tables are combined and added to a query's results only if the values of the joined fields meet certain specified criteria, usually equality.

input member A member whose value is loaded directly from the data warehouse instead of being calculated from other data. *See also* calculated member.

input set The set of data provided to a multidimensional expression (MDX) value expression upon which the expression operates. For more information about set value expressions, see your OLE DB documentation.

input source Any table, view, or schema diagram used as an information source for a query.

insensitive cursor A cursor that does not reflect data modifications made to the underlying data by other users while the cursor is open. Insensitive cursors are typically used in Transact-SQL batches, stored procedures, and triggers using the INSENSITIVE keyword on the DECLARE CURSOR statement.

INSERT The Transact-SQL statement used to append new rows into a table.

Insert query A query that copies specific columns and rows from one table to another or to the same table.

installation path The drive and directory into which the SQL Server files will be copied. The default is C:\Mssql7, although this can be set at installation time. After installation, this is often referred to as the SQL Server root directory.

int (integer) data type A SQL Server system data type that holds whole numbers from 2,147,483,647 through –2,147,483,648, inclusive. You cannot enter –2,147,483,648 in an integer column, but you can enter –2,147,483,647 – 1. You can store this number, or it can be the result of a calculation. Storage size is 4 bytes.

integrated security *See* Windows NT Authentication.

integrity constraint *See* rule.

integrity rule *See* constraint.

intent lock An lock that indicates that SQL Server wants to acquire a shared or exclusive lock on a more specific resource. An intent lock prevents another transaction from acquiring an exclusive lock on the resource containing that page or row.

interactive structured query language (ISQL) An interactive command-prompt utility provided with SQL Server that allows users to execute Transact-SQL statements or batches from a server or workstation and view the results returned.

International Electrotechnical Commission (IEC) One of two international standards bodies responsible for developing international data communications standards. The International Electrotechnical Commission works closely with the International Organization for Standardization (ISO) to define standards of computing. They jointly published the ISO/IEC SQL-92 standard for SQL.

International Organization for Standardization (ISO) One of two international standards bodies responsible for developing international data communications standards. The International Organization for Standardization works closely with the International Electrotechnical Commission (IEC) to define standards of computing. They jointly published the ISO/IEC SQL-92 standard for SQL.

Internet-enabled A publication setting that enables replication to Internet Subscribers.

interprocess communication (IPC) A system by which threads and processes can transfer data and messages among themselves. Interprocess communication (IPC) is used to offer and receive services from other programs.

IO busy The time, in milliseconds, that SQL Server spent performing input and output operations.

IPC *See* interprocess communication (IPC).

ISO *See* International Organization for Standardization (ISO).

isolation level An option that allows you to customize locking for an entire SQL Server session. When you set the isolation level, you specify the default locking behavior for all SELECT statements in your SQL Server session.

ISQL *See* interactive structured query language (ISQL).

J

job An implementation of an administrative action that contains one or more steps. The term *job* replaces the SQL Server 6.5 term *task*.

join As a verb, to combine the contents of two or more tables and produce a result set that incorporates rows and columns from each table. Tables are typically joined using data that they have in common. As a noun, *join* means the process or result of joining tables, as in the term *inner join,* which indicates a particular method of joining tables.

join condition A comparison clause that specifies how tables are related by their join fields. The most common join condition is equivalence (an equijoin) in which the values of the join fields must be the same.

join operator A comparison operator in a join condition that determines how the two sides of the condition are evaluated and which records are returned.

junction table A table that has associations with two other tables and is used indirectly as an association between those two tables. Also called a linking table. Often junction tables are used to express a many-to-many relationship, which is modeled as two one-to-many relationships.

K

kernel The essential core component of the server that handles several functions, such as task scheduling, disk caching, locking, and executing compiled queries.

key A column or group of columns that uniquely identifies a row (PRIMARY KEY), defines the relationship between two tables (FOREIGN KEY), or is used to build an index.

key column A column whose contents uniquely identify every row in a table.

key range lock A lock used to lock ranges between records in a table to prevent phantom insertions or deletions into a set of records. A key range lock also ensures serializable transactions.

keyset-driven cursor A cursor that shows the effects of updates made to its member rows by other users while the cursor is open, but does not show the effects of inserts or deletes.

keyword A reserved word in SQL Server that performs a specific function, such as to define, manipulate, and access database objects.

L

latency The amount of time that elapses between when a change is completed on the Publisher and when it appears in the destination database on the Subscriber.

latent consistency A replication model that allows a time lag between the moment that original data is altered and time that the replicated copies are updated. An advantage of latent consistency is that it supports local area networks (LANs), wide area networks (WANs), fast and slow communication links, and intermittently connected databases. SQL Server replication is based on a latent consistency model. *See also* immediate consistency.

latent transactional consistency A level of transaction consistency in which all participating sites are guaranteed to have the same data values that were achieved at the publishing site at some point in time. There can, however, be a delay in the data values being reflected at the participating sites, so that at any instant in time, the sites are not assured of having the exact same data values.

leaf level The bottom level of a clustered or nonclustered index. In a clustered index, the leaf level contains the actual data pages of the table. In a nonclustered index, the leaf level either points to data pages or points to the clustered index (if one exists), rather than containing the data itself.

left outer join A type of outer join in which all rows from the first-named table (the left table, which appears leftmost in the JOIN clause) are included. Unmatched rows in the right table do not appear.

level An element of a dimension hierarchy. Levels describe the dimension order from the highest (most summarized) level to the lowest (most detailed) level of data. For example, possible levels for a Geography dimension are: Country, Region, State or Province, City. *See also* dimension; hierarchy.

level hierarchy *See* dimension hierarchy; hierarchy.

library In OLAP Services, a folder that contains shared objects such as shared dimensions that can be used by multiple objects within a database.

library cache *See* procedure cache.

linked server An abstraction of an OLE DB data source that looks like another server to the local SQL Server. A linked server has an associated OLE DB provider that manages the data source. Linked servers allow heterogeneous data access as if the data were local SQL Server data.

linking table *See* junction table.

livelock A request for an exclusive lock that is repeatedly denied because a series of overlapping shared locks keep interfering. SQL Server detects the situation after four denials and refuses further shared locks. A livelock also occurs when read transactions monopolize a table or page, forcing a write transaction to wait indefinitely. *See also* deadlock.

load *See* restore.

local cube A cube created and stored with the extension .CUB on a local computer using PivotTable Service. *See also* PivotTable Service.

local Distributor A server configured as a Publisher that also acts as its own Distributor. In this configuration, the publication and distribution databases reside on the same computer. *See also* remote Distributor.

locale The set of information that corresponds to a specific language and country. A locale indicates specific settings such as decimal separators, date and time formats, and character-sorting order.

local group A Windows NT group containing user accounts and global groups from the domain group it is created in, and any trusted domain. Local groups cannot contain other local groups.

local login identification The identification (ID) that a user must use to log on to a local server. A login ID can have up to 128 characters. The characters can be alphanumeric; however, the first character must be a letter (for example, CHRIS or TELLER8).

local server The server to which the user is logged on. If remote servers are set up for the local server, users can access remote servers from their local server.

local variable A user-defined variable that has an assigned value. A local variable is defined with a DECLARE statement, assigned an initial value with a SELECT or SET statement, and used within the statement batch or procedure in which it was declared.

lock A restriction on access to a resource in a multiuser environment. SQL Server locks users out of a specific record, field, or file automatically to maintain security or prevent concurrent data manipulation problems.

lock escalation The process of converting many fine-grain locks into fewer coarse-grain locks, reducing system overhead.

log file A file or set of files containing a record of a database's transactions.

logical design An implementation-independent design that models the entities, relationships, and attributes in a database.

logical name A name used by SQL Server to identify a file. A logical name for a file must correspond to the rules for identifiers and can have as many as 128 characters.

logical operators The operators AND, OR, and NOT. These operators are used to connect search conditions in WHERE clauses.

login (account) The identity with which a user establishes a connection to SQL Server.

login identification The identification (ID) a user needs to log in to SQL Server. A login ID can have up to 128 characters and must be unique for that server. The characters can be alphanumeric; however, the first character must be a letter, the number sign (#), or underscore (_). With Windows NT Authentication, you do not need to maintain a separate login ID for SQL Server; you can use your Windows NT account.

login security mode A security mode that determines the manner in which a SQL Server validates a login request. There are two types of login security: Windows NT Authentication and Mixed Mode.

Log Reader Agent The transactional replication component that moves transactions marked for replication from the transaction log on the Publisher to the distribution database.

loose consistency A replication model that allows a time lag between the moment that original data is altered and the time that replicated copies of that data are updated. It does not guarantee that all copies will be constantly identical to the original. An advantage of loose consistency is that it supports LANs, WANs, fast and slow communication links, and intermittently connected databases. It also allows better database availability and scales much better in its implementation as compared to tight consistency. SQL Server replication is based on a loose consistency model.

lost update An update in which two transactions read and update the same data item.

M

manual synchronization Synchronization that is accomplished by a user. As with automatic synchronization, the publication server produces files containing the schema and a snapshot of the data from the published table, but with manual synchronization, it is applied to the Subscriber manually, using tape or another medium.

many-to-many relationship A relationship between two tables in which rows in each table have multiple matching rows in the related table. Many-to-many relationships are maintained by using a third table called a junction table.

MAPI Messaging Application Programming Interface. An e-mail application programming interface (API). Both SQL Mail and SQLAgentMail use MAPI.

mapped drive letter A shared resource that can be referred to as if it were a local drive. Local drives are assigned a letter of the alphabet. For example, the server share \\Server1\Quarterly Sales\ could be mapped to drive Q:. In that case a file on that shared resource could be referred to as either \\Server1\Quarterly Sales\Q1-1998.xls or Q:\Q1-1998.xls.

master database The database that controls user databases and the operation of SQL Server as a whole. It is installed automatically with SQL Server and keeps track of user accounts, remote user accounts, and remote servers that this server can interact with. It also tracks on-going processes, configurable environment variables, system error messages, databases on SQL Server, storage space allocated to each database, tapes and disks available on the system, and active locks.

master definition site *See* Publisher.

master device The file installed with earlier versions of SQL Server used to store the master, model, and tempdb system databases and transaction logs and the pubs sample database and transaction log. These databases now reside on their own individual files. *See also* master file.

master file The database file that contains the master database.

master site *See* Distributor.

MDX *See* multidimensional expressions (MDX).

measure A quantitative, numerical column in a fact table. Measures typically represent the values that are analyzed. *See also* dimension.

media description The descriptive text describing the media set.

media family All media in a set written by a single device. For example, an initial medium and all continuation media, if any.

media header Information about the backup media.

media name The descriptive name for the entire backup media set.

media password The password for the entire media set. SQL Server does not support media passwords.

media retention A setting that protects backups from being overwritten until the specified number of days has elapsed.

media set All media involved in a backup operation.

member An item in a dimension representing one or more occurrences of data. A member can be either unique or nonunique. For example, 1997 and 1998 represent unique members in the year level of a Time dimension, whereas January represents nonunique members in the month level because there can be more than one January in the Time dimension if it contains data for more than one year.

MemberKeyColumn The property that specifies the identifiers for dimension members. The MemberKeyColumn specifies a column in a table or an expression that, when evaluated, results in a set of member identifiers. For example, a MonthNumber column in a Time dimension table would contain numbers from 1 through 12, corresponding to the months of the year. *See also* MemberNameColumn; member variable.

MemberNameColumn The property that associates names with identifiers for dimension members specified by the MemberKeyColumn property. For example, a MonthName column in a Time dimension table would contain the names Jan, Feb, Mar, and so on, to correspond to the numbers from 1 through 12 in the MonthNumber column in the same table. These names are returned to the client when queries are evaluated and can be used to make the presented data more readable. *See also* MemberKeyColumn; member variable.

member property Information about the members of a dimension level in addition to that contained in the dimension (for example, the color of a product or the telephone number of a sales representative). For more information about member properties, see your OLE DB documentation.

member variable The value used internally by OLAP Services to identify a dimension member. MemberKeyColumn specifies the member variables for a dimension. For example, a number from 1 through 12 could be the member variable that corresponds to a month of the year. *See also* MemberKeyColumn; MemberNameColumn.

memo A type of column containing long strings of text (typically more than 255 characters). This is the Microsoft Access equivalent of a SQL Server text datatype.

merge In SQL Server OLAP Services, the operation that combines two partitions into a single partition.

Merge Agent In merge replication, the component that applies initial snapshot jobs held in publication database tables to Subscribers. It also merges incremental data changes that have occurred since the initial snapshot was created.

merge replication A type of replication that allows sites to make autonomous changes to replicated data and, at a later time, merge changes made at all sites. Merge replication does not guarantee transactional consistency. *See also* snapshot replication; transactional replication.

message number A number that uniquely identifies an error message.

metadata Data about data. That is, information about the properties of data, such as the type of data in a column (numeric, text, and so on) or the length of a column, information about the structure of data, or information that specifies the design of objects such as cubes or dimensions. Metadata is an important aspect of SQL Server, Data Transformation Services, and OLAP Services.

method A function that performs an action by using a component object model (COM) object, as in SQL-DMO, OLE DB, and ADO.

Microsoft ActiveX Data Objects (ADO) An easy-to-use, application programming interface (API) wrapping OLE DB for use in languages such as Visual Basic, Visual Basic for Applications, Active Server Pages, and Microsoft Internet Explorer Visual Basic Scripting.

Microsoft ActiveX Data Objects (Multidimensional) (ADO MD) A high-level, language-independent set of object-based data access interfaces optimized for multidimensional data applications. Visual Basic and other automation languages use ActiveX Data Objects (Multidimensional) (ADO MD) as the data access interface to multidimensional data storage. ADO MD is a part of ADO 2.0 and later.

Microsoft Management Console (MMC) An extensible, common console framework for management applications. Both SQL Server and OLAP Services use MMC to host their administrative user interfaces, the SQL Server Enterprise Manager and OLAP Manager.

Microsoft ODBC *See* Open Database Connectivity (ODBC).

Microsoft Open Database Connectivity (ODBC) *See* Open Database Connectivity (ODBC).

Microsoft Open Data Services *See* Open Data Services (ODS).

Microsoft Repository A set of Microsoft ActiveX interfaces and information models that are used to define database schema and data transformations as specified by the Microsoft Data Warehousing Framework. DTS supports Repository information stored in the SQL Server msdb database. Repository is the preferred means of storing DTS packages in a data-warehousing scenario because it is the only method of providing data lineage for packages.

mirroring In general NT computing, the continuous duplication of the information on one volume to another. Either the hardware or the Windows NT operating system can provide mirroring capabilities. Mirroring can provide continuous recovery in the event of media failure.

Mixed Mode A login security mode that combines Windows NT Authentication and SQL Server Authentication. It allows users to connect to SQL Server through either a Windows NT user account or a SQL Server login.

mixed security *See* Mixed Mode.

MMC *See* Microsoft Management Console (MMC).

MOLAP (multidimensional OLAP) A storage mode that uses a proprietary multidimensional structure to store a partition's facts and aggregations. A partition's data is completely contained within the multidimensional structure. *See also* HOLAP (hybrid OLAP); ROLAP (relational OLAP).

model database A database installed with SQL Server that provides the template for new user databases. Each time a database is created, SQL Server makes a copy of the model and then extends it to the size requested. A new database cannot be smaller than the model. The model database contains the system tables required for each user database. You can modify the model to add objects that you want in all newly created databases.

modulo An arithmetic operator that provides the integer remainder after a division involving two integers.

money data type A SQL Server system data type that stores monetary values from +922,337,203,685,477.5807 through –922,337,203,685,477.5808 with accuracy to a ten-thousandth of a monetary unit. The storage size is 8 bytes.

multidimensional expressions (MDX) A syntax used for querying multidimensional data. For more information about multidimensional expressions (MDX), see your OLE DB documentation.

multidimensional OLAP *See* MOLAP (multidimensional OLAP).

multidimensional structure A database paradigm that treats data not as relational tables and columns, but as information cubes that contain dimension and summary data in cells, each addressed by a set of coordinates that specifies a position in the structure's dimensions. For example, the cell at coordinates {SALES, 1997, WASHINGTON, SOFTWARE} would contain the summary of software sales in Washington in 1997. *See also* cube.

multithreaded server application An application that creates multiple threads within a single process to service multiple user requests at the same time.

multiuser The ability of a computer to support many users operating at the same time, while providing the computer system's full range of capabilities to each user.

N

named pipe An interprocess communication (IPC) mechanism that SQL Server and Open Data Services use to provide communication between clients and servers. Named pipes permit access to shared network resources.

native format Data stored in a bulk copy data file using SQL Server native data types.

nchar data type A fixed-length data type with a maximum of 4000 Unicode characters. Unicode characters use 2 bytes per character and support all international characters.

nested loops joins The nested loops join, also called nested iteration, uses one join input as the outer input table (shown as the top input in the graphical execution plan) and one as the inner (bottom) input table. The outer loop consumes the outer input table row by row. The inner loop, executed for each outer row, searches for matching rows in the inner input table.

nested query A SELECT statement that contains one or more subqueries.

Net-Library SQL Server uses dynamic link libraries to communicate via a particular network protocol. The same pair of Net-Libraries must be active on both client and server computers to support the desired network protocol.

network adapter An expansion card or other physical device used to connect a computer to a local area network (LAN); also known as NIC (network interface card).

niladic functions Niladic functions allow a system-supplied value to be inserted into a table when no value is specified. ANSI-standard niladic functions are used in DEFAULT constraints.

no guaranteed consistency A level of transaction consistency in which all participating sites can have the same data values, but not necessarily the same data values that could have been achieved if all the work had been done at one site. The act of replicating the data creates the possibility that variations in data values result at one or more sites. *See also* immediate transactional consistency; latent transactional consistency.

no initial snapshot A replication option used when a server subscribes to a publication. This option allows changes to replicated data to be distributed immediately to Subscribers, without delay for synchronization. An initial snapshot is not performed by SQL Server; it is the responsibility of the user setting up replication to ensure that the table schema and data are identical for the published article and the destination table. *See also* automatic synchronization.

noise word Words that do not participate in a full-text query search. For example, *a*, *and*, *the*, and so on.

nonclustered index An index in which the logical order of the index does not match the physical, stored order of the rows on disk. The leaf nodes of a nonclustered index contain index rows. Each index row contains the nonclustered key value and one or more row locators that point to the data row (or rows if the index is not unique) having the key value.

nonrepeatable read When a transaction reads the same row more than one time, and between the two (or more) reads, a separate transaction modifies that row. Because the row was modified between reads within the same transaction, each read produces different values, which introduces inconsistency.

normalization rules Rules that identify certain attributes that must be present (or absent) in a well-designed database, according to commonly accepted relational theory.

Northwind database A sample database provided with SQL Server. If Northwind was not installed with SQL Server, you can install it using the Instnwnd.sql script.

ntext data type A variable-length data type that can hold a maximum of $2^{30} - 1$ (1,073,741,823) characters or $2^{31} - 1$ bytes, which is 2,147,483,647. ntext columns store a 16-byte pointer in the data row, and the data is stored separately.

NTFS *See* Windows NT File System (NTFS).

NULL An entry that has no explicitly assigned value. NULL is not equivalent to zero or blank. A value of NULL is not considered to be greater than, less than, or equivalent to any other value, including another value of NULL.

nullability The capability that determines whether a column can allow null values for the data in that column.

nvarchar data type A variable-length data type with a maximum of 4000 Unicode characters. Unicode characters use 2 bytes per character and support all international characters.

O

object One of the components of a database: a table, index, trigger, view, key, constraint, default, rule, user-defined data type, or stored procedure. Also called a database object. In COM programming, an object has properties and methods and exposes interfaces; for example, the SQL-DMO is a hierarchy of COM objects.

object dependencies The views and procedures that depend on a table or view, and the tables or views that depend on a view or procedure.

Object Linking and Embedding (OLE) An application programming interface (API) for sharing objects among applications. OLE is built on the component object model (COM).

object owner The security account with special permissions for an object, usually the creator of the object. Also called the database object owner.

object permission Permission based on a table or view; controls the ability to execute the SELECT, INSERT, UPDATE, and DELETE statements against the table or view.

ODBC *See* Open Database Connectivity (ODBC).

ODBC driver A dynamic link library (DLL) that an ODBC-enabled application, such as Microsoft Excel, can use to access an ODBC data source. Each ODBC driver is specific to a database management system (DBMS), such as SQL Server, Access, and so on.

ODS *See* Open Data Services (ODS).

ODS Library A set of C functions that makes an application a server. ODS Library calls respond to requests from a client in a client/server network. The library also manages the communication and data between the client and the server. ODS Library follows the tabular data stream (TDS) protocol.

ODS log file A text file used to store Open Data Services (ODS) error messages. The default log file for ODS is Srv.log.

OLAP *See* online analytical processing (OLAP).

OLAP client *See* client application.

OLAP Manager A Microsoft Management Console (MMC) snap-in that provides a user interface for managing the OLAP server and for designing and creating multidimensional databases, cubes, and dimensions. *See also* Microsoft Management Console (MMC); snap-in.

OLAP server The server component of OLAP Services that is specifically designed to create and maintain multidimensional data structures and provide multidimensional data in response to client queries. *See also* PivotTable Service.

OLE *See* Object Linking and Embedding (OLE).

OLE Automation controller A programming environment (for example, Visual Basic) that can drive Automation objects.

OLE Automation objects A component object model (COM) object that provides Automation-compatible interfaces.

OLE Automation server An OLE custom component that provides programmable Automation objects.

OLE DB A COM-based application programming interface (API) for accessing data. OLE DB supports accessing any format of data storage (databases, spreadsheets, text files, and so on) for which an OLE DB provider is available.

OLE DB consumer The application software that calls and uses the OLE DB application programming interface (API).

OLE DB for OLAP A section of OLE DB 2.0 and later that addresses multidimensional structures and OLAP. *See also* Microsoft ActiveX Data Objects (Multidimensional) (ADO MD); OLE DB.

OLE DB provider A software component that exposes an OLE DB interface. Each OLE DB provider is specific to a particular storage mechanism (for example, SQL Server databases, Access databases, or Excel spreadsheets).

OLTP *See* online transaction processing (OLTP).

one-to-many relationship A relationship between two tables in which a single row in the first table can be related to one or more rows in the second table, but a row in the second table can be related only to one row in the first table. A typical one-to-many relationship is between the publishers table and the titles table in the pubs sample database, in which each publisher can be related to several titles, but each title can be related to only one publisher.

one-to-one relationship A relationship between two tables in which a single row in the first table can be related only to one row in the second table, and a row in the second table can be related to only one row in the first table. This type of relationship is unusual.

online analytical processing (OLAP) A technology that uses multidimensional structures to provide rapid access to data for analysis. The source data for OLAP is commonly stored in data warehouses in a relational database. *See also* HOLAP (hybrid OLAP); MOLAP (multidimensional OLAP); ROLAP (relational OLAP).

online redo log *See* transaction log.

online transaction processing (OLTP) A database management system representing the state of a particular business function at a specific point in time. An OLTP database is typically characterized by having large numbers of concurrent users actively adding and modifying data.

Open Data Services (ODS) An application programming interface (API) for the server portion of a client/server system that makes data sources or data services appear to a client as a SQL Server. ODS provides a network interface that handles network protocol processes and a set of server routines that provides the application programming interface.

Open Database Connectivity (ODBC) A database-material application programming interface (API) aligned with the American National Standards Institute (ANSI) and International Organization for Standardization (ISO) standards for a database call-level interface (CLI). ODBC supports access to any database for which an ODBC driver is available.

operator A symbol used to perform mathematical computations and/or comparisons between columns or variables. In SQL Server management, an operator is a person designated to receive e-mail or pager notification of alerts and job disposition.

optimistic locking A method of locking in which data is locked when updated rather than when accessed. Optimistic locking supports higher levels of concurrency than pessimistic locking, in which data is locked when accessed.

optimizer *See* query optimizer.

ordered set A set of members returned in some specific order. The ORDER function in a multidimensional expression (MDX) query returns an ordered set. For more information about the ORDER function, see your OLE DB documentation.

outer join A join that includes all rows from the joined tables regardless of whether there is a matching row between the joined tables.

ownership chain When objects have dependencies, their ownership is referred to as an ownership chain. If dependent objects do not have the same owner, it is known as a broken ownership chain. Broken ownership chains complicate permissions, since all owners must grant permissions to all users of the dependent object.

P

package A Data Transformation Services (DTS) object that defines one or more tasks to be executed in a coordinated sequence to import, export, or transform data.

packet errors The number of network errors that SQL Server detects while reading and writing packets of data over the network.

packets received The number of input packets that SQL Server has read.

packets sent The number of output packets that SQL Server has written.

page In a virtual storage system, a fixed-length block of contiguous virtual addresses copied as a unit from memory to disk and back during paging operations. SQL Server allocates database space in pages. In SQL Server, a page is 8 KB in size.

page lock A lock on 8 KB of RAM (one page) that is allocated as a single unit.

page split The process of moving half the rows in a full page to a new page to make room for a new entry.

parallel query execution Execution of a single query across multiple processors.

parameter A placeholder in a query or stored procedure that can be filled in when the query or stored procedure is executed. Parameters allow you to use the same query or stored procedure many times, each time with different values. Parameters can be used for any literal value, and in some databases for column references as well.

parent A member of the next higher level in a hierarchy that is directly related to the current member. The parent value is usually a consolidation of the values of all of its children. For example, in a Time dimension containing the levels Quarter, Month, and Day, Qtr1 is the parent of January. In referential integrity, the term *parent* is sometime used to describe the "one" table in a parent/child, or one-to-many, relationship. *See also* ancestor; child; descendant; sibling.

partition In general computing terms, a formatted volume of a hard disk drive. In OLAP services, one of the storage containers for data and aggregations of a cube. Every cube contains one or more partitions. For a cube with multiple partitions, each partition can be stored separately in a different physical location. Each partition can be based on a different data source. Partitions are not visible to users; the cube appears to be a single object.

partitioning To divide a table into logical subsets based on characteristics of the data. Partitioning is used to improve application performance or reduce the potential for conflicts in multisite update replication. *See also* filtering; horizontal partitioning; vertical partitioning.

pass-through query A query that is passed uninterpreted to an external server for evaluation. The result set returned by a pass-through query can be used in the FROM clause of a query like an ordinary base table.

pass-through statement A SELECT statement that is passed directly to the source database without modification or delay. In PivotTable Service, the PASSTHROUGH option is part of the INSERT INTO statement. *See also* PivotTable Service.

Performance Monitor *See* Windows NT Performance Monitor.

permissions Authorization that enforces database security. SQL Server permissions specify the Transact-SQL statements, views, and stored procedures each user is authorized to use. The ability to assign permissions is determined by each user's status. There are two types of permissions: object permissions and statement permissions.

permissions validation The process of validating the activities that the user is allowed to perform in the SQL Server database.

persistence Permanent, or persistent, storage of objects and data structures that involves converting complex data structures into a format suitable for file storage.

phantom A phenomenon that occurs when a transaction attempts to select a row that does not exist and a second transaction inserts the row before the first transaction finishes. If the row is inserted, the row appears as a phantom to the first transaction, inconsistently appearing and disappearing.

physical name The path where a backup file or database file is located.

physical reads Reads and writes of the data performed by the database page.

pivot To rotate rows to columns, and columns to rows, in a crosstabular data browser. Also refers to choosing dimensions from the set of available dimensions in a multidimensional data structure for display in the rows and columns of a crosstabular structure.

PivotTable Service An in-process desktop OLAP server that communicates with the OLAP server and provides interfaces for use by client applications accessing OLAP data on the server. PivotTable Service is an OLE DB for OLAP provider. It provides online and offline data analysis functionality.

polling interval The option that sets how often the state of the service (SQL Server or SQL Server Agent) is checked.

populate *See* process.

position The current location of processing in a cursor. For example, after an application fetches the first 10 rows from a cursor, it is positioned on the tenth row of the cursor. Database application programming interfaces (APIs) also have functions, such as the ODBC SQLSetPos function, that allow an application to move directly to a specific position in a cursor without performing a fetch.

positioned update An update, insert, or delete performed on a row at the current position of the cursor. The actual change is made in the rows of the base tables used to build the current row in the cursor. Transact-SQL batches, stored procedures, and triggers use the WHERE CURRENT OF clause to perform positioned updates. Applications use application programming interface (API) functions, such as the ODBC SQLSetPos function, to perform positioned updates.

precalculate To compute combinations of data while a cube is being processed. Data is precalculated in anticipation of ad hoc queries to minimize computation and disk access time when a query is submitted. For example, total quantity sold for a year can be precalculated from individual sales transactions during cube processing. *See also* aggregation.

precision The maximum total number of decimal digits that can be stored, both to the left and right of the decimal point.

predicate An expression that returns a value of TRUE, FALSE, or UNKNOWN. Predicates are used in the search condition of WHERE and HAVING clauses of Transact-SQL statements such as SELECT and UPDATE, and in the conditions of program logic statements such as IF and WHILE.

prefix characters Characters that precede each noncharacter field in a bcp native format data file, indicating the length of the field.

prefix length The number of prefix characters preceding each field in a bcp native format data file.

prefix search Full-text query searching for those columns where the specified character-based text, word, or phrase is the prefix. When using a phrase, each word within the phrase is considered to be a prefix. For example, a prefix search specifying the phrase "sport fish" matches "sport fishing," "sportsman fishing supplies," and so on.

primary dimension table A dimension table in a snowflake schema in a data warehouse that is directly related to the fact table. Additional tables that complete the dimension definition are joined to the primary dimension table instead of to the fact table. *See also* dimension table; snowflake schema.

primary domain controller (PDC) A server in a Windows NT domain that maintains the domain's security database and authenticates user login passwords. It also provides a copy of the domain's security database to backup domain controllers (BDCs), which share the user login authentication load.

primary key (PK) The column or combination of columns that uniquely identifies one row from any other row in a table. A primary key (PK) must be nonnull and must have a unique index. A primary key is commonly used for joins with foreign keys (matching nonprimary keys) in other tables.

private data space A structure passed to Open Data Services event handlers that contains information to make and use a connection to a remote database management system.

private dimension A dimension created for and used by a specific cube. Unlike shared dimensions, private dimensions are available only to the cube in which they are created. *See also* shared dimension.

procedure A collection of stored Transact-SQL statements that can be called from one or more locations in program code.

procedure cache A temporary storage location for the current, executing version of a specific stored procedure.

process In a cube, the series of operations that rebuilds the cube's structure, loads data into a multidimensional structure, calculates summaries, and saves the precalculated aggregations. As a verb, to populate a cube with data and aggregations; one of three processing options for a cube. In a dimension, the operation that loads data from a dimension table in a data warehouse into the levels defined for a dimension and rebuilds the structure of the dimension; one of two processing options for a dimension. *See also* incremental update; refresh data.

producer Any process that collects events in a specific event category and sends the data to a SQL Server Profiler queue.

projection The process of extracting data from fewer than all available columns in a table or set of tables.

protocol A set of rules or standards designed to enable computers to connect with one another and exchange information.

provider An OLE DB provider. A provider is an in-process dynamic link library (DLL) that provides access to a database.

proximity search Full-text query searching for those columns in which the specified words are close to one another.

publication A group of articles available for replication as a unit. A publication can contain one or more published tables or stored procedure articles from one user database. Each user database can have one or more publications.

Publication Access List A list of logins that have access to a publication. The default Publication Access List on a server controls access to all publications on that server not having a custom Publication Access List.

publication database A database source of replicated data that contains tables for replication.

publish To make data available for replication.

Publisher A server that makes data available for replication. A Publisher maintains publication databases and sends copies of all changes of the published data to the Distributor.

pubs database A sample database provided with SQL Server. If pubs was not installed with SQL Server, you can install it using the Instpubs.sql script.

pull subscription A type of subscription in which the initiation of data movement is made at the Subscriber. The Subscriber maintains a subscription by requesting, or pulling, data changes from a Publisher. The Distribution Agent is maintained at the Subscriber, thereby reducing the amount of overhead at the Distributor. *See also* push subscription.

push subscription A subscription in which the initiation of data movement is made at the Publisher. The Publisher maintains a subscription by sending, or pushing, the appropriate data changes to one or more Subscribers. The Distribution Agent is maintained at the Distributor. *See also* pull subscription.

Q

query A specific request for data retrieval, modification, or deletion.

query optimizer The SQL Server component responsible for generating the optimum execution plan for a query.

queue In SQL Server Profiler, a temporary holding place for server events to be captured.

R

RAID (redundant array of independent disks) Sometimes referred to as redundant array of inexpensive disks, a system that uses multiple disk drives (an array) to provide performance and reliability. There are six levels describing RAID arrays, 0 through 5. Each level uses a different algorithm to implement fault tolerance.

range query A query that specifies a range of values as part of the search criteria, such as all rows from within a column valued from 10 through 100.

ranking A value indicating the degree of matching (0 is a very low degree of matching and 1000 is the highest degree of matching) of each value that is determined to match a full-text query.

RDBMS *See* relational database management system (RDBMS).

read-only replica A publication that cannot be updated or changed by the Subscriber.

read-only snapshot *See* read-only replica.

real data type A SQL Server system data type that has 7-digit precision. The approximate range of values is from 3.4E − 38 through 3.4E + 38. Storage size is 4 bytes.

record A group of related fields (columns) of information treated as a unit. A record is more commonly called a row in a SQL database.

recordset The ADO object used to contain a result set. It also exhibits cursor behavior depending on the recordset properties set by an application. ADO recordsets are mapped to OLE DB rowsets.

recovery *See* automatic recovery.

recovery interval The interval that determines checkpoint frequency by specifying the amount of time it should take the system to recover.

redo log file *See* backup file.

referential integrity (RI) An integrity mechanism that ensures that vital data in a database, such as the unique identifier for a given piece of data, remains accurate and usable as the database changes. Referential integrity involves managing corresponding data values between tables when the foreign key of a table contains the same values as the primary key of another table.

reflexive relationship A relationship from a column or combination of columns in a table to other columns in that same table. A reflexive relationship is used to compare rows within the same table. In queries, this is called a self-join.

refresh data The series of operations that clears data from a cube, loads the cube with new data from the data warehouse, and calculates aggregations. Refresh data is used when a cube's underlying data in the data warehouse changes but the cube's structure and aggregation definitions remain the same. One of three processing options for a cube. *See also* incremental update; process.

registry A database repository that contains information about a computer's configuration. It is organized hierarchically and comprises subtrees and their keys, hives, and value entries.

relational data model A method of organizing data into two-dimensional tables made up of rows and columns. The model is based on the mathematical theory of relations, a part of set theory.

relational database A collection of information organized in tables, each of which models a class of objects of interest to the organization (for example, Customers, Parts, Suppliers). Each column in a table models an attribute of the object modeled by the table (for example, LastName, Price, Color). Each row in a table represents one entity in the class of objects modeled by the table (for example, the customer named John Smith or the part numbered 1346). Queries can use data from one table to find related data in other tables.

relational database management system (RDBMS) A system that organizes data into related rows and columns. SQL Server is a relational database management system.

relational OLAP *See* ROLAP (relational OLAP).

relationship A link between tables that references the primary key in one table to a foreign key in another table. The relationship line is represented in a database diagram by a solid line if referential integrity between the tables is enforced, or a dashed line if referential integrity is not enforced for INSERT and UPDATE transactions. The endpoints of a relationship line show a primary key symbol to denote a primary-key-to-foreign-key relationship or an infinity symbol to denote the foreign key side of a one-to-many relationship.

remote data Data stored on a computer other than the computer running SQL Server and accessed by either establishing a linked server or using the ad hoc connector name.

remote Distributor A server configured as a Distributor but on a separate computer from the Publisher. In this configuration, the publication and distribution databases reside on separate computers. *See also* local Distributor.

remote login identification The login identification (login ID) assigned to a user for accessing remote procedures on a remote server. This login ID can be the same as the user's local login ID. A remote login ID can have up to 128 characters. The characters can be alphanumeric; however, the first character must be a letter (for example, CHRIS or TELLER8).

remote procedure call (RPC) In general networking terms, a call that uses IPC mechanisms such as named pipes to establish communications between the client and the server. In SQL Server terms, the invocation of a stored procedure on a remote server from a procedure on a server.

remote server A SQL Server on the network that can be accessed through a user's local server. SQL Server Setup can install, upgrade, or configure remote servers.

remote stored procedure A collection of SQL statements and optional control-of-flow statements stored under a name on a remote server. Remote stored procedures can be called by clients or by SQL Server.

remote stored procedure event An Open Data Services event that occurs when a client or server calls a remote stored procedure.

remote table A table external to the local SQL Server data source.

replica A copy of objects in a publication received when a server subscribes to the publication.

replication Duplication of table schema and data or stored procedure definitions and calls from a source database to a destination database, usually on separate servers.

Replication Monitor A graphical tool in SQL Server Enterprise Manager used to simplify replication monitoring and troubleshooting.

report generator A software component that produces formatted output from a database.

repository The storage container for the metadata managed by OLAP Services. Metadata is stored in tables in a relational database and is used to define the parameters and properties of OLAP server objects. *See also* metadata; Microsoft Repository.

restore To restore an entire database and transaction log, database file(s), or a transaction log from a backup.

restricted publication In replication, a security status. A publication marked Restricted cannot be subscribed to by any registered Subscriber. *See also* unrestricted publication.

results completion message A message sent to a client with srv_senddone indicating that one set of results has been sent to the client.

result set The set of rows returned from a SELECT statement. The format of the rows in the result set is defined by the column-list of the SELECT statement.

retention In replication, the period of time for which a transaction is maintained in the distribution database. In backup media, a specified time period during which backups cannot be overwritten.

return parameters Output parameters returned by an ODS Library function to the client.

reusable bookmark A bookmark that can be consumed from a rowset for a given table and used on a different rowset of the same table to position on a corresponding row.

revoke To remove a previously granted or denied permission from a user account in the current database. The user account may then acquire the permission through membership in groups or roles.

RI *See* referential integrity (RI).

right outer join A type of outer join in which all rows in the second-named table (the right table, the one that appears rightmost in the JOIN clause) are included. Unmatched rows in the left table are not included.

ROLAP (relational OLAP) A storage mode that uses tables in a relational database to store multidimensional structures. *See also* HOLAP (hybrid OLAP); MOLAP (multidimensional OLAP).

role An administrative unit within SQL Server that contains SQL Server logins, Windows NT logins, groups, or other roles. *See also* group; SQL Server role.

roll back To remove partially completed transactions after a database or other system failure. *See also* commit; roll forward.

roll forward To recover from disasters, such as media failure, by reading the transaction log and reapplying all readable and complete transactions. *See also* roll back.

root directory *See* installation path.

rotate *See* pivot.

row A data structure that is a collection of elements (columns), each with its own name and type. A row can be accessed as a collective unit of elements, or the elements can be accessed individually. A row is equivalent to a record. *See also* column.

row aggregate A function (SUM, AVG, MAX, MIN, or COUNT) used on a group or aggregate of data.

row aggregate function A function that generates summary values that appear as additional rows in the query results (unlike aggregate function results that appear as new columns). A row aggregate function allows you to see detail and summary rows in one set of results. Row aggregate functions (SUM, AVG, MIN, MAX, and COUNT) are used in a SELECT statement with the COMPUTE clause.

row-level locking *See* row lock.

row lock A lock on a single row in a table.

rowset The OLE DB object used to contain a result set. It also exhibits cursor behavior depending on the rowset properties set by an application.

rule A database object that is bound to a column or user-defined data type that specifies what data can be entered in that column. Every time a user enters or modifies a value (with an INSERT or UPDATE statement), SQL Server checks it against the most recent rule bound to the specified column—for example, for limit checking or list checking. Data entered before the creation and binding of a rule is not checked. Rules are supported primarily for backward compatibility.

S

sa *See* system administrator.

sample data Artificially generated data presented instead of actual data when a cube is queried before it has been processed. Sample data enables you to view the effects of structural changes while modifying a cube.

savepoint A marker that the user includes in a user-defined transaction. When transactions are rolled back, they can be rolled back only to the savepoint.

scalability A characteristic of a system that provides increased performance with the addition of resources. SQL Server is scalable. For example, it can use memory or additional processors to accommodate more user connections.

scalar aggregate A function applied to all of the rows in a table (producing a single value per function). An aggregate function in the select list with no GROUP BY clause applies to the whole table and is an example of a scalar.

scalar function A function that operates on a single value and then returns a single value. Scalar functions can be used wherever an expression is valid.

scalar subquery A SELECT statement that evaluates to a single value for each result set row. Scalar subqueries can be used in place of expressions if they return a single value.

scheduled backup An automatic backup accomplished by SQL Server Agent when defined and scheduled as a job.

scheduled table refresh *See* snapshot replication.

schema A description of a database generated by the data definition language (DDL) of the database management system (DBMS). In OLAP Services, a schema is a description of multidimensional objects such as cubes, dimensions, and so forth.

schema script *See* table schema script.

script A collection of Transact-SQL statements used to perform an operation. Transact-SQL scripts are stored as files, usually with the .SQL extension.

scroll The ability to move around with a cursor in directions other than forward-only. Users can move up and down with the cursor.

search condition In a WHERE or HAVING clause, conditions to be met for the specified action to occur on the specified data.

Security Identifier (SID) A unique value that identifies a user who is logged on to the security system. Security IDs (SIDs) can identify either one user or a group of users.

Security Principal An entity (for example, a user, group, or computer) that has been assigned an ID for security purposes.

segment In SQL 7, segments are replaced by filegroups. *See also* filegroup.

SELECT The Transact-SQL statement used to request a selection, projection, join, query, and so on from a SQL Server database.

select list The information (columns, expressions, and so on) to return from the specified tables in a query.

Select query A query that returns rows into a result set from one or more tables. A Select query can contain specifications for those columns to return, the rows to select, the order to put the rows in, and how to group (summarize) information.

selection An extraction of data from a subset of all rows of a table or set of tables.

self-join A join that compares rows within the same table. In database diagrams, a self-join is called a reflexive relationship.

sensitive cursor A cursor that can reflect data modifications made to underlying data by other users while the cursor is open. Updates, deletes, and inserts made by other users are reflected in the sensitive cursor. Sensitive cursors are typically used in Transact-SQL batches, stored procedures, and triggers by omitting the INSENSITIVE keyword on the DECLARE CURSOR statement.

sequence *See* identity column.

sequential file A file whose records are arranged in the order in which they are placed in the file.

serializable A transaction isolation level that ensures a database changes from one predictable state to another. If multiple concurrent transactions can be executed serially, and the results are the same, the transactions are considered serializable.

server A computer on a local area network (LAN) that controls access to resources, such as files, printers, and communication devices. *See also* OLAP server.

server cursor A cursor that is implemented on the server. The cursor itself is built at the server, and only the rows fetched by an application are sent to the client.

server name The name a client uses to identify a server running SQL Server. The server names on a client are managed by using the Client Network Utility. It is also the name used by one SQL Server when making a remote stored procedure call to another SQL Server.

server process ID A unique integer assigned to every server process, including user connections.

server state polling The polling interval, used to set how often the state of the service is checked.

service A process that performs a specific system function and often provides an application programming interface (API) for other processes to call. It runs independently on a computer running Windows NT, unlike a program that requires a logged-on user to start or stop the program.

session-level setting A setting that applies to the current connection. Settings can apply to the entire server, the database, or the individual user connection.

setup initialization file A text file, using the Windows .INI file format, that stores configuration information allowing SQL Server to be installed without a user having to be present to respond to prompts from the Setup program.

severity level number The severity level of an error. Valid levels are from 1 through 25. Only the system administrator can add a message with a severity level from 19 through 25.

shared dimension A dimension created within a database that can be used by any cube in the database. *See also* private dimension.

Shared Global Allocation Map (SGAM) Pages that record what extents are currently used as mixed extents and have at least one unused page. Each SGAM covers 64,000 extents, or nearly 4 GB of data. The SGAM has one bit for each extent in the interval it covers. If the bit is 1, the extent is being used as a mixed extent and has free pages; if the bit is 0, the extent is not being used as a mixed extent, or it is a mixed extent whose pages are all in use.

shared lock A lock created by nonupdate (read) operations. Other users can read the data concurrently, but no transaction can acquire an exclusive lock on the data until all of the shared locks have been released.

showplan A report showing the execution plan for a SQL statement. SET SHOWPLAN_TEXT and SET SHOWPLAN_ALL produce textual showplan output. SQL Server Query Analyzer and SQL Server Enterprise Manager can display showplan information as a graphical tree.

sibling A member in a dimension hierarchy that is a child of the same parent as a specified member. For example, in a Time dimension with Year and Month levels, the members January 1997 and February 1997 are siblings. *See also* ancestor; child; descendant; parent.

single-user mode A startup mode that restricts connections. Only a single user can connect, and the CHECKPOINT mechanism (which guarantees that completed transactions are regularly written from the disk cache to the database device) is not started.

slice A subset of the data in a cube, specified by limiting one or more dimensions by members of the dimension. For example, facts for a particular year constitute a slice of multiyear data.

smalldatetime data type A SQL Server system data type that holds dates and times of day less precisely than datetime. Storage size is 4 bytes, consisting of one small integer for the number of days after January 1, 1900, and one small integer for the number of minutes past

midnight. Dates range from January 1, 1900, through June 6, 2079, with accuracy to the minute.

smallint data type A SQL Server system data type that holds whole numbers from +32,767 through –32,768, inclusive. Storage size is 2 bytes.

smallmoney data type A SQL Server system data type that stores monetary values from +214,748.3647 through –214,748.3648 with accuracy to a ten-thousandth of a monetary unit. Storage size is 4 bytes. When smallmoney values are displayed, they are rounded up two places.

SMP *See* symmetric multiprocessor.

snap-in A program that runs within Microsoft Management Console (MMC) and that provides specific added functionality. The OLAP Manager is a snap-in. *See also* Microsoft Management Console (MMC); OLAP Manager.

Snapshot Agent The replication component that prepares snapshot files of published tables and stored procedures, stores the files on the Distributor, and records information about synchronization status in the distribution database.

snapshot cursor *See* static cursor.

snapshot replication A type of replication that takes a snapshot of current data in a publication at a Publisher and replaces the entire replica at a Subscriber on a periodic basis, in contrast to publishing changes when they occur. *See also* merge replication; transactional replication.

snowflake schema An extension of a star schema such that one or more dimensions are defined by multiple tables. In a snowflake schema, only primary dimension tables are joined to the fact table. Additional dimension tables are joined to primary dimension tables. *See also* star schema.

sort order A set of rules that determines how SQL Server compares, collates, and presents character data in response to database queries. Sort order is a serverwide setting that affects how strings are compared.

source database *See* publication database.

sparsity The relative percentage of a multidimensional structure's cells that do not contain data. OLAP Services stores only cells that contain data. A sparse cube requires less storage than a dense cube of identical structure design. *See also* data explosion; density.

SPID *See* server process ID.

SQL *See* structured query language (SQL).

SQL-92 The latest version of the standard for SQL, published in 1992. The international standard is ISO/IEC 9075:1992 Database Language SQL. The American National Standards Institute (ANSI) also published a corresponding standard (Data Language SQL X3.135-1192), so SQL-92 is sometimes referred to as ANSI SQL in the United States.

SQL-DMF SQL Distributed Management Framework. An integrated framework of objects, services, and components used to manage SQL Server. SQL-DMF lessens the need for user-attended maintenance tasks, such as database backup and alert notification, by providing services that interact directly with SQL Server. At its most basic level, SQL-DMF provides direct access to the SQL Server engine and services from the command line through Transact-SQL. The second tier of the framework is a set of distributed management objects (DMOs) that provides an object interface to the SQL Server engine and services. The top level of the framework is a graphical administration tool, SQL Server Enterprise Manager, which provides an easy way to manage a multiserver environment. The framework also provides services for replication, scheduling, and alerting.

SQL Executive *See* SQL Server Agent.

SQL Mail A component of SQL Server that includes extended stored procedures and allows SQL Server to send and receive mail messages through the built-in Windows NT mail application programming interface (MAPI). A mail message can consist of short text strings, the output from a query, or an attached file.

SQL script *See* script.

SQL Server Agent A service used to create and manage local or multiserver jobs, alerts, and operators. Job schedules are defined in the Job Properties dialog box. SQL Server Agent communicates with SQL Server to execute the job according to the job's schedule.

SQL Server Authentication A login security mode that allows users to connect to SQL Server using SQL Server logins. SQL Server performs the authentication.

SQL Server Books Online The SQL Server online documentation set. SQL Server Books Online is an installation option presented by the Setup program. If you select this option, files are copied to your hard disk, and the SQL Server Books Online icon is added to the Microsoft SQL Server 7.0 program group.

SQL Server Client Network Utility A utility whose most basic purpose is to change the default client Net-Library. The SQL Server Client Network Utility is also used for managing the client configuration for DB-Library, Net-Libraries, and custom-defined network connections.

SQL Server Enterprise Manager A graphical MMC snap-in that allows for easy, enterprise-wide configuration and management of SQL Server and SQL Server objects. You can also use SQL Server Enterprise Manager to manage logins, permissions, and users; create scripts; manage databases; back up databases and transaction logs; and manage tables, views, stored procedures, triggers, indexes, rules, defaults, and user-defined data types.

SQL Server Event Forwarding Server *See* forwarding server.

SQL Server login An account stored in SQL Server that allows users to connect to the SQL Server.

SQL Server Performance Monitor integration The integration of Windows NT Performance Monitor with SQL Server, providing up-to-the-minute activity and performance statistics.

SQL Server Profiler A SQL Server tool that captures a continuous record of server activity in real time. SQL Server Profiler can monitor many different server events and event categories, filter those events with user-specified criteria, and output a trace to the screen, a file, or another SQL Server.

SQL Server Query Analyzer A SQL Server utility that allows you to enter Transact-SQL statements and stored procedures in a graphical user interface. SQL Server Query Analyzer also provides capability for graphically analyzing queries.

SQL Server role A named set of security accounts. A SQL Server role can contain Windows NT users, Windows NT groups, SQL Server users, or other SQL Server roles from the same database.

SQL Server Service Manager A SQL Server utility that provides a graphical way to start, pause, and stop the MS DTC, MSSQLServer, and SQLServerAgent services. SQL Server is integrated with the service control management of Windows NT, so you can start, pause, and stop SQL Server, MS DTC, and SQLServer-Agent from the Services application in Control Panel or from the Server Manager application.

SQL Server user A security account that maps to a SQL Server login and controls the permissions on activities performed in a database.

SQL statement A SQL or Transact-SQL statement, such as SELECT or DELETE, that performs some action on data.

SQL Transfer Manager *See* Data Transformation Services (DTS).

standalone installation An installation of SQL Server on a computer that is not connected to a network. A standalone installation may be used to install SQL Server on a computer that will soon be but is not yet connected to a network (for example, one that does not yet have a network adapter card installed.) Or a standalone installation might be performed on a computer that is intended as a development system that will have no need for network connections.

standard security SQL Server 7 no longer uses standard security, although SQL Server may authenticate users under Mixed Mode.

star join A join between a fact table (typically a large fact table) and at least two dimension tables. The fact table is joined with each dimension table on a dimension key. SQL Server considers special index manipulation strategies on these queries to minimize access to the fact table.

An example of a schema participating in a star join query could be a sales table, the fact table (with millions of rows), a product table, with the description of several hundred products, and a store table with several dozen store names. (In this example, the product and store tables are dimension tables). A query for selecting sales data for a small set of stores and a subset of products restricted by attributes not present in the sales database is an ideal candidate for the star join query optimization.

star schema A relational database structure in which data is maintained in a single fact table at the center of the schema with additional dimension data stored in dimension tables. Each dimension table is directly related to the fact table by a key column. *See also* snowflake schema.

statement block *See* blocks.

statement permission Permission that controls the execution of Transact-SQL statements that create database objects or perform certain administrative tasks. Can be granted, revoked, or denied.

static cursor A cursor that shows the result set exactly as it was at the time the cursor was opened. Static cursors do not reflect updates, deletes, or inserts made to underlying data while the cursor is open. Sometimes called a snapshot cursor.

static SQL statement In Embedded SQL for C, a SQL statement that is built at the time the application is compiled. It is created as a stored procedure when the application is compiled, and the stored procedure is executed when the application is run.

statistics refresh The interval, in minutes and seconds, for refreshing SQL server statistics information. The default is 30 seconds.

status code A 4-byte integer that indicates the status of a result set returned to the client. The status code is sent to the client by using srv_senddone.

step object A Data Transformation Services (DTS) object that coordinates the flow of control and execution of tasks in a DTS package. A task that does not have an associated step object is never executed. *See also* data transformation; task object.

store-and-forward database *See* distribution database.

stored procedure A precompiled collection of Transact-SQL statements and optional control-of-flow statements stored under a name and processed as a unit. Stored procedures are stored within a database, can be executed with one call from an application, and allow user-declared variables, conditional execution, and other powerful programming features. SQL Server–supplied stored procedures are called system stored procedures. *See also* system stored procedure.

string functions Functions that perform operations on binary data, character strings, or expressions. Built-in string functions return values commonly needed for operations on character data.

structured query language (SQL) A database query and programming language originally developed by IBM for mainframe computers. It is widely used for accessing data and for querying, updating, and managing relational database systems. There is now an ANSI-standard SQL definition for all computer systems.

structured storage file *See* COM-structured storage file.

subquery A SELECT statement nested inside another SELECT, INSERT, UPDATE, or DELETE statement, or inside another subquery.

subscribe To agree to receive a publication. A destination database on a Subscriber subscribes to replicated data from a publication database on a Publisher.

Subscriber A server that receives copies of published data.

subscription database The database that receives tables and data replicated from a publication database.

surrogate key A unique identifier for a row within a database table. A surrogate, or candidate, key can be made up of one or more columns. By definition, every table must have at least one surrogate key (in which case it becomes the primary key for a table automatically). However, it is possible for a table to have more than one surrogate key (in which case one of them must be designated as the primary key). Any surrogate key that is not the primary key is called the alternate key.

symmetric multiprocessor A computer with more than one processor, where each processor can access memory, handle interrupts, and access I/O just like every other processor in the computer.

synchronization The process of maintaining the same schema and data in a publication at a Publisher and in the replica of a publication at a Subscriber. *See also* initial snapshot.

synchronous transaction A replication feature that allows a Subscriber to modify replicated data and send it to the Publisher by using two-phase commit. Synchronous transactions can be performed using either transactional replication or snapshot replication.

sysname A system-supplied user-defined data type that is a synonym for nvarchar(128) and is used to reference database object names.

system administrator The person responsible for the overall administration of a SQL Server. The system administrator (sa) login is the only login authorized to perform all functions in SQL Server. Certain critical administrative functions can be performed only by the sa login. Members of the sysadmin fixed server role operate outside the protection system (SQL Server does not check permission for these members). The members are also treated as the owner of whatever database they are using.

system catalog A collection of system tables found only in the master database. These tables describe server information such as logins and configuration options.

system databases Four databases that are provided on a newly installed SQL Server installation:

- The master database, which controls user databases and the operation of SQL Server
- The tempdb database, used for temporary tables
- The model database, used as a template for creating user databases
- The msdb database, used by the SQL Server Agent to manage jobs and alerts

In addition, you can also install sample databases, pubs and Northwind, which are provided as learning tools and are the basis for most of the examples in the SQL Server documentation. Although installed by the Setup program, neither pubs nor Northwind are system databases, since SQL Server does not require them to operate.

system functions Functions that return specific information from the SQL Server installation. System functions allow access to database or server information from within an expression, such as from a WHERE clause or a SELECT statement.

system stored procedure A SQL Server–supplied, precompiled collection of Transact-SQL statements. System stored procedures are provided as shortcuts for retrieving information from system tables or as mechanisms for accomplishing database administration and other tasks that involve updating system tables. The names of all system stored procedures begin with sp_. System stored procedures are located in the master database and are owned by the system administrator, but many of them can be run from any database. If a system stored procedure is executed in a database other than master, it operates on the system tables in the database from which it is executed. You can write stored procedures (called user-defined stored procedures), which can be executed from any database.

system tables Tables that store SQL Server configuration information and definitions of all of the objects, users, and permissions in SQL Server databases. Server-level configuration information is stored in system tables found only in the master database. Every database contains system tables defining the users, objects, and permissions contained by the database.

The master database and its system tables are created during SQL Server Setup. System tables in a user database are created automatically when the database is created.

SQL Server contains system stored procedures to report and manage the information in system tables. Users should use these system stored procedures rather than accessing the system tables directly. Users should not directly update any system table.

T

table An object in a database that stores data as a collection of rows and columns.

table creation script *See* table schema script.

table data file A file containing a snapshot of the data of a published table used during synchronization as the source of data inserted into the destination table. The filename extension of a data snapshot is .BCP. The file is stored in the working folder of the distribution database, a subfolder in \Mssql7\Repldata by default. *See also* table schema script.

table-level constraint A constraint that allows various forms of data integrity to be defined on one column (column-level constraint) or on several columns (table-level constraint) when the table is defined or altered. Constraints support domain integrity, entity integrity, and referential integrity, as well as user-defined integrity.

table lock A lock on a table, including all data and indexes.

table scan The means by which SQL Server searches a table sequentially without using an index. SQL Server starts at the beginning of the table and reads every row in the table to find the rows that meet the search criteria of the query.

table schema script A script containing the schema of a published table used during synchronization to create the destination table. The filename extension of a schema script is .SCH. The file is stored in the working folder of the distribution database, a subfolder in \Mssql7\Repldata by default. *See also* table data file.

tabular data stream (TDS) The SQL Server internal client/server data transfer protocol. TDS allows client and server products to communicate regardless of operating system platform, server release, or network transport.

tape backup A backup operation to any tape device supported by Windows NT. If you are creating a tape backup file, you must first install the tape device by using Windows NT. The tape device must be physically attached to the SQL Server you are backing up.

task *See* job.

task object A Data Transformation Services (DTS) object that defines pieces of work to be performed as part of the data transformation process. For example, a task can execute a SQL statement or move and transform heterogeneous data from an OLE DB source to an OLE DB destination using the DTS data pump. *See also* data transformation; step object.

taskpad A graphical way of presenting actions that can be performed on a selected item in the console tree. In MMC, a taskpad is implemented as a view on the selected item in the console tree, and that view is represented as a DHTML page in the details pane.

TDS *See* tabular data stream (TDS).

tempdb database The database that provides a storage area for temporary tables, temporary stored procedures, and other temporary working storage needs. No special permissions are required to use tempdb (that is, to create temporary tables or to execute commands that may require storage space in the tempdb database). All temporary tables are stored in tempdb, regardless of what database the user who creates them is using.

temporary stored procedure A procedure placed in the temporary database, tempdb, and erased at the end of the session. A temporary stored procedure is created by prefacing the procedure name (in the CREATE statement) with a number sign—for example,

```
CREATE PROCEDURE #author_sel AS
SELECT * FROM authors
```

The first 13 characters of a temporary stored procedure name (excluding the number sign) must be unique in tempdb. Because all temporary objects belong to the tempdb database, you can create a temporary stored procedure with the same name as a procedure already in another database.

temporary table A table placed in the temporary database, tempdb, and erased at the end of the session. A temporary table is created by prefacing the table name (in the CREATE statement) with a number sign—for example,

```
CREATE TABLE #authors (au_id Exchar (11))
```

The first 13 characters of a temporary table name (excluding the number sign) must be unique in tempdb. Because all temporary objects belong to the tempdb database, you can create a temporary table with the same name as a table already in another database.

text data type A SQL Server system data type specifying variable-length columns that can hold 2,147,483,647 characters. The text data type cannot be used for variables or parameters in stored procedures.

theta join A join based on a comparison of scalar values (=, > , >= , < , <= , < >, !<, !>).

thread A mechanism that allows one or more paths of execution through the same instance of an application. Each device requires one thread, and each remote site requires two threads. SQL Server uses the native thread services of Windows NT. There are separate threads for each network, a separate thread for database checkpoints, and a pool of threads for all users.

tight consistency A replication model that guarantees that all copies will be identical to the original. It is usually implemented using two-phase commit, and it requires a high-speed LAN. It also reduces database availability and is less scalable in its implementation than loose consistency.

Time dimension A dimension that breaks time down into levels such as Year, Quarter, Month, and Day. In OLAP Services, a special type of dimension created from a date/time column.

timestamp data type A SQL Server system data type that is a monotonically increasing counter whose values are always unique within a database. A timestamp is the date and time the data was last modified.

tinyint data type A SQL Server system data type that holds whole numbers from 0 through 255, inclusive. Storage size is 1 byte.

tool A SQL Server application with a graphical user interface used to perform common tasks.

total errors The number of errors that SQL Server detected while reading and writing.

total reads The number of disk reads made by SQL Server.

total writes The number of disk writes made by SQL Server.

trace file A file used by SQL Server Profiler to record monitored events.

transaction A group of database operations combined into a logical unit of work that is either wholly committed or rolled back. A transaction is atomic, consistent, isolated, and durable.

transactional replication A type of replication that marks selected transactions in the Publisher's database transaction log for replication and then distributes them asynchronously to Subscribers as incremental changes, while maintaining transactional consistency. *See also* merge replication; snapshot replication.

transaction log A database file in which all changes to the database are recorded. It is used by SQL Server during automatic recovery.

transaction processing A processing method in which transactions are executed immediately after they are received by the system.

transaction rollback Rollback of a user-specified transaction to the last savepoint inside a transaction or to the beginning of a transaction.

Transact-SQL The standard language for communicating between applications and SQL Server. The Transact-SQL language is an enhancement to structured query language (SQL), the ANSI-standard relational database language. It provides a comprehensive language for defining tables; for inserting, updating, or deleting information stored in tables; and for controlling access to data in those tables. Extensions such as stored procedures make Transact-SQL a full programming language.

Transact-SQL cursor A server cursor defined by using the Transact-SQL DECLARE CURSOR syntax. Transact-SQL cursors are intended for use in Transact-SQL batches, stored procedures, and triggers.

transformation *See* data transformation.

trigger A stored procedure that executes automatically when data in a specified table is modified. Triggers are often created to enforce referential integrity or consistency among logically related data in different tables.

trusted connection An authenticated connection between a client and a server. Windows NT Authentication requires network protocols that support trusted connections.

T-SQL *See* Transact-SQL.

tuple An ordered collection of members from different dimensions. For example, (Boston, [1995]) is a tuple formed by members of two dimensions: geography and time. A single member is a degenerated case of a tuple and can be used as an expression without the parentheses. For more information about tuples, see your OLE DB documentation. *See also* axis.

two-phase commit A protocol that ensures that transactions that apply to more than one server are completed on all servers or on none.

type conversion function A function that transforms expressions from one data type into another.

U

unattended installation A process that allows you to install SQL Server 7 without having to respond to prompts for information from the Setup program. Instead, you create an initialization file, save the initialization file on a storage device accessible to the computer that will be set up, and start Setup using some required options. During Setup, the configuration parameters are read from the initialization file.

UNC *See* universal naming convention (UNC).

underlying object An object (a table or another view) from which a view is derived. A view can have more than one underlying object.

underlying table A table from which a view is derived. A view can have more than one underlying table or underlying view. Also called a base table.

unenforced relationship A link between tables that references the primary key in one table to a foreign key in another table, and which does not check the referential integrity during INSERT and UPDATE transactions. An unenforced relationship is represented in a database diagram by a dashed line.

unhandled event forwarding server *See* forwarding server.

Unicode A set of letters, numbers, and symbols that SQL Server recognizes in the nchar, nvarchar, and ntext data types. It is related to but separate from character sets. Unicode has more than 65,000 possible values compared to a character set's 256, and takes twice as much space to store. Unicode includes characters for most languages.

Unicode collation A sort order for Unicode data. It is a set of rules that determines how SQL Server compares, collates, and presents Unicode data in response to database queries.

Unicode format Data stored in a bulk copy data file using Unicode characters.

Union query A query that combines two tables by performing the equivalent of appending one table to the other.

UNIQUE constraints Constraints that enforce entity integrity on a nonprimary key. UNIQUE constraints ensure that no duplicate values are entered and that an index is created to enhance performance.

uniqueidentifier data type A data type containing a unique identification number stored as a 16-byte binary string, used for storing a globally unique identifier (GUID).

unique index An index in which no two rows are permitted to have the same index value, thus prohibiting duplicate index or key values. The system checks for duplicate key values when the index is created and checks each time data is added with an INSERT or UPDATE statement.

universal naming convention (UNC) A naming convention that consists of the following format:

\\servername\sharename\path\file_name

unrestricted publication In replication, a security status. A publication marked Unrestricted (the default) can be subscribed to by any registered Subscriber. *See also* restricted publication.

update An addition, deletion, or change to data.

update lock A lock placed on resources (such as rows, pages, or tables) that can be updated. Update locks are used to prevent a common form of deadlock that occurs when multiple sessions are locking resources and are potentially updating them later.

Update query A query that changes the column values of one or more rows in a table.

update replication Any replication technology that allows you to update replicated data. *See also* merge replication; synchronous transaction.

update statistics A process that recalculates information about the distribution of key values in specified indexes. These statistics are used by the query optimizer to determine the most efficient way to execute a query.

user (account) Used to control permissions for activities performed in a database. User accounts are created in a database and assigned to a login ID for allowing a user to access that database. The abilities a user has within a database depend on the permissions granted to the user account and on the permissions granted to any roles of which the user account is a member. A user account name can have up to 128 characters and must be unique within the database. The characters can be alphanumeric, but the first character must be a letter, the number sign (#), or an underscore (_) (for example, #CHRIS or USER8). A user account is also called a username or a user ID.

user databases A database created by a user. Each user database is created with a copy of the tables from the model database. The system tables in a user database are copied from the model database automatically when a database is created.

user-defined data type A data type, based on a system-supplied SQL Server data type, created by the user for custom data storage. Rules and defaults can be bound to user-defined data types (but not to system data types). *See also* base data type.

user-defined event A server process created internally by Open Data Services and not as the result of a client action. The srv_define_event function creates a user-defined event.

username A name known to a database and assigned to a login ID for the purpose of allowing a user to access that database. The abilities a user has within a database depend on the permissions granted to the username as well as to any groups of which the username is a member. A username can have up to 128 characters and must be unique within the database. The characters can be alphanumeric, but the first character must be a letter or the symbols # or _ (for example, #CHRIS or USER8).

utility A SQL Server application run from a command prompt to perform common tasks.

V

value expression A multidimensional expression (MDX) that returns a value. Value expressions can operate on sets, tuples, members, levels, numbers, or strings. For example, set value expressions operate on member, tuple, and set elements to yield other sets. For more information about MDX, see your OLE DB documentation.

varbinary data type A SQL Server system data type that holds up to 8000 bytes of variable-length binary data.

varchar data type A SQL Server system data type that holds any combination of up to 8000 letters, symbols, and numbers.

variables Defined entities that are assigned values. A local variable is defined with a DECLARE @localvariable statement and assigned an initial value within the statement batch where it is declared with either a SELECT or SET @localvariable statement.

vector aggregate Functions applied to all rows that have the same value in a specified column or expression by using the GROUP BY clause and, optionally, the HAVING clause (producing a value for each group per function).

vertical filtering To create an article that replicates only selected columns from the base table. Subscribers receive only the subset of vertically filtered data. The primary key column(s) in a table cannot be filtered out of an article in a transactional publication. You can use vertical filtering to partition your base table vertically. *See also* horizontal filtering; vertical partitioning.

vertical partitioning To segment a single table into multiple tables based on selected columns. Each of the multiple tables has the same number of rows but fewer columns. *See also* horizontal filtering; vertical filtering.

view An alternate way of looking at data from one or more tables in the database. A view is a virtual table, usually created as a subset of columns from one or more tables, which is expressed as a SELECT statement. Depending on the definition, data in base tables can be modified through views.

virtual cube A logical cube composed of dimensions and measures of one or more physical cubes. Virtual cubes are similar to views in a relational database. Virtual cubes combine data from the underlying physical cubes and require no additional data storage.

virtual dimension A logical dimension based on the properties of members of a physical dimension. Members of a virtual dimension are derived from the values of one of the properties of a member of the physical dimension. For example, a virtual dimension Color could be derived from a product dimension containing member properties Color, Size, and Style; it could contain members Blue, Red, and Green, which are values for the property Color. *See also* dimension; member; member property.

virtual log file A segment of a transaction log file. Each transaction log file is divided logically into virtual log files. Virtual log files are the unit of truncation for the transaction log. When a virtual log file no longer contains log records for active transactions, it can be truncated and the space becomes available to log new transactions.

W

wildcard characters Characters, including underscore (_), percent (%), and brackets ([ ]), used with the LIKE keyword for pattern matching.

Windows Distributed interNet Applications Architecture (Windows DNA) The all-encompassing application architecture used by Microsoft Corporation.

Windows NT Authentication A login security mode that allows users to connect to SQL Server through a Windows NT user account.

Windows NT Event Viewer A Windows NT application that allows you to view events, filter certain events, and retain event logs.

Windows NT File System (NTFS) An advanced file system designed for use specifically within the Windows NT operating system. It supports file system recovery, extremely large storage media, long filenames, and various features for the Portable Operating System Interface for Unix (POSIX) subsystem. It also supports object-oriented applications by treating all files as objects with user-defined and system-defined attributes.

Windows NT Performance Monitor A Windows NT utility that provides a way for system administrators to monitor the performance of SQL Server. SQL Server statistics include lock performance, current size of transaction logs, user connections, and server performance. You can even set alerts to initiate a specified action when a specified threshold is reached.

Windows NT user A security account that maps to a Windows NT login and controls permissions on activities performed in a database.

wizard A series of pages, displayed in a secondary window, that automates tasks. A wizard is generally used to help you perform complex or infrequent tasks.

word generation The process of determining other forms of the word(s) specified. The Microsoft Search Service currently implements inflectional word generation. For example, if the word *swim* is specified, SQL Server also searches for *swim*, *swam*, and *swimming*.

write-ahead log A transaction logging method in which the log is always written prior to the data.

write-back The facility that enables users to apply changes to data in a cube. User-initiated changes to cube data are logged to a separate partition table associated with the cube and applied automatically as cube data is viewed. To the user it appears as if the data in the cube has changed.

Index

The **intelligent** way to practice for the MCP exam.

If you took the Microsoft, Certified Professional (MCP) exam today, would you pass? With the READINESS REVIEW MCP exam simulation on CD-ROM, you get a low-risk, low-cost way to find out! Use this electronic assessment tool to take randomly generated, 60-question practice tests covering actual MCP objectives. Test and retest with different question sets each time, then consult the companion study guide to review all featured exam items and identify areas for further study. READINESS REVIEW—it's the smart way to prep!

MCSE Readiness Review—Exam 70-058: Networking Essentials

U.S.A. **$29.99**
U.K. $27.99 [V.A.T. included]
Canada $42.99
ISBN 0-7356-0536-X

MCSE Readiness Review—Exam 70-067: Microsoft® Windows NT® Server 4.0

U.S.A. **$29.99**
U.K. $27.99 [V.A.T. included]
Canada $42.99
ISBN 0-7356-0538-6

MCSE Readiness Review—Exam 70-073: Microsoft Windows NT® Workstation 4.0

U.S.A. **$29.99**
U.K. $27.99 [V.A.T. included]
Canada $42.99
ISBN 0-7356-0537-8

MCSE Readiness Review—Exam 70-087: Microsoft Internet Information Server 4.0

U.S.A. **$29.99**
U.K. $27.99 [V.A.T. included]
Canada $44.99
ISBN 0-7356-0541-6

MCSE Readiness Review—Exam 70-098: Supporting and Implementing Microsoft Windows® 98

U.S.A. **$29.99**
U.K. $27.99 [V.A.T. included]
Canada $44.99
ISBN 0-7356-0671-4

Microsoft Press® products are available worldwide wherever quality computer books are sold. For more information, contact your book or computer retailer, software reseller, or local Microsoft® Sales Office, or visit our Web site at mspress.microsoft.com. To locate your nearest source for Microsoft Press products, or to order directly, call 1-800-MSPRESS in the U.S. (in Canada, call 1-800-268-2222).

Prices and availability dates are subject to change.

Microsoft®

mspress.microsoft.com

http://mspress.microsoft.com/reslink/

ResourceLink—your online IT library!

Access the full line of Microsoft Press® Resource Kits for the Windows® and BackOffice® families, along with MCSE Training Kits and other IT-specific resources at mspress.microsoft.com/reslink/. Microsoft Press ResourceLink is the essential online information service for IT professionals. Get the latest technical updates, support alerts, insider tips, and downloadable utilities—direct from Microsoft. If you evaluate, deploy, or support Microsoft® technologies and products, the information you need to optimize their performance—and your own—is online and ready for work at ResourceLink.

For a complimentary 30-day trial CD packed with Microsoft Press
IT products, order through our Web site: mspress.microsoft.com/reslink/

mspress.microsoft.com

Gain work-ready expertise as you prepare for the Microsoft Certified Professional (MCP) exam

**Microsoft® Windows NT®
Technical Support Training Kit**
ISBN   1-57231-373-0
U.S.A. $99.99
U.K.   £93.99 [V.A.T. included]
Canada $134.99

**Networking Essentials,
Second Edition**
ISBN   1-57231-527-X
U.S.A. $99.99
U.K.   £93.99 [V.A.T. included]
Canada $140.99

Microsoft TCP/IP Training
ISBN   1-57231-623-3
U.S.A. $99.99
U.K.   £92.99 [V.A.T. included]
Canada $140.99

**Microsoft Certifed Systems
Engineer Core Requirements
Training Kit**
ISBN   1-57231-905-4
U.S.A. $299.99
U.K.   £249.99 [V.A.T. included]
Canada $434.99

**Microsoft SQL Server 7.0 Database
Implementation Training Kit**
ISBN   1-57231-826-0
U.S.A. $99.99
U.K.   £93.99 [V.A.T. included]
Canada $149.99

**Microsoft® SQL Server 7.0 System
Administration Training Kit**
ISBN   1-57231-827-9
U.S.A. $99.99
U.K.   £93.99 [V.A.T. included]
Canada $149.99

**Microsoft Windows® 98
Training Kit**
ISBN   1-57231-730-2
U.S.A. $99.99
U.K.   £93.99 [V.A.T. included]
Canada $144.99

Build real-world systems administration skills—and prepare for the MCP exams—with Microsoft Official Curriculum training kits from Microsoft Press. Use their modular design, self-paced lessons, and hands-on labs to master the intricacies of planning, installing, managing, and optimizing Microsoft Windows and BackOffice® technologies—how, when, and where you study best.

mspress.microsoft.com

Microsoft Press® products are available worldwide wherever quality computer books are sold. For more information, contact your book or computer retailer, software reseller, or local Microsoft Sales Office, or visit our Web site at mspress.microsoft.com. To locate your nearest source for Microsoft Press products, or to order directly, call 1-800-MSPRESS in the U.S. (in Canada, call 1-800-268-2222).

Prices and availability dates are subject to change.

Microsoft Press Resource Kits—
powerhouse resources to minimize costs
while maximizing performance

Microsoft® Windows NT® Server 4.0 Resource Kit
ISBN   1-57231-344-7
U.S.A. $149.95
U.K.   £140.99 [V.A.T. included]
Canada $199.95

Microsoft Windows NT Workstation 4.0 Resource Kit
ISBN   1-57231-343-9
U.S.A. $69.95
U.K.   £64.99 [V.A.T. included]
Canada $94.95

Microsoft Internet Information Server Resource Kit
ISBN   1-57231-638-1
U.S.A. $49.99
U.K.   £46.99 [V.A.T. included]
Canada $71.99

Microsoft Windows® 98 Resource Kit
ISBN   1-57231-644-6
U.S.A. $69.99
U.K.   £64.99 [V.A.T. included]
Canada $100.99

Microsoft Internet Explorer Resource Kit
ISBN   1-57231-842-2
U.S.A. $49.99
U.K.   £46.99 [V.A.T. included]
Canada $71.99

Microsoft BackOffice® Resource Kit, Second Edition
ISBN   1-57231-632-2
U.S.A. $199.99
U.K.   £187.99 [V.A.T. included]
Canada $289.99

Direct from the Microsoft product groups, the resources packed into these bestselling kits meet the demand for hardcore use-now tools and information for the IT professional. Each kit contains precise technical reference, essential utilities, installation and rollout tactics, planning guides, and upgrade strategies. Use them to save time, reduce cost of ownership, and maximize your organization's technology investment.

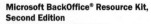

mspress.microsoft.com

Microsoft Press® products are available worldwide wherever quality computer books are sold. For more information, contact your book or computer retailer, software reseller, or local Microsoft Sales Office, or visit our Web site at mspress.microsoft.com. To locate your nearest source for Microsoft Press products, or to order directly, call 1-800-MSPRESS in the U.S. (in Canada, call 1-800-268-2222).

Prices and availability dates are subject to change.